SECOND EDITION

METHODS OF META-ANALYSIS

This Book Is Dedicated to the Memory of John E. ("Jack") Hunter
1939–2002

Brilliant Colleague and Dear Friend. He Enriched All the Lives He Touched.

SECOND EDITION

METHODS OF META-ANALYSIS

Correcting Error and Bias in Research Findings

JOHN E. HUNTER
Michigan State University
FRANK L. SCHMIDT
University of Iowa

SAGE Publications
International Educational and Professional Publisher
Thousand Oaks ■ London ■ New Delhi

For information:

Sage Publications, Inc.
2455 Teller Road
Thousand Oaks, California 91320
E-mail: order@sagepub.com

Sage Publications Ltd.
1 Oliver's Yard
55 City Road
London EC1Y 1SP
United Kingdom

Sage Publications India Pvt. Ltd.
B-42, Panchsheel Enclave
New Delhi 110 017
India

Printed in the United States of America

Library of Congress Cataloging-in-Publication Data

Hunter, John E. (John Edward), 1939-
Methods of meta-analysis: Correcting error and bias in research findings / by
John E. Hunter, Frank L. Schmidt.—2nd ed.
p. cm.
Includes bibliographical references and indexes.
ISBN 978-1-4129-0912-9 (cloth)—ISBN 978-1-4129-0479-7 (pbk.)
1. Social sciences—Statistical methods. 2. Meta-analysis. I. Schmidt, Frank L. II. Title.
HA29.H847 2004
300′.72—dc22 2003026057

07 10 9 8 7 6 5 4 3

Acquisitions Editor:	Lisa Cuevas-Shaw
Editorial Assistant:	Margo Crouppen
Production Editor:	Diane S. Foster
Copy Editor:	Mattson Publishing Services
Typesetter:	C&M Digitals (P) Ltd.
Proofreader:	Scott Oney
Indexer:	Molly Hall
Cover Designer:	Janet Foulger

Brief Contents

Detailed Contents

List of Tables

Chapter 1

Chapter 2

Chapter 3

Chapter 4

Chapter 5—No Tables

Chapter 6

Chapter 7

Chapter 8

Chapter 9

Chapter 10—No Tables

Chapter 11—No Tables

Chapter 12—No Tables

Chapter 13

Chapter 14—No Tables

Appendix—No Tables

List of Figures

Chapter 1

Chapter 2

Chapter 12—No Figures

Chapter 13

Chapter 14—No Figures

Appendix—No Figures

Preface to Second Edition

Meta-analysis has made tremendous progress in acceptance and impact since the publication of the last edition of this book in 1990. As detailed in Chapter 1, it is now widely used and highly influential within the research enterprise. The 1990 edition of this book has also been influential, having been cited thousands of times and having sold many copies. New developments since 1990, however, now require that the book be updated and extended. This book is different from the last edition in several ways.

An important addition is the treatment of indirect range restriction. Indirect range restriction is by far the most common type of range restriction in real data. Yet, until recently, quantitative procedures for correcting for the most common form of indirect range restriction were not available. The new procedures now available are discussed in Chapters 2 through 5. One major implication is that procedures used in the past have undercorrected for range restriction.

Also new in this edition are extended discussions of fixed-effects versus random-effects models in meta-analysis. Fixed-effects meta-analysis models are still widely used in some areas, but it is increasingly being recognized that they are almost always inappropriate and lead to biased results, as stated by the National Research Council (1992). All the meta-analysis methods in this book—and in both our earlier books (Hunter & Schmidt, 1990a; Hunter, Schmidt, & Jackson, 1982)—are random-effects models. These discussions appear in Chapters 3, 4, 5, and 9. The relative accuracy of different random-effects models is also discussed in Chapter 5.

Exercises are now provided at the end of Chapters 3, 4, 7, and 9. These include bare-bones meta-analysis of correlations, meta-analysis of correlations correcting each correlation individually, artifact distribution meta-analysis of correlations, meta-analysis of d values correcting each individually, and second-order meta-analysis.

Equations are now numbered in all chapters to allow easier reference by those citing the book.

A key feature of our meta-analysis methods is the correction for measurement error, usually accomplished using reliability coefficients. Over the last 12 years, we have observed confusion in published meta-analyses about the appropriate type of reliability coefficient in particular circumstances. Therefore, we now provide a more detailed discussion of the different types of reliability estimates, the types of measurement error each controls for, and the circumstances under which each should be used. This treatment can be found in Chapter 3.

We now describe (and apply) a Windows-based package of six meta-analysis programs created to facilitate application of the methods presented in this book. Over the years, we have received many requests for Windows-based programs in preference to our DOS-based programs, and we have now responded to this request. In addition to being Windows-based, these programs contain numerous technical improvements not included in the earlier DOS-based programs. Probably the most important of these is the ability to correct for indirect range restriction, but there are many others. These accuracy-enhancing refinements are now discussed in detail in Chapters 4 and 5. This software package is described in some detail in the Appendix at the end of the book and is available commercially from the second author. In Chapter 11, we have added a discussion of other available software for meta-analysis.

As a new and seemingly radical data analysis method, meta-analysis attracted considerable criticism in its early days. The 1990 edition of this book devoted considerable space (in Chapters 5 and 13) to criticisms directed against meta-analysis. As of today, it is now widely agreed that these criticisms were either mistaken or have been successfully addressed, and so we have omitted discussion of them. However, interested readers can still reference this discussion in the 1990 edition.

We have attempted to layer the content of this book, so that it will be suitable for two different audiences. For those who are less technically inclined or are just too busy to pursue technical issues, we present the basic principles and methods and simple illustrative examples of applications of these methods. We have also, as noted previously, made available a package of six Windows-based meta-analysis programs (sold separately) that make it easy to apply these methods. Throughout the book, we indicate when each of these programs should be used. For those more interested in the technical foundations of the methods, we present technical material, derivations, and references for additional reading. An example illustrating our attempt at layering is our treatment of indirect range restriction, new in this edition. In Chapters 2 through 4, we present general definitions and discussion of indirect range restriction, give the key equations needed in applications, and refer the reader to the appropriate computer programs for making corrections for indirect range restriction. Then, in Chapter 5, in an extended technical discussion that may be skipped by nontechnical readers, we present the statistical and psychometric foundations for these methods. Hence, we hope that different readers with different interests and objectives can read and use this book at different levels.

Recently, an edited book devoted entirely to the history, impact, and examination of our meta-analysis methods appeared (Murphy, 2003). This book is an excellent source of additional information beyond that contained in this book. In particular, Chapter 2 of that book, by the authors of this book, presents the history of the development of these methods.

The methods presented in this book differ from other approaches to meta-analysis in a wide variety of technical ways. However, all of these differences stem from one central difference, a difference in how the purpose of meta-analysis is viewed. The avowed purpose of other methods of meta-analysis is to describe and summarize the results of studies in a research literature (Rubin, 1990). The purpose of our methods is very different. In our view, the purpose of meta-analysis is to estimate what the results would have been had all the studies been conducted without methodological limitations or flaws. The results of perfectly conducted studies would reveal the underlying construct-level relationships, and it is these relationships that we as scientists are interested in, as Rubin (1990) has noted. Our methods estimate these relationships. We are much less interested in attaining an accurate description and summary of necessarily flawed studies. This critical distinction is developed in more detail near the end of Chapter 1 and in Chapter 14.

John E. (Jack) Hunter died on June 26, 2002, as the revision for this edition was getting under way. The story of his life is sketched in Schmidt (2003). To me, he was not only an inspired collaborator of 30 years, but a best friend, too. The great loss to psychology and the other social sciences is in addition to my personal loss. There will never be another such. This book is dedicated to his memory. Because of his death, all errors and omissions in this edition are mine. I would like to believe that he would approve of the book.

—Frank Schmidt

Preface to First Edition

Scientists have known for centuries that a single study will not resolve a major issue. Indeed, a small sample study will not even resolve a minor issue. Thus, the foundation of science is the cumulation of knowledge from the results of many studies.

There are two steps to the cumulation of knowledge: (1) the cumulation of results across studies to establish facts, and (2) the formation of theories to organize the facts into a coherent and useful form. The focus of this book is on the first of these, the resolution of the basic facts from a set of studies that all bear on the same relationship. For many years this was not an important issue in the social sciences because the number of studies dealing with a given issue was small. But that time has passed. There are now hundreds of studies that have sought to measure the extent to which we can predict job performance in clerical work from cognitive ability, hundreds of studies that seek to measure the effect of psychotherapy, and so on.

With as many as a hundred or more studies on a relationship, one might think that there would be a resolution of the issue. Yet most review studies traditionally have not concluded with resolution, but with a call for more research on the question. This has been especially frustrating to organizations that fund research in the behavioral and social sciences. Many such organizations are now questioning the usefulness of research in the social sciences on just this ground. If research never resolves issues, then why spend millions of dollars on research?

In this book we will review all the methods that have been proposed for cumulating knowledge across studies, including the narrative review, counting statistically significant findings, and the averaging of quantitative outcome measures. Our critique will show that the narrative review has often worked poorly. We will note how significance counting can be done correctly in those limited conditions in which it is appropriate. Most of the book will be devoted to methods of averaging results across studies (as advocated by Glass, 1976, and Schmidt & Hunter, 1977). We will refer to the averaging methods as "meta-analysis" (we view the Glass procedure as only one such method). Most methods of meta-analysis have been concerned with one artifactual source of variation across studies: sampling error. Following the lead of work in personnel selection on "validity generalization," we will extend meta-analysis to consider two other major problems that create artifactual variation across studies: error of measurement, and range variation (restriction of range in personnel selection). We will also consider other artifacts, such as the effects of dichotomization of continuous variables, and errors in data.

The main focus of the book will be on methods of distinguishing between variance across studies due to artifacts (such as sampling error, error of measurement, and restriction in range) and variance across studies due to real moderator variables. We will also present a historical review of cumulation methods after the current methods have been described.

The Meta-Analysis Dilemma for Behavioral and Social Scientists

Meta-analysis is rapidly increasing in importance in the behavioral and social sciences, a development we predicted in our 1982 meta-analysis book. The increasing importance of meta-analysis and the reasons for it are discussed in Chapter 1. But most behavioral and social scientists will not need this presentation to be convinced; the evidence is in the journals they read. It is not merely the use of meta-analysis that has increased; the number of different techniques and methods in meta-analysis has also increased dramatically, particularly since some mathematical statisticians have turned their attention in this direction. The result has been a proliferation of complex and highly technical and statistical journal articles on proposed new techniques in meta-analysis. Books on meta-analysis that are equally forbidding have also been published. A survey of primary authors of reviews in *Psychological Bulletin*—a group that should be more familiar with meta-analysis than most of their colleagues—obtained the following responses to this question (Jackson, 1984):

How familiar are you with meta-analysis at this time?

1. Very familiar; I have used it. 12%
2. Fairly familiar; I could use it without much further study. 21%
3. Somewhat familiar; I know the basic principles. 35%
4. Not very familiar; I could not state the basic principles. 31%

Clearly, even many authors of research reviews are unfamiliar with meta-analysis. The percentage that is completely unfamiliar with even basic meta-analysis principles is almost certainly much larger than 31% in the social sciences in general.

These developments have placed many researchers and teachers of methodological courses in a difficult position: they need to know and understand meta-analysis to be effective in their work, yet they do not have the time, inclination, or sometimes the training, to plough through the highly technical material now available on meta-analysis. Many need to apply meta-analysis in their own research. But even those with no plans to apply meta-analysis must be familiar with it to understand the research literature in their fields. Today, it is a rare research literature that is still unaffected by applications of meta-analysis; it will be even less common in the future (see Chapter 1). Thus, the need for familiarity with meta-analysis is now almost universal. But with the "fuller development" of meta-analysis methods of recent years, many of the published articles, and many chapters and sections in books, are now devoted to elaboration and exploration of methods that are really of only statistical interest; that is, they are devoted to methods that, despite their statistical elegance, will rarely be used in reality, because better methods are available or because the data conditions required for their application are virtually never met. For those who are primarily researchers rather than methodologists, reading and evaluating such articles is probably not the best use of their time.

In this book we have attempted to sort the wheat from the chaff. We have made judgments about which meta-analysis methods are the most useful and informative for researchers in integrating research findings across studies. For these methods, we have attempted to present a simple, clear and thorough presentation. The goal is that the reader will not only understand but be able to apply these methods based on the material in this book. We have not attempted to be encyclopedic; we do not cover all meta-analysis methods in detail. In the case of those methods that are less informative or practical than other available methods, we present only a general conceptual description and references for further reading. Methods for the cumulation of p values across studies are one such example. Our interest has been to spare the reader the difficult and time-consuming task of wading through complex statistical material that has little future applications value. We hope this will leave more of the reader's time and energy for the technical material that is truly useful.

In short, our goal has been to write a meta-analysis book that is (1) simply and clearly enough written that it is understandable by most researchers in the behavioral and social sciences, and (2) focused on the meta-analysis methods that we believe are the most useful and informative in integrating research, rather than exhaustively treating all methods, both trivial and important. Thus, this book attempts to provide a solution to the dilemma faced by many researchers today. To the extent that this purpose is achieved, this book will have been successful.

Brief History of This Book

Gene V. Glass published the first journal article on meta-analysis in 1976. In that article, he laid out the essential rationale and defined many of the basic features of meta-analysis as it is known and used today. He also coined the term "meta-analysis." Unaware of Glass's work, we developed our meta-analysis methods in 1975 and applied them to empirical data sets from personnel selection research. But, instead of submitting our report immediately for publication, we entered it in the James McKeen Cattell Research Design contest sponsored by Division 14 (The Society for Industrial and Organizational Psychology) of the American Psychological Association. Although our development and initial applications of meta-analysis won the Cattell award for 1976, a one-year delay in publication resulted (Schmidt & Hunter, 1977). But Glass's (1976) article was not only first in time, it was also the first to emphasize meta-analysis as a fully general set of methods that should be applied to the integration of literatures in all areas of research. Although our article mentioned this as a possibility for the future, our major emphasis was on solving the problem of the apparent substantial variability of test validities in the personnel selection literature (see Chapter 4). However, we were aware of and discussed the potential of our methods for broader application. So when Lee J. Cronbach suggested to us in correspondence in early 1978 that our methods might be usefully generalized to research literatures in many different areas of the behavioral and social sciences, we had already begun to think about a possible book. That book was published in 1982 (Hunter, Schmidt, & Jackson, 1982). (Again, Glass was first; he and his associates published their book on meta-analysis in 1981 [Glass, McGaw, & Smith, 1981]). Since then, the methods presented in our 1982 book have been widely applied, particularly in the industrial-organizational research literature (see Hunter & Hirsh, 1987), but also in other areas. However, our 1982 work was intended to be a short introductory book on meta-analysis; as a result, some potentially useful material was omitted. And since then there have been many new developments in meta-analysis methodology and numerous new applications of interest. As a result, we began to receive requests from colleagues and researchers for an expanded and updated treatment of meta-analysis. This book is our attempt to respond to that need.

Other Characteristics of This Book

There are six other characteristics of this book that should be mentioned.

First, this is the only meta-analysis book focused specifically on the areas of Industrial-Organizational (I/O) Psychology and Organizational Behavior (OB). Other books focus on research in other areas: social psychology (Rosenthal, 1984; Cooper, 1984) or research in education (Hedges & Olkin, 1985; Glass et al., 1981). Wolf (1986) is a very short (56 pages) overview of meta-analysis. In keeping with this substantive emphasis, we have used examples from the I/O and OB research literatures.

Second, this book is different from other books on meta-analysis because of its presentation of methods unique to our approach to meta-analysis. Specifically, our methods allow one to determine how much of the variance in findings across studies is due to sampling error, measurement artifacts, and other artifacts, and to adjust for the effects of these artifacts, yielding an estimate of the true population variability of study outcomes. This true variance is often either remarkably small or zero, indicating that many of the apparent disagreements among different studies are illusory. Our methods also allow correction of correlations and study effect sizes for the attenuating effects of measurement error and other artifacts. The meta-analysis methods used to make these corrections are typically based on psychometric principles, and thus these methods can collectively be referred to as psychometric meta-analysis. There are no comparable methods in the Glass et al. (1981), Rosenthal (1984), or Cooper (1984) books. This distinction is discussed by Bangert-Drowns (1986) in his review of meta-analysis methods. The Glass et al. (1981) method focuses on magnitudes of effect sizes, like our method, but does not correct the variance of effect sizes for variance produced by artifacts. Rosenthal (1984) focuses primarily on the cumulation of p values (significance levels) across studies, with some emphasis on mean effect sizes, but very little emphasis at all on the variance of effect sizes. Cooper (1984) focuses primarily on methods for locating and organizing primary studies and has only a limited treatment of statistical methods of combining results across studies. His statistical methods are similar to those of Rosenthal (1984). The Light and Pillemer (1984) book focuses heavily on the use of qualitative information in conjunction with meta-analysis methods that are similar to those of Glass and Rosenthal.

Third, this book examines in detail the severe distorting effects of statistical, measurement, and other methodological artifacts on the outcomes of the *individual* study. In addition to its contribution to the question of how best to combine findings across studies, this examination illustrates how untrustworthy empirical data in any study can be and usually are. In our judgment, there is a strong cult of overconfident empiricism in the behavioral and social sciences. There is an excessive faith in data as the source of scientific truths and an inadequate appreciation of how misleading most social science data are when accepted at face value and interpreted naively. The commonly held belief that research progress will be made if only we "let the data speak" is sadly erroneous. Because of the effects of the artifacts discussed in this book, it would be more accurate to say that data come to us encrypted, and to understand their meaning we must first break the code. One purpose of this book is to contribute to that process.

Fourth, we have attempted to write this book in a simple, direct and readable style. We believe there is a need for a book that can be read and understood by behavioral and social scientists who are not mathematical statisticians or even methodological specialists. The essential concepts in meta-analysis are not complex or difficult. We reject the position that to be correct and authoritative, discussions of meta-analysis must be written in the arcane language of mathematical statistics. Where appropriate and needed, we cite such references for further reading. More difficult statistical material (demonstration, proofs, and so on) has been put in special sections; those who are interested will find the detailed treatment there, while the average reader can skip over these materials. This book is intended to be a clear nontechnical presentation that makes important methodological tools available to a wider group of users. This was a deliberate choice. We recognize the dilemma in mode of presentation. Authors who present methodological material in highly complex technical language avoid the criticism that they are oversimplifying complex issues and questions. On the other hand, their presentations have little impact because they are not widely read; and when they are read, they are often misunderstood and misquoted. Authors who present matters in simpler, more direct language can communicate to a much wider audience; however, critics often charge that they have ignored many complexities and special cases. Also, there is among some an unfortunate tendency to believe that anything that can be communicated clearly in relatively nontechnical language must be unimportant and/or inherently too simple to be of much real scientific significance. We will take that chance.

However, none of this means that this book is a simplified presentation of methods that have appeared elsewhere earlier in less accessible form. This book is not a presentation of the existing literature. It contains much new and original material on meta-analysis methods—material that cannot be found in journals or in books (including our 1982 meta-analysis book). It also contains considerable new material of a conceptual (as opposed to methodological) nature.

A fifth feature of this book is the extensive use of examples to illustrate meta-analysis methods. To keep the examples simple and to avoid large data sets, the examples are usually based on hypothetical (but realistic) data.

Finally, we have included information on meta-analysis computer programs (in IBM BASIC) in the Appendix. These are programs that we have written and used in some of our own research. These programs can be run on any IBM PC or clone. We have found these programs to be useful, and others who have used them have, too.

Organization of the Book

In normal science writing, historical review is presented first. However, in our case the historical review is very difficult for novices. In effect, the new methods can only be compared to earlier methods if the new methods are first understood. Therefore, we will first present the methods of psychometric meta-analysis in some detail. Later in the book (Chapter 11), we will present our review and critique of earlier methods.

In the course of conducting a meta-analysis, the steps would be as follows: (1) search for and gather studies, (2) extract and code information from the studies, and (3) apply meta-analysis to the information extracted. We will discuss all three steps, but not in their natural chronological order. The reason for this is that to know what is good or bad procedure in early steps, you must know what you are going to do in the third step. Thus, we will cover meta-analysis methods first, then return to issues of defining the study domain, deciding what to code, and writing up the meta-analysis report. Finally, we will go back one step further and present a list of recommendations for changes in publication practices for primary studies that we believe are necessary for optimal cumulation of results across studies.

—John Hunter
—Frank Schmidt

Acknowledgments

Jack Hunter died shortly after work began on this edition of the book. Yet his input, stemming from our conversations and earlier joint papers, was absolutely critical. His contributions to this revision must be given first place in any acknowledgments. I would like to thank all of our colleagues and students whose persistent curiosity and questions about meta-analysis stimulated the development of many of the ideas in this book. I would also like to thank them for urging us to write this new, expanded treatment of psychometric meta-analysis and for encouraging its completion once we had started. The wait has been long, but I hope they will be happy with the final product. Special thanks go to Huy Le, Mike McDaniel, Deniz Ones, Hannah Rothstein, and Vish Viswesvaran for their insightful comments on draft chapters. I also benefited from stimulating conversations or correspondence on issues and questions related to meta-analysis with the following individuals, among other colleagues: Nambury Raju, Will Shadish, Jorge Mendoza, Herman Aguinis, Bruce Thompson, the late Jacob Cohen, Phil Bobko, John Callender, Fritz Drasgow, Larry Hedges, Roger Millsap, Betsy Becker, Paul Sackett, and Kevin Murphy. I would like to thank our editors, Lisa Cuevas-Shaw, Margo Crouppen, and Diane Foster, and our copy editors, Frances Andersen and Geri Mattson, for their patience, professionalism, and support. I would also like to thank Deborah Laughton, then with Sage, who so strongly encouraged this revision. Finally, I would like to thank Irma Herring for her dedication, skill, and professionalism in preparing this manuscript, even when the work extended to weekends and after hours. It could not have been done without her.

PART I

Introduction to Meta-Analysis

1

Integrating Research Findings Across Studies

Before we delve into an abstract discussion of methods, we would like to consider a concrete example. The next section presents a set of studies to be reviewed, then a sample narrative review, followed by a critique of this review. It has been our experience that personal experience with the problems of such a review greatly quickens the learning process.

General Problem and an Example

A major task in all areas of science is the development of theory. In many cases, the theorists have available the results of a number of previous studies on the subject of interest. Their first task is to find out what empirical relationships have been revealed in these studies so they can take them into account in theory construction. In developing an understanding of these relationships, it is often helpful in reviewing the studies to make up a table summarizing the findings of these studies. Table 1.1 shows such a summary table put together by a psychologist attempting to develop a theory of the relationship between job satisfaction and organizational commitment. In addition to the observed correlations and their sample sizes, the psychologist has recorded data on (1) sex, (2) organization size, (3) job level, (4) race, (5) age, and (6) geographical location. The researcher believes variables 1, 2, 3, and 4 may affect the extent to which job satisfaction gets translated into organizational commitment. The researcher has no hypotheses about variables 5 and 6, but has recorded them because they were often available.

As an exercise in integrating findings across studies and constructing theory, we would like you to spend a few minutes examining and interpreting the data in Table 1.1. We would like you to jot down the following:

Table 1.1 Correlations between organizational commitment and job satisfaction

Study	*N*	*r*	*Sex*	*Size of Organization*	*White vs. Blue Collar*	*Race*	*Under vs. Over 30*	*North vs. South*
1	20	.46*	F	S	WC	B	U	N
2	72	.32**	M	L	BC	Mixed	Mixed	N
3	29	.10	M	L	WC	W	O	N
4	30	.45**	M	L	WC	W	Mixed	N
5	71	.18	F	L	BC	W	O	N
6	62	.45**	F	S	BC	W	U	N
7	25	.56**	M	S	BC	Mixed	U	S
8	46	.41**	F	L	WC	W	Mixed	S
9	22	.55**	F	S	WC	B	U	N
10	69	.44**	F	S	BC	W	U	N
11	67	.34**	M	L	BC	W	Mixed	N
12	58	.33**	M	S	BC	W	U	N
13	23	.14	M	S	WC	B	O	S
14	20	.36	M	S	WC	W	Mixed	N
15	28	.54**	F	L	WC	W	Mixed	S
16	30	.22	M	S	BC	W	Mixed	S
17	69	.31**	F	L	BC	W	Mixed	N
18	59	.43**	F	L	BC	W	Mixed	N
19	19	.52*	M	S	BC	W	Mixed	S
20	44	−.10	M	S	WC	W	O	N
21	60	.44**	F	L	BC	Mixed	Mixed	N
22	23	.50**	F	S	WC	W	Mixed	S
23	19	−.02	M	S	WC	B	O	S
24	55	.32**	M	L	WC	W	Mixed	Unknown
25	19	.19	F	S	WC	B	O	N
26	26	.53**	F	S	BC	B	U	S
27	58	.30*	M	L	WC	W	Mixed	S
28	25	.26	M	S	WC	W	U	S
29	28	.09	F	S	BC	W	O	N
30	26	.31	F	S	WC	Mixed	U	S

*$p < .05$.
**$p < .01$.

1. The tentative conclusions you reached about the relationship between job satisfaction and organizational commitment and the variables that do and do not moderate that relationship
2. An outline of your resulting theory of this relationship

A Typical Interpretation of the Example Data

A typical report on the findings shown in Table 1.1 would run like this: The correlation between occupational commitment and job satisfaction varies from study to study with the correlation varying between −.10 and .56. Although

Table 1.2 Existence of correlation between organizational commitment and job satisfaction under various conditions as shown by the studies in Table 1.1

Sex

	M	F	
Not Significant	7	4	11
Significant	8	11	19
	15	15	30

$\chi^2 = 1.29$

Organization Size

	S	L	
Not Significant	9	2	11
Significant	9	10	19
	18	12	30

$\chi^2 = 3.44$

Job Level

	WC	BC	
Not Significant	8	3	11
Significant	8	11	19
	16	14	30

$\chi^2 = 2.62$

Race

	W	B	Mix	
Not Significant	7	3	1	11
Significant	13	3	3	19
	20	6	4	30

$\chi^2 = 1.64$

Age

	Young	Old	Mix	
Not Significant	2	7	2	11
Significant	7	0	12	19
	9	7	14	30

$\chi^2 = 16.12$

Geographical Location

	N	S	
Not Significant	6	5	11
Significant	11	7	18
	17	12	29

$\chi^2 = .12$

19 out of 30 studies found a significant correlation, 11 of 30 studies found no relationship between commitment and satisfaction. Why are commitment and satisfaction correlated within some organizations and not within others?

Table 1.2 presents a breakdown of the findings according to the features of the organization and the nature of the work population being studied. For example, for male work populations, commitment and satisfaction were correlated in 8 studies and not correlated in 7 (i.e., correlated in 53% of the studies), while for women there was a correlation in 11 of 15 cases (or in 73% of the studies). Correlation was found in 83% of the large organizations, but in only 50% of the small organizations. Correlation was found in 79% of the blue-collar populations, but in only 50% of the white-collar populations. Correlation was found in 67% of the populations that were all white or mixed race, while correlation was found in only 50% of those work populations that were all black. Correlation was found in 83% of the cases in which the workforce was all under 30 or a mixture of younger and older workers, while not a single study with only older workers found a significant correlation. Finally, 65% of the studies done in the North found a correlation, while only 58% of the southern studies found a correlation.

Table 1.3 Analysis of correlations from studies based on younger or mixed-age subjects

Sex

	M	F	
Not Significant	3	1	4
Significant	8	11	19
	11	12	23

$\chi^2 = 1.43$

Organization Size

	S	L	
Not Significant	4	0	4
Significant	9	10	19
	13	10	23

$\chi^2 = 3.72$

Job Level

	WC	BC	
Not Significant	3	1	4
Significant	8	11	19
	11	12	23

$\chi^2 = 1.43$

Race

	W	B	Mix	
Not Significant	3	0	1	4
Significant	13	3	3	19
	16	3	4	23

$\chi^2 = .81$; $df = 2$

Geographic Area

	N	S	
Not Significant	1	3	4
Significant	11	7	18
	12	10	22

$\chi^2 = 1.72$

Each of the differences between work populations could be taken as the basis for a hypothesis that there is an interaction between that characteristic and organizational commitment in the determination of job satisfaction. However, some caution must be urged because the only chi-square value that is significant in Table 1.2 is that for age. That is, the difference in the frequency of correlation between older and younger workers is significant ($\chi^2 = 16.52$; $df = 2$; $p < .01$), while the other differences can only be regarded as trends.

If the studies done on older workers are removed, then significant correlation is found for 19 of the remaining 23 studies. If these 23 cases are examined for relationship to organizational characteristics, then all of the chi squares are nonsignificant. These results are shown in Table 1.3. However, the chi square for size of organization is very close ($\chi^2 = 3.72$; 3.84 required). Within the 23 studies with younger or mixed-age work populations, all 10 correlations for large organizations were significant.

There are 13 studies of younger or mixed-age work populations in small organizations. None of the chi-square values even approaches significance on this set of studies, although with 13 cases the power of the chi-square test is low. These results are shown in Table 1.4. Within this group of studies, there is a tendency for correlation between organizational commitment and job satisfaction

Table 1.4 Analysis of correlations from studies based on younger and mixed-age subjects in small organizations

Sex

	M	F	
Not Significant	3	1	4
Significant	3	6	9
	6	7	13

$\chi^2 = 1.93$

Job Level

	WC	BC	
Not Significant	3	1	4
Significant	9	10	19
	12	11	23

$\chi^2 = 1.93$

Race

	W	B	Mix	
Not Significant	3	0	1	4
Significant	5	3	1	9
	8	3	2	13

$\chi^2 = 1.84$

Geographical Location

	N	S	
Not Significant	1	3	4
Significant	4	4	8
	5	7	12

$\chi^2 = .69$

to be more likely found among women, among blue-collar workers, in all-black work populations, and in the North.

Conclusions of the Review

Organizational commitment and job satisfaction are correlated in some organizational settings, but not in others. In work groups in which all workers are over 30, the correlation between commitment and satisfaction was never significant. For young or mixed-age work populations, commitment and satisfaction are always correlated in large organizations. For young or mixed-age work populations in small organizations, correlation was found in 9 of 13 studies with no organizational feature capable of perfectly accounting for those cases in which correlation was not found.

These findings are consistent with a model that assumes that organizational commitment grows over about a 10-year period to a maximum value at which it asymptotes. Among older workers, organizational commitment may be so uniformly high that there is no variation. Hence, among older workers there can be no correlation between commitment and job satisfaction. The finding for large organizations suggests that growth of commitment is slower there, thus generating a greater variance among workers of different ages within the younger group.

Critique of the Sample Review

The preceding review was conducted using standard review practices that characterize many narrative review articles not only in psychology, but in sociology, education, and the rest of the social sciences as well. Yet every conclusion in the review is false. The data were constructed by a Monte Carlo run in which the population correlation was always assumed to be .33. After a sample size was randomly chosen from a distribution centering about 40, an observed correlation was chosen using the standard distribution for r with mean $\rho = .33$ and variance

$$\frac{(1 - \rho^2)^2}{N - 1}$$

That is, the variation in results in Table 1.1 is entirely the result of sampling error. Each study is assumed to be conducted on a small sample and hence will generate an observed correlation that will depart by some random amount from the population value of .33. The size of the departure depends on the sample size. Note that the largest and smallest values found in Table 1.1 are all from studies with very small samples. The larger sample size studies tend to be found in the central part of the range; that is, they tend to show less of a random departure from .33.

The moderator effects appear to make sense, yet they are purely the results of chance. The values for the organizational characteristics were assigned to the studies randomly. The fact that one of the six was highly significant is due solely to capitalization on sampling error.

The crucial lesson to be learned from this exercise is this: "Conflicting results in the literature" may be entirely artifactual. The data in Table 1.1 were generated by using one artifact for generating false variation across studies, sampling error. There are other artifacts that are found in most sets of studies: Studies vary in terms of the quality of measurement in their scales; researchers make computational or computer errors; people make typographical errors in copying numbers from computer output or in copying numbers from handwritten tables onto manuscripts or in setting tables into print; people study variables in settings with greater or smaller ranges of individual differences; and so on. In our experience (to be described later), many of the interactions hypothesized to account for differences in findings in different studies are nonexistent; that is, they are apparitions composed of the ectoplasm of sampling error and other artifacts.

Problems With Statistical Significance Tests

In the data set given in Table 1.1, all study population correlations are actually equal to .33. Of the 30 correlations, 19 were found to be statistically significant. However, 11 of the 30 correlations were not significant. That is, the significance test gave the wrong answer 11 out of 30 times, an error rate of 37%. In oral presentations, many express shock that the error rate can be greater than 5%. The significance test was derived in response to the problem of sampling error, and many believe that the use of significance tests guarantees an error rate of 5% or less. This is just not true. Statisticians have pointed this out for many years; the possibility of high error rates is brought out in discussions of the "power" of statistical tests. However, statistics teachers are all well aware that this point is missed by most students. The 5% error rate is guaranteed only if the null hypothesis is true. If the null hypothesis is false, then the error rate can go as high as 95%.

Let us state this in more formal language. If the null hypothesis is true for the population and our sample data lead us to reject it, then we have made a Type I error. If the null hypothesis is false for the population and our sample data lead us to accept it, then we have made a Type II error. The statistical significance test is defined in such a way that the Type I error rate is at most 5%. However, the Type II error rate is left free to be as high as 95%. The question is which error rate applies to a given study. The answer is that the relevant error rate can only be known if we know whether the null hypothesis is true or false for that study. If we know that the null hypothesis is true, then we know that the significance test has an error rate of 5%. Of course, if we know that the null hypothesis is true and we still do a significance test, then we should wear a dunce cap, because if we know the null hypothesis to be true, then we can obtain a 0% error rate by ignoring the data. That is, there is a fundamental circularity to the significance test. If you do not know whether the null hypothesis is true or false, then you do not know whether the relevant error rate is Type I or Type II; that is, you do not know if your error rate is 5% or some value as high as 95%. There is only one way to guarantee a 5% error rate in all cases: Abandon the significance test and use a confidence interval.

Consider our hypothetical example from Table 1.1. However, let us simplify the example still further by assuming that the sample size is the same for all studies, say $N = 40$. The one-tailed significance test for a correlation coefficient is $\sqrt{N-1}\ r \geq 1.64$; in our case, $\sqrt{39}r \geq 1.64$ or $r \geq .26$. If the population correlation is .33 and the sample size is 40, the mean of the sample correlations is .33, while the standard deviation is $(1 - \rho^2)/\sqrt{N-1} = (1 - .33^2)/\sqrt{39} = .14$. Thus, the probability that the observed correlation will be significant is the probability that the sample mean correlation will be greater than .26 when it has a mean of .33 and a standard deviation of .14:

$$P\{r \geq .26\} = P\left\{\frac{r - .33}{.14} \geq \frac{.26 - .33}{.14}\right\} = P\{z \geq -.50\} = .69$$

That is, if all studies were done with a sample size of 40, then a population correlation of .33 would mean an error rate of 31% (i.e., $1 - .69 = .31$).

Suppose we alter the population correlation in our hypothetical example from .33 to .20. Then the probability that the observed correlation will be significant drops from .69 to

$$P\{r \geq .26\} = P\left\{z \geq \frac{.26 - .20}{.15} = .39\right\} = .35$$

That is, the error rate rises from 31% to 65%. In this realistic example, we see that the error rate can be over 50%. A two-to-one majority of the studies can find the correlation to be not significant despite the fact that the population correlation is always .20.

Error rates of over 50% have been shown to be the usual case in the personnel selection research literature. Thus, reviewers who count the number of significant findings are prone to incorrectly conclude that a given procedure does not predict job performance. Furthermore, as Hedges and Olkin (1980) pointed out, this situation will only get worse as more studies are done. The reviewer will become ever more convinced that the majority of studies show no effect and that the effect thus does not exist. Statistical power has been examined in many research literatures in psychology, starting with Cohen (1962) and extending up to the present. In most literatures, the mean statistical power is in the .40 to .60 range and is as low as .20 in some areas (Hunter, 1997; Schmidt, 1996; Schmidt & Hunter, 2003; Sedlmeier & Gigerenzer, 1989).

If the null hypothesis is true in a set of studies, then the base rate for significance is not 50% but 5%. If more than 1 in 20 studies finds significance, then the null hypothesis must be false in some studies. We must then avoid an error made by some of the reviewers who know the 5% base rate. Given 35% significant findings, some have concluded that "because 5% will be significant by chance, this means that the number of studies in which the null hypothesis is truly false is $35 - 5 = 30\%$." Our hypothetical example shows this reasoning to be false. If the population correlation is .20 in every study and the sample size is always 40, then there will be significant findings in only 35% of the studies, even though the null hypothesis is false in all cases.

The typical use of significance test results leads to gross errors in traditional review studies. Most such reviews falsely conclude that further research is needed to resolve the "conflicting results" in the literature. These errors in review studies can only be eliminated if errors in the interpretation of significance tests can be eliminated. Yet those of us who have been teaching power to generation after generation of graduate students have been unable to change the reasoning processes and the false belief in the 5% error rate (Sedlmeier & Gigerenzer, 1989).

This example illustrates a critical point. The traditional reliance on statistical significance tests in interpreting studies leads to false conclusions about what the study results mean; in fact, the traditional approach to data analysis makes it virtually impossible to reach correct conclusions in most research areas (Hunter, 1997; Schmidt, 1996).

A common reaction to this critique of traditional reliance on significance testing goes something like this: "Your explanation is clear but I don't understand how so many researchers (and even some methodologists) could have been so wrong so long on a matter as important as the correct way to analyze data? How could psychologists and others have failed to see the pitfalls of significance testing?" Over the years, a number of methodologists have addressed this question (Carver, 1978; Cohen, 1994; Guttman, 1985; Meehl, 1978; Oakes, 1986; Rozeboom, 1960). For one thing, in their statistics classes young researchers have typically been taught a lot about Type I error and very little about Type II error and statistical power. Thus, they are unaware that the error rate is very large in the typical study; they tend to believe the error rate is the alpha level used (typically .05 or .01). In addition, empirical research suggests that most researchers believe that the use of significance tests provides them with many nonexistent benefits in understanding their data. Most researchers believe that a statistically significant finding is a "reliable" finding in the sense that it will replicate if a new study is conducted (Carver, 1978; Oakes, 1986; Schmidt, 1996). For example, they believe that if a result is significant at the .05 level, then the probability of replication in subsequent studies (if conducted) is $1.00 - .05 = .95$. This belief is completely false. The probability of replication is the statistical power of the study and is almost invariably much lower than .95 (e.g., typically .50 or less). Most researchers also falsely believe that if a result is nonsignificant, one can conclude that it is probably just due to chance, another false belief, as illustrated in our example. There are other widespread but false beliefs about the usefulness of information provided by significance tests (Carver, 1978; Oakes, 1986). A recent discussion of these beliefs can be found in Schmidt (1996).

Another fact is relevant at this point: The physical sciences, such as physics and chemistry, do not use statistical significance testing in interpreting their data (Cohen, 1990). It is no accident, then, that these sciences have not experienced the debilitating problems described here that are inevitable when researchers rely on significance tests. Given that the physical sciences regard reliance on significance testing as unscientific, it is ironic that so many psychologists defend the use of significance tests on grounds that such tests are the objective and scientifically correct approach to data analysis and interpretation. In fact, it has been our experience that psychologists and other behavioral scientists who attempt to defend significance testing usually equate null hypothesis statistical significance testing with scientific hypothesis testing in general. They argue that hypothesis testing is central to science and that the abandonment of significance testing would amount to an attempt to have a science without hypothesis testing. They falsely believe that significance testing and hypothesis testing in science is one and the same thing. This belief is tantamount to stating that physics, chemistry, and the other physical sciences are not legitimate sciences because they are not built on hypothesis testing. Another logical implication of this belief is that prior to the introduction of null hypothesis significance testing by Fisher (1932) in the 1930s, no legitimate scientific research was possible. The fact is, of course, that there are many ways to test scientific hypotheses—and that significance testing is one of the least effective methods of doing this (Schmidt & Hunter, 1997).

Is Statistical Power the Solution?

Some researchers believe that the only problem with significance testing is low power and that if this problem could be solved there would be no problems with reliance on significance testing. These individuals see the solution as larger sample sizes. They believe that the problem would be solved if every researcher, before conducting each study, would calculate the number of subjects needed for "adequate" power (usually taken as power of .80) and then use that sample size. What this position overlooks is that this requirement would make it impossible for most studies ever to be conducted. At the start of research in a given area, the questions are often of the form, "Does Treatment A have an effect?" (e.g., Does interpersonal skills training have an effect? Does this predictor have any validity?). If Treatment A indeed has a substantial effect, the sample size needed for adequate power may not be prohibitively large. But as research develops, subsequent questions tend to take the form, "Is the effect of Treatment A larger than the effect of Treatment B?" (e.g., Is the effect of the new method of training larger than that of the old method? Is Predictor A more valid than Predictor B?). The effect size then becomes the *difference* between the two effects. Such effect sizes will often be small, and the required sample sizes are therefore often quite large—1,000 or 2,000 or more (Schmidt & Hunter, 1978). And this is just to attain power of .80, which still allows a 20% Type II error rate when the null hypothesis is false—an error rate most would consider high. Many researchers cannot obtain that many subjects, no matter how hard they try; either it is beyond their resources or the subjects are just unavailable at any cost. Thus, the upshot of this position would be that many—perhaps most—studies would not be conducted at all.

People advocating the power position say this would not be a loss. They argue that a study with inadequate power contributes nothing and therefore should not be conducted. Such studies, however, contain valuable information when combined with others like them in a meta-analysis. In fact, precise meta-analysis results can be obtained based on studies that *all* have inadequate statistical power individually. The information in these studies is lost if these studies are never conducted.

The belief that such studies are worthless is based on two false assumptions: (1) the assumption that every individual study must be able to justify a conclusion on its own, without reference to other studies, and (2) the assumption that every study should be analyzed using significance tests. One of the contributions of meta-analysis has been to show that no single study is adequate by itself to answer a scientific question. Therefore, each study should be considered as a data point to be contributed to a later meta-analysis. In addition, individual studies should be analyzed using not significance tests but point estimates of effect sizes and confidence intervals.

How, then, *can* we solve the problem of statistical power in individual studies? Actually, this problem is a pseudoproblem. It can be "solved" by discontinuing the significance test. As Oakes (1986, p. 68) noted, statistical power is a legitimate concept only within the context of statistical significance testing. If significance testing is not used, then the concept of statistical power has no place and is not meaningful. In particular, there need be no concern with statistical power when point estimates and confidence intervals are used to analyze data in studies and meta-analysis is used to integrate findings across studies.

Our critique of the traditional practice of reliance on significance testing in analyzing data in individual studies and in interpreting research literatures might suggest a false conclusion, namely, that if significance tests had never been used, the research findings would have been consistent across different studies examining a given relationship. Consider the correlation between job satisfaction and job performance. Would these studies have all had the same findings if researchers had not relied on significance tests? Absolutely not: The correlations would have varied widely (as indeed they did). The major reason for such variability in correlations is simple sampling error—caused by the fact that the small samples used in individual research studies are randomly unrepresentative of the populations from which they are drawn. Most researchers severely underestimate the amount of variability in findings that is caused by sampling error.

The law of large numbers correctly states that large random samples are representative of their populations and yield parameter estimates that are close to the real (population) values. Many researchers seem to believe that the same law applies to small samples. As a result, they erroneously expect statistics computed on small samples (e.g., 50 to 300) to be close approximations to the real (population) values. In one study we conducted (Schmidt, Ocasio, Hillery, & Hunter, 1985), we drew random samples (small studies) of $N = 30$ from a much larger data set and computed results on each $N = 30$ sample. These results varied dramatically from "study" to "study"—and all this variability was due solely to sampling error (Schmidt, Ocasio, et al., 1985). Yet when we showed these data to researchers, they found it hard to believe that each "study" was a random draw from the larger study. They did not believe simple sampling error could produce that much variation. They were shocked because they did not realize how much variation simple sampling error produces in research studies.

If there is an alternative analysis, then maybe it is time to abandon the significance test. There are two alternatives to the significance test. At the level of review studies, there is meta-analysis. At the level of single studies, there is the confidence interval.

Confidence Intervals

Consider Studies 17 and 30 from our hypothetical example in Table 1.1. Study 17, with $r = .31$ and $N = 69$, finds the correlation to be significant at the .01 level. Study 30, with $r = .31$ and $N = 26$, finds the correlation to be not significant. That is, two authors with an identical finding, $r = .31$, come to opposite conclusions. Author 17 concludes that organizational commitment is highly related to job satisfaction, while Author 30 concludes that they are independent. Thus, two studies with identical findings can lead to a review author claiming "conflicting results in the literature."

The conclusions are quite different if the results are interpreted with confidence intervals. Author 17 reports a finding of $r = .31$ with a 95% confidence interval of $.10 \leq \rho \leq .52$. Author 30 reports a finding of $r = .31$ with a 95% confidence interval of $-.04 \leq \rho \leq .66$. There is no conflict between these results; the two confidence intervals overlap substantially. On the other hand, the fact recorded by the significance test is still given in the two confidence intervals. Study 17 finds that $\rho = 0$ is not a reasonable possibility, while Study 30 finds that $\rho = 0$ cannot be ruled out. Thus, the two separate studies do not draw conclusions inconsistent with the significance test. The two studies considered together, however, lead to the correct conclusion if confidence intervals are used.

Consider now Studies 26 and 30 from Table 1.1. Study 26 finds $r = .53$ with $N = 26$, which is significant at the .01 level. Study 30 finds $r = .31$ with $N = 26$, which is not significant. That is, we have two studies with the same sample size but apparently widely divergent results. Using significance tests, one would conclude that there must be some moderator that accounts for the difference. This conclusion is false.

Had the two studies used confidence intervals, the conclusion would have been different. The confidence interval for Study 26 is $.25 \leq \rho \leq .81$ and the confidence interval for Study 30 is $-.04 \leq \rho \leq .66$. It is true that the confidence interval for Study 30 includes $\rho = 0$, while the confidence interval for Study 26 does not; this is the fact registered by the significance test. The crucial thing, however, is that the two confidence intervals show an overlap of $.25 \leq \rho \leq .66$. Thus, consideration of the two studies together leads to the correct conclusion that it is possible that both studies could imply the same value for the population correlation ρ. Indeed, the overlapping intervals include the correct value, $\rho = .33$.

Two studies with the same population value can have nonoverlapping confidence intervals, but this is a low-probability event (about 5%). But, then, confidence intervals are not the optimal method for looking at results across studies; that distinction belongs to meta-analysis.

Confidence intervals are more informative than significance tests for two reasons. First, the interval is correctly centered on the observed value rather than on the hypothetical value of the null hypothesis. Second, the confidence interval gives the author a correct image of the extent of uncertainty in small-subsample studies. It may be disconcerting to see a confidence interval as wide as $-.04 \leq \rho \leq .66$, but that is far superior to the frustration produced over the years by the false belief in "conflicting results."

Confidence intervals can be used to generate definitions for the phrase "small sample size." Suppose we want the confidence interval for the correlation coefficient to define the correlation to the first digit, that is, to have a width of $\pm.05$. Then, for small population correlations, the minimum sample size is approximately 1,538. For a sample size of 1,000 to be sufficient, the population correlation must be at least .44. Thus, under this standard of accuracy, for correlational studies "small sample size" includes all studies with less than a thousand persons and often extends above that.

There is a similar calculation for experimental studies. If the statistic used is the d statistic (by far the most frequent choice), then small effect sizes will be specified to their first digit only if the sample size is 3,076. If the effect size is larger, then the sample size must be even greater than 3,076. For example, if the difference between the population means is .3 standard deviations or more, then the minimum sample size to yield accuracy to within $\pm.05$ of .30 is 6,216. Thus, given this standard of accuracy, for experimental studies, "small sample size" begins with 3,000 and often extends well beyond that.

Since the publication of the first edition of this book in 1990, recognition of the superiority of confidence intervals and point estimates of effect sizes over significance tests has grown exponentially. The report of the task force on significance testing of the American Psychological Association (APA; Wilkinson & The APA Task Force on Statistical Inference, 1999) stated that researchers should report effect size estimates and confidence intervals. The latest (5th) edition of the APA *Publication Manual* stated that it is almost always necessary for primary studies to report effect size estimates and confidence intervals (American Psychological Association, 2001). Twenty-one research journals in psychology and education now require that these statistics be reported (Thompson, 2002). Some have argued that information on the methods needed to compute confidence intervals is not widely available. However, there are now at least two helpful and informative statistics textbooks designed around point estimates of effect size and confidence intervals instead of significance testing (Lockhart, 1998; Smithson, 2000). Thompson (2002) presented considerable information on computation of confidence intervals and cited many useful references that provide more detail (e.g., Kirk, 2001; Smithson, 2001). The August 2001 issue of *Educational and Psychological Measurement* was devoted entirely to methods of computing and interpreting confidence intervals. There are now many other such publications (e.g., Borenstein, 1994, is an excellent reference on this).

Confidence intervals give a correct picture of the extent of uncertainty that surrounds results computed from small-sample studies (Hunter, 1997; Schmidt, 1996). However, the only way to eliminate uncertainty is either to run large-sample single studies or to use meta-analysis to combine results across many small-sample studies. Given the limited resources available to social scientists, this means that the only possible answer in most areas is meta-analysis.

Meta-Analysis

Is there a quantitative analysis that would have suggested that all the differences in Table 1.1 might stem from sampling error? Suppose we compute the variance of the correlations, weighting each by its sample size. The value we obtain is .02258 ($SD = .150$). We can also compute the variance expected solely on the basis of sampling error. The formula for the sampling error variance of each individual correlation r_i is

$$(1 - .331^2)^2/(N_i - 1)$$

where .331 is the sample-size-weighted mean of the correlations in Table 1.1. If we weight each of these estimates by its sample size (as we did when we computed the observed variance), the formula for variance expected from sampling error is

$$S_e^2 = \frac{\sum_{i=1}^{i=30}[N_i(1 - .331^2)^2/N_i - 1]}{\sum N_i}$$

This value is .02058 ($SD = .144$). The ratio of variance expected from sampling error to actual (observed) variance is $.02058/.02258 = .91$. Thus, sampling error alone accounts for an estimated 91% of the observed variance in the correlations. The best conclusion is probably that the relationship between job satisfaction and organizational commitment is constant across sexes, races, job levels, ages, geographical locations, and size of organization. (The remaining 9% of the variance, a tiny value of only .00203, is probably due to other statistical artifacts—as discussed later.) The best estimate of this constant value is .331, the sample-size-weighted mean of the 30 correlations. Our analysis indicates that this relationship holds across ages, sexes, races, geographical locations, job levels, and different-sized organizations. When people in oral presentations analyzed the data from these 30 studies qualitatively, different people came to different conclusions. In contrast, all researchers applying the quantitative method used here would (barring arithmetic errors) come to exactly the same conclusion.

For theoretical purposes, the value .331 is not the one we want, because it is biased downward by unreliability in both measures. That is, the effect of measurement error is to reduce all the observed correlations, and hence the mean correlation, below the actual correlation between the two constructs. What we are interested in scientifically is the construct-level correlation. Suppose from information in the 30 studies we estimate the average reliability of job satisfaction measures at .70 and the average reliability of organizational commitment measures at .60. Then the estimated correlation between true scores on the measures is $.331/\sqrt{.70(.60)} = .51$. This is the best estimate of the construct-level correlation.

Most artifacts other than sampling error that distort study findings are systematic rather than random. They usually create a downward bias on the obtained study r or d value. For example, all variables in a study must be measured and all measures of variables contain measurement error. (There are no exceptions to this rule.) The effect of measurement error is to downwardly bias every correlation or d value. Measurement error can also contribute *differences* between studies: If the measures used in one study have more measurement error than those used in another study, the observed rs or ds will be smaller in the first study. Thus, meta-analysis must correct both for the downward bias and for the artifactually created differences between different studies. Corrections of this sort are discussed in Chapters 2 to 7.

Traditional review procedures are inadequate to integrate conflicting findings across large numbers of studies. As Glass (1976, p. 4) pointed out, the results of hundreds of studies "can no more be grasped in our traditional narrative discursive review than one can grasp the sense of 500 test scores without the aid of techniques for organizing, depicting and interpreting data." In such areas as the effects of class size on student learning, the relationship of IQ to creativity, and the effects of psychotherapy on patients, literally hundreds of studies can accumulate over a period of only a few years. Glass (1976) noted that such studies collectively contain much more information than we have been able to extract from them to date. He pointed out that because we have not exploited these gold mines of information, "we know much less than we have proven." What is needed are methods that will integrate results from existing studies to reveal patterns of relatively invariant underlying relationships and causalities, the establishment of which will constitute general principles and cumulative knowledge.

At one time in the history of psychology and the social sciences, the pressing need was for more empirical studies examining the problem in question. In many areas of research, the need today is not for additional empirical data but for some means of making sense of the vast amounts of data that have been accumulated. Because of the increasing number of areas within psychology and the other social sciences in which the number of available studies is quite large and the importance to theory development and practical problem solving of integrating conflicting findings to establish general knowledge, meta-analysis has come to play an increasingly important role in research. Such methods can be built around statistical and psychometric procedures that are already familiar to us. As Glass (1976, p. 6) stated,

> Most of us were trained to analyze complex relationships among variables in the primary analysis of research data. But at the higher level, where variance, nonuniformity and uncertainty are no less evident, we too often substitute literary exposition for quantitative rigor. The proper integration of research requires the same statistical methods that are applied in primary data analysis.

Role of Meta-Analysis in the Behavioral and Social Sciences

The small-sample studies typical of psychological research produce seemingly contradictory results, and reliance on statistical significance tests causes study results to appear even more conflicting. Meta-analysis integrates the findings across such studies to reveal the simpler patterns of relationships that underlie research literatures, thus providing a basis for theory development. Meta-analysis can correct for the distorting effects of sampling error, measurement error, and other artifacts that produce the illusion of conflicting findings.

The goal in any science is the production of cumulative knowledge. Ultimately, this means the development of theories that explain the phenomena that are the focus of the scientific area. One example would be theories that explain how personality traits develop in children and adults over time and how these traits affect their lives. Another would be theories of what factors cause job and career satisfaction and what effects job satisfaction in turn has on other aspects of one's life. Before theories can be developed, however, we need to be able to precisely calibrate the relationships between variables. For example, what is the relationship between peer socialization and level of extroversion? The relationship between job satisfaction and job performance?

Unless we can precisely calibrate such relationships among variables, we do not have the raw materials out of which to construct theories. There is nothing for a theory to explain. For example, if the relationship between extroversion and popularity of children varies capriciously across different studies from a strong positive to a strong negative correlation and everything in between, we cannot begin to construct a theory of how extroversion might affect popularity. The same applies to the relationship between job satisfaction and job performance.

The unfortunate fact is that most research literatures do show conflicting findings of this sort. Some studies find statistically significant relationships and some do not. In many research literatures, this split is approximately 50–50 (Cohen, 1962, 1988; Schmidt, Hunter, & Urry, 1976; Sedlmeier & Gigerenzer, 1989). This has been the traditional situation in most areas of the behavioral and social sciences. Hence, it has been very difficult to develop understanding, theories, and cumulative knowledge.

The Myth of the Perfect Study

Before meta-analysis, the usual way in which scientists attempted to make sense of research literatures was by use of the narrative subjective review. In many research literatures, however, there were not only conflicting findings, there were also large numbers of studies. This combination made the standard narrative subjective review a nearly impossible task—one shown by research on human information processing to be far beyond human capabilities. How does one sit down and make sense of, say, 210 conflicting studies?

The answer as developed in many narrative reviews was what came to be called the myth of the perfect study. Reviewers convinced themselves that most—usually the vast majority—of the studies available were "methodologically deficient" and should not even be considered in the review. These judgments of methodological deficiency were often based on idiosyncratic ideas: One reviewer might regard the Peabody Personality Inventory as "lacking in construct validity" and throw out all studies that used that instrument. Another might regard use of that same inventory as a prerequisite for methodological soundness and eliminate all studies *not* using this inventory. Thus, any given reviewer could eliminate from consideration all but a few studies and perhaps narrow the number of studies from 210 to, say, 7. Conclusions would then be based on these 7 studies.

It has long been the case that the most widely read literature reviews are those appearing in textbooks. The function of textbooks, especially advanced-level textbooks, is to summarize what is known in a given field. No textbook, however, can cite and discuss 210 studies on a single relationship. Textbook authors would often pick out what they considered to be the one or two "best" studies and then base textbook conclusions on just those studies, discarding the vast bulk of the information in the research literature. Hence, the myth of the perfect study.

In fact, there are no perfect studies. All studies contain measurement error in all measures used, as discussed later. Independent of measurement error, no study's measures have perfect construct validity. Furthermore, there are typically other artifacts that distort study findings. Even if a hypothetical (and it would have to be hypothetical) study suffered from none of these distortions, it would still contain sampling error—typically a substantial amount of sampling error—because sample sizes are rarely very large. Hence, no single study or small selected subgroup of studies can provide an optimal basis for scientific conclusions about cumulative knowledge. As a result, reliance on "best studies" did not provide a solution to the problem of conflicting research findings. This procedure did not even successfully deceive researchers into believing it was a solution—because different narrative reviewers arrived at different conclusions because they selected a different subset of "best" studies. Hence, the "conflicts in the literature" became "conflicts between the reviews."

Some Relevant History

By the mid-1970s, the behavioral and social sciences were in serious trouble. Large numbers of studies had accumulated on many questions that were important to theory development or social policy decisions. Results of different studies on the same question typically were conflicting. For example, are workers more productive when they are satisfied with their jobs? The studies did not agree. Do students learn more when class sizes are smaller? Research findings were conflicting. Does participative decision making in management increase productivity? Does job enlargement increase job satisfaction and output? Does psychotherapy really help people? The studies were in conflict. As a consequence, the public and government officials were becoming increasingly disillusioned with the behavioral and social sciences, and it was becoming more and more difficult to obtain funding for research. In an invited address to the American Psychological Association in 1970, then Senator Walter Mondale expressed his frustration with this situation:

> What I have *not* learned is what we should do about these problems. I had hoped to find research to support or to conclusively oppose my belief that quality integrated education is the most promising approach. But I have found very little conclusive evidence. For every study, statistical or theoretical, that contains a proposed solution or recommendation, there is always another, equally well documented, challenging the assumptions or conclusions of the first. No one seems to agree with anyone else's approach. But more distressing I must confess, I stand with my colleagues confused and often disheartened.

Then, in 1981, the Director of the Federal Office of Management and Budget, David Stockman, proposed an 80% reduction in federal funding for research in the behavioral and social sciences. (This proposal was politically motivated in part, but the failure of behavioral and social science research to be cumulative created the vulnerability to political attack.) This proposed cut was a trial balloon sent up to see how much political opposition it would arouse. Even when proposed cuts are much smaller than a draconian 80%, constituencies can usually be counted on to come forward and protest the proposed cuts. This usually happens, and many behavioral and social scientists expected it to happen. But it did not. The behavioral and social sciences, it turned out, had no constituency among the public; the public did not care (see "Cuts Raise New Social Science Query," 1981). Finally, out of desperation, the American Psychological Association took the lead in forming the Consortium of Social Science Associations to lobby against the proposed cuts. Although this superassociation had some success in getting these cuts reduced (and even, in some areas, getting increases in research funding in subsequent years), these developments should make us look carefully at how such a thing could happen.

The sequence of events that led to this state of affairs was much the same in one research area after another. First, there was initial optimism about using social science research to answer socially important questions. Do government-sponsored job-training programs work? We will do studies to find out. Does Head Start really help disadvantaged kids? The studies will tell us. Does integration increase the school achievement of black children? Research will provide the answer. Next, several studies on the question are conducted, but the results are conflicting. There is some disappointment that the question has not been answered, but policymakers—and people in general—are still optimistic. They, along with the researchers, conclude that more research is needed to identify the supposed interactions (moderators) that have caused the conflicting findings. For example, perhaps whether job training works depends on the age and education of the trainees. Maybe smaller classes in the schools are beneficial only for lower IQ children. It is hypothesized that psychotherapy works for middle-class but not working-class patients. That is, the conclusion at this point is that a search for moderator variables in needed.

In the third phase, a large number of research studies are funded and conducted to test these moderator hypotheses. When they are completed, there is now a large body of studies, but instead of being resolved, the number of conflicts increases.

The moderator hypotheses from the initial studies are not borne out, and no one can make sense out of the conflicting findings. Researchers conclude that the question that was selected for study in this particular case has turned out to be hopelessly complex. They then turn to the investigation of another question, hoping that this time the question will turn out to be more tractable. Research sponsors, government officials, and the public become disenchanted and cynical. Research funding agencies cut money for research in this area and in related areas. After this cycle has been repeated enough times, social and behavioral scientists themselves become cynical about the value of their own work, and they publish articles expressing doubts about whether behavioral and social science research is capable, *in principle,* of developing cumulative knowledge and providing general answers to socially important questions. Examples of this include Cronbach (1975), Gergen (1982), and Meehl (1978).

Clearly, at this point, there was a critical need for some means of making sense of the vast number of accumulated study findings. Starting in the late 1970s, new methods of combining findings across studies on the same subject were developed. These methods were referred to collectively as *meta-analysis,* a term coined by Glass (1976). Applications of meta-analysis to accumulated research literatures (e.g., Schmidt & Hunter, 1977) showed that research findings were not nearly as conflicting as had been thought and that useful and sound general conclusions could, in fact, be drawn from existing research. The conclusion was that cumulative theoretical knowledge is possible in the behavioral and social sciences, and socially important questions can be answered in reasonably definitive ways. As a result, the gloom and cynicism that had enveloped many in the behavioral and social sciences has been lifting.

In fact, meta-analysis has even produced evidence that cumulativeness of research findings in the behavioral sciences is probably as great as that in the physical sciences. We have long assumed that our research studies are less replicable than those in the physical sciences. Hedges (1987) used meta-analysis methods to examine variability of findings across studies in 13 research areas in particle physics and 13 research areas in psychology. Contrary to common belief, his findings showed that there was as much variability across studies in physics as there was in psychology. Furthermore, he found that the physical sciences used methods to combine findings across studies that were "essentially identical" to meta-analysis. The research literature in both areas—psychology and physics—yielded cumulative knowledge when meta-analysis was properly applied. Hedges's major finding is that the frequency of conflicting research findings is probably no greater in the behavioral and social sciences than in the physical sciences. The fact that this finding has been so surprising to many social scientists points up the fact that we have long overestimated the consistency of research findings in the physical sciences. In the physical sciences also, no research question can be answered by a single study, and physical scientists must use meta-analysis to make sense of their research literature, just as we do (and, as noted earlier, the physical sciences do not use significance tests).

Other changes have also been produced by meta-analysis. The relative status of reviews has changed dramatically. Journals that formerly published only primary studies and refused to publish reviews now publish meta-analytic reviews in large numbers. In the past, research reviews were based on the narrative subjective method, and they had limited status and gained little credit for one in academic raises or promotions. Perhaps this was appropriate because such reviews rarely contributed to cumulative knowledge. The rewards went to those who did primary research. Not only is this no longer the case, but there has been a more important development. Today, many discoveries and advances in cumulative knowledge are being made not by those who do primary research studies, but by those who use meta-analysis to discover the latent meaning of existing research literatures. A behavioral or social scientist today with the needed training and skills can make major original discoveries and contributions by mining the untapped veins of information in accumulated research literatures.

The meta-analytic process of cleaning up and making sense of research literatures not only reveals the cumulative knowledge that is there, but also provides clearer directions about what the remaining research needs are. That is, we also learn what kinds of primary research studies are needed next. However, some have raised the concern that meta-analysis may be killing the motivation and incentive to conduct primary research studies. Meta-analysis has clearly shown that no single primary study can ever resolve an issue or answer a question. Research findings are inherently probabilistic (Taveggia, 1974), and, therefore, the results of any single study could have occurred by chance. Only meta-analytic integration of findings across studies can control sampling error and other artifacts and provide a foundation for conclusions. And yet meta-analysis is not possible unless the needed primary studies are conducted. In new research areas, this potential problem is not of much concern. The first study conducted on a question contains 100% of the available research information, the second contains roughly 50%, and so on. Thus, the early studies in any area have a certain status. The 50th study, however, contains only about 2% of the available information, and the 100th, about 1%. Will we have difficulty motivating researchers to conduct the 50th or 100th study? If we do, we do not believe this will be due to meta-analysis. When the narrative review was the dominant method of research integration, reviewers did not base their conclusions on single studies, but on multiple studies. So no researcher could reasonably hope then—as now—that his or her single study could decide an issue. In fact, meta-analysis represents an improvement for the primary researcher in one respect—all available relevant studies are included in a meta-analysis and hence every study has an effect. As we saw earlier, narrative reviewers often threw out most relevant studies and based their conclusions on a handful of their favorite studies. Also, it should be noted that those who raise this question overlook a beneficial effect that meta-analysis has had: It prevents the diversion of valuable research resources into truly unneeded research studies. Meta-analysis applications have revealed that there are questions on which additional research would waste scientifically and socially valuable resources. For example, already as of 1980, 882 studies based on a total sample of 70,935 had been conducted relating measures of perceptual speed to the job performance of clerical workers. Based on these studies, our meta-analytic estimate of this correlation is .47 ($SD_\rho = .22$; Pearlman, Schmidt, & Hunter, 1980). For other abilities, there were often 200 to 300 cumulative studies. Clearly, further research on these relationships is not the best use of available resources.

Role of Meta-Analysis in Theory Development

As noted earlier, the major task in the behavioral and social sciences, as in other sciences, is the development of theory. A good theory is simply a good explanation of the processes that actually take place in a phenomenon. For example, what actually happens when employees develop a high level of organizational commitment? Does job satisfaction develop first and then cause the development of commitment? If so, what causes job satisfaction to develop and how does it affect commitment? How do higher levels of mental ability cause higher levels of job performance? Only by increasing job knowledge? Or also by directly improving problem solving on the job? The social scientist is essentially a detective; his or her job is to find out why and how things happen the way they do. To construct theories, however, we must first know some of the basic facts, such as the empirical relationships among variables. These relationships are the building blocks of theory. For example, if we know there is a high and consistent population correlation between job satisfaction and organization commitment, this will send us in particular directions in developing our theory. If the correlation between these variables is very low and consistent, theory development will branch in different directions. If the relationship is highly variable across organizations and settings, we will be encouraged to advance interactive or moderator-based theories. Meta-analysis provides these empirical building blocks for theory. Meta-analytic findings tell us what it is that needs to be explained by the theory. Meta-analysis has been criticized because it does not directly generate or develop theory (Guzzo, Jackson, & Katzell, 1986). This is akin to criticizing word processors because they do not generate books on their own. The results of meta-analysis are indispensable for theory construction; but theory construction itself is a creative process distinct from meta-analysis.

As implied in the language used in our discussion, theories are causal explanations. The goal in every science is explanation, and explanation is always causal. In the behavioral and social sciences, the methods of path analysis (see, e.g., Hunter & Gerbing, 1982) and structural equation modeling (SEM) can be used to test causal theories when the data meet the assumptions of the method. The relationships revealed by meta-analysis—the empirical building blocks for theory—can be used in path analysis and SEM to test causal theories. Experimentally determined relationships can also be entered into path analyses along with observationally based relationships. It is only necessary to transform d values to correlations (see Chapters 6 and 7). Thus, path analyses can be "mixed." Path analysis and SEM cannot demonstrate that a theory is correct but can disconfirm a theory, that is, show that it is not correct. Path analysis can therefore be a powerful tool for reducing the number of theories that could possibly be consistent with the data, sometimes to a very small number, and sometimes to only one theory (Hunter, 1988). For an example, see Hunter (1983f). Every such reduction in the number of possible theories is an advance in understanding.

Application of path analysis or SEM requires either the correlations among the theoretically relevant variables (correlation matrix) or the covariances among the variables (variance-covariance matrix). Meta-analysis can be used to create correlation matrices for the variables of interest. Because each meta-analysis can

Figure 1.1 Path model and path coefficients (from Schmidt, Hunter, & Outerbridge, 1986)

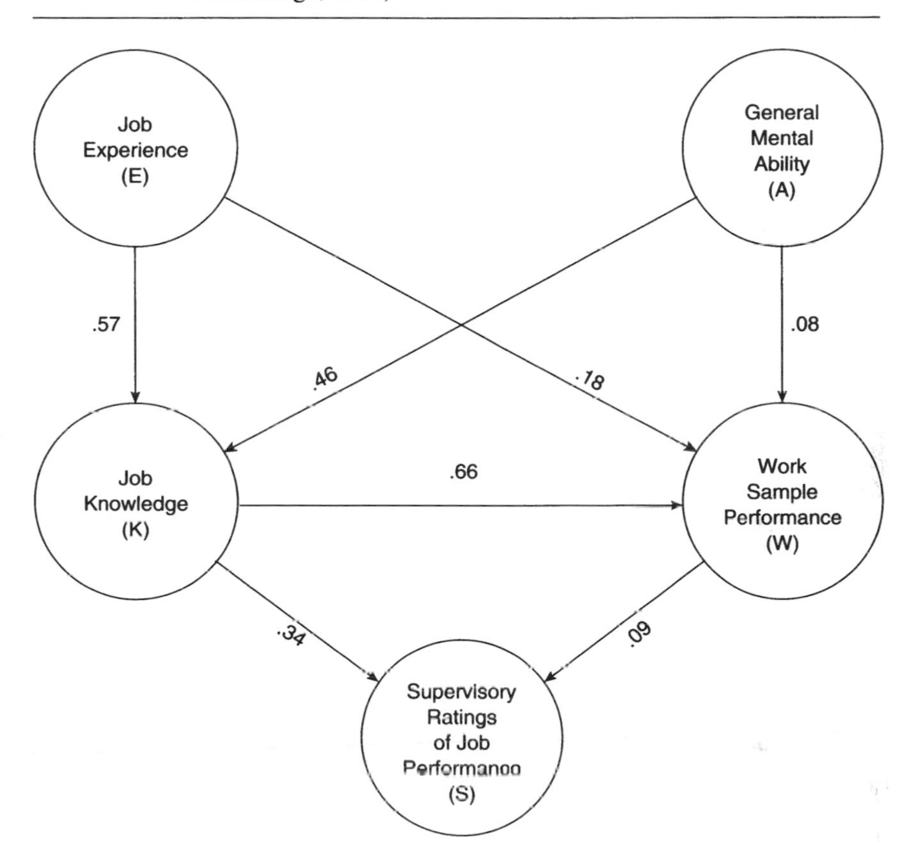

estimate a different cell in the correlation matrix, it is possible to assemble the complete correlation matrix, even though no single study has included every one of the variables of interest (see, e.g., Viswesvaran & Ones, 1995). If these correlations are appropriately corrected for the biasing effects of artifacts such as measurement error, it is then possible to apply path analysis or SEM to test causal (or explanatory) theories (Cook et al., 1992, pp. 315–316). One example of this is Schmidt, Hunter, and Outerbridge (1986). This study used meta-analysis to assemble the correlations among the variables of general mental ability, job experience, job knowledge, work sample performance, and supervisory evaluations of job performance. (These correlations were homogeneous across studies.) The path analysis results are shown in Figure 1.1. This causal model fit the data quite well. As can be seen in Figure 1.1, both job experience and general mental ability exert strong causal influence on the acquisition of job knowledge, which, in turn, is the major cause of high performance on the job sample measure. The results also indicate that supervisors based their ratings more heavily on employees' job knowledge than on actual performance capabilities. This causal model (or theory) of job performance has since been supported in other studies (Schmidt & Hunter, 1992).

Becker (1989) and Becker and Schram (1994) discussed the possibilities of using meta-analysis in this manner. Becker (1992) used this approach in examining a model of the variables affecting the achievement in science of male and female high school and college students. In that case, there were insufficient studies available to obtain meta-analytic estimates of some of the needed correlations; nevertheless, progress was made and the information needed from future research was pinpointed. Becker (1996) and Shadish (1996) provided additional discussion. Although there are technical complexities that must be dealt with in using meta-analysis in this manner (Cook et al., 1992, pp. 328–330), it is a promising approach to accelerating cumulative knowledge in the social sciences. Recent examples of application of this approach include Colquitt, LePine, and Noe (2002), Hom, Caranikas-Walker, Prussia, and Griffeth (1992), and Whiteside and Becker (2000).

Increasing Use of Meta-Analysis

The use of meta-analysis has grown dramatically since the publication of the first edition of this book in 1990. Figure 1.2 shows the increase over the period 1974 to 2000 in articles in the PsycINFO database with the term "meta-analysis" in the title or abstract. The increase is from 0 in the 1974–1976 period to 835 in the 1998–2000 period. Although the rate of growth appears to have tapered off in the late 1990s, there has been no decline in the high absolute number of meta-analyses. Also, the numbers in Figure 1.2 are underestimates to some extent, because some authors of meta-analyses use other terms—such as "research synthesis" or "systematic review"—in place of the term "meta-analysis." In February 2004, an Internet search of the term "meta-analysis" yielded over 522,000 hits; just five years earlier, this number was only about 2,500. These statistics provide a picture of the rapid growth of meta-analysis.

Meta-Analysis in Industrial-Organizational Psychology

There have been numerous applications of meta-analysis in industrial-organizational (I/O) psychology. The most extensive and detailed application of meta-analysis in I/O psychology has been the study of the generalizability of the validities of employment selection procedures (Schmidt, 1988; Schmidt & Hunter, 1981, 1998). The findings have resulted in major changes in the field of personnel selection. Validity generalization research is described in more detail in Chapter 4.

The meta-analysis methods presented in this chapter have been applied in other areas of I/O psychology and organizational behavior (OB). Between 1978 and 1998, there have been approximately 80 published nonselection applications. The following are some examples: (a) correlates of role conflict and role ambiguity (Fisher & Gittelson, 1983; Jackson & Schuler, 1985); (b) relationship of job satisfaction to absenteeism (Hackett & Guion, 1985; Terborg & Lee, 1982); (c) relationship between job performance and turnover (McEvoy & Cascio, 1987);

Figure 1.2 Number of articles in PsycINFO database with "meta-analysis" in title or abstract, 1974–2000

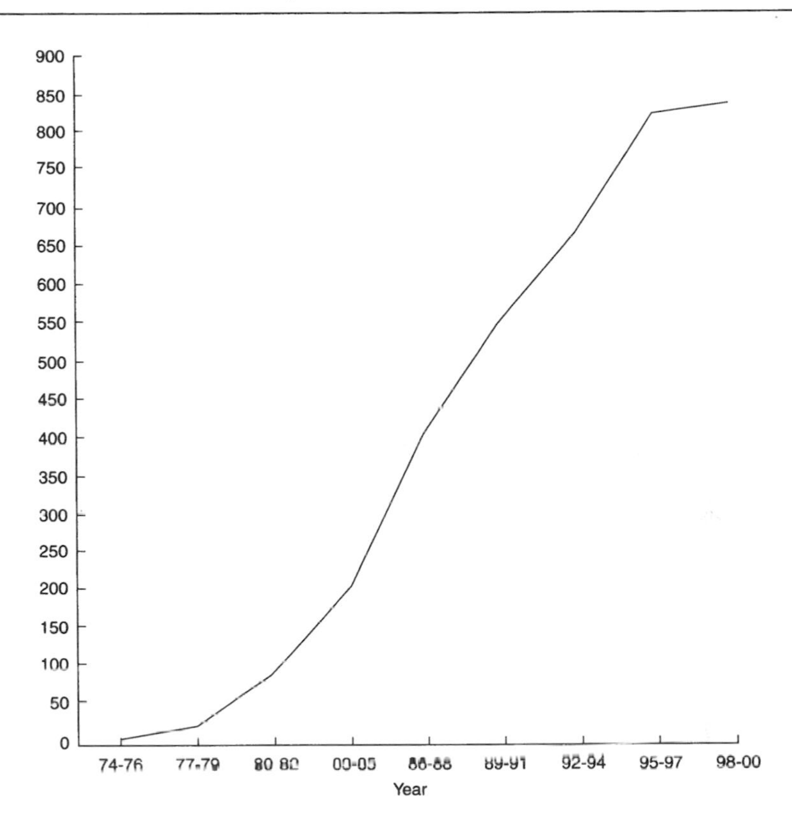

(d) relationship between job satisfaction and job performance (Iaffaldono & Muchinsky, 1985; Petty, McGee, & Cavender, 1984); (e) effects of nonselection organizational interventions on employee output and productivity (Guzzo, Jette, & Katzell, 1985); (f) effects of realistic job previews on employee turnover, performance, and satisfaction (McEvoy & Cascio, 1985; Premack & Wanous, 1985); (g) evaluation of Fiedler's theory of leadership (Peters, Harthe, & Pohlman, 1985); and (h) accuracy of self-ratings of ability and skill (Mabe & West, 1982). Most meta-analyses in I/O psychology have used the methods presented in this book. Table 1.5 shows the breakdown by methods for the top two I/O journals for the period 1974 to 2000. During this period, 116 meta-analyses were published in these two journals. In addition, each publication typically reported 15 to 20 separate meta-analyses, so the total number of meta-analyses was much larger.

The applications have been to both correlational and experimental literatures. As of the mid-1980s, sufficient meta-analyses had been published in I/O psychology that a review of the meta-analytic studies in this area was also published. This lengthy review (Hunter & Hirsh, 1987) reflected the fact that this literature had already become quite large. It is noteworthy that the review denoted considerable space to the development and presentation of theoretical propositions; this was possible because the clarification of research literatures produced by meta-analysis

Table 1.5 Substantive meta-analyses published in the top two journals in industrial/organizational psychology by methods used, 1974–2000

Method	*Journal of Applied Psychology*	*Personnel Psychology*
Hunter-Schmidt	77%	82%
Hedges-Olkin	2%	6%
Rosenthal-Rubin	5%	0%
Glass	1%	0%
Mixed	15%	12%
Total percentage	100%	100%
Total numbers	83	33

provided a foundation for theory development that previously did not exist. It is also noteworthy that the findings in one meta-analysis were often found to be theoretically relevant to the interpretation of the findings in other meta-analyses. A second review of meta-analytic I/O psychology has since been published (Tett, Meyer, & Roese, 1994).

In view of the large number of meta-analyses now available in the I/O and OB literatures, some readers may wonder why the examples we use in this book to illustrate meta-analysis principles and methods do not employ data from those meta-analyses. The primary reason is that the amount of data (the number of correlations or d statistics) is usually so large as to result in cumbersome examples. For pedagogical reasons, we have generally employed examples consisting of small numbers of studies in which the data are hypothetical. As explained in the following chapters, meta-analyses based on such small numbers of studies would not ordinarily yield results that would be optimally stable. (We discuss second-order sampling error in Chapter 9.) However, such examples provide the means to simply and clearly illustrate the principles and methods of meta-analysis, and we believe this is the crucial consideration.

Wider Impact of Meta-Analysis on Psychology

Some have viewed meta-analysis as merely a set of improved methods for doing literature reviews. Meta-analysis is actually more than that. By quantitatively comparing findings across diverse studies, meta-analysis can discover new knowledge not inferable from any individual study and can sometimes answer questions that were never addressed in any of the individual studies contained in the meta-analysis. For example, no individual study may have compared the effectiveness of a training program for people of higher and lower mental ability; by comparing mean d-value statistics across different groups of studies, however, meta-analysis can reveal this difference. That is, moderator variables (interactions) never studied in any individual study can be revealed by meta-analysis. Even though it is much more than that, meta-analysis is indeed an improved method for synthesizing or integrating research literatures. The premier review journal in psychology is *Psychological Bulletin.* In viewing that journal's volumes from 1980 to 2000, the impact of meta-analysis is apparent. Over this time period, a steadily increasing percentage of the reviews published in this journal are meta-analyses and a steadily decreasing percentage are traditional narrative subjective reviews. It is not uncommon for narrative review manuscripts to be returned by editors to the authors with the request that meta-analysis be applied to the studies reviewed. Most of the remaining narrative reviews published today in *Psychological Bulletin* focus on research literatures that are not well enough developed to be amenable to quantitative treatment.

Most of the meta-analyses appearing in *Psychological Bulletin* have employed fixed-effects methods, resulting, in many cases, in overstatement of the precision of the meta-analysis findings. (See Chapters 5 and 9 for discussions of fixed vs. random meta-analysis models.) Despite this fact, these meta-analyses produce findings and conclusions that are far superior to those produced by the traditional narrative subjective method. Many other journals have shown the same increase over time in the number of meta-analyses published. Many of these journals had traditionally published only individual empirical studies and had rarely published reviews up until the advent of meta-analysis in the late 1970s. These journals began publishing meta-analyses because meta-analyses came to be viewed not as "mere reviews" but as a form of empirical research in themselves. As a result of this change, the quality and accuracy of conclusions from research literatures improved in a wide variety of journals and in a corresponding variety of research areas in psychology. This improvement in the quality of conclusions from research literatures has expedited theory development in many areas in psychology.

The impact of meta-analysis on psychology textbooks has been positive and dramatic. Textbooks are important because their function is to summarize the state of cumulative knowledge in a given field. Most people—students and others—acquire most of their knowledge about psychological theory and findings from their reading of textbooks. Prior to meta-analysis, textbook authors faced with hundreds of conflicting studies on a single question subjectively and arbitrarily selected a small number of their preferred studies from the literature and based the textbook conclusions on only those few studies. Today, most textbook authors base their conclusions on meta-analysis findings (Myers, 1991), making their conclusions and their textbooks much more accurate. We cannot overemphasize the importance of this development in advancing cumulative knowledge in psychology.

Because multiple studies are needed to solve the problem of sampling error, it is critical to ensure the availability of all studies on each topic. A major problem is that many good replication articles are rejected by the primary research journals. Journals currently put excessive weight on innovation and creativity in evaluating studies and often fail to consider either sampling error or other technical problems such as measurement error. Many journals will not even consider "mere replication studies" or "mere measurement studies." Many persistent authors eventually publish such studies in journals with lower prestige, but they must endure many letters of rejection and publication is often delayed for a long period of time.

To us, this clearly indicates that we need a new type of journal—whether hard copy or electronic—that systematically archives all studies that will be needed for later meta-analyses. The American Psychological Association's Experimental Publication System in the early 1970s was an attempt in this direction. However, at that time, the need subsequently created by meta-analysis did not yet exist; the system apparently met no real need at that time and hence was discontinued. Today, the need is so great that failure to have such a journal system in place is retarding our efforts to reach our full potential in creating cumulative knowledge in psychology and the social sciences. The Board of Scientific Affairs of the American Psychological Association is currently studying the feasibility of such a system.

Impact of Meta-Analysis Outside Psychology

Impact in Medicine

The impact of meta-analysis may be even greater in medical research than in the behavioral and social sciences (Hunt, 1997, Chap. 4). Hundreds of meta-analyses have been published in leading medical research journals such as the *New England Journal of Medicine* and the *Journal of the American Medical Association.* (As of 1995, the medical literature contained between 962 and 1,411 meta-analyses, depending on the method of counting; Moher & Olkin, 1995.) In medical research, the preferred study is the randomized controlled trial (RCT), in which participants are assigned randomly to receive either the treatment or a placebo, with the researchers being blind as to which treatment the participants are receiving. Despite the strengths of this research design, it is usually the case that different RCTs on the same treatment obtain conflicting results. This is partly because the underlying population effect sizes are often small and partly because (contrary perhaps to our perceptions) RCTs are often based on small sample sizes. In addition, the problem of information overload is even greater in medicine than in the social sciences; over a million medical research studies are published every year. No practitioner can possibly keep up with the medical literature in his or her area.

The leader in introducing meta-analysis to medical research was Thomas Chalmers. In addition to being a researcher, Chalmers was also a practicing internist who became frustrated with the inability of the vast, scattered, and unfocused medical research literature to provide guidance to practitioners. Starting in the mid-1970s, Chalmers developed his initial meta-analysis methods independently of those developed in the social and behavioral sciences. Despite being well conducted, his initial meta-analyses were not well accepted by medical researchers, who were critical of the concept of meta-analysis. In response, he and his associates developed "sequential meta-analysis"—a technique that reveals the date by which enough information had become available to show conclusively that a treatment was effective. Suppose, for example, that the first RCT for a particular drug had been conducted in 1975 but had a wide confidence interval, one that spanned zero effect. Now, suppose three more studies had been conducted in 1976, providing a total of four studies to be meta-analyzed—and the confidence interval for the meta-analytic mean of these studies was still wide and still included 0. Now, suppose five more RCTs had been conducted in 1977, providing nine studies for a meta-analysis up to this date. Now, if that meta-analysis yielded a confidence interval that excluded 0, then we conclude that, given the use of meta-analysis, enough information was already available in 1977 to begin using this drug. Chalmers and his associates then computed, based on the meta-analysis finding and statistics on the disease, how many lives would have been saved to date had use of the drug begun in 1977. It turned out that, considered across different treatments, diseases, and areas of medical practice, a very large number of lives would have been saved had medical research historically relied on meta-analysis. The resulting article (Antman, Lau, Kupelnick, Mosteller, & Chalmers, 1992) is widely considered the most important and influential meta-analysis ever published in medicine. It was even reported and discussed widely in the popular press (for example, *The New York Times*, Science Section). It assured a major role for meta-analysis in medical research from that point on (Hunt, 1997, Chap. 4).

Chalmers was also one of the driving forces behind the establishment of the Cochrane Collaboration, an organization that applies sequential meta-analysis in medical research in real time. This group conducts meta-analyses in a wide variety of medical research areas—and then updates each meta-analysis as new RCTs become available. That is, when a new RCT becomes available, the meta-analysis is rerun with the new RCT included. Hence, each meta-analysis is always current. The results of these updated meta-analyses are available on the Internet to researchers and medical practitioners around the world. It is likely that this effort has saved hundreds of thousands of lives by improving medical decision making. The Cochrane Collaboration Web site is www.update-software.com/ccweb/cochrane/general.htm.

Impact in Other Disciplines

Meta-analysis has also become important in research in finance, marketing, sociology, and even wildlife management. In fact, it would probably be difficult to find a research area in which meta-analysis is unknown today. In the broad areas of education and social policy, the Campbell Collaboration is attempting to do for the social sciences what the Cochrane Collaboration (on which it is modeled) has done for medical practice (Rothstein, 2003; Rothstein, McDaniel, & Borenstein, 2001). Among the social sciences, perhaps the last to assign an important role to meta-analysis has been economics. However, meta-analysis has recently become important in economics, too (see, e.g., Stanley, 1998, 2001; Stanley & Jarrell, 1989, 1998). There is even a doctoral program in meta-analysis in economics (http://www.feweb.vu.nl/re/Master-Point/). Meta-analysis is also beginning to be used in political science (see, e.g., Pinello, 1999).

Meta-Analysis and Social Policy

By providing the best available empirically based answers to socially important questions, meta-analysis can influence public policy making (Hoffert, 1997; Hunter & Schmidt, 1996). This can be true for any public policy question for which there is a relevant research literature—which today includes virtually all policy questions. Examples range from the Head Start program to binary chemical weapons (Hunt, 1997, Chap. 6). The purpose of the recently established Campbell Collaboration, described previously, is specifically to provide policy-relevant information to policymakers in governments and other organizations by applying meta-analysis to policy-relevant research literatures. For over 20 years, the U.S. General Accounting Office (GAO), a research and evaluation arm of the U.S. Congress, has used meta-analysis to provide answers to questions posed by senators and representatives. For example, Hunt (1997, Chap. 6) described how a GAO meta-analysis of the effects of the Women, Infants, and Children (WIC) program, a federal nutritional program for poor pregnant women, apparently changed the mind of Senator Jesse Helms and made him a (reluctant) supporter of the program. The meta-analysis found evidence that the program reduced the frequency of low-birth-weight babies by about 10%.

This meta-analysis was presented to Senator Helms by Eleanor Chelimsky, for years the director of the GAO's Division of Program Evaluation and Methodology. In that position, she pioneered the use of meta-analysis at GAO. Chelimsky (1994) stated that meta-analysis has proven to be an excellent way to provide Congress with the widest variety of research results that can hold up under close scrutiny under the time pressures imposed by Congress. She stated that GAO has found that meta-analysis reveals both what is known and what is not known in a given topic area and distinguishes between fact and opinion "without being confrontational." One application she cited as an example was a meta-analysis of studies on the merits of producing binary chemical weapons (nerve gas in which the two key ingredients are kept separate for safety until the gas is to be used). The meta-analysis did not support the production of such weapons. This was not what the Department of Defense (DOD) wanted to hear, and DOD disputed the methodology and the results. The methodology held up under close scrutiny, however, and in the end Congress eliminated funds for these weapons.

By law, it is the responsibility of GAO to provide policy-relevant research information to Congress. So the adoption of meta-analysis by GAO is a clear example of the impact that meta-analysis can have on public policy. Although most policy decisions probably depend as much on political as on scientific considerations, it is possible for scientific considerations to have an impact with the aid of meta-analysis (Hoffert, 1997).

Meta-Analysis and Theories of Data

Every method of meta-analysis is of necessity based on a theory of data. It is this theory (or understanding) of data that determines the nature of the resulting meta-analysis methods. A complete theory of data includes an understanding of sampling error, measurement error, biased sampling (range restriction and range enhancement), dichotomization and its effects, data errors, and other causal factors that distort the raw data we see in research studies. Once a theoretical understanding of how these factors affect data is developed, it becomes possible to develop methods for correcting for their effects. In the language of psychometrics, the first process—the process by which these factors (artifacts) bias data—is modeled as the attenuation model. The second process—the process of correcting for these artifact-induced biases—is called the disattenuation model. If the theory of data on which a method of meta-analysis model is based is incomplete, that method will fail to correct for some or all of these artifacts and will thus produce biased results. For example, a theory of data that fails to recognize measurement error will lead to methods of meta-analysis that do not correct for measurement error. Such methods will then perforce produce biased meta-analysis results. Some current methods of meta-analysis do not, in fact, correct for measurement error (see Chapter 11).

Sampling error and measurement error have a unique status among the statistical and measurement artifacts with which meta-analysis must deal: They are always present in all real data. Other artifacts, such as range restriction, artificial dichotomization of continuous variables, or data transcription errors, may be absent in a particular set of studies being subjected to meta-analysis. There is always sampling error, however, because sample sizes are never infinite. Likewise, there is always measurement error, because there are no perfectly reliable measures. In fact, as we will see in subsequent chapters, it is the requirement of dealing simultaneously with both sampling error and measurement error that makes even relatively simple meta-analyses seem complicated. We are used to dealing with these two types of error separately. For example, when psychometric texts (e.g., Lord & Novick, 1968; Nunnally & Bernstein, 1994) discuss measurement error, they assume an infinite (or very large) sample size, so that the focus of attention can be on measurement error alone, with no need to deal simultaneously with sampling error. Similarly, when statistics texts discuss sampling error, they implicitly assume perfect reliability (the absence of measurement error), so that they and the reader can focus solely on sampling error. Both assumptions are highly unrealistic because all real data simultaneously contain both types of error. It is admittedly more complicated to deal with both types of error simultaneously, yet this is what meta-analysis must do to be successful (see, e.g., Cook et al., 1992, pp. 315–316, 325–328).

The question of what theory of data underlies a method of meta-analysis is strongly related to the question of what the general purpose of meta-analysis is. Glass (1976, 1977) stated that the purpose is simply to summarize and describe the studies in a research literature. As we will see in this book, our view (the alternative view) is that the purpose is to estimate as accurately as possible the construct-level relationships in the population (i.e., to estimate population values or parameters), because these are the relationships of scientific interest. This is an entirely different task; this is the task of estimating what the findings would have been if all studies had been conducted perfectly (i.e., with no methodological limitations). Doing this requires correction for sampling error, measurement error, and other artifacts (if present) that distort study results. Simply describing the contents of studies in the literature requires no such corrections but does not allow estimation of the parameters of scientific interest.

Rubin (1990) critiqued the common, descriptive concept of the purpose of meta-analysis and proposed the alternative offered in this book. He stated that, as scientists, we are not really interested in the population of imperfect studies per se, and hence an accurate description or summary of these studies is not really important. Instead, he argued that the goal of meta-analysis should be to estimate the true effects or relationships—defined as "results that would be obtained in an infinitely large, perfectly designed study or sequence of such studies." According to Rubin,

> Under this view, we really do not care *scientifically* about summarizing this finite population (of observed studies). We really care about the underlying scientific process—the underlying process that is generating these outcomes that we happen to see—that we, as fallible researchers, are trying to glimpse through the opaque window of imperfect empirical studies. (p. 157; emphasis in original)

This is an excellent summary of the purpose of meta-analysis as we see it and as embodied in the methods presented in this book.

Conclusions

Until recently, psychological research literatures were conflicting and contradictory. As the number of studies on each particular question became larger and larger, this situation became increasingly frustrating and intolerable. This situation stemmed from reliance on defective procedures for achieving cumulative knowledge: the statistical significance test in individual primary studies in combination with the narrative subjective review of research literatures. Meta-analysis principles have now correctly diagnosed this problem and have provided the solution. In area after area, meta-analytic findings have shown that there is much less conflict between studies than had been believed; that coherent, useful, and generalizable conclusions can be drawn from research literatures; and that cumulative knowledge is possible in psychology and the social sciences. These methods have also been adopted in other areas such as medical research. A prominent medical researcher, Thomas Chalmers (as cited in Mann, 1990), has stated, "[Meta-analysis] is going to revolutionize how the sciences, especially medicine, handle data. And it is going to be the way many arguments will be ended" (p. 478). In concluding his oft-cited review of meta-analysis methods, Bangert-Drowns (1986, p. 398) stated:

> Meta-analysis is not a fad. It is rooted in the fundamental values of the scientific enterprise: replicability, quantification, causal and correlational analysis. Valuable information is needlessly scattered in individual studies. The ability of social scientists to deliver generalizable answers to basic questions of policy is too serious a concern to allow us to treat research integration lightly. The potential benefits of meta-analysis method seem enormous.

2

Study Artifacts and Their Impact on Study Outcomes

The goal of a meta-analysis of correlations is a description of the distribution of actual (i.e., construct level) correlations between a given independent and a given dependent variable. If all studies were conducted perfectly, then the distribution of study correlations could be used directly to estimate the distribution of actual correlations. However, studies are never perfect. As a result, the relationship between study correlations and actual correlations is more complicated.

There are many dimensions along which studies fail to be perfect. Thus, there are many forms of error in study results. Each form of error has some impact on the results of a meta-analysis. Some errors can be corrected and some cannot. We refer to study imperfections as "artifacts" to remind ourselves that errors in study results produced by study imperfections are artifactual or man-made errors and not properties of nature. In later chapters, we present formulas that correct for as many artifacts as possible. Correction of artifacts requires auxiliary information such as study sample sizes, study means and standard deviations, estimates of reliability, and so on.

The complexity of formulas depends on two things: (1) the extent of variation in artifacts and (2) the extent of variation in actual correlations. Formulas for meta-analysis would be simplest if artifacts were homogeneous across studies, that is, if all studies had the same sample size, all had the same reliability for the independent and dependent variables, all had the same standard deviations, and so forth. If artifacts were homogeneous, then the primary calculations would all be simple averages and simple variances. In actuality, artifacts vary from study to study; hence, more complicated weighted averages are necessary.

If there is nonartifactual variation in actual construct-level correlations, that variation must be caused by some aspect of the studies that varies from one study to the next, that is, a "moderator" variable. If the meta-analyst anticipates variation in actual correlations, then studies will be coded for aspects that are thought to be potential moderators. For example, studies can be coded as based on white-collar or blue-collar workers. If the variation in actual correlations is large, then the key question is this: Is the moderator variable one of those we have identified as potential moderators? If we find that some coded study characteristics are large moderators, then the overall meta-analysis is not particularly important. The key meta-analyses will be those carried out on the moderator study subsets where the variation in actual correlations is much smaller in magnitude (and perhaps 0).

Study Artifacts

We have identified 11 artifacts that alter the size of the study correlation in comparison to the actual correlation. These artifacts are listed in Table 2.1 along with typical substantive examples from the personnel selection research literature. The most damaging artifact in narrative reviews has been sampling error. Sampling error has been falsely interpreted as conflicting findings in almost every area of research in the social sciences. However, some of the other artifacts induce quantitative errors so large as to create qualitatively false conclusions (Hunter & Schmidt, 1987a, 1987b) or to greatly alter the practical implications of findings (Schmidt, 1992, 1996; Schmidt & Hunter, 1977, 1981). This is especially important to consider when several artifacts work in conjunction.

Sampling Error

Sampling error affects the correlation coefficient additively and nonsystematically. If the actual correlation is denoted ρ and the sample correlation r, then sampling error is added to the sample correlation in the formula

$$r = \rho + e \tag{2.1}$$

The size of the sampling error is primarily determined by the sample size. Because the effect is unsystematic, the sampling error in a single correlation cannot be corrected. Sampling error and the corrections for it in meta-analysis are discussed in detail in Chapters 3 and 4 (for correlations) and in Chapters 6 and 7 (for d values).

Error of Measurement

Note that the distinction between artifacts 2 and 3 versus artifacts 8 and 9 in Table 2.1 represents the distinction between simple or unsystematic error of measurement and systematic error (or departures from perfect construct validity). Simple error of measurement is the random measurement error assessed as unreliability of the measure. Error of measurement has a systematic multiplicative effect on the correlation. If we denote the actual correlation by ρ and the observed correlation by ρ_o, then

$$\rho_o = a\rho \tag{2.2}$$

Table 2.1 Study artifacts that alter the value of outcome measures (with examples from personnel selection research)

1. Sampling error:
   Study validity will vary randomly from the population value because of sampling error.
2. Error of measurement in the dependent variable:
   Study validity will be systematically lower than true validity to the extent that job performance is measured with random error.
3. Error of measurement in the independent variable:
   Study validity for a test will systematically understate the validity of the ability measured because the test is not perfectly reliable.
4. Dichotomization of a continuous dependent variable:
   Turnover, the length of time that a worker stays with the organization, is often dichotomized into "more than . . ." or "less than . . ." where . . . is some arbitrarily chosen interval such as one year or six months.
5. Dichotomization of a continuous independent variable:
   Interviewers are often told to dichotomize their perceptions into "acceptable" versus "reject."
6. Range variation in the independent variable:
   Study validity will be systematically lower than true validity to the extent that hiring policy causes incumbents to have a lower variation in the predictor than is true of applicants.
7. Attrition artifacts: Range variation in the dependent variable:
   Study validity will be systematically lower than true validity to the extent that there is systematic attrition in workers on performance, as when good workers are promoted out of the population or when poor workers are fired for poor performance.
8. Deviation from perfect construct validity in the independent variable:
   Study validity will vary if the factor structure of the test differs from the usual structure of tests for the same trait.
9. Deviation from perfect construct validity in the dependent variable:
   Study validity will differ from true validity if the criterion is deficient or contaminated.
10. Reporting or transcriptional error:
    Reported study validities differ from actual study validities due to a variety of reporting problems: inaccuracy in coding data, computational errors, errors in reading computer output, typographical errors by secretaries or by printers. Note: These errors can be very large in magnitude.
11. Variance due to extraneous factors that affect the relationship:
    Study validity will be systematically lower than true validity if incumbents differ in job experience at the time their performance is measured (because job experience affects job performance).

where a is the square root of the reliability. Because a is a number less than 1 in magnitude, the size of the correlation is systematically reduced by error of measurement. For a fairly high reliability such as $r_{xx} = .81$ (a typical reliability of a test of general cognitive ability), the correlation is multiplied by $\sqrt{.81}$ or .90, that is, reduced by 10%. For a low reliability of .36 (the average reliability of a supervisor global rating of job performance on a one-item rating scale), the correlation is multiplied by $\sqrt{.36}$ or .60, a reduction of 40%.

There is a separate effect for error of measurement in the independent variable and error of measurement in the dependent variable. Thus, for error in both variables—the usual case—we have

$$\rho_o = ab\rho \qquad (2.3)$$

where a is the square root of the reliability of the independent variable and b is the square root of the reliability of the dependent variable. For a test of general cognitive ability predicting the immediate supervisor's rating on a single global item, the correlation would be multiplied by (.90) (.60) = .54. That is nearly a 50% reduction.

Dichotomization

Despite its considerable disadvantages, dichotomization of continuous variables is quite common in the literature (MacCallum, Zhang, Preacher, & Rucker, 2002). If a continuous variable is dichotomized, then the point biserial correlation for the new dichotomized variable will be less than the correlation for the continuous variable. If the regression is bivariate normal, the effect of dichotomizing one of the variables is given by

$$\rho_o = a\rho$$

where a depends on the extremeness of the split induced by the dichotomization. Let P be the proportion in the "high" end of the split and let $Q = 1 - P$ be the proportion in the "low" end of the split. Let c be the point in the normal distribution that divides the distribution into proportions P and Q. For example, $c = -1.28$ divides the distribution into the bottom 10% versus the top 90%. Let the normal ordinate at c be denoted $\phi(c)$. Then

$$a = \phi(c)/\sqrt{PQ} \qquad (2.4)$$

The smallest reduction in the correlation occurs for a median, or 50–50, split, where $a = .80$, a 20% reduction in the correlation.

If both variables are dichotomized, there is a double reduction in the correlation. The exact formula is more complicated than just the product of an "a" for the independent variable and a "b" for the dependent variable. The exact formula is that for the tetrachoric correlation. However, Hunter and Schmidt (1990b) showed that the double product is a very close approximation under the conditions holding in most current meta-analyses. Thus, the attenuation produced by double dichotomization is given by

$$\rho_o = ab\rho$$

If both variables are split 50–50, the correlation is attenuated by approximately

$$\rho_o = (.80)(.80)\rho = .64\rho$$

that is, by 36%. For splits more extreme than 50–50, there is even greater attenuation. If one variable has a 90–10 split and the other variable has a 10–90 split, then the double-product estimate of attenuation is

$$\rho_o = (.59)(.59)\rho = .35\rho$$

That is, there is a 65% reduction in the correlation. If the actual correlation is greater than $\rho = .30$, then the reduction is even greater than that predicted by the double-product formula (Hunter & Schmidt, 1990b).

Range Variation in the Independent Variable

Because the correlation is a standardized slope, its size depends on the extent of variation in the independent variable. At one extreme, in a population in which there is perfect homogeneity (no variance) in the independent variable, the correlation with any dependent variable will be 0. At the other extreme, if we fix the amount of error about the regression line and then consider populations in which the variance of the independent variable progressively increases, the population correlations increase eventually to an upper limit of 1.00. If correlations from different studies are to be compared, then differences in the correlations due to differences in spread (variance) in the independent variable must be controlled. This is the problem of range variation in the independent variable.

The solution to range variation is to define a reference population and express all correlations in terms of that reference population. We will now discuss how this is done when range restriction (or range enhancement) is produced by direct truncation on the independent variable measure (direct range restriction). For example, suppose only the top 30% on an employment test are hired (range restriction). Or suppose a researcher includes only the top and bottom 10% of subjects on an attitude measure (range enhancement). (We will discuss *indirect* range restriction later.) If the regression of the dependent variable onto the independent variable is linear and homoscedastic (bivariate normality is a special case of this), and there is direct truncation on the independent variable, then there is a formula (presented in Chapter 3) that computes what the correlation in a given population would be if the standard deviation were the same as in the reference population. This same formula can be used in reverse to compute the effect of studying the correlation in a population with a standard deviation different from that of the reference population. The standard deviations can be compared by computing the ratio of standard deviations in the two groups. Let u_X be the ratio of the study population standard deviation divided by the reference group population. That is, $u_X = SD_{\text{study}}/SD_{\text{ref}}$. Then the study population correlation is related to the reference group population by

$$\rho_o = a\rho$$

where

$$a = u_X/[(u_X^2 - 1)\rho^2 + 1]^{1/2} \tag{2.5}$$

This expression for the multiplier contains the actual correlation ρ in the formula. In practice, it is the attenuated correlation ρ_o that is observed. A useful algebraic identity in terms of ρ_o was derived by Callender and Osburn (1980):

$$a = [u_X^2 + \rho_o^2(1 - u_X^2)]^{1/2} \tag{2.6}$$

The multiplier a will be greater than 1.00 if the study standard deviation is larger than the reference standard deviation. The multiplier a will be less than 1.00 if the study standard deviation is smaller than the reference standard deviation.

There are two cases in which range variation produced by direct selection appears in the empirical literature: (1) scientifically produced artificial variation and (2) variation that arises from situation constraints. Scientific variation can be produced by manipulation of the data. The most frequent of these infrequent cases are those in which the scientist creates an artificially high variation by deliberately excluding middle cases (Osburn, 1978). For example, a psychologist studying anxiety might use an anxiety inventory test to preselect as "High" or "Low" those in the top 10% and bottom 10%, respectively. The correlation between anxiety and the dependent variable calculated in this selected group will be larger than the correlation in the original (reference) population. The increase in the correlation would be determined by the increase in the standard deviation of the independent variable. If the original population standard deviation were 1.00, then the standard deviation in a group composed of the top and bottom 10% would be 1.80. For this artificially inflated range variation, the multiplier would be

$$a = 1.80/[(1.80^2 - 1)\rho^2 + 1]^{1/2}$$
$$= 1.80/[1 + 3.24\rho^2]^{1/2}$$

For example, if the reference correlation were .30, the multiplier would be 1.58 and the study correlation would be .48, a 58% increase in the correlation. In a small-sample study, this increase in the study correlation would greatly increase the statistical power and, hence, make the significance test work much better. That is, the significance test would have higher statistical power to detect the correlation (Osburn, 1978).

In field studies, the range variation is usually range restriction. For example, suppose a football team measures the speed of applicants running the 40-yard dash. If only those in the top half were selected, then the standard deviation among those considered would be only 60% as large as the standard deviation among all applicants. The applicant correlation between speed and overall performance would be reduced by the multiplier

$$a = .60/[(.60^2 - 1)\rho^2 + 1]^{1/2}$$
$$= .60/[1 - .64\rho^2]^{1/2}$$

If the correlation were $\rho = .50$ for applicants, the multiplier would be .65, and the correlation among those selected would be reduced to

$$\rho_o = a\rho = .65(.50) = .33$$

a 34% reduction in the correlation.

In addition to the direct range restriction or enhancement discussed here, range restriction can also be indirect. For example, suppose subjects who volunteer (sign up) to participate in a study are self-selected—for example, they are mostly on the high end of the extroversion distribution. Their standard deviation (SD) on an extroversion measure is lower than that of the general population. This is indirect range restriction. Suppose we know that people in a certain job were not hired using the test we are studying but we have no record of how they were hired. Yet we find that their *SD* on the test we are studying is smaller than the *SD* for the applicant population, indicating the presence of range restriction. Again, this is a case of indirect range restriction. In indirect range restriction, people are not selected directly based on scores on the independent variable but on other variables that are correlated with the independent variable. Occasionally, we know or can find the scores on the related variables they were selected on—but this is rare. As in the preceding examples, we typically do not know how the range restriction was produced—but we know that it occurred because the sample *SD* is smaller than the population *SD*. Most range restriction in real data is, in fact, of this sort (Hunter, Schmidt, & Le, 2002; Linn, Harnisch, & Dunbar, 1981b; Mendoza & Mumford, 1987).

Indirect range restriction of this sort reduces correlations more than direct range restriction (Hunter et al., 2002; Mendoza & Mumford, 1987). To determine how large this reduction is, we can still use the formula for the attenuation factor "*a*," given previously, but we now have to use a different ratio of *SD*s. Instead of the ratio of observed *SD*s (called u_X), we must use the ratio of true score *SD*s (called u_T). This ratio must be computed using a special formula. This ratio is also used in the formula for correcting for indirect range restriction. Both direct and indirect range restriction and their associated formulas are discussed in Chapters 3 to 5. Formulas for correcting for this type of indirect range restriction have been developed only recently and were not included in the 1990 edition of this book. Mendoza and Mumford (1987) were the first to derive formulas for correcting for this (ubiquitous) form of indirect range restriction. Developments relating these corrections to meta-analysis were presented by Hunter et al. (2002). The availability of these formulas greatly increases the accuracy of meta-analyses involving range restriction.

Attrition Artifacts: Range Variation on the Dependent Variable

Range variation on the dependent variable is usually produced by attrition artifacts. For example, in personnel selection the study correlation is computed on current workers (i.e., incumbents) because data on job performance is available only on those hired. However, workers with poor performance are often fired or quit voluntarily. Those who participate in the study will be only those still on the job. This population will differ from applicants because of that attrition.

There is one special case of attrition artifacts that can be eliminated with statistical formulas: the case in which there is no range restriction on the independent variable. If there is selection on the dependent variable, this will cause induced selection on any independent variable correlated with it. Assume that there is no selection other than this form of induced selection. In such a case, attrition artifacts can be treated statistically as range variation on the dependent variable. Statistically, the independent and dependent variables are symmetrically related to the correlation coefficient. The special case of attrition artifacts described previously exactly reverses this symmetry. Thus, the formulas are the same, except that the standard deviation ratio u is defined by the dependent variable rather than by the independent variable (i.e., it becomes u_Y instead of u_X). In such a case, range restriction on the dependent variable may be either direct or indirect. If it is direct, the correction formulas for direct range restriction should be used. If indirect, the correction formulas for indirect range restriction should be used.

In personnel selection, most studies are affected by both range restriction on the independent variable and by attrition artifacts on the dependent variable (in addition to terminating poor performers, employers also promote good performers). However, at present, there are no exact statistical methods for simultaneously correcting for both range restriction and attrition artifacts, even in the case of direct range restriction. The underlying mathematical problem is that selection on one variable changes the regression for the other variable in a complex way so that the regression is no longer linear and homoscedastic. For example, when there is selection on the predictor, the (reverse) regression of the predictor onto job performance is no longer linear and homoscedastic.

However, Alexander, Carson, Alliger, and Carr (1987) proposed an approximation method for making such a "double" correction for range restriction. These authors noted that after one has selected directly on the independent variable, the regression of the independent variable onto the dependent variable (the "reverse regression") is no longer linear and homoscedastic. Thus, the slope of that regression line will not remain the same when direct restriction is introduced on the dependent variable. They conjectured, however, that it might not change much. The same is true for homoscedasticity: The conditional variance will not remain exactly the same after the second truncation, but perhaps it does not change by much. If both changes are small, then the assumption of no change would yield an approximation equation for correction of range restriction, which might be accurate enough for practical purposes. They derived their equation for a special case of double range restriction: double truncation. That is, they assumed that the range restriction is direct on both variables and is caused by a double threshold: Any data point is lost if the independent variable is less than an x cutoff value or if the dependent variable is less than a y cutoff value. Thus, in the study population—what they call the "doubly truncated population"—the only people remaining are those for whom both variables are above the respective thresholds. In the case of personnel selection, this would correspond to a situation in which hiring was done using only the test and using it with a fixed threshold, and where termination from the job was based on a specific fixed performance-level threshold. There is probably no actual selection situation that fits the double-truncation model, but it is a good mathematical beginning point. Alexander et al. (1987) tested their correction approximation for various double-truncation combinations. They varied each cutoff value independently from -2.0 standard deviations below the mean (which eliminates only the bottom 2.5% of cases) to $+2.0$ standard deviations (where 97.5% of cases are eliminated). They varied the untruncated population correlation from $-.90$ to $+.90$. The accuracy of this method is quite good: 84% of their estimated values are within 3% of the correct value. The worst fit is for the population correlation of .50. For that value, the corrected correlations are as much as 6% too high in 8.6% of the combinations. The combinations where the fit is poorer are the combinations where there is high selection on both variables and where the two cutoff scores are about equal. This would be predicted by the fact that the formula works perfectly for direct range restriction on one variable only. The cases showing the greatest inaccuracy may not be very realistic. If the cutoff is 1.0 standard deviation above the mean for both variables, then the truncated population usually represents little more than 3% of the untruncated population. Elimination of 97% of the original population would probably rarely occur in real data.

The findings for absolute accuracy are even more promising. Alexander et al. (1987) found that 90% of corrected correlations differ by no more than .02 from the actual correlation. In fact, if the corrected correlation is rounded to two places, the estimated corrected correlation is within .02 in 94% of cases. In no case was their formula off by more than .03. The poorest fit is for a population correlation of .60 where 17% of cases were off by .03. The cases of poor absolute fit were essentially the same as the cases with poor percentage fit: the cases of equally severe selection on both variables. The method of Alexander et al. is certainly accurate enough for practical purposes. The obvious next question is: Does the formula remain accurate for the more common and therefore more realistic case of indirect selection? Our calculations indicate that the formula is even more accurate in that case. The contribution of Alexander et al. appears to be a major breakthrough in this area.

Imperfect Construct Validity in the Independent Variable

This section is considerably longer than the other sections on study artifacts. In our judgment, however, this is unavoidable because it is essential to develop an understanding of how study outcomes are distorted by departures from perfect construct validity. This section and the following section are of necessity based on path analysis. We have tried to make the discussion as simple as possible, and we believe most readers will be able to follow it. Readers who have difficulty may want to skip ahead to the section titled "Computational and Other Errors in the Data." However, we hope that such readers will return to these sections later when they no longer seem so difficult.

The independent variable used in a given study may suffer from either of two kinds of error of measurement: random error or systematic error. The effect of random error was discussed under the label "error of measurement." The extent to which a measure is free of random error is measured by the coefficient of reliability of that measure. This section will treat systematic error under the label "imperfect construct validity." The phrase "construct invalidity" would also be correct grammatically, but there are many who would react to the word "invalidity" in an absolute sense. That is, some would react to the word "invalidity" as if it meant "completely invalid" and would disregard the study. Actually, it is infrequent that a study independent variable is so construct invalid that the study should be disregarded. Instead, imperfect construct validity may be dealt with adequately in any of three ways: (1) by using a statistical correction formula, (2) by treating variations in measurement strategy as a potential moderator variable, or (3) (for minor departures from perfect validity) by ignoring the imperfection. If the imperfection is ignored, then the study correlation is attenuated by an amount proportional to the quantitative departure from perfect construct validity. If there is variation across studies in the extent of construct validity and it is ignored, that variation contributes to uncontrolled artifact variation in the residual variance computed as the final step in meta-analysis. That is, ignored variation in construct validity would have the same appearance as a real moderator variable.

Construct validity is a quantitative question, not a qualitative distinction such as "valid" or "invalid"; it is a matter of degree. In most cases, construct validity can be quantified as a correlation coefficient, namely, the correlation between the variable intended and the variable as measured. We will define the construct validity of the independent variable measure as the correlation between the intended independent variable and the actual independent variable used in the study when both variables are measured without random error (measurement error). This definition is used to distinguish between the effects of random and systematic error. The error in the actual study used will be assessed by a correlation called the "operational quality" of the measure. The operational quality is determined in part by the extent of construct validity and in part by the reliability of the study variable.

The effect of systematic error on the correlation between independent and dependent variables depends not only on the extent of construct validity of the study independent variable, but on the qualitative structure of the causal relationships among the three variables: the intended or desired independent variable, the study independent variable, and the dependent variable. In certain cases, the effect of systematic error is simple: The correlation between independent and dependent variable is multiplied by the construct validity of the study independent variable. However, there are cases where this simple relationship does not hold. In such cases, the meta-analyst may not be able to use the study.

Consider an example in which we want to examine the relationship between general cognitive ability and performance in recreational activities. Because performance in recreational activities depends on learning, we hypothesize that people with high cognitive ability will perform better than average. We find a survey study of a large bowling league in which one of the variables is the bowling performance average. The study has no measure of general cognitive ability, but it does have a measure of amount of education. Suppose we use the education variable as an imperfect indicator for cognitive ability. In the language of econometrics, we use education as a "proxy variable" for ability. How good a proxy is amount of education for cognitive ability? One answer would be the correlation between education and ability. However, there are two other considerations that enter into this decision. First, there is the question of which correlation to use: the correlation between ability and actual education or the correlation between ability and the study measure of education. This is the issue of distinguishing between construct validity and reliability. Second, there is the issue of the relationship between the proxy variable and the dependent variable. For certain kinds of relationships, the effect of using a proxy variable is easily quantified and can be computed from the coefficient of construct validity. For other relationships, the effect may be much more complicated. In such complicated cases, use of the proxy variable may be problematic.

Figure 2.1 Path model showing the causal nature of imperfect construct validity in using education as a proxy variable for general cognitive ability

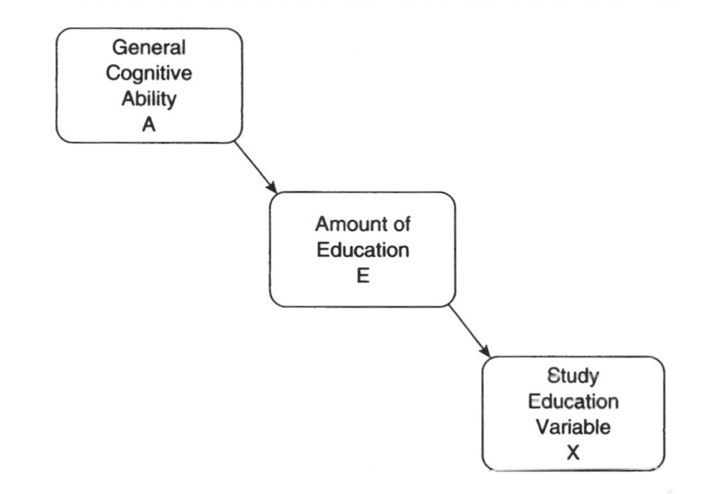

To show the distinction between systematic and random error of measurement, suppose the study does not have a perfect measure of education. Although we would like a measure of the exact amount of education, the study recorded only the measure

$X = 0$ if the person did not finish high school,
$X = 1$ if the person finished high school but not college,
$X = 2$ if the person finished college.

There are, then, two kinds of error in the study variable. There is the systematic error produced by using education instead of ability and there is the random error produced by using an imperfect measure of education. This situation is illustrated in the path diagram in Figure 2.1.

In Figure 2.1, general cognitive ability is the independent variable that we wanted to measure. Thus, the ability variable in the path diagram is implicitly assumed to be perfectly measured. Figure 2.1 shows an arrow from general cognitive ability to amount of education where amount of education is assumed to be perfectly measured. This represents the assumption that ability is one of the causal determinants of amount of education. If ability were the sole cause of differences in the amount of education, then ability and education would be perfectly correlated and there would be no problem in using education as a proxy for ability. In fact, the correlation between ability and education is only about .50, and there is thus a considerable discrepancy between the two measures. The size of the correlation between ability and education determines the size of the path coefficient from ability to education and, hence, measures the extent of systematic error in substituting education for ability. The correlation between ability and education where both are perfectly measured is the construct validity of education as a measure of ability. The construct validity of education as a measure of ability is the first path coefficient in Figure 2.1.

Figure 2.1 also shows an arrow from amount of education to the study education variable X. Qualitatively, this arrow represents the introduction of random error into the measure of education. Quantitatively, the path coefficient measures the amount of random error. The path coefficient for this arrow is the correlation between actual amount of education and the study education measure. This correlation is less than 1.00 to the extent that the study measurement procedure introduces random error into the estimate of education. The square of the correlation between actual and estimated education is the reliability of the study measure of education.

The total discrepancy between the intended independent variable of ability and the study measure of education is measured by the correlation between the two. According to path analysis, the correlation between ability and the study measure of education is the product of the two path coefficients. That is,

$$r_{AX} = r_{AE}\, r_{EX} \tag{2.7}$$

Let us define the phrase "the operational quality of the proxy variable" to be the correlation between the intended variable and the study proxy variable. Then we have shown that the operational quality is the product of two numbers: the construct validity of the proxy variable, r_{AE}, and the square root of the reliability of the proxy variable, $r_{EX} = \sqrt{r_{XX}}$.

The key semantic issue in the definition of the phrase "construct validity" is to choose between two correlations: the correlation between the intended variable and the proxy variable as perfectly measured, or the correlation between the intended variable and the study variable as measured with random error. The substantial and conceptual meaning of the phrase "construct validity" is represented by the correlation between intended and proxy variables measured without random error. Thus, we label that correlation as "construct validity." On the other hand, the total impact of substitution depends also on the amount of random error in the study variable, and, hence, we need a name for that correlation as well. The name used here is "operational quality." We can thus say that the operational quality of the study proxy variable depends on the construct validity of the proxy variable and the reliability of the study measure. In a simple case such as that of Figure 2.1, the operational quality is the product of the construct validity and the square root of the reliability of the proxy measure.

We can now consider the main question: What is the effect of systematic error in the measure of cognitive ability on the observed correlation between ability and performance? This is answered by comparing two population correlations: the desired correlation between cognitive ability and performance versus the correlation between the study measure of education and performance. To answer this question, we must know the causal relationship among education, ability, and performance. Consider the causal model shown in Figure 2.2.

Figure 2.2 shows an arrow from cognitive ability to bowling performance. This arrow represents the hypothesized effect of differences in learning ability on differences in performance. Figure 2.2 shows no causal arrow from education to performance. This corresponds to the assumption that the material learned in

Figure 2.2 Path model showing the assumed causal structure of ability, education, and performance

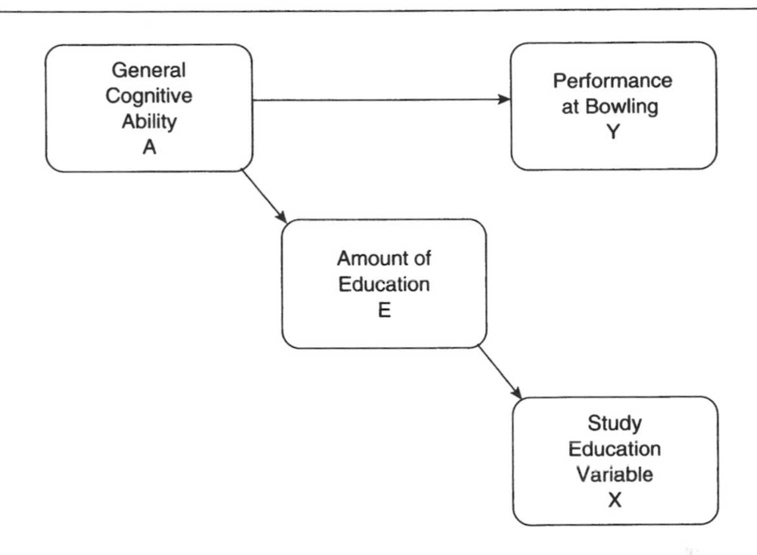

mastery of bowling does not depend on the specific material learned in school. Thus, among people matched on cognitive ability, there would be no correlation between amount of education and performance at bowling. According to this path model, ability is a common causal antecedent to both performance and education. Therefore, the correlation between the study education variable X and the performance measure Y is the product

$$r_{XY} = r_{AE}\, r_{EX}\, r_{AY} \tag{2.8}$$

Thus, the desired population correlation r_{AY} is multiplied by two other correlations: the construct validity of education as a measure of ability, r_{AE}, and the square root of the reliability of the study education measure, r_{EX}. Denote the product of these two correlations by a. That is, define a by

$$a = r_{AE}\, r_{EX} \tag{2.9}$$

Then a is the operational quality of the study independent variable as a measure of cognitive ability. The desired population correlation r_{AY} is related to the study population r_{XY} by

$$r_{XY} = a r_{AY} \tag{2.10}$$

Because a is a fraction, this is an attenuation formula. The observed correlation is attenuated by the factor a. That is, the lower the operational quality of the study independent variable, the greater the attenuation of the study correlation between independent and dependent variables.

The total attenuation of the effect size is given by the net attenuation factor, which is the operational quality of the study independent variable. However, this net attenuation factor is itself the product of two other attenuation factors. One factor

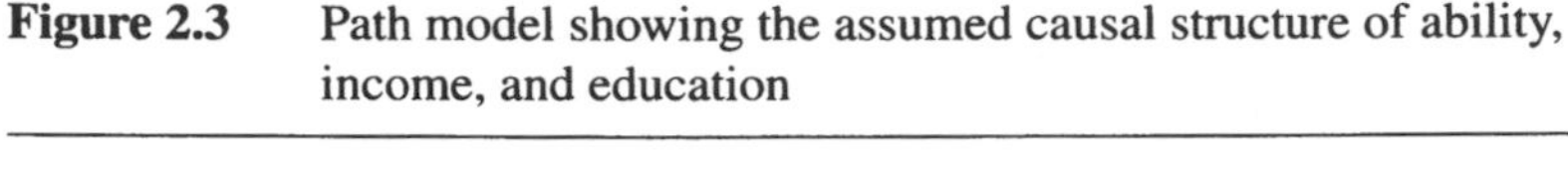

Figure 2.3 Path model showing the assumed causal structure of ability, income, and education

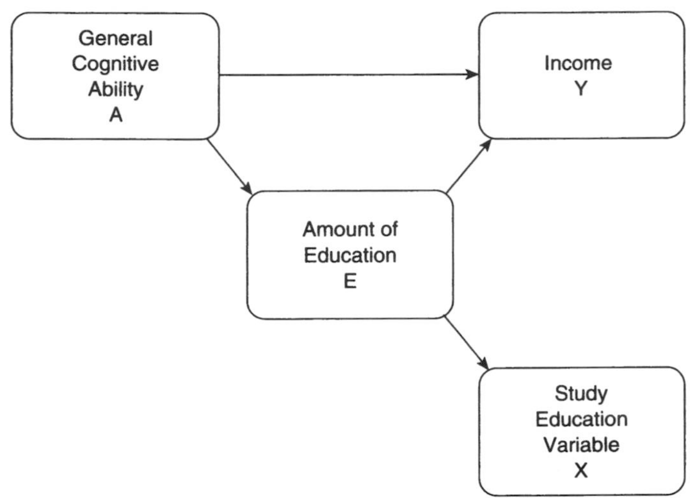

is the square root of the study variable reliability. This is the familiar attenuation factor for random error of measurement. The second factor is the construct validity of the study variable as a measure of the intended independent variable. Thus, one factor measures the effect of random error while the second factor measures the effect of systematic error.

The previous example shows that under certain conditions the effect of systematic error on the study effect size is to multiply the desired population effect size by the operational quality of the study proxy variable. A second example will show that this simple formula does not always work. Finally, we will present a third example, which shows a different causal structure for which the same simple attenuation formula can be used.

Consider now a meta-analysis on the relationship between general cognitive ability and income. Suppose the study has no measure of ability, but has the same imperfect measure of amount of education as considered in the first example. The causal structure for these variables will differ from the causal structure in Figure 2.2. The assumed causal model for ability, education, and income is shown in Figure 2.3.

Figure 2.3 shows an arrow from general cognitive ability to income. This corresponds to the fact that once people are working at the same job, differences in cognitive ability are a prime determinant of job performance and, hence, of how high the person rises in the job and of income level. However, Figure 2.3 also shows an arrow from amount of education to income. The amount of education determines what job the person starts in and, hence, sets limits on how high the person will rise. This arrow from education to income distinguishes the structure of the causal models in Figures 2.2 and 2.3. The path coefficients for the arrows to the dependent variable are no longer simple correlations but are beta weights, the multiple regression weights for cognitive ability, b_{AY}, and education, b_{EY}, in jointly predicting income. The study effect size correlation r_{XY} is given by path analysis to be

$$\begin{aligned} r_{XY} &= r_{EX}(b_{EY} + r_{AE}b_{AY}) \\ &= r_{AE}r_{EX}b_{AY} + r_{EX}b_{EY} \end{aligned} \tag{2.11}$$

By contrast, the simple education formula would have been

$$r_{XY} = r_{AE}\, r_{EX}\, r_{AY} \tag{2.12}$$

In both models, the effect of random error of measurement is the same. In both models, it is true that

$$r_{XY} = r_{EX}\, r_{EY} \tag{2.13}$$

The difference between the models lies in the structure of the correlation between education and income. If education has a causal impact on income, as in Figure 2.3, then the correlation between education and income is

$$r_{EY} = r_{AE}\, b_{AY} + b_{EY} \tag{2.14}$$

whereas in the simpler model the correlation would have been

$$r_{EY} = r_{AE}\, r_{AY} \tag{2.15}$$

The larger the causal impact of education on income, the greater the difference between the models. The most extreme case would be one in which the assumption (known to be false) is made that there is no direct causal impact of ability at all. That is, assume that the beta weight for ability is 0, that is, $b_{AY} = 0$. Then, for the complex model,

$$r_{EY} = r_{AY}/r_{AE} \tag{2.16}$$

instead of

$$r_{EY} = r_{AY}\, r_{AE} \tag{2.17}$$

That is, in this extreme case the effect of substitution would be to divide the effect size correlation by the construct validity rather than to multiply the effect size correlation by the construct validity!

The key to the product rule in the previous examples is the assumption that the only causal connection between the dependent variable and the proxy variable is the intended independent variable. In the first example, the intended independent variable (ability) is causally prior to the proxy variable, and the proxy variable has no link to the dependent variable. It is also possible to have the proxy variable be causally prior to the intended variable. However, the product rule will fail if there is any path from the proxy variable to the dependent variable that does not go through the intended variable.

Consider a third example. Suppose we hypothesize that teachers with a strong knowledge of their subject matter will do a better job of teaching due in part to having more time saved by eliminating look-up tasks, and in part to having

Figure 2.4 Path model showing the assumed causal structure of teacher's specialized knowledge, teacher's overall GPA, teacher's grade point in selected education courses, and student performance

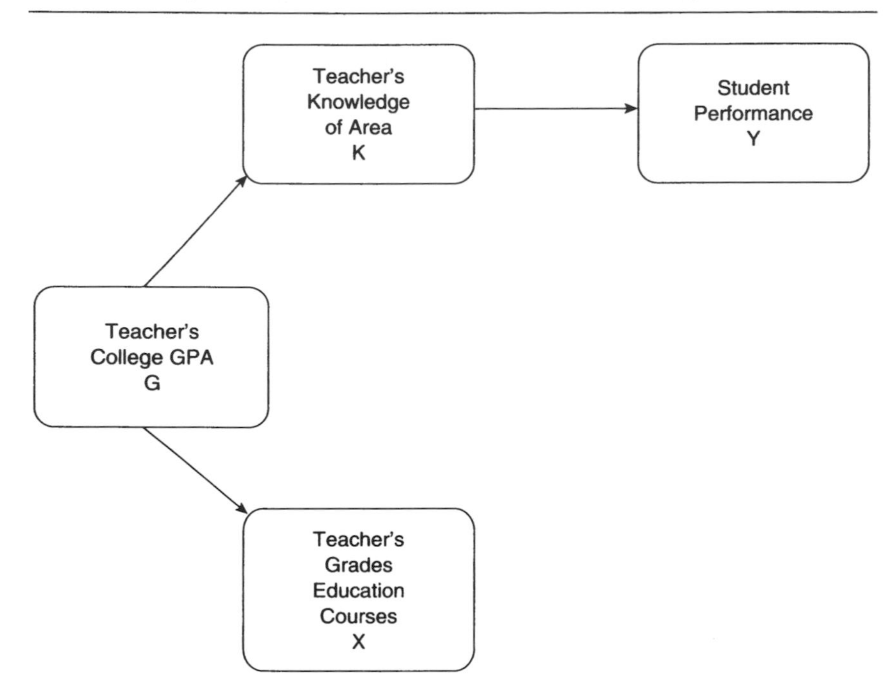

more cognitive options for presentation, and so on. A large metropolitan high school system has national test scores for students that can be averaged for each class. Thus, we have a dependent variable for student performance. However, it is impractical to construct knowledge tests for all the teaching areas. Assume that the amount learned in a specialty is primarily a function of how well the teacher learns and how much the teacher studies in general. Learning in general would be measured by college grade point average (GPA). So, instead of a specialized knowledge test, we use the teacher's college grade point average as a proxy variable for knowledge of area. The total grade point is not available, but a code for grades in key education courses is stored in the computer. The design for this construct validity problem is shown as a path diagram in Figure 2.4.

Figure 2.4 shows an arrow from teacher's GPA to teacher's knowledge of area. Thus, the proxy variable is causally prior to the intended independent variable. There is no other path from GPA to the dependent variable. The path coefficient from GPA to knowledge is the construct validity of GPA as a measure of specialized knowledge. This path coefficient measures the extent of systematic error in the GPA measure. There is an arrow from overall GPA to GPA in the key education courses. The size of this path coefficient measures the extent of random error in the study variable. The correlation between the study grade point variable X and the performance measure Y is the product

$$r_{XY} = r_{KG}\, r_{GX}\, r_{KY} \tag{2.18}$$

Thus, the desired population correlation r_{KY} is multiplied by two other population correlations: the construct validity of GPA as a measure of knowledge (r_{KG}) and the square root of the reliability of the study GPA measure (r_{GX}). Denote the product of these two correlations by a. That is, define a by

$$a = r_{KG} \, r_{GX} \tag{2.19}$$

Then a is the operational quality of the study independent variable as a measure of specialized knowledge. The desired population correlation r_{KY} is related to the study population r_{XY} by

$$r_{XY} = a \, r_{KY} \tag{2.20}$$

Because a is a fraction, this is an attenuation formula. The observed correlation is attenuated by the factor a. That is, the lower the operational quality of the study independent variable, the greater the attenuation of the study correlation between independent and dependent variable.

We can now summarize the two most common cases in which construct validity of the independent variable can be quantified and where systematic error of measurement is easily corrected. The imperfect construct validity will be correctable if the imperfect measure or proxy variable stands in one of two causal relationships to the intended independent variable and the dependent variable. Consider the path diagrams in Figure 2.5. Figure 2.5a shows the imperfect variable as causally dependent on the intended independent variable and as having no other connection to the dependent variable. Figure 2.5b shows the imperfect variable as causally antecedent to the intended independent variable and as having no other connection to the dependent variable. The key to both path diagrams is the assumption that there is no extraneous causal path from the imperfect variable to the dependent variable that does not go through the intended independent variable.

Figure 2.5a shows the case in which the intended independent variable is antecedent to the study independent variable. This case can be described by saying that the study variable is influenced by "extraneous factors."

This is the most common case for a proxy variable. For example, many employers use educational credentials as a proxy variable for general cognitive ability (Gottfredson, 1985). Although cognitive ability is an important determinant of amount of education, education is influenced by many other variables (such as family wealth) as well. The path diagram in Figure 2.5a assumes that these other influences are not correlated with the dependent variable (say job performance) and, hence, are "extraneous factors" from the point of view of using the study variable as a proxy variable.

Figure 2.5b shows the case in which the study variable is causally antecedent to the intended variable. For example, the intended variable in a study of political values might be "political sophistication." The study variable might be general cognitive ability. Although cognitive ability is an important determinant of sophistication, it does not measure other causal determinants of political sophistication such as political socialization by politically active parents.

Figure 2.5 Path models for cases in which the effect of imperfect construct validity is to attenuate the desired effect size correlation by multiplying the effect size by the construct validity of the proxy variable ($r_{XX'}$ in both cases)

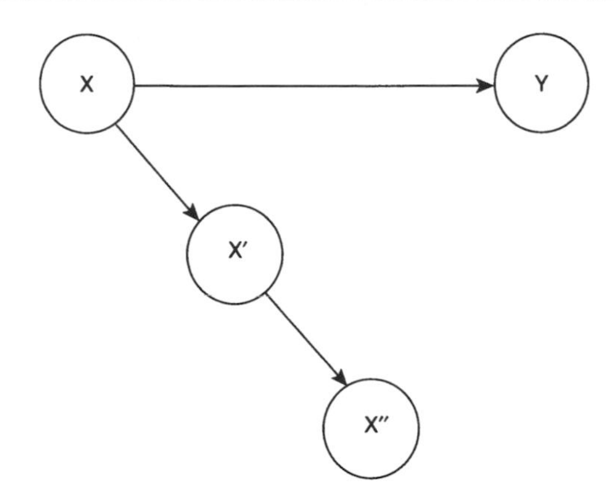

Figure 2.5a Extraneous factors in the study independent variable

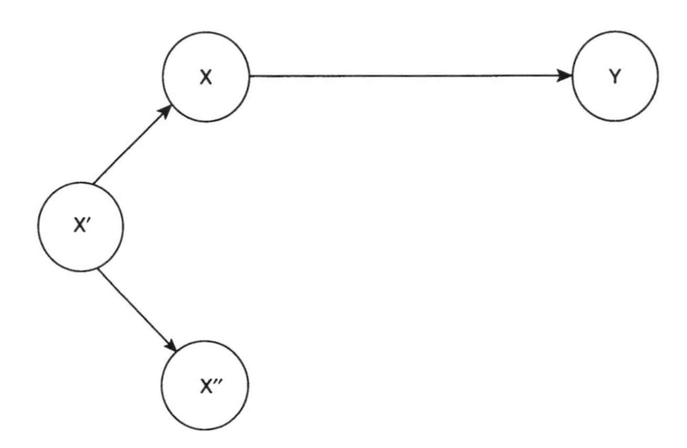

Figure 2.5b The study as a causal antecedent of the intended independent variable

In either Figure 2.5a or 2.5b, the correlation between the observed study independent variable X'' and the dependent variable Y can be written as a triple product:

$$r_{X''Y} = r_{X''X'}\, r_{X'X}\, r_{XY} \tag{2.21}$$

In the notation of the article by Gottfredson (1985), this triple product would be

$$r_o = abr \tag{2.22}$$

where

$a = r_{X''X'} =$ the square root of the reliability of X'' and
$b = r_{X'X} =$ the construct validity of X'.

If X' were a perfect measure of X, then the value of b would be 1.00 and the triple product would reduce to the equation for random error of measurement. If the measure is imperfect, then b will be less than 1.00 and the triple product will represent a reduction beyond that caused by error of measurement. That is, ab will be less than a to the extent that X' is not perfectly construct valid.

Note that, in this path diagram, X is assumed to be perfectly measured. Thus, path coefficient b is the correlation between X' and X corrected for attenuation due to random error of measurement. Note that parameter a is the usual square root of the reliability of X'' that would be used to correct $r_{X''Y}$ for attenuation due to error in X''. The presence of the third factor b represents the difference between a model of imperfect construct validity and a model of random error of measurement.

As an example, suppose education is used as a proxy for general cognitive ability and assume that the "extraneous" factors in education are unrelated to the dependent variable. Assume that the correlation between ability and education is .50 and that the reliability of the study education measure is .90. The multipliers would be given by $a = \sqrt{.90} = .95$ and $b = .50$. The study correlation would be related to the actual correlation by

$$r_o = abr = (.95)(.50)\,r = .48r.$$

In this example, there would be little error if random error were ignored (a 5% error) but a large error if imperfect construct validity were ignored.

Imperfect Construct Validity in the Dependent Variable

There can also be deviations from perfect construct validity in the dependent variable. Some deviations can be corrected, but some cannot.

Figure 2.6 shows one case in which the effect of imperfect validity can be quantified. Figure 2.6a shows the abstract case in which the study variable is causally taken from personnel selection research.

Consider the example in Figure 2.6b: the use of supervisor ratings to measure job performance in a personnel selection validation study. The ideal measure would be an objective measure of job performance such as a construct-valid, perfectly reliable, work sample test. Instead, the study uses supervisor perception (ratings) as the measure. The ideal rating would be a consensus judgment across a population of supervisors. Instead, the observed study variable is the rating of the immediate supervisor. Thus, the idiosyncrasy of that supervisor's perceptions is a part of the error of measurement in the observed ratings. Extraneous factors that may influence human judgment include friendship, physical appearance, moral and/or lifestyle conventionality, and more.

Figure 2.6 Correctable imperfect construct validity in the dependent variable

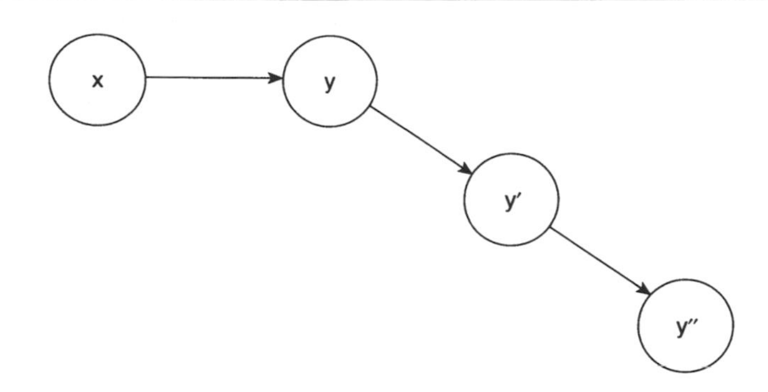

Figure 2.6a Extraneous factors in the study measure of the intended dependent variables

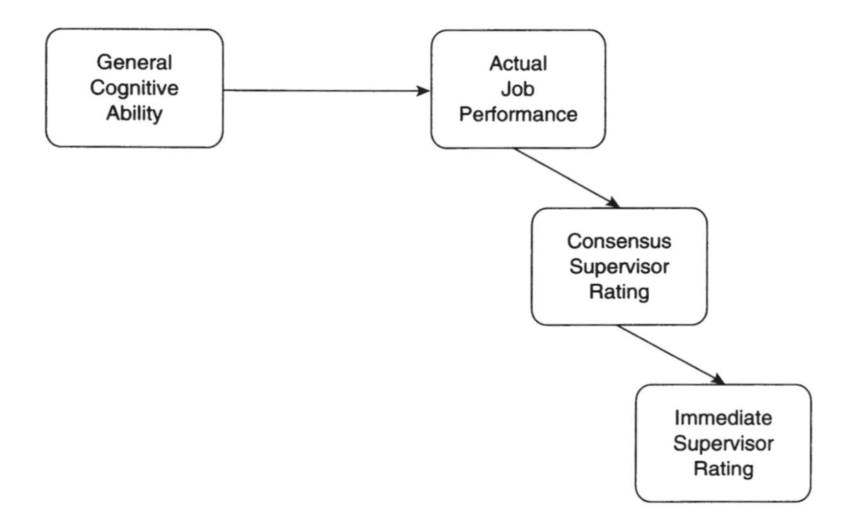

Figure 2.6b Using supervisor ratings as a measure of job performance

The triple-product rule for this quantifiable form of imperfect construct validity is given by the following path analysis:

$$\rho_{xy''} = \rho_{xy}\rho_{yy'}\rho_{y'y''} \tag{2.23}$$

That is,

$$\rho_o = ab\rho.$$

where

$\rho_o =$ the observed correlation,
$a = r_{y'y''} =$ the square root of the reliability of y'',
$b = r_{yy'} =$ the construct validity of y, and
$\rho =$ the true score correlation between ability and actual job performance.

In the case of the example in Figure 2.6b, cumulative empirical data from a meta-analysis indicates that the correlation between actual job performance and consensus ratings is only .52 (Hunter, 1986). The reliability of the immediate supervisor rating depends on the quality of the rating instrument. For a summating rating, the reliability would average .47 (Rothstein, 1990); for a single global rating, the reliability would average .36 (Hunter & Hirsh, 1987; King, Hunter, & Schmidt, 1980). The reduction in validity from using a single global rating measure would be given from $a = \sqrt{.36} = .60$ and $b = .52$, that is,

$$\rho_o = ab\rho = (.60)(.52)\rho = .31\rho,$$

a reduction of 69% in the observed correlation.

In this example, the new factors in the dependent variable were not only extraneous to the intended dependent variable, but were also uncorrelated with the independent variable. However, in some cases, the extraneous variable is related to both the dependent *and* the independent variables. Such cases are more complex, and it is not always possible to correct for the effect of the extraneous variable on the construct validity of the dependent variable. These cases are beyond the scope of this book.

Computational and Other Errors in the Data

The most difficult artifact in meta-analysis is data errors. Bad data can arise from any step in the scientific process. The raw data may be incorrectly recorded or incorrectly entered into the computer. The computer may correlate the wrong variable because the format was incorrectly specified or because a transformation formula was incorrectly written. The sign of the correlation may be wrong because the analyst reverse-scored the variable, but the person who read the output did not know that, or because the reader thought the variable had been reverse-scored when it had not. When computer output is put into tables, the correlation can be incorrectly copied; the sign may be lost or digits may be reversed; or, when the table is published, the typesetter may miscopy the correlation.

These types of errors are much more frequent than we would like to believe (Tukey, 1960; Wolins, 1962). Tukey maintained that all real data sets contain errors. Gulliksen (1986) made the following statement:

> I believe that it is essential to check the data for errors before running my computations. I always wrote an error-checking program and ran the data through it before computing. I find it very interesting that in every set of data I have run, either for myself or someone else, there have always been errors, necessitating going back to the questionnaires and repunching some cards, or perhaps discarding some subjects. (p. 4)

Further, some errors are likely to result in outliers, and outliers have a dramatic inflationary effect on the variance. In a normal distribution, for example, the *SD* is 65%, determined by the highest and lowest 5% of data values (Tukey, 1960). Data errors of various kinds probably account for a substantial portion of the observed variance in correlations and d values in many research literatures.

The upshot of this is that virtually every meta-analysis with a large number of correlations and some meta-analyses with a small number of studies will contain some data errors. If the bad data could be located, they could be thrown out. However, the only bad data that can be identified are correlations that are so far out of the distribution that they are clearly outliers. Outlier analysis works best where study samples are at least moderate in size. If sample sizes are small, it is difficult to distinguish true outliers from extremely large sampling errors. (Outlier analysis is discussed in Chapter 5.)

Thus, even if the present list of artifacts were complete (it is not) and even if all known artifacts were controlled (rarely possible), there would still be variation in study outcomes due to data errors. In actual meta-analyses, there is always attenuation and false variation due to unknown and uncontrolled artifacts in addition to bad data. These considerations led Schmidt and Hunter (1977) to propose their "75% rule," which asserted as a rule of thumb that if in any data set known and correctable artifacts account for 75% of the variance in study correlations, it is likely that the remaining 25% is due to uncontrolled artifacts. It is unwise to assume that all unexplained variance is due to real moderator variables, because it is never possible to correct for all artifacts that cause variation across studies (see, e.g., Schmidt et al., 1993).

Extraneous Factors Introduced by Study Procedure

The measurement process or observation procedure of the study might cause variation on the dependent variable due to a variable that would not have existed (or that would have been constant) had the study been done perfectly. As an example, consider the effect of job experience in a concurrent validity study of job performance. In personnel selection, applicants can be considered as a cohort. When applicants are compared, they are implicitly being compared as if they were to start work simultaneously. In a concurrent validity study, performance is measured on all current workers, workers with different amounts of experience on the job. This means that workers will differ in performance in part because they differ in job experience (Schmidt, Hunter, & Outerbridge, 1986). This would not be true of applicants hired at the same time. Thus, the differences in experience constitute an extraneous variable created by the study observation procedure.

The abstract path diagram for this process is shown in Figure 2.7a, while Figure 2.7b shows the case for job experience. If there had been no extraneous variable introduced into the situation, the observed correlation would be equivalent to the partial correlation between the independent variable and the dependent variable with the extraneous variable held constant. Because the extraneous variable is not correlated with the independent variable, the formula for the partial correlation is

$$\rho_{xy\bullet z} = \rho_{xy} / \sqrt{1 - \rho_{zy}^2} \quad (2.24)$$

Figure 2.7 Path diagrams for an extraneous variable produced by the study procedure

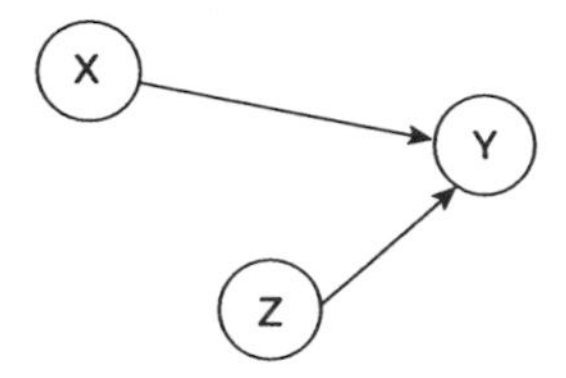

Figure 2.7a Path diagram for an extraneous variable *Z* introduced by study procedure

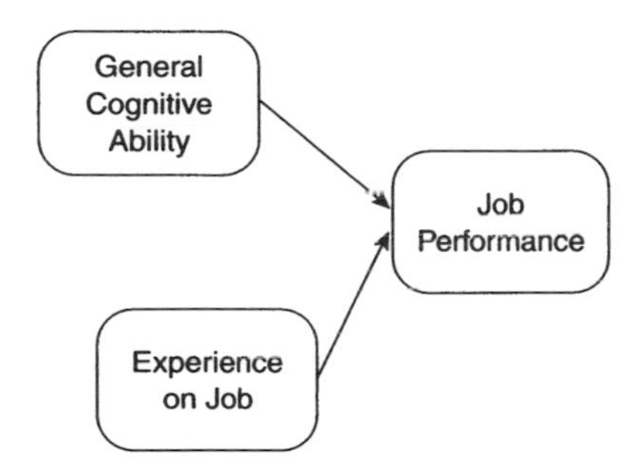

Figure 2.7b Experience differences as an extraneous variable produced by concurrent validation procedure

This can be regarded as a correction for attenuation due to experience. If we reverse the equation, we obtain the attenuation formula. Let a be the reciprocal of the denominator of the equation for the partial correlation, that is,

$$a = 1/\sqrt{1 - \rho_{zy}^2} \tag{2.25}$$

Then

$$\rho_o = a\rho \tag{2.26}$$

The reader may ask why we do not just compute the partial correlation in each individual study. In fact, that would solve the problem. That is, if experience were recorded in the study and the partial correlation were used as the study correlation, then there would be no need for further statistical correction. This would also eliminate the increase in sampling error produced by statistical correction. This correction is similar to that for dichotomization. If the right correlation were given in the original research report (or if the additional correlations necessary to compute it were given), then there would be no need to use after-the-fact statistical correction. This is typically not the case, however, and so correction is needed.

Bias in the Sample Correlation

From time to time, statistically sophisticated observers have noted that the sample correlation is not an "unbiased" estimate of the population correlation, where the word "unbiased" is used in the strict sense of mathematical statistics. From this, they have often then leaped to two false conclusions: (1) that the bias is large enough to be visible and (2) that use of the Fisher z transformation eliminates the bias (see, e.g., James, Demaree, & Mulaik, 1986). However, Hunter, Schmidt, and Coggin (1996) showed that, for sample sizes greater than 20, the bias in the correlation coefficient is less than rounding error. Even in meta-analysis, the bias for smaller sample size domains (i.e., $N < 20$) would be trivial in comparison to distortions due to sampling error. They also showed that the positive bias in the Fisher z transformation is always larger than the negative bias in r (especially if the population correlations vary across studies). Thus, it is always less accurate to use the Fisher z transformation. As we will see in Chapters 5 and 9, use of the Fisher z transformation can cause serious inaccuracies in random-effects meta-analysis models—the meta-analysis model of choice for almost all real data (Hunter & Schmidt, 2000; Schmidt & Hunter, 2003). Further, it would be a very rare case in which it would be worthwhile to correct the bias in the correlation coefficient at all. However, so the reader can make his or her own decision, we include the attenuation formula and correction here.

The average sample correlation is slightly smaller than the population correlation. Assume that the population correlation has already been attenuated by all other artifacts. Then the bias in the sample correlation is given to a close approximation (Hotelling, 1953) by

$$E(r) = \rho - \rho(1 - \rho^2)/(2N - 2) \tag{2.27}$$

In our present multiplier notation, we would write

$$\rho_o = a\rho$$

where the attenuation multiplier is

$$a = 1 - (1 - \rho^2)/(2N - 2) \tag{2.28}$$

and ρ_o is the expected sample correlation.

The bias is greatest and, therefore, the bias multiplier is smallest if $\rho = .50$, so that

$$a = 1 - .375/(N - 1) \tag{2.29}$$

In personnel selection research, the average sample size is 68 and the multiplier is, therefore, $1 - .006 = .994$, which differs only trivially from 1.00. Because the typical attenuated correlation is less than .25 in value, the bias in the typical personnel selection research study would be less than the difference between the average sample correlation of .2486 and the population correlation of .25, a difference less than rounding error.

Only in meta-analyses with an average sample size of 10 or less would the bias be visible at the second digit. If correction is desired, then the preceding attenuation formula can be used with the average study correlation as the estimate of ρ. That is, $\hat{\rho} = r/a$, where r is the observed correlation. For population correlations less than .50, the attenuation factor is closely approximated by the linear multiplier $(2N - 2)/(2N - 1)$, and the correction for bias is effected by multiplying the observed correlation by $(2N - 1)/(2N - 2)$.

Sampling Error, Statistical Power, and the Interpretation of Research Findings

An Illustration of Statistical Power

Traditional methods of interpreting research literatures lead to disastrous errors (Schmidt, 1992, 1996; Schmidt, Ocasio, Hillery, & Hunter, 1985). For example, consider research on the validity of nontest procedures for predicting job performance as measured by supervisory ratings. Hunter and Hunter (1984) found that the average observed correlation for reference checks was .20 and for interests, it was .08. Consider a predictor of job performance that has a mean observed validity of .10. Suppose this is the population correlation and it is constant across all settings. The attenuated population value of .10 may seem small, but after correction for downward biases due to artifacts, it might correspond to an operational validity of .20 and, hence, might have practical value (Schmidt, Hunter, McKenzie, & Muldrow, 1979). If 19 studies were conducted and arranged by order of observed validity, the results would be as shown in Table 2.2. Table 2.2 presents findings for studies based on three sample sizes: (1) the classic recommended minimum of $N = 30$; (2) the median N of 68 found by Lent, Auerbach, and Levin (1971a) for studies published in the Validity Information Exchange in *Personnel Psychology;* and (3) $N = 400$, a sample size considered by many psychologists to be "large."

Clearly, the correlations in Table 2.2 vary over a wide range. Bearing in mind that the actual value of the correlation is always .10, we will now examine two traditional interpretations of these "findings": (1) that of the naive reviewer who takes observed correlations at face value and does not use significance tests and (2) that of the "more sophisticated" reviewer who applies significance tests.

If the studies are each based on 30 people, the naive reviewer reaches the following conclusions:

1. Six of the 19 studies (or 32%) find negative validities. That is, 32% of the studies show that job performance is predicted in reverse rank order of actual job performance.
2. Using a liberal standard of .20 for "moderate" correlations, in only 32% of the settings does the validity reach even a moderate level.
3. Overall conclusion: In most cases, the procedure is not related to job performance.

If the naive reviewer is faced with 19 studies, each based on $N = 68$, he or she concludes as follows:

1. Four of the 19 studies (or 21%) find negative validity.
2. In only 21% of the settings (4 of 19) does the validity reach the moderate level of .20.
3. Overall conclusion: In most cases, the procedure is not related to job performance.

Table 2.2 Nineteen studies

	$N = 30$	$N = 68$	$N = 400$
Study 1	.40**	.30**	.18**
Study 2	.34*	.25*	.16**
Study 3	.29	.23*	.15**
Study 4	.25	.20*	.14**
Study 5	.22	.18	.13**
Study 6	.20	.16	.13**
Study 7	.17	.15	.12**
Study 8	.15	.13	.11**
Study 9	.12	.12	.11**
Study 10	.10	.10	.10**
Study 11	.08	.08	.08*
Study 12	.05	.07	.09*
Study 13	.03	.05	.08*
Study 14	−.00	.04	.08
Study 15	−.02	.02	.07
Study 16	−.05	−.00	.06
Study 17	−.09	−.03	.05
Study 18	−.14	−.05	.04
Study 19	−.20	−.10	.02

**Significant by two-tailed test.
*Significant by one-tailed test.

If each study is based on $N = 400$, the naive reviewer arrives at the following conclusions:

1. No studies find negative validity.
2. No studies report validity even as high as the "moderate" .20 level.
3. Overall conclusion: The selection method predicts performance poorly in all settings and almost not at all in many settings.

Naive reviewers do not even begin to reach correct judgments unless the typical study has a sample size of 400 or more. Even at $N = 400$, there is enough sampling error to produce validity coefficients that differ in magnitude by a factor of .18/.02, or 9 to 1.

It has been a traditional belief that the use of significance tests enhances the accuracy of study interpretations (Hunter, 1997; Schmidt, 1996). So let us examine the interpretations of a reviewer who applies significance tests to the studies in Table 2.2. If the studies are each based on $N = 30$, the reviewer reaches the following conclusions:

1. Only 2 of the 19 studies (11%) find significant validity.
2. The procedure is not valid almost 90% of the time; that is, it is "generally invalid."

When each study is based on $N = 68$, the reviewer concludes as follows:

1. Only 4 of the 19 studies (21%) find significant validity.
2. Thus, in the overwhelming majority of cases, the procedure is invalid.

The reviewer's conclusions from the $N = 400$ studies are as follows:

1. Only 13 of the 19 studies (68%) find significant validity.
2. Thus, in 32% of the settings, the procedure does not work.
3. Conclusion: The method predicts job performance in some settings, but not in others. Further research is needed to determine why it works in some settings, but not in others.

These conclusions based on significance tests are *not* more accurate that those of the naive reviewer. With small sample sizes ($N < 400$), the conclusions are no more accurate using the significance test, and, even with a sample size of 400, reviewers relying on traditional interpretations of significance tests do not reach correct conclusions from cumulative research. The reason the significance tests lead to errors of interpretation is that they have a very high error rate. An error is the failure to detect the constant underlying correlation of .10 in a study. The percentage of time that the statistical test will make this error in our example is

	$N = 30$	$N = 68$	$N = 400$
Two-tailed test	92%	88%	48%
One-tailed test	86%	80%	36%

These error rates are very high. The percentage of the studies in which the significance test does *not* make this error is called its statistical power. Statistical power is 100% minus the error rate. For example, when one-tailed tests are used in our 19 studies, and $N = 68$ in each study, the error rate is 80%. The statistical power is $100\% - 80\% = 20\%$. That is, the significance test is correct only 20% of the time. The next section examines statistical power in more detail.

A More Detailed Examination of Statistical Power

The problems created by low statistical power in individual studies are central to the need for meta-analysis. This section explores the question of statistical power in more detail.

Suppose the population correlation between supervisory consideration and job satisfaction is .25 in all settings. This is the correlation prior to corrections for unreliability (measurement error). Now, suppose studies are conducted in a large number of settings, each with $N = 83$. For simplicity, assume that the same instruments are used in all studies to measure these two variables, so reliabilities are constant across studies. Assume also that the subjects in each study are a random sample from the population of all possible employees, and range variation and the other artifacts discussed previously do not vary across studies. Then the average observed correlation across all these studies will be .25, the true value. However, there will be substantial variability due to sampling error; the *SD* of the correlations will be

$$SD_r = \sqrt{\frac{(1 - .25^2)^2}{83 - 1}} = .103$$

This distribution of correlations is shown on the right in Figure 2.8a. The other distribution in Figure 2.8a is the one that would have resulted if the true population correlation had been $\rho = 0$, instead of $\rho = .25$. This null distribution is the basis of the statistical significance test. Its mean is 0. The *SD* of the null distribution is not the same as the *SD* of the real distribution, because the true value of ρ is 0,

$$SD_{\text{NULL}} = \sqrt{\frac{(1 - 0^2)^2}{83 - 1}} = .110$$

The .05 significance value for a one-tailed test is the point in the null distribution where only 5% of the correlations would be larger than that value. The 5% significance level is thus 1.645 *SD*s above the mean of the null distribution, that is, above 0. Therefore, to be significant, a study r must be at least as large as $1.645(.110) = .18$. If the true ρ really were 0, only 5% of study correlations would be as large as .18 or larger. That is, the Type I error rate would be 5%. Because $\rho = .25$, and not 0, however, there can be no Type I errors, only Type II errors. What percentage of the study rs will be .18 or larger? If we convert .18 to a z score in the r distribution, we get

$$z = \frac{.18 - .25}{.103} = -.68$$

The percentage of values in a normal distribution that is above .68 standard deviations below the mean is .75, as can be determined from any normal curve table. Therefore, the statistical power is .75; 75% of all these studies will obtain a statistically significant correlation. In Figure 2.8a, this represents the area to the right of .18 in the observed r distribution. That area contains 75% of the observed rs. For the remaining 25% of the studies, the traditional conclusion would be that the correlation, being nonsignificant, is 0. This represents the area to the left of .18 in the observed r distribution. That area contains 25% of the observed rs. This conclusion is false; the correlation is always .25, and it has only that one value. Thus, the probability of Type II error (concluding there is no relationship where there is) is .25.

The studies in this example have higher statistical power than many real studies. This is because the true correlation (.25) is larger than is often the case for real-world population correlations. Also, the sample size ($N = 83$) is larger here than is often the case in real studies, further increasing statistical power. For example, the mean validity coefficient for a typical employment test measuring verbal or quantitative aptitude is about .20 before correction for range restriction and criterion unreliability, and sample sizes in the literature are often smaller than 83.

Figure 2.8b illustrates a case that is more representative of many real studies. In Figure 2.8b, the true value of the correlation (the population correlation) is .20, and each study is based on a sample size of $N = 40$. The standard deviation of the observed correlations across many such studies is

$$SD_r = \sqrt{\frac{(1 - .20^2)^2}{40 - 1}} = .154$$

Figure 2.8 Statistical power: Two examples

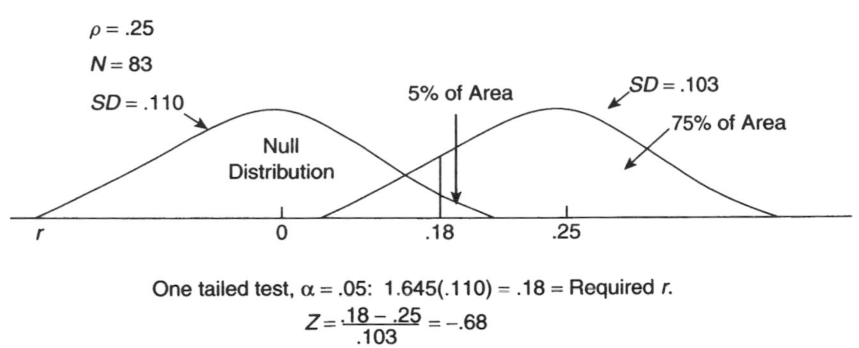

One tailed test, $\alpha = .05$: $1.645(.110) = .18 =$ Required r.

$$Z = \frac{.18 - .25}{.103} = -.68$$

P(Type II Error) = .25; Statistical Power = .75

Figure 2.8a Statistical power greater than .50

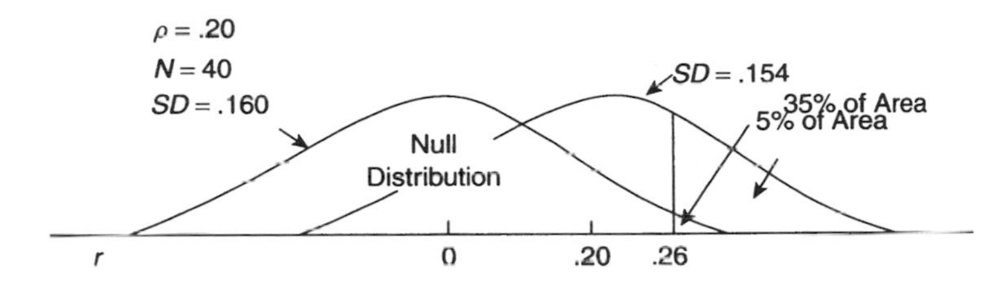

One tailed test, $\alpha = .05$: $1.645(.160) = .26 =$ Required r.

$$Z = \frac{.26 - .20}{.154} = .39$$

P(Type II Error) = .65; Statistical Power = .35

Figure 2.8b Statistical power less than .50

The *SD* in the null distribution is

$$SD_{\text{NULL}} = \sqrt{\frac{(1 - 0^2)^2}{40 - 1}} = .160$$

To be significant at the .05 level (again, using a one-tailed test), a correlation must be above the zero mean of the null distribution by $1.645(.160) = .26$. All correlations that are .26 or larger will be significant; the rest will be nonsignificant. Thus, to be significant, the correlation must be larger than its true value! The actual value of the correlation is always .20; observed values are larger (or smaller) than the true value of .20 only because of random sampling error. To get a significant correlation, we must be lucky enough to have a positive random sampling error. Any study in which r is equal to its real value of .20—that is, any study that is perfectly accurate in estimating r—will lead to the false conclusion that the correlation is 0! What percentage of the correlations will be significant? When we convert .26 to a z score in the observed r distribution, we get

$$z = \frac{.26 - .20}{.154} = .39$$

The percentage of values in a normal distribution that is above a z score of .39 is 35%. In Figure 2.8b, this 35% is the area above the value of .26 in the observed r distribution. So only 35% of all these studies will get a significant r, even though the true value of r is always .20; it is never 0. Statistical power is only .35. The majority of studies—65%—will falsely indicate that $\rho = 0$; 65% of all studies will reach a false conclusion.

A vote-counting procedure has often been used in the past (see Chapter 11) in which the majority outcome is used to decide whether a relationship exists. If a majority of the studies show a nonsignificant finding, as here, the conclusion is that no relationship exists. This conclusion is clearly false here, showing that the vote-counting method is defective. Even more surprising, however, is the fact that the larger the number of studies that are conducted, the greater is the certainty of reaching the false conclusion that there is no relationship (i.e., that $\rho = 0$)! If only a few studies are conducted, then just by chance a majority might get significant correlations, and the vote-counting method might not result in an erroneous conclusion. For example, if only five studies are done, then by chance three might get significant correlations. If a large number of studies are conducted, however, we are certain to zero in on approximately 35% significant and 65% nonsignificant. This creates the paradox of the vote-counting method: If statistical power is less than .50, and if the population correlation is not 0, then the more research studies there are, the more likely the reviewer is to reach the false conclusion that $\rho = 0$ (Hedges & Olkin, 1980).

These examples illustrate statistical power for correlational studies, but they are equally realistic for experimental studies. In experimental studies, the basic statistic is not the correlation coefficient, but the standardized difference between the means of two groups, the experimental and control groups. This is the difference between the two means in standard deviation units and is called the d-value statistic (see Chapters 6, 7, and 8). The d statistic is roughly twice as large as the correlation. Thus, the example in Figure 2.8a corresponds to an experimental study in which $d = .51$; this is a difference of one-half a standard deviation, a fairly substantial difference. It corresponds to the difference between the 50th and 69th percentiles in a normal distribution. The corresponding sample sizes for Figure 2.8a would be $N = 42$ in the experimental group and $N = 41$ in the control group (or vice versa). These numbers are also relatively large; many studies have far less in each group.

The example in Figure 2.8b translates into a more realistic analogue for many experimental studies. Figure 2.8b corresponds to experimental studies in which there are 20 subjects each in the experimental and control groups. We have seen many studies, especially laboratory studies in organizational behavior and decision making, in which there were 20 or fewer (sometimes 5 or 10) in each group. The ρ of .20 corresponds to a d value of .40, a value as large or larger than many observed in real studies.

Thus, these two examples illustrating the low statistical power of small-sample studies and the errors in conclusions that result from traditional use of significance tests in such studies generalize also to experimental studies. Because the properties of the d statistic are somewhat different, the exact figures given here for statistical power will not hold; statistical power is actually somewhat lower in the experimental studies. However, the figures are close enough to illustrate the point.

How would meta-analysis handle the studies shown in Figures 2.8a and 2.8b? First, meta-analysis calls for computing the mean r in each set of studies. For the studies in Figure 2.8a, the mean r would be found to be .25, the correct value. For Figure 2.8b, the computed mean would be .20, again the correct value. These $\bar{r}$s would then be used to compute the amount of variance expected from sampling error. For the studies in Figure 2.8a, this would be

$$S_e^2 = \frac{(1 - \bar{r}^2)^2}{N - 1}$$

and

$$S_e^2 = \frac{(1 - .25^2)^2}{83 - 1} = .0107$$

This value would then be subtracted from the amount of variance in the observed correlations to see whether any variance over and above sampling variance was left. The observed variance is $(.10344)^2 = .0107$. Thus, the amount of real variance in the correlations across these studies is $S_\rho^2 = .0107 - .0107 = 0$. The meta-analytic conclusion is that there is only one value of $\rho (\rho = .25)$ and all the apparent variability in rs across studies is sampling error. Thus, meta-analysis leads to the correct conclusion, while the traditional approach led to the conclusion that $\rho = 0$ in 25% of the studies and varied all the way from .18 to approximately .46 in the other 75% of the studies.

Likewise, for the studies in Figure 2.8b, the expected sampling error is

$$S_e^2 = \frac{(1 - .20^2)^2}{40 - 1} = .0236$$

The variance actually observed is $(.1537)^2 = .0236 = S_r^2$. Again, $S_r^2 - S_e^2 = 0$, and the meta-analytic conclusion is that there is only one value of ρ in all the studies—$\rho = .20$—and all the variability in rs across different studies is just sampling error. Again, meta-analysis leads to the correct conclusion, while the traditional use of statistical significance tests leads to false conclusions. The principle here is identical for the d statistics. Only the specific formulas are different (see Chapter 7).

The examples in Figures 2.8a and 2.8b are hypothetical, but they are not unrealistic. In fact, the point here is that real data often behave in the same way. For example, consider the real data in Table 2.3. These data are validity coefficients obtained in a study of nine different job families in Sears, Roebuck and Company (Hill, 1980). For any of these seven tests, validity coefficients are significant for some job families but not for others. For example, the arithmetic test has significant validity coefficients for job families 1, 2, 5, 8, and 9; the validity is not significant

Table 2.3 Validity coefficients from the Sears study

		Sears Test of Mental Alertness			*Sears Clerical Battery*			
Job Family	*N*	*Linguistic*	*Quantitative*	*Total Score*	*Filing*	*Checking*	*Arithmetic*	*Grammar*
1. Office Support Material Handlers	86	.33*	.20*	.32*	.30*	.27*	.32*	.25*
2. Data Processing Clerical	80	.43*	.51*	.53*	.30*	.39*	.42*	.47*
3. Clerical-Secretarial (Lower Level)	65	.24*	.03	.20	.20	.22	.13	.26*
4. Clerical-Secretarial (Higher Level)	186	.12*	.18*	.17*	.07	.21*	.20	.31*
5. Secretarial (Top Level)	146	.19*	.21*	.22*	.16*	.15*	.22*	.09
6. Clerical With Supervisory Duties	30	.24	.14	.23	.24	.24	.31	.17
7. Word Processing	63	.03	.26*	.13	.39*	.33*	.14	.22*
8. Supervisors	185	.28*	.10	.25*	.25*	.11	.19*	.20*
9. Technical, Operative, Professional	54	.24*	.35*	.33*	.30*	.22*	.31*	.42*

*$p < .05$.

for job families 3, 4, 6, and 7. One interpretation of these findings—the traditional one—is that the arithmetic test should be used to hire people in job families 1, 2, 5, 8, and 9, because it is valid for these job families but not for the others. This conclusion is erroneous. Application of the meta-analysis methods that we present in this book shows that for the tests in Table 2.3 all the variation in validities across job families is due to sampling error. The nonsignificant validities are due only to low statistical power.

Another example in which sampling error accounts for all the variation in study outcomes in real data is given in Schmidt, Ocasio, et al. (1985). In that extensive study, observed correlation coefficients varied across different studies all the way from $-.16$ to .61, a range of .78 correlation points. Yet the true value of ρ was constant in every study at .22. (In fact, each study was a random sample from a single large study.) Sampling error in small-sample studies creates tremendous variability in study outcomes. Researchers have for decades underestimated how much variability is produced by sampling error.

Of course, sampling error does not explain all the variation in all sets of studies. In most cases, other artifacts also operate to cause variance in study outcomes, as discussed earlier in this chapter. And, in some cases, even the combination of sampling error and other artifacts (such as measurement error and range restriction differences between studies) cannot explain all the variance. However, these artifacts virtually always account for important amounts of variance in study outcomes.

When and How to Cumulate

In general, a meta-analytic cumulation of results across studies is conceptually a simple process.

1. Calculate the desired descriptive statistic for each study available and average that statistic across studies.
2. Calculate the variance of the statistic across studies.
3. Correct the variance by subtracting the amount due to sampling error.
4. Correct the mean and variance for study artifacts other than sampling error.
5. Compare the corrected standard deviation to the mean to assess the size of the potential variation in results across studies in qualitative terms. If the mean is more than two standard deviations larger than 0, then it is reasonable to conclude that the relationship considered is always positive.

In practice, cumulation usually involves a variety of technical complexities that we will examine in later chapters.

Cumulation of results can be used whenever there are at least two studies with data bearing on the same relationship. For example, if your study at Crooked Corn Flakes contains a correlation between job status and job satisfaction, then you might want to compare that correlation with the correlation found in your earlier study at Tuffy Bolts. However, to correct for sampling error with two correlations, it is possible to use a strategy different from the corrected variance procedures presented in Chapters 3 and 4. One can simply compute confidence intervals around each correlation, as discussed in Chapter 1. If the two confidence intervals overlap, then the difference between the two correlations may be due solely to sampling error (cf. Schmidt, 1992, 1996), and the average is the best estimate of their common value.

Cumulation of results should ideally be based on a large number of studies located by exhaustive search procedures (see Chapter 12 and Cooper, 1998). However, cumulation is also valid for "convenience" samples of studies that just happen to lie at hand, as long as they are a random sample of existing studies. This is particularly true if the corrected standard deviation suggests that all the variation across studies is due to sampling error. If all the variation is due to sampling error, then the accuracy of the mean value in relationship to the one true population value is determined by the total number of subjects across studies. Even a relatively small number of studies may have a large cumulative sample size.

If a convenience sample of studies has a small corrected standard deviation, then one concludes that there is little or no variation in the results across the population of studies that is implicitly sampled. However, the investigator may have *systematically* excluded studies that others would have put in the same population of studies. In this case, the basis for the exclusion might be a real moderator variable, and the population of excluded results might cluster around a different population correlation value. Reliance on a convenience sample always involves some risk.

A major issue in meta-analysis has been the question of representativeness of the studies included in the meta-analysis. This has been referred to as potential source bias, availability bias, or publication bias. For example, it has long been alleged that published studies have larger correlations and effect sizes than unpublished ones, partly because the published studies are better designed, but partly because editorial reviewers have a substantial preference for studies with statistically significant results. Research areas in which the true effect size is 0 are rare. Lipsey and Wilson (1993) found this was the case in less than 1% of the 302 research areas they examined. If the true effect size *is* 0, and if some studies with Type I errors get published, and most studies without Type I errors do not get published, an assessment limited to published studies would lead to the conclusion that a relationship exists when, in fact, none does. Even if the true effect size is not 0, there may still be an upward bias in the estimation of its *size* (although, by definition, there could be no Type I errors).

Two studies provide some evidence that unpublished studies do have smaller effect sizes. Smith and Glass (1977) analyzed the standardized effect sizes of 375 studies on psychotherapy. They found that studies published in books had an average d value of .80, those published in journals had an average effect size of .70, dissertations averaged .60, and unpublished studies averaged .50. Rosenthal and Rubin (1978a, 1978b) found that, in a sample of interpersonal expectancy effect studies, the average d value of 32 dissertations was .35 and the average of 313 nondissertations was .65. Neither set of authors reported an assessment of the relative methodological quality of the published and unpublished studies. Most of the difference between the average effect size of the published and unpublished studies may be due to differences in the methodological quality (e.g., levels of measurement error). If the attenuation effects of artifacts were properly corrected for, differences might disappear (see Schmidt & Hunter, 1977, pp. 536–537). Methods for testing for, detecting, and correcting source bias in meta-analysis are discussed in Chapter 13.

Undercorrection for Artifacts in the Corrected Standard Deviation

The corrected standard deviation of results across studies should always be regarded as an overestimate of the true standard deviation. Procedures developed to date correct for only some of the artifacts that produce spurious variation across studies. There are other artifacts that have similar effects. The largest of these is computational or reporting errors. If you have 30 correlations ranging from .00 to .60 and one correlation of −.45 (a case we encountered in one of our studies), then it is virtually certain that the outlier resulted from some faulty computational or reporting procedure, for example, failing to reverse the sign of a variable that is reverse scored, or using the wrong format in a computer run, or a typographical error, and so on. Other artifacts that create spurious variation across studies include differences in the reliability of measurement, differences in the construct validity of measurement (such as criterion contamination or criterion deficiency in personnel selection studies), differences in the variances of measured variables in different studies (such as differences in restriction in range in personnel selection studies), and differences in the amount or strength of the treatment (in experimental studies). Indeed, the relevant question in many settings is this: Is all the variation across studies artifactual? In the personnel selection area, this has been the conclusion in a number of areas, such as single-group validity, differential validity by race or ethnic group, specificity of ability test validity across setting or time, and amount of halo in ratings made using different methods (cf. Schmidt & Hunter, 1981; Schmidt, Hunter, Pearlman, & Hirsh, 1985; Schmidt et al., 1993). However, it is very important to *test* the hypothesis that all variation is artifactual—and not just *assume* a priori that this is the case, as fixed-effects meta-analysis models do. The models and procedures presented in this book are all random-effects models and they test this hypothesis empirically. The distinction between fixed-effects and random-effects meta-analysis models is presented in Chapters 5 and 9.

Some artifacts can be quantified and corrected for. Corrections for differences in reliability and restriction in range were first made by Schmidt and Hunter (1977) and Schmidt, Hunter, Pearlman, and Shane (1979); these are described in Chapters 3 and 4. Differences in the construct validity of measures can be corrected using similar techniques if there is an integrated study available that provides a path analysis relating the alternate measures to each other (see the discussion earlier in this chapter). Quantitative differences in treatment effects (such as magnitude of incentive) can be coded and corrected after the initial cumulation establishes the relationship (if any) between that aspect of the treatment and the study outcome (see Chapters 6 and 7).

However, these corrections depend on additional information that is frequently not available. For example, reliabilities and standard deviations are often not included in correlational studies. They are not even considered in most experimental studies. And, alas, computational and reporting errors will never be fully quantified and eliminated.

If there is large, real variation in results across studies, then any conclusion based solely on the summary result entails a certain amount of error. This is the familiar problem of ignoring interactions or moderator effects. However, errors of even greater magnitude can be made if variation caused by artifacts is attributed to nonexistent methodological and substantive moderators. For example, before the era of meta-analysis, one well-known psychologist became so discouraged by the variation in results in several research areas that he concluded it was unlikely that any finding in psychology would ever hold from one generation to the next, because each cohort would always differ on some social dimension that would alter research outcomes (Cronbach, 1975). Such a position reflects the reification of sampling error variance and other artifactual variance (Schmidt, 1992, 1996; Schmidt & Hunter, 2003). Such reification leads not only to epistemological disillusionment, but also to immense wasted effort in endlessly replicating studies when enough data already exist to answer the question (Schmidt, 1996).

If there is a large corrected standard deviation, it may be possible to explain the variation across studies by breaking the studies into groups on the basis of relevant differences between them. This breakdown can be an explicit subdivision of studies into categories, or it can be an implicit breakdown using regression methods to predict study outcomes from study characteristics. Both of these will be considered in detail in Chapters 3, 4, and 7. However, we will show in the next section that such a breakdown should be attempted only if there is a substantial corrected variance. Otherwise, the search for moderators can introduce serious errors into the interpretation of the studies by virtue of capitalization on sampling errors.

Coding Study Characteristics and Capitalization on Sampling Error in Moderator Analysis

The process of meta-analysis was defined by Glass and his associates (Glass, McGaw, & Smith, 1981) as a composite process: (1) cumulation of descriptive statistics across studies; (2) the coding of perhaps 50 to 100 study characteristics, such as date of study, number of threats to internal validity, and so forth; and (3) regression of study outcome onto the coded study characteristics. Such coding can be 90% to 95% of the work in the research integration process. Yet this coding work may be entirely wasted. In our own research, in which we have made corrections for sampling error and other artifacts, we have usually found little appreciable variation across studies remaining after these corrections. That is, it is our experience that there is often no important variation in study results after sampling error and other artifacts are removed (despite the fact that it is never possible to correct for *all* artifacts causing variation across studies). In such cases, all observed correlations with study characteristics would be the result of capitalization on sampling error due to the small number of studies.

If there is little variation other than sampling error, then the dependent variable (study outcome: the r or d statistic) has low reliability. For example, if 90% of between-study variance in correlations is due to artifacts, then the reliability of the study outcome variable is only .10, and therefore the maximum correlation between any study characteristic and study outcome is the square root of .10, which is .31. Therefore, large observed correlations between study characteristics and study outcomes could occur only because of sampling error. Correlating study characteristics with study outcome statistics (rs or d values) leads to massive capitalization on chance when the correlations that are large enough to be statistically significant are identified ex post facto. Sampling error is very large because the *sample size* for this analysis is not the number of persons in the studies but the *number of studies*. For example, the multiple regression of study outcome onto 40 study characteristics (typical of current meta-analyses) with only 50 studies as observations (typical of current meta-analyses) would lead by capitalization on sampling error to a multiple correlation near 1.00. Indeed, some studies have more study characteristics than studies, a situation in which the multiple correlation is always 1.00 by fiat.

Many meta-analyses are conducted in the following manner. The researchers first examine their 40 study characteristics to find the 5 that are most highly correlated with study outcomes. Then they use multiple regression with those 5, using a shrinkage formula (if one is used at all) for 5 predictors. Picking the best 5 out of 40, however, is approximately the same as doing a step-up regression from 40 predictors, and hence one should use 40 in the shrinkage formula rather than 5 (Cattin, 1980). In many cases, the proper shrinkage correction would show the actual multiple correlation to be near 0.

Table 2.4 Expected values of the multiple R of study characteristics with study outcomes when all study characteristics correlate zero with study outcomes and with each other

Number of Study Characteristics in Regression Equation	*Total Number of Study Characteristics*	*Number of Studies*							
		20	*40*	*60*	*80*	*100*	*200*	*400*	*800*
2		.49	.34	.28	.24	.21	.15	.11	.07
3	6	.51	.36	.29	.25	.22	.16	.11	.08
4		.53	.37	.30	.26	.23	.16	.12	.08
2		.53	.37	.30	.26	.23	.17	.12	.08
3	8	.57	.40	.33	.28	.25	.18	.13	.09
4		.61	.42	.35	.30	.27	.19	.13	.09
2		.57	.40	.32	.28	.25	.18	.12	.09
3	10	.62	.43	.35	.31	.27	.19	.13	.10
4		.66	.46	.38	.33	.29	.21	.14	.10
2		.61	.43	.35	.30	.27	.19	.13	.09
3	13	.67	.47	.38	.33	.29	.21	.14	.10
4		.72	.50	.41	.36	.32	.22	.16	.11
2		.64	.45	.36	.32	.28	.20	.14	.10
3	16	.71	.49	.40	.35	.31	.22	.16	.11
4		.77	.54	.44	.38	.34	.24	.17	.12
2		.68	.48	.37	.34	.30	.21	.15	.11
3	20	.76	.53	.43	.37	.33	.23	.16	.12
4		.83	.58	.47	.41	.36	.26	.18	.13
2		.70	.49	.40	.35	.31	.22	.15	.11
3	25	.79	.55	.45	.39	.34	.24	.17	.12
4		.86	.60	.49	.43	.38	.27	.19	.13
2		.73	.51	.41	.36	.32	.22	.16	.11
3	30	.82	.57	.46	.40	.36	.25	.18	.13
4		.90	.63	.51	.44	.39	.28	.20	.14
2		.75	.52	.42	.37	.33	.23	.16	.11
3	35	.84	.59	.48	.42	.37	.26	.18	.13
4		.93	.65	.53	.46	.41	.29	.20	.14
2		.76	.53	.43	.38	.33	.24	.17	.12
3	40	.87	.61	.50	.43	.38	.27	.19	.13
4		.97	.68	.55	.48	.42	.30	.21	.15
2		.80	.55	.45	.39	.35	.24	.17	.12
3	50	.90	.63	.51	.44	.39	.28	.20	.14
4		1.00	.70	.57	.49	.44	.31	.22	.15

NOTE: Actual multiple $R = 0$ in all cases in this table.

Table 2.4 illustrates how severe the problem of capitalization on chance is when only those study characteristics that correlate highest with study outcomes are retained and entered into the regression analysis. Table 2.4 depicts a situation in which every study characteristic correlates 0 with study outcomes and all study characteristics correlate 0 with each other. Thus, the true value of all multiple correlations in Table 2.4 is 0; all multiple correlations in the table are produced solely by capitalization on sampling error. Consider a typical example. Suppose the number of study characteristics coded is 20 and the 4 that correlate highest with study correlations are retained and used in the regression analysis. If the number of studies is 100, then the expected multiple R is .36, a value that is highly "statistically significant" ($p = .0002$). If there are 60 studies, then the spurious multiple R will, on average, be .47. If there are only 40 studies, it will be .58. Remember that in every cell in Table 2.4 the true multiple R is 0. The values in Table 2.4 are *mean* values; they are not the largest values. Approximately half the time the observed multiple Rs will be *larger* than the values in Table 2.4. The situation in which 4 study characteristics out of 20 are retained is representative of some actual meta-analyses. However, larger numbers of study characteristics are often coded; for example, it is not unusual for 40 to 50 characteristics to be coded. If 40 are coded and 4 are retained, the spurious multiple R can be expected to be .68 with 40 studies, .55 with 60 studies, and .48 with 80 studies. The reason the multiple R is spuriously large is that the retained study characteristic correlations are biased upward from their true value of 0 by capitalization on (chance) sampling error. For example, if there are 60 studies and 40 study characteristics are coded but only the top 4 are retained, then the correlation for the retained 4 will average .23. These retained characteristics then yield a bogus multiple R of .55.

Thus, it is apparent that the problem of capitalization on chance in conventional moderator analysis in meta-analysis is extremely severe. Many moderators identified in published meta-analyses using regression and correlation methods are probably not real. Those that were identified purely empirically, and were not predicted a priori by a theory or hypothesis, are particularly likely to be illusions created by capitalization on sampling error.

On the other hand, those moderators that *are* real are unlikely to be detected because of low statistical power. The discussions of statistical power earlier in this chapter apply to correlations between study characteristics and study outcomes just as well as to other correlations. The sample size—the number of studies—is usually small (e.g., 40–100), and the study characteristic correlations are likely to be small because much of the variance of observed study outcome statistics (rs and d values) is sampling error variance and other artifactual variance. Thus, statistical power to detect real moderators will typically be quite low. Hence, the real moderators are unlikely to be detected, and, at the same time, there is a high probability that capitalization on sampling error will lead to the "detection" of nonexistent moderators. This is indeed an unhappy situation.

To take all variation across studies at face value is to pretend that sampling error does not exist. Because most studies are done with small samples (e.g., less than 500 subjects), the sampling error is quite large in comparison to observed outcome values. Thus, to ignore sampling error is to guarantee major statistical errors at some point in the analysis. The classical reviewer's error is to report the range of outcome values; the range is determined by the two most extreme sampling errors in the set of studies. The error in many current meta-analyses is capitalization on chance and low statistical power in relating variation across studies in r or d values to coded study characteristics.

We do not claim to have the answer to the problems of capitalization on chance and low statistical power in moderator analysis. In our judgment, there is no solution to this problem within statistics. It is well known within statistics that the statistical test does not solve the problem; the Type I error versus Type II error trade-off is unavoidable. Thus, if issues are to be resolved solely on statistical grounds, then the answer to subtle questions can only be to gather more data, often vast amounts of data. A more workable alternative is to develop theories that allow new data to be drawn indirectly into the argument. This new data may then permit an objective resolution of the issue on theoretical grounds (see Chapter 11).

A Look Ahead in the Book

The two most common research designs for empirical studies are the correlational study and the two-group intervention study (i.e., an experimental study with independent treatment and control groups). Strength of relationship in correlational designs is usually measured by the correlation coefficient. We present methods for cumulating the correlation coefficient in Chapters 3 and 4. Some have argued that the slope or covariance should be cumulated, rather than the correlation. However, slopes and covariances are comparable across studies only if exactly the same instruments are used to measure the independent and dependent variables in each study. It is a rare set of studies in which this is true. Thus, only in rare cases can the slope or covariance be cumulated because it is in the same metric in all studies. Furthermore, the strength of relationship represented by a slope or covariance can only be known when these numbers are compared to the standard deviations, that is, only when the correlation coefficient is computed. We examine the cumulation of slopes and intercepts in detail in Chapter 5.

The statistic most commonly reported in experimental studies of treatment effects is the t-test statistic. However, t is not a good measure of strength of effect because it is multiplied by the square root of the sample size and, hence, does not have the same metric across studies. When sample size is removed from the t statistic, the resulting formula is the effect size statistic d. We will consider the effect size statistic d in Chapters 6 to 8. We will also consider its correlational analogue, the point biserial correlation. It is often better to convert d values to point biserial correlations, conduct the meta-analysis on these correlations, and then transform the final result back to the d-value statistic. Some would argue for use of proportion of variance instead of r or d, but proportion of variance accounted for (or explained) has many defects. For example, it does not preserve the sign or direction of the treatment effect. Also, as a consequence of the loss of sign, the squared effect measure mean is biased. Proportion of variance indexes are discussed and critiqued further in Chapter 5.

Chapters 3 to 5 on the correlation coefficient and 6 to 8 on d values assume that each entry is based on a statistically independent sample. However, it is frequently possible to obtain more than one relevant estimate of a correlation or effect size from the same study. How, then, should multiple estimates of a relationship from within the same study contribute to a cumulation across studies? This question is taken up in Chapter 10.

PART II

Meta-Analysis of Correlations

3

Meta-Analysis of Correlations Corrected Individually for Artifacts

Introduction and Overview

In Chapter 2, we examined 11 study design artifacts that can affect the size of the correlation coefficient. At the level of meta-analysis, it is possible to correct for all but one of those artifacts: reporting or transcriptional error. Except for outlier analysis, we know of no way to correct for data errors. Outlier analysis can detect some but not all bad data and is often problematic in meta-analysis (as discussed in Chapter 5). Sampling error can be corrected for, but the accuracy of the correction depends on the total sample size that the meta-analysis is based on. The correction for sampling error becomes perfect as total sample size approaches infinity. Our discussion of meta-analysis in this chapter and in Chapter 4 will implicitly assume that the meta-analysis is based on a large number of studies. If the number of studies is small, then the formulas presented here still apply, but there will be nontrivial sampling error in the final meta-analysis results. This is the problem of "second order" sampling error, which is discussed in Chapter 9.

The 10 potentially correctable study design artifacts are listed in Table 3.1. To correct for the effect of an artifact, we must have information about the size and nature of the artifact. Ideally, this information would be given for each study (i.e., each correlation) individually for each artifact. In that case, each correlation can be corrected individually, and the meta-analysis can be conducted on the corrected correlations. This type of meta-analysis is the subject of this chapter.

Artifact information is often available only on a sporadic basis and is sometimes not available at all. However, the nature of artifacts is such that, in most research domains, the artifact values will be independent across studies. For example, there is no reason to suppose that reliability of measurement will be either higher or lower if the sample size is large or small. If the artifacts are independent of each other and independent of the size of the true population correlation, then it is possible to base meta-analysis on artifact distributions. That is, given the independence

Table 3.1 Study artifacts that alter the value of outcome measures (with examples from personnel selection research)

1. Sampling error:
   Study validity will vary randomly from the population value because of sampling error.
2. Error of measurement in the dependent variable:
   Study validity will be systematically lower than true validity to the extent that job performance is measured with random error.
3. Error of measurement in the independent variable:
   Study validity for a test will systematically understate the validity of the ability measured because the test is not perfectly reliable.
4. Dichotomization of a continuous dependent variable:
   Turnover, the length of time that a worker stays with the organization, is often dichotomized into "more than ..." or "less than ..." where ... is some arbitrarily chosen interval such as one year or six months.
5. Dichotomization of a continuous independent variable:
   Interviewers are often told to dichotomize their perceptions into "acceptable" versus "reject."
6. Range variation in the independent variable:
   Study validity will be systematically lower than true validity to the extent that hiring policy causes incumbents to have a lower variation in the predictor than is true of applicants.
7. Attrition artifacts: Range variation in the dependent variable:
   Study validity will be systematically lower than true validity to the extent that there is systematic attrition in workers on performance, as when good workers are promoted out of the population or when poor workers are fired for poor performance.
8. Deviation from perfect construct validity in the independent variable:
   Study validity will vary if the factor structure of the test differs from the usual structure of tests for the same trait.
9. Deviation from perfect construct validity in the dependent variable:
   Study validity will differ from true validity if the criterion is deficient or contaminated.
10. Reporting or transcriptional error:
    Reported study validities differ from actual study validities due to a variety of reporting problems: inaccuracy in coding data, computational errors, errors in reading computer output, typographical errors by secretaries or by printers.
    Note: These errors can be very large in magnitude.
11. Variance due to extraneous factors that affect the relationship:
    Study validity will be systematically lower than true validity if incumbents differ in experience at the time they are assessed for performance.

assumption, it is possible to correct for artifacts at the level of meta-analysis even though we cannot correct individual correlations. This type of meta-analysis is the subject of Chapter 4. Finally, if no information is available on an artifact, then the meta-analysis cannot correct for that artifact. Note that this does not mean that the artifact does not exist or that it has no impact. It merely means that the meta-analysis does not correct for that artifact. If no correction is made for an artifact, then the estimated mean and standard deviation of true effect size correlations are not corrected for the effect of that artifact. The estimates will be inaccurate to the extent that uncorrected artifacts have a substantial impact in that research domain.

Although there are 10 potentially correctable artifacts, they will not all be discussed at the same level of detail. First, sampling error is both nonsystematic and of devastating effect in narrative reviews of the literature. Thus, sampling error will be discussed first and in considerable detail. The systematic artifacts will then be considered one by one. Here, too, there will be differences in the length of the presentation. This does not mean that some are less important than others. Rather, it is a matter of mathematical redundancy. Most of the artifacts have the effect of attenuating the true correlation by a multiplicative fraction, and hence, these artifacts all have a very similar mathematical structure. Once we look at error of measurement and range variation in detail, the others are mathematically similar and, hence, can be treated more briefly. However, it is important to remember that an artifact that may have little or no effect in one research domain may have a large effect in another. For example, there are research domains where the dependent variable has never been dichotomized; hence, there need be no correction for that artifact at all. In research on employee turnover, however, almost every study dichotomizes the dependent variable, and the dichotomization is based on administrative conventions that often lead to very extreme splits. Thus, none of the artifacts in Table 3.1 can be routinely ignored, no matter how short our treatment of that artifact may be and regardless of whether it can be corrected or not.

Consider the effect of sampling error on the study correlation. At the level of the single study, sampling error is a random event. If the observed correlation is .30, then the unknown population correlation could be higher than .30 or lower than .30, and there is no way that we can know the sampling error or correct for it. However, at the level of meta-analysis, sampling error can be estimated and corrected for. Consider first the operation of averaging correlations across studies. When we average correlations, we also average the sampling errors. Thus, the sampling error in the average correlation is the average of the sampling errors in the individual correlations. For example, if we average across 30 studies with a total sample size of 2,000, then sampling error in the average correlation is about the same as if we had computed a correlation on a sample of 2,000. That is, if the total sample size is large, then there is very little sampling error in the average correlation. The variance of correlations across studies is another story. The variance of correlations is the average *squared* deviation of the study correlation from its mean. Squaring the deviation eliminates the sign of the sampling error and, hence, eliminates the tendency for errors to cancel themselves out in summation. Instead, sampling error causes the variance across studies to be systematically larger than the variance of population correlations that we would like to know. However, the effect of sampling error on the variance is to add a known constant to the variance, which is the sampling error variance. This constant can be subtracted from the observed variance. The difference is then an estimate of the desired variance of population correlations.

To eliminate the effect of sampling error from a meta-analysis, we must derive the distribution of population correlations from the distribution of observed correlations. That is, we would like to replace the mean and standard deviation of the observed sample correlations by the mean and standard deviation of the population correlations. Because sampling error cancels out in the average correlation across studies, our best estimate of the mean population correlation is simply the mean of the sample correlations. However, sampling error adds to the variance of correlations across studies. Thus, we must correct the observed variance by subtracting the sampling error variance. The difference is then an estimate of the variance of population correlations across studies.

Once we have corrected the variance across studies for the effect of sampling error, it is possible to see if there is any real variance in results across studies. If there is a large amount of variance across studies, then it is possible to look for moderator variables to explain this variance. To test our hypothesized moderator variable, we break the set of studies into subsets using the moderator variable. For example, we might split the studies into those done on large corporations and those done on small businesses. We then do separate meta-analyses within each subset of studies. If we find large differences between subsets, then the hypothesized variable is indeed a moderator variable. The meta-analysis within subsets also tells us how much of the residual variance within subsets is due to sampling error and how much is real. That is, the meta-analysis tells us whether or not we need look for a second moderator variable.

Although it is pedagogically useful for us to present the search for moderator variables immediately after presenting the method for eliminating the effects of sampling error, that search is actually premature. Sampling error is only one source of artifactual variation across studies. We should eliminate other sources of variance before we look for moderator variables. Another important source of correctable variation across studies in most domains is variation in error of measurement across studies. That is, a variable such as job satisfaction can be measured in many ways. Thus, different studies will often use different measures of the independent variable or different measures of the dependent variable. Alternate measures will differ in the extent to which they are affected by error of measurement. Differences in amount of measurement error produce differences in the size of the correlations. Differences in correlations across studies due to differences in error of measurement often look like differences due to a moderator variable. Thus, we obtain a true picture of the stability of results across studies only if we eliminate the effects of measurement error. The same is true of other study design artifacts. However, measurement error is always present in every study, while other artifacts, such as dichotomization or range restriction, are sometimes present and sometimes not present.

Correctable artifacts other than sampling error are systematic rather than unsystematic in their impact on study correlations. Let us discuss error of measurement as one example of a correctable systematic artifact. At the level of the individual person, error of measurement is a random event. If Bill's observed score is 75, then his true score could be either greater than 75 or less than 75, and there is no way of knowing which. However, when we correlate scores across persons, the random effects of error of measurement produce a systematic effect on the correlation coefficient. Error of measurement in either variable causes the correlation to be lower than it would have been with perfect measurement. We will present a formula for "attenuation" that expresses the exact extent to which the correlation is lowered by any given amount of error of measurement. This same formula can be algebraically reversed to provide a formula for "correction for attenuation." That is, if we know the amount of error of measurement in each variable, then we can correct the observed correlation to provide an estimate of what the correlation would have been had the variables been perfectly measured.

The amount of error of measurement in a variable is measured by a number called the reliability of the variable. The reliability is a number between 0 and 1 that measures the percentage of the observed variance that is true score variance. That is, if the reliability of the independent variable is .80, then 80% of the variance in the scores is due to the true score variation, and, by subtraction, 20% of the variance is due to variation in errors of measurement. To correct for the effect of error of measurement on the correlation, we need to know the amount of error of measurement in both variables. That is, to correct the correlation for attenuation, we need to know the reliability of both variables.

Error of measurement can be eliminated from a meta-analysis in either of two ways: at the level of single studies or at the level of averages across studies. If the reliability of each variable is known in each study, then the correlation for each study can be separately corrected for attenuation. We can then do a meta-analysis on the corrected correlations. This type of meta-analysis is the subject of this chapter. However, many studies do not report the reliability of their instruments. Thus, reliability information is often only sporadically available. Under such conditions, we can still estimate the distribution of the reliability of both the independent and the dependent variables. Given the distribution of observed correlations, the distribution of the reliability of the independent variables, and the distribution of the reliability of the dependent variable, it is possible to use special formulas to correct the meta-analysis to eliminate the effects of error of measurement. Meta-analysis based on such artifact distributions is the subject of the next chapter.

If each individual correlation is corrected for attenuation, then the meta-analysis formulas will differ slightly from the formulas for meta-analysis on uncorrected correlations. The average corrected correlation estimates the average population correlation between true scores. The observed variance of the corrected correlations can be corrected for sampling error simply by subtracting a constant—the sampling error variance. However, the sampling error in a corrected correlation is larger than the sampling error in an uncorrected correlation. Therefore, a different formula must be used to compute the sampling error variance for corrected correlations.

The other correctable artifact most studied in psychometric theory (and in personnel selection research) is range restriction (though our formulas also handle the case of range enhancement or range variation). In many contexts, the standard deviation of the independent variable is approximately the same across studies (i.e., is the same to within sampling error—which will produce *some* variation in standard deviations). In such cases, the meta-analysis need not correct for range variation. However, if the standard deviation of the independent variable differs radically from study to study, then there will be corresponding differences in the correlation from study to study. These differences across studies will look like differences produced by a moderator variable. Thus, if there are big differences in the standard deviation of the independent variable across studies, then a true picture of the stability of results will appear only if the effects of range variation are eliminated. To do this, we compute the value that the correlation would have had had the study been done on a population with some reference level of variance on the independent variable.

Range deviation can be corrected at the level of the single study. If we know the standard deviation of the independent variable in the study, and if we know the standard deviation in the reference population, then there are range correction formulas that will produce an estimate of what the correlation would have been had the standard deviation of the study population been equal to the standard deviation of the reference population. As noted in the previous chapter, these correction procedures are different for direct and indirect range variation. If we correct a correlation for range departure, then the corrected correlation will have a different amount of sampling error than an uncorrected correlation. Therefore, a meta-analysis on corrected correlations must use a different formula for the sampling error variance.

In an ideal research review, we would have complete information about artifacts on each study. For each study, we would know the extent of range departure and the reliabilities of both variables. We could then correct each correlation for both range departure and error of measurement. We would then do a meta-analysis of the fully corrected correlations.

Discussion of other correctable artifacts will be taken up when the needed mathematical tools have been presented. Skipping these artifacts at this time is by no means intended to imply that they are less important. For example, in turnover studies, dichotomization has an even larger attenuating effect on study correlations than does error of measurement.

The remainder of this chapter is presented in four main sections. First, we give a complete treatment of meta-analysis with correction for sampling error only. Second, we present a detailed treatment of error of measurement and range departure, both in terms of the corrections for single studies and in terms of the effect of the correction on sampling error. Third, we describe a more abbreviated treatment of each of the other correctable artifacts. Fourth, we present meta-analysis for the case of individually corrected correlations, that is, meta-analysis as it is done when full information is available on the artifact values in each study. Examples of published studies of this sort include Carlson, Scullen, Schmidt, Rothstein, and Erwin (1999), Judge, Thorensen, Bono, and Patton (2001), and Rothstein, Schmidt, Erwin, Owens, and Sparks (1990).

At present, we know of no research domain where the information has been available to correct for every one of the correctable artifacts listed in Table 3.1. Some meta-analysis methods (e.g., Glass, McGaw, & Smith, 1981) do not even correct for sampling error; they take each study outcome at face value (see Chapter 11). In personnel selection research, correction is typically made only for sampling error, error of measurement, and range restriction. Most current meta-analyses have made no correction for dichotomization or imperfect construct validity. Furthermore, there will probably be more correctable artifacts defined and quantified over the coming years. And even if all correctable artifacts were corrected, there is still reporting error and other data errors.

It is important to keep in mind that even a fully corrected meta-analysis will not correct for all artifacts. Even after correction, the remaining variation across studies should be viewed with skepticism (see Chapters 2 and 5). Small residual variance is probably due to uncorrected artifacts rather than to a real moderator variable.

Bare-Bones Meta-Analysis: Correcting for Sampling Error Only

We will now present a detailed discussion of sampling error. To keep the presentation simple, we will ignore other artifacts. The resulting presentation is thus written as if the study population correlations were free of other artifacts. In later sections, we will discuss the relationship between sampling error and other artifacts. This section also presents the mathematics of a meta-analysis in which sampling error is the only artifact corrected. Alas, there are those who do not believe that other artifacts exist. There are also those who believe that if there are artifacts in the original studies, then those same artifacts *should be* reflected in the meta-analysis. They believe that the purpose of meta-analysis is only to describe observed results and that meta-analysis should not correct for known problems in research design (see Chapter 11). However, most scientists believe that the goal of cumulative research is to produce better answers than can be obtained in isolated studies (Rubin, 1990). From that point of view, the purpose of meta-analysis is to estimate the relationships that would have been observed if studies had been conducted perfectly (Rubin, 1990), that is, to estimate construct-level relationships (see Chapters 1, 11, and 14). Given this purpose for meta-analysis, a meta-analysis that does not correct for as many artifacts as possible is an unfinished meta-analysis. We hold that view. If a meta-analysis corrects only for sampling error, then it is the mathematical equivalent of the ostrich with its head in the sand: It is a pretense that if we ignore other artifacts then their effects on study outcomes will go away.

Estimation of Sampling Error

If the population correlation is assumed to be constant over studies, then the best estimate of that correlation is not the simple mean across studies but a weighted average in which each correlation is weighted by the number of persons in that study. Thus, the best estimate of the population correlation is

$$\bar{r} = \frac{\Sigma[N_i r_i]}{\Sigma N_i} \tag{3.1}$$

where r_i is the correlation in study i and N_i is the number of persons in study i. The corresponding variance across studies is not the usual sample variance, but the frequency-weighted average squared error

$$s_r^2 = \frac{\Sigma[N_i(r_i - \bar{r})^2]}{\Sigma N} \tag{3.2}$$

Two questions are often asked about this procedure. First, is the weighted average always better than the simple average? Hunter and Schmidt (1987a) presented a detailed discussion of this. Their analysis showed that it is a very rare case in which an unweighted analysis would be better. Second, why do we not transform the correlations to Fisher z form for the cumulative analysis? The answer is that the Fisher z transformation produces an estimate of the mean correlation that is upwardly biased and less accurate than an analysis using untransformed correlations (see Chapter 5; also, Hall & Brannick, 2002; Hunter, Schmidt, & Coggin, 1996).

The frequency-weighted average gives greater weight to large studies than to small studies. If there is no variance in population correlations across studies, then the weighting always improves accuracy. If the variance of population correlations is small, then the weighted average is also always better. If the variance of population correlations across studies is large, then as long as sample size is not correlated with the size of the population correlation, the weighted average will again be superior. That leaves one case in which the weighted average could prove troublesome. For example, in one meta-analysis, we found 13 studies on the validity of bio-data in predicting job success. One of these studies was done by an insurance consortium with a sample size of 15,000. The other 12 studies were done with sample sizes of 500 or less. The weighted average will give the single insurance study over 30 times the weight given to any other study. Suppose that the insurance study were deviant in some way. The meta-analysis might then be almost entirely defined by one deviant study. In a situation such as this, we recommend two analyses: a first analysis with the large-sample study included and a second analysis with the large-sample study left out. We have not yet had to figure out what to do should the two analyses show a major discrepancy. (In our case, they did not.) (See the related discussion of fixed- vs. random-effects meta-analysis models in Chapters 5 and 9. In particular, see the discussion of methods of weighting studies in random vs. fixed models of meta-analysis.)

What about the Fisher z transformation? In our original work, we carried out calculations with and without use of Fisher's z. For preliminary calculations done by hand, we averaged the correlations themselves, but on the computer we used what we thought to be the superior Fisher z transformation. For several years, we noticed no difference in the results for these two analyses, but in our validity generalization study for computer programmers (Schmidt, Gast-Rosenberg, & Hunter, 1980), the difference was notable. The average validity using the Fisher z transformation was larger (by about .03) than the average validity when correlations were averaged without this transformation. Careful checking of the mathematics then showed that it is the Fisher transformation that is biased. The Fisher z transformation gives larger weights to large correlations than to small ones, hence the positive bias. This problem is discussed in more detail in Chapter 5. (See "Accuracy of Different Random-Effects Models.")

Although the Fisher z transformation produces an upward bias when it is used in averaging correlations, the transformation does serve its original purpose quite well. The original purpose was not to create a method for averaging correlations. Fisher's purpose was to create a transformation of the correlation for which the standard error (and, therefore, confidence intervals) would depend solely on the sample size and not on the size of the statistic. The standard error of the Fisher z statistic is $1/(N-3)^{1/2}$, and so this goal was achieved. This means that, unlike the case for the correlation, it is unnecessary to have an estimate of the population value to compute the standard error and confidence intervals.

There has been considerable confusion in the literature produced by the fact that there is a slight bias in the correlation coefficient (a bias that can be corrected, as noted in Chapter 2 and below). There is a widespread false belief that the Fisher z eliminates that bias. The fact is that the Fisher z replaces a small underestimation, or negative bias, by a typically small overestimation, or positive bias, a bias that is always greater in absolute value than the bias in the untransformed correlation. This bias is especially large if there is variation in the population correlations across studies (Hunter et al., 1996; Schmidt & Hunter, 2003). In this case, the bias in Fisher's z can cause estimates of the mean correlation to be biased upward by substantial amounts (Field, 2001; Hall & Brannick, 2002; Schmidt & Hunter, 2003). This appears to be the reason that the random-effects meta-analysis methods of Hedges and Olkin (1985) overestimate the mean correlation (Field, 2001; Hall & Brannick, 2002). (See Chapters 5 and 9 for more detail on this issue.) It appears that meta-analysis is never made more accurate by using the Fisher z transformation and can be made substantially less accurate under certain conditions.

It is well-known that the variance of any variable can be computed using either N or $N-1$ in the denominator. The formulation in Equation (3.2) corresponds to use of N in the denominator. The advantage of using N in the denominator is that it leads to a more accurate estimate of the variance in the sense of statistical efficiency. That is, root mean square error is lower, an important consideration in meta-analysis. Use of $N-1$ instead of N leads to a slight reduction in bias but at the expense of a reduction in overall accuracy.

Correcting the Variance for Sampling Error and a Worked Example

Consider the variation in correlations across similar studies on a research question. The observed variance s_r^2 is a confounding of two things: variation in population correlations (if there is any) and variation in sample correlations produced by sampling error. Thus, an estimate of the variance in population correlations can be obtained only by correcting the observed variance s_r^2 for sampling error. The following mathematics shows that sampling error across studies behaves like error of measurement across persons and that the resulting formulas are comparable to standard formulas in classical measurement theory (reliability theory).

We begin with a treatment of sampling error in an isolated study. In an isolated study, the correlation is based on a sample: a specific sample of the population of people who might have been in that place at that time, a sample of the random processes in each person's head that generate error of measurement in test responses or supervisor ratings and so on, and a sample of time variation in person and situational parameters. This is represented in statistics by noting that the observed correlation is a sample from a population distribution of correlation values that might have been observed if the study were replicated except for the random factors. These replications are hypothetical in the sense that a real study usually contains only one such sample. However, the replications are not hypothetical in that they do represent real variation. There have been thousands of actual experiments testing the theory of statistical sampling error, and all have verified that theory. Sampling error in an isolated study is unobservable but present nonetheless.

For any study, then, there is a real population correlation ρ (which is usually unknown) that can be compared to the study correlation r. The difference between them is the sampling error, which we will denote by e. That is, we define sampling error e by the formula

$$e = r - \rho$$

or

$$r = \rho + e.$$

The distribution of observed correlations for the (usually hypothetical) replications of the study is always centered about the population correlation ρ, although the sampling error varies randomly. If we ignore the small bias in the correlation coefficient (or if we correct for it as discussed later), then the average sampling error will be 0 and the standard deviation of the sampling error will depend on the sample size. The sampling error in a particular correlation can never be changed (and, in particular, is not changed when a statistical significance test is run). On the other hand, if replications of the study could be done, then sampling error could thus be reduced. Because the average error is 0, the replicated correlations can be averaged, and the average correlation is closer to the population correlation than the individual correlations. The sampling error in the average correlation is the average of the individual sampling errors and is thus much closer to 0 than the typical single sampling error. The average correlation has smaller sampling error in much the same way as a correlation based on a larger sample size. Thus, replicating studies can potentially solve the problem of sampling error.

Whereas replication is not possible in most individual studies, replication does take place across different studies. Consider the ideal special case: a meta-analysis for a research domain in which there is no variation in the population correlations across studies and in which all studies are done with the same sample size. This case is mathematically identical to the hypothetical replications that form the basis of the statistics of isolated correlations. In particular, the average correlation across studies would have greatly reduced sampling error. In the case in which the population correlation varies from one study to another, the replication is more complicated, but the principle is the same. Replication of sampling error across studies enables us to use averaging to reduce the impact of sampling error. If the number of studies is large, the impact of sampling error can be virtually eliminated.

How big is the typical sampling error? Because sampling error has a mean of 0, the mean sampling error does not measure the size of the sampling error. That is, because a negative error of $-.10$ is just as bad as a positive error of $+.10$, it is the absolute value of the error that counts. To assess the size of errors without the algebraic sign, the common statistical practice is to square the errors. The average squared error is the variance, and the square root of that is the standard deviation of the errors. It is the standard deviation of sampling error that is the best representation of the size of errors. Consider, then, the isolated study. In the common case in which the underlying distribution is the bivariate normal distribution, the standard deviation of the sampling error is given by

$$\sigma_e = (1 - \rho^2)/\sqrt{(N - 1)}$$

where N is the sample size. Technically, our use of this formula throughout this book is tantamount to the assumption that all studies are done in contexts where the independent and dependent variables have a bivariate normal distribution, but the statistics literature has found this formula to be fairly robust in the face of departures from normality. However, under conditions of range restriction, this formula underestimates sampling error variance to some extent. That is, actual sampling variance is greater than the value predicted by the formula, leading to undercorrections for sampling error variance. Using computer simulation, Millsap (1989) showed this for direct range restriction, and Aguinis and Whitehead (1997) showed it for indirect range restriction. This means that corrections for sampling error variance are undercorrections, leading to overestimates of SD_ρ, particularly in validity generalization studies. This could create the appearance of a moderator where none exists. However, in research areas where there is no range restriction, this problem does not occur.

The effect of averaging across replications is dramatic in terms of sampling error variance. If the sample size in each replication is N and the number of studies is K, then the sampling error variance in the average of K correlations is the variance of the average error e, that is,

$$\text{Var}(\bar{e}) = \text{Var}(e)/K \tag{3.3}$$

In other words, the effect of averaging across K studies is to divide the sampling error variance by K. Because the total sample size in K studies is K times the sample size in a single study, this means that to increase the sample size by a factor of K is to reduce the sampling error variance by a factor of K. This is exactly the same rule as that for increasing the sample size of a single study. Thus, replication can reduce sampling error in the same way as using larger samples.

In practice, the effect of increasing sample size is not quite as impressive as the previous formula would suggest. Unfortunately, it is not the variance but the standard deviation (standard error) that counts. The standard deviation of the average error is divided only by the square root of the number of studies. Thus, to cut the standard error in half, we must average four studies rather than two studies. This is important in judging the number of missing studies in a meta-analysis when that number is small. For example, if an investigator randomly misses 10 out of 100 potential studies, the sampling error variance is increased by 10%, but the sampling error standard error is increased by only 5%. Thus, missing a few studies randomly usually does not reduce the accuracy of a meta-analysis by nearly as much as might be supposed.

We come now to the meta-analysis of correlations taken from different studies. The power of meta-analysis to reduce the problem of sampling error lies in the fact that sampling errors are replicated across studies. The ultimate statistical error in meta-analysis will depend on two factors: the size of the average sample size for the individual studies and the number of studies in the meta-analysis. For the mean correlation, it is the total sample size that determines the error in the meta-analysis. For the estimate of the variance of correlations, the computations are more complicated but the principle is similar.

Let the subscript i denote the study number. Then the error variable e_i represents the sampling error in the sample correlation in study i; that is, we define e_i by

$$r_i = \rho_i + e_i$$

Then the mean of the error within hypothetical replications is 0. The average error across studies is

$$E(e_i) = 0$$

The variance across hypothetical replications of any one study is denoted by

$$\sigma_{e_i}^2 = \frac{(1 - \rho_i^2)^2}{N_i - 1} \tag{3.4}$$

In going across studies, this hypothetical and unobserved variation becomes real and potentially observable variation. This is similar to the case of observing a sample of people or scores from a distribution of people or scores. It differs from the usual case in statistics because the sampling error variance differs from one study to the next. Nonetheless, the critical fact is that the variance of sampling error becomes visible across studies. The formula

$$r_i = \rho_i + e_i$$

is analogous to the true score, error score formula from measurement error theory:

$$X_p = T_p + e_p$$

where X_p and T_p are the observed and true scores for person p. In particular, sampling error (signed sampling error, not sampling error variance) is unrelated to population values across studies (cf. Schmidt, Hunter, & Raju, 1988). Thus, if we calculate a variance across studies, then the variance of sample correlations is the sum of the variance in population correlations and the variance due to sampling error, that is,

$$\sigma_r^2 = \sigma_\rho^2 + \sigma_e^2$$

The implication of this formula is that the variance of observed correlations is larger than the variance of population correlations, often much larger. The reason it is larger is because squared sampling errors are always positive and do not cancel out when averaged. Thus, the average squared deviation of observed correlations is systematically larger than the average squared deviation of population correlations because sampling error makes a systematically positive contribution to the squared deviation.

The formula $\sigma_r^2 = \sigma_\rho^2 + \sigma_e^2$ has three variances. If any two of the variances are known, the third can be computed. In particular, if the sampling error variance σ_e^2 were known, then the desired variance of population correlations would be

$$\sigma_\rho^2 = \sigma_r^2 - \sigma_e^2$$

Of these three variances, only the variance of observed correlations is estimated using a conventional variance, that is, average squared deviation of given numbers. If we knew the value of the sampling error variance, then it would not matter that we could not compute it as a conventional variance. The fact is that the sampling error variance need not be given as an empirical number; it is given by statistical formula. The sampling error variance across studies is just the average of the sampling error variances within studies. If study correlations are weighted by sample size N_i, then the error variance across studies is

$$\sigma_e^2 = \text{Ave}\, \sigma_{e_i}^2 = \frac{\sum[N_i \sigma_{e_i}^2]}{\sum N_i} = \frac{\sum[N_i[(1-\rho_i^2)^2]/[N_i - 1]]}{\sum N_i} \quad (3.5)$$

This formula is used in our Windows-based meta-analysis computer program package. (See the Appendix for a description and availability.) However, Law, Schmidt, and Hunter (1994b) and Hunter and Schmidt (1994b) showed via computer simulation that this formula is more accurate if ρ_i is estimated by $\bar{r}$. That is, in computing the sampling error variance for each individual study, $\bar{r}$ is used in place of r_i. This modification is used in our computer programs. (See Chapter 5 for further discussion of this.)

Approximation formulas are available for use in hand calculations of meta-analysis. In Equation (3.5), the fraction $N_i/(N_i - 1)$ is close to unity. If we take this fraction as unity, and we use the approximation that average $(\rho^2) \cong (\text{average } \rho)^2$, then we have the almost perfect approximation

$$\sigma_e^2 = \frac{(1-\bar{r}^2)^2 K}{T} \quad (3.6)$$

where K is the number of studies and $T = \sum N_i$ is the total sample size. The corresponding estimate of the variance of population correlations is thus

$$\text{est } \sigma_\rho^2 = \sigma_r^2 - \sigma_e^2 = \sigma_r^2 - \frac{(1-\bar{r}^2)^2 K}{T}$$

There is an even better estimate of the sampling error variance. Consider the special case in which all studies have the same sample size N. The ratio $N_i/(N_i - 1)$ is then simply the constant $N/(N-1)$, which factors out of the summation. We then have

$$\sigma_e^2 = \text{Ave}\,(1-\rho_i^2)^2/(N-1)$$

If we estimate ρ_i by the average correlation across studies (Hunter & Schmidt, 1994b; Law et al., 1994b), we have the approximation

$$\sigma_e^2 = (1-\bar{r}^2)^2/(N-1) \quad (3.7)$$

This formula is exactly analogous to the formula for sampling error in the single study

$$\sigma_e^2 = (1 - \rho^2)^2/(N - 1)$$

The relationship between the first approximation and the second approximation stems from the fact that

$$K/T = 11/(T/K)(T/K) = 1/N$$

That is, the previous approximation with K in the numerator and T in the denominator is equivalent to having average sample size in the denominator. Thus, the improvement is to use $N - 1$ instead of N, a small change for typical sample sizes of 100, but a noticeable improvement in those unusual meta-analyses conducted in research areas with very small sample sizes. For example, psychotherapy studies have a typical sample size of about 20.

Consider again the typical case where sample size varies from one study to the next. Let the average sample size be denoted by $\bar{N}$, that is,

$$\bar{N} = T/K$$

Our first approximation could be written as

$$\sigma_e^2 = (1 - \bar{r}^2)^2/\bar{N}$$

while the second improved approximation is

$$\sigma_e^2 = (1 - \bar{r}^2)^2/(\bar{N} - 1)$$

Mathematical work not presented here (Hunter & Schmidt, 1987a) shows that the second approximation is accurate both when the population correlations are all the same (Hunter & Schmidt, 1994b)—when it is optimal—and also when there is variation in population correlations (when complicated weighting schemes based on knowledge of the distribution of sample size—not usually known in a meta-analysis—would improve the estimate slightly; Law et al., 1994b). The corresponding estimate of the variance of population correlations is

$$\sigma_\rho^2 = \sigma_r^2 - \sigma_e^2 = \sigma_r^2 - (1 - \bar{r}^2)^2/(\bar{N} - 1)$$

This equation allows an empirical test of the hypothesis $\sigma_\rho^2 = 0$.

An Example: Socioeconomic Status and Police Performance

Bouchard (1776, 1860, 1914, 1941) postulated that differences in upbringing would produce differences in response to power over other people. His theory was that because lower-class parents obtain obedience by beating their children to a pulp while middle-class parents threaten them with loss of love, lower-class children would grow into adults who are more likely themselves to use physical force to gain compliance. He tested his theory by looking at the relationship between socioeconomic status of origin of police officers and brutality in police departments. His independent measure was socioeconomic status measured in terms of six classes, ranging from 1 = upper, upper class to 6 = lower, lower class. His brutality measure was the number of complaints divided by the number of years employed. Only patrol officers were considered in the correlations, which are shown in Table 3.2. The meta-analysis of these data is as follows:

$$\bar{r} = \frac{100(.34) + 100(.16) + 50(.12) + 50(.38)}{100 + 100 + 50 + 50} = \frac{75.00}{300} = .25$$

$$\sigma_r^2 = \frac{100(.34 - .25)^2 + 100(.16 - .25)^2 + 50(.12 - .25)^2 + 50(.38 - .25)^2}{100 + 100 + 50 + 50}$$

$$= \frac{3.31}{300} = .011033$$

The average sample size is

$$\bar{N} = T/K = 300/4 = 75$$

Thus, the sampling error variance is estimated to be

$$\sigma_e^2 = (1 - \bar{r}^2)^2/(\bar{N} - 1) = (1 - .25^2)^2/74 = .011877$$

The estimate of the variance of population correlations is thus

$$\sigma_\rho^2 = \sigma_r^2 - \sigma_e^2 = \sigma_r^2 - (1 - \bar{r}^2)^2/(\bar{N} - 1)$$

$$= .011033 - .011877 = -.000844.$$

Because the estimated variance is negative, the estimated standard deviation is 0, that is,

$$\sigma_\rho = 0$$

Some readers have been bothered by this example. They ask, "How can a variance be negative, even if only −.0008?" The answer is that the estimated variance of population correlations is not computed as a conventional variance, that is, the average squared deviation of given numbers. Rather, it is computed as the difference between the given variance of observed correlations and the statistically given sampling error variance. Although there is little error in the statistically given sampling error variance, the variance of observed correlations is a sample estimate. Unless the number of studies is infinite, there will be some error in that empirical estimate. If the population difference is 0, then error will cause the estimated difference to be positive or negative with probability one-half. Thus, in our case, sampling error caused the variance of observed correlations to differ slightly from the expected value, and that error caused the estimating difference to be negative. There is no logical contradiction here. In analysis of variance and in Cronbach's generalizability theory, estimation of components of variance using expected mean square formulas also produces negative observed estimates for similar reasons. Such estimates are always taken as 0. This question is discussed further in Chapter 9. (See discussion of second-order sampling error.)

Table 3.2 Correlations between socioeconomic status and police brutality (U.S.)

Location	*Date*	*Sample Size*	*Correlation*
Philadelphia	1776	100	.34*
Richmond, VA	1861	100	.16
Washington, DC	1914	50	.12
Pearl Harbor	1941	50	.38*

*Significant at the .05 level.

Consider the empirical meaning of our results. Bouchard claimed that his results varied dramatically from city to city. His explanation was that Washington, D.C., and Richmond are southern cities, and southern hospitality is so strong that it reduces the incidence of brutality in the lower classes and, hence, reduces the correlation in those cities. However, our analysis shows that all the variation in his results is due to sampling error and that the correlation is always .25.

Moderator Variables Analyzed by Grouping the Data and a Worked Example

A moderator variable is a variable that causes differences in the correlation between two other variables. For example, in the police brutality study discussed previously, Bouchard postulated that geographic region (North vs. South) would be a moderator variable for the relationship between socioeconomic status and brutality. If there is true variation in results across studies, then there must be such a moderator variable (or possibly more than one) to account for such variance. On the other hand, if the analysis shows that the variation in results is due to sampling error, then any apparent moderating effect is due to capitalization on sampling error. This was the case in Bouchard's work.

If the corrected standard deviation suggests substantial variation in population correlations across studies, then a moderator variable derived from a theory or hypothesis can be used to group the observed correlations into subsets. Within each subset, we can calculate a mean, a variance, and a variance corrected for sampling error. A moderator variable will reveal itself in two ways: (1) the average correlation will vary from subset to subset, and (2) the corrected variance will *average* lower in the subsets than for the data as a whole. These two facts are mathematically dependent. By a theorem in analysis of variance, we know that the total variance is the mean of the subset variances plus the variance of the subset means. Thus, the mean uncorrected within-subset variance must decrease to exactly the extent that the subset means differ from one another. This means that if the average correlation varies across subsets, then the average standard deviation of the subsets *must* be less than the standard deviation in the combined data set.

An Example: Police Brutality in Transylvania

In order to justify a European sabbatical, Hackman (1978) argued that Bouchard's work on police brutality needed a cross-cultural replication. So he gathered data in four cities in Transylvania, carefully replicating Bouchard's measurement on socioeconomic status and brutality. His data are given along with Bouchard's in Table 3.3.

Analysis of the Whole Set

$$\bar{r} = \frac{100(.34) + \cdots + 100(.19) + \cdots + 50(.23)}{100 + \cdots + 100 \ldots + 50} = \frac{105.00}{600} = .175$$

$$\sigma_r^2 = \frac{100(.34 - .175)^2 + \cdots + 50(.23 - .175)^2}{100 + \cdots + 50} = \frac{9.995}{600} = .016658$$

$$N = T/K = 600/8 = 75$$

$$\sigma_e^2 = \frac{(1 - .175^2)^2}{74} = .012698$$

$$\sigma_\rho^2 = .016658 - .012698 = .00396$$

$$\sigma_\rho = .063$$

The corrected standard deviation of .063 can be compared with the mean of .175 : .175/.063 = 2.78. That is, the mean correlation is nearly 2.8 standard deviations above 0. Thus, if the study population correlations are normally distributed, the probability of a zero or below-zero correlation is virtually nil. So the qualitative nature of the relationship is clear: The population correlation is positive in all studies.

However, the variation is not trivial in amount relative to the mean. This suggests a search for moderator variables. The moderator analysis is as follows:

United States	*Transylvania*
$\bar{r} = .25$	$\bar{r} = .10$
$\sigma_r^2 = .011033$	$\sigma_r^2 = .011033$
$\sigma_e^2 = .011877$	$\sigma_e^2 = .013245$
$\sigma_\rho^2 = -.000844$	$\sigma_\rho^2 = -.002212$
$\sigma_\rho = 0$	$\sigma_\rho = 0$

Analysis of the subsets shows a substantial difference in mean correlations, $\bar{r} = .25$ in the United States and $\bar{r} = .10$ in Transylvania. The corrected standard deviations reveal that there is no variation in results within the two countries.

In this case, there was only one moderator. When there are multiple moderators, the moderators may be correlated, and hence, they will be confounded if examined sequentially one at a time. In these cases, it is important to conduct moderator analyses hierarchically to avoid such confounding. (See Chapter 9.)

Hackman explained the difference between the two countries by noting that vampires in the United States live quiet, contented lives working for the Red Cross, while vampires in Transylvania must still get their blood by tracking down and killing live victims. Vampires in Transylvania resent their low station in life and focus their efforts on people of high status, whom they envy. Middle-class policemen who work at night are particularly vulnerable. Thus, there is less variance in social class among the policemen in Transylvania, and this restriction in

Table 3.3 Correlations between socioeconomic status and police brutality (U.S. and Transylvania)

Investigator	*Location*	*Sample Size*	*Correlation*
Bouchard	Philadelphia	100	.34*
Bouchard	Richmond, VA	100	.16
Bouchard	Washington, DC	50	.12
Bouchard	Pearl Harbor	50	.38*
Hackman	Brasov	100	.19
Hackman	Targul-Ocna	100	.01
Hackman	Hunedoara	50	−.03
Hackman	Lupeni	50	.23

*Significant at the .05 level.

range reduces the correlation. According to this hypothesis, correcting for range restriction would make the two mean correlations equal (at .25). Later in this chapter, we will examine range corrections that can be used to test this hypothesis.

After a heated exchange at the Academy of Management convention, Bouchard bared his fangs and showed Hackman that American vampires can still be a pain in the neck. Bouchard then noted that the difference in the results reflected the fact that his studies were done at times when the country was going to war. This increase in aggressive excitement increased the general level and the variance of brutality and, thus, increased its reliability of measurement and, hence, the level of correlation. According to this hypothesis, correcting for measurement error in the brutality measure would reveal that the two mean correlations are really equal at the level of true scores. This hypothesis can be tested using the corrections for measurement error discussed later in this chapter.

Correcting Feature Correlations for Sampling Error and a Worked Example

Suppose some study feature is coded as a quantitative variable y. Then that feature can be correlated with the outcome statistic across studies. For example, if correlations between dependency and school achievement varied as a function of the age of the child, then we might code average age in study i as y_i. We could then correlate age of children with size of correlation across studies. An example of this method is given by Schwab, Olian-Gottlieb, and Heneman (1979). However, such a correlation across studies is a confounding of the correlation for population values with y and the noncorrelation of the sampling error with y. This is directly analogous to the role of error of measurement in attenuating correlations based on imperfectly measured variables. Thus, the observed correlation across studies will be smaller than would be the case had there been no sampling error in the correlations.

To avoid confusion between the basic statistic r, which is the correlation over persons within a study, and correlations between r and study features over studies, the correlations over studies will be denoted by "Cor." For example, the correlation between the correlation r and the study feature y across studies will be denoted $\text{Cor}(r, y)$. This is the observed correlation across studies, but the desired correlation across studies is that for population correlations, ρ_i. The desired correlation across studies is $\text{Cor}(\rho, y)$. Starting from the formula $r_i = \rho_i + e_i$, we calculate a covariance over studies and use the principle of additivity of covariances to produce

$$\sigma_{ry} = \sigma_{\rho y} + \sigma_{ey} = \sigma_{\rho y} + 0 = \sigma_{\rho y}$$

If this covariance across studies is divided by standard deviations across studies, then we have

$$\begin{aligned} \text{Cor}(r, y) &= \frac{\sigma_{ry}}{\sigma_r \sigma_y} = \frac{\sigma_{\rho y}}{\sigma_r \sigma_y} \\ &= \frac{\sigma_{\rho y}}{\sigma_\rho \sigma_y} \frac{\sigma_\rho}{\sigma_r} \\ &= \text{Cor}(\rho, y) \frac{\sigma_\rho}{\sigma_r} \end{aligned}$$

However, the covariance of r_i with ρ_i is

$$\sigma_{r\rho} = \sigma_{\rho\rho} + \sigma_{e\rho} = \sigma_{\rho\rho} + 0 = \sigma_\rho^2$$

Hence, the correlation across studies is

$$\text{Cor}(r, \rho) = \frac{\sigma_{r\rho}}{\sigma_r \sigma_\rho} = \frac{\sigma_\rho^2}{\sigma_r \sigma_\rho} = \frac{\sigma_\rho}{\sigma_r} \tag{3.8}$$

Thus, the observed correlation across studies is the product of two other correlations, the desired correlation and reliability-like correlation:

$$\text{Cor}(r, y) = \text{Cor}(\rho, y)\,\text{Cor}(r, \rho)$$

The desired correlation is then the ratio

$$\text{Cor}(\rho, y) = \frac{\text{Cor}(r, y)}{\text{Cor}(r, \rho)} \tag{3.9}$$

which is precisely the formula for correction for attenuation due to error of measurement if there is measurement error in one variable only. What is the correlation between r and ρ over studies? We have the variance of r as estimated by s_r^2. We need only the variance of ρ, which was estimated in the previous section of this chapter. Thus, the "reliability" needed for use in the attenuation formula is given by

$$\begin{aligned} \text{Reliability of } r &= \{\text{Cor}(r, \rho)\}^2 \\ &= \frac{\sigma_\rho^2}{\sigma_r^2} = \frac{\sigma_r^2 - (1 - \bar{r}^2)^2/(\bar{N} - 1)}{\sigma_r^2} \end{aligned} \tag{3.10}$$

Hence,

$$\text{Cor}(\rho, y) = \frac{\text{Cor}(r, y)}{[\sigma_r^2 - (1 - \bar{r}^2)^2/(\bar{N} - 1)]/[\sigma_r^2]^{1/2}} \tag{3.11}$$

An Example: The Tibetan Employment Service

Officials in the Tibetan Employment Service have been using a cognitive ability test for some years to steer people into various jobs. Although they have relied on content validity for such assignments, they have also been gathering criterion-related validity data to test their content validity system. In their content validity system, test development analysts rate each occupation for the extent to which it requires high cognitive ability, with ratings from 1 = low to 3 = high. They have concurrent validity studies on six occupations chosen to stratify the full range of the content validity continuum. These data are shown in Table 3.4. The analysis is as follows:

$$\bar{r} = .30$$

$$\sigma_r^2 = .048333$$

$$\bar{N} = T/K = 600/6 = 100$$

$$\sigma_e^2 = .008365$$

$$\sigma_\rho^2 = .048333 - .008365 = .039968$$

$$\sigma_\rho = .20$$

$$\text{Rel}(r) = \frac{\sigma_\rho^2}{\sigma_r^2} = \frac{.0400}{.0483} = .83$$

The percentage of variance due to sampling error is 17%. Let y_i be the cognitive rating of the ith occupation. Then

$$\text{Cor}(r, y) = .72$$

$$\text{Cor}(\rho, y) = \frac{.72}{\sqrt{.83}} = .79$$

The study found very large variation in validity, even after correction for sampling error. The correlation was .72 between rating and observed correlation and rose to .79 after correction for sampling error. In this case, only 17% of the variance of the correlations was due to artifacts, so the reliability of the study correlations was .83 (i.e., $1 - .17$). Ordinarily, reliability would be much lower and, hence, the correction would be much larger. For example, if 70% of the variance were due to artifacts, then the reliability would be only $1 - .70 = .30$. The correction factor would be $1/(.30)^{1/2} = 1.83$.

Table 3.4 Tibetan employment service test validities

Occupation	*Cognitive Rating*	*Validity (Correlation)*	*Sample Size*
Monastery Abbot	3	.45*	100
Magistrate	3	.55*	100
Holy Man	2	.05	100
Farmer	2	.55*	100
Bandit	1	.10	100
Yak Chip Collector	1	.10	100

*Significant at the .05 level.

In this example, we have corrected only for unreliability in the dependent variable (the validity correlations). However, as in all studies, the independent variable also contains measurement error, and so we should also correct for unreliability in the ratings of the cognitive requirements of the jobs, as pointed out by Orwin and Cordray (1985). Suppose in this particular case, the reliability of these ratings was found to be .75. Then the true score correlation between ratings and test validity would be

$$\mathrm{Cor}(\rho, y) = \frac{.72}{\sqrt{.83\,(.75)}} = .91$$

So it is apparent that in a real analysis of this sort, it is critical to correct for measurement error *in both measures* (Orwin & Cordray, 1985). Otherwise, construct-level relationships will be underestimated.

Artifacts Other Than Sampling Error

Error of Measurement and Correction for Attenuation

Variables in science are never perfectly measured. Indeed, sometimes the measurement is very crude. Since the late 1890s, we have known that the error of measurement attenuates the correlation coefficient. That is, error of measurement systematically lowers the correlation between *measures* in comparison to the correlation between the variables themselves. This systematic error is then exaggerated by the unsystematic distortions of sampling error. In this section, we will review the theory of error of measurement and derive the classic formula for correction for attenuation. Measurement error has a special status among systematic artifacts: It is the only systematic artifact that is always present in every study in a meta-analysis.

We will then look at the impact of error of measurement on sampling error and confidence intervals. In particular, we will derive the confidence interval for individual corrected correlations. From this base, we will later consider the impact of error of measurement as it varies in amount from one study to another.

Let us denote by T the true score that would have been observed on the independent variable had we been able to measure it perfectly. We then have

$$x = T + E_1$$

where E_1 is the error of measurement in the independent variable. Let us denote by U the true score that would have been observed on the dependent variable had we been able to measure it perfectly. We then have

$$y = U + E_2$$

where E_2 is the error of measurement in the dependent variable. Let us use the traditional notation by denoting the reliabilities by r_{xx} and r_{yy}, respectively. We then have

$$r_{xx} = \rho_{xT}^2$$
$$r_{yy} = \rho_{yU}^2$$

The desired correlation is the population correlation between perfectly measured variables, that is, ρ_{TU}, but the observed correlation is the sample correlation between observed scores r_{xy}. There are two steps in relating the one to the other: the systematic attenuation of the population correlation by error of measurement and the unsystematic variation produced by sampling error.

The systematic attenuation can be computed by considering the causal pathways from x to T to U to y. According to the rules of path analysis, ρ_{xy} is the product of the three paths from x to y, that is,

$$\begin{aligned}\rho_{xy} &= \rho_{xT}\rho_{TU}\rho_{Uy} = \rho_{xT}\rho_{yU}\rho_{TU}\\ &= \sqrt{r_{xx}}\sqrt{r_{yy}}\rho_{TU}\end{aligned}$$

At the level of population correlations, this leads to the classic formula for correction for attenuation:

$$\rho_{TU} = \frac{\rho_{xy}}{\sqrt{r_{xx}}\sqrt{r_{yy}}} \tag{3.12}$$

At the level of observed correlations, we have

$$r_{xy} = \rho_{xy} + e$$

where e is the sampling error in r_{xy} as before. Thus,

$$\sigma_r^2 = \sigma_\rho^2 + \sigma_e^2$$

where the sampling error variance is given by the formulas of earlier sections.

If we correct the observed correlation using the population correlation formula, then we have

$$\begin{aligned}r_c &= \frac{r_{xy}}{\sqrt{r_{xx}}\sqrt{r_{yy}}} = \frac{\sqrt{r_{xx}}\sqrt{r_{yy}}\rho_{TU} + e}{\sqrt{r_{xx}}\sqrt{r_{yy}}}\\ &= \rho_{TU} + \frac{e}{\sqrt{r_{xx}}\sqrt{r_{yy}}}\end{aligned} \tag{3.13}$$

We can write a new equation for the corrected correlation

$$r_c = \rho_c + e_c \tag{3.14}$$

where e_c is the sampling error in the corrected correlation r_c and where the population value $\rho_c = \rho_{TU}$. The error variance for the corrected correlation can then be computed from the error variance for uncorrected correlations and the reliabilities of the two variables:

$$e_c = \frac{e}{\sqrt{r_{xx}}\sqrt{r_{yy}}}$$

$$\sigma_{e_c}^2 = \frac{\sigma_e^2}{r_{xx}r_{yy}} \tag{3.15}$$

Thus, if we correct the observed correlation for attenuation, we increase the sampling error correspondingly. In particular, to form the confidence interval for a corrected correlation, we apply the correction formula to the two endpoints of the confidence interval for the uncorrected correlation. That is, in the case of correction for attenuation, just as we divide the point estimate of the correlation by the product of the square roots of the reliabilities, so, too, we divide each endpoint of the confidence interval by the same product.

An Example of Correction for Attenuation

Suppose that if organizational commitment and job satisfaction were perfectly measured, the correlation between true scores would be $\rho_{TU} = .60$. Suppose instead that we measure organizational commitment with reliability $r_{xx} = .45$ and that we measure job satisfaction with reliability $r_{yy} = .55$. Then the population correlation between observed scores would be

$$\rho_{xy} = \sqrt{r_{xx}}\sqrt{r_{yy}}\rho_{TU} = \sqrt{.45}\sqrt{.55}\rho_{TU}$$
$$= .50(.60) = .30$$

That is, the effect of error of measurement in this example is to reduce the correlation between true scores by 50%—from a true score population correlation of .60 to a study population correlation of .30 between observed scores. If we apply the correction formula, we have

$$\rho_{TU} = \frac{\rho_{xy}}{\sqrt{r_{xx}}\sqrt{r_{yy}}} = \frac{.30}{\sqrt{.45}\sqrt{.55}} = \frac{.30}{.50} = .60$$

That is, correction for attenuation works perfectly for population correlations; it is perfectly accurate when sample size is infinite.

Consider the impact of sampling error. If the sample size for the study is $N = 100$, then the standard error of the observed correlation (from $\rho_{xy} = .30$) is $(1 - .30^2)/\sqrt{99} = .091$. Thus, it would not be uncommon to observe a correlation of .20 in the actual study. If we compare the observed correlation of .20 with the desired correlation of .60, then we see that there is a massive error. However, this error can be broken into two components: the systematic error of attenuation and the unsystematic error due to sampling error. The systematic error reduced the correlation from .60 to .30. The unsystematic error is the difference between an observed r of .20 and the population attenuated correlation .30.

Let us correct for attenuation and look at the error in the corrected correlation:

$$r_c = \frac{r_{xy}}{\sqrt{r_{xx}}\sqrt{r_{yy}}} = \frac{.20}{\sqrt{.45}\sqrt{.55}} = \frac{.20}{.50} = .40$$

The sampling error in the corrected correlation is the difference between the estimated .40 and the actual .60. Thus, we have

$$r = \rho_{xy} + e = \rho_{xy} - .1 = .30 - .10 = .20$$
$$r_c = \rho_c + e_c = \rho_c - .2 = .60 - .20 = .40$$

Therefore, as we doubled the observed attenuated correlation to estimate the unattenuated correlation, we doubled the sampling error as well. On the other hand, we reduced the systematic error from .30 to 0. We can combine both types of error and look at total error. Total error has been reduced by 50%:

$$\text{Total error for } r = .60 - .20 = .40$$
$$\text{Total error for } r_c = .60 - .40 = .20$$

The standard error for the observed correlation would be calculated as

$$\frac{1 - .20^2}{\sqrt{99}} = .096$$

The 95% confidence interval for the observed correlation is given by $r \pm 1.96\sigma_e = .20 \pm 1.96(.096)$ or $.01 \leq \rho \leq .39$, which does include the actual value of $\rho_{xy} = .30$. We then correct each endpoint of the confidence interval to obtain

Lower Endpoint	*Upper Endpoint*
$r_1 = .01$	$r_1 = .39$
$r_{1c} = \frac{.01}{\sqrt{.45}\sqrt{.55}}$	$r_{2c} = \frac{.39}{\sqrt{.45}\sqrt{.55}}$
$= \frac{.01}{.50} = .02$	$= \frac{.39}{.50} = .78$

Let us compare the confidence intervals of corrected and uncorrected correlations:

$$.01 \leq \hat{\rho}_{xy} \leq .39$$

$$.02 \leq \hat{\rho}_{TU} \leq .78$$

We see that the center of the confidence interval changes from the uncorrected correlation .20 to the corrected correlation .40. At the same time, the width of the confidence interval doubles, reflecting the increased sampling error in the corrected correlation.

This point can be made dramatically with confidence intervals. If measurement of both variables were perfectly reliable, then the population correlation would be .60, and the standard error would be $(1 - .60^2)/\sqrt{99} = .064$. This is much smaller than the standard error for a correlation of .30, which is .091. Thus, if we can reduce error of measurement substantively, then we can obtain larger observed correlations *and smaller confidence intervals.* Substantive elimination of error of measurement is vastly superior to elimination by statistical formula after the fact.

We could have obtained the same confidence interval in a different way. Suppose we erected the confidence interval around the corrected correlation using the sampling error formula for e_c. The center of the confidence interval is then $r_c = .40$. The sampling error variance is then given by

$$\sigma_{e_c}^2 = \frac{\sigma_e^2}{r_{xx}r_{yy}} = \frac{\sigma_e^2}{(.45)(.55)} = \frac{(1 - .2^2)^2/99}{.2475} = .0376$$

That is, the sampling error standard deviation for the corrected correlation is $\sigma_{e_c} = (.0376)^{1/2} = .19$. The confidence interval is then given by $.40 \pm 1.96\sigma_{e_c}$ or $.02 \leq \rho_{TU} \leq .78$. This is the same confidence interval obtained earlier.

Statistical Versus Substantive Correction

If we use statistical formulas to correct for attenuation, we obtain larger corrected correlations with a wider confidence interval. There are two conclusions that might be drawn from this fact. (1) *False conclusion:* Because correcting for attenuation increases the amount of sampling error, maybe we should not correct for attenuation. *Key fact:* If we do not correct for attenuation, then we do not eliminate the *systematic* error. In our example, the error in the uncorrected correlation was $.60 - .20 = .40$. Thus, the error in the corrected correlation was only half as large as the error in the uncorrected correlation. (2) *True conclusion:* We could greatly improve our statistical accuracy if we could reduce the error of measurement substantively, that is, by using better measurement procedures in the first place.

Using the Appropriate Reliability Coefficient

In making corrections for measurement error, the researcher should make every effort to use the appropriate type of reliability coefficient. Different methods of computing reliability coefficients assess different kinds (sources) of measurement error. Estimation of the appropriate reliability coefficient requires the specification of the kinds of measurement error in the specific research domain and requires the gathering of data that allows each kind of measurement error to be reflected in the reliability coefficient. In most current meta-analyses, the unit of analysis is the person (or rat or pigeon or . . .) and the variable measured is some behavior of the person. For this case, there is an extensive theory of reliability developed by psychometricians and there has been extensive testing of that theory (see, e.g., Cronbach, 1947; Stanley, 1971; Thorndike, 1951). This is the case discussed in this book. However, meta-analyses are being conducted in other areas. For example, Rodgers and Hunter (1986) conducted a meta-analysis in which the measures were business unit productivity measures. Another example of this is Harter, Schmidt, and Hayes (2002). In both meta-analyses, the unit of measurement was not the individual employee but the business unit (e.g., individual stores or individual bank branches), and in both meta-analyses special reliability estimation procedures had to be used. However, such cases are the exception. Suppose the unit of analysis in the study is persons, the usual case. The measure is usually obtained in one of three ways: the behavior is directly recorded (as in test scores or closed-ended questionnaire answers, here called "response data"), assessed by an observer (here called a "judgment or rating"), or observed and recorded by an observer (here called "coded response data"). The reliability considerations differ by case.

Response Data. Response data behavior is used for measurement of a given variable under the assumption that the variable to be measured is the primary causal agent that determines that behavior. Error of measurement is present to the extent that the behavior is determined by other causal agents. At least three kinds of error have been identified by psychometric theory: random response error, specific error, and transient error (cf. Le & Schmidt, 2002; Le, Schmidt, & Lauver, 2003; Schmidt & Hunter, 1996, 1999b; Schmidt, Le, & Ilies, 2003; Stanley, 1971; Thorndike, 1949, 1951). The ubiquitous error agent is randomness in behavior. Except for highly practiced responses, such as giving one's name, most human acts have a sizeable random element. This is called "random response error." Random response error can be thought of as noise in the human nervous system (Schmidt &

Hunter, 1999b; Thorndike, 1949, 1951). Sometimes the behavior is influenced by something peculiar about the measurement situation, for example, an idiosyncratic response to one of the specific words used in an opinion item. The influence of such situation- or stimulus-specific agents is called "specific error" (or specific factor error). Specific factor error is associated with individual items in a measure. (It is actually the person by item interaction.) Each different scale for measuring a variable also has specific factor measurement error unique to that scale. Sometimes the behavior is affected by an influence that varies randomly over time, such as mood or illness. The influence of a time-varying factor is called "transient error." Each of these three forms of error of measurement enters differently into the designs traditionally used to measure reliability (Schmidt et al., 2003; Stanley, 1971; Thorndike, 1951).

One design makes error visible by obtaining multiple responses in a given measurement session—eliciting behaviors to various situations or stimuli (e.g., items) that are equivalent in the extent of causal influence from the variable to be measured. The independent responses allow for independent sampling of the random response error and independent sampling of the specific error. Thus, reliability computed from this design detects and measures the extent of random response error and specific error. However, if there is transient error, this design will not detect it; thus, the reliability coefficient will be too large by the relative amount of transient error. This form of reliability is properly called "parallel forms reliability" and is improperly called "internal consistency reliability," although better language would substitute the phrase "reliability estimate" for the word "reliability." This form of reliability is usually assessed using Cronbach's alpha coefficient or the KR-20 coefficient (the equivalent coefficient for items answered dichotomously). Cronbach (1947) referred to this type of reliability as the coefficient of equivalence (CE).

Another common design is the test-retest design. A behavior is measured with the same scale at two points in time that are far enough apart so that the transient error factor is not repeated, but close enough in time so that there is no significant change in the variable to be measured. The two measures will allow for new (independent) sampling from the random response error distribution and new (independent) sampling from the transient error distribution. However, if there is specific error, this design will not detect it; thus, the reliability coefficient will be too large by the relative amount of specific error. Specific factor measurement error is not detected because the same specific errors occur at time 1 and time 2 due to use of the same scale (instrument) at both times. This form of reliability is called "test-retest reliability," although better language would substitute the phrase "reliability estimate" for the word "reliability." Cronbach (1947) referred to this type of reliability estimate as the coefficient of stability (CS).

If all three kinds of measurement error are present, then the correct reliability will be obtained only by a design in which both the situational determinants of specific error and the temporal determinants of transient error are resampled. This is the "delayed parallel forms" design. Cronbach (1947) referred to this type of reliability estimate as the coefficient of equivalence and stability (CES). Given two forms of the measure and two occasions, it is possible to separately estimate the extent of each of the three kinds of error (cf. Cronbach, 1947; Schmidt et al., 2003; Stanley, 1971; Thorndike, 1949, 1951). If all three kinds of error are present, then the delayed parallel forms reliability (CES) will be smaller than either the parallel forms reliability estimate or the test-retest reliability estimate. The effect of using the wrong reliability estimate is to underestimate the impact of error of measurement. Thus, correction using the wrong reliability means that some source of error is not calibrated and, as a result, the correlation is not corrected for attenuation due to that error source. That is, correction using the wrong reliability means that the corrected correlation will correspondingly underestimate the actual correlation between constructs. This will, of course, cause a downward bias in estimates of mean correlations in the meta-analysis. If a primary researcher or a meta-analyst is forced to use CE or CS estimates of reliability because CES estimates are not available, the study or meta-analysis should point out that full correction for measurement error was not possible and that the results reported are therefore conservative (i.e., have a downward bias). The report should also point out that such an incomplete correction for measurement error yields results that are much more accurate than failure to make any correction for measurement error.

Judgments by Raters. If a construct such as job performance is assessed by an observer such as the person's immediate supervisor, then there are two sources of error in the measurement: error in the judgment and idiosyncrasy in rater perception (called "halo"; cf. Hoyt, 2000; Schmidt, Viswesvaran, & Ones, 2000; Viswesvaran, Ones, & Schmidt, 1996; Viswesvaran, Schmidt, & Ones, in press). First, the judgment is itself a response by the rater and is, thus, subject to random response error and potentially subject to specific error in rating scale items and to transient error. These latter sources are the only sources of error assessed by data methods that consider only data from one rater. Second, in no research area has human perception of other people proved to be without idiosyncrasy. In fact, in most areas, there are large differences in the perceptions of different raters. This idiosyncratic bias associated with each rater (halo) is not part of the construct being assessed and, thus, is measurement error (Hoyt, 2000; Viswesvaran et al., 1996, in press). This form of measurement error functions as specific factor error associated with each rater. It is also referred to as halo error. Thus, the proper reliability estimate must take differences in perception into account as well as randomness in the judgment made by each judge. The appropriate way to estimate reliability for judgments is to correlate judgments made independently by different raters. The correlation between judges will be reduced to the extent that there is either random measurement error in the judgments or differences in perception (halo error). If two judgments (say, "quality of work" and "quantity of work") are each made by two raters, then it is possible to separately estimate the effect of random response error, item-specific error (specific to these two rating scale items), and idiosyncrasy error (also called "halo"; Viswesvaran et al., 1996, in press). If there is transient error, and if the cause of the transient error is independent in the two judges (the usual case), then this correlation will be appropriately lowered by transient error also, although transient error will not be distinguishable from idiosyncrasy (halo) error. In this case, the reliability is called "inter-rater reliability," although it, too, would better be called a reliability estimate. Inter-rater reliability is the CES (delayed parallel forms reliability) for ratings. Studies of this sort have found average inter-rater reliabilities of about .50 for supervisory ratings of job performance (cf. Rothstein, 1990; Schmidt et al., 2000; Viswesvaran et al., 1996). Intra-rater reliability, estimated by correlating ratings made by the same rater at two different times, is much higher (around .85; Viswesvaran et al., 1996) but is a gross overestimate of actual reliability.

Coded Response Data. Some behaviors are too complicated to be directly recorded. Thus, the data used represent a coding by an observer of the behavior. For example, we might code the extent of need for achievement expressed in a story inspired by a picture shown to the subject. Differences between the codings by different observers are called "coding error." A critical error often made in this context is to consider as error only the discrepancy between coders. While coding error is one important source of error in the measurement, there are also random response error, specific error, and transient error in the behavior coded. For example, suppose that coders were so well trained that they agreed to a correlation of .95 in their assessments of the amount of achievement motivation contained in the stories. However, suppose that from one week to the next, there is only a correlation of .40 between the achievement imagery in successive stories told by the same person. The "reliability" of .95 would not reflect this instability (random response error and transient error) in inventing stories and would, thus, greatly overestimate the actual reliability in question. For a more complete treatment of measurement error in coded response data, see Schmidt and Hunter (1996, 1999b).

What are the implications of these facts about measurement errors and reliability estimates for meta-analysis? Unlike other systematic artifacts, measurement error is always present. Accurate corrections for measurement error are critical to accurate meta-analysis results (Cook et al., 1992, pp. 215–216). The use of inappropriate reliability estimates to make corrections for measurement error in meta-analysis leads to some loss of accuracy of results. For example, recent research indicates that there is transient measurement error in commonly used psychological measures (e.g., personality and ability measures) (Schmidt et al., 2003). This means that the common practice of using coefficient alpha and KR-20 reliability estimates to correct for measurement error in meta-analysis typically leads to undercorrections and, hence, produces a downward bias in estimates of mean correlations, because coefficient alpha and KR-20 reliabilities do not detect or remove the effects of transient error. Likewise, use of test-retest reliability estimates will also lead to undercorrections, because of failure to control for specific factor measurement errors. Whether one is correcting each coefficient individually (as described in this chapter) or using distributions of reliability coefficients (as described in Chapter 4), all relevant sources of measurement error should be considered and, to the extent possible given available data, appropriate reliability estimates should be used (Schmidt et al., 2003).

Unfortunately, most available estimates of reliability are alpha coefficients or KR-20 estimates (i.e., estimates of the CE) and so do not take transient error into account. Estimates of the CES coefficient are rare in the literature and not common even in test manuals. Estimates of the amount of transient error in a variety of scales are around 4% to 5% (see, e.g., Schmidt et al., 2003). (These values are larger for trait measures of affectivity.) Hence, CE estimates can be adjusted or corrected for transient error by subtracting .04 or .05 from these reliability estimates, as suggested in Schmidt et al. (2003). Such adjustment figures, however, are not (yet) available for all types of scales. Therefore, it is important to bear in mind that in research, as in other areas, "the perfect is the enemy of the good." It would be a false argument to state that unless ideal estimates of reliability can be used, no correction for measurement error should be made. As noted earlier, use of coefficient alpha estimates (CE estimates) when CES estimates (delayed parallel forms estimates) are more appropriate still leads to final results that are much more accurate than failure to make any correction for the biasing effects of measurement error. However, in such a case, the researcher should point out that only a partial correction for measurement error was possible and the resulting corrected values therefore contain a downward bias.

Another important implication is that when ratings are used, use of intra-rater reliabilities will lead to very severe undercorrections for measurement error. To avoid this, inter-rater reliabilities should always be used, and (except in very special cases) intra-rater reliabilities should not be used. Also, in artifact distribution meta-analysis (discussed in Chapter 4), one should never use a *mixture* of intra- and inter-rater reliabilities in the reliability artifact distribution. Fortunately, inter-rater estimates (unlike CES estimates for tests and scales) are widely available (cf. Rothstein, 1990; Viswesvaran et al., 1996).

In the case of coded response data, it is critical that the reliability estimates be based on two separate administrations of the measure. That is, the first coder should code responses obtained at time 1 and the second coder should code responses from the same individuals obtained at time 2. The correlation between these two codings provides the only accurate estimate of the reliability of coded response data. If both coders code responses obtained on a single occasion, the resulting correlation grossly overestimates reliability, resulting in a large downward bias in meta-analysis estimates.

The use of inappropriate reliability estimates has been a problem in some applications of meta-analysis. It is important to remember that different types of reliability estimates are not all equally appropriate.

Restriction or Enhancement of Range

If studies differ greatly in the range of values present on the independent variable, then the correlation will differ correspondingly. Correlations are directly comparable across studies only if they are computed on samples from populations with the same standard deviation on the independent variable. Range correction formulas are available that take a correlation computed on a population with a given standard deviation and produce an estimate of what the correlation would have been had the standard deviation been different. That is, range correction formulas estimate the effect of changing the study population standard deviation from one value to another. To eliminate range variation from a meta-analysis, we can use range correction formulas to project all correlations to the same reference standard deviation.

As noted in Chapter 2, range restriction (or range enhancement) can be either direct or indirect—and range correction procedures are different for the two cases.

Direct range restriction occurs when there is direct truncation on the independent variable. For example, if only those in the top 50% of test scores are hired, and no one with a lower test score is hired, we have direct range restriction. Likewise, it is direct range *enhancement* if an experimenter selects as subjects only those in the top 10% and the bottom 10% of scores on, say, a measure of conscientiousness to participate in a study. The statistic we need to know to correct for direct range restriction is the ratio of the observed *SD* in the restricted sample to the observed *SD* in the unrestricted sample, that is, s_x/S_x. This ratio is referred to as u_X; that is, $u_X = s_x/S_x$. If we know this ratio, we can use the Thorndike Case II (Thorndike, 1949) direct range restriction formula to correct for range restriction. By using the reciprocal of this statistic, that is, S_x/s_x, we can use this same formula to correct for direct range enhancement. This ratio is referred to as U_X; that is, $U_X = S_x/s_x$.

Indirect range restriction occurs when people are selected on a third variable that correlates with the independent variable. For example, if we are evaluating the validity of a new engineering aptitude test in an engineering college and all our engineering students were originally admitted based on a college entrance examination, then there will be indirect range restriction on the engineering aptitude test. If selection into the college is based only on the entrance examination (direct range restriction on that exam), and if we know the restricted and unrestricted *SD* on that examination, there is a formula for correcting for this sort of indirect range restriction (called the Thorndike Case III indirect range restriction correction formula; Thorndike, 1949). However, this situation is very rare, because selection on the third variable (here the college entrance exam) is rarely direct (because other variables are also used in selection) and because, even if it is, we rarely have the needed statistics on the third variable. Thus, this correction formula can rarely be applied. For this reason, we do not develop applications of this formula.

The type of indirect range restriction that is most common is the situation in which people have been selected on an unknown (unrecorded) combination of variables and that combination (or composite) of variables is correlated with the independent variable, producing indirect range restriction on the independent variable (Linn, Harnisch, & Dunbar, 1981a). A common example is the case in which people have been hired based on some unknown combination of, say, an interview, an application blank, and a background check, and we find that the *SD* on the test we are studying is considerably smaller in this selected (incumbent) group than the *SD* in an application population (the unrestricted *SD*), indicating there is indirect range restriction on our independent variable. That is, we find u_x is less than 1.00. Linn et al. (1981a) showed that students admitted to law schools were an example of this sort of indirect range restriction. Another example is the case in which people who volunteer to participate in a study have a lower *SD* on extroversion scores (the independent variable); that is, u_x is again less than 1.00. Here, indirect range restriction is produced by some unknown combination of self-selection variables. Most range restriction in real data is, in fact, caused by this sort of indirect range restriction (Hunter, Schmidt, & Le, 2002; Linn et al., 1981a; Mendoza & Mumford, 1987; Thorndike, 1949). As in the case of direct selection, we can also have indirect range *enhancement*. For example, the *SD* on extroversion of those volunteering for the study might be *larger* than the *SD* of extroversion in the reference population. However, in the case of indirect selection, range enhancement appears to be relatively rare.

The key statistic we must know to correct for indirect range restriction of this sort is not u_X but u_T, where u_T is the ratio of *true score SDs*. That is, $u_T = s_T/S_T$. As we will see, there are special formulas for computing u_T from u_X and other information. If we have indirect range enhancement (instead of range restriction), the statistic we need is $U_T = S_T/s_T$. The correction for indirect range restriction is made using the same correction formula used to correct for direct range restriction, but with u_T used in that formula in place of u_X. Likewise, to correct for range enhancement, U_T is substituted in that formula for U_X. Procedures for correcting for this type of range restriction—the most commonly occurring type of range restriction—have been developed only recently (Hunter et al., 2002; Mendoza & Mumford, 1987) and were not included in the 1990 edition of this book. The availability of these corrections greatly increases the accuracy of meta-analyses involving range restriction corrections. More detailed information on indirect range restriction can be found in Chapter 5.

For each study, we need to know the standard deviation of the independent variable s_x. Range departure is then measured by relating that standard deviation to the reference standard deviation S_x. The comparison used is the ratio of the standard deviation in the study group to the reference standard deviation, that is, $u_X = s_x/S_x$. The ratio u_X is less than 1 if the study has restriction in range (the usual case) and greater than 1 if the study has enhancement of range. The correlation in the study will be greater than or less than the reference correlation depending on whether the ratio u_X is greater than or less than 1, respectively. In direct range restriction, the correction for range restriction depends on the value of u_X. In indirect range restriction, the correction depends on u_T, which is a function of u_X and r_{xx_a}, the reliability of the independent variable in the unrestricted population. These corrections depend on two assumptions. First, the relationship in question must be linear (or at least approximately so). Second, the variance of the independent variable must be equal (or at least approximately so) at each level of the dependent variable. This latter condition is known as homoscedasticity (Gross & McGanney, 1987). As we will see in Chapter 5, one additional assumption is required for the correction for indirect range restriction.

As noted previously, the major computational difference between direct and indirect range restriction is that in direct range restriction we use u_X in making range corrections and in indirect range restriction we use u_T. The correction formula is otherwise identical. (There are also some differences, described in this chapter, in the order in which corrections for measurement error are made.) The extra steps involved in computing u_T make the mathematics of correcting for indirect range restriction somewhat more complicated than is the case for direct range restriction and, therefore, make the presentation somewhat more mathematically complicated and lengthy. However, once u_T is computed and substituted for u_X, the correction equation is the same. Likewise, the computation of sampling error variance and confidence intervals for range-corrected correlations is also identical in form. Therefore, to simplify our presentation, we will present most of the following discussion in terms of direct range restriction corrections and will forgo the presentations for indirect range restriction corrections at this point.

(We will return to the topic of indirect range restriction later in this chapter.) Before proceeding, we present the necessary formulas for computing u_T:

$$u_T = s_T / S_T$$

$$u_T = \left[\frac{u_X^2 - (1 - r_{XX_a})}{r_{XX_a}} \right]^{1/2} \tag{3.16}$$

where r_{XX_a} is the reliability of the independent variable in the unrestricted group. If only the reliability in the *restricted* group (r_{XX_i}) is known, r_{XX_a} can be computed as follows:

$$r_{XX_a} = 1 - \frac{s_{X_i}^2 \, (1 - r_{XX_i})}{s_{X_a}^2} \tag{3.17a}$$

$$r_{XX_a} = 1 - u_X^2 \, (1 - r_{XX_i}) \tag{3.17b}$$

This equation can be reversed to give r_{XX_i} for any value of r_{XX_a}:

$$r_{XX_i} = 1 - U_X^2 \, (1 - r_{XX_a}) \tag{3.17c}$$

where $U_X = 1/u_X$. (Equation [3.16] is derived in Chapter 5, where it appears as Equation [5.31].)

In this section, we will use the direct range restriction model to explore range departure in the context of a single study in which population correlations are known. In the following section, we will consider the effect of correcting a sample correlation for range departure. We will find that the sampling error of the corrected correlation differs from that of the uncorrected correlation, and we will show how to adjust the confidence interval correspondingly. We will then briefly note the relationship between the ratio u_X and the "selection ratio" in personnel selection research. After this treatment of range correction in single studies, we will consider the effect of range correction in meta-analysis. At that point, we will treat both indirect and direct range restriction.

We cannot always study the population that we wish to use as a reference point. Sometimes we study a population in which our independent variable varies less than in the reference population (restriction in range) and sometimes we study a population in which it varies more widely than in the reference population (enhancement of range). In either case, the same relationship between the variables produces a different correlation coefficient. In the case of enhancement of range, the study population correlation is systematically larger than the reference population correlation. This problem is compounded by sampling error and by error of measurement.

Consider personnel selection research. The reference population is the applicant population, but the study is done with people who have already been hired (because we can get job performance scores only for those on the job). If the people hired were a random sample of the applicants, then the only problems would be sampling error and measurement error. Suppose, however, the test we are studying has been used to select those who are hired. For example, suppose those hired are those who are above the mean on the test; that is, we have direct range restriction. Then the range of test scores among the job incumbents is greatly reduced in comparison to the applicant population. We would thus expect a considerable reduction in the size of the population correlation in the incumbent population compared to the applicant population. If test scores are normally distributed in the applicant population, then the standard deviation for people in the top half of the distribution is only 60% as large as the standard deviation for the entire population. Thus, if the standard deviation were 20 in the applicant population, it would be only $.60(20) = 12$ in the incumbent population of those hired. The degree of restriction in range would thus be $u_X = 12/20 = .60$.

The formula for the correlation produced by a direct selection change in distribution in the independent variable is called the formula for restriction in range, although it works for enhancement, too, as we shall see. Let ρ_1 be the reference population correlation and let ρ_2 be the study population correlation. Then

$$\rho_2 = \frac{u_X \rho_1}{\sqrt{(u_X^2 - 1)\rho_1^2 + 1}} \tag{3.18}$$

where

$$u_X = \frac{\sigma_{x_2}}{\sigma_{x_1}}$$

is the ratio of standard deviations in the two populations. In the case of direct restriction in range, we have $u_X < 1$ and, hence, $\rho_1 > \rho_2$. In the case of direct range enhancement, we have $u_X > 1$ and, hence, $\rho_2 > \rho_1$.

In the case of our personnel selection example, we have $u_X = .60$ and, hence,

$$\rho_2 = \frac{.60\rho_1}{\sqrt{(.60^2 - 1)\rho_1^2 + 1}} = \frac{.60\rho_1}{\sqrt{1 - .64\rho_1^2}}$$

For example, if the correlation between test and job performance in the applicant population were .50, then the correlation in the study population would be

$$\rho_2 = \frac{.60(.50)}{\sqrt{(1 - .64(.50)^2}} = \frac{.60(.50)}{.92} = .33$$

That is, if the study were done on only the top half of the distribution on the independent variable, then the population correlation would be reduced from .50 to .33. If undetected, this difference between .50 and .33 would have profound implications for the interpretation of empirical studies.

Suppose, however, we have the data, that is, $\rho_2 = .33$ and $u_X = .60$, and we wish to correct for restriction in range. We could reverse the roles of the two populations. That is, we could regard the applicant population as an enhancement of the incumbent population. We could then use the same formula as before with the ρs reversed, that is,

$$\rho_1 = \frac{U_X \rho_2}{\sqrt{(U_X^2 - 1)\rho_2^2 + 1}} \tag{3.19}$$

where

$$U_X = \frac{\sigma_{x_1}}{\sigma_{x_2}} = \frac{1}{u_X}$$

is the ratio of standard deviations in the opposite order. This formula is called the correction for restriction in range, although it also works for correction for enhancement. In the personnel example, we plug in $\rho_2 = .33$ and $U = 1/u_X = 1/.60 = 1.67$ to obtain

$$\rho_1 = \frac{1.67(.33)}{\sqrt{(1.67^2 - 1)(.33)^2 + 1}} = \frac{1.67(.33)}{1.09} = .50$$

Thus, at the level of population correlations (i.e., when N is infinite), we can use the formula for restriction in range to move back and forth between populations of different variance with perfect accuracy. If range restriction were indirect, substituting u_T and U_T for u_X and U_X, respectively, would allow us to do this same thing.

The situation is more complicated if there is sampling error. If we apply the formula for correction for restriction in range to a sample correlation, then we get only an approximate estimate of the reference group population correlation. Moreover, the corrected correlation will have a different amount of sampling error. This situation is analogous to that in correction for attenuation due to measurement error. There is a trade-off. In order to eliminate the systematic error associated with restriction in range, we must accept the increase in sampling error produced by the statistical correction. If we could correct substantively, that is, if the study could be done on the reference population, then there would be no increase in sampling error. In fact, in the case of restriction in range, the study done on the applicant population (if it could be done) would have the larger correlation and, hence, the smaller confidence interval.

The confidence interval for the corrected correlation is easy to obtain. The correction formula can be regarded as a mathematical transformation. This transformation is monotone (but not linear) and, hence, it transforms confidence intervals. Thus, the confidence interval is obtained by correcting the endpoints of the confidence interval using the same formula that is used to correct the correlation. That is, the same range correction formula that is applied to the correlation is applied to the endpoints of the confidence interval.

Consider the personnel example with direct range restriction in which the population correlations are .50 for the applicant population and .33 for the study population. If the sample size is 100, then the standard error for a correlation of $\rho = .33$ is $\sigma_c = (1 - .33^2)/\sqrt{99} = .09$. If the sample correlation came out low, it might be something such as .28, which is low by .05. Corrected for restriction in range of $U_X = 1.67$, we have

$$r_c = \frac{1.67(.28)}{\sqrt{(1.67^2 - 1)(.28^2) + 1}} = \frac{.47}{1.07} = .44$$

The standard error of the observed r of .28 is .093. The 95% confidence interval on the observed r of .28 is

Lower Endpoint	*Upper Endpoint*
$r_1 = .10$	$r_2 = .46$
$r_{c_1} = \frac{1.67(.10)}{\sqrt{(1.67^2 - 1).10^2 + 1}}$	$r_{c_2} = \frac{1.67(.46)}{(1.67^2 - 1).46^2 + 1}$
$= .16$	$= .65$

Thus, the confidence interval for the corrected correlation is $.16 \leq \rho_c \leq .65$, which includes the actual value of $\rho_c = .50$. This confidence interval is much wider than the confidence interval for the uncorrected correlation and wider yet than the confidence interval that would have been found had the study been done in the reference population itself.

In this example, the range restriction is direct. We remind the reader that if the range restriction were indirect, one would use u_T in place of u_X. Otherwise, the procedures would be identical.

Range Correction and Sampling Error

There is no difficulty in obtaining a confidence interval for a corrected correlation using the range correction formula; we simply correct the two endpoints of the confidence interval for the uncorrected correlation. However, it is not so easy to compute the standard error of the corrected correlation. Correction for attenuation due to measurement error is a linear operation; the uncorrected correlation is just multiplied by a constant. Thus, the sampling error and the error standard deviation are multiplied by the same constant. However, the range correction formula is not linear, and there is no exact formula for the resulting standard error. (The nature of the nonlinearity is that, for the same value of u_X, the correction increases smaller correlations by a greater percentage increase than it increases larger correlations.) The extent of nonlinearity depends on the size of the numbers involved, that is, the extent to which U_X is different from 1 and the extent to which the uncorrected correlation has a square much greater than 0. If the nonlinearity is not too great, then we can approximate the sampling error by pretending that we have just multiplied the uncorrected correlation by the constant

$$\alpha = \frac{r_c}{r}$$

The sampling error would then be approximately

$$\sigma_{e_c}^2 = \alpha^2 \sigma_e^2 \tag{3.20}$$

To see the extent of this approximation, let us consider our personnel research example. We center our confidence interval for the corrected correlation about the corrected correlation itself, that is, around $r_c = .44$. The error standard deviation for the uncorrected correlation is $(1 - .28^2)/\sqrt{99} = .093$, and the ratio of corrected to uncorrected correlations is $.44/.28 = 1.57$. Hence, the estimated standard error for the corrected correlation is $(1.57)(.093) = .146$. The corresponding confidence interval is $.15 \leq \rho_c \leq .73$. This implied confidence interval differs only slightly from the confidence interval obtained by correcting the endpoints, that is, $.16 \leq \rho_c \leq .65$.

There is a more accurate estimate of the standard error that can be obtained using Taylor's series as suggested by Raju and Brand (2003) and Raju, Burke, and Normand (1983). For large sample size, the sampling error in the corrected correlation induced by the sampling error in the uncorrected correlation is proportional to the derivative of the correction function. Whereas the correlation is multiplied by the constant α, the standard deviation is multiplied by the number $a\alpha$, where

$$a = 1/[(U_X^2 - 1)r^2 + 1] \tag{3.21}$$

The variance would be multiplied by $a^2\alpha^2$. In the personnel selection example, we have $\alpha = 1.57$ and

$$a = 1/[(1.67^2 - 1)(.28)^2 + 1] = 1/1.0352 = .8770$$

Thus, the standard error is multiplied by .8770(1.57) = 1.38 instead of 1.57. The standard error of the corrected correlation is therefore estimated as (.8870)(1.57)(0.93) = .130. The confidence interval found using the improved estimate of the standard error is

$$.19 < \rho < .69$$

This is in comparison to the correct interval obtained by correcting the confidence interval endpoints, which was

$$.16 < \rho < .65$$

This improved estimate of the standard deviation is barely worth the trouble for hand calculations, although it is easy to introduce into computer programs, and we have done so. The Windows-based meta-analysis program VG6 (see the Appendix for a description) contains this refinement. Again, we note that if the range restriction were indirect, U_T would be used in the preceding formula for a in place of U_X. (Bobko & Reick, 1980, also presented an equation for the standard error of a correlation corrected for range restriction; their formula appears different on the surface but produces the same results as our procedure. The same is true for the formulas presented by Cureton, 1936; Kelly, 1947; and Raju & Brand, 2003. Mendoza, Stafford, & Stauffer, 2000, presented a method of estimating the confidence interval for a corrected correlation without estimating its *SE*. See also Forsyth & Feldt, 1969.)

An Example: Confidence Intervals. Consider a personnel selection validation study with direct range restriction and using job performance ratings by a single supervisor. Given an observed correlation of .30 with a sample size of 100, the confidence interval for the uncorrected validity coefficient is $P\,[.12 \leq \rho \leq .48] = .95$. From King, Hunter, and Schmidt (1980), we know that the reliability of the supervisor ratings in the applicant pool is at most .60. If the selection ratio is 50%, then the formulas in Schmidt, Hunter, and Urry (1976) (presented later in this chapter) show that the ratio of the standard deviation of the applicant group to that of the incumbent population (U_X) is 1.67. The point correction of the observed validity coefficient is therefore

$$r_1 = \frac{1.67r}{\sqrt{(1.67^2 - 1)r^2 + 1}} = .46$$

$$r_2 = \frac{r_1}{\sqrt{.60}} = .60$$

The confidence interval for the corrected validity is obtained by applying the same corrections to the endpoints of the confidence interval for the uncorrected validity:

Lower Endpoint

$$r_1 = \frac{1.67(.12)}{\sqrt{(1.67^2 - 1).12^2 + 1}} = .20$$

$$r_2 = \frac{.20}{\sqrt{.60}} = .26$$

Upper Endpoint

$$r_1 = \frac{1.67(.48)}{\sqrt{(1.67^2 - 1).48^2 + 1}} = .67$$

$$r_2 = \frac{.67}{\sqrt{.60}} = .86$$

Hence, the confidence interval for the corrected validity is

$$P\{.26 \leq \rho \leq .86\} = .95$$

Direct Range Restriction and the Selection Ratio. In personnel research, restriction in range sometimes comes about in a very particular way: People are hired from the top down using the test that is to be validated. Only those hired appear in the validation study. Thus, those who appear in the study are chosen from the top portion of the reference population distribution of test scores (direct range restriction). Because the test score distribution in applicant populations is typically a normal or nearly normal distribution, the range restriction parameter u_X can be computed indirectly from the selection ratio.

The selection ratio is defined as the proportion of applicants selected by the test. For example, if all applicants in the top tenth of the distribution are offered employment, then the selection ratio is 10%. The test selection ratio will be equal to the percentage of applicants offered jobs if hiring is based solely on test scores from the top down (Schmidt, Hunter, McKenzie, & Muldrow, 1979).

Let p be the selection ratio as a proportion (i.e., as a fraction such as .10, rather than as a percentage). If we are hiring from the top of a normal distribution, then, corresponding to any selection ratio p, there is a cutoff score C such that

$$P[x \geq C] = p \tag{3.22}$$

If that cutoff score is given in standard score form, then it can be looked up using any normal distribution table. Once the cutoff score is known, then we can compute the mean and variance in test scores among those selected in standard score form using the following formulas:

$$\mu_x = \frac{\varphi(C)}{p} \tag{3.23}$$

where $\varphi(C)$ is the value of the unit normal density function at the cutoff (also called the "normal ordinate") and

$$\sigma_x^2 = 1 - \mu_x(\mu_x - C) = 1 - \mu_x^2 + C\mu_x \tag{3.24}$$

Because the applicant population has a variance of 1 in standard scores, the number σ_x is equal to the parameter u in the range restriction formula.

For example, if the selection ratio is 10%, then the normal distribution table shows that a cutoff score of 1.28 is required to select the top tenth. The mean standard score among those selected will be

$$\mu_x = \frac{1}{p}\frac{1}{\sqrt{2\pi}}e^{-C^2/2} = 10\frac{1}{2.507}e^{-.82} = 1.76$$

The variance among those selected is

$$\sigma_x^2 = 1 - 1.76^2 + 1.28(1.76) = .1552$$

The standard deviation—and, hence, the parameter u_X—is then the square root of .1552, which is .39. That is, with a selection ratio of 10%, the standard deviation in the study population will be only 39% as large as the standard deviation in the applicant population.

It is important to note that the procedures described in this particular section apply only to direct range restriction. If range restriction is indirect, estimates of u_X will be somewhat inaccurate.

Dichotomization of Independent and Dependent Variables

The mathematics of dichotomization is very similar to that of correction for attenuation and will thus be developed succinctly. Some aspects of dichotomization were discussed in Chapter 2; a more detailed treatment is presented in Hunter and Schmidt (1990b) and MacCallum, Zhang, Preacher, and Rucker (2002). The key fact is that the impact of dichotomizing a continuous variable is to multiply the population correlation by an attenuating factor. This systematic attenuation can be corrected by dividing the attenuated correlation by the same factor. That is, if we know the factor by which the study correlation was attenuated, then we can restore the study correlation to its original value by dividing by that same attenuation factor. If we divide a variable by a constant, then the mean and the standard deviation are divided by that same constant. Thus, the corrected correlation coefficient has a mean that is divided by the attenuation factor and a sampling error that is divided by the attenuation factor. Thus, the sampling error in the corrected correlation is larger than the sampling error in the uncorrected correlation. However, there is no other way to eliminate the systematic error introduced by the dichotomization.

Consider an example. Suppose the independent variable is split at the median. Then the attenuation factor is .80, and thus, the population correlation is reduced by 20%. If ρ is the true population correlation and ρ_o is the attenuated population correlation, then

$$\rho_o = .80\rho$$

This equation is algebraically reversible. To undo multiplication by .80, we divide by .80:

$$\rho_o/.80 = (.80\rho)/.80 = \rho$$

That is,

$$\rho = \rho_o/.80$$

is the formula for correction for dichotomization. The formula works perfectly for population correlations and works to eliminate the systematic error in the sample correlation.

The study sample correlation r_o is related to the study population correlation in the usual manner:

$$r_o = \rho_o + e_o$$

where e_o is the usual sampling error. If we correct the point biserial correlation to eliminate the attenuation due to dichotomization, then the corrected correlation r_C is given by

$$\begin{aligned} r_C &= r_o/.80 = (\rho_o + e_o)/.80 = \rho_o/.80 + e_o/.80 \\ &= (.80\rho)/.80 + e_o/.80 \\ &= \rho + e_o/.80 \end{aligned}$$

Let us denote by e_C the sampling error in the corrected correlation. We then have

$$r_C = \rho + e_C$$

Thus, the population correlation corresponding to the corrected sample correlation is the desired true correlation; that is, the systematic part of the sample correlation is restored to its pre-dichotomization value ρ. However, the sampling error e_C is not the usual sampling error associated with a population correlation of ρ. Rather, e_C is the sampling error associated with a corrected correlation. Had there been no dichotomization to begin with, the standard deviation of the sampling error (the standard error) would have been

$$\sigma_e = (1 - \rho^2)/\sqrt{(N-1)}$$

Instead, the standard deviation of the sampling error in the corrected correlation σ_{e_C} must be computed from the sampling error of the uncorrected correlation σ_{eo}. The sampling error standard deviation of the uncorrected correlation is

$$\begin{aligned} \sigma_{eo} &= (1 - \rho_o^2)/\sqrt{(N-1)} \\ &= [1 - (.80\rho)^2]/\sqrt{(N-1)} \\ &= [1 - .64\rho^2]/\sqrt{(N-1)} \end{aligned}$$

The sampling error standard deviation of the corrected correlation is

$$\sigma_{e_C} = \sigma_{eo}/.80 = 1.25\sigma_{eo}$$

Consider an example. Suppose the population correlation for the original continuous variables is $\rho = .50$. The population correlation with the independent variable split at the median is

$$\rho_o = .80\rho = .80(.50) = .40$$

If the sample size is $N = 100$, then the sampling error standard deviation for non-dichotomized variables is

$$\sigma_e = (1 - .50^2)/\sqrt{99} = .0754$$

The sampling error standard deviation of the uncorrected correlation is

$$\sigma_{eo} = (1 - .40^2)/\sqrt{99} = .0844$$

The sampling error standard deviation of the corrected correlation is

$$\sigma_{ec} = \sigma_{eo}/.80 = .0844/.80 = .1055.$$

Whereas 95% of sample correlations for non-dichotomized variables will be spread over

$$.35 < r < .65$$

the corrected correlations spread over the range

$$.29 < r_C < .71$$

For a more extreme split, the cost of correction will be higher. For a 90–10 split, the attenuation factor is .59, and the contrasting probability intervals are much different from each other:

$$.35 < r < .65 \text{ if no dichotomization}$$
$$.20 < r_C < .80 \text{ if one variable is split 90–10}$$

The situation is even more extreme if both variables are dichotomized. Consider a case from personnel selection. Hunter and Hunter (1984) found an average correlation of .26 between (continuous) reference recommendations and job performance ratings. Suppose (hypothetically) that there were no errors of measurement in the study and that, for purposes of communicating to the employer, the company psychologist decided to dichotomize the two variables. He dichotomizes the reference variable into "generally positive" versus "generally negative." He finds that 90% of past employers give positive ratings while 10% give negative ratings. He splits the supervisor performance ratings at the median to produce "above average" versus "below average." The effect of the double dichotomization (Hunter & Schmidt, 1990b) is to attenuate the correlation of .26 to

$$\rho_o = (.59)(.80)\rho = .472\rho = (.472)(.26) = .12$$

The corrected correlation is thus

$$r_C = r_o/.472 = 2.12\, r_o$$

That is, the observed correlation must be more than doubled to correct the attenuation produced by the dichotomization. The sampling error is correspondingly increased. For a sample size of $N = 100$, the 95% confidence intervals in sample correlations are $.08 < r < .44$ if the variables are not dichotomized and $-.15 < r_C < .67$ for a 10–90 and a 50–50 split.

Furthermore, it is not likely that the reference evaluations in a local validation study will have reliability as high as that in the Hunter and Hunter (1984) data. The reference check studies reviewed by Hunter and Hunter checked across three or more past employers and used professionally developed scales to assess employer ratings. The correlation of .26 is corrected for the attenuation due to error of measurement in the performance ratings only. Suppose the validation study asks for references from just one past employer and uses performance ratings by the immediate supervisor. If good rating scales are used in both cases, the reliability of each variable would be expected to be at most .60. Because both reliabilities are equal, the square roots are also equal at .77. The attenuation factor for error of measurement is thus

$$\rho_o = a_1 a_2\ \rho = (.77)(.77)\rho = .60\rho = (.60)(.26) = .156$$

This correlation is then attenuated by double dichotomization

$$\rho_{oo} = a_3 a_4\ \rho_o = (.59)(.80)\rho_o = .472\rho_o = .472(.156) = .074$$

The net attenuation for both error of measurement and dichotomization is

$$\rho_{oo} = (.60)(.472)\rho = .2832\rho$$

This value of .2832 is thus the attenuation factor for the correction of the sample correlation. That is, the corrected correlation r will be

$$r_C = r_{oo}/.2832 = 3.53\ r_{oo}$$

That is, one must more than triple the observed sample correlation to correct for the attenuation produced by both error of measurement and double dichotomization. The sampling error is similarly increased. For a sample size of $N = 100$, the 95% probability intervals are

$$.08 < r < .44 \text{ if perfect measurement and no dichotomization}$$

and

$$-.43 < r_C < .95 \text{ if the correlation is corrected for measurement error and dichotomization in both variables.}$$

Hence, it is clear that the combination of dichotomization and measurement error can greatly reduce the amount of information conveyed by a sample (study) correlation.

Imperfect Construct Validity in Independent and Dependent Variables

We define the construct validity of a measure as its true score correlation with the actual construct or trait it is supposed to measure. The case of construct validity is similar to the case of error of measurement if the path analysis permits a simple multiplicative attenuation (see Chapter 2 for the required conditions). If error of measurement is treated separately, then the impact of imperfect construct validity is to multiply the true population correlation by an attenuation factor equal to the construct validity of the variable. If there is imperfect construct validity in both variables, and if both proxy variables satisfy the path analysis requirements, then the effect is a double attenuation, that is, multiplication by the product of the two construct validities. Because the attenuation effect is systematic, it can be algebraically reversed. To reverse the effect of multiplying the correlation by a constant, we divide the correlation by the same constant. Thus, to restore the correlation to what it would have been had the variables been measured with perfect construct validity, we divide the study correlation by the product of the two construct validities. Note that, for perfect construct validity, we divide by 1.00, which leaves the correlation unchanged. So perfect construct validity is a special case of imperfect construct validity.

For example, let the construct validity of the independent variable be a_1 and let the construct validity of the dependent variable be a_2. The impact of imperfect construct validity is to multiply the true correlation by the product $a_1 a_2$. That is,

$$\rho_o = a_1 a_2 \rho$$

The correction formula divides by the same attenuation factors

$$\rho_o / a_1 a_2 = (a_1 a_2 \rho) / a_1 a_2 = \rho$$

The corrected sample correlation is thus

$$r_C = r_o / a_1 a_2 = (1/a_1 a_2) r_o$$

which multiplies the sampling error by the same factor $(1/a_1 a_2)$.

The attenuating effect of imperfect construct validity combines with the attenuating effect of other artifacts. Consider another example:

$a_1 = .90 =$ the square root of the reliability of X; $r_{XX} = .81$,
$a_2 = .90 =$ the square root of the reliability of Y; $r_{YY} = .81$,
$a_3 = .90 =$ the construct validity of X,
$a_4 = .90 =$ the construct validity of Y,
$a_5 = .80 =$ the attenuation factor for splitting X at the median,
$a_6 = .80 =$ the attenuation factor for splitting Y at the median.

The total impact of the six study imperfections is

$$\rho_o = (.9)(.9)(.9)(.9)(.8)(.8)\rho = .42\rho$$

Thus, even minor imperfections add up. Had the true correlation been .50, the study population correlation would be

$$\rho_o = .42\rho = .42(.50) = .21$$

a reduction of over one-half. The formula for the corrected correlation is

$$r_C = r_o / .42 = 2.38\, r_o$$

Thus, to restore the systematic value of the study correlation, we must more than double the correlation.

Attrition Artifacts

As noted in Chapter 2, attrition artifacts can usually be treated as range variation on the dependent variable. If there is range variation on the dependent variable, but not on the independent variable, then the mathematical treatment is identical to the treatment of range variation on the independent variable; we merely interchange the role of variables X and Y. To our knowledge, there are no meta-analysis methods that correct for range restriction on both the independent and the dependent variables. However, as noted in Chapter 2, the approximation methods for doing this developed by Alexander, Carson, Alliger, and Carr (1987) are fairly accurate and could be adapted for use in meta-analysis. To date, this has not been done. The combined accuracy enhancements produced by use of indirect range restriction corrections (Hunter et al., 2002) and the Alexander et al. (1987) methods could be important, especially in the area of validity generalization. The more accurate validity estimates are likely to be substantially larger (Hunter et al., 2002).

Extraneous Factors

As discussed in Chapter 2, easily correctable extraneous factors in the research setting usually enter into the causal model for the research design in much the same form as the extraneous factors in the measurement of a proxy variable for the dependent variable. At the level of the study, it would be possible to correct the study effect correlation by partialing out the extraneous factor. If the extraneous factor was not controlled in the original analysis, then the attenuation factor is

$$a = \sqrt{(1 - \rho_{EY}^2)} \tag{3.25}$$

where ρ_{EY} is the correlation between the extraneous factor and the dependent variable. The impact on the study effect correlation is to attenuate the population correlation by the multiplicative factor

$$\rho_o = a\rho$$

This formula can be algebraically reversed

$$\rho = \rho_o / a$$

to yield the correction formula for the sample correlation

$$r = r_o / a$$

The sampling error is divided by the same factor and increases correspondingly.

The mathematics is otherwise identical to that for attenuation due to error of measurement. The impact of extraneous factors can combine with the impact of other artifacts. The compound impact is to multiply the attenuation factors for the other factors by the attenuation factor for the extraneous factor.

Bias in the Correlation

As noted in Chapter 2, the purely statistical bias in the sample correlation as an estimate of the population correlation is normally trivial in magnitude, and it is rarely worthwhile to correct for it. This is why this bias is not listed in Table 3.1 (or in Table 2.1 in Chapter 2). However, we provide the computations to check the size of the bias in any given application. The impact of bias is systematic and can be captured to a close approximation by an attenuation multiplier. If the population correlations are less than .70 (usually the case), then the best attenuation multiplier for meta-analysis is the linear attenuation factor (Hunter et al., 1996):

$$a = 1 - 1/(2N - 1) = (2N - 2)/(2N - 1) \tag{3.26}$$

This attenuation factor is most useful in meta-analysis because it is independent of the population correlation ρ. For applications with population correlations larger than .70 (a rare condition), the more accurate attenuation factor is

$$a = 1 - (1 - \rho^2)/(2N - 1) \tag{3.27}$$

Note that, if the preceding nonlinear attenuator is used, then correction for bias due to an extraneous variable should always be the last artifact corrected. In the case of multiple artifacts, the "ρ" in the attenuation formula will be the population correlation already attenuated for all other artifacts.

The impact of bias on the population correlation is a systematic reduction,

$$\rho_o = a\rho$$

The correction formula follows from the algebraic reversal of this equation,

$$\rho = \rho_o / a$$

to yield

$$r_C = r_o / a$$

The sampling error is divided by the same factor and increases correspondingly. The sampling error *variance* is divided by a^2.

Multiple Simultaneous Artifacts

Table 3.1 lists 11 artifacts, 9 of which are potentially correctable by the use of multiplicative artifact attenuation factors. The other two artifacts are sampling error, which is corrected by a different strategy, and bad data, which can be corrected only if the bad data can be identified and corrected or thrown out (see Chapter 5). This section considers the compound of all the multiplicative artifacts. It is implicitly understood that range variation on both the independent and dependent variable is not simultaneously considered (Hunter & Schmidt, 1987b). Thus, the analysis would contain at most eight multiplicative artifacts. Note again that the artifact attenuation is caused by the real imperfections of the study design. The attenuation of the true correlation will thus occur whether we can correct for it or not.

Consider again the six artifact examples from the section on construct validity. The artifact attenuation factors are

$a_1 = .90 =$ the square root of the reliability of X; $r_{XX} = .81$,
$a_2 = .90 =$ the square root of the reliability of Y; $r_{YY} = .81$,
$a_3 = .90 =$ the construct validity of X,
$a_4 = .90 =$ the construct validity of Y,
$a_5 = .80 =$ the attenuation factor for splitting X at the median,
$a_6 = .80 =$ the attenuation factor for splitting Y at the median.

The total impact of the six study imperfections is determined by the total attenuation factor

$$A = (.9)(.9)(.9)(.9)(.8)(.8) = .42$$

If the true correlation for the study is $\rho = .50$, the attenuated study correlation is only

$$\rho_o = .42\rho = .42(.50) = .21$$

If the sample size is $N = 26$, then the linear bias attenuation factor is

$$a_l = 1 - 1/(2N - 1) = 1 - 1/25 = .96$$

The total attenuation factor for all seven artifacts is thus

$$A = .42(.96) = .40$$

and the attenuated study population correlation is

$$\rho_o = .40\rho = .40(.50) = .20$$

With a sample size of 26, the sampling error variance of the uncorrected correlation is

$$\text{Var}(e_o) = [1 - .20^2]^2/(26 - 1) = .0368$$

The sampling error variance of the corrected correlation is

$$\text{Var}(e_C) = \text{Var}(e_o)/A^2 = .0368/.40^2 = .2304$$

Thus, the sampling error standard deviation is $\sqrt{.2304} = .48$. The 95% probability interval for the observed *corrected* correlation (r_C) is

$$-.44 < r_C < 1.44$$

If the sample size were increased to $N = 101$, the probability interval for the corrected correlation would shrink to

$$.03 < r_C < .97$$

The preceding example is an extreme case, but not unrealistic. All artifact values were derived from the empirical literature. This example shows that there is only limited information in the best of small-sample studies. When that information is watered down with large methodological artifacts, then there may be almost no information in the study. Ideally, studies with approximately perfect methodology would eliminate these artifacts substantively and, hence, eliminate the need for statistical correction. However, most methodological artifact values are determined by the feasibility limitations of field research. Thus, researchers frequently have little leeway for improvement. This means that there will nearly always be a need for statistical correction and, hence, there will nearly always be a need to greatly reduce sampling error.

Meta-Analysis of Individually Corrected Correlations

The examples of the preceding sections show that individual studies usually contain only very limited information. The random effects of sampling error are unavoidable. Furthermore, the other artifacts in study designs are often caused by factors outside the control of the investigator. Thus, the information in most studies is diluted by statistical artifacts such as those listed in Table 3.1, and perhaps still further by artifacts yet to be delineated and quantified in future research. Solid conclusions can thus only be built on cumulative research combining the information across studies. The traditional narrative review is clearly inadequate for this complex task (see Chapter 11). Thus, there is no alternative to meta-analysis. If one pretends that the only study artifact is sampling error, then the meta-analysis techniques given earlier in this chapter are used. However, if other artifacts are acknowledged and if information about the artifacts is available, then the values estimated by meta-analysis will be much more accurate if the study artifacts are corrected.

There are three kinds of artifacts in Table 3.1. First, there are bad data: recording, computing, reporting, and transcriptional errors. If the error is so large that the resulting correlation is an outlier in the meta-analysis, then the deviant result can be detected and eliminated (see Chapter 5). Otherwise, bad data go undetected and, hence, uncorrected. Second, there is the nonsystematic and random effect of sampling error. That effect can be eliminated in meta-analysis or at least greatly reduced. Third, the table contains nine artifacts that are systematic in nature. These we call the "correctable artifacts." For each correctable artifact, there is a quantitative factor that must be known in order to correct the study correlation for that artifact. Given the necessary artifact values for the research domain in question, meta-analysis can correct for that artifact.

There are three cases in meta-analysis: (1) Artifact values are given in each individual study for all artifacts, (2) artifact values are only sporadically given for any artifact in the various studies, and (3) artifact values are given for each study on some artifacts but are only available sporadically on other artifacts. The case of individually available artifact information is treated in this chapter. The case of sporadically available information is covered in Chapter 4, as is the last case of mixed artifact information (i.e., the case in which artifact information is available for each study for some but not all artifacts).

We now consider the case where artifact information is available on nearly all individual studies. The missing artifact values can be estimated by inserting the mean value across the studies where information is given. This is done automatically by our VG6 computer program, described later. At that point, each artifact value is available for each study. There are then three phases to the meta-analysis: (1) performing the computations for each of the individual studies, (2) combining the results across studies, and (3) computing the estimated mean and variance of true effect size correlations in the designated research domain.

Individual Study Computations

The computations for each study are the computations used in correcting the correlation for artifacts. We begin with the observed study correlation and the sample size for that study. We next collect each piece of artifact information for that study. These values are placed in a table and may be read into a computer file. This analysis can be performed by the Windows-based program VG6 (described in the Appendix).

We next do the computations to correct for artifacts. Under most conditions, the effect of each correctable artifact is to reduce the correlation by an amount that can be quantified as a multiplicative factor less than 1.00, which we call the "attenuation factor." Under these conditions, the net impact of all the correctable artifacts can be computed by simply multiplying the separate artifact attenuation factors. This results in a compound artifact attenuation factor. Dividing the observed study correlation by the compound attenuation factor corrects the study correlation for the systematic reduction caused by those artifacts.

For each study, we first compute the artifact attenuation factor for each artifact. Denote the separate attenuation factors by a_1, a_2, a_3, and so forth. The compound attenuation factor for the several artifacts is the product

$$A = a_1 a_2 a_3 \ldots \tag{3.28}$$

We can now compute the corrected study correlation r_C. We denote the study observed correlation by r_o and the corrected correlation by r_C. The corrected correlation is then

$$r_C = r_o / A \tag{3.29}$$

This estimate of r_C has a slight downward (i.e., negative) bias (Bobko, 1983), but the degree of underestimation is very small.

For purposes of estimating sampling error, it is necessary to estimate the mean uncorrected correlation. This is the sample size weight average of the observed correlations. The sampling error variance in the corrected correlation is computed in two steps. First, the sampling error variance in the uncorrected correlation is computed. Then the sampling error variance in the corrected correlation is computed from that. The sampling error variance in the uncorrected correlation, $\text{Var}(e_o)$, is

$$\text{Var}(e_o) = [1 - \bar{r}_o^2]^2 / (N_i - 1)$$

where $\bar{r}_o$ is the mean uncorrected correlation across studies (Hunter & Schmidt, 1994b; Law et al., 1994b) and N_i is the sample size for the study in question. The sampling error variance in the corrected correlation is then given by

$$\text{Var}(e_C) = \text{Var}(e_o)/A^2 \qquad (3.30)$$

where A is the compound artifact attenuation factor for that study. For simplicity, denote the sampling error variance by ve. That is, define ve by

$$ve = \text{Var}(e_C)$$

The preceding computation of sampling error variance is corrected for all artifacts. However, we can refine our estimate of the contribution of the range correction to sampling error. Because the attenuation factor for range variation contains the correlation itself, the corresponding sampling error increase is only in proportion to the derivative of the attenuation instead of the attenuation factor itself. This difference is small in many cases. However, a more accurate estimate can be computed using a more complicated formula for sampling error variance. Compute a first estimate of ve using the preceding formula. Label the first estimate ve'. The improved estimate is then

$$ve = a^2 ve'$$

where a is computed as

$$a = 1/[(U_X^2 - 1)r_o^2 + 1]$$

in the case of direct range restriction. In the case of indirect range restriction, use the same formula for a but substitute U_T for U_X. Consider an extreme example: Suppose only the top half of the ability distribution had been selected in a personnel selection study (i.e., direct range restriction). The study population standard deviation is smaller than the reference population standard deviation by the factor $u_X = .60$. The reciprocal of u_X would be $U_X = 1/.60 = 1.67$. If the study correlation (r_{0_i}) were .20, then $a = .94$, and the refining factor would be $a^2 = .88$. That is, the sampling error variance for that study would be 12% smaller than estimated using the simple attenuation factor. (See Bobko, 1983, for an equation for ve that yields values essentially identical to the equation for ve presented here.) Thus, for each study i, we generate four numbers: the corrected correlation r_{c_i}, the sample size N_i, the compound attenuation factor A_i, and the sampling error variance ve_i. These are the numbers used in the meta-analysis proper.

Combining Across Studies

Meta-analysis reduces sampling error by averaging sampling errors. Thus, an important step in meta-analysis is the computation of certain critical averages: the average correlation, the variance of correlations (the average squared deviation from the mean), and the average sampling error variance. To do this, we must decide how much weight to give to each study.

What weights should be used? The first step in the meta-analysis is to average certain numbers across studies. This averaging can be done in several ways. In averaging corrected correlations, a simple or "unweighted" average gives as much weight to a study with a sample size of 12 as to a study with a sample size of 1,200. Yet the sampling error variance in the small-sample study is 100 times greater than that in the large-sample study. Schmidt and Hunter (1977) noted this problem and recommended that each study be weighted by its sample size. Hunter, Schmidt, and Jackson (1982, pp. 41–42) noted that this is an optimal strategy when there is little or no variation in population correlations across studies—the "homogeneous" case (Hunter & Schmidt, 2000). They noted that there can be a problem if correlations differ a great deal across studies. The problem is potentially acute if the meta-analysis contains one study with very large sample size while all the other studies have much smaller sample size. If the large-sample-size study is deviant in some way, then, because it dominates the meta-analysis, the meta-analysis will be deviant. This case arises rarely in practice.

The homogeneous case was considered in technical detail in Hedges and Olkin (1985, Chapter 6). They noted the key mathematical theorem for that case. If the population correlations do not differ from one study to the next, then the optimal weights are obtained by weighting each study inversely to its sampling error variance. In the case of correlations that are not corrected for any artifacts, the sampling error variance is

$$\mathrm{Var}(e_i) = (1 - \rho_i^2)^2/(N_i - 1)$$

The optimal weight for this homogeneous case would thus be

$$w_i = (N_i - 1)/(1 - \rho_i^2)^2$$

Because the population correlation ρ_i is not known, this optimal weight cannot be used. Although Hedges and Olkin (1985) did not note it, even in the homogeneous case, the substitution of the observed study correlation r_{oi} for the study population correlation ρ_i does not lead to the most accurate alternative weights. As noted earlier in this chapter, a more accurate alternative is to substitute the mean observed correlation $\bar{r}_o$ for each study population ρ_i (Hunter & Schmidt, 1994b; Law et al., 1994b; see Chapter 5). Because the resulting multiplicative term

$$1/(1 - \bar{r}_0^2)^2$$

is the same for all studies, it can be dropped. That is, the corresponding weighting can be more easily accomplished by using the weight

$$w_i = N_i - 1$$

As Hedges and Olkin noted, this differs only trivially from the Schmidt and Hunter (1977) recommendation to weight each study by sample size:

$$w_i = N_i \tag{3.31}$$

The previous discussion is cast in terms of the homogeneous case (i.e., the case where $S_\rho^2 = 0$). However, as noted earlier in this chapter, these weights are also very accurate for the heterogeneous case (where $S_\rho^2 > 0$), so long as the sample size is not correlated with the size of ρ_i (the population correlation). Except for that rare situation, weighting by N_i is very accurate for the heterogeneous case as well as for the homogeneous case (see, e.g., Hall & Brannick, 2002). This is important because some have maintained that one should not weight by N_i in the heterogeneous case. (See the discussion of fixed- vs. random-effects meta-analysis models in Chapters 5 and 9.)

When studies differ greatly on one or more of the artifacts corrected, then more complicated weighting will make better use of the information in the studies. Studies with more information should receive more weight than studies with less information. For example, studies in which one or both of the variables is dichotomized with extreme splits should receive much less weight than a study with a near-even split. The same is true if one study has very low reliability while a second study has high reliability.

The sampling error variance of the corrected correlation is

$$\text{Var}(e_C) = [(1 - \rho_i^2)^2/(N_i - 1)]/A_i^2$$

Thus, the weight for each study would be

$$\begin{aligned} w_i &= A_i^2[(N_i - 1)/(1 - \rho_i^2)^2] \\ &= [(N_i - 1)A_i^2]/(1 - \rho_i^2)^2 \end{aligned}$$

Because the study population correlation ρ_i is not known, some substitution must be made. As noted previously, the most accurate substitution is to substitute the mean observed correlation $\bar{r}_o$ for each study population correlation ρ_i (Hunter & Schmidt, 1994b; Law et al., 1994b). Because $\bar{r}_o$ is a constant, this has the effect of eliminating the term with ρ_i and thus yields the weights

$$w_i = (N_i - 1)A_i^2$$

This, in turn, differs only trivially from the simpler weights

$$w_i = N_i A_i^2 \tag{3.32}$$

That is, the weight for each study is the product of two factors: the sample size N_i and the square of the artifact attenuation factor A_i. The attenuation factor is squared because to multiply a correlation by the factor $1/A_i$ is to multiply its sampling error variance by $1/A_i^2$. This weighting scheme has the desired effect: The more extreme the artifact attenuation in a given study, the less the weight assigned to that study. That is, the more information contained in the study, the greater its weight.

Consider two studies with sample size 100. Assume that (1) both variables are measured with perfect reliability and without range restriction, (2) the population correlation ρ is the same in both studies, and (3) the dependent variable is dichotomized in both studies. In Study 1, there is a 50–50 split so the true population correlation ρ is reduced to a study population correlation of .80 ρ. In Study 2, there is a 90–10 split so the true population correlation ρ is reduced to a study population correlation of .59 ρ. To correct for the attenuation due to artificial dichotomization, the Study 1 observed correlation r_{o1} must be multiplied by the reciprocal of .80, that is, $1/.80 = 1.25$:

$$r_1 = 1.25 r_{o1}$$

Thus, the sampling error variance is multiplied by the square of 1.25, that is, $1.25^2 = 1.5625$. To correct for the attenuation due to artificial dichotomization, the Study 2 observed correlation r_{o2} must be multiplied by the reciprocal of .59, that is, $1/.59 = 1.695$:

$$r_2 = 1.695 r_{o2}$$

Thus, the sampling error variance is multiplied by the square of 1.695, that is, $1.695^2 = 2.8730$. Before the dichotomization and the correction, the sampling error in both correlations was the same: the sampling error implied by equal sample sizes of 100 and equal population correlations of ρ_i. However, after the correction for dichotomization, the second study has sampling error variance that is $2.8730/1.5625 = 1.839$ times larger than the sampling error variance in the first study. Thus, the second study deserves only $1/1.839 = .544$ times as much weight in the meta-analysis. The weights assigned to the studies by the formula

$$w_1 = N_i A_i^2$$

do just that:

$$w_1 = 100(.802)^2 = 100(.64) = 64$$

and

$$w_2 = 100(.592)^2 = 100(.35) = 35$$

where $64/35 = 1.83$. Thus, to use round numbers, the study with twice the information is given twice the weight (1.00 vs. .544).

In summary, there are three typical types of weights that might be used in averaging. First, one could ignore the differences in quality (information content) between studies and give as much weight to high-error studies as to low-error studies. This is the case of equal weights and is represented by $w_i = 1$. Second, one might consider the effect on quality of unequal sample size but ignore the effects of other artifacts. This leads to the sample size weights recommended by Schmidt and Hunter (1977): $w_i = N_i$. Third, one might consider the weights that take into account both N_i and other artifacts: $w_i = N_i A_i^2$.

We recommend the use of these last weights, because they give less weight to those studies that require greater correction and, hence, have greater sampling error. These weights are used in our Windows-based program for meta-analysis of correlations corrected individually (described in the Appendix).

Final Meta-Analysis Estimation

Once the researcher has corrected each study correlation for artifacts and has decided on the weights, there are three meta-analysis averages to be computed using the corrected rs:

$$\bar{r}_C = \Sigma w_i r_{C_i} / \Sigma w_i \qquad (3.33)$$

$$\text{Var}(r_C) = \Sigma w_i [r_{C_i} - \bar{r}_C]^2 / \Sigma w_i \tag{3.34}$$

$$\text{Ave}(ve) = \Sigma\, w_i ve_i / \Sigma\, w_i \tag{3.35}$$

The mean actual correlation is then estimated by the mean corrected correlation:

$$\bar{\rho} = \bar{r}_C \tag{3.36}$$

The variance of actual correlations is given by the corrected variance of corrected correlations:

$$\text{Var}(\rho) = \text{Var}(r_C) - \text{Ave}(ve) \tag{3.37}$$

The standard deviation is estimated by the square root of the variance estimate if it is positive. If the standard deviation is actually 0, then the variance estimate will be negative half the time by chance. As discussed earlier in this chapter, a negative variance estimate suggests that the actual variance is 0 (see also Chapter 9).

An Example: Validity Generalization

We will now consider a hypothetical, but realistic validity generalization example for a test of verbal aptitude. The reliability of this test computed in the applicant group (unrestricted group) is $r_{XX_a} = .85$. The 12 studies shown in Table 3.5a have been conducted on job incumbents who have earlier been hired using a variety of procedures of which we have no record; hence, any range restriction would be indirect. The observed validities range from .07 to .49, and only 7 of the 12 validity estimates are statistically significant. The u_X values in the second column in Table 3.5a are all less than 1.00, indicting there has been indirect range restriction. Using Equation (3.16), we convert these u_X values into u_T values, which are shown in the table. The first column of job performance reliabilities (r_{yy_i}) represents the restricted values (i.e., those computed in the incumbent samples). These are the r_{yy} values that are needed for the computations in this example. The r_{yy_a} values—the estimated criterion reliabilities in the *applicant* group—are presented for only general informational purposes. (These values are computed using Equation [5.20] in Chapter 5.) The test reliabilities in Table 3.5a are the restricted (incumbent group) values (i.e., r_{XX_i}). Note that, because of the effects of the indirect range restriction, the r_{XX_i} values are less than the applicant pool value of $r_{XX_a} = .85$. (Test reliabilities are computed from the $r_{XX_a} = .85$ value using Equation [3.17c].) We first correct each observed correlation for measurement error in both variables and then correct for range restriction, using the u_T values in the range restriction correction formula. These corrected correlations are shown in the last column in Table 3.5a. The underlying true score (construct level) correlation used to generate these hypothetical data is $\rho = .57$. However, the true score correlation overestimates operational validity, because in actual test use we must use observed test scores to predict future job performance and cannot use applicants' (unknown) true scores. Hence, the underlying true validity used to generate this example is $\rho_{xy_t} = \sqrt{.85}(.57) = .53$. In the case of indirect range restriction, meta-analysis must correct for measurement error in both variables prior to the range restriction correction. (The technical reasons for this are given in Chapter 5 and in Hunter et al., 2002.) Thus, the meta-analysis results are those for true score (constant level) correlations. The mean and *SD* for operational validities are then obtained ex post facto as follows:

$$\text{Mean operational validity:} \quad \rho_{xy_t} = \sqrt{r_{XX_a}}\,(\rho) \tag{3.38}$$

$$SD \text{ of operational validity:} \quad SD_{\rho_{xy_t}} = \sqrt{r_{XX_a}}SD_\rho \tag{3.39}$$

A Worked Example: Indirect Range Restriction

We now proceed with the meta-analysis of the data in our example. Our calculations are the same as those in the computer program VG6-I (for indirect range restriction). (See the Appendix for availability of the software package containing this program.) We weight each study as follows:

$$w_i = N_i A_i^2$$

The worksheet for these calculations is shown in Table 3.5b. The attenuation factor for each study is most easily computed as the ratio of the uncorrected correlation to the corrected correlation. For Study 1,

$$A_1 = .35/.80 = .43$$

Thus, the study weight shown in the next to the last column is

$$w_1 = 68(.43)^2 = 68(.18) = 12.6$$

The sample size weighted-average uncorrected sample correlation is $\bar{r} = .28$. Thus, the sampling error variance of the uncorrected correlation in Study 1 is

$$\text{Var}(e) = (1 - .28^2)^2/67 = .012677$$

Because all studies in this hypothetical example have the same sample size, this is the estimate of sampling error variance in the uncorrected correlations for every study (not shown in Table 3.5b).

The sampling error variance in the *corrected* correlations can be estimated in two ways. We could use the simple estimate that ignores the nonlinearity of the range restriction correction:

$$\text{Var}(ve) = \text{Var}(e)/A^2$$

For Study 1, this value is

$$\text{Var}(ve) = .012677/(.43)^2 = .068561$$

This estimate is recorded in the column "Simple Error Variance" in Table 3.5b. However, a more accurate estimate is obtained by using the correction factor computed using the derivative of the correction transformation:

$$a = 1/[(U_T^2 - 1)r_o^2 + 1]$$

For Study 1, the standard deviation ratio is

$$U_T = 1/u_T = 1/.468 = 2.1368$$

So the correction factor is

$$a = 1/[(2.1368^2 - 1)(.35)^2 + 1] = 1/1.4368 = .6960$$

Thus, the refined estimate of sampling error variance in Study 1 is

$$\text{Var}(ve) = a^2(.068561) = .033212$$

as shown in the column "Refined Error Variance" in Table 3.5b.

Again, we note that the corrected correlations are denoted by r_C. The three weighted averages are

$$\bar{\rho} = \bar{r}_C = .574$$

$$\text{Var}(r_C) = .034091$$

$$\text{Var}(e) = .048120 \text{ (Simple method)}$$

$$\text{Var}(e) = .035085 \text{ (Refined method)}$$

The estimated mean true score correlation (.574) is very close to the actual value (.570). Because all population correlations were assumed to be the same, the variance of population correlations is actually 0. Thus, the sampling error variance should equal the observed variance. For the simple estimation method, we have

$$\text{Var}(\rho) = \text{Var}(r_C) - \text{Var}(e) = .034091 - .048120 = -.014029$$

which correctly suggests a standard deviation of 0 but which is a poorer estimate than we would like. For the refined estimation method, we have

$$\text{Var}(\rho) = \text{Var}(r) - \text{Var}(e) = .034091 - .035085 = -.000994$$

The value $-.000994$ is much closer to the true value of 0 and, again, correctly indicates that the true value is 0.

Meta-analysis correcting each correlation individually can be carried out on the computer using the program VG6. (See the Appendix for a description of the software package.) This program has separate subroutines for direct and indirect range restriction. In the case of indirect range restriction, as in our example here, the reliabilities entered into the program should be those in the restricted group. (If unrestricted independent variable reliabilities are entered, the program will convert them to restricted group values, using Equation [3.17].) Reliability corrections for both variables are made prior to the correction for range restriction (see Chapter 5 and Hunter et al., 2002). If range restriction is direct, the reliability correction for the dependent variable can be made prior to the range restriction correction, but the correction for unreliability in the independent variable must be made after the range restriction correction, using the reliability (r_{XX_a}) in the unrestricted population. The reason for this is that direct range restriction on the independent variable causes true scores and measurement errors to be (negatively) correlated in the selected sample, hence violating the critical assumption underlying reliability

Table 3.5 A meta-analysis on hypothetical personnel selection studies with indirect range restriction

Table 3.5a Hypothetical validity and artifact information

Study	s_X/S_X (u_X)	s_T/S_T (u_T)	*Test Reliability* (r_{XX_i})	*Criterion Reliability* (r_{yy_i})	(r_{yy_a})	*Sample Size*	*Observed Correlation*	*Corrected Correlation* *n*
1	.580	.468	.55	80	.86	68	.35**	.80
2	.580	.468	.55	60	.61	68	.07	.26
3	.580	.468	.55	80	.81	68	.11	.34
4	.580	.468	.55	60	.70	68	.31*	.81
5	.678	.603	.67	80	.81	68	.18	.39
6	.678	.603	.67	60	.67	68	.36**	.75
7	.678	.603	.67	80	.84	68	.40**	.73
8	.678	.603	.67	60	.61	68	.13	.33
9	.869	.844	.80	80	.82	68	.49**	.68
10	.869	.844	.80	60	.61	68	.23	.38
11	.869	.844	.80	80	.81	68	.29*	.42
12	.869	.844	.80	60	.63	68	.44*	.70

**$p < .01$ (two-tailed).
*$p < .05$ (two-tailed).
NOTE: r_{yy_a}, the criterion reliability in the applicant group, is not used in the example. It is shown only for informational purposes.

Table 3.5b Meta-analysis worksheet

Study	*Sample Size*	*Attenuation Factor*	*Simple Error Variance*	*Refined Error Variance*	*Study Weight*	*Corrected Correlation*
1	68	.43	.0686	.0332	12.6	.80
2	68	.27	.1739	.0863	5.0	.26
3	68	.32	.1238	.1138	7.0	.34
4	68	.38	.0878	.0488	9.8	.81
5	68	.47	.0574	.0319	15.0	.39
6	68	.48	.0550	.0365	15.7	.75
7	68	.55	.0419	.0256	20.6	.73
8	68	.39	.0833	.0785	10.3	.33
9	68	.72	.0244	.0203	35.3	.68
10	68	.60	.0352	.0337	24.5	.38
11	68	.69	.0266	.0233	32.3	.42
12	68	.63	.0319	.0274	27.0	.70

NOTE: Figures in this table apply to the *corrected* correlations.

theory (see Chapter 5; Hunter et al., 2002; Mendoza & Mumford, 1987). Under these conditions, the reliability of the independent variable in the selected sample is undefined and undefinable; hence, this correction must be made after the range restriction correction has been made, using an estimate of r_{XX_a} obtained in the unrestricted sample. Mendoza and Mumford (1987) were the first to point out this important fact. Hunter et al. (2002) incorporated this consideration into their meta-analysis procedures. Of course, if the meta-analysis is a validity generalization study, there is no need to correct for unreliability in the independent variable, and this correction is simply omitted. (An example of a validity generalization meta-analysis correcting correlations individually under conditions of direct range restriction is presented in Chapter 3 of the 1990 edition of this book.) For further details, see Chapter 5.

Returning to our example, the mean corrected correlation of .57 that we obtained does not estimate the true validity, because it has been corrected for measurement error in the independent variable (the predictor test). The value .57 is the mean true score correlation, not the mean operational validity (ρ_{xy_t}). Because we know the reliability of this test in the applicant pool (unrestricted) group (i.e., $r_{XX_a} = .85$, as noted at the beginning of our example), we can easily calculate the needed operational validity estimates as follows:

$$\rho_{xy_t} = \sqrt{r_{XX_a}}\rho$$

$$\rho_{xy_t} = \sqrt{.85}(.574) = .53$$

$$SD_{\rho_{xy_t}} = \sqrt{.85}\, SD_\rho$$

$$SD_{\rho_{xy_t}} = \sqrt{.85}(0) = 0$$

Again, both these values are correct. Although we need the operational validity estimate for applied work in personnel selection, it is the construct-level correlation of .57 that is needed for theoretical research (theory testing). Most meta-analyses outside the area of personnel selection are theoretical in orientation.

Next, for comparison purposes, we present sampling error corrections for the observed correlations (bare-bones meta-analysis) as well as for the fully corrected correlations (complete meta-analysis). The comparative results are as follows:

Uncorrected Correlations	*Fully Corrected Correlations*
$\bar{r}_o = .28$	$\bar{r} = .57$
$\sigma^2_{ro} = .017033$	$\sigma^2_r = .034091$
$\sigma^2_e = .012677$	$\sigma^2_e = .035085$
$\sigma^2_\rho = .004356$	$\sigma^2_\rho = -.000994$
$SD_\rho = .07$	$SD_\rho = .0$

These results may be checked using the Windows-based program VG6-I (see the Appendix for availability). Program results are the same as those calculated here. The results for uncorrected correlations show an incorrect mean of .28 (vs. the true value of .57) and a standard deviation of .07 (vs. an actual standard deviation of 0). The bare-bones meta-analysis is very inaccurate in comparison to the actual effect size correlation used to generate these hypothetical data. However, the error in the uncorrected correlation meta-analysis is exactly consistent with the known artifacts. The average attenuation factor is .494 (using the weights that would be used for the meta-analysis of uncorrected correlations, i.e., weighting by sample size). The mean correlation would then be expected to be reduced from .57 to .494(.57) = .282, which matches the mean uncorrected correlation. A check of Table 3.5b shows considerable variation in the attenuation factors due to variation in the artifact values across studies. In the bare-bones meta-analysis of the standard deviation, this variation of .07 across studies is all artifactual; that is, even after correction for sampling error, the uncorrected correlations vary across studies due to differences in range restriction and criterion unreliability.

If the variance beyond sampling error in uncorrected correlations is interpreted to mean that there are real moderator variables present, that is a major substantive error of interpretation. However, if it is correctly noted that no correction for artifacts other than sampling error was made and that the remaining variation might be due to such artifacts, then the substantive error would be avoided. The moral of this story is this: Even meta-analysis will not save a review from critical errors if there is no correction for study artifacts beyond sampling error. Such artifacts are present in virtually every research domain.

This method of meta-analysis, in which each study correlation is individually corrected for attenuating artifacts, can often not be used. The reason is obvious: Many study sets fail to provide all the needed artifact information. For examples of large-scale meta-analyses in which this method could be and was applied, see Carlson et al. (1999) and Rothstein et al. (1990). These studies were both consortium validation efforts in which numerous employers participated. Quite a number of such consortium studies have been conducted over the last 15 to 20 years (e.g., Dunnette et al., 1982; Dye, 1982; Peterson, 1982). The meta-analysis methods described in this chapter could be applied to the data from these studies. Another example of a meta-analysis in which correlations were corrected individually is the study by Judge et al. (2001) relating job satisfaction to job performance.

When there is no range restriction (and, hence, no corrections for range restriction), meta-analysis correcting each correlation individually is much simpler than the example presented here. When there is no range restriction, sampling error and measurement error are often the only artifacts for which corrections can be made. In such cases, one need not consider the impact of range restriction on the reliabilities. That is, the distinction between reliabilities in the restricted and unrestricted groups does not exist. Also, there is no need for the special step used in our example to compute the "refined" estimate of sampling error variance for the corrected correlations. Hence, such meta-analyses are much easier to compute using a calculator. However, for these simpler meta-analyses, the same computer program (VG6) can still be used. In terms of data input to the program, the only difference is that all values of u_X or u_T are entered as 1.00 (indicating no range restriction). The program output presents the same final estimates (e.g., $\bar{\rho}$ and SD_ρ) as it does for the case in which there is range restriction.

In addition to the methods described in this chapter, Raju, Burke, Normand, and Langlois (1991) also developed procedures for conducting meta-analysis on correlations corrected individually for artifacts. Their procedures take into account sampling error in the reliability estimates. These procedures have been incorporated into a computer program called MAIN (Raju & Fleer, 1997), which is available from Nambury Raju. At present, this program is set up to assume that range restriction is direct, but it could be modified in the future to incorporate the corrections for indirect range restriction described in this chapter. As of this writing, the computer program Comprehensive Meta-Analysis (published by Biostat; www.metaAnalysis.com) does not contain a subprogram for meta-analysis of individually corrected correlations. However, it is planned that this feature will be added in later versions of the program. Further discussion of available software for meta-analysis can be found in Chapter 11.

Summary of Meta-Analysis Correcting Each Correlation Individually

Correlations are subject to many artifactual sources of variation that we can control in a meta-analysis: the random effect of sampling error and the systematic attenuation produced by correctable artifacts such as error of measurement, dichotomization, imperfect construct validity, or range variation. Sampling error and error of measurement are found in every study; hence, a full meta-analysis should always correct for both. Some domains are not subject to significant amounts of range variation across studies, but in areas with high degrees of subject selection, such as personnel selection research, the effects of range restriction can be as large as the effects of error of measurement. The attenuation produced by dichotomization is even larger than the effects produced by error of measurement in most domains. (However, measurement error is *always* present while dichotomization is often not present.) Failure to correct for these artifacts results in massive underestimation of the mean correlation. Failure to control for variation in these artifacts results in a large overstatement of the variance of population correlations and, thus, in a potential false assertion of moderator variables where there are none.

All meta-analyses can be corrected for sampling error. To do this, we need only know the sample size N_i for each sample correlation r_i. Meta-analysis correcting for only sampling error has come to be called "bare-bones" meta-analysis. However, in this analysis, the correlations analyzed are the correlations between imperfectly measured variables (which are therefore systematically lowered by error of measurement); the correlations may be computed on observed rather than reference populations (so that these correlations are biased by range variation); the correlations may be greatly attenuated by dichotomization; and the correlations may be much smaller than they would have been had the construct validity in each study been perfect. Thus, the mean correlation of a bare-bones meta-analysis is a biased estimate of the desired mean correlation, that is, the correlation from a study conducted without the imperfections that stem from limited scientific resources (Rubin, 1990). Furthermore, although the variance in a bare-bones meta-analysis is corrected for sampling error, it is still biased upward because it contains variance due to differences in reliability, differences in range (if any), differences in extremity of split in dichotomization (if any), and differences in construct validity. Thus, the "bare-bones" variance is usually a very poor estimate of the real variance.

For any artifact, if the needed artifact information is available from each study, then each correlation can be separately corrected for that artifact. The corrected correlations can then be analyzed by meta-analysis to eliminate sampling error. This chapter presented detailed procedures for this form of meta-analysis: meta-analysis of correlations corrected individually for the effects of artifacts.

In most sets of studies to be subjected to meta-analysis, such complete artifact information will not be available. Such study sets do occur, however, and may become more frequent in the future as reporting practices improve. In three cases to date known to us where this information has been available (Carlson et al., 1999; Dye, 1982; Rothstein et al., 1990), this form of meta-analysis has found virtually all between-study variance in correlations to be due to artifacts. However, if the fully corrected variance of correlations across studies is far enough above 0 to suggest that there is a moderator variable, then appropriate potential moderator variables can be checked by analyzing subsets of studies (as was done in Judge et al., 2001). That is, a separate meta-analysis is conducted within each subset of studies. Alternatively, study characteristics that are potential moderators can be coded and correlated with study correlations. This chapter described methods for both these approaches to moderator analysis. See also the last section in Chapter 8.

In many sets of studies, information on particular artifacts is available in some studies, but not in others. Because some (often much) artifact information is missing, it is not possible to fully correct each study correlation for the attenuating effects of every artifact. Nevertheless, it is possible to conduct accurate meta-analyses that correct the final meta-analytic results for all artifacts. This is accomplished using distributions of artifact effects compiled from studies that do provide information on that artifact. These methods of meta-analysis are the subject of the next chapter.

Exercise 3.1

Bare-Bones Meta-Analysis: Correcting for Sampling Error Only

These are real data. Psychological Services, Inc. (PSI), of Los Angeles, a selection consulting company, conducted a consortium study that 16 companies participated in. These firms were from all over the United States and from a variety of industries.

The job was mid-level clerical work, and one scale studied was the composite battery score of four clerical tests. The criterion was ratings of job performance based on rating scales specially developed for this study. The same scales were used in all 16 companies.

Following are the sample sizes and observed correlations. Conduct a meta-analysis that corrects only for sampling error (i.e., a bare-bones meta-analysis). Remember to use $\bar{r}$ in the formula for sampling error variance. Give and explain the following:

1. The mean observed correlation.
2. The observed *SD* and variance.
3. The expected sampling error variance.
4. The corrected *SD* and variance.
5. The percentage of variance accounted for by sampling error.
6. What observed *SD* would you expect for these correlations if all observed variance were due to sampling error?
7. What additional corrections need to be made (beyond those that are part of this exercise) before this meta-analysis could be considered complete? Why? What effects would these corrections correct for?

For maximum learning, you should carry out this exercise using a calculator. However, it can also be carried out using either of our computer programs for correlations corrected individually (VG6-D and VG6-I). Both programs provide bare-bones meta-analysis results. See the Appendix for a description of these programs.

Observed PSI Data

Company	*N*	*Observed Validity of Sum of the Four Tests*
1	203	.16
2	214	.19
3	225	.17
4	38	.04
5	34	.13
6	94	.38
7	41	.36
8	323	.34
9	142	.30
10	24	.20
11	534	.36
12	30	.24
13	223	.36
14	226	.40
15	101	.21
16	46	.35

Exercise 3.2

Meta-Analysis Correcting Each Correlation Individually

Find the following journal article in a library and make a personal copy of it:

Brown, S. H. (1981). Validity generalization and situational moderation in the life insurance industry. *Journal of Applied Psychology, 66,* 664–670.

Brown analyzed his data as if it were unmatched. That is, even though he had a criterion reliability value and a range restriction value specifically for each observed validity coefficient, he did not correct each observed coefficient individually. Instead, he used an unmatched data approach; that is, he used artifact distribution meta-analysis. (See Chapter 4.) In fairness to him, at the time he conducted his analysis, we had not yet published a description of methods for correcting each correlation individually.

Assume that range restriction in his data is direct and conduct new meta-analyses of his data correcting each observed validity individually. In the first meta-analysis, weight each study only by sample size (original weighting method). (This analysis cannot be run using the VG6-D program, because it does not weight by N_i.) Then do the meta-analysis again, weighting each study by $N_i A_i^2$ as described in this chapter. The analysis weighting by $N_i A_i^2$ can be done using the program VG6-D (i.e., the program for correcting correlations individually; specify that range restriction is *direct*). This program is described in the Appendix. For each set of analyses, report the following separately for the Group A and Group B companies and for the combined data:

1. Mean true validity
2. Standard deviation of true validities
3. Value at the 10th percentile
4. Percentage variance accounted for
5. Observed standard deviation of corrected validities
6. Standard deviation predicted from artifacts
7. Number of studies (companies)
8. Total N across the studies

Present these items in columns 1 through 8, in the order given here (with the columns labeled). (Each meta-analysis is then one row of your table.)

Compare your values to those obtained by Brown in each case. (Note: Brown did not compute values at the 10th percentile, but you can compute values for his data from information he gives in the study. Be careful to use the correct SD_ρ in this calculation: Use SD_ρ for true validity, not SD_ρ for true score correlations.) How different are the conclusions reached when these two different methods of meta-analysis are applied to the same data? What effect does weighting each study by other artifact indexes in addition to sample size have on the results? Why do you think this is the case? Do your results support Brown's original conclusions?

Worksheet–Exercise 3.2

Weighted by Sample Size

	1	2	3	4	5	6	7	8
	Mean True Validity	*SD* True Validity	10th Percentile	% Var. Accounted For	SD_{obs} Corrected Validities (SD_{rc})	*SD* Pred. From Artifacts	*K*	*N*
Overall								
Group A								
Group B								

Weighted by $N_i A_i^2$

	1	2	3	4	5	6	7	8
	Mean True Validity	*SD* True Validity	10th Percentile	% Var. Accounted For	SD_{obs} Corrected Validities (SD_{rc})	*SD* Pred. From Artifacts	*K*	*N*
Overall								
Group A								
Group B								

Data From Brown (1981)

	1	2	3	4	5	6	7	8
	Mean True Validity	*SD* True Validity	10th Percentile	% Var. Accounted For	SD_{obs} Validities	*SD* Pred. From Artifacts	*K*	*N*
Overall								
Group A								
Group B								

4

Meta-Analysis of Correlations Using Artifact Distributions

The preceding chapter assumed that the correlation in each individual study could be corrected for artifacts. However, often every study in meta-analysis does not provide all the information required to correct for attenuation on all the study artifacts that impact on that study. In any given meta-analysis, there may be several artifacts for which artifact information is only sporadically available. Indeed, this may be the case for all artifacts other than sampling error. For example, suppose measurement error and range restriction are the only relevant artifacts beyond sampling error. In such a case, the meta-analysis is conducted in three stages. First, the studies are used to compile information on four distributions: the distribution of the observed correlations, the distribution of the reliability of the independent variable, the distribution of the reliability of the dependent variable, and the distribution of range departure. That is, there are then four means and four variances compiled from the set of studies, using each study to provide whatever information it has. Second, the distribution of correlations is corrected for sampling error. Third, the distribution corrected for sampling error is then corrected for error of measurement, range variation, and perhaps other artifacts. This fully corrected distribution is the final result of the meta-analysis (unless the data are analyzed by subsets to test for moderator variables). Thus, the broad conceptual outline of meta-analysis based on artifact distributions is very simple. However, there are numerous statistical considerations involved in the third step here. These are examined in this chapter.

In the first section of this chapter, we consider the case in which information on all artifacts (except sampling error) is only sporadically available in the studies. That is, except for sample size, there is no artifact on which information is given in every study. Thus, for every artifact except sampling error, correction is accomplished by use of a distribution of artifact values that is compiled across the studies that do provide information on that artifact. In fact, information on some artifacts may be drawn from studies that do not present any study correlations. For example, the reliabilities of scales measuring the independent and dependent variables (e.g., widely used scales for job satisfaction or work commitment) may be obtained from such studies.

In the second section of this chapter, we consider the mixed case. In the mixed case, every study presents information on one or more artifacts, while information on other artifacts is missing from many but not all of the studies. For example, all studies may present information on reliability of the independent variable and on dichotomization of the dependent variable, but only sporadic information on other artifacts. In this case, correlations are first corrected individually for the artifacts for which there is complete information. Next, meta-analysis is performed on these partially corrected correlations. Finally, the results of that interim meta-analysis are corrected using artifact distributions. This step yields the final meta-analysis results (unless there is a subsequent search for moderators).

As noted in previous chapters, this book, unlike the 1990 edition, includes meta-analysis procedures for the case of indirect range restriction. When there is range restriction *and* when that range restriction is indirect, many of the formulas given in the 1990 edition for artifact distribution meta-analysis are not appropriate. Instead, new procedures must be used. These are presented in this chapter and are discussed in more detail in Chapter 5. When there is no range restriction or when there is direct range restriction, the procedures for artifact distribution meta-analysis remain the same as those presented in the 1990 edition. These procedures are retained in the present book.

Another important note concerns the reliability estimates used in making corrections for biases induced in data by measurement error. It is important to use appropriate types of reliability estimates. Use of inappropriate types of reliability estimates leads to incomplete corrections for measurement error. If this is the case, the meta-analysis report should explain that the biasing effects of measurement error were only partially corrected. A detailed guide for selecting appropriate reliability estimates is presented in Chapter 3. We refer the reader to that guide.

Full Artifact Distribution Meta-Analysis

In full artifact distribution meta-analysis, there is no artifact other than sampling error for which information is given in all studies. In this form of meta-analysis, the initial or interim meta-analysis is a meta-analysis of the uncorrected (observed) study correlations. The questions are these: How can the mean and standard deviation of uncorrected correlations be corrected for the impact of artifacts? How do we restore the mean observed correlation to the value that it would have had had the studies been conducted without design imperfections? How do we subtract the variance in study correlations produced by variation in artifact values across studies? The answer lies in the algebra of the correctable artifacts. Because most correctable artifacts can be quantified in the form of a multiplicative factor, certain average products can be computed as the product of averages. This enables us to correct the means and variances of the interim meta-analysis even though we cannot correct the individual values that go into that analysis. These methods are appropriate for all meta-analyses of correlations except those involving indirect range restriction.

The algebraic formulas used in this meta-analysis make certain assumptions, namely, that artifact parameters are (1) independent of the actual correlation and (2) independent of each other. Examination of the substantive nature of artifacts suggests that the independence assumptions are reasonable; most artifact values are less a matter of scientific choice and more a function of situational and resource constraints. The constraints for different artifacts usually have little to do with each other. (See Pearlman, Schmidt, & Hunter, 1980, and Schmidt, Pearlman, & Hunter, 1980, for a discussion of the reasons artifacts will usually be independently distributed.) Furthermore, Raju, Anselmi, Goodman, and Thomas (1998), in a computer simulation study, found that violation of independence has minimal effect on meta-analysis results unless artifacts are correlated with actual correlations, an unlikely event. However, two caveats should be noted here. First, the assumption of independence among artifacts does not hold if there is indirect range restriction. The technical reasons for this are presented in Chapter 5. When there is indirect range restriction, artifacts are, in fact, substantially correlated, and so a different procedure—the interactive meta-analysis procedure (described later in this chapter)—must be used. Second, even in the absence of indirect range restriction, the assumption of artifact independence, strictly speaking, applies only to the universe of studies and not necessarily to the sample of studies included in the meta-analysis. For the studies in hand, independence would be satisfied only to within second-order sampling error. That is, the independence assumptions will become more valid as the number of studies increases. By chance, there could be meta-analyses with a small number of studies for which the independence assumptions are violated to a sizeable degree. However, in meta-analyses on a small number of studies, the problem of second-order sampling error is usually more serious (see Chapter 9).

Suppose there is sporadic information on some artifact, say the reliability of the independent variable. Some studies report the reliability while other studies do not. Indeed, as we noted previously, we may obtain reliability estimates for some scales in studies that never used the dependent variable studied in the meta-analysis, that is, studies outside the original research domain for the meta-analysis. Data on the construct validity of the independent variable are likely to come predominantly from studies outside the research domain for the meta-analysis. For the studies available, we can use the artifact information (e.g., the reliability of our independent variable as reported in that study) to compute the attenuation factor for that artifact (the square root of the reported reliability). These attenuation factor values can then be compiled across studies to generate a distribution for that artifact.

Consider then the nature of the meta-analysis to be done. We have the study values to do a meta-analysis of uncorrected correlations. For each of several correctable artifacts, we have a mean and standard deviation of the artifact attenuation factor. These artifact distribution values are then used to correct the initial meta-analysis for the effects of those artifacts. The fact that we can combine analyses of the artifacts done separately into an analysis of how they operate jointly stems from the independence assumption and the fact that the compound attenuation factor is simply the product of the separate attenuation factors.

The Mean Correlation

For a meta-analysis of uncorrected correlations, we write the fundamental equation for sampling error as

$$r_{oi} = \rho_{oi} + e_i$$

where r_{oi} and ρ_{oi} are the uncorrected study sample correlation and study population correlation, respectively. The average of the uncorrected study correlations across studies is related to average population correlations and to average sampling error by

$$\text{Ave}(r_{oi}) = \text{Ave}(\rho_{oi}) + \text{Ave}(e_i)$$

for whatever set of weights is used to combine study values. Across a large enough set of studies, the average sampling error will be 0. Thus, for a large meta-analysis, the mean sample correlation is equal to the mean population correlation

$$\text{Ave}(r_{oi}) = \text{Ave}(\rho_{oi})$$

We know that the mean uncorrected correlation will be smaller than the mean of actual correlations because the study correlations have been attenuated by artifacts such as error of measurement. The question is: Just how much has the mean correlation been attenuated? Because the effect of the correctable artifacts is systematic, it is reasonable to hope that the answer to this question will be an algebraic equation such that the artifact impact can be reversed algebraically. We will now derive that equation.

Although the compound artifact multiplier A_i is not known for most studies, it is a definite number and can thus be entered into our equations as if it were known. The equation for the study population correlation is

$$\rho_{oi} = A_i \rho_i$$

where ρ_i is the actual effect size correlation for that study. When we average study correlations, we have

$$\text{Ave}(\rho_{oi}) = \text{Ave}(A_i \rho_i)$$

That is, the average study correlation is the average of the products of the actual study correlation and the artifact attenuation factor for that study. If the two variables in a product are independent, then the average product is the product of the averages. That is, suppose two variables X and Y are independent. Then

$$\text{Ave}(X_i Y_i) = \text{Ave}(X_i)\text{Ave}(Y_i)$$

If the extent of the artifact impact in a study is independent of the size of the study effect size correlation, then

$$\text{Ave}(\rho_{oi}) = \text{Ave}(A_i \rho_i) = \text{Ave}(A_i)\text{Ave}(\rho_i) \tag{4.1}$$

If the average artifact attenuation factor $\text{Ave}(A_i)$ were known, then this equation could be algebraically reversed to produce

$$\text{Ave}(\rho_i) = \text{Ave}(\rho_{oi})/\text{Ave}(A_i) \tag{4.2}$$

Note that this equation is exactly analogous to the formula for the correction of an individual correlation:

$$\rho_i = \rho_{oi}/A_i$$

That is, given the independence assumption, we can use the average attenuation factor to correct the average correlation for artifacts.

Thus, we have the answer to the question: How much is the average uncorrected correlation attenuated by artifacts? If the number of studies is large enough to eliminate sampling error, then

$$\text{Ave}(r_{oi}) = \text{Ave}(A_i)\text{Ave}(\rho_i)$$

and, hence,

$$\text{Ave}(\rho_i) = \text{Ave}(r_{oi})/\text{Ave}(A_i)$$

Where the number of studies is not large enough to completely eliminate sampling error, we use the same equation to estimate the mean actual correlation. However, that estimate will now be off by (second order) sampling error. The sampling error in the estimation equation will be exactly determined by the average sampling error. The sampling error in our estimation formula is

$$\text{Error} = \text{Ave}(e_i)/\text{Ave}(A_i)$$

To the extent that the numerator of this equation is small, the sampling error in our estimate will be small.

The Average Attenuation Factor

If artifact information is sporadic, it is possible that the compound attenuation factor cannot be known for any study. How, then, do we estimate the average across studies? The key lies in the independence of the artifacts. The causes of extreme values in one artifact are different from the causes of extreme values in another. Thus, any one attenuation factor is independent of any other. It is this fact that enables us to compute the average compound attenuation factor from the average of the component attenuation factors considered separately.

When each study correlation is corrected individually, the compound artifact attenuation factor is the product of the component artifact attenuation factors.

That is, if we write the separate single artifact attenuation factors as $a, b, c, \ldots,$ then the compound attenuation factor A is given by the product

$$A = abc \ldots$$

Because the artifacts are independent, the average compound attenuation factor is the product of the averages of the component attenuation factors

$$E(A) = E(a)E(b)E(c) \ldots \tag{4.3}$$

Artifact information is given for one artifact at a time. Thus, we usually collect information on artifact values a and b and c and so on separately. The mean of each artifact is denoted $E(a)$ or $E(b)$ or $E(c)$ and so on, where the average is computed across the studies where the information is present. The mean of the compound attenuation factor is the product of the averages for the separate attenuation factors.

The Final Correction

This is the last step needed to compute the mean effect size correlation. We compute the mean compound attenuation factor as the product of the separate mean attenuation factors for the individual artifacts. Then we divide the mean uncorrected correlation by that mean compound attenuation factor. That is, our estimate of the average unattenuated study effect correlation is

$$\text{Ave}(\rho) = \text{Ave}(r)/E(A) \tag{4.4}$$

The Standard Deviation of Correlations

The meta-analysis of uncorrected correlations provides an estimate of the variance of study population correlations. However, these study population correlations are themselves uncorrected. They have been attenuated by the study artifacts and are thus systematically reduced in magnitude. Furthermore, the variation in artifact extremity across studies causes the study correlations to be attenuated by different amounts in different studies. This produces variation in the size of the study correlations that could be mistaken for variation due to real moderator variables. Thus, the variance of population study correlations computed from a meta-analysis of uncorrected correlations is erroneous for two different reasons. It is smaller than it should be because of the systematic reduction in the magnitude of the study correlations, and it is larger than it should be because of variation in artifact extremity across studies. Both problems must be solved to estimate the standard deviation of true correlations across studies. We will show how this is done for our multiplicative model, the model that best lends itself to mathematical presentation. Other methods of estimating the standard deviation of true score correlations will be discussed later in this chapter.

Let us begin with some notation. An actual study correlation free of study artifacts is denoted ρ_i and the compound artifact attenuation factor for that study is denoted A_i. The attenuated study correlation ρ_{oi} is computed from the actual study correlation by

$$\rho_{oi} = A_i \rho_i$$

The study sample correlation r_{oi} departs from the study population correlation ρ_{oi} by sampling error e_i defined by

$$r_{oi} = \rho_{oi} + e_i = A_i \rho_i + e_i \quad (4.5)$$

Consider now a meta-analysis on the uncorrected correlations from all the studies in the meta-analysis. We know that the variance of sample correlations is the variance of population correlations plus the sampling error variance. That is,

$$\text{Var}(r_o) = \text{Var}(\rho_o) + \text{Var}(e)$$

Because the sampling error variance can be computed by statistical formula, we can subtract it to yield

$$\text{Var}(\rho_o) = \text{Var}(r_o) - \text{Var}(e)$$

That is, the meta-analysis of uncorrected correlations (bare-bones meta-analysis) produces an estimate of the variance of attenuated study population correlations—the actual study correlations after they have been reduced in magnitude by the study imperfections.

At the end of a meta-analysis of uncorrected correlations, we have the variance of attenuated study population correlations $\text{Var}(\rho_o)$, but we want the variance of actual unattenuated correlations $\text{Var}(\rho)$. The relationship between these is

$$\text{Var}(\rho_o) = \text{Var}(A_i \rho_i)$$

That is, $\text{Var}(\rho_o)$ is the variance of a variable that is the product of two other variables. We know that the A_i and ρ_i variables are independent. We can use this fact to compute the variance of the product. We will derive the formula for the variance of a product later, but for the moment let us use the final result. Let us denote the average actual study correlation by $\bar{\rho}$ and denote the average compound attenuation factor by $\bar{A}$. Then, to a close approximation,

$$\text{Var}(A_i \rho_i) = \bar{A}^2 \text{Var}(\rho_i) + \bar{\rho}^2 \text{Var}(A_i) \quad (4.6)$$

We can then rearrange this equation algebraically to obtain the desired equation for the variance of actual study correlations free of artifact:

$$\text{Var}(\rho_i) = [\text{Var}(A_i \rho_i) - \bar{\rho}^2 \, \text{Var}(A_i)]/\bar{A}^2 \quad (4.7)$$

That is, starting from the meta-analysis of uncorrected correlations, we have

$$\text{Var}(\rho) = [\text{Var}(\rho_o) - \bar{\rho}^2 \text{Var}(A_i)]/\bar{A}^2 \quad (4.7a)$$

The right-hand side of this equation has four numbers:

1. $\text{Var}(\rho_o)$: the population correlation variance estimated in the meta-analysis of uncorrected correlations (the bare-bones meta-analysis)
2. $\bar{\rho}$: the mean of unattenuated or actual study population correlations whose estimate was derived in the preceding section
3. $\bar{A}$: the mean compound attenuation factor that was estimated as part of the process of estimating the mean unattenuated correlation $\text{Ave}(\rho)$
4. $\text{Var}(A_i)$: the variance of the compound attenuation factor, which has not yet been estimated

How do we compute the variance of the compound attenuation factor A? We are given the distribution of each component attenuation factor. These must be combined to produce the variance of the compound attenuation factor. The key to this computation lies in two facts: (1) The compound attenuation factor is the product of the component attenuation factors and (2) the attenuation factors are independent. That is, because the compound attenuation factor A_i for any single study is

$$A_i = a_i b_i c_i \ldots$$

the variance of the A_i across studies is the variance of a product variable across studies

$$\text{Var}(A_i) = \text{Var}(a_i b_i c_i \ldots)$$

We can also express this without the subscripts:

$$\text{Var}(A) = \text{Var}(a\,b\,c \ldots)$$

The variance of the compound attenuation factor is the variance of the product of independent component attenuation factors. We will derive the formula for the variance of the product later. Here let us simply use the result.

For each separate artifact, we have a mean and a standard deviation for that component attenuation factor. From the mean and the standard deviation, we can compute the "coefficient of variation," which is the standard deviation divided by the mean

$$CV = SD/\text{Mean}$$

For each artifact, we now compute the *squared* coefficient of variation. For the first artifact attenuation factor a, we compute

$$v_1 = \text{Var}(a)/[\text{Ave}(a)]^2$$

ond artifact attenuation factor b, we compute

$$v_2 = \text{Var}(b)/[\text{Ave}(b)]^2$$

For the third artifact attenuation factor c, we compute

$$v_3 = \mathrm{Var}(c)/[\mathrm{Ave}(c)]^2$$

and so on. Thus, we compute a squared coefficient of variation for each artifact. These are then summed to form a total

$$V = v_1 + v_2 + v_3 + \ldots \tag{4.8}$$

Recalling that $\bar{A}$ denotes the mean compound attenuation factor, we write the formula for the variance of the compound attenuation factor (to a close approximation) as the product

$$\mathrm{Var}(A) = \bar{A}^2 V \tag{4.9}$$

We now have all the elements to compute the variance in actual study correlations $\mathrm{Var}(\rho)$. The final formula is

$$\mathrm{Var}(\rho) = [\mathrm{Var}(\rho_o) - \bar{\rho}^2 \mathrm{Var}(A_i)]/\bar{A}^2$$

$$\mathrm{Var}(\rho) = [\mathrm{Var}(\rho_o) - \bar{\rho}^2 \bar{A}^2 V]/\bar{A}^2 \tag{4.10}$$

Decomposition of Variance

Buried in the preceding derivation is a decomposition of the variance of uncorrected correlations. Let us pull that decomposition together here:

$$\mathrm{Var}(r) = \mathrm{Var}(\rho_o) + \mathrm{Var}(e)$$

$$\mathrm{Var}(\rho_o) = \mathrm{Var}(A\rho) = \bar{A}^2 \mathrm{Var}(\rho) + \bar{\rho}^2 \mathrm{Var(A)}$$

$$\mathrm{Var}(A) = \bar{A}^2 V$$

That is,

$$\mathrm{Var}(r) = \bar{A}^2 \mathrm{Var}(\rho) + \bar{\rho}^2 \bar{A}^2 V + \mathrm{Var}(e)$$

$$\mathrm{Var}(r) = S_1^2 + S_2^2 + S_3^2 \tag{4.11}$$

where (1) S_1^2 is the variance in uncorrected correlations produced by the variation in actual unattenuated effect size correlations, (2) S_2^2 is the variance in uncorrected correlations produced by the variation in artifacts, and (3) S_3^2 is the variance in uncorrected correlations produced by sampling error.

In this decomposition, the term S_1^2 contains the estimated variance of effect size correlations. This estimated variance is corrected for those artifacts that were corrected in the meta-analysis. This is usually not all the artifacts that affect the study value. Thus, S_1^2 is an upper bound estimate of the component of variance in uncorrected correlations due to real variation in the strength of the relationship and not due to artifacts of the study design. To the extent that there are uncorrected artifacts, S_1^2 will overestimate the real variation, possibly greatly overestimating that variation.

Schmidt and Hunter (1977) noted this overestimation and recommended that if the term S_1^2 is less than 25% of the total variance, $\mathrm{Var}(r)$, then it is probably true that the remaining variance is artifactual and is due to remaining artifacts that it was not possible to correct for (e.g., data errors, variations in construct validity of measures, etc.). This is the often-cited "75% rule." In that article, we were arguing that in any given meta-analysis it is probably the case that the unknown and uncorrected artifacts account for 25% of the variance. Thus, if the estimate of real variance is not at least this large, there may be no real variance.

The 75% rule has been widely misinterpreted. Some authors have mistakenly interpreted this to be a rule for judging whether the variance is explained by second-order sampling error (see Chapter 9). Consider a meta-analysis in a research domain where the number of studies is small. If the number of studies in the meta-analysis is small, there is sampling error in the observed variance of sample correlations, that is, second-order sampling error (see Chapter 9). Thus, by chance, the observed value of $\text{Var}(r)$ may be larger than would be predicted by the sampling error variance formula. Some authors have falsely assumed that the 75% rule is intended to be a statistical test for such chance fluctuation.

Variance of a Product: Two Variables

This section and the following two sections are mathematical in nature. They demonstrate the derivation of the formulas that were used in the preceding two sections. Readers uninterested in these derivations may want to skip ahead to the section "A Worked Example: Error of Measurement." Formulas for the variance of a product were invoked at several points in the preceding development. We now proceed to derive those formulas. First, we note an identity for the variance that will be heavily used in these computations. Consider any variable X. The identity for the variance of X is

$$\text{Var}(X) = E(X^2) - [E(X)]^2 \tag{4.12}$$

That is, the variance equals the mean of the square minus the square of the mean. This identity can also be used in the reverse direction:

$$E(X^2) = [E(X)]^2 + \text{Var}(X) \tag{4.13}$$

Consider first the product of two independent variables a and b. We first compute the mean of the square, after which we subtract the square of the mean. The expected square is

$$E[(ab)^2] = E[a^2b^2]$$

Because a and b are independent, the squares a^2 and b^2 are independent. Thus, the mean of the product equals the product of the means:

$$E[a^2\,b^2] = E(a^2)E(b^2)$$

The reverse identity for variables a and b separately is

$$E(a^2) = [E(a)]^2 + \text{Var}(a)$$
$$E(b^2) = [E(b)]^2 + \text{Var}(b)$$

These are then substituted into the expected square of the product

$$E[a^2b^2] = \{[E(a)]^2 + \text{Var}(a)\}\{[E(b)]^2 + \text{Var}(b)\}$$
$$= E(a)^2E(b)^2 + E(a)^2\text{Var}(b) + E(b)^2\text{Var}(a) + \text{Var}(a)\text{Var}(b)$$

The mean of the product is the product of the means:

$$E(ab) = E(a)E(b)$$

Thus, the square of the mean is

$$[E(ab)]^2 = [E(a)E(b)]^2 = E(a)^2E(b)^2$$

This is subtracted from the mean square to produce the variance. The variance of the product of two independent variables is thus

$$\text{Var}(ab) = E(a)^2\,\text{Var}(b) + E(b)^2\,\text{Var}(a) + \text{Var}(a)\text{Var}(b) \tag{4.14}$$

For our purposes, we will argue that the last term, $\text{Var}(a)\text{Var}(b)$, is so small that it can be dropped with no visible error. This would leave the formula used to compute $\text{Var}(A\rho)$.

All the variables considered in this part of the book are fractions. The mean of a fraction variable is a fraction and its variance is a smaller fraction. Thus, we will argue that the product $\text{Var}(a)\text{Var}(b)$ is so small that it makes no visible contribution to the variance of the product.

As an illustration, consider the attenuation factor for the reliability of the independent variable. Suppose the 95% interval for that reliability is

$$.64 < r_{XX} < .81$$

Then the 95% interval for the square root of the reliability is

$$.80 < \sqrt{r_{XX}} < .90$$

Thus, the mean is about .85 and the standard deviation is about .025, yielding a coefficient of variation of

$$CV = SD/\text{Mean} = .025/.85 = .0294$$

That is, for this attenuation factor, the mean is 34 times larger than the standard deviation. The comparison is even more striking when we square the mean and the standard deviation. The squared coefficient of variation is

$$CV^2 = \text{Var}/\text{Mean}^2 = .025^2/.85^2 = .00625/.7225 = .000865$$

That is, the squared mean is 1,156 times larger than the variance.

Suppose now that a is the attenuation factor for error of measurement in the independent variable and that b is the attenuation factor for error of measurement in the dependent variable. If both have the distribution given in the previous paragraph, then the variance of the product is

$$\begin{aligned}\text{Var}(ab) &= E(a)^2\,\text{Var}(b) + E(b)^2\text{Var}(a) + \text{Var}(a)\text{Var}(b)\\ &= (.64)(.0025) + (.64)(.0025) + (.0025)(.0025)\\ &= .0016 + .0016 + .00000625\end{aligned}$$

The last term is less than 1/200 of either of the first two terms and would make little difference if dropped. If we drop the product of the variances, the estimated variance of the product is .0032. If the last term is tacked on, the figure for the variance of the product is .00320625. This tiny difference is invisible unless calculations are carried out to six digits. This illustrates our argument that virtually no error is incurred in dropping the product of the variances from the formula for the variance of the product.

Variance of the Product: Three Variables

Consider the product of three variables, a, b, and c. If these variables are independent, then the mean of the product is the product of the means, that is,

$$E[abc] = E[a]E[b]E[c]$$

If all three variables are independent, then so are their squares. Hence,

$$E[a^2b^2c^2] = E[a^2]E[b^2]E[c^2]$$

We can now derive a formula for the variance of a triple product if all three variables are independent:

$$\begin{aligned}\sigma^2_{abc} &= E[(abc)^2] - (E[abc])^2\\ &= E[a^2b^2c^2] - (E[a]E[b]E[c])^2\\ &= E[a^2]E[b^2]E[c^2] - \bar{a}^2\bar{b}^2\bar{c}^2\\ &= (\bar{a}^2 + \sigma^2_a)(\bar{b}^2 + \sigma^2_b)(\bar{c}^2 + \sigma^2_b) - \bar{a}^2\bar{b}^2\bar{c}^2\\ &= \bar{a}^2\bar{b}^2\bar{\sigma}^2_c + \bar{a}^2\bar{c}^2\bar{\sigma}^2_b + \bar{b}^2\bar{c}^2\bar{\sigma}^2_a\\ &\quad + \bar{a}^2\sigma^2_b\sigma^2_c + \bar{b}^2\sigma^2_a\sigma^2_c + \bar{c}^2\sigma^2_a\sigma^2_b\\ &\quad + \sigma^2_a\sigma^2_b\sigma^2_c \qquad (4.15)\end{aligned}$$

The terms in this variance have been listed in a special order. The first three terms have two means and one variance, the next three terms have one mean and two variances, and the last term is the product of the three variances. The order is important because, in our context, the variables a, b, and c are all fractions and have means much larger than variances. Thus, the last four terms in our formula are negligible in size and can be dropped.

The resulting formula for the variance of the product is

$$\text{Var}(abc) = \bar{a}^2\bar{b}^2\,\text{Var}(c) + \bar{a}^2\bar{c}^2\,\text{Var}(b) + \bar{b}^2\bar{c}^2\,\text{Var}(a) \qquad (4.16)$$

This can be written in a form that shows a pattern of substitution. Consider the product of the squares:

$$E(abc)^2 = \bar{a}^2\bar{b}^2\bar{c}^2$$

If one substitutes a variance for a squared mean for each of the variables in turn, one gets the terms in the variance of the product:

$$\text{Var}(abc) = \text{Var}(a)\,\bar{b}^2\bar{c}^2 + \bar{a}^2\,\text{Var}(b)\bar{c}^2 + \bar{a}^2\bar{b}^2\,\text{Var}(c)$$

For example, the term for the b variable substitution can be written as

$$\begin{aligned}\bar{a}^2\,\text{Var}(b)\bar{c}^2 &= [\bar{a}^2\bar{b}^2\bar{c}^2]\,[\text{Var}(b)/\bar{b}^2]\\ &= [\overline{abc}]^2\,[\text{Var}(b)/\bar{b}^2]\end{aligned}$$

The second term, $\text{Var}(b)/\bar{b}^2$, is the square of the coefficient of variation of factor b. Denote the squared coefficient of b by v_2 and denote the squared coefficients of a and c by v_1 and v_3, respectively. Let A be the triple product, $A = \overline{abc}$. Then we have shown that the variance of the product is given by

$$\text{Var}(abc) = A^2(v_1 + v_2 + v_3)$$

This is the formula used to derive the variance of the compound attenuation factor.

Variance of a Product: General Case

The preceding derivation extends immediately to any number of factors. For example, the variance of the product of four variables is

$$\begin{aligned}\text{Var}(abcd) = \text{Var}(a)\,\bar{b}^2\bar{c}^2\bar{d}^2 + \bar{a}^2\,\text{Var}(b)\bar{c}^2\bar{d}^2 + \bar{a}^2\bar{b}^2\\ \text{Var}(c)\bar{d}^2 + \bar{a}^2\bar{b}^2\bar{c}^2\,\text{Var}(d)\end{aligned}$$

That is, in each term there is the substitution of a variance for a squared mean. If the squared quadruple product $A^2 = [\overline{abcd}]^2$ is factored out, then each such substitution is represented by the square of the coefficient of variation. Thus,

$$\text{Var}(abcd) = A^2(v_1 + v_2 + v_3 + v_4) = A^2V \qquad (4.17)$$

using the notation

$$V = v_1 + v_2 + v_3 + v_4$$

Formulas for full artifact distribution meta-analysis were first developed in the specialized area of personnel selection research under the rubric "validity generalization" (Schmidt & Hunter, 1977). However, there is a certain quirk in research in personnel selection; specifically, there are reasons for not correcting for error of measurement in the predictor (independent) variable, as noted in Chapter 3 and as explained later in this chapter. As a result, the formulas from validity generalization must be modified to be useful in the broader general context of research integration in the social and behavioral sciences generally. We will develop three sets of formulas here. First, we will consider the most common case: error of measurement in both variables x and y, but no restriction in range. We will then develop a set of formulas for the case in which all three of these artifacts are to be corrected for. These formulas apply only to direct range restriction. As noted earlier, different procedures must be used when range restriction is indirect. Later in this chapter, we will present the methods to be used when range restriction is indirect. We will also present the validity generalization formulas that have been used in the literature. Most of these methods are appropriate only when range restriction is direct and will underestimate mean validities and overestimate SD_ρ when used with data in which range restriction is indirect. This has, in fact, been the case in most published validity generalization studies.

A Worked Example: Error of Measurement

Variables in the social sciences are often only poorly measured. Thus, results must be corrected to eliminate error of measurement. Suppose error of measurement is the only artifact that attenuates the studies in a given area. (Or, alas, more realistically, assume that it is the only artifact on which information is available.) The attenuation model for this study is

$$\rho_o = ab\rho$$

where

$$a = \sqrt{r_{XX}}$$
$$b = \sqrt{r_{YY}}$$

Table 4.1 presents the basic computations for the meta-analysis of a hypothetical set of studies of the correlation between organizational commitment and job satisfaction. Table 4.1a presents the basic findings and the artifact information for eight studies. The studies are listed in three groups. The first pair of studies presents no correlational data pertaining to organizational commitment or job satisfaction, but these studies do contain reliability data on organizational commitment. The first is the classic study in which Ermine presented his measure of organizational commitment. The second study is one in which Ferret used "the key items from Ermine" and then correlated commitment with other variables (not including job satisfaction). The second pair of studies contains only reliability information on job satisfaction scales. Finally, the last four studies contain only correlational information (although each study had the item data and, hence, could have computed at least coefficient alpha reliability coefficients for that study). In Table 4.1a, we see that two of the correlations were statistically significant and two were not.

Table 4.1b presents the meta-analysis worksheet. The column for a presents the attenuation factor for the first correctable artifact, that is, the square root of the reliability of the independent variable. The column for b presents the attenuation factor for the second correctable artifact, that is, the square root of the reliability of the dependent variable. At the bottom of the table, the mean and standard deviation of each entry is given.

Table 4.1 Organizational commitment and job satisfaction (hypothetical results)

Table 4.1a Basic information

	Organizational Commitment Reliability (r_{xx})	*Job Satisfaction Reliability* (r_{yy})	*Sample Size* (N_i)	*Sample Correlation* (r_{xy})
Ermine (1976)	.70			
Ferret (1977)	.50			
Mink (1976)		.70		
Otter (1977)		.50		
Polecat (1978)			68	.01
Stoat (1979)			68	.14
Weasel (1980)			68	.23*
Wolverine (1978)			68	.34**

*Significant at the .05 level.
**Significant at the .01 level.

Table 4.1b Meta-analysis worksheet

Study	*a*	*b*	*N*	r_o
1	.84			
2	.71			
3		.84		
4		.71		
5			68	.01
6			68	.14
7			68	.23
8			68	.34
Ave	.775	.775	68	.180
SD	.065	.065	0	.121

Consider first the meta-analysis of the uncorrected correlations:

$$\bar{\rho}_{xy} = \bar{r} = .18,$$

$$\sigma_r^2 = .014650,$$

$$\sigma_e^2 = \frac{4(1 - .18^2)^2}{4(67)} = .013974,$$

$$\sigma_{\rho_{xy}}^2 = \sigma_r^2 - \sigma_e^2 = .014650 - .013974 = .000676,$$

$$\sigma_{\rho_{xy}} = .026.$$

This analysis of sampling error shows that there is little variation in the correlations across studies. The 95% credibility interval is $.13 \leq \rho_{xy} \leq .23$. Thus, the two studies that fail to find statistical significance make Type II errors.

To correct for the artifacts, we first compute the mean compound artifact attenuation factor:

$$\bar{A} = \text{Ave}(a)\,\text{Ave}(b) = \bar{a}\,\bar{b} = (.775)(.775) = .600625$$

From this, we compute the mean actual study correlation, that is, the study correlation restored to its preattenuated value:

$$\rho = \text{Ave}(\rho_i) = \text{Ave}(r)/\bar{A} = .18/.600625 = .2997$$

Next, we compute the sum of the squared coefficients of variation:

$$V = .065^2/.775^2 + .065^2/.775^2 = .014069$$

The variance due to artifact variation is thus

$$S_2^2 = \bar{\rho}^2\bar{A}^2V = (.2997^2)(.600625^2)(.014069) = .000456$$

The variance in true score correlations is thus

$$\begin{aligned}\text{Var}(\rho) &= [\text{Var}(\rho_o) - \bar{\rho}^2\bar{A}^2V]/\bar{A}^2\\ &= [.000676 - .000456]/(.600625^2)\\ &= .000610\end{aligned}$$

The standard deviation of population correlations is thus estimated to be the square root of .000610, or $SD_\rho = .0247$. In round numbers, the actual study correlations are estimated to have a mean of .30 and a standard deviation of .025. If the effect size correlations have a normal distribution, then the 95% credibility interval is

$$.25 < \rho < .35$$

It is important to remember that only two study artifacts were corrected here: the error of measurement in the independent and the dependent variables. Thus, the residual variation attributed to the actual correlations contains variation due to uncorrected artifacts such as imperfect construct validity or bad data and so on. Therefore, the true standard deviation may be less than the .025 nominal estimate.

Let us consider the impact of artifacts in this example. The impact of sampling error on the mean correlation was assumed to be negligible (although that would not really be true with a total sample size of only 272). However, the impact of sampling error on the variance across studies is massive. The variance of the sample correlations is .01465, of which sampling error is .013974, variance due to variation of reliability is .000137, and "else" is .000539. That is, 95% of the variance in correlations across studies is due to sampling error, 1% is due to variation in reliability, and 4% is due to unspecified other determinants.

Variation in reliabilities causes only 1% of the variation in observable correlations, but the impact of measurement error on the mean correlation is very large. Error of measurement caused the *mean* correlation to be depressed from .30 to .18, a 40% reduction.

A Worked Example: Unreliability and Direct Range Restriction

Suppose we have artifact information on three artifacts: error of measurement in the independent variable, error of measurement in the dependent variable, and direct range restriction on the independent variable. The three attenuation artifacts are

$$a = \sqrt{r_{XX_a}}$$
$$b = \sqrt{r_{YY_a}}$$
$$c = [(1 - u_X^2)\bar{r}^2 + u_X^2]^{1/2} \quad \text{(Callender \& Osburn, 1980)}$$

where r_{xx_a} and r_{yy_a} are the reliabilities in the unrestricted group and $\bar{r}$ is the average observed correlation. The attenuation formula is

$$\rho_o = abc\rho$$

Table 4.2 presents both the artifact information in raw form and the computed attenuation factors for each artifact for 16 hypothetical studies. The example in Table 4.2 was created by assuming that the population correlation between true scores on the two variables in the reference population is always $\rho = .60$. The first five columns of Table 4.2 are the data extracted from the 16 hypothetical studies. The last three columns are the values of a, b, and c, computed from the values of r_{XX_a}, r_{YY_a}, and u_X, respectively.

The four means and variances needed are

$$\bar{r} = .175, \quad \bar{a} = .75, \quad \bar{b} = .75, \quad \bar{c} = .525,$$
$$\sigma_r^2 = .015100, \quad \sigma_a^2 = .0025, \quad \sigma_b^2 = .0025, \quad \sigma_c^2 = .009025.$$

Table 4.2 Sixteen hypothetical studies

Study	*N*	r_{xx_a}	r_{yy_a}	u_x	r_{xy}	*a*	*b*	*c*
1	68	.49	–	.40	.02	.70	–	.43
2	68	–	64	–	.26*	–	.80	–
3	68	.49	.64	–	.33*	.70	.80	–
4	68	–	–	.60	.09	–	–	.62
5	68	.49	–	–	.02	.70	–	–
6	68	–	.49	.40	.24*	–	.70	.43
7	68	.49	.49	–	.30*	.70	.70	–
8	68	–	–	.60	.06	–	–	.62
9	68	.64	–	.40	.28*	.80	–	.43
10	68	–	.64	–	.04	–	.80	–
11	68	.64	.64	–	.12	.80	.80	–
12	68	–	–	.60	.34*	–	–	.62
13	68	.64	–	–	.26*	.80	–	–
14	68	–	.49	.40	.02	–	.70	.43
15	68	.64	.49	–	.09	.80	.70	–
16	68	–	–	.60	.33*	–	–	.62

*Significant at the .05 level (two-tailed test).
NOTE: r_{xx_a} and r_{yy_a} are the values in the unrestricted populations.

We first use the mean and variance of the observed correlations to correct for sampling error:

$$\bar{\rho}_{xy} = \bar{r} = .175$$
$$S_e^2 = \frac{(1 - .175^2)^2}{68 - 1} = .013974$$
$$\sigma_{\rho_{xy}}^2 = \sigma_r^2 - \sigma_e^2 = .015100 - .013974 = .001126$$

These values can then be corrected to eliminate the effects of error of measurement and range variation. First, we compute the mean compound attenuation factor A:

$$\bar{A} = (.75)(.75)(.525) = .2953$$

This can be used to correct the mean uncorrected correlation:

$$\text{Ave}(\rho_i) = .175/.2953 = .5926$$

We then compute the sum of the squared coefficients of variation:

$$V = [.05/.75]^2 + [.05/.75]^2 + [.095/.525]^2 = .041633$$

The variance due to variation in artifacts is

$$S_2^2 = \bar{\rho}^2 \bar{A}^2 V = (.5926^2)(.2953^2)(.041633) = .001275$$

The residual variance in the uncorrected population correlations is thus

$$S_{\text{res}}^2 = \text{Var}(\rho_o) - S_2^2 = .001126 - .001275 = -.000149$$

This is very close to 0. Because it is negative, it is taken as 0.

The estimated variance of true correlations is thus

$$\text{Var}(\rho) = S_{\text{res}}^2 / A^2 = 0/.2953^2 = 0$$

The estimated standard deviation is thus 0. Because this example was constructed assuming no real variation, the standard deviation should be 0, and it is. Thus, the final meta-analysis results are $\bar{\rho} = .59$ and $SD_\rho = 0$. These results are almost identical to the true values (the values used to generate the data): $\bar{\rho} = .60$ and $SD_\rho = 0$. The slight difference indicates the extent to which artifact distribution meta-analysis is an approximation rather than an exact calculation.

A Worked Example: Personnel Selection With Fixed Test (Direct Range Restriction)

Personnel selection is a special case because, in the practical use of the test for hiring, the predictor test is used in imperfect form. Thus, the relevant population correlation for purposes of assessing the practical impact of the test is corrected for error of measurement in the dependent variable but not in the independent variable. The validity of the test is given by the applicant population correlation between uncorrected test scores and job performance true scores. This means we should correct for measurement error in the job performance measure and correct for restriction in range, but not correct for error of measurement in the test. (Of course, in the *theory* of personnel selection, we would want fully corrected correlations.)

Personnel selection research is vexed by all the artifacts shown in Table 3.1. In particular, restriction in range on the independent variable is created by selective hiring. Suppose all studies in a meta-analysis use exactly the same test so there is no variation across studies in the reliability of the independent variable, r_{XX_a}, the reliability of the test in the applicant (unrestricted) group. Suppose $r_{XX_a} = .80$.

Suppose error of measurement in the dependent variable (job performance) and range restriction are the only other artifacts for which artifact information is available. Suppose also that range restriction on the independent variable is direct. The attenuation factors would then be

$$b = \sqrt{r_{YY_a}}$$
$$c = [(1 - u_X^2)\bar{r}^2 + u_X^2]^{1/2}$$

where r_{YY_a} is the reliability of the job performance measure in the applicant pool (the unrestricted group) and $\bar{r}$ is the average uncorrected correlation across studies. The attenuation formula is

$$\rho_o = bc\rho$$

Tabled 4.3 presents hypothetical data for 12 personnel selection studies of this type. (Note that these data are different from those in Table 3.5; the range restriction values are different.) The multiplicative model illustrated here requires the criterion reliability values in the applicant (unrestricted) group (r_{yy_a}). Ordinarily, only criterion reliability values for incumbents (the restricted group) would be available (i.e., r_{yy_i} values). Hence, we must use Equation (5.20) in Chapter 5 to transform r_{yy_i} values to r_{yy_a} values. This has been done in Table 4.3. Notice that all criterion unreliabilities are slightly higher in the applicant group. (Later in this chapter and in Chapter 5, we present other procedures for artifact distribution meta-analysis that do allow use of r_{yy_i} in correcting for direct range restriction.) Because complete artifact information is given in Table 4.3 for each observed correlation, the artifact distribution method ordinarily would not be used; instead, each correlation would be corrected individually, using the methods presented in Chapter 3. Here, however, we present an artifact distribution analysis for these data to illustrate the mechanics of artifact distribution meta-analysis using the multiplicative model presented earlier in this chapter. The last two columns of Table 4.3 show the attenuation factors. The necessary means and variances are as follows:

$$\bar{b} = .85342 \qquad \bar{c} = .67656 \qquad \bar{r} = .28$$
$$\sigma_b^2 = .003301 \qquad \sigma_c^2 = .018478 \qquad \sigma_r^2 = .017033$$
$$\sigma_e^2 = .012677$$
$$\sigma_{\rho_o}^2 = .004357$$

Table 4.3 Meta-analysis of personnel selection validities (direct range restriction)

			Criterion Reliability					
Study	*Selection Ratio*	u_X	(r_{yy_i})	(r_{yy_a})	*Sample Size*	*Observed Correlation*	*b*	*c*
1	.20	.468	.80	.86	68	.35**	.928	.529
2	.20	.468	.60	.61	68	.07	.779	.529
3	.20	.468	.80	.81	68	.11	.899	.529
4	.20	.468	.60	.70	68	.31*	.838	.529
5	.50	.603	.80	.81	68	.18	.900	.643
6	.50	.603	.60	.67	68	.36**	.821	.643
7	.50	.603	.80	.84	68	.40**	.919	.643
8	.50	.603	.60	.61	68	.13	.782	.643
9	.90	.844	.80	.82	68	.49**	.904	.857
10	.90	.844	.60	.61	68	.23	.780	.857
11	.90	.844	.80	.81	68	.29*	.898	.857
12	.90	.844	.60	.63	68	.44*	.793	.857

*$p < .05$ (two-tailed test).
**$p < .01$ (two-tailed test).

The compound attenuation factor is

$$\bar{A} = (\bar{b})(\bar{c})$$

$$\bar{A} = .85342\,(.67656) = .57739$$

Thus, the mean actual correlation is estimated as

$$\text{Ave}(\rho_i) = .28/.57739 = .486$$

The sum of the squared coefficients of variation is

$$V = [.003301/.85342^2] + [.018478/.67656^2] = .044900$$

The variance in the uncorrected correlations caused by variation in artifacts is

$$S_2^2 = .486^2\,(.57739)^2(.044900) = .003520$$

The residual variance in uncorrected correlations is

$$S_{\text{res}}^2 = .004357 - .003520 = .000836$$

The variance of actual study correlations is thus estimated as

$$\text{Var}(\rho) = S_{\text{res}}^2/\bar{A}^2 = .000836/.57739^2 = .002509$$

Hence, the standard deviation is estimated to be $(.002509)^{1/2} = .0500$.

The final estimates are thus $\bar{\rho}_{xy_t} = .49$ and $SD_\rho = .05$. The mean value of .49 is close to the correct value of .50, and the SD_ρ estimate is not much different from the correct value of 0. The deviation of our SD_ρ estimate from the correct value of 0 reflects in part rounding error in carrying out the calculations and in part the fact that the meta-analysis methods are approximations. (Computer simulation studies on this and related methods have consistently shown a tendency to slightly overestimate SD_ρ; see Law, Schmidt, & Hunter, 1994b. Hence, these methods can be said to be "conservative.")

The data in Table 4.3 are "matched data." That is, all artifact information is available for every correlation. Therefore, we can meta-analyze these data using the methods described in Chapter 3. That is, we can correct each correlation individually and then do the meta-analysis on the corrected correlations. We can do this by applying the VG6-D (for direct range restriction) program (discussed in Chapter 3 and described in the Appendix) to the data in Table 4.3. In doing this, we enter 1.00s for the reliability of the predictor because we are not correcting for measurement error in the predictor. The program output states that $\bar{\rho}_{xy_t} = .50$ and $SD_\rho = 0$. The estimate of the mean value is correct to two decimal places. The estimated SD_ρ of 0 is the exactly correct value and is more accurate than the .05 value obtained in our worked example based on the multiplicative model for artifact distribution meta-analysis. This is as would be expected because correction of each correlation individually is a more exact method. We can also compare our example results with those produced by the program INTNL-D, a program for artifact distribution meta-analysis that is mathematically different from the multiplicative model used in our example. INTNL-D (for direct range restriction) and INTNL-I (for indirect range restriction) are discussed later in this chapter (and are described in the Appendix). The methods used by these programs are too complex to apply to a worked example. As explained later, the INTNL programs are based on estimation methods very different from the methods we used in our Table 4.3 worked example. Yet the results are very similar: $\bar{\rho}_{xy_t} = .49$ and $SD_\rho = .03$. The SD_ρ value of .03 is closer to the correct value of 0 than the estimate of .05 obtained in our worked example, suggesting that the INTNL program is slightly more accurate than the multiplicative method we used in our worked example and is nearly as accurate as the method of correcting each correlation individually.

Suppose the type of range restriction affecting the data in Table 4.3 was actually indirect range restriction—and we had falsely assumed it was direct range restriction. In that case, the mean true validity estimates given previously would be underestimates. How large would this underestimation be? We can answer this question by running the data in Table 4.3 through the program INTNL-I (for indirect range restriction). We enter u_X values, which the program converts internally to u_T values, using Equation (3.16). As noted earlier, the unrestricted reliability for the single test used in these studies is $r_{XX_a} = .80$. We enter this value into INTNL-I. (Note that in this program one cannot enter 1.00s for r_{XX_a} values when one does not want to correct for predictor unreliability—because this "convenient fiction" will cause u_X values to be the same as u_T values, because r_{XX_a} values are used in the formula that converts u_X to u_T, Equation [3.16]. This problem does not occur when range restriction is direct, i.e., when applying INTNL-D.) Running the program, we obtain the following results:

$$\bar{\rho}_{xy_t} = .67$$

$$SD_\rho = 0$$

SD_ρ is 0, the correct value. However, $\bar{\rho}_{xy_t}$ is now .67 (vs. the earlier .50), which is 34% larger. Looked at another way, use of corrections for direct range restriction when the range restriction is actually indirect leads to a 25% underestimate of mean true validity. Hence, it is critical to accuracy of estimates of mean actual correlations to correctly specify and apply the type of range restriction correction.

Personnel Selection With Varying Tests

The test used for prediction is usually only specified in terms of the construct to be measured, for example, arithmetic reasoning. There are many arithmetic reasoning tests available that are (nearly) equivalent in general content but different in reliability. This variation in reliability contributes to the variation in correlations across studies if the review covers all studies using a given type of test rather than a fixed test.

There have been two responses to this in the literature. In our earliest work, we ignored the variation in the reliability of the predictor (as did Callender & Osburn, 1980). Later, we used a hybrid solution. We corrected the variance across studies for all artifacts, but we corrected the mean correlation only for restriction in range and for error of measurement in job performance. That is, we did not correct the mean for the attenuating effect of error of measurement in the predictor variable. This gives the mean and standard deviation for a distribution of operational validities in which the reliability of the predictor is always fixed at the average value for the study population. If the results are applied in a context in which the actual test used has a reliability equal to the average reliability, then our results can be used as such. However, if the results are to be used in a context in which the reliability is different from the average, then the user should modify our reported results. The mean validity and the standard deviation must first be corrected for attenuation using the square root of the mean test reliability. Then the resulting true score validity and true score standard deviation must be attenuated using the square root of the reliability of the actual test to be used (Schmidt, Gast-Rosenberg, & Hunter, 1980).

For example, suppose the validity generalization (VG) results were $\bar{\rho}_{xy_t} = .50$ and $SD_{\rho_{xy_t}} = .10$ and suppose the mean unrestricted reliability in the meta-analysis was $r_{xx_a} = .80$. Now suppose you want to use these results but your test has an $r_{xx_a} = .90$.

First, you correct the VG results to obtain the true score correlation results:

$$\bar{\rho} = \frac{.50}{\bar{a}} = \frac{.50}{\sqrt{.80}} = .56$$

$$SD_{\rho} = \frac{.10}{\bar{a}} = \frac{.10}{\sqrt{.80}} = .11$$

Next, you attenuate the true scores results so they correspond to a test reliability of $r_{xx_a} = .90$:

$$\bar{\rho}_{xy_t} = .56\sqrt{.90} = .53$$

$$SD_{\rho_{xy_t}} = .11\sqrt{.90} = .10$$

These are the values tailored to your test with a reliability of .90. With a test reliability of .90, mean operational validity is .53 and its standard deviation is .10.

Hence, it can be seen that using a more reliable test increases the mean operational validity from .50 to .53, a 6% increase.

There is a more straightforward procedure. Simply compute and report the fully corrected mean and standard deviation in the first place (including correction for error of measurement in the independent variable and including any other artifacts that information is available for). (The procedures presented in this chapter do this as a matter of course.) Then report two means and two standard deviations: (1) the fully corrected mean and standard deviation and (2) a mean and standard deviation attenuated to the level of the mean reliability of the predictor variable. Then if the user's mean predictor reliability is the same as the mean predictor reliability in the meta-analysis, result 2 can be used as is. If the user's predictor reliability is different, however, the user must attenuate the true score results to correspond with the reliability of his or her predictor. For example, suppose the true score results were as above: $\bar{\rho} = .56$, $SD_\rho = .11$, and mean r_{xx_a} is .80. Now suppose the reliability of the user's test is .60. Then, when that test is used, the mean operational validity and its *SD* are as follows:

$$\bar{\rho}_{xy_t} = .56\sqrt{.60} = .43$$

$$SD_{\rho_{xy_t}} = .11\sqrt{.60} = .09$$

As can be seen, the lower predictor reliability substantially reduces the operational validity (from .50 to .43, a 14% reduction).

Personnel Selection: Findings and Formulas in the Literature

One major application of artifact distribution meta-analysis has been the examination of the validity of tests and other methods used in personnel selection. Meta-analysis has been used to test the hypothesis of situation-specific validity. In personnel selection, it had long been believed that validity was specific to situations; that is, it was believed that the validity of the same test for what appeared to be the same job varied from employer to employer, region to region, across time periods, and so forth. In fact, it was believed that the same test could have high validity (i.e., a high correlation with job performance) in one location or organization and be completely invalid (i.e., have zero validity) in another. This belief was based on the observation that obtained validity coefficients for similar tests and jobs varied substantially across different studies. In some studies, there was a statistically significant relationship, and in others, there was no significant relationship—which was falsely taken to indicate no relationship at all. This puzzling variability of findings was explained by postulating that jobs that appeared to be the same actually differed in important ways in what was required to perform them. This belief led to a requirement for local or situational validity studies. It was held that validity had to be estimated separately for each situation by a study conducted in the setting; that is, validity findings could not be generalized across settings, situations, employers, and the like (Schmidt & Hunter, 1981). In the late 1970s, meta-analysis of validity coefficients began to be conducted to test whether validity might not, in fact, be generalizable (Schmidt & Hunter, 1977; Schmidt, Hunter, Pearlman, & Shane, 1979), and, thus, these meta-analyses were called "validity generalization" studies. These studies indicated that all or most of the study-to-study variability in observed validities was due to artifacts of the kind discussed in this book and that the traditional belief in situational specificity of validity was therefore erroneous. Validity findings did generalize.

Early applications of validity generalization (VG) methods were mostly limited to ability and aptitude tests (e.g., Pearlman et al., 1980; Schmidt, Hunter, Pearlman, et al., 1979), but applications to a wide variety of different selection procedures soon followed: work sample tests (Hunter & Hunter, 1984); behavioral consistency and traditional evaluations of education and experience (McDaniel, Schmidt, & Hunter, 1988a); assessment centers (Gaugler, Rosenthal, Thornton, & Bentson, 1987); integrity tests (Ones, Viswesvaran, & Schmidt, 1993); employment interviews (McDaniel, Whetzel, Schmidt, & Maurer, 1994); job knowledge tests (Dye, Reck, & Murphy, 1993); biographical data measures (Carlson, Scullen, Schmidt, Rothstein, & Erwin, 1999; Rothstein, Schmidt, Erwin, Owens, & Sparks, 1990); personality scales (Mount & Barrick, 1995); college grade point average (Roth, BeVier, Switzer, & Shippmann, 1996); and others (Schmidt & Hunter, 1998). In general, validities for these procedures also proved to be generalizable, although interpretation of generalizability was sometimes more complex (see, e.g., Schmidt & Rothstein, 1994). The findings from most of this research are summarized in Schmidt and Hunter (1998).

Selection programs based on validity generalization were introduced by many organizations during the 1980s and 1990s. Examples include the petroleum industry (through the American Petroleum Institute), the electric utility industry (through the Edison Electric Institute), the life insurance industry (through the Association of Insurance Companies), AT&T, Sears, the Gallup Organization, the state of Iowa, ePredix, the Pentagon, and the U.S. Office of Personnel Management (OPM). During this period, VG methods were also used in developing and supporting commercial employment tests (e.g., Psychological Services Incorporated [PSI] and the Wonderlic Company included VG results in their test manuals).

VG methods and findings also affected professional standards. The 1985 edition of the AERA-APA-NCME *Standards for Educational and Psychological Testing* recognized validity generalization and the importance of meta-analysis (p. 12). In the most recent edition of this document (the fifth edition; AERA-APA-NCME, 1999), validity generalization plays an even larger role (see pp. 15–16 and Standards 1.20 and 1.21). The 1987 edition of the *Principles for the Validation and Use of Personnel Selection Procedures*, published by the Society for Industrial/Organizational Psychology (SIOP), devoted nearly three pages to validity generalization (pp. 26–28). The current SIOP *Principles* (2003) incorporated newer research and further developments in validity generalization. A report by the National Academy of Sciences (Hartigan & Wigdor, 1989) devoted an entire chapter (Chapter 6) to validity generalization and endorsed its methods and assumptions.

Although, to our knowledge, no up-to-date definitive review is available, validity generalization seems to have fared well in the courts. Sharf (1987) reviewed cases up through the mid-1980s. The most recent case we are aware of is *U.S. Department of Justice v. City of Torrance, CA*. In that 1996 decision, all basic VG findings were accepted by the court, and the court's rejection of the DOJ challenge to the Torrance police and fire tests appears to be based mostly on the court's acceptance of VG and related findings. In addition to U.S. court cases, the use of validity generalization as the basis for selection systems was upheld in Canada in 1987 (*Maloley v. Canadian Civil Service Commission*). A comprehensive review of court decisions related to validity generalization would probably be useful at this point.

The procedures used in most published validity generalization studies were developed for the case of direct range restriction. At the time these procedures were developed, there was no known procedure for correcting for indirect range restriction resulting from selection on a composite of unknown (unrecorded) variables, the type of range restriction that is nearly universal in personnel and educational selection (Linn, Harnisch, & Dunbar, 1981b; Thorndike, 1949). As a result, published estimates of mean operational validities are underestimates to some extent, and published estimates of SD_ρ are overestimates to some extent. (See Chapter 5 and Hunter, Schmidt, & Le, 2002.) Hence, published results must be described as presenting a conservative picture of validity and validity generalizability. Of the VG procedures used in the literature, only one—the interactive procedure—can be used in the case of indirect range restriction. (This is the INTNL-I program mentioned earlier.) Hence, we will discuss this procedure in more detail and provide an example applying it to data in which range restriction is indirect.

The formulas used in the validity generalization literature to compute $\bar{\rho}$ are basically the same as those presented earlier in this chapter. (The one difference that exists was discussed in the preceding section.) However, the formulas used to estimate the variance of the corrected validities contain somewhat different terms, resulting from the fact that each was derived using a slightly different set of assumptions. This is not to imply that any of the formulas are more (or less) "correct" than any of the others. The different formulas for the estimation of the same parameter (S_ρ^2) are all correct relative to their derivational assumptions (Schmidt, Hunter, & Pearlman, 1981). (This is the same situation that holds in the case of the various formulas derived to estimate the shrinkage of multiple correlations; each is correctly derived, given the assumptions of the derivation [Cattin, 1980].) Nor does it necessarily imply that any one formula is more accurate than another; as it turns out, computer simulation studies have shown that all are quite accurate (Callender & Osburn, 1980; Law, Schmidt, & Hunter, 1994a, 1994b; Mendoza & Reinhardt, 1991; Raju & Burke, 1983).

The first method that appeared in the literature was our noninteractive method (Pearlman et al., 1980; Schmidt, Gast-Rosenberg, et al., 1980; Schmidt, Hunter, Pearlman, et al., 1979). The formulas for this method are

$$\bar{\rho}_{xy_t} = \frac{\bar{r}}{\bar{b}\bar{c}} \tag{4.18}$$

and

$$\sigma^2_{\rho_{xy_t}} = \frac{(\sigma_r^2 - \sigma_e^2) - \bar{\rho}_{TU}^2(\sigma_b^2 + \bar{b}\sigma_a^2 + \bar{a}^2\bar{b}^2\sigma_c^2)}{\bar{b}^2\bar{c}^2} \tag{4.19}$$

where

$\bar{r}$ = the mean observed correlation,
ρ_{xy_t} = the mean true validity,

ρ_{TU} = the fully corrected (true score) correlation between the two variables,
$a = (r_{xx_a})^{1/2}$,
$b = (r_{yy_a})^{1/2}$,
$c = [(1 - u_x^2)\bar{r}^2 + u_x^2]^{1/2}$,
$\sigma^2_{\rho_{xy_t}}$ = the variance of validities corrected for range restriction and for measurement error in the job performance measure (y), but not in the predictor (x).

Other terms are as defined in previous sections. This procedure corrects for variance in validities due to variability in r_{xx_a}, but not the attenuating effect of mean r_{xx_a}. The reasons for this were given in the previous section. (To correct for the attenuation effects of r_{xx_a}, one need only include the term $\bar{a}$ in the denominator product term in Equations [4.18] and [4.19].) Further details on this formula and its assumptions are given in Schmidt, Gast-Rosenberg, et al. (1980). Although shown repeatedly in computer simulation studies to be quite accurate, in recent years the interactive procedure (described later) has been more commonly used. The interactive procedure has the advantage that it can be used with indirect range restriction (the noninteractive procedure cannot.)

Callender and Osburn (1980) derived the following equation for $\sigma^2_{\rho_{xy_t}}$:

$$\sigma^2_{\rho_{xy_t}} = \frac{(\sigma_r^2 - \sigma_e^2) - \bar{\rho}^2_{xU}(\bar{c}^2\sigma_b^2 + \bar{b}^2\sigma_c^2 + \sigma_b^2\sigma_c^2)}{(\bar{b}^2 + \sigma_b^2)(\bar{c}^2 + \sigma_c^2)} \tag{4.20}$$

Their estimate of the mean is again

$$\bar{\rho}_{xy_t} = \frac{\bar{r}}{\bar{b}\bar{c}}$$

All terms are as defined earlier for the noninteractive method. Callender and Osburn called this method the "independent multiplicative method." It is based on the same algebra of products of independent variables as the equations presented earlier in this chapter. In fact, Callender and Osburn (1980) originated this approach to derivation of meta-analysis equations and we borrowed their approach to develop the multiplicative equations presented earlier in this chapter. This equation has been used in several published validity generalization studies. It can be used only when range restriction is direct.

Raju and Burke (1983) derived two equations (TSA-1 and TSA-2) for $\sigma^2_{\rho_{xy_t}}$, both based on Taylor series approximations. These equations do not assume that a, b, and c are independent, as does the method of Callender and Osburn and the equations presented earlier in this chapter. TSA-1 assumes that a^2, b^2, and u are independent, while TSA-2 assumes that a, b, and u are independent. This change reduces inaccuracies resulting from the dependence of c on a and b. These equations were derived under the assumption of direct range restriction and would have to be modified to accommodate indirect range restriction. The symbolism used in these equations is different and more complex than that used in the other equations, and space precludes their reproduction here. These equations have proven to be quite accurate and have been used in published validity generalization studies.

Raju and Drasgow (2003) presented methods for meta-analysis and validity generalization based on maximum likelihood statistics. As of this writing, these methods have not been applied to data or evaluated via computer simulation. This work is under way.

The noninteractive, the multiplicative, the two TSA procedures, and the interactive procedure (discussed next) have all been shown by computer simulation studies to be more than accurate enough for operational use when range restriction is direct (Callender & Osburn, 1980; Law et al., 1994a, 1994b; Mendoza & Reinhardt, 1991; Raju & Burke, 1983). The interactive procedure with accuracy-enhancing refinements appears to be somewhat more accurate than other methods under most realistic conditions (Law et al., 1994a, 1994b). Computer simulation studies conducted to date to evaluate the accuracy of the interactive method when modified for indirect range restriction show that it produces accurate estimates of both the mean and the standard deviation (Le, 2003).

The interactive procedure was first presented by Schmidt, Gast-Rosenberg, et al. (1980) and was further developed in Schmidt, Hunter, and Pearlman (1981) and Law et al. (1994a, 1994b). Calculational procedures for the interactive procedure are complex and must be done via a computer program. The interactive procedure differs from the noninteractive procedure in that variances due to between-study differences in criterion reliability, test reliability, and range restriction are computed simultaneously rather than sequentially. This composite step can be summarized as follows:

1. Compute the sample size weighted mean of the observed correlations ($\bar{r}$) and correct this value for range restriction, criterion unreliability, and test unreliability, using mean values of these artifacts (i.e., $\bar{u}$, $\bar{a}$, and mean $\bar{b}$). The result is $\bar{\rho}_{TU}$, the estimated mean true score correlation.

2. Create a three-dimensional matrix, the cells of which represent all possible combinations from the artifact distributions of range restriction u values, criterion unreliability, and test unreliability. For example, if there are 10 different u values in that artifact distribution, 15 different values of r_{xx_a}, and 9 different values of r_{yy_a}, the number of cells is $(10)(15)(9) = 1{,}350$. Typically, the number of cells is large enough to make it impractical to do the calculations described in steps 3 and 4 below by calculator. For this reason, the interactive procedure is applied only via computer software.

3. For each cell, attenuate $\bar{\rho}_{TU}$ to compute the expected value of the observed coefficient for that combination of artifacts. The fully corrected mean correlation ($\bar{\rho}_{TU}$) will be attenuated to a different value in each cell.

4. Compute the variance of the resulting coefficients across cells, weighting each cell value by its cell frequency. Cell frequency is determined by artifact-level frequencies; because range restriction values are assumed to be uncorrelated with (applicant pool) reliabilities, and the reliabilities of independent and dependent variables are also assumed to be independent, the joint (cell) frequency is the product of the three marginal frequencies. (Recall that, in each artifact distribution, each artifact value has an associated frequency.) This computed variance of cell correlations is the variance in observed coefficients that would be created by criterion and test reliability differences and range restriction differences if the

true score correlation (ρ_{TU}) were constant and N were infinite. This variance can be symbolized as the variance of a four-way product: $\sigma^2_{abc\rho_{TU}}$. Because ρ_{TU} is a constant, however, this becomes $\rho^2_{TU}\sigma^2_{abc}$.

The formula for the interactive model estimate of σ^2_{ρ} can therefore be expressed as

$$\sigma^2_{\rho_{TU}} = \frac{(\sigma^2_r - \sigma^2_e) - \bar{\rho}^2_{TU}\sigma^2_{abc}}{\bar{a}^2\bar{b}^2\bar{c}^2} \quad (4.21)$$

All terms except σ^2_{abc} are as defined earlier. When used in validity generalization research with direct range restriction, $\bar{a}$ is set to 1.00, because there is no correction for the attenuating effect of mean predictor unreliability. When used under conditions of indirect range restriction, all three corrections are initially made (see Chapter 5), with the results then being later appropriately attenuated to estimate operational (true) validity. The equation for the mean true score correlations is $\rho_{TU} = \bar{r}/\bar{a}\bar{b}\bar{c}$.

Because the order in which corrections must be made is different for direct and indirect range restriction, there are two separate interactive computer programs: INTNL-D for direct range restriction and INTNL-I for indirect range restriction. These programs and their availability are described in the Appendix. The master program asks the user to indicate whether there is range restriction and if so whether it is direct or indirect. It then selects the correct subprogram. When range restriction is indirect, in computing $\bar{\rho}_{TU}$, the reliability corrections must be made *prior to* the range restriction correction, using reliability values for the restricted group. In attenuating $\bar{\rho}_{TU}$ to estimate variance caused by artifacts beyond sampling error, this order must be reversed. The technical reasons for this are given in Chapter 5. INTNL-I makes the corrections in this order. When range restriction is direct, in computing $\bar{\rho}_{TU}$, the correction for dependent variable reliability can be made either before or after the range restriction correction; however, it is usually made before because the reliability estimates available for the dependent variable are usually for the restricted group. In direct range restriction, predictor reliability is undefined in the restricted group because the direct selection on x induces a correlation between true scores and measurement errors in the selected group (Hunter et al., 2002; Mendoza & Mumford, 1987), thus violating the central assumption of reliability theory. Hence, in estimating $\bar{\rho}_{TU}$, the correction for measurement error in the predictor must be made *after* the range restriction correction and must be made using an estimate of reliability in the unrestricted group. Again, see Chapter 5 for full technical development of these issues. In estimating $\bar{\rho}_{TU}$, the program INTNL-D corrects first for dependent variable reliability, then corrects for range restriction, and corrects last for independent variable reliability. In attenuating $\bar{\rho}_{TU}$ to estimate variance caused by artifacts beyond sampling error, this order is reversed.

The interactive procedure has four important advantages over other procedures for artifact distribution meta-analysis. First, unlike other procedures, it takes into account the slight interaction between the effects of measurement error and range restriction. (Hence the name of the procedure.) This interaction occurs because the effect of measurement error on the observed correlation is greater in studies in which there is less range restriction (cf. Schmidt, Gast-Rosenberg, et al., 1980). (This interaction occurs because of the nonlinear nature of the effect of range restriction.) The direct nature of the calculation of artifact effects on observed rs in the interactive procedure allows this interaction to be reflected in the estimate of variance caused by artifacts beyond sampling error (i.e., in the term $\bar{\rho}_{TU}^2 \sigma_{abc}^2$ in Equation [4.21]). The models discussed earlier that are based on products of artifact attenuation factors do not take this interaction into account.

Second, the interactive procedure avoids the problem of lack of independence among the artifact attenuation factors a, b, and c, at least in the case of direct range restriction. Recall from our discussion earlier in this chapter that c cannot be completely independent of a and b because the formula for c *contains* both a and b. Other procedures we have discussed (except for those of Raju & Burke, 1983) assume that a, b, and c are independent, and because this is not strictly true, there is a slight reduction in their accuracy. The interactive procedure, however, does not assume that a, b, and c are independent. Instead, it assumes that a, b, and u_X are independent. That is, it substitutes u_X for c in the independence assumption. Because there is no mathematical dependency among any of the terms a, b, and u_X, there is no reason they cannot be independent. In fact, it is usually reasonable to assume they are. This leads to some improvement in accuracy for the interactive procedure. (Note: The independence assumption applies to values of a and b in the unrestricted population. Obviously, range restriction [u_X] reduces a and b values in the restricted group, and these values are not independent of u_X.)

Third, the interactive procedure can be used when range restriction is indirect. The only change needed is that u_T values must be entered instead of u_X values when the range restriction corrections are made. (The formula for computing u_T was given in Chapter 3; see Equation [3.16].) The application of the interactive procedure to indirect range restriction is slightly less accurate in estimating S_ρ^2 than it is in the case of direct range restriction because a $(a = \sqrt{r_{XX_a}})$ is not independent of u_T, as can be seen in Equation (3.16). This prediction was verified via computer simulation studies by Le (2003). However, these simulation studies showed that the interactive procedure, when adapted for indirect range restriction, produced reasonably accurate estimates of both the mean and the standard deviation. The other procedures we have discussed probably produce less accurate results under conditions of indirect range restriction. This prediction stems from the fact that, under conditions of indirect range restriction, the values of a, b, and c become much more highly intercorrelated (i.e., dependent) than they are under direct range restriction (see Chapter 5 and Hunter et al., 2002), and this severe violation of the independence assumption causes inaccuracies. The methods of Raju and Burke (1983) may be an exception. It is possible that these methods can be successfully adapted to the case of indirect range restriction (Hunter et al., 2002).

Finally, a fourth advantage of the interactive method is that certain accuracy-enhancing statistical refinements have been developed for it and have been included in the INTNL computer programs; we discuss these refinements later in this chapter and in Chapter 5.

A Worked Example: Indirect Range Restriction (Interactive Method)

We now present an example illustrating the application of the interactive procedure to data with indirect range restriction. The data are shown in Table 4.4. These are the same data presented in Table 3.5. In Chapter 3, we meta-analyzed these data by correcting each correlation individually. Here, we will analyze the same data, treating the artifact information as distributions—that is, as not being matched to specific observed rs. Because complete artifact information is given in Table 4.4 for each observed correlation, the artifact distribution method ordinarily would not be used; instead, each correlation would be corrected individually, as was done in Chapter 3. However, we present the artifact distribution analysis of these data here because the results can be directly compared to those obtained in Chapter 3 with the same data.

Observed values of u are always u_X values. These are shown in the first data column in Table 4.4. In correcting for indirect range restriction, we must convert u_X values to u_T values, using Equation (3.16). The computer program INTNL-I makes this conversion automatically if you enter u_X values. To make this conversion, we (or the program) must have an estimate of r_{XX_a}, the reliability of the independent variable (predictor) in the unrestricted population. Again, the computer program INTNL-I computes r_{XX_a} automatically from the r_{XX_i} and u_X values entered. In this data set, the same test was used in all studies, and its r_{XX_a} is .85. The calculated u_T values are shown in the second data column in Table 4.4. For the reasons given in Chapter 5 and in Hunter et al. (2002), when correcting for indirect range restriction, we must correct observed rs for measurement error *in both variables* before applying the range correction formula. That means, of course, that one must

Table 4.4 Indirect range restriction: Hypothetical data for an artifact distribution meta-analysis of 12 personnel selection studies

Study	s_X/S_X (u_X)	s_T/S_T (u_T)	*Test Reliability* (r_{XX_i})	*Criterion Reliability* (r_{yy_i})	*Sample Size*	*Observed Correlation*
1	.580	.468	.55	.80	68	.35**
2	.580	.468	.55	.60	68	.07
3	.580	.468	.55	.80	68	.11
4	.580	.468	.55	.60	68	.31*
5	.678	.603	.67	.80	68	.18
6	.678	.603	.67	.60	68	.36**
7	.678	.603	.67	.80	68	.40**
8	.678	.603	.67	.60	68	.13
9	.869	.844	.80	.80	68	.49**
10	.869	.844	.80	.60	68	.23**
11	.869	.844	.80	.80	68	.29*
12	.869	.844	.80	.60	68	.44*

*$p < .05$ (two-tailed test).
**$p < .01$ (two-tailed test).

have available the restricted group reliabilities for both variables. The criterion reliabilities shown in Table 4.4 are for the restricted group, as is usually the case. The single test used in all 12 studies has an unrestricted group reliability of $r_{XX_a} =$ .85. However, range restriction reduces this value in the incumbent groups in the individual studies (Sackett, Laczo, & Arvey, 2002). The restricted group r_{XX_i} values have been computed using the formula for this given in Chapter 3 (Equation [3.17c]) and have been entered into Table 4.4 in the column headed r_{XX_i}.

The formula used is

$$r_{XX_i} = U_X^2 (1 - r_{XX_a})$$

where $U_X^2 = S_{X_a}^2 / s_{X_i}^2$. Note that $S_{X_a}^2$ = the variance of X in the unrestricted group and $s_{X_i}^2$ = the variance of X in the restricted group.

Entering these data into the INTNL-I computer program yields the following results:

$\bar{r} = .28$,
$S_r^2 = .017033$,
$S_e^2 = .012677$,
$S_{\rho_{xy}}^2 = S_r^2 - S_e^2 = .004356$,
Percentage variance accounted for by sampling error = 74.4%,
Percentage variance accounted for by all artifacts = 99.3%.

The estimated true score correlation is

$$\bar{\rho} = .581$$
$$SD_\rho = .0182$$

The mean true validity is

$$\bar{\rho}_{xy_t} = .531$$
$$SD_{\rho_{xy_t}} = .0168$$

In Chapter 3, we meta-analyzed this same data set (Table 3.5), correcting each correlation individually. We can compare the present results to those obtained in Chapter 3 using the program VG6-I. In Chapter 3, the estimated mean true score ρ was .57 versus .58 here for artifact distribution meta-analysis. In Chapter 3, the estimate for mean true validity was .530 versus .531 here. In Chapter 3, both SD_ρ and $SD_{\rho_{xy_t}}$ were estimated at 0 (the correct value). Here, $SD_\rho = .0182$ and $SD_{\rho_{xy_t}} = .0168$. These values are close to the correct value of 0, but are slight overestimates. Our estimate here of the total percentage of variance accounted for by artifacts is 99.3% versus the correct value of 100% obtained in Chapter 3. These comparisons show that the INTNL-I artifact distribution meta-analysis program is quite accurate, although not quite as accurate as correcting each coefficient individually. However, the information necessary to correct each correlation individually is often not available, and so artifact distribution meta-analysis must be used.

Refinements to Increase Accuracy of the SD_ρ Estimate

All quantitative estimates are approximations. Even if these estimates are quite accurate, it is always desirable to make them more accurate if possible. The most complex task performed by meta-analysis methods is the estimation of the *SD* of the population correlations (SD_ρ). One way to make this estimate more accurate is to find a more accurate estimate of the sampling error variance of the correlation coefficient in meta-analysis. Hunter and Schmidt (1994b) showed analytically that using mean *r* ($\bar{r}$) in place of *r* in the sampling error variance formula for the correlation coefficient increases the accuracy of this estimate in the homogeneous case (i.e., the case in which $SD_\rho = 0$). Because of the complexity of the math, no such analytic demonstration was possible for the heterogeneous case (i.e., the case in which $SD_\rho > 0$). We therefore tested the heterogeneous case using computer simulation and found that there, too, use of mean *r* improved accuracy over the traditional sampling error variance formula (Law et al., 1994b). Aguinis (2001), again using computer simulation, provided an even more complete and thorough demonstration of this fact. This finding that the traditional formula underestimates the amount of sampling error variance and that its accuracy can be improved by using $\bar{r}$ in the formula instead of the observed *r* from the individual study at hand is important, because the traditional formula has been accepted throughout statistics since around 1900. However, in studies with range restriction, even the more accurate formula still underestimates (and undercorrects for) sampling error variance. Millsap (1989) showed that the presence of direct range restriction increases sampling error variance and therefore causes the formula to underestimate the amount of sampling variance. Aguinis and Whitehead (1997) showed the same thing for indirect range restriction. Hence, final corrected SD_ρ estimates are still overestimated in validity generalization studies (and other meta-analyses with range restriction), and validity generalizability is correspondingly underestimated. (However, in non-VG meta-analyses there may be no range restriction, and, if so, this problem does not occur.)

The preceding improvement increases the accuracy of the estimate of the residual *SD* (SD_{res})—the *SD* of observed *r*s after variation due to artifacts has been subtracted out. Another opportunity to improve accuracy occurs at the step in which the residual *SD* is corrected to estimate SD_ρ or the *SD* of operational (true) validities ($SD_{\rho_{xyt}}$). This opportunity occurs with respect to the correction for range restriction. One can think of the range restriction correction as multiplying the observed correlation by a constant. For example, if the correction increases the *r* by 30%, then the constant of correction is 1.30. In our earlier methods, if the constant of correction for range restriction for *the mean r* was, say, 1.30, we applied that same constant to all the values in the residual distribution. That is, we assumed (as an approximation) that the range restriction correction would increase all values of *r* by 30%. Actually, the range restriction correction (unlike the measurement error correction) is nonlinear: It increases small *r* values by *more* than 30% (in this example) and large values by *less* than 30% (in this example). Hence, applying the constant of range restriction correction of the mean *r* to all *r*s resulted in overestimation of SD_ρ. We therefore added a refinement that computed the range restriction correction independently for each separate *r* value in the residual distribution, and we tested this refinement using computer simulation methods. This study (Law et al., 1994a) showed that doing this increased the accuracy of estimates of SD_ρ. Both these accuracy-increasing refinements were then added to the interactive meta-analysis program and that program was then used to reanalyze the extensive database from Pearlman et al. (1980). This research (Schmidt et al., 1993) showed that validity was more generalizable than Pearlman et al. (1980) had concluded. Specifically, the true validity *SD*s were substantially smaller, 90% credibility values were considerably larger, and the percentage of variance accounted for by artifacts was substantially larger. These developments show that the accuracy of even well-established methods—methods that are very accurate by the standards of psychological research—can nevertheless be improved. The findings also further undercut the theory of situational specificity of validity. In fact, the average amount of variance accounted for was so large (87%) and the average SD_ρ value was so small (.097) that Schmidt et al. (1993) interpreted their findings as fully disconfirming the situational specificity hypothesis (the hypothesis that $SD_\rho > 0$) for aptitude and ability tests. They reasoned that the tiny amount of remaining variance (.0094, on average) could be explained by the six sources of artifactual variance that could not be corrected for (see pp. 8–11 of that article; see also Chapter 5). (Note: Because the focus in this study was on SD_ρ and because of space limitations, mean true validity estimates were not reported in this study; however, they can be found in Hunter and Schmidt [1996].)

It is important to note here that a conclusion that all observed variance is explained by artifacts is not required for validity generalizability. Even if $SD_\rho > 0$, validity still generalizes so long as the 90% credibility value (see pages 205-206) in the resulting true validity distribution is greater than 0. However, the fact that in a large validity database (over 600 studies) created over a span of six decades by a wide variety of researchers, essentially all validity variance can be accounted for by statistical and measurement artifacts is a striking scientific finding. It illustrates the extent to which nature can indeed be parsimonious at its fundamental (deep structure) level despite surface appearances of great variability or complexity.

Accuracy of Corrections for Artifacts

In some validity generalization studies (e.g., Hirsh, Northrop, & Schmidt, 1986; Schmidt, Hunter, & Caplan, 1981a, 1981b), the artifact values used in the artifact distributions were taken directly from the studies that contributed validities to the meta-analysis; that is, the procedure described earlier in this chapter was used. In other studies, however, the information on artifacts from the studies analyzed was too sparse. In those studies, artifact distributions were used that were estimated based on familiarity with the personnel selection literature in general. For example, a distribution of u_X values ($u_X = s_X/S_X$) was constructed that was believed to be typical of this research literature as a whole. Later, when it was possible to compare some of these artifact distributions to empirically cumulated distributions from bodies of research studies, the constructed artifact distributions were found to fairly closely match the empirical distributions (Schmidt, Hunter, Pearlman, & Hirsh, 1985, Q&A No. 26; Alexander, Carson, Alliger, & Cronshaw, 1989).

The results produced by VG methods would exaggerate the magnitude and generalizability of validity if the artifact distributions used and the corrections made overcorrect for the effects of artifacts. Computer simulation studies do not (and cannot) determine whether the artifact distributions are realistic or not; instead, such studies use these artifact distributions along with initial true validity values to generate simulated observed validities and then determine whether the procedures can accurately recapture the initial true validity distributions. So the question can be raised: Are the artifact distributions that have typically been used likely to overcorrect for the effects of artifacts?

This question has usually been focused on criterion reliabilities and u_X values. To our knowledge, no one has questioned the artifact distribution values used for the reliability of predictors—because in VG no correction is made to mean validity for unreliability in the predictors.

Overcorrection could occur in two different ways. First, the mean validity could be overcorrected. That is, if one's estimate of criterion (dependent variable) reliability were too low, or one's estimate of the mean level of range restriction were too severe, then the corrected mean validity estimate (mean true validity estimate) would be too large. Second, even if mean artifact values and corrections were correct, if one's artifact distributions were too variable, then the amount of variance in observed validities attributed to differences between studies in criterion reliability and range restriction would be too great. It appears clear that this second form of overcorrection cannot be a source of serious distortion in results. Hunter and Schmidt (1990a, pp. 224–226) summarized the research showing that even if the artifact distributions are too variable, the effect on the VG final results is negligible. This finding stems from the fact that between-study differences in artifact levels account for very little variance; most between-study variance in validities results from sampling error variance. In addition, empirical studies of range restriction values and criterion reliabilities have found levels of variability similar to those used in VG studies (Alexander et al., 1989; Viswesvaran, Ones, & Schmidt, 1996).

This leaves the question of whether there is overcorrection of mean validity for criterion reliability and range restriction. Criteria include both measures of job performance and measures of training performance. Training performance measures are usually quite reliable, and, to our knowledge, there has been no criticism of the high reliabilities (and corresponding small corrections) we have estimated for training performance measures. The criterion measure of job performance used in most validity studies is supervisory ratings of job performance. Almost invariably, one supervisor produces these ratings; it is very rare, for example, that the ratings used are the average ratings from two or more supervisors. Also, it is almost always the case that some of the employees in the sample are rated by one rater, others by another rater, and still others by a third rater, and so on, introducing differences in rater leniency effects into the variance of ratings. That is, almost never are all subjects in the study rated by the same rater. Starting with our first VG study, whenever rating reliabilities were not available from the studies in the VG analysis, we have estimated the mean inter-rater reliability of ratings of this sort at .60. This value was based on our reading of the literature. However, later large-sample and meta-analytic research studies of ratings found smaller mean reliabilities—values at or near .50 (Rothstein, 1990; Viswesvaran et al., 1996). Hence, it is very unlikely that there has been overcorrection for criterion unreliability. In fact, it is likely that there has been undercorrection. (Use of the .60 figure when the correct figure is .50 results in a 9% undercorrection.)

In passing, we note that Murphy and DeShon (2000) argued that inter-rater reliability is inappropriate for ratings of job performance and stated that intra-rater reliability should be used instead. This position entails the rejection of the classical measurement model in I/O research. Schmidt, Viswesvaran, and Ones (2000) presented the reasons this position is mistaken. These two articles provide a thorough exploration of the issues involved in this question. This issue is explored further in Viswesvaran, Schmidt, and Ones (in press).

The final question is whether there is overcorrection for range restriction. There are two ways in which the mean correction for range restriction could be erroneous. First, the mean u_X value used could be too small, leading to an overcorrection for range restriction. When empirical estimates of u_X values were not available, we have typically estimated the mean u_X value at .60 to .70, with these values being based on our reading of the literature. However, as the data became available, we compared these values to quantitative averages from real studies. In the large VG study that Hunter conducted for the U.S. Department of Labor on over 400 GATB (General Aptitude Test Battery) test validity studies, the average u_X value was .67 (Hunter, 1983b; Hunter & Hunter, 1984). A later empirical study by Alexander et al. (1989) that included available published and unpublished data found an average u_X value of .70. Hence, the empirical evidence indicates that the mean u_X values we have used are close to the appropriate values. These u_X values are for cognitive ability and aptitude measures. Average values of u_X are larger for personality measures (Barrick & Mount, 1991; Ones & Viswesvaran, 2003).

The second way in which range restriction corrections can be erroneous is that the range correction formula used can over- or undercorrect. The correction equation we have used has been Thorndike's (1949) Case II formula. This is also the formula used in the models of Callender and Osburn (1980) and Raju and Burke (1983). This formula assumes direct range restriction (truncation) on the predictor. That is, it assumes that all applicants below a certain score on the predictor are rejected for hire and all others are hired. It has long been known that if range restriction is indirect rather than direct this formula will undercorrect (see, e.g., Linn et al., 1981b), and we have repeatedly pointed out this undercorrection (Schmidt, Hunter, & Pearlman, 1981; Schmidt, Hunter, et al., 1985, p. 751; Schmidt et al., 1993, p. 7). It is clear that if some or all of the primary validity studies in a VG study are characterized by indirect range restriction, the use of this range correction formula will lead to undercorrection, even if one's u_X values are accurate. This is important because range restriction is indirect in almost all studies (Thorndike, 1949, p. 175). For example, in the General Aptitude Test Battery (GATB) database of the U.S. Department of Labor, *all* of the 515 validity studies were concurrent and hence range restriction was indirect. Range restriction is often indirect even in predictive studies: The tests to be validated are often given to *incumbents*, with the criterion measures being taken months or years later, making the study technically predictive. In our research over the years, we have rarely seen a study in which there had been direct selection on the predictor(s) being validated—the only kind of study for which the Case II range correction formula would not undercorrect.

If the Case II range correction formula used in all VG models (ours, Callender and Osburn's, and Raju and Burke's) undercorrects, then why has this undercorrection not shown up in computer simulation studies? As noted most recently by Hall and Brannick (2002), computer simulation studies have shown that these VG methods are quite accurate. In fact, estimates of $\bar{\rho}$ seem to be particularly accurate. The answer is that all computer simulation studies have assumed (and programmed in) only direct range restriction. With the exception of Le (2003), there have to date been no computer simulation studies of VG methods based on indirect range restriction. Hence, the earlier simulation studies, by definition, cannot detect the undercorrection that occurs when range restriction is indirect.

How large is this underestimation of mean true validity? All VG models have, in effect, implicitly assumed that it is relatively small. Linn, Harnisch, and Dunbar (1981b) attempted to calibrate empirically the size of the undercorrection in the case of the Law School Admissions Test (LSAT) and concluded that it is probably substantial. Because they were unable to develop an analytical solution, however, their estimates were only suggestive. However, an analytical solution has been developed for the most common case of indirect range restriction: the one in which incumbents have been selected on unknown and unmeasured variables (or on a composite of such variables; Hunter et al., 2002; Mendoza & Mumford, 1987). An example would be a validity study in which there is no formal record of how incumbents were selected but in which $u_X < 1.00$, indicating the presence of range restriction; this example is, in fact, the usual case. Unlike the formula we derived (also derived by Mendoza & Mumford, 1987), other equations for correction for indirect range restriction require knowledge of scores on the measure that produced the indirect range restriction; because of this requirement, it is rarely possible to use these equations (e.g., Thorndike's Case III) with real data.

Our findings indicate that the undercorrection of $\bar{\rho}$ for range restriction is substantial (Hunter et al., 2002). For example, application of the new equation to the GATB database (Hunter & Hunter, 1984) indicates that the mean true validity of measures of general mental ability has been underestimated by 25% to 30% (Hunter et al., 2002). Hence, the implications of the traditional undercorrection are important. It will probably take a number of years to explore the full implications of this development. Further discussion of this issue can be found in Chapter 5.

In summary, the evidence indicates that artifact values used for both criterion reliability and range restriction (the u_X values) do not lead to overcorrection of mean true validities. In fact, there has probably been an undercorrection for criterion unreliability when the criterion was job performance. In addition, even when u_X values are accurate, the Case II range restriction correction equation used in all published studies to date undercorrects validities for range restriction, resulting in substantial underestimates of mean true validities.

Mixed Meta-Analysis: Partial Artifact Information in Individual Studies

Artifacts differ in terms of the information given in studies. The sample size is almost always given so we can correct for sampling error variance. The same is true for dichotomization whenever it occurs. The degree of split for dichotomization is usually given in the research report. For example, a study may state that 70% were in the successful group and 30% were in the unsuccessful group or that 20% quit their jobs and 80% did not. Thus, it is usually possible to correct individual study correlations for the attenuating effects of dichotomization. Reliability is reported more frequently since meta-analysis has become known, but it is uncommon in older studies and frequently not given even in recent studies. Thus, error of measurement is usually corrected using artifact distributions. The problems are even more serious with the other artifacts, such as range variation, construct validity, attrition artifacts, and extraneous factors. Information is often extremely sporadic. Thus, there are research domains where some correctable artifacts can be corrected for in each individual study while others can be corrected only using artifact distributions. This is the "partial information" case to be treated in this section.

There are three ways to conduct meta-analysis in such an area. First, the easiest way is to ignore the fact that information on one or more of the artifacts is available for all studies. One would then use only the distributions of the artifact multipliers and compute the meta-analysis using the artifact distribution methods described earlier in this chapter. Averages across studies would be based on simple sample size weights $w_i = N_i$. As we saw earlier in the analysis of the data in Table 4.3, this procedure yields approximate results that are quite accurate.

Second, one could improve accuracy by weighting each study in accordance with the known amount of sampling error produced by attenuation due to dichotomization (or any other individually correctable artifact). That is, one could give low weight to the low-quality studies and high weight to the high-quality studies. For each study, one would compute the attenuation multiplier A_i as if it were to be corrected. Then one would weight each study by

$$w_i = N_i A_i^2$$

These weights are used in computing both the mean and the variance of study correlations and in computing the artifact mean and variance for the artifacts that contribute to the artifact multiplier A_i. In the case where dichotomization is the only artifact with information given on individual studies, this can be approximated by using a study weight that depends on the split in that study. Let the proportions for the split in study i be given by P_i and $Q_i = 1 - P_i$. Then the approximation weights would be

$$w_i = N_i P_i Q_i$$

For two studies with sample size 100, a study with a 50–50 split would receive weight

$$w = 100(.50)(.50) = 25$$

while a study with a 90–10 split would receive weight

$$w = 100(.90)(.10) = 9$$

The ratio $25/9 = 2.78$ differs somewhat from the ratio 1.84 for optimal weights.

Third, the optimal strategy is to do a two-step meta-analysis. In the first step, the individually known artifacts are corrected. In the second step, the sporadically given artifacts are corrected. This method will now be presented.

First, the individually known artifacts are used to do a meta-analysis using individual study correction. This meta-analysis produces a mean correlation corrected for the individually known artifacts and a variance corrected for those artifacts and for sampling error. Denote the partially corrected mean and variance by *PR* and *PV*, respectively. The methods of artifact distributions can then be used to correct for the remaining artifacts.

The first step is to correct the mean correlation. This is done by computing the average attenuation factor for the remaining artifacts and using that factor to correct the partially corrected mean correlation from the first meta-analysis. Consider each sporadically available artifact separately. For each artifact, compute the mean and standard deviation of the corresponding attenuation factor. Combine the effects of the separate sporadic artifacts by multiplication; the mean compound attenuation factor is the product of the means of the separate artifacts. If the sporadic artifacts are designated $a, b, c, \ldots$, then the mean of the compound attenuation factor A is given by

$$\text{Ave}(A_i) = \text{Ave}(a_i)\,\text{Ave}(b_i)\,\text{Ave}(c_i)\ldots$$

Denote the average by $\bar{A}$. The fully corrected mean correlation is then the partially corrected mean correlation *PR* divided by the compound sporadic artifact attenuation factor A, that is,

$$\text{Ave}(\rho) = PR/\bar{A}$$

Denote the fully corrected mean correlation by $\bar{R}$; that is, define $\bar{R}$ by

$$\bar{R} = \text{Ave}(\rho) = (PR/\bar{A})$$

The next step is to correct the partially corrected variance *PV* for the effects of the sporadic artifacts. First, estimate the variance in the partially corrected correlations due to sporadic artifact variance. Compute the sum of the squared coefficients of variation across the separate sporadic attenuation factors:

$$V = [\text{Var}(a)/\text{Ave}(a)^2] + [\text{Var}(b)/\text{Ave}(b)^2] + \ldots$$

The variance in partially corrected study correlations accounted for by variation in sporadic artifacts is the product

$$S_4^2 = \bar{R}^2\bar{A}^2V$$

The unexplained variance in partially corrected study correlations is

$$S_5^2 = PV - S_4^2$$

Note that some, if not all, of this residual variance is due to uncontrolled artifacts, such as recording, computational, and transcriptional errors and other bad data.

The upper bound estimate of the variance of actual correlations can then be computed from the residual variance. Because some of the residual variance is due to uncontrolled artifacts, the residual variance is an upper bound for the unexplained variance in study correlations. This number is the numerator of the estimate of the variance of actual correlations. Because this number is an upper bound estimate, the ratio is also an upper bound estimate. The variance of actual correlations should be less than the ratio

$$\mathrm{Var}(\rho) = S_5^2/\bar{A}^2$$

An Example: Dichotomization of Both Variables

Tenure is the length of time that a person stays with an employer. Termination from the firm can be voluntary or involuntary. We focus here on voluntary termination—people who leave the job of their own accord. There are many factors that determine tenure, but one of the main factors is performance. People with low performance are frequently under pressure from supervisors and/or peers for a variety of problems that they cause others. This pressure often leads to quitting. So we consider a hypothetical meta-analysis of the correlation between performance and tenure.

If working conditions are poor, workers may quit for that reason, thus reducing the correlation between tenure and performance. Thus, we postulate that the correlation between performance and tenure will be higher in jobs with good working conditions than in jobs with poor working conditions, and we code the studies for working conditions as a potential moderator variable.

Table 4.5a presents the basic information for 24 hypothetical studies. Information is available on all studies for both the independent and the dependent variable as to whether or not the variable was dichotomized. If it was dichotomized, the resulting split is given. On the other hand, reliability information is sporadic for both variables. No information was available on other potential artifacts, such as imperfect construct validity or extraneous factors. In these data, there is no range restriction, so complications caused by the distinction between direct and indirect range restriction do not arise. (In particular, there are no problems with the assumptions of independence of artifacts.)

Table 4.5b presents the artifact information recorded as attenuation factors. Note that if a variable is not dichotomized, then the dichotomization attenuation factor is 1.00. To multiply by 1 is to leave the correlation unchanged (unattenuated by that factor).

Table 4.5c presents the worksheet for the first meta-analysis of the studies, a meta-analysis that uses individual study correction for the dichotomization artifact on both independent and dependent variables. The corrected correlations are corrected for dichotomization but not for error of measurement. Thus, they are

Table 4.5 Hypothetical meta-analysis of performance and turnover

Table 4.5a Basic study information

Study Number	*Sample Size*	*Ratings Split*	*Tenure Split*	*Ratings Reliability*	*Tenure Reliability*	*Sample Correlation*
Jobs with good working conditions						
1	50	50–50	90–10	.47	–	.46*
2	50	50–50	90–10	–	.81	.08
3	50	Not	90–10	.64	–	.46*
4	50	Not	90–10	–	.81	.18
5	50	50–50	50–50	.47	–	.44*
6	50	50–50	50–50	–	.81	.16
7	50	Not	50–50	.64	–	.52*
8	50	Not	50–50	–	.81	.24
9	50	50–50	Not	.47	–	.51*
10	50	50–50	Not	–	.81	.24
11	50	Not	Not	.64	–	.68*
12	50	Not	Not	–	.81	.40*
Jobs with poor working conditions						
13	50	50–50	90–10	.47	–	.23
14	50	50–50	90–10	–	.64	−.05
15	50	Not	90–10	.64	–	.27
16	50	Not	90–10	–	.64	−.01
17	50	50–50	50–50	.47	–	.26
18	50	50–50	50–50	–	.64	−.02
19	50	Not	50–50	.64	–	.32*
20	50	Not	50–50	–	.64	.04
21	50	50–50	Not	.47	–	.29*
22	50	50–50	Not	–	.64	.01
23	50	Not	Not	.64	–	.36*
24	50	Not	Not	–	.64	.08

NOTE: Not = not dichotomized.
$*p < .05$

partially corrected correlations. Over all 24 studies the mean and variance of the partially corrected correlations are

$$PR = .364$$

$$PV = \text{Var}(r) - \text{Ave}(ve) = .251823^2 - .031494 = .031921$$

From Table 4.5b, we compute the mean and variance of each sporadic attenuation factor, that is, the mean and variance of the attenuation factors for error of measurement of the two variables:

$$\text{Ave}(a) = .745, \qquad \text{Var}(a) = .003025,$$

$$\text{Ave}(b) = .850, \qquad \text{Var}(b) = .002500.$$

The mean compound attenuation factor for the sporadic factors is

$$\bar{A} = \text{Ave}(a)\text{Ave}(b) = (.745)(.850) = .63325$$

Table 4.5b Attenuation factors

Study Number	*Sample Size*	*Ratings Split*	*Tenure Split*	*Ratings Reliability*	*Tenure Reliability*	*Sample Correlation*
Jobs with good working conditions						
1	50	.80	.59	.69	–	.46
2	50	.80	.59	–	.90	.08
3	50	1.00	.59	.80	–	.46
4	50	1.00	.59	–	.90	.18
5	50	.80	.80	.69	–	.44
6	50	.80	.80	–	.99	.16
7	50	1.00	.80	.80	–	.57
8	50	1.00	.80	–	.90	.29
9	50	.80	1.00	.69	–	.51
10	50	.80	1.00	–	.90	.24
11	50	1.00	1.00	.80	–	.68
12	50	1.00	1.00	–	.90	.40
Jobs with poor working conditions						
13	50	.80	.59	.69	–	.23
14	50	.80	.59	–	.80	−.05
15	50	1.00	.59	.80	–	.27
16	50	1.00	.59	–	.80	−.01
17	50	.80	.80	.69	–	.26
18	50	.80	.80	–	.80	−.02
19	50	1.00	.80	.80		.32
20	50	1.00	.80	–	.80	.04
21	50	.80	1.00	.69	–	.29
22	50	.80	1.00	–	.80	.01
23	50	1.00	1.00	.80	–	.36
24	50	1.00	1.00	–	.80	.08

Thus, the fully corrected mean correlation is

$$\bar{R} = \text{Ave}(\rho_i) = PR/\bar{A} = .364/.63325 = .5748$$

The sum of the squared coefficients of variation for the sporadic artifacts is

$$V = [.003025/.745^2] + [.002500/.850^2] = .008910$$

The residual variance is

$$S_5^2 = PV - \bar{R}^2\bar{A}^2V = .031921 - .5748^2(.63325^2)\,.008910 = .030741$$

The standard deviation of actual correlations is thus .175. This is a fairly large standard deviation, even in comparison to a mean correlation of .575. This is consistent with the hypothesis of a major moderator variable. Working conditions were hypothesized a priori to be a moderator of the correlation between performance and tenure. To test this hypothesis, we can perform a meta-analysis within each set of studies separately.

Table 4.5c Worksheet for the interim meta-analysis

Study Number	*Sample Size*	*Ratings Split*	*Tenure Split*	*Compound Atten.*	*Uncorr. Correl.*	*Corrected Correl.*	*Error Variance*	*Study Weight*
Jobs with good working conditions								
1	50	.80	.59	.472	.46	.97	.076846	11.1
2	50	.80	.59	.472	.08	.17	.076846	11.1
3	50	1.00	.59	.59	.46	.78	.049181	17.4
4	50	1.00	.59	.59	.18	.31	.049181	17.4
5	50	.80	.80	.64	.44	.69	.041797	20.5
6	50	.80	.80	.64	.16	.25	.041797	20.5
7	50	1.00	.80	.80	.57	.71	.026750	32.0
8	50	1.00	.80	.80	.29	.36	.026750	32.0
9	50	.80	1.00	.80	.51	.64	.026750	32.0
10	50	.80	1.00	.80	.24	.30	.026750	32.0
11	50	1.00	1.00	1.00	.68	.68	.017120	50.0
12	50	1.00	1.00	1.00	.40	.40	.017120	50.0
Ave					.414	.519	.031494	
SD					.172227	.204412		
Jobs with poor working conditions								
13	50	.80	.59	.472	.23	.49	.076846	11.1
14	50	.80	.59	.472	−.05	−.11	.076846	11.1
15	50	1.00	.59	.59	.27	.46	.049181	17.4
16	50	1.00	.59	.59	−.01	−.02	.049181	17.4
17	50	.80	.80	.64	.26	.41	.041797	20.5
18	50	.80	.80	.64	−.02	−.03	.041797	20.5
19	50	1.00	.80	.80	.32	.40	.026750	32.0
20	50	1.00	.80	.80	.04	.05	.026750	32.0
21	50	.80	1.00	.80	.29	.36	.026750	32.0
22	50	.80	1.00	.80	.01	.01	.026750	32.0
23	50	1.00	1.00	1.00	.36	.36	.017120	50.0
24	50	1.00	1.00	1.00	.08	.08	.017120	50.0
Ave					.167	.208	.031494	
SD					.146216	.191532		
Overall					.290	.364		
SD					.201923	.251823		

Jobs With Good Working Conditions

The meta-analysis of partially corrected correlations is obtained from the averages and standard deviations in the top part of Table 4.5c:

$$PR = \text{Ave}(r) = .519$$

$$PV = \text{Var}(r) - \text{Var}(e) = .204412^2 - .031494 = .010290$$

The mean and standard deviation of each sporadic artifact can be computed from the top part of Table 4.5b:

$$\text{Ave}(a) = .745, \qquad \text{Var}(a) = .003025,$$

$$\text{Ave}(b) = .900, \qquad \text{Var}(b) = 0.$$

The mean compound attenuation factor for the sporadic artifacts is

$$\bar{A} = \text{Ave}(a)\,\text{Ave}(b) = (.745)(.900) = .6705$$

The fully corrected mean correlation is thus

$$\bar{R} = \text{Ave}(\rho) = PR/\bar{A} = .519/.6705 = .774$$

The sum of the squared coefficients of variation for the sporadic artifacts is

$$V = [.003025/.745^2] + [0/.900^2] = .005487$$

The residual variance is

$$S_5^2 = PV - \bar{R}^2\bar{A}^2V = .010290 - .774^2\,(.6705^2)\,.005487 = .008812$$

The fully corrected variance is thus

$$\text{Var}(\rho_i) = S_5^2/\bar{A}^2 = .008812/.6705^2 = .019601$$

The standard deviation is thus estimated to be .14.

Within the studies conducted on jobs with good working conditions, the mean correlation is, therefore, .77 and the standard deviation is .14.

Jobs With Poor Working Conditions

The meta-analysis of partially corrected correlations is obtained from the averages and standard deviations in the bottom part of Table 4.5c:

$$PR = \text{Ave}(r) = .208$$

$$PV = \text{Var}(r) - \text{Var}(e) = .191532^2 - .031494 = .005191$$

The mean and standard deviation of each sporadic artifact can be computed from the top part of Table 4.5b:

$$\text{Ave}(a) = .745, \qquad \text{Var}(a) = .003025,$$

$$\text{Ave}(b) = .800, \qquad \text{Var}(b) = 0.$$

The mean compound attenuation factor for the sporadic artifacts is

$$\bar{A} = \text{Ave}(a)\,\text{Ave}(b) = (.745)(.800) = .5960$$

The fully corrected mean correlation is thus

$$\bar{R} = \text{Ave}(\rho_i) = PR/\bar{A} = .208/.5960 = .349$$

The sum of the squared coefficients of variation for the sporadic artifacts is

$$V = [.003025/.745^2] + [0/.800^2] = .005487$$

The residual variance is

$$S_5^2 = PV - \bar{R}^2\bar{A}^2V = .005191 - .349^2\,(.5960^2)\,.005487 = .004954$$

The fully corrected variance is thus

$$\text{Var}(\rho_i) = S_5^2/\bar{A}^2 = .004954/.5960^2 = .013945$$

The standard deviation is thus estimated to be .118.

Thus, within the studies conducted on jobs with poor working conditions, the mean correlation is .35 and the standard deviation is .12.

The Moderator Variable Evaluated

For jobs with good working conditions, the mean correlation is .77 with a standard deviation of .14. If the distribution of correlations within this condition is normal, then the 95% credibility interval would be

$$.49 < \rho < 1.00 \quad \text{(good working conditions)}$$

For jobs with poor working conditions, the mean correlation is .35 with a standard deviation of .12. If the distribution of correlations within this condition is normal, then the 95% credibility interval would be

$$.21 < \rho < .59 \quad \text{(poor working conditions)}$$

The mean correlations are quite different, .77 versus .35. This finding suggests that working conditions are a moderator variable. There is residual variation within each set of studies, although we cannot know how much of this remaining variance is due to unknown and uncorrected artifacts. As is indicated by the credibility intervals, the two distributions overlap, but this could be explained by the fact that the moderator variable (working conditions) is actually a continuum that was split at the median. Thus, the upper end of one set is the bottom end of the other. It may be that much of the residual variation could be explained by coding finer gradations in working conditions.

In computing these meta-analyses, we used the overall mean uncorrected r of .290 in the sampling error variance calculations for both subset meta-analyses. The results could be computed using the separate mean rs shown in Table 4.5c (.414 and .167 for good and poor working conditions). This would produce slightly more accurate results. We leave this as an exercise for the reader.

Finally, we note that the meta-analysis of the partically corrected correlations in Table 4.5c can be conducted using the INTNL computer program (see Appendix A) if the appropriate adjusted Ni are entered. See page 280 for how to compute these adjusted Ni values.

Summary of Artifact Distribution Meta-Analysis of Correlations

Ideally, artifact information on every artifact would be available for every correlation in every study. However, publication practice has not yet reached this level of completeness in reporting research. Typically, artifact information is available at three levels. For some artifacts, information is available for all or nearly all studies. This information can be used to correct studies individually. For some artifacts, information is available on a random subset of studies, enough to estimate the distribution of artifact values across studies. Although individual studies cannot be corrected, the meta-analysis results can be corrected for those artifacts. For some artifacts, no information is available and no correction can be made. We recommend that meta-analysis be conducted in two stages, corresponding to the artifact information available.

The first-stage meta-analysis corrects for those artifacts for which information is available for all or nearly all studies. In some research domains, that will be a bare-bones meta-analysis. That is, one will be able to correct only for the artifact of sampling error. The methods for this first-stage bare-bones meta-analysis were presented in Chapter 3. The main product of the first-stage meta-analysis is the estimate of the mean and standard deviation of population correlations corrected for those artifacts controlled in the first-stage meta-analysis. If a moderator variable was hypothesized, then there will be a meta-analysis for each corresponding subset of studies.

The purpose of the second-stage meta-analysis is to correct the first-stage meta-analysis for those artifacts where information is available on a sporadic basis. The phrase "those artifacts" means the sporadic artifacts in this context. There are two phases to the second-stage meta-analysis: analysis of each artifact separately, followed by an analysis for the compound effect of the artifacts.

Phase 1: Cumulating Artifact Information

For each sporadic artifact, the artifact information is used to generate the artifact multiplier for those studies where it can be computed. These values are then cumulated across studies. That is, we compute a mean and a standard deviation for each artifact multiplier. For each artifact distribution, we also compute the coefficient of variation, the standard deviation divided by the mean, and the square of the coefficient of variation, here denoted v.

Phase 2a: Correcting the Mean Correlation

The compound impact of the artifacts on the mean correlation is computed by the compound multiplier. That is, the mean attenuated correlation is the product of the mean true correlation and the mean compound artifact multiplier. The mean compound multiplier is the product of the means of the separate artifact multipliers. To correct for the compound effect of the sporadic artifacts, we take the mean correlation from the first-stage meta-analysis and divide it by the mean compound multiplier.

Phase 2b: Correcting the Standard Deviation of Correlations

The compound effect of the artifacts on the variance of correlations is more complicated. On the one hand, the attenuating effect of artifacts tends to reduce the variation of population correlations. On the other hand, the variation in artifacts across studies causes an artifactual increase in the variance of correlations across studies. Computationally, we first correct for artifact variation. From the variance found in the first-stage meta-analysis, we subtract a term computed from the sum of the squared coefficients of variation of the separate artifacts. We then correct for the attenuation effect by dividing the reduced variance by the square of the mean compound multiplier. That number is the desired variance of correlations corrected for all artifacts with available artifact information.

The main product of the second-stage meta-analysis is the mean and standard deviation of population correlations corrected for those artifacts for which sporadically available artifact information has been gathered. To the extent that important artifacts have not been corrected, the mean will be an underestimate and the standard deviation will be an overestimate. If the artifacts not corrected have only a small impact, and if we are lucky enough to have little bad data in the research domain, then the mean and the standard deviation will be reasonably accurate estimates of the true correlation distribution. In any case, the estimates will be much more accurate than the bare-bones meta-analysis results and far more accurate than the single-study uncorrected correlations that form the basis of many current scientific inferences.

Exercise 4.1

Artifact Distribution Meta-Analysis

The data presented in this exercise are real data from a selection validity study conducted in one of the largest retailing firms in the United States. Save all your calculations and results from this exercise. The results will be used in the exercise at the end of Chapter 9.

I. First, do a bare-bones meta-analysis of these data (correct *only for* sampling error). You can do this either with a calculator or using the INTNL program (i.e., the program labeled "Correlations—Using Artifact Distributions" in the software package described in the Appendix). You will learn more if you use a calculator. For each test, give

1. The average observed validity ($\bar{r}$)
2. The observed variance of validities (S_r^2)
3. The variance expected from sampling error (S_e^2)
4. The residual variance (S_{res}^2)
5. The residual standard deviation (SD_{res})
6. The percentage of variance accounted for

II. We can correct the results of the bare-bones meta-analysis to get the final meta-analysis results. We will do this in two ways: First, we will assume that the range restriction is direct—direct selection on test scores (Thorndike's Case II). Second, we will assume that the range restriction is indirect, being based on some unknown (unrecorded) combination of variables (e.g., the employees were hired based on some unrecorded procedure that, for example, might have included an application blank, an interview, etc.).

A. *Direct Range Restriction (Case II).* Assume that $u_X = s/S = .65$ in every job family for every test. Assume that the reliability of the job performance measure (supervisory ratings) is .50 (restricted sample value) in each job family. (Note: This means you must make the correction for ratings unreliability first, then the range restriction correction.) Because both of these values are constant across all job families, you can estimate mean true validity ($\bar{\rho}_{xy_\infty}$) and the standard deviation of true validity (SD_ρ) by just correcting $\bar{r}$ and SD_{res}. (That is, after correcting $\bar{r}$ to estimate $\bar{\rho}_{xy_\infty}$, you can get an approximate estimate of SD_ρ as $SD_\rho = [\,\bar{\rho}_{xy_\infty}/\,\bar{r}\,]\ SD_{\text{res}}$.) Compute these estimates in this way. Also, compute the 90% credibility value. Enter your results into the table (under "Direct Range Restriction—Hand Calculations").

You can also use the INTNL-D program with artifact distributions. This is the program labeled "Correlations—Using Artifact Distributions" in the software described in the Appendix; specify that range restriction is direct when asked by the program. Run the INTNL-D program and enter the results into the accompanying table (under "Direct Range Restriction—Program Calculations").

B. *Indirect Range Restriction.* Here the employees have been selected by some unknown means, not on the test itself. The reliability of the job performance ratings remains the same, at .50. The value of u_X remains the same at .65 for all tests in all job families. Here you must convert u_X to u_T, using Equation (3.16) in Chapter 3. You then use u_T to make the correction for range restriction. In the case of indirect range restriction, you need to know the reliability of the test—which is not needed in Case II. Assume the reliability of each test is .70 in the incumbent (i.e., restricted) group. (From this value, you can compute the reliability in the unrestricted group using Equation [3.17a] or [3.17b].) You need test reliability for two reasons. First, you need it to compute u_T. Second, you need to enter test reliability into the INTNL-I program, if you use the program. This is the program labeled "Correlations—Using Artifact Distribution"; when asked by the program, specify that range restriction is indirect. (For direct range restriction, you just enter 1.00s for test reliability. For indirect range restriction, however, you must enter the .70 values.) The program will ask you whether the .70 values are from the restricted or unrestricted groups. To get your final estimates, you take the *true score* values of $\bar{\rho}$ and SD_ρ and attenuate them by the square root of the *unrestricted* test reliability. This gives the two values for the true validity distribution. (The program provides these values.) (Note that this last step would not be necessary in a nonselection meta-analysis.)

After converting u_X to u_T, do this part of the exercise either using the program INTNL-I or by calculator (or both ways, if you wish). If you use the program, follow the instructions given previously. If you use a calculator, you must first correct r for unreliability in both measures, using *restricted* sample values of reliability, then correct for range restriction, and then attenuate by the square root of *unrestricted* test reliability. Follow the same procedure in computing SD_ρ. You will learn more if you use a calculator rather than the computer program.

Enter your results in the appropriate section of the table. For example, if you use INTNL-I, enter your results under "Indirect Range Restriction—Program Calculations."

III. Now interpret your results:

A. Bare-Bones Meta-Analysis. How different across the different tests are the figures for $\bar{r}$, SD_{res}, and percentage variance accounted for? How do you interpret these differences?

B. In the data corrected for direct range restriction, compare $\bar{\rho}_{xy_\infty}$ and SD_ρ computed via the simple-approximation method to these values computed via the computer program. How different are these values? Why are these values different? How acceptable is the accuracy of the simple approximation?

C. Compare the results obtained when correcting for direct versus indirect range restriction. Do you consider these differences in $\bar{\rho}_{xy_\infty}$ and SD_ρ large or not? Based on the material in this chapter, explain why these differences occur. Suppose the range restriction in these data is indirect. How serious are the consequences of falsely assuming that it is direct?

D. Compare the percentage variance accounted for from the bare-bones analysis to that from the program-calculated direct and indirect range restriction corrections. How different are these? Why are they not more different in this particular data set?

		Test of Mental Alertness			*Clerical Battery*			
Job Family	*N*	*Linguistic*	*Quantitative*	*Total*	*Filing*	*Checking*	*Arithmetic*	*Grammar*
1. Office Support Material Handlers	86	.33*	.20	.32*	.30*	.27*	.32*	.25*
2. Data Processing Clerical	80	.43*	.53*	.51*	.30*	.39*	.42*	.47*
3. Clerical-Secretarial (Lower Level)	65	.24*	.03	.20	.20	.22	.13	.26*
4. Clerical-Secretarial (Higher Level)	186	.12*	.18*	.17*	.07*	.21*	.20	.31*
5. Secretarial (Top Level)	146	.19*	.21*	.22*	.16*	.13*	.22*	.09
6. Clerical With Supervisory Duties	30	.24	.14	.23	.24	.24	.31	.17
7. Word Processing	63	.03	.26*	.13	.39*	.33*	.14	.22*
8. Supervisors	185	.28*	.10	.25*	.25*	.11	.19*	.20*
9. Technical, Operative, Professional	95	.24*	.35*	.33*	.30*	.22*	.31*	.42*
Total Group (*Pooled Correlations*)		.25*	.25*	.29*	.23*	.24*	.27*	.27*

*$p < .05$.

			Tests						
		MA Results	*Linguistic*	*Quant.*	*L & Q Total*	*Filing*	*Checking*	*Arithmetic*	*Grammar*
Calculate Either Way	Bare-Bones Meta-Analysis	$\bar{r}$							
		S_r^2							
		S_e^2							
		S_{res}^2							
		SD_{res}							
		% Var.							
Hand Calculations	Direct Range Restriction	$\bar{\rho}$							
		SD_ρ							
		90% CV							
	Indirect Range Restriction	$\bar{\rho}$							
		SD_ρ							
		90% CV							
Program Calculations	Direct Range Restriction	$\bar{\rho}$							
		SD_ρ							
		90% CV							
		% Var.							
	Indirect Range Restriction	$\bar{\rho}$							
		SD_ρ							
		90% CV							
		Var.							

5

Technical Questions in Meta-Analysis of Correlations

This chapter discusses technical questions that arise in the meta-analysis of correlations. These include the question of whether r or r^2 should be used in meta-analysis, and the question of whether meta-analysis of regression slopes and intercepts is preferable to meta-analysis of correlations. In earlier chapters, we have stated that estimates of SD_ρ must always be considered to be upper bound values. This chapter presents and discusses five technical factors and shows how they contribute to inflation in SD_ρ estimates.

Next, this chapter discusses the important distinction between fixed and random models for meta-analysis and concludes that random models should always be used, as recommended by the National Research Council (1992). We then discuss the distinction between credibility intervals and confidence intervals in meta-analysis and present methods for computing confidence intervals for estimates of $\bar{\rho}$. Finally, we present an extended technical treatment of the distinction between direct and indirect range restriction and the differing corrections that are appropriate in each case.

In the previous edition of this book, this chapter also discussed numerous criticisms of meta-analysis procedures for correlations. This edition omits that discussion.

r Versus r^2: Which Should Be Used?

Chapter 3 focuses on the correlation coefficient as the statistic to be cumulated across studies. Some have argued, however, that it is the squared correlation—r^2—that is of interest, not r itself. They argue that r^2 is the proportion of variance in one variable that is accounted for by the other variable, and this is the figure that provides the true description of the size of the relationship. Further, the advocates of r^2 typically hold that relationships found in the behavioral and social sciences are very small. For example, they maintain that $r = .30$ is small because $r^2 = .09$, indicating that only 9% of the variance in the dependent variable is accounted for. Even $r = .50$ is considered small: Only 25% of the variance is explained.

The "percentage of variance accounted for" is statistically correct but substantively erroneous. It leads to severe underestimates of the practical and theoretical significance of relationships between variables. This is because r^2 (and all other indexes of percentage of variance accounted for) are related only in a very nonlinear way to the magnitudes of effect sizes that determine their impact in the real world.

The correlation is the standardized slope of the regression of the dependent variable on the independent variable. If x and y are in standard score form, then $\hat{y} = rx$. Thus, r is the slope of the line relating y to x. As such, it indexes the predictability of y from x. For example, if $r = .50$, then, for each increase of 1 *SD* in x, there is an increase of .50 *SD* in y. The statistic r^2 plays no role in the regression equation. The same principle applies in raw score regression; here the slope again is based on r, not r^2. The slope is $B = r\ (SD_y/SD_x)$. The raw score regression equation is

$$\hat{Y} = \left\{ r\frac{SD_y}{SD_x} \right\} X + C$$

where C is the raw score intercept.

The problem with all percentage variance accounted for indexes of effect size is that variables that account for small percentages of the variance often have very important effects on the dependent variable. Variance-based indexes of effect size make these important effects appear much less important than they actually are, misleading both researchers and consumers of research. Consider an example. According to Jensen (1980) and others, the heritability of IQ true scores is about .80. This means that 80% of the (true) variance is due to heredity and only 20% is due to environmental differences, yielding a ratio of "importance" of .80/.20 or 4 to 1. That is, based on percentage of variance accounted for indexes, heredity is 4 times more important than environment in determining intelligence. However, this picture is very deceptive. (For purposes of this example, we assume heredity and environment are uncorrelated; that is close to true, and in any event the principle illustrated here is not dependent on this assumption.) The functional relationships between these two variables and intelligence are expressed by their respective standard score regressions, not by the figures of .80 and .20. The correlation between IQ and heredity is $\sqrt{.80} = .894$, and the correlation between environment and intelligence is $\sqrt{.20} = .447$. Thus, the functional equation for predicting IQ from each (when all variables are in standard score form) is

$$\hat{Y}_{IQ} = .894(H) + .447(E)$$

Thus, for each 1 *SD* increase in heredity (H), there is a .894*SD* increase in *IQ*, and for each 1 *SD* increase in environment (E), there is a .447*SD* increase in *IQ*. This is the accurate statement of the power of H and E to produce changes in *IQ*; that is, it is the true statement of their effects on IQ. The relative size of these effects is $.894/.447 = 2$. That is, the true impact of heredity on intelligence is only twice as great as that of environment, not 4 times as great, as implied by the percentage of variance accounted for indexes. The variance-based indexes underestimate the causal impact of environment relative to heredity by a factor of 2. Further, the absolute causal importance of environment is underestimated. The correct interpretation shows that if environment could be improved by 2 *SD*s, the expected increase in IQ (where $SD_{IQ} = 15$) would be $.447(2.00)(15) = 13.4$. This would correspond to an increase from 86.6 to 100, which would have very important social implications. This correct analysis shows the true potential impact of environment, while the variance-based statement that environment accounts for only 20% of IQ variance leaves the false impression that environment is not of much importance. (Note: The fact that no one seems to know *how* to increase environment by 2 *SD*s is beside the point here.)

This is not an unusual case. For example, the Coleman Report (1966) concluded that, when other variables were controlled for, money spent per student by school districts accounted for only a small percentage of the variance of student achievement. The report concluded that financial resources and facilities, such as libraries and labs, were not very important because they provide little "leverage" over student achievement. Later analyses, however, showed that this small percentage of variance corresponded to a standardized regression coefficient for this variable that was much larger, and demonstrated that improvements in facilities could yield increases in student achievement that were significant socially and practically (Mosteller & Moynihan, 1972).

Variance-based interpretations have led to the same sort of errors in personnel selection. There it was said that validity coefficients of, for example, .40 were not of much value because only 16% of the variance of job performance was accounted for. A validity coefficient of .40, however, means that, for every 1 *SD* increase in mean score on the selection procedure, we can expect a .40 *SD* increase in job performance—a substantial increase with considerable economic value. In fact, a validity coefficient of .40 has 40% of the practical value to an employer of a validity coefficient of 1.00—perfect validity (Schmidt & Hunter, 1998; Schmidt, Hunter, McKenzie, & Muldrow, 1979).

Variance-based indexes of effect size are virtually always deceptive and misleading and should be avoided, whether in meta-analysis or in primary research. In meta-analysis, such indexes have an additional disadvantage: They obscure the *direction* of the effect. Being nondirectional, they do not discriminate between an r of .50 and an r of $-.50$; both would enter the meta-analysis as $r^2 = .25$.

To illustrate that r, and not r^2, is the appropriate index of effect size and to show that "small" rs (e.g., .20–.30) indicate substantial relationships, Rosenthal and Rubin (1979b, 1982c) presented the binomial effect size display (BESD). Although this technique requires that both variables be dichotomous (e.g., treatment vs. control or "survived" vs. "died") and requires 50% on each side of each dichotomy, it does forcefully illustrate the practical importance of "small" correlations. For example, a correlation of .32 ($r^2 = .10$) between treatment with a particular drug and patient survival corresponds to a reduction in the death rate from 66% to 34% (Rosenthal, 1984, p. 130). Thus, a relationship that accounts for only 10% of the variance means a reduction in the death rate of almost 50%. Small correlations can indicate large impacts. The BESD uses a special case—that of truly dichotomous variables—to illustrate the same principle we have presented using the more general regression analysis method.

r Versus Regression Slopes and Intercepts in Meta-Analysis

On the surface, it often appears that some hypotheses or theories could be tested as effectively or more effectively by cumulating raw score slopes and intercepts rather than correlations. For example, a theory advanced by Hackman and Oldham (1975) states simply that the relationship between the "motivating potential" of a job and the job satisfaction of incumbents will be stronger for those incumbents with high "growth need strength" (GNS) than for those low in GNS. Because the theory is not explicit, it seems plausible a priori that it could be tested by cumulation of either regression slopes or correlations. Although some hypotheses or theories specify correlation- or regression-based relationships, most are like the Hackman-Oldham theory. Some have advocated that all such theories should be tested using (raw score) regression analyses. What is the relative feasibility and usefulness of meta-analysis based on slopes and intercepts versus correlations? We show next that the disadvantages of using raw score regression slopes and intercepts rather than correlations outweigh the advantages.

Range Restriction

Correlations are affected by range restriction and, therefore, need to be corrected to a common *SD* for the independent variable to remove the resulting differences and the overall attenuation. When range restriction on the independent variable is direct, it has no effect on estimates of raw score slopes and intercepts, and therefore, there is no need for range corrections. This appears to be an important advantage, but unfortunately, range restriction is nearly always indirect, and thus, slopes and intercepts are affected. As noted in Chapters 3 and 4 and as discussed in detail later in this chapter, direct range restriction is rare; most range restriction is indirect.

Measurement Error

Correlations are attenuated by unreliability in the measures of both independent and dependent variables, and they have to be corrected for unreliability in both. These corrections were described in Chapter 3. Raw score regression slopes and intercepts are also attenuated by measurement error, but only measurement error in the independent variable. They are not affected by unreliability in the dependent variable, and thus, one need neither know that reliability nor make that correction. The correction for unreliability in the independent variable is (Hunter & Schmidt, 1977)

$$\hat{B}_T = B/r_{XX}$$

and

$$\hat{C}_T = \bar{Y} - (B/r_{XX})\bar{X}$$

where $\hat{B}_T$ is the estimated true score slope, $\hat{C}_T$ is the estimated true score intercept, and r_{XX} is the reliability of the independent variable. From these equations, it is apparent that measurement error reduces the observed slope and increases the observed intercept; these corrections reverse those effects. Thus, uncorrected slopes and intercepts can be just as deceptive as uncorrected correlations, underestimating true relationships. In addition, the corrections, with their corresponding increase in sampling error, are often about the same in magnitude. Although B is corrected only for measurement error in the independent variable, division is by r_{XX}, not $\sqrt{r_{XX}}$, and thus, the correction is larger. Both range restriction and reliability corrections increase sampling error; for this reason, it would be better if such corrections were unnecessary. However, this statement is far more important for single studies than for meta-analyses; a major strength of meta-analysis is that, unlike single studies, it corrects for the effects of sampling error. Thus, even if fewer or smaller corrections sometimes have to be made to the slope and intercept, meta-analysis cancels out this advantage.

Comparability of Units Across Studies

A major disadvantage of regression slopes and intercepts is that they are usually not comparable across studies and, thus, cannot be meaningfully cumulated in a meta-analysis. The formulas for the bivariate regression slope (B) and intercept (C) are

$$B = r\frac{SD_y}{SD_x}$$

and

$$C = \bar{Y} - B\bar{X}$$

The values for B are comparable across studies only when all studies have used exactly the same scales to measure X and Y. For example, if X is job satisfaction, then every study must have used the same job satisfaction scale, say, the JDI. If Y is life satisfaction, again the same scales must have been used in all studies. If different scales are used, slopes are not comparable, even if those scales correlate 1.00 corrected for unreliability. For example, suppose one study uses a shortened form of the same job satisfaction scale used by another study. Even though the two scales measure the same construct, the short form will have a smaller SD, and that scale difference alone will greatly increase the observed slope. In personnel selection, suppose two studies both use rating scales to measure job performance and use the same test (X). If one study uses a rating scale with 20 subscales and the other a scale with only 7, the SD_y in the first study might be twice as large, causing the slope to be twice as large. This problem makes it impossible to meaningfully compare slopes across the two primary studies. In meta-analysis, it is usually impossible to use slopes and intercepts as the statistic to be cumulated for this reason. The correlation coefficient, on the other hand, is in the same units in all studies and can be cumulated across studies; it is scale independent.

This problem of noncomparable scales is unique to the behavioral and social sciences. In the physical sciences, even if different studies use different scales, all studies can be put on a common scale and the slopes and intercepts can then be cumulated. Pounds can be converted to kilograms, inches to centimeters, quarts to liters, and vice versa. These scales are fully translatable to each other because each has a rational zero point; each is some constant times the other. We can define zero weight, but it is difficult to define zero verbal ability; thus, our studies cannot be converted to the same units of measurement. Instead, we must convert all to the same scale-free unit, the correlation (or the d value; see Chapters 6 and 7). This important distinction between the physical and social sciences has been overlooked by those who have criticized the correlation coefficient and advocated the use of slopes instead (e.g., the Society to Abolish the Correlation Coefficient).

It is sometimes maintained that this comparability problem can be solved by simply standardizing the independent and dependent variables within each study, creating equal standard deviations across studies; but in bivariate regression the resulting standardized regression weights are then equal to the correlation. There is then no point in not starting with r.

Comparability of Findings Across Meta-Analyses

If all available studies have been conducted using the same measurement scales (a very rare event), then one can apply meta-analysis to slopes and intercepts. Methods for doing this have been developed in detail by Raju, Fralicx, and Steinhaus (1986) and have been discussed by Callender (1983). For example, virtually all the studies testing the Hackman-Oldham theory have used the same scales—the original scales developed by Hackman and Oldham. Also, where a consortium study is carried out in many organizations, the same scales are usually used in all organizations. The problem, then, is that the results of such a meta-analysis cannot be compared to other meta-analyses. For example, we cannot ask whether the strength of the relationship between job satisfaction and job performance is the same in the consortium study as in other meta-analyses in the literature. These latter meta-analyses will be in correlation units (or, more rarely, in some *different* raw score unit). As we noted in Chapter 1, the development of theories requires that the results of different meta-analyses can be brought together and integrated into a coherent explanation. Thus, noncomparability of meta-analyses is a serious drawback to cumulation of slopes and intercepts. What it means is that, even in those rare cases in which meta-analysis of slopes and intercepts is statistically possible, one must still do a meta-analysis in correlations to have a set of findings that can be linked to the wider developing nomological net (Callender, 1983).

Intrinsic Interpretability

In addition to the problems mentioned previously, slopes and intercepts are very difficult to interpret. It is easy to grasp the meaning of the correlation—it is the standardized regression coefficient of y or x:

$$\hat{y} = rx$$

For every increase of 1 unit (1 *SD*) on x, there is an increase of r *SD*s on y. If $r = .50$, increasing x by 1.00 *SD* increases y by .50 *SD*. Suppose, however, the raw score regression equation is

$$\hat{Y} = 3.8X + 13.2$$

It is very hard to see whether this is a strong relationship or a weak one. For every 1-unit increase in X, we get a 3.8-unit increase in Y. But is this a large or small increase? Perhaps SD_y is just very large, so that an increase of 3.8 is actually a small increase. After all, the scaling is arbitrary. To make sense of this equation, one must somehow translate it into standard score units—and then one is back to the correlation!

In summary, the disadvantage of conducting meta-analysis using slopes and intercepts rather than correlations is substantial. Ordinarily, meta-analysts will have few occasions to prefer slopes and intercepts over correlations.

Technical Factors That Cause Overestimation of SD_ρ

Throughout this book, we have stressed that much of the variation in correlations across studies is caused by the operation of statistical and measurement artifacts. These artifacts were defined in Chapter 2, and methods for correcting for many of them were presented in Chapters 3 and 4. This section discusses five additional factors that contribute to overestimation of SD_ρ, the standard deviation of population correlations. These factors lead to an overestimation of the amount of variability in actual correlations. These factors are (1) the presence of non-Pearson correlations in the meta-analysis, (2) the presence of outliers (extremely large or small correlations) in the meta-analysis, (3) the use of study observed correlations in the formula for sampling error variance, (4) the undercorrection for sampling error variance when there is range restriction, and (5) the failure to allow for the nonlinearity in range corrections in meta-analyses based on artifact distributions. The first three of these factors apply in all meta-analyses; the fourth applies only when some or all of the correlations have been affected by range restriction; the fifth applies only to meta-analyses that use artifact distributions. However, most meta-analyses to date have used artifact distributions.

Presence of Non-Pearson *r*s

It is well-known that commonly used non-Pearson correlation coefficients, such as the biserial and tetrachoric, have larger standard errors than do Pearson *r*s. Thus, the formula for the sampling error variance of the Pearson correlation underestimates the amount of sampling error variance in these correlations. When such correlations are included in a meta-analysis, they are treated as if their standard errors were those of Pearson *r*s. This deflates the estimated variance accounted for by artifacts and inflates the estimate of SD_ρ in any distribution of correlations in which biserial and tetrachoric correlations are present. More accurate results can be obtained if non-Pearson *r*s are deleted prior to the meta-analysis. Of course, such deletion is more feasible when the total number of correlations is large to begin with. In large sets of validity studies, we have found that deleting non-Pearson rs increased the average percentage of variance accounted for by sampling error by almost five percentage points (Schmidt et al., 1993). It should be noted that Spearman's rho is the Pearson r between ranks and has the same sampling error variance as the Pearson r. Hence, it should not be deleted.

Presence of Outliers and Other Data Errors

The use of least squares statistical methods to estimate the mean and variance of the distribution of correlations is based on the assumption that the data contain no aberrant values (i.e., outliers). When this assumption does not hold, the statistically optimal properties (efficiency and unbiasedness) of least squares estimates disappear. Under these circumstances, least squares estimates become very inaccurate because of their extreme sensitivity to outliers (Huber, 1980; Tukey, 1960; see also Barnett & Lewis, 1978; Grubbs, 1969). The presence of even a single outlier can produce a radical increase in the observed standard deviation and a somewhat smaller distortion of the mean. Data sets in any research area are likely to contain data points that are erroneous due to computational, transcriptional, and other errors (Gulliksen, 1986; Wolins, 1962). Even when such errors do not result in outliers, they still produce additional artifactual variance beyond that produced by sampling error and other artifacts. Based on his extensive experience with data sets of all kinds, Tukey (1960) judged that virtually all data sets contain outliers and other errors. One of our best-known psychometricians expressed the following sentiment (Gulliksen, 1986):

> I believe that it is essential to check the data for errors before running my computations. I always wrote an error-checking program and ran the data through it before computing. I find it very interesting that in every set of data I have run, either for myself or someone else, there have always been errors, necessitating going back to the questionnaires and repunching some cards, or perhaps discarding some subjects. (p. 4)

Unfortunately, the failure to conduct such checks is very widespread. In the physical sciences (e.g., physics and chemistry), extreme values have been routinely eliminated for centuries (Hedges, 1987). The behavioral and social sciences have recently begun to recognize the need for such "trimming" prior to data analysis. Tukey (1960) and Huber (1980) recommended deletion of the most extreme 10% of data points—the largest 5% and the smallest 5% of values. In one study (Schmidt et al., 1989), we found that deletion of only the top and bottom 2% resulted in a five-percentage-point increase in the average percentage of variance accounted for by artifacts. However, in the case of meta-analysis methods that estimate SD_ρ, the identification and elimination of outliers is a complicated and problematic process. When sample sizes are small to moderate (the usual case), extreme values can occur simply because of large sampling errors. Such values are not true outliers and should not be eliminated from the data, because the formula for sampling error variance assumes and allows for such occasional large sampling errors. Elimination of such nonoutlier extreme values can result in overcorrection for sampling error and underestimation of SD_ρ. Because of this, we have generally not removed any but the most extreme "outliers" in conducting our meta-analyses. Huffcutt and Arthur (1995) developed a procedure for identifying and removing outliers in meta-analysis. However, for the reasons discussed here, the use of such procedures is problematic.

Use of r Instead of $\bar{r}$ in the Sampling Error Formula

The formula for the sampling error variance in a correlation coefficient is

$$S_e^2 = \frac{(1 - \rho_{xy}^2)^2}{N - 1}$$

where N is the sample size and ρ_{xy} is the population (uncorrected) correlation. ρ_{xy} is, of course, unknown, and to use this formula, some method must be found to estimate it. In single studies, the estimate of ρ_{xy} typically used—because it is the only one available—is the observed correlation in the study at hand. In our early meta-analyses of employment test validities, we followed this tradition: The value used to estimate the sampling error variance in every study was the observed correlation in that study. Subsequent simulation studies and studies with real data have shown that this procedure is not optimal. The mean observed r ($\bar{r}_{\text{obs}}$)—a good estimate of ρ_{xy}—is typically about .20 in this literature. Sample sizes are usually small, so there are substantial departures in both directions from ρ_{xy}. When the sampling error is large and positive (e.g., +.20, so that $r = .40$), the estimated S_e^2 is substantially reduced (by 23% in this example). However, this effect is not symmetrical. When the sampling error is large and negative (e.g., −.20, so that $r = .00$), the estimated S_e^2 is increased by only a small amount (by 9% in this example). Thus, on balance, the sampling error in a set of correlations is substantially underestimated. The smaller the sample size in the studies analyzed, the greater this underestimation will be. Also, the smaller the (attenuated) population correlation, the greater the underestimation will be (because smaller ρ_is have larger sampling error variances, sample sizes being equal). The result is underestimation of the amount of variance accounted for by sampling error and overestimation of SD_ρ. This distortion can be eliminated by using the $\bar{r}$ for the set of studies rather than individual rs in the formula for sampling error. The $\bar{r}$ contains little sampling error, and extreme values are very unlikely. The result is more accurate estimates of SD_ρ. Hunter and Schmidt (1994b) showed analytically that use of $\bar{r}$ enhances accuracy in the homogeneous case (where $SD_\rho = 0$). Law, Schmidt, and Hunter (1994b) used computer simulation to show this was also true in the heterogeneous case (where $SD_\rho > 0$). As a result, the methods presented in this book all use $\bar{r}$ in the formula for the sampling error variance of correlations, as do the computer programs available to apply these methods. (See the Appendix for a description of this software package.)

Millsap (1988), in a Monte Carlo study, used r rather than $\bar{r}$ in the formula for sampling error variance. In his study, all ρs were equal so S_ρ^2 was 0, and the variance of the observed rs was solely sampling error variance, that is, $S_r^2 = S_e^2$. However, he found that his formula-derived estimates of S_e^2 were slightly smaller than the

S_r^2 figures, and this difference was larger for smaller sample sizes. He attributed this finding to inaccuracy in the formula (the formula is an approximation), but the phenomenon described in this section is in large part the explanation for his findings. He also found that the negative bias in his formula-derived estimates of sampling error variance was larger when scale reliability was lower. This finding is explained by the fact that lower reliability leads to lower values of ρ_i, the operative population correlation (see Chapter 3). Lower ρ_i values have larger sampling error variances for any fixed sample size, thus intensifying the process described previously. Thus, contrary to Millsap's (1988) conclusion, it was not unreliability (measurement error) per se that caused the increase in the underestimation, but rather the reduced value of the population correlation and the resulting increase in sampling error.

Undercorrection for Sampling Error Variance in the Presence of Range Restriction

The formula for sampling error variance assumes that the independent and dependent variables are at least approximately normally distributed. Where there is direct range restriction (truncation) on one or both variables, this assumption is violated. For example, in personnel selection, there may be direct restriction on the test (the independent variable). For example, job offers may be made only to those applicants above the mean test score. Millsap (1989), using computer simulation studies, found that under such conditions the sample (or study) correlations have larger sampling error variances than indicated by the sampling error variance formula. That is, the formula underestimates the true amount of sampling error, leading to undercorrections for sampling variance and, therefore, overestimation of the residual variance and SD_ρ. The undercorrection is largest when sample sizes are 60 or less. As an example, if $N = 60$ and $\rho = .40$ in all studies, and all variance is, in fact, due only to sampling error, then the estimated residual *SD* (SD_{res}) will, on average, be .046. The estimated SD_ρ value will typically be about .09. The correct value in both cases is, of course, 0. Thus, many nonzero estimates of SD_ρ in the literature could be due, in whole or in large part, to this effect because many are in the .08 to .12 range (see, e.g., Schmidt et al., 1993). Aguinis (2001) reported results similar to Millsap's. In most studies, range restriction is indirect rather than direct. Aguinis and Whitehead (1997) showed that indirect range restriction produces a similar downward bias in estimates of sampling error variance. There is no known procedure to adjust for the underestimation of sampling error variance caused by either direct or indirect range restriction.

Nonlinearity in the Range Correction

In artifact distribution–based methods of meta-analysis, the mean ($\bar{\rho}$) and standard deviation (SD_ρ) of true correlations are estimated from the mean ($\bar{r}_{\text{res}}$) and standard deviation (SD_{res}) of the residual distribution. The residual distribution is the distribution of observed correlations expected across studies if *N* were always infinite (i.e., no sampling error) and reliability, range restriction, and other artifacts were always constant at their respective mean values. The estimated mean of this distribution is the mean observed r (i.e., $\bar{r}_{\text{res}} = \bar{r}$). To correct the residual distribution for the mean level of unreliability, we could divide every value in that distribution by the mean of the square roots of reliabilities. Because that value is a constant, however, we can instead just divide both $\bar{r}_{\text{res}}$ and SD_{res} by that constant and get the same result. This is what artifact distribution–based procedures do in correcting for measurement error. However, these procedures do exactly the same thing in correcting the residual distribution for the effects of mean range restriction—and here things do not work out quite so neatly. Using the mean level of range restriction (in the form of the ratio of the restricted to the unrestricted predictor standard deviations), current procedures correct $\bar{r}_{\text{res}}$. This increases $\bar{r}_{\text{res}}$ by some factor, say 1.50. Then SD_{res} is multiplied by this same factor to estimate the SD of a distribution in which each r has been corrected for the mean level of range restriction. (In Chapter 4, this is expressed as division of SD_{res} by $\bar{c}$.) Unlike the reliability correction, however, the range restriction correction is not linear in r. The range correction is not the same for every value of r in the residual distribution: It is larger for smaller rs and smaller for larger rs. Thus, the approximation based on the assumption of linearity in artifact distribution–based meta-analysis procedures leads to overestimates of SD_ρ. Simulation studies (Callender & Osburn, 1980; Raju & Burke, 1983) demonstrated that our original interactive procedure—theoretically, our most sophisticated method; see Chapter 4 and Schmidt, Gast-Rosenberg, and Hunter (1980)—yields estimates of SD_ρ that are too large by about .02. The same is true for the Callender-Osburn and Raju-Burke procedures. This overestimation occurs in simulated data in which sample sizes are infinite and sources of artifactual variance, such as computational errors, outliers, and non-Pearson rs, do not exist. This overestimation stems from failure to take into account the nonlinearity of range restriction corrections. This nonlinearity can be taken into account by correcting each value in the residual distribution separately for the mean level of range restriction. To take this nonlinearity into account, the following method can be used (Law et al., 1994a, 1994b). After determining the mean and SD of the residual distribution, identify 60 additional values in that distribution by moving out from the mean in .1 SD units to 3 SD above and below the mean. Then correct each of these values individually for range restriction, using the mean of the s/S ratio. The formula used to correct each value is

$$R = \frac{r(S/s)}{\{([S/s]^2 - 1)r^2 + 1\}^{1/2}}$$

where

r = the value of the correlation in the residual distribution,
R = the range-corrected value,
S = the unrestricted standard deviation (as discussed later in this chapter, for indirect range restriction, the true score value of S is used),
s = the restricted standard deviation (as discussed later in this chapter, for indirect range restriction, the true score value of s is used).

Each range-corrected r is then corrected for the mean effect of unreliability. The relative frequency of each value of r is indexed by the normal curve ordinate associated with its z score in the residual distribution. These frequencies are applied to the corresponding corrected correlations (ρ_i). The frequency-weighted mean of the distribution of the corrected correlations ($\bar{\rho}$) is then determined, and the following (relative) frequency-weighted variance formula is used to find S_ρ^2:

$$S_\rho^2 = \frac{\sum f_i(\hat{\rho}_i - \bar{\rho})^2}{\sum f}$$

where f_i is the relative frequency associated with $\hat{\rho}_i$.

Law et al. (1994a, 1994b) showed via computer simulation that this refinement improves accuracy. Schmidt et al. (1993) found that in empirical data sets the estimated true standard deviations resulting from this improved procedure were smaller than the analogous values derived from the original procedure. Our current computer programs based on the interactive model for artifact distribution–based meta-analysis of correlations (INTNL-D and INTNL-I) incorporate this refinement. (These programs are described in Chapter 4 and in the Appendix.) The interactive model is described in Chapter 4. The letters INT in the program label refer to the interactive model. The letters NL stand for "nonlinear," that is, the nonlinear correction (estimation) procedure described here.

Other Factors Causing Overestimation of SD_ρ

Every research area can be expected to have additional factors that cause overestimation of SD_ρ in that particular research literature. The meta-analyst should be alert to this fact and should describe these factors even if no correction can be made for them. This section presents some examples from the meta-analysis of employment test validities. In that literature, some studies used ratings of job performance that had earlier been made for administrative purposes (e.g., pay raises, promotions, etc.), while other studies were based on special ratings that were used solely for the research study. Administrative ratings are known to be strongly influenced by nonperformance considerations (McDaniel, Whetzel, Schmidt, & Maurer, 1994; Schmidt & Zimmerman, in press) and to yield smaller observed correlations with selection procedures than research ratings. This difference is a source of artifactual variance in the observed correlations that could not be corrected for; it thus causes SD_ρ to be an overestimate. Another artifactual source of variance stemmed from the fact that some studies assessed job performance using content-valid work sample measures, while other studies used supervisory ratings of job performance. Work samples are by far the better measure of job performance. We now know that employment tests correlate more highly with work sample measures than with ratings of job performance (Hunter, 1983f; Nathan & Alexander, 1988). This difference between studies inflates estimates of SD_ρ. Another factor causing SD_ρ to be overestimated is inclusion of two or more correlations from the same study whenever the study contains two different tests measuring the same ability in the same sample (e.g., two different tests measuring spatial ability). These correlations are not independent, and the result is inflation of both the observed

SD (SD_r) and SD_ρ (see Chapter 10). Finally, we now know that differences between employees in amount of job experience reduce the observed validities of employment tests (McDaniel, Schmidt, & Hunter, 1988b; Schmidt, Hunter, Outerbridge, & Trattner, 1986). Thus, studies in which employees vary widely in job experience can be expected to report smaller correlations on average than studies in which employees vary little in time on the job. The result is additional variation in correlations across studies that is not corrected for. Again, the effect is to inflate the estimate of SD_ρ.

The specific nature of the factors that cause SD_ρ to be overestimated will vary from one research literature to another. However, they will virtually always be present. Even if no method can be found to correct for their effects, these factors should be described clearly in the meta-analysis report. As we emphasized in Chapter 2, it is important that every meta-analyst and every reader of meta-analyses constantly bear in mind the fact that all estimates of SD_ρ are likely to be overestimates. Even after the meta-analysis is completed, there is still less actual variation across studies than there appears to be.

Fixed- and Random-Effects Models in Meta-Analysis

Recently, two questions have received considerable attention in meta-analysis: (1) the relative appropriateness of fixed- versus random-effects meta-analysis models (Cook et al., 1992, Chap. 7; Hedges & Vevea, 1998; Hunter & Schmidt, 2000; Overton, 1998); and (2) the relative accuracy of different random-effects models (Field, 2001; Hall & Brannick, 2002).

Fixed- Versus Random-Effects Models. The basic distinction here is that fixed-effects models assume a priori that exactly the same ρ (or δ) value underlies all studies in the meta-analysis (i.e., $SD_\rho = 0$), while random-effects models allow for the possibility that population parameters (ρ or δ values) vary from study to study. A major purpose of random-effects models is to estimate this variance. The random-effects model is the more general one: Fixed-effects models are a special case of random-effects models in which $SD_\rho = 0$. In fact, when a random-effects model is applied to data in which $SD_\rho = 0$, it becomes mathematically a fixed-effects model. Application of a random-effects model can result in an estimated SD_ρ of 0, indicating that a fixed-effects model would be appropriate for those data. Application of a random-effects model can detect the fact that $SD_\rho = 0$; however, application of a fixed-effects model cannot estimate SD_ρ if $SD_\rho > 0$. That is, random-effects models allow for any possible value of SD_ρ, while fixed-effects models allow for only one value: $SD_\rho = 0$.

All the models presented in this book, in the two predecessor books (Hunter & Schmidt, 1990a; Hunter, Schmidt, & Jackson, 1982), and in related publications are random-effects models (Hedges & Olkin, 1985, p. 242; Hunter & Schmidt, 2000; Schmidt & Hunter, 1999a). These models all assume that population parameters may vary across studies and attempt to estimate that variance. The basic model is subtractive: The estimate of population variance is the variance that is left after variance due to sampling error and other artifacts is subtracted out. Some authors—for example, Field (2001), Hall and Brannick (2002), and Hedges and Vevea (1998)—pointed out that the weights these procedures apply to studies in computing means and variances across studies are somewhat different from those traditionally applied in random-effects models. This is true. The rationale for our study weighting approach (weighting by sample size and, where possible, by the product of sample size and the square of artifact attenuation factors) is presented in Chapters 2 and 3. While traditional random-effects weights produce slightly more accurate estimates of the mean, weighting by sample size produces more accurate estimates of population *SD*s (SD_ρ or SD_δ values), the accuracy of which is critical to meta-analysis. This question is addressed empirically in the studies discussed later that examine the accuracy of different models. These studies show that our random-effects models are quite accurate—and more accurate than random-effects models with more traditional random-effects study weights. Similar to the models in this book and in Hunter and Schmidt (1990a) and related publications, the Callender-Osburn and Raju-Burke models are also random-effects models and also weight studies by sample size. All these models have been shown in computer simulation studies to produce very accurate estimates of mean correlations.

Hedges and Olkin (1985) and Hedges and Vevea (1998) presented both fixed- and random-effects models. However, as a practical matter, their random-effects models have almost never been used in the literature. For example, all the applications of the Hedges-Olkin methods of meta-analysis appearing in *Psychological Bulletin* through 1999 have used their fixed-effects models (Hunter & Schmidt, 2000). (But see Shadish, Matt, Navarro, & Phillips, 2000.) None has used their random-effects models. (All applications of the Rosenthal-Rubin models in that journal have also used fixed-effects models.) Hedges and Olkin (1985) recommended that, when the fixed-effects model is proposed for use, the chi-square homogeneity test should be applied. They stated that only if this test is nonsignificant should one conclude that $SD_\rho = 0$ and proceed to apply the fixed-effects model. The National Research Council (1992) pointed out that this chi-square test has low power to detect variation in population values and therefore recommended against the use of fixed-effects models and in favor of random-effects models. Hedges and Pigott (2001) later showed that the power of the chi-square test is too low to allow its use in detecting between-study variation in population parameters. Not only does the chi-square test often fail to detect real heterogeneity, many users of the Hedges-Olkin fixed-effects model apply that model even when the chi-square test *is* significant, indicating the fixed-effects model is not appropriate (Hunter & Schmidt, 2000). If the fixed-effects model is applied when it is not appropriate (i.e., when $SD_\rho > 0$), confidence intervals are erroneously narrow and all significance tests have Type I biases (National Research Council, 1992). These Type I biases are typically quite large (Hunter & Schmidt, 2000; Overton, 1998). For example, the actual alpha level can easily be .35 or more when the nominal alpha level is .05. Reported confidence intervals can be only half their actual width. The upshot of this is that most of the meta-analyses appearing in *Psychological Bulletin* and other journals, because they are based on fixed-effects models, are potentially inaccurate and should be recomputed using random-effects models (Hunter & Schmidt, 2000).

A more detailed discussion of fixed- versus random-effects models of meta-analysis can be found in Chapter 9.

Accuracy of Different Random-Effects Models

Fixed-effects models have never been used in validity generalization research and have rarely been used in any research in industrial/organizational psychology. So the key question in these areas is which of the random-effects models is the most accurate. Actually, because fixed-effects models should not be used (National Research Council, 1992), this is the key question in all research areas. This question has been addressed over the years by the many computer simulation studies in the *Journal of Applied Psychology* and *Personnel Psychology* comparing the accuracy of our noninteractive and interactive models, the Callender-Osburn model, the two Raju-Burke models, and other models. The studies by Law et al. (1994a, 1994b) discussed earlier are examples of such studies. The general finding is that all these random-effects models are quite accurate by the standards of social science. Law et al. (1994a) showed that the addition of the two accuracy-increasing features discussed earlier in this chapter makes our interactive model (the INTNL program, described in the Appendix) slightly more accurate than the others under most realistic conditions.

One reason so few researchers conducting meta-analyses in social psychology and other non-I/O areas have used the Hedges-Olkin random-effects models is that the book by Hedges and Olkin (1985) developed its fixed-effects models more completely than its random-effects models. Recently, however, Hedges and Vevea (1998) presented a more complete development and discussion of their random-effects model. This has stimulated interest in comparing the accuracy of the Hedges-Vevea (1998) and the Hunter-Schmidt (1990a) random-effects models.

Field (2001) compared the accuracy of the Hedges-Vevea (H-V) and the Hunter-Schmidt (H-S) random-effects models in estimating $\bar{\rho}$. (Strangely, Field did not compute or compare estimates of SD_ρ, nor did he include or compare the Raju-Burke models or the Callender-Osburn model.) He found that when the studies were homogeneous (i.e., $SD_\rho = 0$), the two models had similar accuracy in estimating $\bar{\rho}$ (see his Table 1). However, he found that when the studies were heterogeneous (e.g., $SD_\rho > 0$), the H-V model overestimated $\bar{\rho}$, often by substantial amounts, while the H-S method slightly underestimated these values. For example, when the actual mean was .30, the H-V estimates ranged from .40 to .43, while the H-S estimates were all .29 (all estimates rounded to two places). When the actual mean was .50, the H-V estimates ranged from .64 to .71, while the H-S estimates ranged from .47 to .49. The overestimation produced by the H-V model was much larger than the underestimation produced by the H-S model. We believe that the overestimation produced by the H-V model stems from biases induced by use of Fisher's z transformation (Hunter & Schmidt, 1990a, pp. 213–218; Hunter, Schmidt, & Coggin, 1996; Schmidt, Hunter, & Raju, 1988). (See the discussion of Fisher's z transformation in Chapter 3.) Field also concluded this. Our procedures (like those of the Raju-Burke and Callender-Osburn models) do not use Fisher's z transformation. All calculations are performed directly on the correlation coefficients.

Hall and Brannick (2002) also used computer simulation to compare the H-V (1998) and H-S (1990a) random-effects models. Like Field, they also did not examine the Raju-Burke or Callender-Osburn random-effects models. However, Hall and Brannick did examine the accuracy of SD_ρ estimates, in addition to $\bar{\rho}$ estimates. Because the H-V method estimates SD_ρ in Fisher's z units, and because there is no way to transform a Fisher's z SD estimate into correlation units, they compared the two methods on the basis of credibility intervals, rather than directly on SD_ρ values. They produced credibility intervals in correlation units for the H-V method by back-transforming the endpoints of the Fisher's z credibility intervals into correlation units. They also separately examined situations in which artifacts attenuated correlations and those in which it was assumed there were no artifacts other than sampling error (i.e., assumed perfect measurement and no range restriction). (The Field study, by contrast, did not examine any artifacts beyond sampling error.) Whether the studies were homogeneous or heterogeneous, when there were no artifacts other than sampling error, Hall and Brannick (2002) found that the H-V method tended to overestimate $\bar{\rho}$ values, while the H-S model produced small underestimates—findings similar to Field's, although the H-V model overestimation was less severe in the Hall-Brannick study.

However, when measurement error and range restriction were present, the H-V model produced very large *underestimates* of $\bar{\rho}$—as would be expected because that model contains no means of correcting for the effects of these artifacts. So Hall and Brannick added the H-S artifact correction methods to the H-V model and then re-evaluated that model. With the H-S artifact correction methods grafted on, the accuracy of the H-V model was much improved. However, it still tended to overestimate $\bar{\rho}$—although not by as large a percentage as in the no-artifact condition. They concluded that the H-S model was generally more accurate than the H-V model.

A major finding in Hall and Brannick (2002) pertained to the credibility intervals produced by the two methods. Hall and Brannick placed considerable stress on credibility values, because they are used to determine the decision as to whether validity generalizes or not. They found that even when the H-V models included the artifact correction modules, the H-S method generally produced more accurate credibility values. The H-V credibility intervals tended to be too wide (compared to the known real values) and to be shifted to the left (see their Figure 1). Again, we believe that this is due to distortions introduced by use of the Fisher's z transformation. The H-S credibility intervals were quite close to the actual values. For these reasons, Hall and Brannick (2002) recommended use of the H-S random-effects model over the H-V random-effects model.

One final comment on the Field (2001) and Hall-Brannick (2002) studies seems appropriate. Both of these studies assumed normal (or at least symmetrical) distributions of ρ values. This assumption is reasonable, but if certain negatively skewed distributions of population correlation values are assumed, the Fisher's z transformation may produce less estimation error. However, the assumption of such a distribution may be unrealistic. It may be difficult to identify a substantive basis for positing such a distribution. This is an issue for future research.

Although they were not included in these studies, there is good reason to believe that the Raju-Burke (1983) TSA models and the Callender-Osburn (1980) model would perform similarly to the H-S model and would likewise prove more accurate than the H-V model. Again, the use of Fisher's z is the key to this difference in accuracy. These studies also support the conclusion that use of sample size to weight studies in a random-effects model—rather than more traditional random-effects study weights (Mosteller & Colditz, 1996) used in the H-V model—does not negatively affect accuracy and may improve accuracy.

Finally, we note that the Hunter-Schmidt random-effects model that both Field (2001) and Hall and Brannick (2002) compared to the Hedges-Vevea random-effects model is not our most accurate random-effects model. The model these authors evaluated, our multiplicative model for artifact distribution meta-analysis, is presented and described in detail in Chapter 4. This model is derived based on the algebra of the products of independent variables (just as the Callender-Osburn, 1980, model is). Unlike our interactive model, this model does not include the accuracy-enhancing refinements discussed earlier in this chapter and in Chapter 4. In preparing Law et al. (1994b), we found through computer simulation that our multiplicative model was not as accurate as our interactive model, even when the accuracy-enhancing refinements were added to it. Because of length concerns by the editor, we did not include the simulation tests of our multiplicative model in Law et al. (1994b), although we did include the somewhat similar Callender-Osburn multiplicative model. Hence, we believe that our interactive random-effects model (i.e., the INTNL program described in Chapter 4 and in the Appendix) will compare even more favorably with the Hedges-Vevea random-effects model. (Apparently, the reason Field, 2001, and Hall & Brannick, 2002, used the H-S model multiplicative rather than our interactive model is that the Hunter-Schmidt, 1990a, book does not contain a detailed mathematical description of the interactive model; this description being omitted because it was available in earlier journal publications.)

Credibility Versus Confidence Intervals in Meta-Analysis

The distinction in meta-analysis between credibility intervals and confidence intervals is very important. Credibility intervals are formed by use of SD_ρ, not by use of the standard error of $\bar{\rho}$. For example, the 80% credibility interval around a $\bar{\rho}$ value of .50 is $.50 \pm 1.28SD_\rho$. If SD_ρ is .10, this credibility interval is .37 to .63. The interpretation of this interval is that 80% of the values in the ρ distribution lie in this interval. The credibility interval refers to the distribution of parameter values, while the confidence interval refers to *estimates* of a single value—the value of $\bar{\rho}$. Confidence intervals express the likely amount of error in our estimate of $\bar{\rho}$ *due to sampling error.* The amount of sampling error is indexed in the standard error of $\bar{r}$ or $\bar{\rho}$ (depending on what artifact corrections are made). The standard error depends on sample size and, hence, sampling error. However, credibility values do not depend on sampling error at all—because variance due to sampling error (and other artifacts) has been removed from the estimate of SD_ρ. The concept of credibility intervals has been viewed by some as Bayesian, because it is based on the idea that parameter values (values of ρ) vary across studies. The concept of credibility values is also critically linked to random-effects meta-analysis models, because random-effects meta-analysis models (unlike fixed-effects models) allow for possible variation in parameters across studies. (In fixed-effects models, all credibility intervals would, by definition, have a width of 0.) The distinction between credibility intervals and confidence intervals is discussed in Hunter and Schmidt (2000), Schmidt and Hunter (1999a), and Whitener (1990).

All the intervals presented in the examples of meta-analysis given in Chapters 3 and 4 are credibility intervals. In meta-analysis, credibility intervals are usually more critical and important than confidence intervals. However, for certain questions, confidence intervals are also relevant to the question at hand (as was the case in Viswesvaran, Ones, & Schmidt, 2002).

Computing Confidence Intervals in Meta-Analysis

The two most important parameters estimated for random-effects models of meta-analysis are $\bar{\rho}$ and SD_ρ. It is perhaps easy to forget that these quantities are *estimates* of the parameters, not the parameters themselves, because in VG and meta-analysis reports they are rarely topped with a circumflex ($\wedge$). Technically, these values should be written as $\hat{\bar{\rho}}$ and $\widehat{SD}_\rho$ but typically are not in the interests of simplifying the symbolism. Every estimate has a standard error (*SE*), known or unknown. Hunter and Schmidt (2000), Schmidt and Hunter (1999a), and Schmidt, Hunter, and Raju (1988) provided formulas for the *SE* of mean observed r, but this is not the same statistic. We have derived equations for the *SE*s of $\hat{\bar{\rho}}$ and $\widehat{SD}_\rho$ (Hunter & Schmidt, 1987a, 1987b) but have not emphasized these statistics. As noted previously, the use made of the *SE* of the mean in statistics is in placing confidence intervals around the mean. In meta-analysis, unless the corrected *SD* is very small, confidence intervals around the mean are not as important as *credibility* intervals—because it is the whole distribution, and not the just the mean, that is important. Our focus has therefore been on credibility intervals. Second, *SE*s are rarely given for *SD* estimates in statistical models. This can be seen in the fact that almost all researchers know by heart the formula for the *SE* of the mean ($SD/\sqrt{n}$) but few can even remember seeing the formula for the *SE* of an *SD*. (How many times have you seen a confidence interval placed around a reported *SD*? Or seen an *SD* tested for statistical significance, which also requires the *SE* estimate?) Other random-effects models—the Hedges-Vevea (1998) model, the Raju-Burke (1983) models, the Callender-Osburn (1980) model—also do not provide the *SE* formula for estimates of SD_ρ and SD_δ.

The formulas for the $SE_{\bar{\rho}}$ are complex, but the following simple approximations are fairly accurate. If correlations are corrected individually (see Chapter 3), then

$$SE_{\bar{\rho}} = SD_{r_c}/\sqrt{k}$$

where $SE_{\bar{\rho}}$ is the *SE* of $\bar{\rho}$, SD_{r_c} is the *SD* of the correlations after each has been individually corrected for measurement error and other artifacts, and k is the number of studies. (It is important to note that $SD_{r_c} \neq SD_\rho$. SD_{r_c} is much larger than SD_ρ, because SD_{r_c} has not been corrected for sampling error—and r_c

values typically have much sampling error.) If artifact distribution meta-analysis (see Chapter 4) is used, then

$$SE_{\bar{\rho}} \cong [(\bar{\rho}/\bar{r})\, SD_r] / \sqrt{k}$$

where $SE_{\bar{\rho}}$ is the *SE* of $\bar{\rho}$, $\bar{\rho}$ is the estimate of mean corrected correlation, $\bar{r}$ is the mean observed (uncorrected) correlation, SD_r is the *SD* of the observed (uncorrected) correlations, and k is the number of studies. These formulas have been used in published studies (e.g., Judge & Bono, 2000, used the first equation). In the case of artifact distribution meta-analysis, an (equivalent) alternative to the second equation can be used to compute confidence intervals for $\bar{\rho}$. First, use the formulas presented by Schmidt, Hunter, and Raju (1988) to compute $SE_{\bar{r}}$, the *SE* of the mean observed correlation. Second, use $SE_{\bar{r}}$ to compute the confidence interval (CI) around $\bar{r}$. Third, correct the endpoints of this CI for mean levels of measurement error and range restriction to yield the CI for $\bar{\rho}$. Estimates produced in this manner are slightly more accurate than those produced by the second equation. When there is range restriction, that equation tends to overestimate SE_{ρ} because of the nonlinearity of the range restriction equation. This latter method was used in Viswesvaran et al. (2002). The formulas for the *SE* of SD_{ρ} are both more complicated and less useful and we do not present them here because of space limitations. See Raju and Drasgow (2003) and Smithson (in press) for treatments of this question.

Range Restriction in Meta-Analysis: New Technical Analysis

This section presents a detailed statistical analysis of direct and indirect range restriction in meta-analysis. Most of this information is new and did not exist at the time the 1990 edition of this book was published. Much of the material in this section is more technical than the rest of this book. However, it is necessary in that it provides the technical basis for the range restriction corrections described and illustrated in Chapters 3 and 4. These corrections are also used in the four computer programs for meta-analysis described in Chapters 3 and 4 and in the Appendix to this book.

A recent paper by Stauffer (1996) and an article by Mendoza and Mumford (1987) have made it clear that in the past meta-analysis procedures and range correction methods in general have not dealt optimally with range restriction and corrections for range restriction. Like most statistical techniques, range restriction was first considered in a context of perfectly reliable measurement. If the independent variable (predictor) is perfectly measured, then the procedure for correcting for indirect range restriction is the same as the procedure for correcting for direct range restriction. Because it is mathematically much easier to understand direct range restriction, most researchers have first learned how to correct for direct restriction and have then applied the correction equation for direct restriction to cases of both direct and indirect range restriction. However, when the independent variable is not perfectly measured, then the procedure is not the same and much of the underlying rationale is also different. The present treatment resulted from a thorough review of that reasoning. The resulting implications are particularly important for meta-analysis findings in the areas of educational and employment selection. For example, it is likely that there has been considerable underestimation of the predictive validity of cognitive abilities. As we show later, the correlation between cognitive abilities and job performance is considerably larger than indicated by current estimates in the literature. The implications are likewise important for other research areas in which range restriction is a factor.

Mendoza and Mumford (1987) focused on the differences in the mathematics of direct and indirect range restriction at the level of the individual study. Our treatment differs from that of Mendoza and Mumford (1987) in that it explicates the implications of these differences for meta-analysis methods. We discuss meta-analysis in three contexts: (1) domains with no range restriction, (2) domains with direct range restriction, and (3) domains with indirect range restriction.

All the existing methods of artifact distribution meta-analysis (Callender & Osburn, 1980; Raju & Burke, 1983; see Chap. 4) are random-effects meta-analysis models (Hall & Brannick, 2002; Hunter & Schmidt, 2000). These methods are accurate in research domains without range restriction. The multiplicative methods presented in Chapter 4 and the Callender-Osburn (1980) method are the simplest for such domains and they work perfectly there. When the data are characterized by direct range restriction, existing models are reasonably but not perfectly accurate. The original interactive method of Schmidt, Gast-Rosenberg, et al. (1980) assumes direct range restriction, as do the Callender-Osburn (1980) and Raju-Burke (1983) methods. Because of the nonlinearity of the range restriction attenuation equation, none of these methods is perfectly accurate. All generate very accurate estimates of the mean correlation, but all tend to slightly overestimate the standard deviation of population correlations (SD_ρ). As discussed earlier in this chapter, refined versions of these methods have been derived to reduce these errors (Law et al., 1994a, 1994b), but some slight overestimation of SD_ρ remains. Until publication of this book, there was no existing meta-analysis model for indirect range restriction.

Domains With No Range Restriction

When there is no range restriction, the artifacts are the *simple artifacts*. Each artifact multiplier can be and is computed entirely separately from other artifacts. This reflects the fact that each artifact depends on a different study imperfection and has a causal structure independent of that for other artifacts. We will see later that this is not true in the case of range restriction. Hence, this section builds the foundation for our later consideration of the complex artifact of range restriction.

Consider a research domain in which all populations are equivalent in terms of variation on both the independent and the dependent variable. In this case, range restriction does not occur, but other artifacts are present. For example, no important variable in the social sciences is measured perfectly; all have at least some degree of measurement error. Measurement error is random at the level of individual subject scores, but has a systematic effect at the level of population statistics. In particular, the correlation between measures of two variables is reduced in size to the extent that there is measurement error in the independent variable and to the extent that there is measurement error in the dependent variable.

Suppose we measure effect size using a correlation. In a hypothetical methodologically perfect study, the correlation computed in the study would be the actual effect size. By analogy with reliability theory, we call this the "true" effect size where the word "true" means "estimated without error." The psychometric literature typically considers a study with exactly one imperfection—the designated artifact—and computes the study population correlation for the imperfect study. For most artifacts, the correlation in the methodologically imperfect study will be smaller than the correlation for the perfect study. Thus, the imperfect study result is said to be "attenuated" (biased downward) in comparison to the perfect study result. If the artifact can be measured, it may be possible to derive a formula for the attenuation produced by that artifact. The usual form for the attenuation formula is a multiplication where the perfect correlation is multiplied by a fraction that is small to the extent that the artifact is large:

Single artifact attenuation formula:
Notation:
ρ = the result from the perfect study,
ρ_0 = the result from the imperfect study,
a = the quantitative measure of the artifact size.
Attenuation formula:

$$\rho_0 = a\rho \qquad (5.1)$$

Random Measurement Error

For example, consider random error of measurement in the independent variable. If T is the true score and X is the observed score, then the true effect size is ρ_{TY} and the imperfect study result is ρ_{XY}. The artifact multiplier a is the correlation between true score and observed score for the independent variable; that is, a is r_{XT}. By historical accident, this multiplier was not named in the original theories; instead, the name "reliability" was given to the square of this multiplier. That is, by name we have "reliability," the square of the desired multiplier, usually denoted as r_{XX}. Because $r_{XX} = a^2$, reliability theory formulas are riddled with square roots. We call the multiplier the "quality" of the variable in order to have a language without square roots.

Random error of measurement:

$$\text{Independent variable: } a_1 = \sqrt{r_{XX}}$$

$$\text{Dependent variable: } a_2 = \sqrt{r_{YY}}$$

Systematic Error of Measurement

Consider systematic error of measurement, that is, imperfect construct validity. A measure has imperfect construct validity to the extent that the correlation between its true scores (T) and the construct intended to be measured (C) is less than 1.00 (i.e., $r_{CT} < 1.00$). If only the independent variable has imperfect construct validity, then the critical question is the causal nature of the contaminating variable causing the imperfect construct validity for the independent variable measurement. If that contaminant is causally unrelated to the dependent variable, then the study correlation r_{XY} will be attenuated and the attenuation multiplier will be the construct validity of the independent variable $a = r_{C_1T}$, where C_1 is the intended construct, that is, the intended independent variable.

If only the dependent variable is contaminated, the effects are congruent with the effects for the independent variable. If the contaminant for the dependent variable is causally unrelated to the independent variable, then the study correlation r_{XY} is attenuated and the attenuation multiplier is the construct validity of the dependent variable, r_{C_2P}, where C_2 is the intended construct (the intended dependent variable) and P is the true score underlying the observed scores Y.

If both variables are contaminated, then there is one additional assumption necessary to get a simple attenuation formula: the assumption that the two contaminants are causally unrelated to each other. If this assumption holds, the attenuation factor is $r_{C_1T}r_{C_2P}$. Note that this attenuation process is separate from (and in addition to) that for random measurement error.

Artificial Dichotomization

Suppose a quantitative variable is artificially dichotomized. That is, we start with a quantitative measure but reduce it to a binary variable by splitting. This is usually done explicitly to make the analysis easier to present. For example, the researcher might split at the median and call those above the median "high" and those below the median "low." Sometimes, however, dichotomization is done implicitly and unintentionally. For example, many behaviorist researchers in attitude theory would use behavior to represent prejudice. The behavior is binary (the subject does it or not), but the prejudice is not. Rather, the behavior acts as a threshold for prejudice. Those above the threshold act in a prejudiced way, while those below that threshold act in a nonprejudiced way. Hence, this is an implicit dichotomization of the dependent variable.

As long as only one of the variables is dichotomized, the result is a simple attenuation formula where the multiplier is computed from the split probabilities using the theory of the biserial correlation. If both variables are dichotomized, the multiplier for the effect of both is computed from the theory of the tetrachoric correlation, which is a mathematically complicated theory. Hunter and Schmidt (1990b) showed that, to a close approximation, the effect for both is approximately the product of the multipliers for each separately. (They discuss the cases in which this approximation is less accurate.)

Multiple Artifacts

Consider a study in which several of these artifacts are present. The simple artifacts combine their effects in a simple multiplicative way. One can start with a perfect study and add the artifacts one at a time. After the last artifact is entered, the resulting formula will be the formula for the combined effects of the artifacts. The reader might worry that one would get different results if one considers the artifacts in a different order but for the simple artifacts this is *not* true. The final result is the same for any order.

Multiple simple artifacts:

Start with no artifacts:

$$\rho = \text{result for perfect study}$$

Add artifact 1:

$$\rho_1 = a_1\rho$$

Add artifact 2:

$$\begin{aligned}\rho_2 &= a_2\rho_1 = a_2(a_1\,\rho)\\ &= a_1a_2\rho\end{aligned}$$

Add artifact 3:

$$\begin{aligned}\rho_3 &= a_3\rho_2 = a_3(a_1a_2\rho)\\ &= a_1a_2a_3\rho\end{aligned}$$

Final result:

$$\rho_0 = A\rho \text{ where } A = a_1a_2a_3 \tag{5.2}$$

The final result is a formula for the attenuation produced by the combination of artifacts for that study. For simple artifacts, the final result is an attenuation formula with the same form as the form for a single artifact. The true effect size is multiplied by an overall artifact multiplier A. The combined multiplier A is the product of the multipliers for the individual artifacts.

This formula for simple artifacts makes the Callender-Osburn (1980) approach to artifact distribution meta-analysis very effective. Hunter and Schmidt (1990a and the present book) extended the Callender-Osburn approach to any number of artifacts and showed that the extended formula completely solves the problem of meta-analysis in domains with only simple artifacts (see Chapter 4). However, range restriction is not a simple artifact of this form.

Meta-Analysis for Simple Artifacts

Artifact distribution meta-analysis for simple artifacts can be conducted most easily with an extension of the Callender-Osburn (1980) multiplicative method, as illustrated in Chapter 4. The key points are reviewed here.

A Single Simple Artifact

For a simple artifact, we have independence between the artifact multiplier and the correlation which is attenuated. Thus, we have the following.

Attenuation is as follows:

$$\rho_0 = a\rho$$

$$E(\rho_0) = E(a)E(\rho) \quad (5.3)$$

$$V_{\rho_0} = \bar{a}^2 V_\rho + \bar{\rho}^2 V_a + V_a V_\rho \quad (5.4)$$

where V_{ρ_0} is the variance of the population attenuated correlations, V_ρ is the variance of the unattenuated population correlations, and V_a is the variance of the attenuation factor. (All variances are between-study variances.)

Meta-analysis corrections and final results are

$$\bar{\rho} = \bar{\rho}_0/\bar{a} \quad (5.5)$$

and

$$V_\rho = \lfloor V_{\rho_0} - \bar{\rho}^2 V_a \rfloor / \lfloor \bar{a}^2 + V_a \rfloor \quad (5.6)$$

where $\bar{\rho}$ is the estimated mean population unattenuated correlation and V_ρ is the variance of the population unattenuated correlations (i.e., S^2_ρ).

Multiple Simple Artifacts

For several simple artifacts, we use the same equations for artifact distribution meta-analysis with the compound multiplier A substituted for the single artifact multiplier a. Complications arise in computing the mean and standard deviation of the compound multiplier A. We usually have information only about one artifact at a time, for example, the mean and standard deviation for that artifact. If the artifacts are independent of each other, then the mean and standard deviation of the compound multiplier can be computed from the means and standard deviations of the single artifacts.

The mean is simple to compute. Because of independence, the mean of the product is the product of the means:

$$E(A) = E(a_1)E(a_2)\ldots$$

Computing the variance is more complicated. We first compute the squared coefficient of variation for each single artifact. Define

$$v_i = V_{a_i}/\bar{a}^2$$

We use these to compute V:

$$V = v_1 + v_2 + v_3 + \ldots$$

The variance is then

$$V_A = \bar{A}^2 V \tag{5.7}$$

This approximation is a sum and can be used to define the percentages of variance accounted for by each artifact, as illustrated in Chapter 4.

Direct Range Restriction

Range restriction is a special case of biased sampling. We want to estimate the parameters for one population, but our primary data are gathered on a different population. Under certain conditions, we can compute the statistical estimates for the desired population from the statistical estimates from the studied population.

It turns out that, under conditions of direct range restriction, corrections for artifacts must be made in a particular order. The same thing is true for indirect range restriction, but the required order of corrections is different. These requirements for specific sequences in which corrections are made affect both approaches to meta-analysis: correction of each correlation individually (Chapter 3) and artifact distribution meta-analysis (Chapter 4). The 1990 edition of this book dealt with only direct range restriction and did not fully address the order in which corrections should be made under conditions of direct range restriction. In this book, this has been corrected for direct range restriction, and, in addition, we have added an extended treatment of indirect range restriction, including the sequence of artifact corrections required for indirect range restriction. To put things in perspective, making artifact corrections in the wrong order usually produces only minor errors in results. However, use of corrections for direct range restriction when, in fact, the range restriction actually affecting the data is indirect range restriction results in substantial underestimation of $\bar{\rho}$ values (up to 25% or more underestimation), as shown later.

Range Restriction as a Single Artifact

For direct range restriction on the independent variable, the population for which we want to estimate the parameter is the full population. However, we have data only for those with selected scores on the independent variable. In most cases, the people left out of the study are those with either very high or very low scores. Thus, the studied population can be described as having a restricted range on the independent variable in comparison to the full population of interest.

Consider a city governed by a civil service law. Suppose promotion from one level to another within a job classification is required to be based solely on a job knowledge test, a condition of direct range restriction. That is, people are promoted top down based solely on their job knowledge test scores. We want to know how well the knowledge test predicts job performance for promotion applicants. The problem is that we can get job performance data only for those who are actually promoted, which means that we get no data on people with low test scores.

We now have two populations. The full population is the population of applicants, which is the population of interest. The studied population is the population of people promoted, called the incumbent population. We now have two correlations, one for each population. The usefulness of the test depends on the correlation between knowledge and performance in the applicant population, and so that is the correlation we want to know. However, our data give us only the correlation for the incumbent population.

The question for psychometric theory was to find a way to estimate the correlation for the full (applicant) population. One key finding concerns the regression of the dependent variable (performance) on the independent variable (the test) in the applicant population. If the regression of Y on X is linear and homoscedastic in the applicant population, then it will be linear and homoscedastic in the incumbent population. Furthermore, the raw score (unstandardized) slope and conditional standard deviation will be the same. The reason for this finding is that direct range restriction changes the frequency of any given value of X but it does *not* change the mean and standard deviation on Y for those at that value of X. If people with X below 70 are not promoted, then the data for the people promoted (the data for $X > 70$) are the same as the data for those people in the applicant population, because they are the same people.

If the regression is linear and homoscedastic, then the best way to compare the two populations is to compare the two standard deviations. The ratio of the standard deviations tells how much the incumbent population is restricted in comparison to the applicant population.

Direct range restriction on the predictor X:

Applicant population: SD_{X_a} = standard deviation on X (unrestricted *SD*)
Incumbent population: SD_{X_i} = standard deviation on X (restricted *SD*)
u_X = comparison ratio = SD_{X_i}/SD_{X_a}

Note that the comparison ratio is a fraction. The standard deviation will be smaller in the restricted population.

The attenuation formula for direct range restriction can be written in the same form as that for simple artifacts, but the multiplier is more complicated than for simple artifacts.

Notation:
Applicant population: ρ = correlation between X and Y
Incumbent population: ρ_0 = correlation between X and Y
Attenuation formula:

$$\rho_0 = a\rho \text{ where } a = \frac{u_X}{\sqrt{1 + (u_X^2 - 1)\rho^2}} \tag{5.8}$$

The complication can be seen in the denominator for the multiplier a. The presence of ρ in the denominator means that the multiplier depends not only on the degree of restriction but on the level of correlation as well. *This is what distinguishes range restriction from the simple artifacts. For a simple artifact, the multiplier is determined entirely by the extent of the artifact. For range restriction, the multiplier is determined not only by the extent of the artifact but also by the size of the true correlation.*

Correction for Direct Range Restriction

For a simple artifact, correction for attenuation is very easy. We just reverse the multiplication process:

Simple artifact:

$$\text{Attenuation: } \rho_0 = a\rho$$

$$\text{Correction: } \rho = \rho_0/a \tag{5.9}$$

This works for range restriction in principle but not in practice. The problem is that, in order to compute the multiplier a, you must already know ρ.

The conventional formula for correction for direct range restriction algebraically reverses the nonlinear algebra of the attenuation formula.

Correction for range restriction:

Define:

$$U_X = 1/u_X$$

$$\rho = b\rho_0 \tag{5.10}$$

where

$$b = \frac{U_X}{\sqrt{1 + (U_X^2 - 1)\rho_o{}^2}}$$

Correction:

$$\rho = b\rho_0$$

The reciprocal parameter $U_X = 1/u_X$ is the comparison ratio of standard deviations in the opposite order: applicant over incumbent. The formula for b is the same in algebraic form as the formula for attenuation due to range restriction; substitution of the parameter U_X for u_X makes it go in the opposite direction.

Meta-Analysis for Range Restriction as a Single Artifact

Range restriction is not a simple artifact, and the meta-analysis methods used for simple artifacts will not work exactly for range restriction. The problem term in Equation (5.8) is $(u_X^2 - 1)\,\rho^2$. This term is small if either u_X is close to 1 or if ρ^2 is small. The ratio u_X will be close to 1 if there is very little range restriction. The squared correlation ρ^2 will be small if ρ is modest. There are many domains where these two conditions are met. Unfortunately, both conditions can fail to be met in employment and educational selection. For example, general mental ability (GMA) has a high correlation with job performance (Schmidt & Hunter, 1998), and range restriction on GMA is substantial in most samples of job incumbents. There are almost certainly other research areas in which these conditions are not met. This causes a problem for artifact distribution meta-analysis methods. The Taylor series methods of Raju and Burke (1983) and the interactive method of Schmidt, Gast-Rosenberg, et al. (1980) were derived to solve this problem. These methods do provide a good approximation unless range restriction is very extreme.

Two Populations in Direct Range Restriction

It is critical to remember that we have two populations. This means that for any statistic there will usually be two different values, one for each population. For both variables, the means and standard deviations will differ between the two populations. This duality is especially important for the consideration of other artifacts because the artifact values might differ between the two populations.

Consider the reliability of the dependent variable. Direct selection on X will produce indirect selection on Y. This means that the reliability of Y will be smaller in the incumbent population than in the applicant population.

Consider artificial dichotomization. Because the median differs between the two populations, a median split in each group means a different cutoff in each population. Furthermore, if the distribution of X is normal in the applicant population, it will not be normal in the incumbent population; it will be the top of the normal distribution of the applicant population. Biserial correlation computations assume normality of X and will thus be in error when computed on the incumbent population (Hunter & Schmidt, 1990b).

Error of Measurement in the Independent Variable in Direct Range Restriction

Because the standard deviation of the predictor differs between the two populations, the reliability of X will differ between the two populations. However, there is a more serious problem here. The substantive nature of the direct selection process makes the meaning of "reliability" unclear for the incumbent data (Mendoza & Mumford, 1987).

Consider the applicant population. If we analyze applicant data, then we can make all the usual assumptions. In particular, we can safely make the critical assumption that true scores and errors will be uncorrelated. This assumption is required for all estimates of reliability (see Chapter 3). For published tests, we can usually find the applicant population reliability listed in the test manual; that is, the reliability computed on an unrestricted sample.

For the incumbent population, things are much different. Most researchers would assume that they could analyze the incumbent data to compute the reliability in the incumbent group. However, there is a severe problem in doing this: True scores and errors of measurement are correlated in the incumbent data for the scores that the incumbents were selected on (Mendoza & Mumford, 1987). We will show by example that in the incumbent data there is strong negative correlation between true scores and errors. Hence, reliability cannot be estimated in the incumbent group for the scores that were used in selection.

Before presenting the example, it is worth considering two very different designs to generate incumbent test data. The usual design takes the test data from the file, that is, uses the test scores that were used in the selection process. This is where the problems occur. Consider an alternative design that might initially appear to be a waste of time: Administer the test again at the time when the performance data are gathered. If the test is given again, then the new scores will have new errors of measurement. These new errors will be uncorrelated with the true scores, and therefore the usual methods of estimating reliability will be appropriate. Also, if one uses the well-known statistical formula to predict the reliability in the incumbent population from reliability in the applicant population (Equation 5.36), it is this reliability that is predicted, that is, the reliability in the new test data. This reliability estimate will not be correct for the original scores that were used in selection.

Consider the incumbent data for the first administration of the test. In the *applicant* population, the true scores and errors are uncorrelated. We will now use an example to show that, in the *incumbent* population, the measurement errors in these test scores are negatively correlated with the true scores.

For simplicity, we consider an applicant reliability of .50. This makes the measurement error variance (V_e) the same size as the true score variance (V_T). That is, if we use the classical equation $X = T + e$ for notation, then $V_e = V_T$.

$$\text{Special case: } r_{XX} = .50$$

$$V_e = V_T$$

$$V_X = V_T + V_e = 2V_T = 2V_e$$

Suppose we set the selection cutoff score at the median of the applicant population. That is, suppose we promote the top half of the applicants. If we delete the bottom half of a normal distribution, then the standard deviation in the restricted group (top half) is only 60% as large as the original standard deviation. That is, if the applicant standard deviation was $SD = 10$, then the incumbent standard deviation would be $SD = 6$. The variance is smaller by the square of .60 or .36. That is, if the applicant variance is 100, then the incumbent variance is 36.

At this point, the mathematics is made much easier if we introduce a new variable that has no substantive meaning whatsoever. This new variable is introduced solely for its mathematical convenience. Denote it by B. We will then compute its variance and its correlation with X. Define

$$B = T - e$$

Applicant population:

$$V_B = V_T + V_e$$

$$r_{BX} = 0$$

Because the reliability is .50, the new variable B is uncorrelated with the old variable X. This can be shown as follows:

$$r_{BX} = r_{(T+e)(T-e)} = \frac{\text{Cov}_{TT} - \text{Cov}_{ee}}{2(S_T^2 + S_e^2)} = \frac{S_T^2 - S_e^2}{2(S_T^2 + S_e^2)} = \frac{0}{2(S_T^2 + S_e^2)} = 0$$

In the applicant population, both variables are normally distributed and are independent (because they are uncorrelated).

Consider selection. B is independent of X. Thus, when we select on X, there will be no selection on B. Thus, in the incumbent population, the variance of B will be unchanged. We now use a trick to enable us to compute the correlation between T and e in the incumbent population. Assume the applicant standard deviation on X is 10. Note that, in our example, V_T and V_e are equal before selection, so selection operates symmetrically on them. That means that the two variances will still be equal after selection.

Incumbent population:

$$V_e = V_T$$

$$V_X = V_T + V_e + 2\text{Cov}_{Te} = 36$$

$$V_B = V_T + V_e - 2\text{Cov}_{Te} = 100$$

Add variances:

$$V_X + V_B = 2V_T + 2V_e = 36 + 100 = 136$$

$$V_T + V_e = (1/2)2(V_T + V_e) = (1/2)136 = 68$$

Because $V_e = V_T$, we have

$$V_T + V_T = V_e + V_e = 68$$

$$V_T = V_e = 68/2 = 34$$

Subtract variances:

$$V_X - V_B = 4\,\text{Cov}_{Te} = 36 - 100 = -64$$

$$\text{Cov}_{Te} = -16$$

Compute r_{Te}:

$$r_{Te} = \text{Cov}_{Te}/(SD_T SD_e) = -16(\sqrt{34}\sqrt{34}) = -16/34 = -.47$$

To summarize the example, in the whole applicant population, the measurement errors are uncorrelated with true scores. However, in the selected subpopulation of incumbents, the errors are correlated $-.47$. This large negative correlation makes impossible any reliability calculation computed on the incumbent data, because all procedures for estimating reliability assume that $r_{Te} = 0$. In fact, it is a problem to even define reliability in this context (Mendoza & Mumford, 1987). For example, the number r_{XT} now depends on the random measurement errors as well as on the true score variance. The conventional definition of reliability as the square of r_{XT}^2 is erroneous in this context.

For values of reliability other than .50, the general principle is the same. The trick variable B is more complicated for other values, but there is a trick variable for every value of the reliability. The problem vanishes only for a hypothetical perfect measure where there is no measurement error.

The Solution. The solution to this problem is to introduce the attenuation due to measurement error on the independent variable before considering range restriction (Mendoza & Mumford, 1987; Mendoza, Stafford, & Stauffer, 2000; Stauffer & Mendoza, 2001). That is, because range restriction is not a simple artifact, it is critical to consider the order in which range restriction is introduced into the attenuation process.

Applicant population:
Notation:
P = the performance rating true score,
T = the predictor true score,

$$\rho_{XP_a} = a\rho_{TP_a} \tag{5.11}$$

where $a = \sqrt{r_{XX_a}}$ and r_{XX_a} = the reliability of predictor scores in the applicant (unrestricted) population.

Incumbent population:

$$\rho_{XP_i} = a\rho_{XP_a} \tag{5.12}$$

where

$$\begin{aligned} a &= u_X/\sqrt{\{1 + (u_X^2 - 1)\,\rho_{XP_a}^2\}} \\ &= u_X/\sqrt{\{1 + (u_X^2 - 1)\,r_{XX_a}\rho_{TP_a}^2\}} \end{aligned} \tag{5.13}$$

The artifact multiplier for range restriction is complicated. The denominator contains not only ρ_{TP_a}, but also r_{XX_a}. That is, the value of the artifact multiplier depends not only on the extent of restriction (u_X) but also on the true effect size (ρ_{TP_a}) and the reliability of the independent variable in the unrestricted group (r_{XX_a}; Mendoza & Mumford, 1987; Stauffer & Mendoza, 2001).

Error of Measurement in the Dependent Variable in Direct Range Restriction

From a practical standpoint, the key question is how well the test predicts educational or job performance. No study measures performance perfectly. For measures with high construct validity, researchers should use an objectively scored work sample measure to assess job performance. This is extremely expensive, however, and few studies do this. So most studies use supervisor ratings of job performance, which suffer from both systematic error and considerable random measurement error. For our present purposes, we ignore systematic error and focus solely on random measurement error. That is, for our example we define "performance" to mean the job performance rating true score.

Job performance ratings will have two reliabilities: one for the applicant population and one for the incumbent population. In research domains other than selection, the reliability is usually estimated in the full population. Thus, we would usually know the reliability of the dependent variable in the unrestricted population. If so, then we can compute the attenuation of the correlation by adhering to the order principle for the independent variable: Introduce range restriction last.

Notation: To be consistent, from this point on, we use the following notation:

$Y =$ the performance rating observed score,
$P =$ the performance rating true score,
$X =$ the predictor observed score,
$T =$ the predictor true score,
Subscript $a =$ value estimated in the applicant (unrestricted) population,
Subscript $i =$ value estimated in incumbent (restricted) population,
$a =$ the attenuating factor due to measurement error in the predictor,
$b =$ the attenuating factor due to measurement error in the predictor,
$c =$ the attenuating factor due to range restriction.

Applicant population:

$$\rho_{TY_a} = a\rho_{TP_a} \quad \text{where } a = \sqrt{r_{YY_a}} \tag{5.14}$$

Incumbent population:

$$\rho_o = \rho_{TY_i} \tag{5.15}$$

$$\rho_{TY_i} = c\rho_{TY_a} \tag{5.16}$$

where

$$c = u_X / \sqrt{\{1 + (u_X^2 - 1)\rho_{TY_a}^2\}}$$
$$= u_X / \sqrt{\{1 + (u_X^2 - 1)r_{YY_a}\rho_{TP_a}^2\}}$$

Again, the artifact multiplier for range restriction is complicated. The denominator not only has ρ_{TP_a} in it, but it has r_{YY_a}, too. That is, the value of the artifact multiplier depends not only on the extent of restriction (u_X) but also on the true effect size (ρ_{TP_a}) and the reliability of the dependent variable in the unrestricted group (r_{YY_a}).

Error of Measurement in Both Variables: Direct Range Restriction

For research and theory testing purposes, we want to know the construct-level correlation. Thus, we would like to eliminate the effects of random measurement error in both the predictor and the criterion measure. The key to the attenuation formula is to consider range restriction last.

Applicant population:

$$\rho_{XY_a} = ab\rho_{TP_a} \quad \text{where } a = \sqrt{r_{XX_a}}, b = \sqrt{r_{YY_b}} \tag{5.17}$$

Incumbent population:

$$\rho_{XY_i} = c\, \rho_{XY_a} \tag{5.18}$$

where

$$c = u/\sqrt{\{1 + (u_X^2 - 1)\,\rho_{XY_a}^2\}}$$

$$= u/\sqrt{\{1 + (u_X^2 - 1) r_{XX_a} r_{YY_a} \rho_{TP_a}^2\}}$$

The artifact multiplier for range restriction is even more complicated here. The denominator not only has ρ_{TP_a} in it, but it has both r_{XX_a} and r_{YY_a} as well. That is, the value of the artifact multiplier depends not only on the extent of restriction (u_X) but also on the true effect size (ρ_{TP_a}), the reliability of the independent variable (r_{XX_a}), and the reliability of the dependent variable (r_{YY_a}).

Meta-Analysis in Direct Range Restriction: Previous Work

There have been three research teams that have worked on methods of meta-analysis that include range restriction: ourselves, Callender and Osburn (1980), and Raju and Burke (1983). The model for meta-analysis for all three teams has been the model discussed previously: the model for direct range restriction. There is no problem with that model if range restriction is indeed direct restriction. The problem with this model is that it has been used for domains where the range restriction is indirect. In a later section, we will show that the attenuation formula given previously does not hold for indirect range restriction.

One of the most useful contributions from the Callender-Osburn (1980) study is an equation for estimating the artifact multiplier for range restriction.

$$\text{Notation: } c = u_X/\sqrt{\{1 + (u_X^2 - 1)\, r_{XX_a} r_{YY_a} \rho_{TP_a}^2\}}$$

$$\text{Identity: } c = u_X/\sqrt{\{u_X^2 + \rho_{XY_i}^2 - u_X^2 \rho_{XY_i}^2\}}$$

This algebraic identity discovered by Callender and Osburn is true for the attenuation model for direct range restriction. However, this identity does not hold for indirect range restriction. Furthermore, it can be very inaccurate for indirect range restriction, as shown later.

Educational and Employment Selection

In educational selection, the dependent variable is usually grade point average (often first-year grade point average). In personnel selection, the dependent variable is almost always either job performance or some job behavior such as training performance, accidents, theft, or turnover. Consider performance ratings. All research on performance ratings has been of necessity conducted on incumbents. For example, a review of inter-rater reliability findings (Viswesvaran et al., 1996) found the average inter-rater reliability of a multiscale rating scale to be .47. This is the incumbent reliability and should not be used in the attenuation formula presented as the attenuation model for meta-analysis. The applicant reliability is higher.

In principle, the traditional formula relating reliability in two populations (usually called the "homogeneity formula") could be used to compute the applicant reliability from the incumbent reliability:

u_Y = incumbent SD_Y/applicant SD_Y
r_{YY_i} = incumbent reliability
r_{YY_a} = applicant reliability

$$r_{YY_a} = 1 - u_Y^2(1 - r_{YY_i}) \qquad (5.19)$$

The problem with this formula is that it requires knowledge of the applicant standard deviation for performance ratings (because $u_Y = SD_{Y_i}/SD_{Y_a}$). Because we have data for job performance ratings only for incumbents, this standard deviation cannot be directly estimated from the data. However, there is another formula that can be used to compute r_{YY_a} (Brogden, 1968; Schmidt, Hunter, & Urry, 1976):

$$r_{YY_a} = 1 - \frac{1 - r_{YY_i}}{1 - r_{XY_i}^2[1 - S_{X_a}^2/S_{X_i}^2]} \qquad (5.20)$$

where r_{XY_i} is the observed correlation between X and Y in the incumbent sample. (Callender and Osburn, 1980, p. 549, present a mathematically identical formula.) Consider a realistic case. Let $u_X = SD_{X_i}/SD_{X_a} = .70$, $r_{XY_i} = .25$, and $r_{YY_i} = .47$. Equation (5.20) then yields $r_{YY_a} = .50$. Hence, the reliability of ratings of job performance would be .03 (6%) higher in the absence of range restriction. Equation (5.20) provides an estimate of r_{YY_a}, and this makes possible use of Equation (5.18). However, it is possible to develop a hybrid model that requires only an estimate of r_{YY_i}. This model, described in the next section, is the one on which corrections in meta-analysis programs are based.

A Hybrid Model

In most research domains, it is the reliabilities in the unrestricted group that are known. The conventional method (Equation [5.18]) works for these domains. For domains like personnel psychology, the dependent variable reliability is typically known only for the incumbent population. In this case, we can analyze the data using a different model, one that introduces the criterion measurement artifact *after* range restriction. This is possible because the random measurement errors in the dependent variable (Y) come into being after the selection process and are not affected by the direct selection on the independent variable (X).

Hybrid model for direct range restriction:
Applicant population:

$$\rho_{XP_a} = a\rho_{TP_a} \text{ where } a = \sqrt{r_{XX_a}} \quad (5.21)$$

Incumbent population:

$$\rho_{XP_i} = c\rho_{XP_a} \text{ where } c = u_X / \sqrt{\{1 + (u_X^2 - 1)\,\rho_{XP_a}^2\}} \quad (5.22)$$

$$\rho_{XY_i} = b\rho_{XP_i} \text{ where } b = \sqrt{r_{YY_i}} \quad (5.23)$$

Correction for attenuation in this model proceeds in three steps. We start with ρ_{XY_i} and correct it for criterion unreliability using the incumbent reliability. The corrected correlation is ρ_{XP_i}. This correlation is then be corrected for range restriction. That correlation is ρ_{XP_a}. If the researcher desires true score (construct level) correlations, the value for ρ_{XP_a} is then corrected for predictor unreliability using the applicant reliability r_{XX_a}. The resulting correlation is the desired estimate of ρ_{TP} in the applicant population. This sequence of corrections is used to calculate $\bar{\rho}$ in the artifact distribution meta-analysis program INTNL-D, which is used for direct range restriction and is described in Chapter 4 and in the Appendix to this book.

Meta-Analysis Correcting Correlations Individually: Direct Range Restriction

In addition to artifact distribution–based meta-analysis, meta-analysis can also be conducted correcting each observed correlation individually for measurement error and range restriction. This procedure, described in Chapter 3, is used less frequently because typically not all observed study correlations are reported with u_X values and estimates of reliability for both the independent and dependent variables. However, in such cases, the procedure for correcting each individual study correlation is the one described here. Using the symbolism described previously, this three-step procedure can be combined into one equation.

Correction formula:

$$\rho_{TP_a} = \frac{U_X \rho_{XY_i}}{[r_{XX_a}[r_{YY_i} + U_X^2 \rho_{XY_i}^2 - \rho_{XY_i}^2]]^{\frac{1}{2}}} \quad (5.24)$$

where $U_X = 1/u_X$. The meta-analysis is then performed on the corrected correlations (the ρ_{TP_a} estimates) using the procedures described in Chapter 3. This is the procedure used in the Windows-based program VG6-D described in Chapter 3 and in the Appendix.

Artifact Distribution Meta-Analysis: Direct Range Restriction

Artifact distribution–based meta-analysis can be conducted in the three steps described previously for the hybrid model correction. We start with the results of the "bare bones" meta-analysis, that is, the estimated mean and standard deviation of ρ_{XY_i}. We can then use the multiplicative methods described in Chapter 4 to do three meta-analyses that correspond to the three steps in correction.

The first step is to use the mean and standard deviation of ρ_{XY_i} to compute the mean and standard deviation of ρ_{XP_i}. This is a meta-analysis correcting for the simple artifact of unreliability in the dependent variable. The incumbent reliability information is used in this analysis. Methods for these calculations were presented in the earlier discussion of simple artifacts and in Chapter 4.

The second step is to use the mean and standard deviation of ρ_{XP_i} to compute the mean and standard deviation of ρ_{XP_a}. This is a meta-analysis correcting for range restriction as the only artifact.

The third step is to use the mean and standard deviation of ρ_{XP_a} to compute the mean and standard deviation of ρ_{TP_a}. This is a meta-analysis correcting for the simple artifact of predictor unreliability. The applicant reliability information is used in this analysis. Methods for these calculations were presented in the earlier section on simple artifacts and in Chapter 4.

In addition to these methods for artifact distribution meta-analysis under direct range restriction, Chapter 4 also describes the interactive method. The interactive method is more difficult to present mathematically but has been found to be slightly more accurate in computer simulation methods. Therefore, it is the interactive method that we have programmed. The computer program INTNL-D applies the interactive method for data with direct range restriction. This program follows the required order presented here for disattenuating (correcting) for artifacts (and also the required reverse order when $\bar{\rho}_{TP_a}$ is attenuated in the internal program calculations described in Chapter 4).

Indirect Range Restriction

The range restriction correction formula used in our work in the past (prior to 2002) and in the work of Callender and Osburn (1980) and Raju and Burke (1983) has been Thorndike's (1949) Case II formula. This formula assumes direct range restriction (truncation) on the predictor. It has long been known that if range restriction is indirect rather than direct this formula will undercorrect (see, e.g., Linn, Harnisch, & Dunbar, 1981b), and we repeatedly pointed out this undercorrection (Schmidt, Hunter, & Pearlman, 1981; Schmidt, Hunter, Pearlman, & Hirsh, 1985, p. 751; Schmidt et al., 1993, p. 7). If some or all of the primary studies in a meta-analysis are characterized by indirect range restriction, the use of this range correction formula will lead to undercorrection. Until recently, no procedure was available that could be used to correct for the most common case of indirect range restriction. Hence, the Thorndike (1949) Case II correction formula was used by default. Although we knew that this formula undercorrected, we thought that the undercorrection was modest (e.g., 2% to 5%). It is not.

Historically, a common context in industrial/organizational psychology has been an organization that has been using its own selection methods but is considering moving to the use of cognitive ability tests for future selection and wants to conduct a local validity study. A concurrent validation study is conducted: The test is given to incumbent workers at the same time as performance is measured. Those data are used to estimate the true effect size (operational validity) in the applicant group. Range restriction is indirect in cases of this sort. In fact, range restriction is indirect in almost all validity studies in employment and education (Thorndike, 1949, p. 175). For example, in the U.S. Department of Labor database on the General Aptitude Test Battery (GATB) (Hunter, 1983b; Hunter & Hunter, 1984), all 515 validity studies were concurrent in nature, and hence, range restriction was indirect. Range restriction is often indirect even in predictive studies: The tests to be validated are often given to *incumbents*, with the criterion measures being taken months or years later, making the study technically predictive. In our research over the years, we have rarely seen a study in which there had been direct selection on the predictor(s) being validated—the only kind of study for which the Case II range correction formula for direct range restriction would not undercorrect. (In some cases, selection is based on a composite that includes the predictor and several other variables [e.g., in educational selection, test scores, grade point average, letters of recommendation, and awards]. This situation is closer to indirect than direct range restriction [Linn et al., 1981b].)

If the Case II range correction formula undercorrects, then why has this undercorrection not shown up in computer simulation studies? As noted most recently by Hall and Brannick (2002), computer simulation studies have shown that these methods are quite accurate. In fact, estimates of $\bar{\rho}$ seem to be particularly accurate. The answer is that all computer simulation studies have assumed (and programmed in) only direct range restriction. Except for Le (2003), there have been no computer simulation studies of meta-analysis methods based on indirect range restriction. Hence, these earlier simulation studies, by definition, cannot detect the undercorrection that occurs when range restriction is indirect.

For indirect range restriction, the selection is based on characteristics other than the predictor itself. For example, suppose an organization considers a high school diploma critical to high job performance. If only high school graduates are hired, then the bottom 20% of the intelligence distribution will be very much underrepresented. This would lead to a lower standard deviation of intelligence test scores, an effect very much like the effect of direct selection.

Stauffer (1996) noted that indirect range restriction leads to a change in the slope of the regression line of the dependent variable onto test scores. For direct range restriction, there is no such change. This is important because the Case II formula for range restriction assumes there is no difference in slope between the two populations. We later found that Mendoza and Mumford (1987) had also made this important point earlier.

There is one situation where Stauffer's point would be moot. If the test were perfectly reliable, the slope would not be changed by indirect range restriction and the formulas for direct range restriction would still be appropriate and provide accurate corrected values. We will discuss this (hypothetical) situation in a later section. That is, if the predictor were measured perfectly, then the only effect of indirect range restriction would be to reduce the standard deviation of the predictor, and the Case II direct range restriction correction formula would be accurate. This condition is hypothetical because there is always measurement error.

The difference between direct and indirect restriction is this. Unlike indirect selection, direct selection is produced by direct use of test scores. Because selection is made on observed test scores, errors of measurement are part of the selection process in direct selection. That is, when people are selected on test scores, they are selected partly on their true scores and partly on their measurement errors. For indirect selection, scores on the test of interest are never considered and so errors of measurement in those test scores have no effect on the selection process. The impact of indirect selection is on the predictor true score T; there is no effect on the errors of measurement in the observed scores.

A Causal Model for Indirect Range Restriction

The selection process itself receives little description in the mathematics of the psychometric literature. We suspect that this is the cause of the mathematical errors that have been made in connection with range restriction corrections. We attempt to remedy this omission here.

The selection process is a decision process. The organization has certain information about an applicant. This information is converted into a judgment as to the suitability of the applicant. The organization then hires top down on its suitability judgment "scale."

In recent years, there has been much study of such organization decisions using methods called "policy capturing." The assumption is that there is an evaluation variable that is implicitly constructed by the organization and that variable is what the organization uses to make decisions (Linn et al., 1981b). For selection, we call this variable "suitability," and we denote it by S. Most current research on policy capturing assumes that S is a linear combination of the attribute information available to the organization, but this is not necessary for our model. Indeed, those who have worked with police background investigations have built models that incorporate strong nonlinear facets such as "fatal flaws" (e.g., conviction for a felony).

For direct range restriction, the selection variable S is identical to the predictor observed score X. So, for direct range restriction, our mathematical models do incorporate the selection process itself. For indirect range restriction, S can be very different from X.

We now have five variables in our model: the selection variable S, the predictor true score T, the predictor observed score X, the criterion true score P, and the criterion observed score Y. The path diagram for the applicant population is presented in Figure 5.1.

For indirect range restriction, we assume that the selection process reduces the standard deviation for the predictor variable. This is represented in a path diagram by an arrow from the selection variable S to the predictor variable. We have two predictor variables: the true score T and the observed score X. There is effectively

Figure 5.1 Path diagram for the applicant population in indirect range

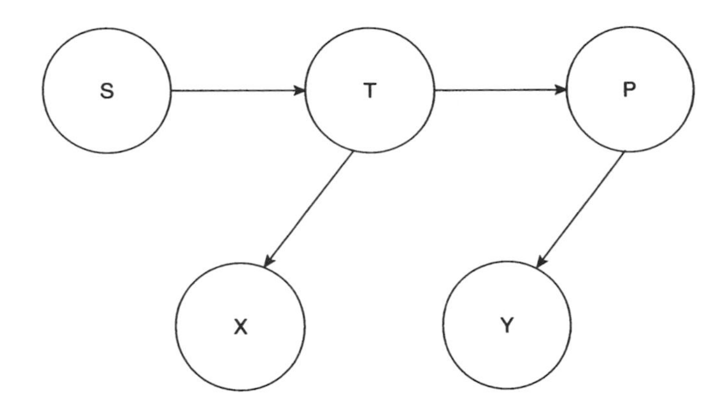

NOTE: S = the suitability composite used by the organization to select applicants; X = the predictor (e.g., test scores); T = true scores on the predictor X; Y = the measure of job performance; and P = the true score on Y.

no way that an organization could predict the errors of measurement in the predictor scores; that is, selection on S cannot be correlated with the measurement errors in X. Thus, in our model, we make the usual assumption that the arrow of causal impact goes from construct to construct rather than from observed score to observed score.

Consider then our path diagram for indirect selection. There is an arrow from S to T. There is also an arrow from T to X, but this arrow represents the predictor measurement process rather than the selection process. Because errors of measurement do not enter the selection process, there is no arrow from S to X.

The consideration of X as a potential predictor is a substantive theory that assumes a causal relationship between the predictor variable and the criterion variable. In most cases, the predictor is considered to be an independent variable for the criterion variable, which is thus the dependent variable. For simplicity, we make this assumption in our diagram, though the causal arrow need not be in this direction.

The criterion variable is also represented by two distinct variables: the true score P and the observed score Y. The causal model for the usual substantive theory represents the causal effect as an arrow from one true score to the other, that is, from T to P. The measurement process is represented by an arrow from P to Y.

Our model now has an arrow from S to T and from T to P. So there is an indirect causal effect of selection on the criterion variable. Our model makes the assumption that there is no other arrow connecting S and P. This corresponds to the assumption that the selection process does not tap any characteristic that would predict the criterion variable for reasons other than those measured by the current predictor variable X. If this assumption is violated, our method for correcting for indirect range restriction will undercorrect. However, the values produced are still more accurate (or less inaccurate) than those produced by use of the correction for direct range restriction.

Range Restriction on S

The most fundamental restriction is on the selection variable S. The organization hires top down on S, creating direct range restriction on S. If S has a normal distribution, we can compute u_S from the selection ratio (the percentage of applicants hired).

Assume that the percentage selected is Q. Then if S is scored in standard scores (z scores), there is a normal cutoff score c, called $P(c)$, which cuts off the top Q applicants. For example, the cutoff score for the top 10% is 1.28. The mean on S for those selected can be computed from the normal density function at c:

$$\text{Cutoff at } c\text{: } \mu_S = \text{Mean} = P(c)/Q \qquad (5.25)$$

$$\text{Example: } c = 1.28 : \mu_S = P(1.28)/.10 = 1.76$$

The variance of those selected can be computed by

$$\text{Cutoff at } c\text{: } s_S^2 = 1 - \mu_S(\mu_S - c) \qquad (5.26)$$

$$\text{Example: } c = 1.28 : s_S^2 = 1 - 1.76(1.76 - 1.28) = .1552$$

The standard deviation of those selected is the range restriction ratio for S:

$$u_S = \sqrt{s_S^2}$$

$$\text{Example: Cutoff at } c\text{: } u_S = \sqrt{.1552} = .39$$

(Note: If all calculations are carried out to six places, this figure is .41.)

Range Restriction on Other Variables in Indirect Range Restriction

The selection process can be regarded as direct selection on S. What effect would this have on the path diagram for the incumbent population? Substantive reasoning shows that the *qualitative* path diagram for the incumbent population would be identical to the diagram for the applicant population. However, the *quantitative* path diagram for standard scores would change drastically. The path coefficient from T to P is the correlation between T and P and that is the target of formulas for correction for range restriction. This path coefficient is smaller in the incumbent population.

Selection reduces the standard deviations of all five variables in the path diagram. The only comparison ratio computed in traditional research is the u ratio for the observed predictor score X, that is, u_X. For direct range restriction, this is appropriate because u_X describes the key impact of selection. Range restriction on the other variables is represented by u_S, u_T, u_P, and u_Y.

The strongest indirect restriction is on the predictor true score T. The range restriction on T is caused directly by the range restriction on S. If the regression of T on S is linear, then we can compute u_T from u_S. Scientists prefer numbers that are descriptively meaningful, so u is defined in terms of the ratio of standard deviations. Statistical formulas care little for scientific preferences and are simple only for variances. One result of this is that the simple formulas for range restriction are formulas for u^2 rather than formulas for u.

The restriction on T is caused directly by the restriction on S. The formulas that relate them can be shown for either applicant population or incumbent population.

Applicant population:

$$\text{Restriction on } T\text{: } u_T^2 = \rho_{ST_a}^2 u_S^2 - \rho_{ST_a}^2 + 1 \tag{5.27}$$

Incumbent population:

$$\text{Restriction on } T\text{: } u_T^2 = u_S^2 / \{u_S^2 - \rho_{ST_i}^2 u_S^2 + \rho_{ST_i}^2\} \tag{5.27a}$$

Similarly, the restriction on X is caused directly by the restriction on T. The formulas that relate them are the following:

Applicant population:

$$\text{Restriction on } X\text{: } u_X^2 = \rho_{TX_a}^2 u_T^2 - \rho_{TX_a}^2 + 1 \tag{5.28}$$

Incumbent population:

$$\text{Restriction on } X\text{: } u_X^2 = u_T^2 / \{u_T^2 - \rho_{TX_i}^2 u_T^2 + \rho_{TX_i}^2\} \tag{5.28a}$$

The restriction on P is caused directly by the restriction on T. The formulas that relate them are the following:

Applicant population:

$$\text{Restriction on } P\text{: } u_P^2 = \rho_{TP_a}^2 u_T^2 - \rho_{TP_a}^2 + 1 \tag{5.29}$$

Incumbent population:

$$\text{Restriction on } P\text{: } u_P^2 = u_T^2 / \{u_T^2 - \rho_{TP_i}^2 u_T^2 + \rho_{TP_i}^2\} \tag{5.29a}$$

The restriction on Y is caused directly by the restriction on P. The formulas that relate them are the following:

Applicant population:

$$\text{Restriction on } Y\text{: } u_Y^2 = \rho_{PY_a}^2 u_P^2 - \rho_{PY_a}^2 + 1 \tag{5.30}$$

Incumbent population:

$$\text{Restriction on } Y\text{: } u_Y^2 = u_P^2 / \{u_P^2 - \rho_{PY_i}^2 u_P^2 + \rho_{PY_i}^2\} \tag{5.30a}$$

Estimation in Indirect Range Restriction

If an explicit policy-capturing study has not been done, then S is not observed and neither is u_S. Fortunately, we do not need this value for our purposes. The critical value is the restriction ratio for the predictor true score T. This is not observed, but it can be computed from the observed value for u_X. Equation (5.28) relates u_X to u_T:

$$\text{Restriction on } X\text{: } u_X^2 = \rho_{TX_a}^2 u_T^2 - \rho_{TX_a}^2 + 1$$

In this equation, $\rho_{TX_a}^2$ is the applicant reliability of the predictor variable, r_{XX_a}. Equation (5.28) can be rewritten as

$$\text{Restriction on } X: u_X^2 = r_{XX_a} u_T^2 - r_{XX_a} + 1$$

This equation can be solved for u_T:

$$u_T^2 = \{u_X^2 - (1 - r_{XX_a})\}/r_{XX_a} \quad (5.31)$$

Equation (5.31) is (the square of) Equation (3.16) in Chapter 3. This formula may appear strange at first, but it is important to remember that the smallest possible value for u_X is *not* 0. For direct range restriction, u_X could go as low as 0 (because SD_{X_i} could be 0 and therefore $SD_{X_i}/SD_{X_a} = u_X = 0$). For indirect range restriction, errors of measurement are not included in the selection process, so selection produces no change in the measurement error variance. Thus, the restricted variance of X is always at least as large as the measurement error variance of X, and the minimum value for u_X is $\sqrt{1 - r_{XX_a}}$.

As an example, consider the U.S. Employment Service (USES) database analyzed by Hunter (1983b; Hunter & Hunter, 1984). The average value for u_X across 425 jobs was .67. The applicant reliability (r_{XX_a}) of the GATB measure of intelligence used was a constant .81. The average value of u_T is

$$u_T^2 = \{.67^2 - (1 - .81)\}/.81 = .3196$$

$$u_T = \sqrt{.3106} = .56$$

The mean value of u_T is .56 and is considerably smaller than the mean value of u_X (mean $u_X = .67$). This means that taking u_X as a measure of range restriction leads to a consistent understatement of the extent of actual range restriction and an underestimation of the attenuating effects of range restriction.

The finding for the example can be generalized: The value of u_T will always show more extreme range restriction than the value of u_X. That is, u_T is always smaller than u_X.

The Correlation Between *S* and *T* in Indirect Range Restriction

The correlation between S and T is a measure of the extent to which the organization indirectly relies on T in its selection scheme when it selects on S. As it happens, that correlation can be computed from the range restriction values for S and T; that is, from u_S and u_T.

The extent of range restriction on the predictor true score depends on the extent of range restriction on S and on the size of the correlation between S and T in the applicant population, as shown in Equation (5.27):

$$\text{Restriction on } T\text{: } u_T^2 = \rho_{ST_a}^2 u_S^2 - \rho_{ST_a}^2 + 1$$

This equation can be solved for ρ_{ST_a}:

$$u_T^2 - 1 = (u_S^2 - 1)\,\rho_{ST_a}^2$$

$$\rho_{ST_a}^2 = (u_T^2 - 1)/(u_S^2 - 1) = (1 - u_T^2)/(1 - u_S^2) \qquad (5.32)$$

Consider the USES example. If an organization selects the top 10%, then the range restriction on S is $u_S = .41$. If its average range restriction on T is $u_T = .56$, then the applicant population correlation between S and T is

$$\rho_{ST_a} = \sqrt{\{[1 - u_T^2]/[1 - u_S^2]\}} = \sqrt{\{[1 - .56^2]/[1 - .41^2]\}}$$

$$= \sqrt{\{.6864/.8319\}} = .76$$

If the average selection ratio for the organizations studied by the USES were .10, then $\rho_{ST} = .76$ would be the average correlation between suitability and intelligence. If the average selection ratio is smaller than 10%, the average correlation would be lower. (The actual average selection ratio S in this data set is, of course, unknown.)

The Attenuation Model in Indirect Range Restriction

The easiest context in which to understand the attenuation model in indirect range restriction is concurrent validation. In such a study, it is clear that selection precedes measurement on both X and Y. Thus, range restriction is the first artifact that affects the data, and measurement error is added later for the incumbent population. (In a predictive validation study, under conditions of indirect range restriction, it is less obvious, but equally true, that the selection causally precedes measurement even though it need not occur first in time.)

Applicant population:
Range restriction on T: u_T

$$\rho_{TP_i} = a\,\rho_{TP_a} \text{ where } a = u_T/\sqrt{\{u_T^2\rho_{TP_a}^2 + 1 - \rho_{TP_a}^2\}} \qquad (5.33)$$

Incumbent population:
Measurement error in the predictor (independent variable):

$$\rho_{XP_i} = a\,\rho_{TP_i} \text{ where } a = \sqrt{r_{XX_i}}$$

Measurement error in the criterion (dependent variable):

$$\rho_{XY_1} = a\,\rho_{XP_i} \text{ where } a = \sqrt{r_{YY_i}}$$

For the educational or employment selection psychologist, this model is fortunate in that the needed dependent variable reliability information is that for the restricted population, and this reliability coefficient can be computed from the data on hand (i.e., the restricted data).

Predictor Measurement Error in Indirect Range Restriction

For predictor measurement error, this model provides an unpleasant surprise: The incumbent reliability may be considerably lower than the applicant reliability. We need a convenient formula relating the two reliabilities. As shown next, the incumbent reliability can be estimated from either range restriction on u_T or range restriction on u_X:

Estimating Incumbent Reliability From u_T

The trick to finding a formula is to shift from thinking about the reliability to thinking about the quality of the predictor (i.e., the square root of the reliability). The quality is a correlation, that is, ρ_{TX}. This correlation will change between applicant and incumbent populations due to range restriction on T. Thus, the formula for the incumbent quality is the same range restriction formula as for the effect size ρ_{TP}.

Applicant population:
Predictor quality: ρ_{TX_a}
Range restriction on T: u_T
Incumbent population:
Predictor quality: ρ_{TX_i}

$$\rho_{TX_i} = a\rho_{TX_a} \text{ where } a = u_T / \sqrt{\{u_T^2 \rho_{TX_a}^2 + 1 - \rho_{TX_a}^2\}} \quad (5.34)$$

Reliability results:
Applicant population reliability: r_{XX_a}
Incumbent population reliability: r_{XX_i}
Formula:

$$r_{XX_i} = \rho_{TX_i}^2 = a^2 r_{XX_a} \quad (5.35)$$

In the case of the USES database, the applicant reliability is $r_{XX_a} = .81$ and the quality is therefore $\rho_{TX_a} = .90$. As noted earlier, $u_T = .56$. Range restriction on T causes the quality to drop to $\rho_{TX_i} = .756$, which means the incumbent reliability is only $(.756)^2 = .57$. That is, a test that has a reliability of .81 in the applicant population has only a modest reliability of .57 in the incumbent population.

There is another subtle problem inherent in the shift from applicant reliability to incumbent reliability: a change in variance. For the USES database, the same test was used in all studies. Thus, the applicant reliability r_{XX_a} is a constant .81. However, the degree of range restriction varied from one study to the next. This causes the incumbent test quality to vary from one study to the next. This means that incumbent reliability varies even though applicant reliability is constant. Variation across studies in range restriction creates variation in incumbent reliabilities. [The computer program INTNL-I (see Chapter 4 and the Appendix) corrects for this variation.]

Estimating Incumbent Reliability From u_X

This can be achieved using the reverse of Equation (5.19):

$$r_{XX_i} = 1 - \frac{S^2_{X_a}(1 - r_{XX_a})}{S^2_{X_i}}$$
$$= 1 - U^2_X(1 - r_{XX_a}) \quad (5.36)$$

where $U_X = 1/u_X$. Equation (5.36) is equivalent to Equation (5.35) and is more convenient to use. In cases in which the independent variable reliability estimates are from the restricted group, one can skip this step and go straight to Equation (5.37).

Meta-Analysis Correcting Each Correlation Individually: Indirect Range Restriction

The following procedures are used in the computer program VG6-I (labeled "Correlations—Correcting Individually"; see the Appendix). When meta-analysis is performed on study correlations corrected individually for the effects of all three artifacts, the first requirement is a procedure for making those corrections. In the case of indirect range restriction, this procedure is as follows.

First, convert r_{XX_a} to r_{XX_i} using Equation (5.35) or (5.36).

Second, correct the observed correlation in the restricted group (ρ_{XY_i}) using r_{XX_i} and r_{YY_i}:

$$\rho_{TP_i} = \rho_{XY_i}/(r_{XX_i} r_{YY_i})^{1/2} \quad (5.37)$$

Third, correct this value for range restriction using $U_T = 1/u_T$ in the equation for range restriction correction in the case of *direct* range restriction:

$$\rho_{TP_a} = \frac{U_T \rho_{TP_i}}{[1 + U^2_T \rho^2_{TP_i} - \rho^2_{TP_i}]^{1/2}} \quad (5.38)$$

This procedure relies on the fact that, in the absence of measurement error, the formula for correcting for direct range restriction is accurate in cases in which range restriction is indirect. In this procedure, the measurement error is first removed and then the formula for correcting for direct range restriction is applied. After each study correlation is corrected in this manner, the meta-analysis is performed on the corrected correlations using the methods described in Chapter 3. Unfortunately, this procedure can often not be used because data from primary studies often do not include the necessary information. As a result, meta-analysis must usually be conducted using distributions of artifacts compiled from the studies that report them (as discussed in Chapter 4).

Artifact Distribution Meta-Analysis for Indirect Range Restriction

The attenuation equations presented earlier act as a model for artifact distribution meta-analysis in the context of indirect range restriction. This model is very different from the model for direct range restriction, which has dominated the literature.

Assume that a bare-bones meta-analysis has been done. The bare-bones meta-analysis converts the mean and standard deviation of sample correlations (r_{XY_i}) into a mean and standard deviation for population attenuated correlations (ρ_{XY_i}) by correcting for sampling error. Thus, we have estimated values for the mean and standard deviation of study population correlations, that is, the mean and standard deviation of ρ_{XY_i} in the notation of this book. That is, the bare-bones meta-analysis provides the mean and standard deviation of attenuated population correlations (ρ_{XY} for the incumbent populations).

The purpose of subsequent steps in the meta-analysis is to remove the effects of three artifacts: range restriction, error of measurement in the criterion (dependent) variable, and error of measurement in the predictor (independent) variable.

The formulas for artifact distribution meta-analysis can be complicated. In the interests of making the equations understandable, it is important to make the equations as simple as possible. This means that there is considerable gain in shifting from reliabilities to qualities. For the researcher, this means compiling data on quality rather than reliability. That is, when a reliability estimate is found in the literature, it should be converted to the corresponding quality by taking the square root. This should be done for both the predictor and the criterion measures.

For indirect range restriction, it is easiest if predictor reliability information is from applicant data. On the other hand, criterion reliability data is easiest to use if it is incumbent reliability data. Both of these conventions fit the usual data-gathering situation for educational and employment selection. That is, typically reliability information is available for the unrestricted population for the independent variable and for the dependent variable in the restricted population.

The crucial value for indirect range restriction is u_T rather than u_X. If an empirical estimate of u_X is accompanied by the corresponding estimate of unrestricted predictor reliability in the applicant group, then the corresponding estimate of u_T can be computed for that source using Equation (5.31). (If values of u_X are given independently from values for the predictor reliability, approximate estimates of u_T can be obtained using the average predictor reliability to convert each value of u_X to an estimated value for u_T.)

The input artifact data for the multiplicative method of meta-analysis is three sets of means and standard deviations: the means and standard deviations of applicant predictor quality, incumbent criterion quality, and range restriction (u_T).

The currently dominant notation for our context is the Callender-Osburn (1980) product notation:

$$\rho_0 = abc\rho_{TP_a}$$

where a is a multiplier for predictor measurement error, b is a multiplier for criterion measurement error, and c is a multiplier for range restriction. This symbolism was proposed for the direct range restriction model but can also be used for the model for indirect range restriction. However, the multipliers are quite different. In the model for direct range restriction, a and b are simple while c is complicated. When we use this notation for indirect range restriction, b is still simple but a is as complicated as c. Indeed, this further complication renders the Callender-Osburn multiplicative method of analysis so inaccurate that it must be abandoned, as explained later.

For direct range restriction, the multiplier *b* is the applicant quality of the criterion variable (ρ_{PY_a}). This is simple mathematics but causes problems in practice because the data on the criterion variable are usually incumbent data. For indirect range restriction, *b* is the incumbent quality of the criterion variable (ρ_{PY_i}). Thus, incumbent data can be used directly to estimate the mean and standard deviation for *b*.

For direct range restriction, the *a* multiplier is the applicant quality of the predictor measure (ρ_{TX_a}). For indirect range restriction, *a* is the *incumbent* quality of the predictor measure (ρ_{TX_i}). In the context of range restriction, that is *not* a simple shift. The formula converting applicant quality to incumbent quality is the same range restriction equation as is used for the effect size. In particular, *a* depends on u_X as well as on the applicant quality. This makes *a* as complicated as *c*.

For direct range restriction, the multiplier *c* is complicated in two ways, as discussed in the earlier section on direct range restriction. First, the range restriction formula is nonlinear, which causes problems in computing means and standard deviations ($\bar{\rho}$ and SD_ρ). Second, the range restriction multiplier is computed *after* measurement attenuation and so the multiplier is affected not only by the effect size but also by the qualities of the predictor and criterion variables.

For indirect range restriction, the multiplier *c* is less complicated, but it is still nonlinear and mathematically difficult for that reason. In fact, because the relevant range restriction parameter is u_T rather than u_X, the nonlinearity is greater. However, because range restriction is the first artifact, the multiplier *c* is *not* affected by measurement error. For indirect range restriction, the multiplier *c* is determined only by range restriction (u_T) and the true effect size. However, the fact that *c* is determined by the true effect size rather than the attenuated effect size means that the nonlinearity of the range restriction equation is again more extreme.

The big problem for the *abc* notation lies in the relationship between the multipliers *a* and *c*. For direct range restriction, *a* is the simple applicant predictor quality (ρ_{TX_a}) and there is only a small correlation between *a* and *c*. For indirect range restriction, the formula for *a* is the same range restriction formula as for *c* and there is a nearly perfect correlation between *a* and *c*. This high correlation between *a* and *c* rules out use of the Callender-Osburn multiplicative method of analysis—because that method assumes independence of *a*, *b*, and *c*. We now demonstrate this high correlation.

A New Format for the Attenuation Formula

It is useful to express the attenuation equation in a different format from the *abc* format.

We first shift from reliability notation to quality notation. The letter "*q*" is used for quality.

$$q_X = \text{quality of predictor } X = \rho_{TX} = \sqrt{r_{XX}}$$

$$q_Y = \text{quality of criterion } Y = \rho_{PY} = \sqrt{r_{YY}}$$

In range restriction models, all parameters have two values, one for each population. Our notation for this is to attach the subscript "a" to values for the applicant population and the subscript "i" to values for the incumbent population. Using this notation, the incumbent attenuation formula can be written as

$$\rho_{XY_i} = q_{X_i} q_{Y_i} \rho_{TP_i} \tag{5.39}$$

The applicant attenuation formula is

$$\rho_{XY_a} = q_{X_a} q_{Y_a} \rho_{TP_a}$$

All three of these values will be different in the two populations. The overall attenuation formula we want is one that relates ρ_{TP_a} and ρ_{XY_i}.

Consider again the attenuation formula for measurement error in the incumbent group:

$$\rho_{XY_i} = q_{Y_i} q_{X_i} \rho_{TP_i}$$

where

$$q_{X_i} = \frac{u_T q_{X_a}}{\sqrt{u_T^2 q_{X_a}^2 + 1 - q_{X_a}^2}}$$

and

$$\rho_{TP_i} = \frac{u_T \rho_{TP_a}}{\sqrt{u_T^2 \rho_{TP_a}^2 + 1 - \rho_{TP_a}^2}}$$

This yields the following attenuation formula:

$$\rho_{XY_i} = q_{Y_i} \frac{u_T q_{X_a}}{\sqrt{u_T^2 q_{X_a}^2 + 1 - q_{X_a}^2}} \frac{u_T \rho_{TP_a}}{\sqrt{u_T^2 \rho_{TP_a}^2 + 1 - \rho_{TP_a}^2}} \tag{5.40}$$

Note the double occurrence of the range restriction expression, first for q_{X_i} and then for ρ_{TP_i}. This produces a major violation of the independence assumptions for these two terms.

The aim of meta-analysis is to estimate the mean and standard deviation of true effect sizes. Computer simulation tests of the model for direct range restriction show that there is little error in estimating the mean effect size. The mean study population correlation ($\bar{\rho}_{XY_i}$) corrected for attenuation using the mean values for the artifact values provides an accurate estimate of $\bar{\rho}_{TP_a}$. Computer simulation studies show that this same correction process is reasonably accurate for the indirect range restriction model, too (Le, 2003).

The major problem in meta-analysis methods under direct range restriction lies in estimating the standard deviation of effect sizes ($SD_{\rho_{TP_a}}$). The problem here is the nonlinearity of range restriction. In the case of the direct range restriction model, no one has been able to develop an exact method. For example, the methods presented and evaluated by Law et al. (1994a, 1994b), although quite accurate, are all approximation methods and slightly overestimate $SD_{\rho_{TP_a}}$. Thus, comparing methods is a matter of comparing approximations, and methods have been continuously tweaked to improve accuracy (as evaluated using computer simulation methods).

Indirect range restriction makes the nonlinearity of the range restriction equation much worse. The fact that we need u_T rather than u_X makes the extent of range restriction more extreme. Because range restriction operates on the true effect size rather than an attenuated effect size the nonlinearity is more extreme than for direct range restriction.

Furthermore, the nonlinearity of the range restriction equation now appears in two factors instead of one; that is, it makes a new appearance in the incumbent quality for the predictor variable. This makes the assumption of independence of artifact attenuation factors more seriously false than in the case of direct range restriction and rules out the use of the multiplicative model in indirect range restriction.

The Mean True Score Correlation. The mean true score correlation in indirect range restriction can be estimated accurately by correction for attenuation. The mean study population correlation is corrected using mean artifact values. We illustrate each step of the procedure by reanalyzing the USES database originally analyzed by Hunter (1983b) and Hunter and Hunter (1984). In that database, the mean study population correlation is .26, the mean applicant quality of the predictor is .90, the mean incumbent quality of the criterion is .69, and the mean range restriction on T is $u_T = .56$.

There are important changes from the model for direct range restriction in order and procedure. The biggest difference is the order of correction. In the direct range restriction attenuation model, the correlation is attenuated for measurement error before range restriction. For indirect range restriction, the correlation is attenuated for range restriction before measurement error.

In all models, correction is in the order opposite to the order in which the artifacts have attenuated the correlation. For indirect range restriction, that means that we correct for measurement error before correcting for range restriction.

The correction for criterion measurement error is straightforward. The data on criterion quality is incumbent data and can thus be used directly. To correct for criterion unreliability, we simply divide the mean study correlation by the mean incumbent quality, as noted earlier. For example, the mean reliability of performance ratings for incumbents on a high-quality rating instrument is .47 (Viswesvaran et al., 1996). Thus, the mean quality is $(.47)^{1/2} = .69$. We divide the mean study correlation of .26 by .69 to get .38.

The correction for predictor measurement error is more complicated. The data on predictor reliability are applicant data. Thus, the applicant quality of $(.81)^{1/2} = .90$ must be converted to incumbent quality using the range restriction formula (i.e., using Equations [5.35] or [5.36]). For the USES data, this reduces the quality of .90 to a considerably lower .76. This is the value used to correct the .38 obtained by correcting for criterion unreliability. The correlation corrected for both sources of error is $.38/.76 = .50$.

After we correct for measurement error, we must correct for range restriction using the mean value for u_T. For the USES data, this means that we correct the .50 using the mean value of u_T which is .56. The correction formula used is that for direct range restriction (i.e., Thorndike's [1949] Case II; our Equation [5.38]). The estimate of mean true score correlation is then .73. (The mean true [operational] validity is then $\sqrt{.81}$ (.73) = .66.)

Hunter (1983b) analyzed the USES data using the direct range restriction model, the inappropriate model. The average true score correlation was estimated to be .57, considerably smaller than the .73 obtained using the correct model. Other published estimates for the average true score correlation between cognitive ability and job performance are underestimates for the same reason, as are published estimates of mean true validity for cognitive ability and other selection methods. That is, all other currently published analyses have inappropriately used the model for direct range restriction and, hence, have produced underestimates of both mean operational validities and mean true score correlations.

The Standard Deviation of True Effect Sizes. The major differences between methods for the direct and indirect range restriction models are in the methods for estimating the standard deviation of effect sizes ($SD_{\rho_{TP_a}}$).

When we attempted to adapt the Callender-Osburn (1980) multiplicative method to this new model, we found that their method for estimating the range restriction artifact (c) does not work for the indirect range restriction model. In any case, poor accuracy can be expected for this method because it does not provide for the extremely high correlation between the multipliers for the true score correlation and the predictor quality, as noted earlier. However, we found via computer simulation studies that a modification of the interactive meta-analysis model for the direct range restriction condition (the INTNL-D program; Law et al., 1994a, 1994b; Schmidt, Gast-Rosenberg, et al., 1980; Schmidt et al., 1993) provides acceptably accurate estimates of $SD_{\rho_{TP_a}}$ for the indirect range restriction case (Le, 2003). Under conditions of direct range restriction, this method (with certain refinements) has proven to be slightly more accurate than other methods (Law et al., 1994a, 1994b; Chap. 4). As discussed in Chapter 4, one reason these $SD_{\rho_{TP_a}}$ estimates (hereafter SD_ρ) are more accurate is that the interactive procedure, unlike the multiplicative methods, does not assume that a, b, and c are independent (uncorrelated). Instead, it assumes that a, b, and u_X are independent. In the direct range restriction model, a^2 is r_{XX_a}, that is, the independent variable reliability in the unrestricted group. Likewise, b^2 is r_{YY_a}, the reliability of the dependent variable in the unrestricted group. In direct range restriction, c cannot be independent of a and b, because the formula for c *contains* both a and b, as noted in Chapter 4. However, there is no such necessary relationship between u_X and a or u_X and b; in fact, there is generally no reason to hypothesize any relationship among these artifact indexes. Hence, the interactive model can be more accurate than the multiplicative model. This same approach is taken in the two Raju-Burke (1983) Taylor series–based models for artifact distribution meta-analysis (TSA-1 and TSA-2). Computer simulation studies have shown these models to be also quite accurate.

In the case of indirect range restriction, the interactive model again assumes that a, b, and u are uncorrelated, but u is now u_T instead of u_X. When range restriction is indirect, however, both a and b are the values in the restricted group, rather than in the unrestricted group. That is, $a^2 = r_{XX_i}$ and $b^2 = r_{YY_i}$. As shown earlier in this section, the value of a depends on the value of u_T when range restriction is indirect.

Hence there is at least some violation of the independence assumptions—one of the three relationships is not independent. The value of b^2 is also affected by the range restriction as reflected in u_T, but this effect is quite weak. This failure of complete independence can be compared to the corresponding failure in the multiplicative model for direct range restriction. There all three relationships among the artifacts violate the independence assumption, yet estimates of SD_ρ are quite accurate (as demonstrated in Chapter 4)—though not as accurate as those from the interactive model for direct range restriction. This violation of the independence assumption in the interactive model for indirect range restriction does not appear to cause significant inaccuracies. The interactive model for indirect range restriction (using the INTNL-I program described in Chapter 4 and in the Appendix) has been tested via computer simulation and has been found to produce accurate estimates of SD_ρ (and $\bar{\rho}$) (Le, 2003).

As noted earlier, the order of corrections for artifacts is different for indirect range restriction. The INTNL-I program first corrects the mean observed correlation ($\bar{r}$) for measurement error in both measures, using the mean of restricted group a and b values. (If only unrestricted reliability values are available for the independent variable, the program converts them to restricted values.) It next corrects the resulting mean correlation for range restriction, using the mean u_T value. The user may input u_X values and have the program compute the needed u_T values, using values of r_{XX_a}. If the user enters only values of r_{XX_i}, the program computes the needed values of r_{XX_a}.

This sequence of corrections produces the estimate of the mean true score correlation. As explained in Chapter 4, this value is then attenuated into a different correlation value for each possible combination of a, b, and u_T, and the variance of these resulting correlation values is the estimate of the amount of variance in the observed correlations that is due to variation in these three artifacts. The order in which these attenuations are carried out is important—and this order is different from the order when range restriction is direct (i.e., in the program INTNL-D). The estimated mean true score correlation is first reduced by the effect of range restriction (using the specific u_{T_i} in the range formula) and then is attenuated for measurement error (i.e., is multiplied by $\sqrt{r_{XX_i} r_{YY_i}}$). Hence, the order of the attenuations is the reverse of the order of corrections.

The first published mathematical treatment of indirect range restriction resulting from selection on unknown variables was published by Mendoza and Mumford (1987). Unaware of this article, we prepared our own analysis years later (Hunter, Schmidt, & Le, 2002), afterward learning about the earlier work by Mendoza and Mumford. It seems amazing that an issue this important has been addressed only recently. Clearly, it would have been desirable for this issue to have been resolved much earlier. As a result of this delay, many mean corrected correlations in meta-analyses in the literature are underestimates, particularly in the area of validity generalization. However, on the bright side, we now have not only a full statistical development of indirect range restriction, but also an accurate computer program for conducting meta-analysis under conditions of indirect range restriction. This will allow more accurate estimates of $\bar{\rho}$ in the future. It will also allow many published meta-analyses to be recomputed, producing more accurate estimates of $\bar{\rho}$ values.

Criticisms of Meta-Analysis Procedures for Correlations

Meta-analysis procedures for correlations have been criticized by James, Demaree, and Mulaik (1986), Kemery, Mossholder, and Roth (1987), Ladd and Cornwell (1986), Spector and Levine (1987), and Thomas (1988). These criticisms are discussed in detail in the first edition of this book (Hunter & Schmidt, 1990a) and are shown not to be significant. To conserve space for new material, this discussion is omitted from this edition.

PART III

Meta-Analysis of Experimental Effects and Other Dichotomous Comparisons

6

Treatment Effects: Experimental Artifacts and Their Impact

This chapter presents a substantive discussion of the evaluation of experiments and interventions. The next chapter (Chapter 7) will present the quantitative methods and formulas for meta-analysis and other more technical material. For purposes of simplicity, we will consider only a two-group experiment. The principles developed here apply equally to more complicated designs.

This presentation will parallel that for correlational studies in Chapter 2. For typical studies, sampling error causes error in treatment effects and causes studies to appear to be inconsistent with each other. If the usual analysis were based on confidence intervals, the large effects of sampling error would be recognized, and spurious differences between studies would be properly attributed to sampling error. Instead, most investigators rely on the statistical significance test, which aggravates rather than reduces the problem. Meta-analysis can disentangle differences due to sampling error from differences due to real moderator variables. Treatment effects are also distorted by other artifacts: error of measurement in the dependent variable, error of measurement in the treatment variable (i.e., differences between the nominal treatment and the actual treatment), dichotomization of a continuous dependent variable, range variation on the dependent variable, lack of perfect construct validity in the dependent variable, lack of perfect construct validity in the treatment variable (e.g., confounding of the intended treatment impact with other unintended impacts), bias in the estimation of the treatment effect, as well as bad data due to reporting errors, computation errors, transcription errors, and so on.

The distortions in treatment effects produced by artifacts were camouflaged by the traditional dichotomous description of treatment effects as either "had an effect" or "had no effect." Most artifacts reduce the size of the treatment effect. Had there been no effect to reduce, the artifact would cause no distortion. Thus, under the null hypothesis of "no effect," artifacts other than sampling error become irrelevant and were traditionally ignored. However, meta-analysis has shown that the nihilistic null hypothesis is rarely true. For example, as discussed in Chapters 2, 3, and 5, Lipsey and Wilson (1993) examined available meta-analyses of over 300 psychological interventions (treatment conditions) and found that only two of the treatments (less than 1%) had essentially no effect. Based on this massive study, one would estimate the prior probability that the null hypothesis is false in studies of psychological treatments at .993. In most research domains, the null hypothesis is not true and the reduction in an effect by artifacts has a real and important effect. Among other things, reduction in the size of the study effect by an artifact increases the error rate of the conventional statistical significance test (which is high in the best of conditions for most studies). Differences in the extent of artifacts between studies cause apparent differences in effects across studies, that is, produce the appearance of situation (or setting) by treatment interactions where there are none.

This chapter will begin with a discussion of the quantification of the treatment effect. We will then present hypothetical across-study data showing the effects of sampling error and the failure of the conventional statistical significance test in the context of the review study. We will then present a substantive discussion of artifacts other than sampling error. These other artifacts can be just as large in size even though they are usually systematic rather than random in nature.

Quantification of the Treatment Effect: The *d* Statistic and the Point Biserial Correlation

A key issue is the description of treatment effects as quantitative or dichotomous. The traditional description is dichotomous: The treatment either had an effect or had no effect. Methodologists have long argued that we should instead describe the treatment effect in quantitative form, that is, estimate the actual size of the treatment. A dichotomous description is poor for several reasons. First, there is a great loss of information, information that can be used (1) to assess the practical importance of a treatment, (2) to compare the effectiveness of treatments, (3) to determine whether a theory has been confirmed or disconfirmed, and (4) to test quantitative theories such as path models. Second, the implicit assumption in dichotomizing the treatment effect is that most treatments have no effect. If this were true, then there would be important information in the statement that the treatment effect is not 0. However, as discussed previously, meta-analyses have now shown that treatments rarely have no effect at all. The conclusion, "The treatment had no effect," is usually erroneous. Thus, the question for a treatment is really not whether it had an effect, but whether the effect is as large as a theory predicts, whether the effect is large enough to be of practical importance, or whether the effect is larger or smaller than some other treatment or some variation of the treatment. These questions can only be answered by quantifying the size of the treatment effect.

The dichotomization of treatment effects is also related to the statistical analysis of treatments. If it were true that most treatments have no effect, then good statistical analysis would focus on Type I error: falsely concluding that there is an effect when there is no such effect. The conventional significance test guarantees that

Type I errors will occur no more than 5% of the time. However, meta-analysis has now shown that this nihilistic null hypothesis is rarely true. If the null hypothesis is false, then all statistical errors will be Type II errors: falsely concluding that there is no effect when there is, in fact, an effect. As we shall see, for typical sample sizes, the Type II error rate is quite high. For sample sizes of 100, the Type II error rate for textbook experiments is around 50% and the Type II error rate for more subtle follow-up research is higher yet. There are many important research domains where the significance test error rate is as high as 85%.

Because the null hypothesis is false in most research domains, the conventional significance test has a very high error rate. This high error rate means that the conventional significance test is actually counterproductive at the level of review studies. The high error rate for the conventional significance test means that results interpreted using the significance test must necessarily look inconsistent across studies. For example, if the significance test is wrong 50% of the time, then half the studies will have a significant treatment effect, but the other half will falsely appear to show no treatment effect.

This is quite evident in comparing the results of meta-analyses to the conclusions of narrative reviews. For most questions studied, meta-analysis shows that the treatment effect was not 0—although treatment effects are sometimes quite small. Narrative reviews, on the other hand, have been inconsistent. Some reviewers are selective; they throw out studies on "methodological" grounds—frequently of an entirely hypothetical nature. They throw out studies until those that remain have consistent results. They then base their conclusions on the remaining studies. Unfortunately, different reviewers will throw out different studies and, hence, come to different—sometimes opposite—conclusions. Comprehensive reviewers make a different error: They usually conclude that treatment effects are sporadic. They conclude that the treatment effect is present in some studies but absent in others.

The natural quantitative description of the treatment effect is just the difference between the means on the dependent variable. Let Y be the dependent variable. Denote the means for the control and experimental groups as follows:

$$\bar{Y}_E = \text{the mean for the experimental group}$$
$$\bar{Y}_C = \text{the mean for the control group}$$

To say, "The treatment increased performance by 3.2 feet," is to say that the difference $\bar{Y}_E - \bar{Y}_C$ is 3.2 feet, that is,

$$\bar{Y}_E - \bar{Y}_C = 3.2$$

If the dependent variable were identically measured in all studies, then the raw score difference between means would be the conventional measure of the treatment effect. However, this is rarely true. Consider the measurement of the job performance of sewing machine operators. One would think that a measure such as "number of garments sewn per week" would be the same variable across studies. However, workers at different places are sewing different kinds of garments. To sew three dresses might be very different from sewing three coats. Thus, typically, the units of the dependent variable vary from one study to the next.

If the dependent variable is the same in two different studies except for units, then it would, in principle, be possible to calibrate the two measures by finding the constant of proportionality between the two units. Consider, however, the problem of matching the units for sewing machine operators in two different studies. In one study, the workers sew dresses, while the workers in the other study sew coats. To transform scores from one metric to the other, the workers at one place would have to sew the other kind of garment. Furthermore, they would have to be given exactly the same training in sewing that other kind of garment to be exactly comparable. This would be prohibitively expensive even if it were possible. Thus, exact calibration of independent variables is also impossible in most research domains.

There is an alternative method of matching across studies, although it depends on a substantive assumption. We can eliminate units within a study by using standard scores instead of raw scores. The treatment effect in standard scores would then be given by

$$d = (\bar{Y}_E - \bar{Y}_C)/\sigma$$

where σ is the standard deviation of the raw scores in that study. The only question is, "Which standard deviation?" This question will be considered in detail in the next chapter. For population data, the natural definition would be to use the population standard deviation of the control group. However, for sample data, the standard deviation is much better estimated by using the "within-group variance," that is, by averaging the experimental and control group standard deviations. This sample statistic is Cohen's (1977) "*d* statistic," which is the most widely used statistic in the meta-analysis of experimental or intervention studies. For the population value, we will use the Greek letter for d, that is, δ.

Suppose the distribution of garment sewing performance per month has a mean of 100 and a standard deviation of 25. If a training program increases performance by 10 garments per day, then the treatment effect in standard scores would be

$$d = 10/25 = .40$$

That is, the treatment effect would be .40 standard deviations.

If the outcome (dependent) variable is a true dichotomy (e.g., patient had the disease vs. patient did not have the disease), then another statistic, the odds ratio, can be used. The odds ratio is frequently used in medical research. We do not present procedures for using the odds ratio in this book because it is rarely appropriate and is rarely used in social science research. Haddock, Rindskopf, and Shadish (1998) provided a discussion of potential uses of the odds ratio in social science research.

There is a closely related measure of treatment effect that will be discussed in detail in the next chapter: the point biserial correlation. The point biserial correlation is actually an ordinary Pearson correlation; the special name comes from the nature of the data on which it is computed. We create a single data set by pooling the data across the control group and the experimental group. We define a treatment variable (sometimes called a "dummy variable" or "contrast variable") by assigning different scores to the people in the two different groups. For example, we might define the variable T by assigning the score 0 to those in the control group and assigning the score 1 to those in the experimental group. The correlation computed on the pooled data between that treatment variable and the dependent variable is the point biserial correlation. The point biserial correlation has the advantage that it can be treated like any other correlation coefficient. In particular, the meta-analysis could be done using the methods of Chapters 3 and 4 on the correlation coefficient. The mathematics is then much easier than that for the d statistic. The correlation is much easier to fit into advanced statistical analyses such as reliability analysis, path analysis, and so on. The point biserial correlation is the second most often used quantification of the treatment effect in meta-analysis. As noted in the next chapter, the two statistics, r and d, can be algebraically transformed back and forth from each other. Thus, it is conceptually arbitrary which statistic is used. However, in this chapter, we will primarily use d. For the usual empirical range of d of $-.41 < d < +.41$, the conversion formulas between r and d are trivial.

$$d = 2r \qquad \text{for} - .21 < r < +.21$$
$$r = .5d \qquad \text{for} - .41 < d +.41$$

How close is this approximation? Consider the worst case, $d = .40$. The approximation $.5d$ yields $r = .20$, while the actual correlation is .196.

The d statistic is comparable across studies if the standard deviation of the dependent variable (measured in any one set of units) is the same across studies. This is a typical finding for standardized variables in psychology in the absence of processes producing range restriction. Although means often differ considerably from one setting to the next, standard deviations often differ little. In a research domain where this is not true, the variation in results due to differing units could only be corrected by making a "correction for range variation" (see Chapter 3).

Sampling Error in *d* Values: Illustrations

Is an argument more effective if it is expressed in intense language or if it is cast in wishy-washy language? A meta-analysis by Hamilton and Hunter (1987) showed the difference in attitude change to be about .20 standard deviations (i.e., $d = .20$ or $r = .10$) favoring strong language. Assume that this is the population value of the d statistic for all studies in a hypothetical meta-analysis. What would the review data look like? That depends on the sample sizes used in the studies collected. For simplicity, suppose all studies had used exactly the same sample size. The study results would be approximately distributed as in Table 6.1. (Note: The distributions in Table 6.1 exactly match the sampling distribution for replicated studies. An actual 19-study meta-analysis would find values that departed from this distribution somewhat because the 19 observed sampling errors would not match the exact population distribution of sampling errors.)

Table 6.1 Hypothetical meta-analysis data for the effect of language intensity on persuasion (results ordered by magnitude)

Study	$N = 30$	$N = 68$	$N = 400$
1	.80**	.60**	.36**
2	.68*	.50**	.32**
3	.58	.46*	.30**
4	.50	.40*	.28**
5	.44	.36	.26**
6	.40	.32	.26**
7	.34	.30	.24**
8	.30	.26	.22**
9	.24	.24	.22**
10	.20	.20	.20**
11	.16	.16	.18*
12	.10	.14	.18*
13	.06	.10	.16
14	−.00	.08	.16
15	−.04	.04	.14
16	−.10	−.00	.12
17	−.18	−.06	.10
18	−.28	−.10	.08
19	−.40	−.20	.04

**Significant by two-tailed test.
*Significant by one-tailed test.
NOTE: In each case, the population effect is given by $\delta = .20$ in all studies and all deviation from that value is entirely due to sampling error. The sample size is the total sample size across control (low intensity) and experimental (high intensity) groups. Thus, "$N = 30$" means "15 in each group."

Case 1: $N = 30$

Suppose 19 studies were done with a total sample size of 30 (15 subjects in each group) in each study. The study treatment effects would distribute themselves as the first column of Table 6.1. Six of the studies would have had negative observed treatment effects. The authors of these studies would believe that intense language is counterproductive and reduces the persuasive effect. On the other hand, six studies would have found treatment effects of $d = .40$ or more, effects as large as textbook examples. These authors would believe that intense language is one of the most powerful persuasive agents known. Both sets of authors would be wrong. Only Study 10—the median study—has an effect size of $d = .20$, the actual population value for all studies.

One classic but crude method of reviewing research is to count the number of studies in the predicted direction. This count is 13 out of 19. This is greater than the 9.5 out of 19 expected by chance, though not significantly so (using a binomial test). However, had there been 190 studies instead of 19, the expected count of studies in the predicted direction would be 130/190, which is significantly greater than the 95 expected by chance. Thus, a count of the studies in the predicted direction would show that intensity increased persuasion more often than chance. However, it would falsely suggest that intensity acted in the *opposite* direction 32% of the time.

The statistical significance test was designed to reduce the impact of sampling error. When the null hypothesis is true, it should reduce errors of inference to 5%. How does the conventional significance test fare in this example? There are two ways to do this significance test. Had each study been analyzed using analysis of variance, it would have been analyzed using a two-tailed significance test, and only the study with $d = .80$ would have been significant. That is, analysis of variance yields the correct inference for only one study, an error rate of 18/19, or 95%. That is, the error rate for the two-tailed significance test is not 5% but 95% in this example.

Had the data been analyzed using the t test, the authors would have had the option of doing a one-tailed test. For a one-tailed test, both Studies 1 and 2 have significant treatment effects. Thus, this significance test yields a correct inference for only 2 of the 19 studies, an error rate of 17/19, or 89%. Thus, for a one-tailed t test, the error rate is not 5% but 89% in this example.

In this example, the two-tailed test (conventional analysis of variance) is correct in only 1 of 19 studies. The one-tailed test is correct in 2 of 19 studies, which doubles the power of the two-tailed test. However, in either case the error rate is far higher than the 5% error rate that most people believe to be the error rate for the statistical significance test.

Why is the error rate higher than 5%? The conventional statistical significance test assumes a nihilistic null hypothesis of $\delta = 0$. If the null hypothesis were true, then the error rate would be only 5%. However, the null hypothesis is false for this research domain (as it is in most research domains), and thus, the error rate is not constrained to be 5%, but will be higher. In this example, the error rate rose to 89% (one-tailed test) or 95% (two-tailed test), which is close to the theoretical maximum error rate.

Consider the position of a reviewer faced with study results such as those in Table 6.1. If the reviewer counts results in the expected direction, then there is a weak indication of results in the expected direction. It is true that nearly a third of the studies go in the wrong direction, but that is counterbalanced by the third of the studies with effects as large as classic textbook effects in social psychology. That reviewer would probably conclude that intense language is more persuasive most of the time but would warn that there are some settings where, for unknown reasons, intense language is counterproductive. This would be a false interpretation of the data.

Suppose the reviewer ignored the size of the treatment effects and considered only a count of the number of significant findings using a two-tailed test. This reviewer would almost certainly conclude that language intensity has no effect on persuasiveness. That, too, would be a false conclusion. Ironically, the reviewer who uses the significance test—the more "sophisticated" method—is even farther off base than the reviewer who naively looks at raw results!

Note that the inferences of reviewers would not materially improve with more data. If the number of studies rose from 19 to 190, the number of studies with results significant by a one-tailed test would rise from 2 to 20. However, the proportion of significant findings would still be the same, $20/190 = 2/19$. Thus, a reviewer who depended on the significance test would still draw the same false conclusions even though there were 10 times as much data.

As we will see, the method of meta-analysis presented in this book will deal with these data correctly. This method would estimate the average treatment effect to be $\delta = .20$ to within the sampling error left by using a total sample size of $N = 19(30) = 570$. If there were 190 studies, the error in estimating the mean effect size would drop to that left by a total sample size of $\bar{N} = 190(30) = 5{,}700$. As more and more studies become available, this method of meta-analysis has less and less error. This method would also have correctly concluded that all or nearly all the variance in observed study effects was due to sampling error.

Is this example far-fetched? The size of the treatment effect for language intensity is that found in actual studies. On the other hand, the sample size of $N = 30$ is lower than the actual studies ($\bar{N} = 56$). However, there are important research domains with sample sizes this low. For example, Allen, Hunter, and Donahue (1988) did a meta-analysis on studies of the effect of psychotherapy on problems of shyness and fear of public speaking. For the studies using systematic desensitization, the average sample size was 23. For the studies using rational-emotive therapy, the average sample size was only 19.

Case 2: $N = 68$

The median sample size of studies in personnel selection is 68 in the pre-1980 literature (Lent, Auerbach, & Levin, 1971a, 1971b). This seems not far from sample sizes in other psychological study domains although there are exceptions both larger and smaller. The average sample size for the language intensity meta-analysis done by Hamilton and Hunter (1987) was $\bar{N} = 56$, which is about the same as the 68 used in Table 6.1. If all 19 studies were done with a sample size of $N = 68$, then the study values would have an expected distribution like that of the second column of Table 6.1.

A reviewer who looked at the results at face value would now see 15 of 19 values in the expected direction and only 4 of 19 negative values. This split is significantly different from a 50–50 split using a binomial comparison. At the same time, the four large values are not quite as large as textbook examples. This reviewer would probably conclude that the studies in the wrong direction were just sampling errors from a zero effect. Thus, the reviewer would probably conclude that language intensity usually increases persuasion, although there are a minority of cases where it does not. This conclusion is false because the effect is actually $\delta = .20$ in all cases.

The conventional two-tailed statistical significance test of analysis of variance registers only the two largest values as significant. Thus, the conventional two-tailed test is correct in only 2 of 19 cases, an error rate of 17/19, or 89%. A reviewer who counted significant findings would probably conclude that language intensity is irrelevant to persuasion. This conclusion would be a grave error in this example.

The one-tailed significance test registers the top four values as significant. Thus, the one-tailed test is correct 4 times, which means that the one-tailed test has twice the power of the two-tailed test in this example. However, the one-tailed test is still wrong in 15 of 19 studies, an error rate of 79%. A reviewer who counts one-tailed significant findings would probably conclude that 4 times in 19 is noticeably greater than the 1 in 20 expected by chance. If not, then if the number of studies were raised to 190, the reviewer would certainly notice that 40 out of 190 is much greater than the $190/20 = 9.5$ expected by chance. The reviewer would probably conclude that language intensity does have an impact in about $(40 - 10)/190$, or 16%, of settings, but has no effect otherwise. This is an improvement over the error made by the reviewer who looks at two-tailed tests, but is worse than the conclusion drawn by the reviewer who ignores the significance test altogether.

The method of meta-analysis presented here would estimate the treatment effect to within the sampling error left by a total sample size of $N = 19(68) = 1{,}292$. If there were 190 studies, the error in the mean effect size would be down to that left by a total sample size of $N = 190(68) = 12,920$. The method would also correctly conclude that all or nearly all of the variance across studies is due to sampling error.

Case 3: $N = 400$

Most psychologists think of a sample size of 400 as if it were ∞. However, pollsters know differently from experience. The typical study results for 19 studies with a sample size of $N = 400$ are shown in the third column of Table 6.1.

A reviewer who looks at the results at face value would now note that all results are in the expected direction, although the smallest results are small indeed. The largest results are still moderate in size. Thus, the reviewer would probably conclude that language intensity always increases persuasion (a correct conclusion) although in some settings the impact is negligible in magnitude (an incorrect conclusion).

A reviewer who counts two-tailed significance tests would find that 10 of 19 study values are significant. This reviewer would probably conclude that language intensity increases persuasion in about half of the settings but does not work in the other half. This conclusion is quite far from the truth.

A reviewer who counts one-tailed significance tests would find that 13 of 19 study values are significant. Thus, in this example, the one-tailed test is 13/10 times more powerful than the two-tailed test, that is, about 30% more powerful. This reviewer would probably conclude that language intensity increases persuasion in about two-thirds of the settings, but does not work in the other third. This conclusion is also quite far from the truth.

Even with a sample size of 400, the reviewer who naively looks at face value results is closer to the truth than a reviewer who counts statistical significance findings. Thus, even with a sample size of 400, the significance test still works so poorly that it is counterproductive in comparison to doing no analysis for sampling error at all.

With an average sample size of 400, our method of meta-analysis would estimate the mean effect size to within the sampling error left by a total sample size of $N = 19(400) = 7{,}600$. The analysis would also correctly conclude that all or nearly all of the variance across studies is due to sampling error.

From the viewpoint of review studies, the statistical significance test does not correctly deal with sampling error. The statistical significance test works only in a research context in which we know the null hypothesis to be true. If we know the null hypothesis to be true, however, then we need not do the test at all. Thus, we should abandon the use of the statistical significance test in doing review studies. There are now many sets of mathematically equivalent meta-analysis formulas that take sampling error into account correctly for mean effect sizes, including the method presented here. Our method will also work when there is real variance in effect sizes across studies. We will estimate the size of the standard deviation of population effect sizes. Some authors stop with a significance test for homogeneity and present no method for estimating the standard deviation if the significance test indicates that the standard deviation is not 0.

Error of Measurement in the Dependent Variable

Ordinary English interprets the phrase "error of measurement" as having two meanings: systematic and unsystematic error. Systematic error is a departure from measuring exactly what was intended. In psychometric theory, this is called "imperfect construct validity." In psychometric theory, the phrase "error of measurement" is used for unsystematic error, also called "random error" or "unreliability." We will follow psychometric terminology here. This section will present the effects of unsystematic or random error of measurement and a later section will cover imperfect construct validity.

In psychology, much of the unsystematic error of measurement is caused by randomness in subject response. This kind of error usually has a mean of 0, that is, is equally likely to be positive or negative, and is uncorrelated with the true value. If we write the observed score on the dependent variable as Y, write the true score as U, and write the error of measurement as e, then

$$Y = U + e$$

where the population mean of e is 0 and the population correlation between e and U is 0.

Because the average error is 0, the mean of errors does not describe the typical size of an error. Rather, the typical size of errors is described by either the error variance—the average squared error—or the error standard deviation. The number σ_e is called the "standard error of measurement" in psychometric theory. The practical impact of error of measurement is relative to the size of differences between people. If two people differ on the dependent variable by 10 points, then errors of size -1 or $+1$ would have little effect on the comparison of those people. On the other hand, if the difference between two subjects were .5, then errors of -1 or $+1$ would completely obscure the comparison. One measure of the relative error of measurement is the "noise to signal" ratio, σ_e/σ_U, although this is not commonly used. Instead, the more useful measure of relative error is the correlation between true and observed score, that is, r_{UY}. By historical convention, the square of this correlation is called the "reliability" of the dependent variable and is denoted r_{UY}^2. That is, we define the reliability of the dependent variable r_{YY} by

$$r_{YY} = r_{YU}^2$$

Different ways of estimating reliability identify and assess different sources of measurement error. It is critical that the researcher use the appropriate reliability estimate. We refer the reader to the extended treatment of this issue presented in Chapter 3. The error standard deviation and the reliability of the dependent variable are related by

$$\sigma_e = \sigma_y\sqrt{(1 - r_{YY})}$$

The size of the reliability depends on the extent of measurement error in the process measured—usually a response in psychology—and on the number of primary measurements used to generate the final response—frequently the number of items on a scale. High-quality measurement often provides reliability in the region of $r_{YY} = .81$. Moderate quality usually falls around $r_{YY} = .64$. Measurement based on a single response frequently has reliability no higher than $r_{YY} = .25$. It should be noted that the reliability of a single response is not determined by the cost of obtaining that response. For example, in equity studies in social psychology, subjects may spend as much as an hour before the criterion act. However, the only measurement of the dependent variable is a single response: the amount of money given to the partner. The reliability of that single response is the correlation between that response and the response that would have been made on some other randomly chosen day. The reliability of single responses is rarely higher than $r_{YY} = .25$.

The size of the reliability depends both on the extent of error in the measurement process and on the extent of individual differences on the dependent variable. For instance, Nicol and Hunter (1973) found that the same semantic differential scale that had a reliability of .90 measuring attitudes toward the polarized issue "law and order" had only a reliability of .20 measuring attitudes toward the issue "pollution."

The observed score for a given person p is related to the true score for that person by

$$Y_p = T_p + e_p$$

If we average scores across persons, the mean score is related to the mean true score by

$$\bar{Y} = \bar{T} + \bar{e}$$

That is, errors of measurement are averaged across persons. The population mean of scores across persons averages the errors of measurement across an ∞ (infinity) of errors and is thus 0. That is, at the population level, error of measurement has no impact on the mean.

The raw score treatment effect is defined as the difference between population means:

$$\text{Raw score } \delta_Y = \bar{Y}_E - \bar{Y}_C$$

Because population mean error of measurement is 0, each mean observed score is equal to the mean true score. Thus,

$$\text{Raw score } \delta_U = U_E - U_C = \bar{Y}_E - \bar{Y}_C = \text{Raw score } \delta_Y$$

That is, random error does not alter the raw score treatment effect. This is the reason that traditional statistics has ignored error of measurement in the treatment of experimental design.

However, it is not the raw score treatment effect but rather the standard score treatment effect that is of primary interest in statistics. For purposes of meta-analysis, it is normally necessary to use standard score treatment effects to achieve comparability across studies. However, the standard score treatment effect is also central to traditional statistics because it is the standard score treatment effect that is assessed by the statistical test for significance. In particular, the power of the conventional significance test depends on the standard score treatment effect.

Error of measurement does not affect the mean of the dependent variable but it *does* affect the variance. The variance of observed scores is related to the variance of true scores by

$$\sigma_Y^2 = \sigma_U^2 + \sigma_e^2$$

That is, error of measurement increases the variance and, hence, the standard deviation of the dependent variable. Consider, then, the experimental versus control group comparison. Adding error does not change the means, but it increases the spread of scores about the mean. This effect is shown in Figure 6.1.

The extent of separation between two groups depends on the extent of overlap between the two distributions. The extent of overlap between the distributions depends on the difference between the means in relation to the extent of spread about the means. The greater the spread about the means, the greater the overlap between the two distributions. Figure 6.1 shows that the extent of overlap is greatly increased by the presence of error of measurement. The lower the reliability, the larger the spread about the means and, hence, the greater the overlap. That is, as the amount of error of measurement increases, the difference is more and more obscure. In terms of statistical power, the more obscure the difference between the means, the more difficult that difference is to detect.

Consider the standardized effect size for true scores and observed scores:

$$\delta_U = (U_E - U_C)/\sigma_U$$
$$\delta_Y = (Y_E - Y_C)/\sigma_Y$$

Because population means are not affected by error of measurement, the numerators are equal. However, error of measurement increases the standard deviation and, hence, the denominators are different. The increase in standard deviation is given by

$$\sigma_Y = \sigma_U/\sqrt{r_{YY}}$$

where we note that to divide by a number less than 1 is to increase the ratio. If this identity is substituted into the equation for δ_Y,we have

$$\delta_Y = \delta_U\sqrt{r_{YY}}$$

That is, the standardized effect size for the observed score is the standardized effect size for the true score multiplied by the square root of the reliability. For example, if the reliability were $r_{YY} = .81$, the effect size would be reduced to

$$\delta_Y = .90\,\delta_U$$

that is, reduced by 10%.

Figure 6.1 Effect of error of measurement on the separation between the control and experimental groups for a case in which the true score treatment effect is $\delta = 1.00$

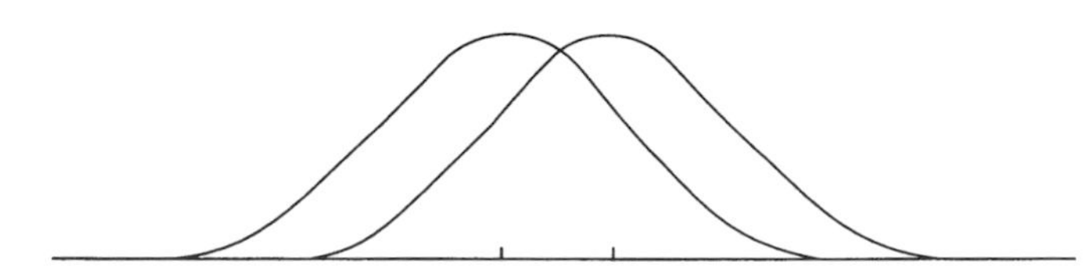

Figure 6.1a Perfect measurement, $r_{yy} = 1.00$

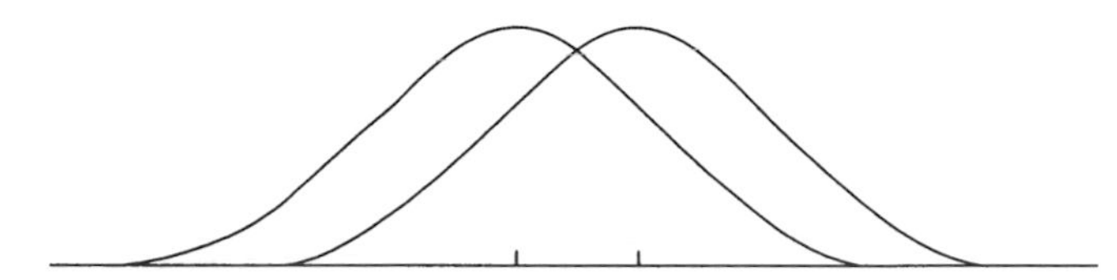

Figure 6.1b Typical good measurement, $r_{yy} = .81$

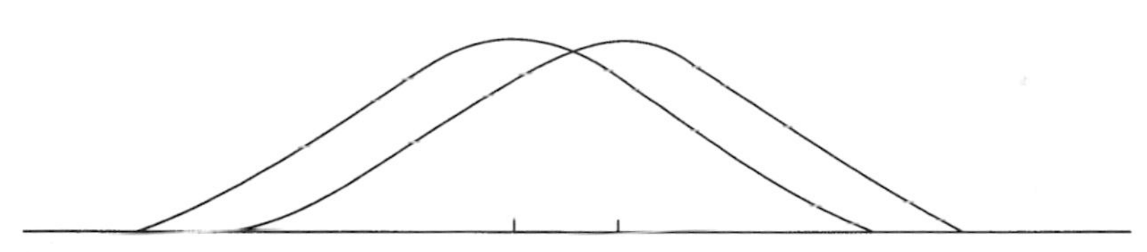

Figure 6.1c Typical moderate measurement, $r_{yy} = .50$

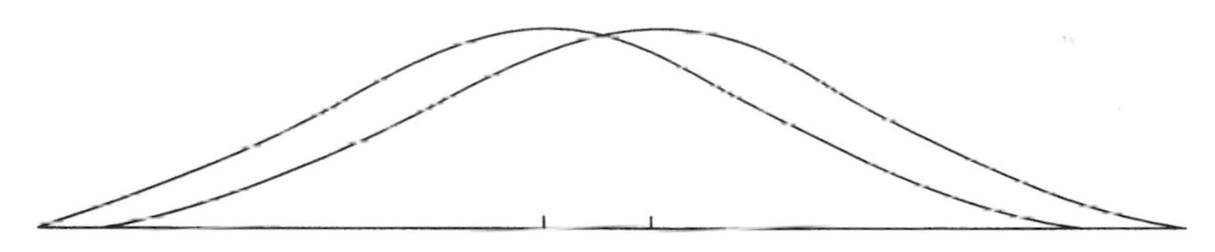

Figure 6.1d Typical poor measurement, $r_{yy} = .25$

If the effect size is reduced by error of measurement, the effect is more difficult to detect by the conventional significance test. This is illustrated in Table 6.2. Table 6.2 computes the power of the conventional significance test for studies of sample size $N = 100$, a value roughly typical for empirical studies. An effect size of $\delta = .40$ is about the size of large introductory textbook examples from the social psychology experimental literature. The effect size of $\delta = .20$ is about the size of effects in the more sophisticated research that follows up textbook examples, that is, research that studies variation in textbook manipulations rather than the crude manipulation itself.

Table 6.2 first shows the reduction in the treatment effect produced by different levels of error of measurement. As the reliability decreases from $r_{YY} = 1.00$ to $r_{YY} = .25$, the treatment effect is reduced by half, for example, from $\delta = .40$ to $\delta = .20$ or from $\delta = .20$ to $\delta = .10$. The probability of detecting the effect using a conventional significance test drops correspondingly. For textbook size effects with $\delta = .40$, the power drops from an already low 51% to 17%, a power level

Table 6.2 Power of the conventional significance test for studies with sample size $N = 100$

I. Reduction in the effect size: the value of δ_y for various values of the reliability of the dependent variable

Reliability	$\delta_U = .10$	$\delta_U = .20$	$\delta_U = .30$	$\delta_U = .40$
1.00	.10	.20	.30	.40
.81	.09	.18	.27	.36
.64	.08	.16	.24	.32
.25	.05	.10	.15	.20

II. Reduction in power: the power of the conventional .05 level statistical significance test for various values of the reliability of the dependent variable, expressed as a percentage

Reliability	$\delta_U = .10$	$\delta_U = .20$	$\delta_U = .30$	$\delta_U = .40$
1.00	7.2	16.6	31.8	51.2
.81	6.5	14.3	26.7	43.2
.64	5.9	12.1	33.0	37.3
.25	4.3	7.2	11.2	16.6

only one-third the size. Stated the other way, the error rate for the significance test rises from 49% to 83%. For sophisticated research, the initial power level is smaller to begin with and, hence, there is less distance to fall. If with perfect measurement the effect size is $\delta = .20$, then, if the dependent variable is based on a single response, the observed effect size would be about $\delta = .10$ and the power would drop from 17% to 7%, a reduction of slightly more than half. The error rate for the significance test rises from 83% to 93%.

The next chapter will show that for population effect sizes the reduction in the treatment effect can be corrected if the reliability of the dependent variable is known. Although the application of that same correction formula to sample values eliminates the systematic effect of error of measurement (Cook et al., 1992, pp. 315–316), the increased sampling error and reduced statistical power cannot be corrected. This shows in the fact that the significance test on the corrected effect size is algebraically equivalent to the significance test on the uncorrected effect size.

Error of Measurement in the Treatment Variable

The treatment variable is defined by group assignment. Because the investigator usually knows exactly which group each subject belongs to, this variable is usually regarded as perfectly measured. However, this definition ignores the interpretation of the results. In interpreting the results, it is not group assignment but the treatment process that is assumed to be the independent variable. From that point of view, the nominal treatment variable may be quite different from the actual treatment variable.

Consider an attitude change experiment directed to the topic of acid rain. The investigator seeks to manipulate the credibility of the source of the change-inducing message. At one point in the instructions, the sentence "The author of the message is ..." is completed either with the phrase "a famous scientist in the area" or with "a marine drill instructor." Assume that the instructions are correctly read to each subject so that we do know correctly and exactly the group assignment of each subject. However, suppose 30% of the subjects are not paying careful attention to the instructions. They do not hear the sentence stating the author of the message. They do not think about the author of the message until they read it. Assume that the subjects who did not hear the author's identity then *assume* one. Suppose half the subjects assume the author to be an expert while half the subjects assume the author to be some know-nothing graduate assistant. Then, in this study, 15% of the control group subjects will assume an expert source and will act as if they had been exposed to the experimental group instructions, while 15% of the experimental group subjects will assume a know-nothing source and will act as if they had been exposed to the control group instruction. In this example, the nominal treatment group variable is the reverse of the actual treatment variable 15% of the time. The observed effect size will be correspondingly reduced.

How much will the treatment effect be reduced? The idea is simple, but the computations are complicated. In our example, where 15% of the subjects were misidentified in each group, we could compute the effect of the treatment variable error by assuming each treatment group to be the pooling of 85% from the corresponding true treatment group and 15% from the other true treatment group. The outcome is easily stated in correlational terms. Denote the nominal treatment variable by X and denote the true treatment variable by T, that is,

$$X = \text{the observed group assignment of the subject,}$$

$$T = \text{the actual treatment value for that subject.}$$

If the correlation between X and T is r_{YT}, then the observed treatment effect correlation r_{XY} is related to the true treatment effect correlation r_{TY} by the equation

$$r_{XY} = r_{XT} r_{TY}$$

The formula for the reduction in the d statistic can be obtained by substituting this product into the formula for r to d conversion.

The product rule for the treatment effect correlation is a special case of the attenuation formula from psychometric theory. Let us denote the "reliability of the treatment" by r_{XX} and define it to be the square of the correlation between true and observed treatment identifications; that is, we define r_{XX} by

$$r_{XX} = r_{XT}^2 \tag{6.1}$$

Then our product formula is a special case of the psychometric formula

$$r_{XY} = \sqrt{r_{XX}} r_{TY} \tag{6.2}$$

In our attitude change example, we assumed 15% misidentification in each group. The correlation between the observed and true treatment is thus $r_{XT} = .70$, and, hence, the observed treatment effect correlation is

$$r_{XY} = .70\, r_{TY}$$

That is, the observed treatment effect correlation is reduced by 30%.

If the treatment effect correlation is reduced, then statistical power will be reduced correspondingly. Suppose in our example that the true treatment effect was $\delta_T = .40$ with a sample size of $N = 100$. The true treatment effect correlation would then be $r_{TY} = .20$. The observed treatment effect correlation would then be $r_{XY} = (.70)(.20) = .14$ and the observed treatment effect would be $\delta_X = .28$. Had there been no error in the treatment identification, the statistical power would have been 51%. Instead, it is 28%, reduced by nearly half.

If the reliability of the treatment variable is known, then the attenuation effect can be corrected. The formula is the usual psychometric formula for correction for attenuation due to error in the independent variable:

$$r_{TY} = r_{XY}/\sqrt{r_{XX}} \tag{6.3}$$

This correction works perfectly at the population correlation level. However, the correction at the sample data level corrects for only the systematic attenuation. It does not correct for the increased sampling error introduced by the measurement error. The significance test on the corrected correlation is algebraically equivalent to the significance test on the uncorrected correlation.

In the previous example of attitude change experiment, errors of measurement in the independent variable had two effects: (1) Within both the experimental and control groups, the within-group variance on the dependent variable was increased; and (2) the raw score mean difference on the dependent variable was reduced, that is, $\bar{Y}_E - \bar{Y}_C$ was reduced. In such a case, the observed d value will be reduced for two reasons: because the numerator is reduced and because the denominator is increased. There are other cases of measurement error in the independent variable in which the numerator, $\bar{Y}_E - \bar{Y}_C$, is unaffected but the denominator, the pooled within-group *SD*, is inflated, leading to artifactually lowered estimates of d.

For example, suppose an experiment is conducted to determine the effect of personal attention and sympathetic listening by work counselors on the job-related attitudes of problem employees. Each member of the experimental group is supposed to get 12 hours of personal interaction (6 two-hour sessions) with a counselor. However, because of interruptions of scheduled sessions, lateness, and other problems, some people in each study get less than that: some 10 and some 11 hours. Because some counselors run past the stopping time without realizing it, other members of the experimental group get more than 12 hours: some 13 and some 14 hours. The average amount of time might be approximately correct: 12 hours. If the impact of treatment strength differences is approximately linear over the range of variation in the study (true in most cases), then the average effect will be determined by the average treatment strength. The individual variations will cancel out, and the mean of the treatment group will be the same as if there had been no variation in treatment. Thus, the numerator of the effect size formula for d (i.e., $\bar{Y}_E - \bar{Y}_C$) will not be affected. However, the individual variations in treatment strength will cause variations in outcome that will contribute to variation in the dependent variable. Thus, the denominator of the effect size will be larger than would be true if there were no variation in treatment strength. If the denominator of the effect size were increased, then the effect size would be reduced. Thus, within-study variation in treatment strength that has no effect on $\bar{Y}_E - \bar{Y}_C$ nevertheless reduces the effect size.

Furthermore, because the extent of within-study variation is likely to differ from one study to the next, failure to correct for attenuation due to treatment variation will lead to artificial variation in effect size across studies. This uncorrected variation could be falsely interpreted as showing the existence of a nonexistent moderator variable.

Variation in the treatment effect increases the experimental group standard deviation, but does not change the control group standard deviation. The increase in the experimental group standard deviation increases the within-group standard deviation and, hence, reduces the observed effect size value. However, this artificial increase in the experimental standard deviation could also cause another error. If there were no true treatment by subject interaction and if there were no variation in the treatment effect, then the control and experimental group standard deviations would be equal. The artificial increase in the experimental group standard deviation might be falsely interpreted as an indication of a treatment by subject interaction. That is, it appears that subjects in the experimental group are reacting differently to the same treatment (causing SD_E to be larger than SD_C), when, in fact, the cause of the larger SD_e is the fact that different subjects in the experimental group are by mistake receiving treatments of different intensity or duration.

If there is no true treatment by subject interaction, then the increase in the experimental group standard deviation can be used to quantify the impact of treatment variation. If there is no interaction, then the desired effect size is

$$\delta = (\bar{Y}_E - \bar{Y}_C)/SD_C \tag{6.4}$$

The observed population effect size is

$$\delta_o = (\bar{Y}_E - \bar{Y}_C)/SD_W \tag{6.5}$$

The two effect sizes differ by

$$\delta_o = a\delta \tag{6.6}$$

where the attenuation factor a is given by

$$a = SD_C/SD_W \tag{6.7}$$

For equal sample sizes, the attenuation factor can be computed from the ratio comparing the experimental and control group standard deviations. Denote the standard deviation comparison ratio by v. That is, define v by

$$v = SD_E/SD_C \tag{6.8}$$

Then the within-group standard deviation is related to v by

$$SD_W = \sqrt{[(SD_C^2 + SD_E^2)/2]} = SD_C\sqrt{[(1 + v^2)/2]} \tag{6.9}$$

Thus,

$$a = SD_C/SD_W = 1/\sqrt{[(1 + v^2)/2]} \tag{6.10}$$

If v is not much larger than 1, then we have the approximation

$$a = 1 - (v^2 - 1)/2 \tag{6.11}$$

In summary, within-study variation in treatment strength causes an inflation in the experimental dependent variable standard deviation. If there is no real treatment by subject interaction, then variation in treatment strength causes the experimental group standard deviation to be artificially larger than the control group standard deviation. If treatment variation is not suspected, then this increase could be falsely interpreted as indicating a treatment by subject interaction. If it is known that there is no interaction, then the attenuation in the effect size can be computed from a comparison ratio of the experimental to control group standard deviation.

Variation Across Studies in Treatment Strength

In the preceding example, the mean raw score treatment effect, $\bar{Y}_E - \bar{Y}_C$, is the same in all studies. In other cases, however, this value may vary across the studies in a meta-analysis—because the amount of treatment given to the experimental group might differ, causing $\bar{Y}_E$ to vary across studies. If these differences are known (i.e., if they are given in each study), they can be coded and treated as a potential moderator variable. If the strength of treatment values is not known, however, then variation in treatment strength will produce variation in effect sizes that cannot be accounted for. This variation could cause an actually homogeneous treatment effect to appear to be heterogeneous and, thus, suggest a nonexistent moderator variable. (Alternatively, the effects of variation in treatment strength will be confounded with the real moderator variable.)

Consider an example. Suppose in a *series* of studies evaluating a new training method, the experimental group was supposed to get 10 hours of training in each study. Due to administrative and communications problems, however, the experimental people in some studies get 8, 9, 11, or 12 hours of training; although, *within* each study, each subject received exactly the same number of hours of training, only some of the studies hit exactly the desired 10 hours. If the mean across studies is 10 hours, then the mean effect size for the meta-analysis will not be affected. However, the variation in training time across studies will create additional variance in effect sizes beyond that created by sampling error. The formulas presented in this book do not correct for this. If the number of training hours is given in each study, this variable can be coded and analyzed as a moderator. However, this information would rarely be given because the deviations from 10 hours all represent errors in carrying out the training plan—errors that the experimenters themselves may not even be aware of.

In the example here, average treatment strength across studies was equal to the target value of 10 hours. This is what would be expected if the measurement error were random. If the mean were discrepant from the goal—say 9 hours instead of 10—then the mean effect size would be affected, as well as the variance. However, in this example, we assume a mean (expected value) of 0 for the measurement errors.

This form of measurement error is analogous to unintended differences between studies in range restriction in correlational studies, that is, differences in range restriction (or enhancement) that might appear despite the fact that researchers took special steps to obtain the same variation in all studies, just as the experimenters attempted here to have exactly the same treatment across studies. In many meta-analyses, the strength of treatment conditions will vary across studies, not because of measurement error, but because the different experimenters did not have a common goal for treatment strength to begin with. This condition is closely analogous to the naturally occurring range variation that occurs across correlational studies. (In the experimental studies, the control group is the same in all studies, anchoring the low end of the independent variables, but the high end of the independent variable varies from study to study, and hence the variance of the independent variable varies from study to study.) As noted and illustrated earlier, this problem can be addressed by a moderator analysis when the needed information on treatment strength is given in individual studies. However, this information will often not be given.

Range Variation on the Dependent Variable

The raw score treatment effect is determined by the nature of the treatment process. Thus, if the same process is used in different settings, it should stay about the same. However, the standard deviation of the study group is not determined by the treatment process but by the nature of the selection of the group in question. Thus, the study population might be more homogeneous in some settings than in others. The standardized treatment effect would vary correspondingly.

Consider an attitude change study done on a polarized political topic. Initial attitudes would be much more homogeneous in a group of Republicans than in a politically unselected population. Assume that the standard deviation among Republicans is only half the size of the standard deviation in a mixed population, say $\sigma = 50$ in the mixed population and $\sigma = 25$ for Republicans. If the change produced by the message is 10 points in raw score form, then a study done on a mixed population would produce a standardized effect size of $10/50 = .20$, while the same study done on a Republican population would produce a standardized effect size of $10/25 = .40$, a standardized effect size twice as large.

From the viewpoint of statistical power, there is a considerable advantage to doing a study using a more homogeneous population. Consider the political attitude example again. The investigator doing the study on a general population would have an effect size of $\delta = .20$, while the same study done on a Republican population would have an effect size of $\delta = .40$. Given a study sample size of $N = 100$, the statistical power for the study on a general population would be 17%, while the power on the homogeneous population would be 51%, three times higher.

The investigator studying the general population could have obtained a similar gain in power by breaking his data down into Republicans and Democrats and then properly merging the results from the two within-group comparisons. This is the gain in power that results from analysis of covariance, or use of the "treatment by levels" design.

For purposes of meta-analysis, let us choose some population as a reference population. We want all effect sizes expressed in terms of that reference population. To do so, we must know the ratio of the standard deviation of the study population to the standard deviation of the reference population. Denote the standard deviations of the two populations by

$$\sigma_P = \text{standard deviation of the reference population,}$$

$$\sigma_S = \text{standard deviation of the study population.}$$

The ratio of study to reference standard deviation is denoted u, that is,

$$u = \sigma_S / \sigma_P$$

If the raw score treatment effect is the same in both populations, then the standardized treatment effect in the study population is given by

$$\delta_S = \delta_P / u$$

That is, the more homogeneous the study population in comparison to the reference population, the larger the study effect size.

To correct for range variation, we need merely use the preceding equation in reverse order, that is,

$$\delta_P = u\delta_S$$

In meta-analysis, this formula could be used to correct each of the study effect sizes to the same reference population value and, thus, eliminate differences in effect size due to differences in homogeneity. However, this correction requires that the same scale of measurement for the dependent variable be used in all studies. This is rarely the case, so this correction can usually not be made.

Dichotomization of the Dependent Variable

In some studies, a continuous dependent variable is dichotomized. For example, in research on the effect of a realistic job preview on subsequent turnover, most investigators do not use the natural dependent variable of tenure, the length of time the worker stays with the firm. Instead, they dichotomize tenure to create a binary "turnover" variable; for example, they might see if a worker stays more than 6 months or not. The loss of information inherent in dichotomization causes a reduction in the effect size and a corresponding loss in statistical power (MacCallum, Zhang, Preacher, & Rucker, 2002). Within a wide range of values, this artificial reduction in effect size can be corrected. However, within a single study, the statistical correction formula does *not* restore the higher level of statistical power.

Denote the treatment variable by T and denote the continuous dependent variable by Y. Denote the dichotomized dependent variable by Y'. The effect of the dichotomization is to replace the correlation r_{TY} by the correlation $r_{TY'}$, which is lower in magnitude. The statistical significance test is then done on the smaller $r_{TY'}$ with correspondingly lower power. What we seek is a correction formula that restores the value $r_{TY'}$ to the value r_{TY}. There is an approximate formula that works at the population level. Application of that formula at the sample level eliminates the systematic error in the correlation, but does not eliminate the larger sampling error that arises from the loss in information due to dichotomization. The formula works well in meta-analysis where the impact of sampling error is greatly reduced.

For a cross-sectional correlation, dichotomization of the dependent variable reduces the correlation by a product rule formula similar to that for attenuation due to error of measurement. The correction formula is known as that which creates a "biserial correlation" from a "point biserial correlation." This formula does not work for treatment correlations because the dependent variable does not have a normal distribution. The treatment effect causes the distribution of the experimental group to be displaced from that of the control group. When the two groups are pooled, the combination distribution is not normal. To see this, consider the extreme case in which the treatment effect is 3 standard deviations in magnitude. The two distributions hardly overlap and the combined distribution is distinctly bimodal—one mode at each of the subgroup means.

However, we will show that the biserial correlation formula works quite well as an approximation over the usual range of effect sizes and distribution splits. This corresponds to the fact that the combined distribution is approximately normal unless the treatment effect is very large. Suppose that in the combined groups the proportion of people in the "high" split is p while the proportion in the "low" split is $q = 1 - p$. For a normal distribution, there would be a z value corresponding to such a split (although the combined distribution is not exactly normal). Call this value the "cutoff" value and denote it by c. The value of the normal density function or "normal ordinate" at c is denoted $\varphi(c)$. The attenuation in the treatment correlation is approximately given by the biserial attenuation formula

$$r_{TY'} = a r_{TY}$$

where

$$a = \varphi(c)/\sqrt{pq}$$

The corresponding correction formula is the biserial formula

$$r_{TY} = r_{TY'}/a$$

The range over which the formula is accurate is shown in Table 6.3. Table 6.3 presents the comparison ratio for the actual continuous variable correlation and the attenuated dichotomous variable correlation corrected using the biserial correction formula. The ratio is in the order corrected/actual and is expressed as a percentage. For example, for a population continuous $d = .40$ and a median split on the combined population $p = .50$, the ratio is 101. That is, whereas the actual continuous treatment correlation is $r_{TY} = .20$, the corrected dichotomized correlation is $1.01(.20) = .202$, an error less than rounding error. The error is always less than rounding error for the range of values $-.51 < d < +.51$ and

Table 6.3 Comparison ratio of corrected/actual correlations—expressed as percentages—where the corrected correlation is the estimated correlation for the continuous dependent variable computed by correcting the dichotomous variable correlation using the biserial correction formula

	Combined proportion "high" on the dependent variable								
d	*.10*	*.20*	*.30*	*.40*	*.50*	*.60*	*.70*	*.80*	*.90*
10	100	100	100	100	100	100	100	100	100
.20	100	100	100	100	100	100	100	100	100
.30	100	100	101	101	101	101	101	100	100
.40	99	100	101	101	101	101	101	100	99
.50	99	101	101	102	102	102	101	101	99
.60	98	101	102	103	103	103	102	101	98
.70	97	101	103	104	104	104	103	101	97
.80	96	101	103	105	105	105	103	101	96
.90	95	101	104	106	106	106	104	101	95
1.00	94	101	105	107	107	107	105	101	94
1.10	93	101	105	108	109	108	105	101	93

NOTE: The statistic d is the population effect size for the continuous variable, that is, approximately twice the value of the population continuous variable treatment correlation.

$.09 < p < .91$, the range of values in most current meta-analyses. For the most extreme case in Table 6.3, $d = 1.10$ and $p = .90$, the actual correlation is .48 and the corrected correlation is $.93(.48) = .45$, an error that is visible but still not large in practical terms.

Imperfect Construct Validity in the Dependent Variable

Suppose there is some systematic error in the measurement of the dependent variable; that is, we measure a dependent variable that is different to some extent from the intended dependent variable. What effect will this have on the effect size and can it be corrected? A full treatment of this problem requires considerable knowledge of path analysis and knowledge of the nature of the dependent variable and its relationships with other variables. However, there are certain common cases that are relatively straightforward.

The most common case is the use of a dependent variable that is an indirect measure of the desired dependent variable. For example, a good assessment of a juvenile delinquency treatment program would require an objective assessment of the subsequent behavior of the clients. Instead, investigators must often rely on indirect measures such as the subsequent arrest record. Figure 6.2 shows the assumed path model of the relationships between the two measures of behavior and the treatment variable.

Let Y be the measure of the client's actual delinquent behavior and let Y' be the arrest record. The desired treatment effect correlation r_{TY} is related to the observed treatment correlation by the product rule

$$r_{TY'} = r_{TY}\, r_{YY'} \tag{6.12}$$

Figure 6.2 Path model for the relationship among the delinquency treatment program, the desired measure of actual posttreatment behavior, and the observed posttreatment arrest record

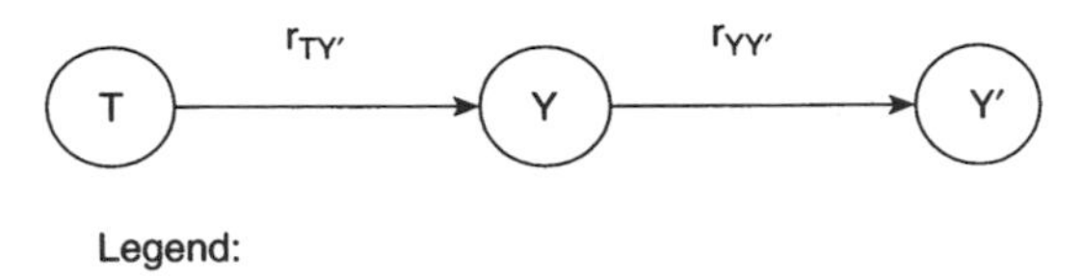

Legend:

T = Delinquency Treatment Variable
Y′ = Posttreatment Behavior
Y = Posttreatment Arrest Record

If the correlation between behavior and arrest were only $r_{YY'} = .30$, then the treatment correlation would be attenuated to

$$r_{TY'} = .30 r_{TY},$$

that is, attenuated by 70%. In this case, the observed correlation could be corrected by reversing the algebraic equation

$$r_{TY} = r_{TY'} / r_{YY'} \tag{6.13}$$

The corrected d statistic would then be obtained by transforming this corrected correlation. In the delinquency example, the correction would be

$$r_{TY} = r_{TY'} / .30$$

The observed correlation must be more than tripled in this case to correct for the imperfect construct validity. If the observed d statistic were $d_{Y'} = .12$, then $r_{TY'} = .06$, which corrects to $r_{TY} = .06/.30 = .20$ and, hence, to $d_Y = .40$.

Although the treatment correlation, or d statistic, can be corrected to eliminate the systematic reduction in the correlation produced by imperfect construct validity, the effect of increased sampling error cannot be corrected. The confidence interval around the corrected correlation is $1/.30 = 3.33$ times as wide as that for the uncorrected correlation, reflecting the increased sampling error caused by the correlation. The significance test for the corrected effect size is algebraically equivalent to the significance test for the uncorrected effect size and, hence, has the same p value.

Imperfect construct validity does not always reduce the size of the effect size. Consider social skills training for supervisors. Assessment of the training program would ideally require measuring the interactive skills of the trainee after the program. Instead, the only available measure might be a measure of how well the person mastered the training program. However, mastery of the material is only antecedent to behavior change; it may take time or special experience for the trainee to put that learning into operation. The path model for this hypothesis is shown in Figure 6.3.

The desired treatment correlation r_{TY} and the observed treatment correlation $r_{TY'}$ are related by the product rule

$$r_{TY} = r_{TY'} \, r_{Y'Y}. \tag{6.14}$$

Figure 6.3 Path model for the assumed relationship among the social skills training of supervisors, program mastery, and subsequent interpersonal behavior on the job

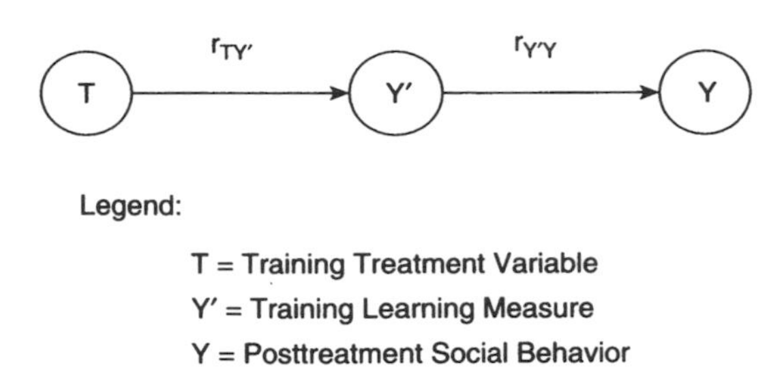

If the correlation between the cognitive learning measure and subsequent social behavior was only $r_{Y'Y} = .30$, then the desired correlation r_{TY} would be lower than the observed correlation $r_{TY'}$:

$$r_{TY} = .30\, r_{TY'}$$

This product rule is itself the correction formula for the treatment correlation. The correction for the *d* statistic is obtained by transforming the corrected treatment correlation to a *d* value.

Imperfect Construct Validity in the Treatment Variable

Imperfect construct validity in the treatment variable is a confounding of the intended treatment effect with an effect due to some other causal agent. This problem can be attacked using path analysis (Hunter, 1986, 1987), and, under certain conditions, it can be corrected in a manner that could be used in meta-analysis. Correction of confounding requires the use of a multiple dependent variable design where an intervening variable is observed that measures the process induced by the confounding causal agent. The desired correlation is then the partial correlation between the treatment variable and the dependent variable with the intervening variable held constant. This approach is a rigorous, quantitative replacement for doing an analysis of covariance with the intervening variable used as a concomitant variable (Hunter, 1988). Detailed treatment of this method is beyond the scope of the present book.

Bias in the Effect Size (*d* Statistic)

The effect size statistic is subject to a statistical phenomenon known by the forbidding title "bias." For sample sizes greater than 20, bias is trivial in magnitude. However, there have been papers arguing that a major problem with meta-analysis is the use of "biased methods." This section will present a correction for bias, although the primary intent of the section is to show that the bias is of trivial magnitude.

Consider a set of perfectly replicated studies, all with the same sample size and the same population effect size. The average sample effect size will differ slightly from the population effect size. This discrepancy is called "bias" in the statistical estimation literature. The size of the bias depends on the sample size. The bias is in different directions for the effect size statistic d and the treatment correlation r. The average d is slightly larger than δ while the average correlation is slightly smaller than ρ.

A complete treatment of bias in the treatment correlation is given by Hunter, Schmidt, and Coggin (1996), who showed that the bias is trivial in all but very small sample studies and small for small-sample studies. Some authors have suggested using the Fisher's z transformation to reduce the bias, but the bias using Fisher's z turns out to be even larger, although in the opposite direction. The bias in the treatment correlation is given by

$$E(r) = a\rho \quad (6.15)$$

where

$$a = 1 - (1 - \rho^2)/(2N - 2) \quad (6.16)$$

How small is this bias? Consider perfectly replicated studies with a population correlation of $\rho = .20$ and a sample size of $N = 100$. The multiplier for the average observed correlation would be $a = 1 - .00485 = .995$. The average correlation would be .199 instead of .200. The trivial size of the bias in the correlation is the reason that bias has traditionally been ignored. However, for very small sample size meta-analyses (average sample size less than 10), or for very fastidious analysts, it is possible to correct the observed treatment correlation for bias. The nonlinear correction corresponding to the preceding equation would be

$$r' = r/a \quad (6.17)$$

where

$$a = 1 - (1 - r^2)/(2N - 2) \quad (6.18)$$

If the meta-analysis is studying treatment correlations below .70 in magnitude, then the correction is very closely approximated by the linear correction

$$r' = r/a$$

where

$$a = (2N - 3)/(2N - 2) \quad (6.19)$$

The linear correction has the advantage that it can be applied *after* the meta-analysis. Just divide both the estimated mean and the estimated standard deviation of population correlations by the multiplier computed with N set at the average sample size. Note that the corrected correlation will be trivially larger than the uncorrected correlation.

A complete treatment of bias in the d statistic is given in Hedges and Olkin (1985). Although the bias is trivial for all but very small sample studies, they recommend routine correction for that bias. Indeed, they use the symbol d only for the corrected statistic. The bias in d is approximately given by

$$E(d) = a\delta \tag{6.20}$$

where

$$a = 1 + 3/(4N - 12) \tag{6.21}$$

How large is this bias? Consider a study with a textbook-sized effect $d = .40$ based on a sample size of $N = 100$. The multiplier is $a = 1 + .0077 = 1.0077$. The average study effect size would be .403 instead of .400. On the other hand, consider a study done with an extremely small sample size, say, $N = 10$ (five subjects in each group). The multiplier would be $a = 1 + .107 = 1.107$ and the average effect size would be .443 rather than .400. The correction is straightforward; just divide by a:

$$d' = d/a \tag{6.22}$$

Note that this is a linear correction. Thus, it could be applied *after* the meta-analysis. Just divide both the estimated mean and the estimated standard deviation of corrected d values by the multiplier a. Again, the N used should be the average N. The corrected effect sizes will be slightly smaller than the uncorrected effect sizes.

Recording, Computational, and Transcriptional Errors

Meta-analysis will inevitably include some studies with bad data. There might be a recording error in gathering the primary data or in entering it into the computer. The study effect size could be erroneous because of computational error or an error in algebraic sign in the effect size. Finally, error can arise in transcription: from computer output to analyst table, from analyst table to manuscript table, from manuscript table to published table. Some have even suggested that a meta-analyst might miscopy a figure, but it is well-known that meta-analysts do not make errors.

Study results should be examined for extreme outliers. This can eliminate the most extreme cases of bad data. However, keep in mind the caveats about outlier analysis in meta-analysis presented in Chapters 3 and 5. Also, even with an outlier analysis, smaller erroneous effect sizes will not be detectable. Thus, any meta-analysis with a very large number of effect sizes will usually have at least a few bad data points.

Because bad data cannot be completely avoided, it is important to consider variation in study results with some caution. A certain percentage of the original observed variation will be due to bad data. A larger proportion of the residual variation—that left after all other study artifacts have been corrected—may be due to bad data.

Multiple Artifacts and Corrections

Unfortunately, there is no rule that says that study results can be distorted by only one artifact. Sampling error will be present in all studies. Error of measurement in the dependent variable will be present in all studies. Imperfect control of the nominal treatment variable will be unavoidable in most studies. Thus, a meta-analysis free of artifact will usually require that effect sizes be corrected for a number of sources of error.

Other than the removal of the most extreme outliers, there is no correction for bad data. Sampling error acts differently from other artifacts in that it is (1) additive and (2) unsystematic. Although a confidence interval for the effect size provides an unbiased estimate of potential sampling error for the single study, there is no *correction* for sampling error at the level of the single study. We will consider correcting the problem of sampling error in meta-analysis in the next chapter.

The artifacts other than sampling error and bad data are systematic in nature and, thus, potentially correctable. The key is to have the necessary information about the size of the artifact process (e.g., knowledge of the extent of unreliability or the extent of range restriction or the extent of imperfect construct validity). You can correct each artifact where there is adequate artifact information, be this one artifact or seven. Every artifact left uncorrected results in a corresponding underestimate of the true effect size. Furthermore, variation in uncorrected artifacts across studies looks like true variance in treatment effect. This may create the appearance of across-setting variation where there is none. If there is true variation in treatment effect, then uncorrected artifacts mask the true differences. That is, variation in apparent effect size due to uncorrected artifacts may override the differences due to true moderator variables and, thus, make it difficult to identify the true moderator variable by examining the studies after the fact.

Correction for artifacts is not difficult if the information on each artifact is given. Consider an example: a study of social skills training for first-line supervisors conducted in a factory setting. The measure of job performance is performance ratings by the immediate manager of each supervisor on a single 100-point graphic rating scale. Because the investigator doubted that performance ratings are measured on a ratio scale (a fact), the investigator decided that parametric statistics could not be used (a statistical error on his part). So the investigator decided to do a sign test on the data. The combined group data were split at the median and a chi-square test was run comparing the proportion of above-average performance among the supervisors with and without the skills training. Assume the treatment effect for training on consensus performance ratings is $d_{TY} = .40$. The true population treatment correlation is thus $r_{TY} = .20$. The inter-rater reliability of performance ratings by a single supervisor on a single rating scale averages .28 (Hunter & Hirsh, 1987; King, Hunter, & Schmidt, 1980). Thus, the effect size is reduced from $d_{TY} = .40$ to

$$d_{TY'} = \sqrt{.28}\, d_{TY} = .53\, d_{TY} = .53\,(.40) = .21$$

For a study with a total sample size of 100, this would reduce statistical power from an already low 51% to a very low 18%. The effect of a dichotomization using a median split for a d value less than .50 is simply to decrease the value by 20%, that is,

$$d_{TY''} = .80\, d_{TY'} = .80\,(.21) = .17$$

This reduces the statistical power from a very low 18% to an even lower 13%. That is, the two artifacts together reduce the effect size from .40 to .17, less than half its proper value. The statistical power is reduced from an already undesirable 51% to only 13%, an increase in the error rate for the significance test from 49% to 87%.

The systematic effect of the artifacts can be eliminated from the study by correction formulas. We have

$$\begin{aligned} d_{TY} &= d_{TY'}/.53 = (d_{TY''}/.80)/.53 = d_{TY''}/.424 \\ &= 2.36\, d_{TY''} \end{aligned}$$

That is, if the artifacts reduce the size of the effect by 58%, we can restore the value by dividing by the corresponding factor .42. However, while this correction eliminates the systematic error in the effect size, it does not eliminate the increased sampling error. A proper statistical test on the corrected effect size gives the same p values as the test on the uncorrected effect size. Thus, statistical correction formulas do not restore the lost statistical power.

Consider the preceding example in abstract form. The effect of the first artifact is to multiply the effect size by a multiplicative factor a_1 as in

$$d' = a_1 d$$

The effect of the second artifact is to multiply by a second factor a_2 as in

$$d'' = a_2 d'$$

The impact of the two factors is

$$d'' = a_2 d' = a_2(a_1)d = a_1 a_2 d$$

namely, to multiply the effect size by a multiplicative factor a, which is the product of the two separate artifact multipliers. That is,

$$d'' = ad$$

where

$$a = a_1 a_2$$

The effect size is then restored to its original value by the correction formula

$$d = d''/a \tag{6.23}$$

The preceding example is typical of correction for multiple artifacts in effect sizes of moderate size. Each artifact reduces the effect size by a multiplicative factor. The net effect is to reduce the effect size by a multiplicative factor that is the product of the separate multipliers. That is, the attenuating effect of several artifacts is to reduce the effect size by the product of the separate attenuating factors. The corresponding correction restores the effect size to its original size by dividing by the attenuation multiplier.

There is one caveat to the preceding discussion: It is exactly true for the treatment correlation but only an approximation for the effect size d. If a treatment effect is so large that the approximation $d = 2r$ breaks down, then the multiplicative formula should be applied only to the treatment correlation. The treatment effect d can then be computed by the usual conversion formula.

For example, consider the social skills training example for a very large treatment effect, say, $d = 1.50$. The observed treatment correlation satisfies the attenuation equation

$$r_{TY''} = .42\, r_{TY}$$

The effect size $d = 1.50$ corresponds to a treatment correlation of .60. The artifacts reduce this correlation from .60 to

$$r_{TY''} = .42(.60) = .25$$

This attenuated treatment correlation corresponds to an attenuated effect size of $d = .52$. The attenuation in the d statistic is from 1.50 to .52, which is by a factor of .35 rather than the factor .42 for the treatment correlation.

The treatment of multiple artifacts is very straightforward for the treatment correlation. The reduction in the size of the treatment correlation by a series of artifacts is effected by multiplication of the correlation by a total multiplier that is the product of the separate artifact attenuation multipliers. The treatment correlation can be restored to its proper size by correcting for those artifacts by dividing by the attenuation multiplier.

For the d statistic, correction for artifacts is only slightly more difficult. If the unattenuated population d value falls in the moderate range $-.50 < d < +.50$, then the formulas for the treatment correlation apply directly to the d statistic. If the population effect size falls outside the moderate range, then the d value can be converted to a correlation, the correlation can be corrected, and the corrected correlation can be converted to a corrected d value.

7

Meta-Analysis Methods for *d* Values

This chapter presents the meta-analysis formulas for effect sizes from experimental studies. In this chapter, we consider only the posttest—only independent-groups experimental designs. In such designs, different people are assigned to different treatment groups, hence the label "independent groups" designs. The next chapter will consider "within subjects" or "repeated measures" designs. Studies with more than two levels for a treatment variable could be handled within the present framework using contrasts, but this is beyond the scope of the present book.

As discussed in textbooks on research design, the key difference between experimental and observational studies is that in experimental studies subjects are randomly assigned to treatments. The control of extraneous influences on study outcomes achieved by random assignment cannot always be fully duplicated by the statistical controls that can be used in observational (nonexperimental) studies. It is random assignment that allows inference of causality in single experimental studies. In this chapter, our primary focus is on experimental studies, but the d statistic can also be used with observational data, and we discuss such usages in some detail. However, the reader should bear in mind the fundamental distinction between experimental and observational research. Even when the two types of research examine the same questions under apparently similar conditions, the obtained results can sometimes be different (see, e.g., Heinsman & Shadish, 1996; Shadish & Ragsdale, 1996).

In Chapters 5 and 9, we present extended discussions of the distinction between random-effects and fixed-effects models of meta-analysis. Fixed-effects models assume a priori that there is no variation in population parameters (in this case, population d values or δ values) across studies. If this assumption is erroneous, meta-analysis results can be very inaccurate. Random-effects models, by contrast, allow for variability across studies in underlying population parameter values and provide methods for estimating the magnitude of this variability. As noted in Chapters 5 and 9, most of the meta-analyses published in *Psychological Bulletin* over the last 25 years are based on fixed-effects models and for that reason may well be inaccurate. *For this reason, we want to emphasize that all the meta-analysis methods presented in this chapter for d values are random-effects models.* No fixed-effects models are presented.

Independent-groups studies could be analyzed using correlations. The size of the treatment effect could be measured by the (point biserial) correlation between treatment and effect. This use of correlation to measure the treatment effect has the advantage of lending itself to multivariate techniques such as partial correlation, multiple regression, and path analysis. However, most meta-analysts have chosen to use a measure of effect size denoted d, the difference between the group means divided by the standard deviation. It matters little because either statistic can be algebraically transformed into the other.

Where the outcome (dependent) variable is dichotomous (e.g., died or lived), another statistic, the odds ratio, can be used. The odds ratio is frequently used in medical research. We do not present meta-analysis methods for the odds ratio statistic in this book, because it is rarely used in social science research. The reason is that our dependent variables are rarely true dichotomies. See Haddock, Rindskopf, and Shadish (1998) for a treatment of the odds ratio in meta-analysis.

The reader who starts this book with this chapter is cautioned that many important issues regarding the d statistic are discussed in Chapter 6. Chapter 6 should be read before this chapter. The reader is also cautioned that this chapter is less detailed than Chapters 3 and 4 because many explanations are identical to the corresponding explanation for the meta-analysis of r and are not repeated here for want of space. That is, to avoid repetition, many conceptual issues discussed in Chapters 3 and 4 are not repeated in this chapter.

The d statistic is affected by all the same artifacts as the correlation, including sampling error, error of measurement, and range variation, but the terminology is the same only for sampling error. Many experimenters believe that error of measurement in the dependent variable is irrelevant in experiments because it averages out in the group means. However, error of measurement enters the variance of the dependent variable and, hence, enters the denominator of d. Thus, the value of d is systematically lowered by error of measurement, and differences across studies in the reliability of the dependent variable produce spurious differences in the value of d.

Error of measurement in the independent variable is also not acknowledged by most experimenters. In their mind, persons are unequivocally assigned to one treatment group or the other. However, those who have used manipulation checks have found that what is nominally the same treatment for all may be a very different thing to different persons. Some hear the instructions while some do not. Some give one meaning to ambiguous instructions while others give another. Error of measurement in the independent and dependent variables was discussed in Chapter 6. It is also discussed in more detail later in this chapter.

Range variation goes under another name in experimental work, namely, "strength of treatment." In dichotomous experiments, the independent variable is scored 0–1, regardless of how strong the treatment is. However, if differences in treatments across studies can be coded, then treatment effects can be projected to a common reference strength and the results of different studies become comparable. However, studies often do not give the information needed to code for treatment strength. The resulting problems are discussed later (see also Chapter 6).

Effect Size Indexes: *d* and *r*

Consider an intervention such as training managers in interpersonal skills. The effect of such an intervention might be assessed by comparing the performance of managers who have had such training (the experimental group) with the performance of comparable managers who have not (the control group). The usual comparison statistic is t (or F, which, in this context, is just the square of t, i.e., $F = t^2$). However, this is a very poor statistic because its size depends on the amount of sampling error in the data. The optimal statistic (which measures size of effect in a metric suitable for path analysis or analysis of covariance or other effects) is the point biserial correlation r. The great advantage of the point biserial correlation is that it can be inserted into a correlation matrix in which the intervention is then treated like any other variable. For example, the partial correlation between the intervention and the dependent variable with some prior individual difference variable held constant is equivalent to the corresponding analysis of covariance (Hunter, 1988).

Path analysis can be used to trace the difference between direct and indirect effects of the intervention (Hunter, 1986, 1987). For example, training might enhance the interpersonal skills of supervisors. This, in turn, might increase their subordinates' satisfaction with the supervisor, which, in turn, might cause a decrease in subordinate absenteeism. If this is the case, then path analysis would show the training to have a direct effect only on the supervisors' interpersonal skills, even though the intervention was also having second-order and third-order indirect effects on subordinate satisfaction and absenteeism, respectively.

The theory of sampling error for the point biserial correlation is identical to the theory for the Pearson correlation given in the previous section, except that the point biserial correlation may need to be corrected for unequal sample sizes in the two groups before cumulation (as discussed later).

When one variable is dichotomous, the usual formula for the Pearson product moment correlation will yield the point biserial correlation r_{pb}. Thus, popular statistical packages, such as SPSS and SAS, can be used to compute the point biserial correlation. There are also other formulas for r_{pb}:

$$r_{pb} = (\sqrt{pq})\,(\bar{Y}_E - \bar{Y}_C)/SD_y \tag{7.1}$$

where $\bar{Y}_E$ is the mean of the experimental group on the continuous (usually the dependent) variable, $\bar{Y}_C$ is the mean for the control group, and p and q are the proportion in the experimental and control groups, respectively. It is important to note that SD_y is *not* the within-group *SD* used in computing d; SD_y is the pooled standard deviation of *all* scores on the dependent variable. The two groups need not be experimental and control groups; they can be any two groups, for example, males and females or high school graduates and nongraduates. Another formula for r_{pb} is

$$r_{pb} = (\bar{Y}_E - \bar{Y}_T)\sqrt{p/q}/SD_y \tag{7.2}$$

where $\bar{Y}_T$ is the total group mean for the continuous variable, and all other terms are as defined previously.

Maximum Value of Point Biserial *r*

Many texts (e.g., Nunnally, 1978) state that the maximum value of r_{pb} is not 1.00 as it is for the Pearson correlation, but rather .79. They further state that this is the maximum value only when $p = q = .50$; otherwise, the maximum value is lower than .79. However, this theorem is false for experiments. The implicit assumption in this theorem is that the two groups were formed by dichotomizing a normally distributed variable, such as mental ability. This is the case treated in Chapter 2 under the rubric "dichotomization." Assume that two variables X and Y have a bivariate normal distribution. If a dichotomous variable X' is formed by splitting the distribution of X, then the correlation between the dichotomous variable X' and Y is equal to the original correlation between X and Y multiplied by a constant, which is at most .79. Hence, the statement that the point biserial correlation is at most .79.

Suppose the two groups in the study are defined as those who are above the median on anxiety versus those below the median on anxiety. The question is: Which group will perform better in an assessment center group exercise? Then, if the continuous anxiety variable had a bivariate normal relationship to the dependent variable, the theorem in Chapters 2 and 3 would apply. If the correlation between the anxiety test and performance on the group task is .30, then the point biserial correlation for the two group mean comparisons will be $(.79)(.30) = .24$.

However, in a typical experiment, the dichotomous variable is defined by treatment groups rather than by splitting some continuous variable. The treatment group is defined by some experimental process. For example, at the end of World War II, some Jews migrated to Israel while other Jews remained in Europe. The two groups were then subjected to the impact of radically different environments. Where the groups are defined by process or treatment differences, the theorem given in Chapter 3 does not apply. Instead, the size of the correlation is determined by the size of the treatment effect. The larger the treatment effect, the higher the correlation. As the treatment effect becomes larger and larger, the implied correlation gets closer and closer to 1.00.

In a purely statistical sense, the difference between the two cases lies in the assumption that the continuous independent variable has a bivariate normal relationship to the continuous dependent variable. That constraint places distinct limits on how far apart the two group means on the dependent variable can be. The largest difference occurs if the continuous variables are perfectly correlated. In this case, the two groups are the top and bottom halves of a normal distribution. The largest difference for such groups occurs if the split is at the mean, a difference of 1.58 standard deviations.

If the groups are defined by a treatment process, then there is no mathematical limit on the size of the difference between the two groups. Consider the impact of education on knowledge of history. Consider first two groups of first graders. One group goes to school for the usual 9 months while the other group goes to school for 10 months. The two distributions are likely to overlap substantially, and the point biserial correlation would be low. On the other hand, consider two groups from a third-world country such as India. One group is raised in a mountain village where children rarely go to school at all, while the other group is educated in Bombay where they go all the way through college. There is likely to be no overlap between the two knowledge distributions. The difference could be 100 or 1,000 standard deviations, and the point biserial correlation could be arbitrarily close to 1.00.

The Effect Size (*d* Statistic)

Glass (1977) and his associates and Cohen (1977) popularized a transform of the point biserial correlation called the effect size statistic d. The effect size d is the difference between the means in standard score form, that is, the ratio of the difference between the means to the standard deviation. The two variants of the effect size statistic are determined by considering two different standard deviations that might be used for the denominator. The standard deviation that will be used here is the pooled within-group standard deviation used in analysis of variance. The alternative is the control group standard deviation as used by Smith and Glass (1977). However, because there is rarely a large difference between the control and experimental group (a comparison that can be separately cumulated), it seems reasonable to use the statistic with the least sampling error. The within-group standard deviation has only about half the sampling error of the control group standard deviation.

If the variance for the experimental group is V_E, the variance for the control group is V_C, and the sample sizes are equal, then the within-group variance V_W is defined by

$$V_W = (V_E + V_C)/2 \tag{7.3}$$

That is, it is the average of the two within-group variances. If the sample sizes are not equal, then a sample size weighted average could be used:

$$V_W = (N_E V_E + N_C V_C)/(N_E + N_C) \tag{7.4}$$

where N_E and N_C are the sample sizes for the experimental group and control group, respectively. This is the maximum likelihood estimate of the population within-group variance. As it happens, the most common current analysis of variance formula is the modified formula popularized by Fisher, who chose to use slightly different formulas for his analysis of variance. He weighted each variance by its degrees of freedom, that is, by $N - 1$ instead of N:

$$V_W = [(N_E - 1)V_E + (N_C - 1)V_C]/[(N_E - 1) + (N_C - 1)] \tag{7.5}$$

In view of this convention, we will use the Fisher formula, although it actually makes little difference.

The effect size statistic d is then defined by

$$d = (Y_E - Y_C)/S_W \tag{7.6}$$

where S_W is the within-group standard deviation, that is, the square root of the within-group variance. That is, d is the difference between the means divided by the within-group standard deviation.

Most researchers are used to comparing group means using the t statistic. However, the t statistic depends on the sample size and, thus, is not a proper measure of the size of the treatment effect. That is, for purposes of testing a difference for statistical significance, it is true that the larger the sample size the more "significant" a given observed difference would be. However, the treatment effect we want to estimate is the population treatment effect, which is defined without reference to sample size. The statistic d can be thought of as a version of t that is made independent of sample size.

The three statistics d, t, and r are all algebraically transformable from one to the other. These transformations are shown here for the special case of equal sample sizes in the two groups, that is, for $N_E = N_C = N/2$, where N is the total sample size for that study. The most common statistic reported is t. Thus, in meta-analysis, we often want to convert t to either d or r. The transformation formulas are

$$d = 2t/\sqrt{N} \tag{7.7}$$

$$r = t/\sqrt{t^2 + N - 2} \tag{7.8}$$

For example, if the total sample size is $N = 100$ and the study value of t is 2.52, then

$$d = (2/\sqrt{100})\,(2.52) = .2(2.52) = .504$$
$$r = 2.52/\sqrt{2.52^2 + 98} = 2.52/\sqrt{104.3504} = .247$$

If the d statistic is given, then it can be transformed to either r or t:

$$r = (d/2)/[(N-2)/N + (d/2)^2]^{1/2} \tag{7.9}$$

$$t = (\sqrt{N}/2)\,d \tag{7.10}$$

For example, reverse the previous case for $N = 100$ and $d = .504$:

$$r = (.504/2)/[98/100 + (.504/2)^2]^{1/2} = .247$$
$$t = (\sqrt{100}/2)\,d = (10/2)\,(.504) = 2.52$$

If the point biserial correlation r is given, then

$$d = \sqrt{[(N-2)/N]}\,2r/\sqrt{(1-r^2)} \tag{7.11}$$

$$t = \sqrt{(N-2)}\,[r/\sqrt{(1-r^2)}] \tag{7.12}$$

For example, given $N = 100$ and $r = .247$, we have

$$d = \sqrt{(98/100)}\,2(.247)/\sqrt{(1-.247^2)} = .505$$

$$t = \sqrt{98}\,(.247)/\sqrt{(1-.247^2)} = 2.52$$

The value for d is off from .504 by rounding error.

The preceding formulas are complicated by the fact that the Fisher estimate of the within-group variance is used. If the maximum likelihood estimate were used, then the formulas relating r and d would be

$$d = 2r/\sqrt{(1 - r^2)} \tag{7.13}$$

$$r = (d/2)/\sqrt{[1 + (d/2)^2]} = d/\sqrt{(4 + d^2)} \tag{7.14}$$

These formulas are also quite accurate approximations for the Fisher estimate, except for very small sample sizes.

The d to r and r to d conversions are especially simple for the usual small treatment effect sizes. If $-.4 < d < +.4$ or $-.2 < r < +.2$, then, to a close approximation, we have

$$d = 2r, \tag{7.15}$$

$$r = d/2. \tag{7.16}$$

The preceding formulas are for the equal sample size case. If the control group and experimental group have different sizes, then the number "2" is replaced by

$$\text{“2”} = 1/\sqrt{(pq)}$$

where p and q are the proportion of persons in the two groups.

Some studies characterize the outcome in statistics other than t, d, or r. Glass, McGaw, and Smith (1981) provided transformation formulas for many such cases. However, the transformed value in such cases will not have the sampling error given by our formulas. In particular, probit transformations yield effect sizes with much larger sampling errors than do our formulas for d and r. This will lead to undercorrections for sampling error variance for such estimates of d and r.

Correction of the Point Biserial *r* for Unequal Sample Sizes

Conceptually, the effect size is normally thought of as independent of the sample sizes of the control and experimental groups. However, in a natural environment, the importance of a difference depends on how often it occurs. Because the point biserial correlation was originally derived for natural settings, it is defined so as to depend on the group sample sizes. As it happens, for a given size treatment effect, the correlation is smaller for unequal sample sizes. For sample size differences as large as 90–10 or 10–90, the correlation is smaller by a factor of .60, that is, 40% smaller. Thus, extremely uneven sampling can cause substantial understatement of the correlation.

In a typical experiment, any large difference between the sample sizes is usually caused by resource limitations rather than fundamental frequencies in nature. Thus, the point biserial correlation that we want is the point biserial correlation that we would have gotten had we been able to do the study with equal sample sizes. That is, we would like to "correct" the observed correlation for the attenuation effect of unequal sampling. The formula for this correction is

$$r_c = ar/\sqrt{[(a^2 - 1)r^2 + 1]} \tag{7.17}$$

where

$$a = \sqrt{[.25/pq]} \tag{7.18}$$

For example, if our study were cut short before we had finished the control group, we might have finished with 90 subjects in the experimental group but only 10 in the control group. We thus have $p = .90$, $q = .10$, and

$$a = \sqrt{.25/[(.90)(.10)]} = \sqrt{2.7777} = 1.6667$$

If the correlation for the unequal groups were .15, then the equal-group correlation would have been

$$r_c = 1.67(.15)/\sqrt{[(1.67^2 - 1)(.15^2) + 1]} = .246$$

Correcting the point biserial correlation in this manner increases its sampling error variance by the factor $(r_c/r)^2$. The sampling error variance of the corrected correlation is

$$S_{e_c}^2 = (r_c/r)^2 \, S_e^2$$

where r_c is the corrected correlation, r is the uncorrected correlation, and S_e^2 is the sampling error of the uncorrected correlation. Note that if r_c is entered into the meta-analysis without taking this into account, the meta-analysis will be conservative; that is, it will undercorrect for sampling error and, hence, overestimate the corrected standard deviation of r, that is, SD_ρ. One way to avoid this is to enter a smaller N, a value of N that corresponds to $S_{e_c}^2$. The needed value for N can be computed by solving Equation 3.7 for N after setting Var(e) equal to $S_{e_c}^2$. In fact, this procedure should be used whenever a correlation or d value has been corrected or adjusted prior to entry into the computer programs.

The effect size d is already expressed independently of the two sample sizes, although this poses certain problems for natural groups of quite uneven sizes (such as persons with and without migraine headache).

Kemery, Dunlap, and Griffeth (1988) criticized this correction formula and offered an alternative that first converts the point biserial correlation to a biserial correlation and then converts the biserial correlation to a point biserial with a 50–50 split. The Kemery et al. formulas yield accurate results only if the underlying distribution of the dichotomized variable is normal. Where this does not hold, the results are not accurate. The normal distribution assumption is usually not appropriate in experiments.

Examples of the Convertibility of *r* and *d*

The d statistic is often used to express the difference between treatment and control groups in experimental studies. Indeed, that is our major focus in this chapter. However, d can also be used to express the difference between any two groups. Differences between naturally occurring groups expressed in d form are often very informative, and the same relationships can be expressed using the point biserial r. For example, females average higher than males on measures of perceptual speed; d is approximately .70. What is the correlation in the population between sex and perceptual speed?

$$r = (d/2)/\sqrt{\{1 + (d/2)^2\}} = .35/1.05948 = .33$$

Thus, the population correlation is .33. Because men and women are about equal in numbers in the population (i.e., $p \cong q \cong .50$), the value of r computed from d is the same as would be computed from representative samples from the population.

As another example, the sex difference on height in the population is approximately $d = 1.50$. This translates into a population correlation between sex and height of $r = .60$.

Consider another example. In the United States, the difference in academic achievement between black and white students is approximately 1 standard deviation, that is, $d = 1.00$. What is the correlation between race and academic achievement? Consider first the formula assuming equal numbers of blacks and whites (Equation 7.4):

$$r = 1.00/\sqrt{4 + 1.00^2} = .45$$

This correlation of .45 is the value that would apply if there were equal numbers of black and white students (i.e., $N_W = N_B$). However, this is not the case; black students are only about 13% of the total. Thus, this value must be adjusted to reflect that fact. The correlation reflecting these unequal frequencies is $r = .32$. Thus, for natural populations, if the two groups have greatly different sizes, the natural correlation is substantially smaller.

In some cases in dealing with naturally occurring groups, one encounters a form of range restriction in d. The effect of this is typically to bias the observed d statistic downward. For example, suppose one is interested in estimating the black-white difference on a cognitive ability test among job applicants but has data only for incumbents. Because incumbents are selected (directly or indirectly) at least in part on cognitive ability, the raw score difference is smaller among incumbents than among applicants. Of course, the variances in each group are also smaller, but the decrease in within-group variances is often not sufficient to prevent an overall downward bias when using the d statistic in the selected (incumbent) group as an estimate of the d statistic in the unselected (applicant group). Bobko, Roth, and Bobko (2001) presented procedures for correcting for such range restriction in d. They provided an equation for correcting when the range restriction is direct (e.g., incumbents have been selected directly on cognitive ability) and another equation for correcting when range restriction is indirect (e.g., incumbents have been selected on some variable correlated with cognitive ability). Because range restriction is almost always indirect (see Chapters 3–5), this latter equation will typically be the more appropriate and more accurate, while the equation for direct range restriction will undercorrect. Unfortunately, the information needed to apply the equation for correcting for indirect range restriction will rarely be available (it requires information on the third variable on which the range restriction took place). However, in these circumstances, use of the correction for direct range restriction will nevertheless provide estimates that are more accurate than those obtained when no correction is made. See also Roth, BeVier, Bobko, Switzer, and Tyler (2001) and Roth, Bobko, Switzer, and Dean (2001).

Problems of Artificial Dichotomization

Throughout this chapter, we focus on true binary variables such as the control group versus experimental group distinction. If the binary variable is created by dichotomizing a continuous variable—as when people are classified as "high anxious" or "low anxious" using a median split on a continuous anxiety measure—then it is important to remember that the word "correlation" becomes ambiguous. There is the correlation between the continuous variable and the dependent variable—ingenuously called the "biserial" correlation—and the correlation between the binary variable and the dependent variable—called the "point biserial" correlation. The conversion formulas given in this chapter apply to the point biserial correlation. To convert from d to the continuous correlation, one would first convert from d to the point biserial correlation using Equation (7.14) in this chapter. Then one would convert the point biserial correlation to the biserial correlation using the formula to correct for dichotomization given in Chapter 3.

In experimental studies, it is common for researchers to define a binary variable such as "anxiety" by a median split on a continuous measure. If the split is the same across studies, there is no problem in simply ignoring the dichotomization for purposes of the initial meta-analysis. The final values for d can be converted to the biserial correlation if desired. However, if the binary variable is created using different splits across studies, then the point biserial correlation and the corresponding d values will vary across studies artifactually because of the variation in split. In the case of "turnover" studies, the variation can be extreme, for example, 50–50 for one author versus 95–5 for another. In such cases, we recommend that the researcher conduct the meta-analysis on correlations and use the correction formulas from Chapters 3 and 4 to correct for dichotomization.

An Alternative to d: Glass's d

Glass has used a variation on the d statistic. He uses the control group standard deviation instead of the within-group standard deviation. His reason for this is that the treatment may have an effect on the experimental group standard deviation as well as on the experimental group mean. That point is well taken; where there is a treatment effect, there may well be a treatment by subject interaction. However, if we wish to check for this, there is a much more effective procedure than altering the definition of d. We can do a meta-analysis that compares the values of the standard deviations directly.

Let v be the ratio of the experimental group standard deviation to the control group standard deviation, that is,

$$v = s_E/s_C \tag{7.19}$$

The value of v will be 1.00 (to within sampling error) if the usual assumptions of the t test are met, that is, if there is no treatment by subject interaction (assuming all subjects in the experimental group received the same strength of treatment; see the discussion in Chapter 6 of measurement error in the independent variable in experiments.) If the meta-analysis produces a mean value other than 1, then this could indicate a treatment by subject interaction. The direction of the departure from 1.00 will provide an inkling as to its nature.

Let us use the symbol d_G to denote the Glass variation on the effect size d. That is, let us define the symbol d_G by

$$d_G = (\bar{Y}_E - \bar{Y}_C)/s_C \tag{7.20}$$

If the meta-analysis shows the value of v to be 1, then the population values of d and d_G are the same. If the meta-analysis shows the value of v to be other than 1, then the meta-analysis value for d can be transformed into the meta-analysis value of d_G by the following identity:

$$d_G = (s_W/s_C)d = d\sqrt{[(1+v^2)/2]} \tag{7.21}$$

For example, suppose our meta-analysis found the average d to be .20 and the average value of v to be 1.50. Then the Glass d_G would be given by

$$d_G = [.20]\sqrt{[(1+1.5^2)/2]} = .255$$

There are two principal advantages to using the within-group standard deviation rather than the control group standard deviation, that is, using d rather than d_G. First, the control group standard deviation (and, hence, d_G) has much more sampling error than does the within-group standard deviation (and, hence, d). Second, most reports have a value for t or F and, hence, permit the computation of d. Many reports do not present standard deviations, and so d_G cannot be computed. Therefore, we have chosen to develop and present meta-analysis formulas only for d.

Sampling Error in the d Statistic

The Standard Error for d

Let us denote the population value of the effect size statistic by δ. The observed value d will then deviate from δ by sampling error. As with correlations, we can write the sampling error formula as

$$d = \delta + e$$

where e is the sampling error. For large samples,

$$E(e) = 0$$

and

$$\text{Var}(e) = (4/N)(1 + \delta^2/8) \tag{7.22}$$

where N is the total sample size. This formula assumes that N_1 and N_2 are not extremely discrepant ($N = N_1 + N_2$); it assumes the larger N_i is not more than 80% of the total N. This formula is accurate for sample sizes of $N = 50$ (25 in each group) or more. However, more accurate approximations are noted in the next few paragraphs.

The important alteration is a more accurate formula for the sampling error variance. The more accurate estimate is

$$\text{Var}(e) = [(N-1)/(N-3)]\,[(4/N)(1+\delta^2/8)] \qquad (7.23)$$

This formula differs from the large-sample formula only by the multiplier $[(N-1)/(N-3)]$. This multiplier differs only slightly from 1.00 for $N > 50$. However, it makes a bigger difference for sample sizes of 20 or less. As with Equation (7.22), Equation (7.23) assumes N_1 and N_2 are not extremely discrepant (i.e., a split no more extreme than 80%–20%).

It will rarely be the case that sample sizes are extremely different in the two groups; as a result Equation (7.23) is typically quite accurate. If the samples sizes in the two groups are very unequal (i.e., if the N in the larger of the two groups is over 80% of the total N), then a more accurate estimate of the sampling error variance of the d statistic is provided by the following equation (Hedges & Olkin, 1985, p. 86):

$$\text{Var}(e) = \frac{N_1 + N_2}{N_1 N_2} + \frac{d^2}{2(N_1 + N_2)} \qquad (7.23\text{a})$$

Laczo, Sackett, Bobko, and Cortina (in press) provided a discussion of cases in which the sample size split is very extreme. This can happen, for example, when computing the standardized difference (d value) between two groups in a workforce when one group (the minority group) is less than 20% of the total sample (i.e., there are more than 5 times as many people in one group than in the other). In such cases, Equation (7.23) underestimates sampling error, resulting in conservative meta-analysis results. That is, the result is an undercorrection for sampling error and an overestimation of the corrected standard deviation of the d values (SD_δ). In such a case, this conservative bias in the meta-analysis can be avoided by using Equation (7.23a). However, even in such a case, the conservative bias resulting from using Equation (7.23) is quite small and has little effect on the final meta-analysis results.

An excellent discussion of sampling error in very small sample size values of d is presented in Hedges and Olkin (1985). However, the reader is warned that the statistic that is traditionally denoted d is called g by Hedges and Olkin. They reserve the symbol d for their approximately unbiased estimator. We will denote the approximately unbiased estimator by d^*. The mean value of d across sample replications is

$$E(d) = a\delta \qquad (7.24)$$

where, to a close approximation,

$$a = 1 + .75/(N-3) \qquad (7.25)$$

For a sample of size $N = 100$, the bias multiplier is

$$a = 1 + .75/97 = 1 + .0077 = 1.01$$

which differs only trivially from 1.00. However, for very small samples—as in therapy research—the bias may warrant correction. For a sample size of $N = 20$, the multiplier a is

$$a = 1 + .75/17 = 1 + .044 = 1.044$$

To correct for the bias, we divide by the bias multiplier. If we denote the (approximately) unbiased estimator by d^*, then

$$d^* = d/a \tag{7.26}$$

This correction mechanically decreases the value of d, and, hence, the sampling error is similarly decreased. If we define sampling error by

$$d^* = \delta + e^*$$

then we have approximately

$$E(e^*) = 0$$

$$\text{Var}(e^*) = \text{Var}(e)/a^2 \tag{7.27}$$

There is a small error in Hedges and Olkin (1985) in this regard. They offer the approximation

$$\text{Var}(e^*) = (4/N)(1 + \delta^2/8)$$

This approximation assumes the further approximation

$$[(N - 1)/(N - 3)]/a^2 = 1$$

This approximation breaks down for sample sizes of 20 or less, where the more accurate approximation

$$[(N - 1)/(N - 3)]/a^2 = 1 + .25/(N - 3)$$

yields the formula that we have given in Equation 7.25.

For a bare-bones meta-analysis, bias can be corrected either study by study or after the meta-analysis has been done. If the meta-analysis is done on the usual d statistic, then the correction for bias would be

$$\text{Ave}(\delta) = \text{Ave}(d^*) = \text{Ave}(d)/a \tag{7.28}$$

where

$$a = 1 + .75/(\bar{N} - 3)$$

where $\bar{N}$ is the average sample size across studies.

The corresponding estimate of the standard deviation of population effect sizes would be

$$\text{Unbiased } SD_\delta = SD_\delta/a \tag{7.29}$$

Thus, to correct for bias after the fact, we merely divide both the mean and the standard deviation by the bias multiplier computed using the average sample size.

The Confidence Interval for δ

The d statistic has mean δ and sampling variance

$$\text{Var}(e) = [(N - 1)/(N - 3)]\ [(4/N)(1 + \delta^2/8)].$$

The square root of the sampling error variance Var(e) is the standard error of d. Denote the standard error by S. Except for very small sample sizes, the d statistic is approximately normally distributed. Thus, the 95% confidence interval for δ is given, to a close approximation, by

$$d = 1.96S < \delta < d + 1.96S.$$

The exact value of the standard error requires knowledge of δ. Because δ is unknown, we estimate the sampling error variance by substituting d for δ. That is, we estimate S^2 by

$$\text{Var}(e) = [(N - 1)/(N - 3)]\ [(4/N)(1 + d^2/8)]. \tag{7.30}$$

The estimated standard error S is then the square root of Var(e).

Cumulation and Correction of the Variance for Sampling Error

At this point, we begin the discussion of the meta-analysis of d. We start with a "bare-bones" meta-analysis, which makes no correction to the mean or variance for artifacts such as error of measurement. This form of meta-analysis corrects only for sampling error variance. We consider a meta-analysis that estimates the distribution of uncorrected population effect sizes δ_i from information about the study sample effect sizes d_i. We will return to the consideration of other artifacts in later sections. However, the reader should note that our final coverage of artifacts for the d statistic will be less extensive than our coverage for correlations. This reflects the greater complexity of correction formulas for d than for r. As noted at the beginning of this chapter, all the meta-analysis methods presented in this chapter are random-effects models. That is, none of the methods presented here assumes a priori that there is no variability in population delta (δ) values, as fixed-effects models do. In fact, a major purpose of the models presented here is to estimate the variability of population δ values across studies. Again, we refer the reader to the discussion of fixed-effects versus random-effects meta-analysis models presented in Chapters 5 and 9.

The simplest way to do a meta-analysis correcting for artifacts such as dichotomization and imperfect construct validity is to do the meta-analysis using r. This is done in four steps.

1. Convert all the ds to rs using the formula given earlier in this chapter. The maximum likelihood formula is

$$r = d/\sqrt{(4 + d^2)} \tag{7.31}$$

2. Use the methods described in Chapters 3 and 4 to conduct the meta-analysis on r, correcting for all possible artifacts.
3. Convert the final results for the mean correlation to a mean effect size using the conversion formula for r to d. The maximum likelihood formula is

$$d = 2r/\sqrt{(1 - r^2)} \tag{7.32}$$

4. Convert the standard deviation of correlations to the standard deviation for effect sizes using the formula

$$SD(\delta) = a\, SD_\rho$$

where

$$a = 2/(1 - r^2)^{1.5} \tag{7.33}$$

For example, suppose the meta-analysis on r yielded a mean treatment correlation of $\text{Ave}(\rho) = .50$ and a standard deviation of $SD(\rho) = .10$. The conversion to mean effect size would be

$$\text{Ave}(\delta) = 2(.50)/\sqrt{[1 - (.50)^2]} = 1.1547$$
$$SD(\delta) = a(.10)$$

where $a = 2/(1 - .25)^{1.5} = 2/.6495 = 3.0792$. That is, $\text{Ave}(\delta) = 1.15$ and $SD(\delta) = .31$.

Bare-Bones Meta-Analysis

The basic cumulation process is the same for d values as for correlations: One computes the frequency-weighted mean and variance of the effect size over studies and then corrects the variance for sampling error. Again, we point out that the model to be presented is a random-effects model. It assumes there may be real variability in effect sizes across studies and attempts to estimate the size of that variability. This is in contrast to all fixed-effects models, which assume a priori that there is no such variability (Hunter & Schmidt, 2000). (See Chapters 5 and 9 for a full discussion.)

Consider any set of weights w_i. There are three averages to be computed: (1) the weighted average of d, (2) the correspondingly weighted variance of d, and (3) the average sampling error variance. If we denote the average value of d by $\bar{d}$, then the averages are as follows:

$$\text{Ave}(d) = \sum w_i d_i / \sum w_i = \bar{d} \tag{7.34}$$

$$\text{Var}(d) = \sum w_i [d_i - \bar{d}]^2 / \sum w_i \tag{7.35}$$

$$\text{Var}(e) = \sum w_i \,\text{Var}(e_i) / \sum w_i \tag{7.36}$$

The tricky computation is the average sampling error variance, Var(e). The problem is that the sampling error variance within each study requires knowledge of the effect size for that study. That is,

$$\text{Var}(e_i) = (4/N_i)(1 + \delta_i^2/8)$$

depends on the population effect size δ_i, which is unknown. A good approximation in most cases is to substitute the mean value of d for δ_i in each study. In the case of the frequency-weighted average, this leads to the equation

$$\text{Var}(e) = (4/\bar{N})(1 + \bar{d}^2/8) \quad (7.37)$$

where $\bar{N}$ is the average sample size. That is, if we denote the total sample size by T and the number of studies by K, then

$$T = \sum N_i$$

$$\bar{N} = T/K$$

The more accurate formula for the sampling error variance is

$$\text{Var}(e) = [(\bar{N} - 1)/(\bar{N} - 3)][(4/\bar{N})(1 + \bar{d}^2/8)] \quad (7.38)$$

where $\bar{N}$ is the average sample size and $\bar{d}$ is the frequency-weighted value of d_i.

The variance of population effect sizes Var(δ) is the observed variance of effect sizes corrected for sampling error. The variance of population effect sizes is found by subtracting the sampling error variance from the observed variance. That is,

$$\text{Var}(\delta) = \text{Var}(d) - \text{Var}(e) \quad (7.39)$$

This difference can be interpreted as subtracting the variance in d due to sampling error. That is, subtracting the average sampling error variance corrects the observed variance for the effect of sampling error. The standard deviation of study population effect sizes is the square root of the variance

$$SD_\delta = \sqrt{\text{Var}(\delta)}$$

Thus, for bare-bones meta-analysis, if the observed distribution of effect sizes is characterized by the values Ave(d) and Var(d), then the study population effect size is characterized by the following:

$$\text{Ave}(\delta) = \text{Ave}(d) \quad (7.40)$$

$$\text{Var}(\delta) = \text{Var}(d) - \text{Var}(e) \quad (7.41)$$

$$SD_\delta = \sqrt{\text{Var}(\delta)} \quad (7.42)$$

If the effect size is really the same across studies, then the variance of population effect sizes is 0. That is, if there is no real variation in population effect sizes, then the observed variance will in expectation exactly equal the variance due to sampling error. Even if there is some variation across studies, the variance may still be small enough to ignore for practical or theoretical reasons. If the variation is large, especially if it is large relative to the mean value, then there should be a search for moderator variables.

A Worked Numerical Example

The reader is cautioned that discussions of examples in this chapter take certain liberties. To present an example and illustrate computations, we must present examples with a small number of studies. This means that the total sample size in the example is not nearly large enough to eliminate the effect of sampling error. That is, the estimates from the meta-analysis will still have sampling error in them. However, in this chapter we want to discuss the results as if the sampling error had been removed. Thus, for each example in this chapter, our discussion will be phrased as if the number of studies were much larger than shown in the example. The estimation of sampling error in the estimates from a meta-analysis will be considered in its own right in Chapter 9. That chapter contains sampling error estimates for many of the examples shown here.

Consider the following example for bare-bones meta-analysis:

N	d
100	−.01
90	.41*
50	.50*
40	−.10

*Significant at the .05 level.

Two of the effect sizes are significant and two are not. By the usual logic, a reviewer would assume from this that there is some moderator variable that causes the treatment to have an effect in some settings but have no effect in others. Could this be sampling error?

The bare-bones meta-analysis is

$$T = 100 + 90 + 50 + 40 = 280$$

$$\bar{N} = T/K = 280/4 = 70$$

$$\begin{aligned} \text{Ave}(d) &= [100(-.01) + 90\,(.41) + 50\,(.50) + 40\,(-.10)]/280 \\ &= 56.9/280 = .20, \end{aligned}$$

$$\begin{aligned} \text{Var}(d) &= [100(-.01 - .20)^2 + 90\,(.41 - .20)^2 \\ &\quad + 50\,(.50 - .20)^2 + 40\,(-.10 - .20)^2]/280 \\ &= 16.479/280 = .058854 \end{aligned}$$

The large-sample estimate of the sampling error variance is

$$\text{Var}(e) = (4/\bar{N})\,(1 + \bar{d}^2/8) = (4/70)(1 + .20^2/8) = .057429$$

Thus, we estimate the distribution of study population effect sizes by

$$\begin{aligned} \text{Ave}(\delta) &= \text{Ave}(d) = .20, \\ \text{Var}(\delta) &= \text{Var}(d) = \text{Var}(e) = .058854 - .057429 = .001425 \\ SD(\delta) &= \sqrt{.001425} = .038 \end{aligned}$$

We now consider an interpretation of this meta-analysis written as if the number of studies were much larger than 4. This meta-analysis has only four studies and a total sample size of 280. Thus, there is actually room for considerable (second order) sampling error in the meta-analysis estimates. This topic is considered in Chapter 9.

Suppose these meta-analysis estimates were very accurate; for example, assume the number of studies to be 400 rather than 4. If population effect sizes were normally distributed, then the middle 95% of population effect sizes would lie in the interval

$$.20 - 1.96D_{\delta} < \delta < .20 + 1.96\,SD_{\delta}$$
$$.13 < \delta < .27$$

For a population effect size to be 0, it would represent a standard score of

$$[0 - .20]/.038 = -5.26$$

This is an extremely unlikely possibility. Thus, in this example, meta-analysis shows the usual review logic to be quite wrong. It is not the case that the treatment has no effect in 50% of settings. There are no settings where the treatment effect is 0. Thus, in the two studies with nonsignificant effect sizes, there was a Type II error. That is, in this example, the error rate for the significance test was 50%.

Consider the use of the more accurate formula for the sampling error variance:

$$\begin{aligned}\text{Var}(e) &= [(\bar{N} - 1)/(\bar{N} - 3)]\ [4/\bar{N}]\ [1 + \bar{d}^2/8] \\ &= [69/67]\ [.057429] = .059143\end{aligned}$$

There is little difference in the estimate of the sampling error variance. However, there is a larger difference in the estimate of the study population effect size variance:

$$\text{Var}(\delta) = \text{Var}(d) - \text{Var}(e) = .058854 - .059143 = -.000289$$

Using the less accurate large-sample formula, the difference between observed variance and variance due to sampling error was .001425; that is, the observed variance was larger than expected on the basis of sampling error. However, the more accurate formula shows that the variance was almost exactly equal to the level expected from sampling error. The fact that the difference is negative shows that with only four studies, there is some second-order sampling error in Var(d) (see Chapter 9). The corresponding estimate of the standard deviation is $SD_{\delta} = 0$. Thus, using the more accurate sampling error formula generates a description of the study population correlations, which is

$$\text{Ave}(\delta) = .20$$
$$SD_{\delta} = 0$$

This estimate indicates that there is no variation in the study population effect sizes. That this is true is known from the fact that the authors generated the data using the same population effect size for all studies. In a real meta-analysis based on only four studies, the same finding would be only provisional.

To correct for bias, we first compute the bias multiplier:

$$a = 1 + .75/(\bar{N} - 3) = 1 + .75/67 = 1.0112$$

The corrected mean and standard deviation are thus

$$\text{Ave}(\delta) = .20/1.0112 = .1978 = .20$$
$$SD_\delta = 0/1.0112 = 0$$

Thus, for an average sample size of 70, the effect of correction for bias is smaller than rounding error.

Another Example: Leadership Training by Experts

Organizational psychologists have long suspected that training in interpersonal or leadership skills improves the performance of managers. Professor Fruitloop decided that he wanted to know the amount of improvement and, therefore, laid out the design of a meta-analysis. He decided that studies should meet two criteria. First, each training program must contain at least three key skills: active listening, negative feedback, and positive feedback. Second, the study should be run under controlled training conditions. To assure this, he used only studies in which the training was done by outside experts (see Table 7.1).

Of the five studies, only one shows a significant effect. Two of the studies show effects in the opposite direction. Thus, using traditional review standards, Fruitloop would be led to conclude that training in interpersonal skills had no impact (or uncertain impact) on performance of supervisors in a majority of settings. Fortunately, however, Fruitloop had heard of meta-analysis. The meta-analysis of the five studies in Table 7.1 is

$$T = 200$$
$$\bar{N} = 40$$
$$\text{Ave}(d) = .20$$
$$\text{Var}(d) = .106000$$

Using the more accurate formula,

$$\text{Var}(e) = [39/37]\,[4/40]\,[1 + .20^2/8] = .105932$$
$$\text{Var}(\delta) = \text{Var}(d) - \text{Var}(e) = .106000 - .105932 = .000068$$
$$SD_\delta = .01$$

For a meta-analysis of five studies with an average sample size of 40, the total sample size is only $T = 200$. Thus, the potential sampling error in the meta-analysis estimates would be about as large as the sampling error in a single study with $N = 200$, and that is very large (though these figures were set up so that such large errors did not occur). Computation of confidence intervals about the estimates from this meta-analysis will be presented in Chapter 9. (See also the related discussion of confidence intervals in Chapter 5.)

Table 7.1 Leadership training (studies with training by outside experts)

Author	*Sample Size*	*Effect Size*
Apple	40	−.24
Banana	40	−.04
Cherry	40	.20
Orange	40	.44
Melon	40	.64*

*Significant at the .05 level.

It is not our purpose here to focus on the sampling error in meta-analysis with a small number of studies. Rather, we used only a small number of studies so that it would be easy for the reader to replicate the computations in order to understand the formulas. For purposes of argument, assume that the residual variance of .000068 is not due to sampling error; that is, accept the standard deviation of .01 as real. A real standard deviation of .01 would mean that there is real variation in the study population effect sizes. Would that mean, however, that there was real variation in actual effect sizes? Certainly not. In a bare-bones meta-analysis, we control for only one artifact: sampling error. No control is included for variation in error of measurement, or variation in the degree of imperfection of construct validity, or variation in the strength of the treatment, and so on. Thus, there are many other artifacts that might have caused variance in the study effect size.

It is even more important to remember that this is a bare-bones analysis in interpreting the size of the treatment effect. Most of the artifacts not controlled have the effect of lowering the observed effect size. Thus, the observed mean of .20 is almost surely an underestimate, and possibly a massive underestimate.

Consider the difference between a narrative review and a meta-analysis, assuming these same results from a meta-analysis of 500 studies. Only 100 of the 500 studies would produce significant results. As many as 200 of the 500 studies would produce results in the wrong direction. Thus, the narrative review would probably conclude that training has an effect in only a minority of settings; on the other hand, 20% of the studies with significant results would find large effect sizes, d values of .60 or more. Thus, a narrative review might well conclude that in those settings where training works, it works quite well.

Using meta-analysis, Fruitloop discovered a very different pattern to population effect sizes. He found that virtually all the variation in observed results was actually due to sampling error. Thus, the available studies actually showed perfect consistency in the effect of training, a uniform effect size of $\delta = .20$. Thus, the effect size is never 0, and it is also never as large as .40, much less .60, the levels observed in isolated studies.

Analysis of Moderator Variables

The impact of an intervention might vary from setting to setting. For example, training programs might vary in quality, in quantity, or in the average learning ability of the trainees. If this were so, then the cumulation formulas would yield nonzero variance for the population effect sizes, that is, a nonzero value for SD_δ. The search for and detection of the moderator variables that account for such variation is identical to the procedure followed in looking for moderator variables in correlational studies. Indeed, the general mathematics is identical for both. In particular, if the number of studies is small and the number of coded study characteristics is large, then blind search is highly prone to capitalization on chance. (See the discussion of this in Chapter 2.) Chapter 9 discusses the hierarchical analysis of moderators in meta-analysis and the effect of second-order sampling error on moderator analysis in meta-analysis.

There are two ways to see if a study characteristic is a moderator variable or not: Use the characteristic to break the data into subsets or correlate the study characteristic with effect size. There have now been enough meta-analyses conducted with both methods to generate an opinion as to which method works better. It is our impression that the correlation method—which is usually touted as "more sophisticated"—is much more often used incorrectly. Thus, for most purposes, we would recommend the subset method be used. (See also the last topic in Chapter 8.)

Finally, we note that meta-analysis can examine moderators only at the study level. For example, if some studies have been conducted on males and some on females, then meta-analysis can examine sex as a potential moderator. However, if every study is based on a combination of males and females and reports only the total group results, sex cannot be tested as a moderator.

Using Study Domain Subsets

If the studies are broken down into subsets, then there is no new computational tool to be learned. The researcher merely performs a separate meta-analysis within each subset. For a bare-bones meta-analysis, there is nothing more to say. However, if artifacts other than sampling error are to be corrected—a critical feature in most research areas—then we have one additional word of advice. Often, artifact information for other artifacts is only sporadically available, and so artifact distribution meta-analysis (discussed later in this chapter) must be used. In most such cases, the artifact distributions are better computed for the entire set of studies rather than computed separately within subsets of studies. The whole domain artifact distribution values are then used in the computation of the within-subsets meta-analyses.

If the data are broken into subsets, then there are two ways that a moderator variable would show itself. First, there should be a difference in the mean effect size between subsets. Second, there should be a reduction in variance within subsets. These are not independent events. We know from an important theorem in analysis of variance that the total variance in effect size is the sum of the variance in mean effect sizes between subsets plus the average within-subset variance. Thus, if there is a large difference between the subset mean effect sizes, then the within-subset variance must be smaller than the overall variance.

This theorem applies equally well to either observed effect sizes or to population effect sizes. If the usual formula for components of variance is applied to the corrected variances rather than to the uncorrected variances, then the result is the same: A large difference between subset means implies a lower value for average within-subset variance than for overall variance. (However, when there are unequal numbers of studies in the two moderator groups and unequal Ns within studies, it becomes difficult to precisely compute the mean within-subset variance, because it becomes difficult to determine the appropriate weight to apply to the two variances. Under these circumstances—which are, in fact, the usual circumstances—it is best to focus solely on differences between the means [here, $\bar{d}_1 - \bar{d}_2$].)

Using Study Characteristic Correlations

Consider instead the correlation approach to the search for moderator variables. In this approach, we compute a correlation over studies between the coded study characteristic and the observed effect size. The effect of sampling error on this correlation is directly analogous to the effect of error of measurement on a correlation between variables over subjects: The correlation is systematically reduced. Thus, to correct a correlation between effect size and study characteristic for the effect of sampling error is to increase that correlation in proportion to the relative size of the real variation in effect size to the artificial variation caused by sampling error. This is directly analogous to correction for attenuation due to measurement error. This correction of $\text{Var}(d)$ for sampling error is comparable to correcting the usual within-experiment variance for error of measurement.

If the observed sample effect size is correlated with a study characteristic, then the correlation will be attenuated by the sampling error in the observed effect size in the same manner that the ordinary correlations across persons are attenuated by error of measurement. Consider the sampling error formula

$$d_i = \delta_i + e_i$$

and consider a study characteristic denoted y_i. Denote the correlation across studies between d and y as $\text{Cor}(d, y)$. The covariance is

$$\text{Cov}(d, y) = \text{Cov}(\delta, y) + \text{Cov}(e, y) \tag{7.43}$$

For a large set of studies, the covariance between sampling error and study characteristics will be 0. Thus, in the research domain as a whole, sampling error does not contribute to the covariance of study characteristic and effect size. However, because

$$\text{Var}(d) = \text{Var}(\delta) + \text{Var}(e)$$

sampling error does contribute to the variance of the effect sizes. Thus, the effect of sampling error is to increase the variance in the denominator of the study characteristic correlation while making no corresponding increase in the numerator. Therefore, the effect of sampling error is to decrease the size of the correlation.

The study characteristic correlation can be corrected for sampling error using a formula that is exactly analogous to the formula for correction of a correlation for error of measurement. To do this, we use the error of measurement to define a "reliability" denoted $\text{Rel}(d)$ and then use it to correct the observed correlation

Cor(d, y) in the usual manner. In measurement theory, the reliability of a variable affected by random error e_p is the ratio of variance of true scores T to observed scores X:

$$r_{XX} = \text{Var}(T)/\text{Var}(X)$$

where

$$\text{Var}(X) = \text{Var}(T) + \text{Var}(e)$$

The analogous formula for meta-analysis is

$$\text{Rel}(d) = \text{Var}(\delta)/\text{Var}(d) \quad (7.44)$$

To correct the over-subject correlation between variables X and Y for error of measurement in X is to divide by the square root of the reliability, that is,

$$r_{TY} = r_{XY}/\sqrt{r_{XX}}$$

The corresponding theorem for meta-analysis is

$$\text{Cor}(\delta, y) = \text{Cor}(d, y)/\sqrt{\text{Rel}(d)} \quad (7.45)$$

This formula generates an estimate of the study characteristic correlation, had all the studies been done with very large samples.

It is important to note that the preceding formula is derived based on the assumption that sampling error will be uncorrelated with any study characteristic. This theorem is true for the research domain and is approximately true for any meta-analysis done with a large number of studies. However, for a meta-analysis done with a small number of studies, the sampling errors in those particular studies may by chance be correlated with some of the study characteristic values for that sample of studies. This is the problem of capitalization on chance (see Chapter 2). As one sorts through potential moderator variables, some study characteristics may have a high-chance correlation with the sampling errors. This variable would then look like a strong moderator variable.

For a meta-analysis with a small number of studies, there is no statistical solution to the problem of capitalization on chance. In a research domain with good theories, there is a possible solution. Test first only that moderator variable predicted by a good theory that is well supported by other research. If that variable does not moderate the effect size, then treat all the remaining potential moderators with a very large grain of salt. If there is a theory that supports the discovered moderator variable, then the researcher should check the literature to see if there is any independent corroboration of that theory. For further discussion of this point, see the last part of Chapter 2.

A Worked Example: Training by Experts Versus Training by Managers

In his dissertation, Jim Russell tested the hypothesis that training of supervisors in interpersonal skills should be conducted by their own managers rather than by

Table 7.2 Training in interpersonal skills by managers versus by experts

Author	*Trainer*	*Sample Size*	*Effect Size*
Apple	Expert	40	−.25
Banana	Expert	40	−.05
Cherry	Expert	40	.20
Orange	Expert	40	.45
Melon	Expert	40	.65*
Cucumber	Manager	40	−.05
Tomato	Manager	40	.15
Squash	Manager	40	.40
Carrot	Manager	40	.65*
Pepper	Manager	40	.85*

*Significant at the .05 level (two-tailed test).

outside experts. That idea derived from the proposition that because managers act as role models for supervisors, the supervisors are much more likely to identify with procedures recommended by managers than with those recommended by outside experts.

Consider again the hypothetical cumulative study done by Fruitloop. Fruitloop discarded all studies done by managers as "lacking in experimental control." Thus, Fruitloop analyzed only studies where the training was done by experts. Suppose instead that all studies were analyzed. The results might look like those in Table 7.2. In this collection of studies, only 3 of 10 have significant effects, and 3 of 10 go in the opposite direction. Thus, traditional review practice would probably conclude that the effect of training in interpersonal skills is problematic at best.

The overall meta-analysis for the studies in Table 7.2 is as follows:

$$
\begin{aligned}
T &= 40 + 40 + \cdots = 400 \\
\bar{N} &= T/10 = 40 \\
\text{Ave}(d) &= .30 \\
\text{Var}(d) &= .116000 \\
\text{Var}(e) &= [39/37][4/40][1 + .30^2/8] = .106591 \\
\text{Var}(\delta) &= .116000 - .106591 = .009409 \\
SD_\delta &= .097
\end{aligned}
$$

For purposes of computational convenience, we have again presented a meta-analysis with only a small number of studies. A set of 10 studies with an average sample size of 40 represents only a total sample size of 400. Thus, there would still be a large potential sampling error in the estimates from the meta-analysis. The formulas for confidence intervals for $\bar{d}$ are presented in Chapter 9. (See also the related discussion in Chapter 5.)

Because we are not interested in such sampling error in this example, let us assume that we obtained similar results not with 10 studies but with 100 studies. The standard deviation of study effect size is .097, which is noticeably greater than 0. The standard deviation of .097 is also large relative to a mean effect size of .30. However, it is not large enough to suggest that there are any settings where the effect size is 0. If variation in effect size were normally distributed (it actually turns out to be dichotomous in this example), the middle 95% of effect sizes would be

$$.30 - 1.96(.097) < \delta < .30 + 1.96(.097)$$

$$.11 < \delta < .49$$

However, this is a large range of possible effects, and a search for a moderator variable is justified, especially because a theoretically based potential moderator has been identified a priori (i.e., managers vs. expert trainers).

Consider again the performance of the statistical significance test on this data set. Only 3 of the 10 effect sizes were significant. Yet the meta-analysis shows that all of the population effect sizes were positive. Thus, the (Type II) error rate for the significance test in this example is 70%. Furthermore, the variation in observed effect sizes covered a massive range: from $-.25$ to $+.85$. In fact, the meta-analysis shows that most of this variation is due to sampling error. Few values would actually be found outside the interval $.11 < \delta < .49$. On the other hand, there is still quite a bit of variability in results; thus, a search for moderator variables is well advised.

In this example, the moderator was hypothesized before the meta-analysis. Thus, we break the studies down into those where the training was done by outside experts versus those where the training was done by managers. The within-subset meta-analyses are as follows:

Training by Experts

$T = 40 + 40 + \cdots = 200$

$\bar{N} = T/10 = 40$

$\text{Ave}(d) = .20$

$\text{Var}(d) = .106000$

$\text{Var}(e) = [39/37][4/40][1 + .20^2/8] = .105932$

$\text{Var}(\delta) = .106000 - .105932 = .000068$

$SD_\delta = .008$

Training by Managers

$T = 40 + 40 + \cdots = 200$

$\bar{N} = T/10 = 40$

$\text{Ave}(d) = .40$

$\text{Var}(d) = .106000$

$\text{Var}(e) = [39/37][4/40][1 + .40^2/8] = .107514$

$\text{Var}(\delta) = .106000 - .107514 = -.001514$

$SD_\delta = 0$

Again, we note that the small number of studies was meant only for computational convenience. Assume that there were not 10, but 1,000 studies, 500 studies of each kind. That is, let us interpret the results of the meta-analysis as if there were little or no sampling error in the estimates.

In this example, breaking studies down by type of trainer shows the moderator effect in two ways. First, there is the wide difference between mean effect sizes: Ave(d) $=$ .20 for training by experts versus Ave(d) $=$ .40 for training by managers. Furthermore, the breakdown by type of trainer eliminates virtually all variation in effect size (beyond that due to sampling error). Thus, training by outside experts always has an effect of .20 standard deviations, while training by managers always has an effect of twice that size, .40 standard deviations.

Note that assuming a normal distribution for effect sizes produced a 95% interval from .11 to .49, suggesting that 2.5% of studies would produce values lower than $\delta = .11$ and that 2.5% of studies would produce values higher than $\delta = .49$. In fact, the distribution was not normal. Instead, half the studies had a population effect size of $\delta = .20$ (those with outside expert trainers) and half had a population effect size of $\delta = .40$ (those with manager trainers). Thus, the assumption of normality overestimated the actual spread of effect sizes.

In this case, there was only one moderator. When there are multiple moderators, the moderators may be correlated, and hence, they will be confounded if examined sequentially one at a time. In such cases, it is important to conduct moderator analysis hierarchically to avoid such confounding. See Chapter 9 for a discussion of hierarchical moderator analysis.

Another Worked Example: Amount of Training

We now present an example in which the impact of training on interpersonal skills varies as a function of the number of hours of training. The data are shown in Table 7.3. The measure of number of hours is the amount of time that the trainee is in actual interaction with the trainer (as opposed to watching the trainer work with someone else).

In this example, the effect size was significant only 1 in 12 times, and the results were positive in 7 of the 12 studies. That is, nearly half the studies found effects in the opposite direction. Traditional review practice would probably conclude that training in interpersonal skills has no effect.

The meta-analysis results are as follows:

All Studies

$T = 40 + 40 + \cdots = 480$

$\bar{N} = 480/12 = 40$

$\text{Ave}(d) = .15$

$\text{Var}(d) = .109717$

$\text{Var}(e) = .105702$

$\text{Var}(\delta) = .004015$

$SD_{\delta} = .063$

Table 7.3 Training in interpersonal skills by hours

Number of Hours	*Sample Size*	*Effect Size*
2	40	−.39
2	40	.54
2	40	.25
2	40	−.05
3	40	−.29
3	40	.00
3	40	.30
3	40	.59
4	40	−.24
4	40	.64*
4	40	.35
4	40	.05

*Significant at the .05 level (two-tailed test).

Again, we duck the issue of the small total sample size of 480 in this example (to which we return in Chapter 9). Suppose there had been not 12, but 1,200 studies. That is, assume that there is essentially no sampling error in the meta-analysis estimates. We describe the distribution of population effect sizes as having a mean of .15 and a standard deviation of .063. How much would study effect sizes vary from one setting to the next? Consider the assumption of a normal distribution of effect sizes. If the variation in effect sizes were normally distributed (it is not), the middle 95% of effect sizes would be

$$.15 - 1.96(.063) < \delta < .15 + 1.96(.063)$$

$$.03 < \delta < .27$$

This would suggest that there are probably no settings in which the training has no effect.

Compare the results of the meta-analysis with the conclusions of a narrative review. Only 100 of the 1,200 studies would have statistically significant effects. This could be interpreted to mean that training only has an effect in about 1 setting in 12. The cumulative analysis shows this to be wrong. At the level of observed study effects, results ranged from −.25 to +.85. The cumulative analysis shows that most of this variation is due to sampling error.

Thus, the meta-analysis reveals a very different story. The average effect size is a weak .15, but most of the variation is due to sampling error. If variation in effect size were normally distributed, then 95% of settings would have effect sizes in the range $.03 < \delta < .27$.

On the other hand, a range in effect of .03 to .27 would be a whopping difference in impact. Thus, it would be very important to know which studies had the large and which studies had the small effects. Thus, we begin the search for a moderator variable. Consider hours of training as a moderator. Because 3 levels of amount of training are represented in the domain of studies, we break the total set of studies into 3 subsets, those with 2 hours, 3 hours, or 4 hours of training. The separate bare-bones meta-analyses follow.

2 Hours Training

$T = 40 + 40 + \cdots = 160$

$\bar{N} = 160/4 = 40$

$\text{Ave}(d) = .10$

$\text{Var}(d) = .108050$

$\text{Var}(e) = .105537$

$\text{Var}(\delta) = .002513$

$SD_\delta = .050$

3 Hours Training

$T = 40 + 40 + \cdots = 160$

$\bar{N} = 160/4 = 40$

$\text{Ave}(d) = .15$

$\text{Var}(d) = .108050$

$\text{Var}(e) = .105702$

$\text{Var}(\delta) = .002348$

$SD_\delta = .048$

4 Hours Training

$T = 40 + 40 + \cdots = 160$

$\bar{N} = 160/4 = 40$

$\text{Ave}(d) = .20$

$\text{Var}(d) = .108050$

$\text{Var}(e) = .105932$

$\text{Var}(\delta) = .002118$

$SD_\delta = .046$

The moderator analysis shows that the amount of training is an important determinant of the effect of training. As the amount grows from 2 to 3 to 4 hours, the mean treatment effect grows from .10 to .15 to .20. That is, the mean treatment effect is proportional to the amount of training time within the range of training times studied. Thus, even greater impact would be projected if still more time were devoted to the training. On the other hand, the nonlinear learning curves in the literature on learning suggest that we could not just project out linearly; rather, diminishing returns would set in at some point.

In this example, the one moderator variable does not explain all the variation in results. The overall standard deviation of .063 dropped to .050, .048, and .046 for the three within-subset analyses. This is a decrease in variation, but it is not 0. Consider the 4-hour training studies. The mean effect size is .20, but the standard deviation is .046. If effect sizes varied normally, the middle 95% of the distribution of effect sizes would be

$$.20 - 1.96(.046) < \delta < .20 + 1.96(.046)$$

$$.11 < \delta < .29$$

Thus, if another moderator variable—perhaps job complexity—could be found, it would add to our understanding of interpersonal training.

However, it should be noted that there may not be another moderator variable. A bare-bones meta-analysis corrects only for the effects of sampling error. Other artifacts that cause variation across studies, such as error of measurement, have not been controlled. Thus, it is possible that the residual variation is due to uncontrolled artifacts rather than real differences in training contexts.

The Correlational Moderator Analysis

The corresponding correlational moderator analysis defines hours of training as a quantitative variable H. This can then be correlated with the observed effect size. The correlation between H and d in Table 7.3 is

$$\text{Cor}(d, H) = .125.$$

The "reliability" is

$$\text{Rel}(d) = \text{Var}(\delta)/\text{Var}(d) = .004015/.109717 = .0366.$$

Thus, the correlation for population effect sizes would be

$$\text{Cor}(\delta, H) = \text{Cor}(d, H)/\sqrt{\text{Rel}(d)} = .125/\sqrt{.0366} = .65.$$

That is, the effect of sampling error was to reduce the correlation of .65 between population effect sizes and hours of training to a correlation of only .125. This example makes it clear that the downwardly biasing effect of sampling error on moderator correlations can be very large.

Correcting *d*-Value Statistics for Measurement Error in the Dependent Variable

It is now generally recognized that the results of meta-analysis are inaccurate unless one corrects for the effects of measurement error (Cook et al., 1992, pp. 315–316). In Chapter 6, we showed that error of measurement in the dependent variable reduces the effect size estimate. If the reliability of measurement is low, the reduction can be quite sizeable. Failure to correct for the attenuation due to error of measurement yields an erroneous effect size estimate. Furthermore, because the error is systematic, a bare-bones meta-analysis on uncorrected effect sizes will produce an incorrect estimate of the true effect size. The extent of reduction in the mean effect size is determined by the mean level of reliability across the studies. Variation in reliability across studies causes variation in the observed effect sizes above and beyond that produced by sampling error. If the true effect size is actually homogeneous across studies, the variation in reliability would produce a false impression of heterogeneity in a bare-bones meta-analysis. A bare-bones meta-analysis will not correct for either the systematic reduction in the mean effect size or the systematic increase in the variance of effect sizes. Thus, even meta-analysis will produce correct values for the distribution of effect sizes only if there is a correction for the attenuation due to error of measurement.

In meta-analysis, there are two ways to eliminate the effect of error of measurement. Ideally, one could compile information on reliability for all or nearly all the individual studies. In this case, each effect size could be individually corrected and the meta-analysis could be done on the corrected effect sizes. However, if information on reliability is only available sporadically, then it may only be possible to generate an estimate of the distribution of reliability across studies. If the level of reliability in studies is independent of the level of effect sizes, then it is possible to correct a bare-bones meta-analysis for the effect of error of measurement. That is, if reliability information is only available in the form of a distribution, then we first do a bare-bones meta-analysis and we then correct the bare-bones meta-analysis estimates for attenuation (the mean effect size) and inflation (the variance of effect sizes) after the fact.

Some authors would rather incur the error of biased estimates than correct for measurement error. They defend this choice by saying that underestimation of effect sizes is acceptable; only overestimation is bad. That is, some believe that only positive errors count and negative errors do not matter. The goal of science, however, should be to obtain unbiased estimates of all scientifically important parameters (Rubin, 1990). In addition, theoretical work often requires the comparison of effect sizes. If some of the effect sizes have been underestimated, the comparison may be wrong and, thus, lead to false inferences. It is our belief that the history of science shows that negative errors (negative biases) are just as damaging as positive errors. Thus, we believe that correction is always desirable.

The problem in meta-analysis is that some studies do not report the reliability of the measures used. Sometimes this problem can be eliminated by going to studies outside the research domain that use the same measure and report its reliability. If none of the studies that use a given measure ever report a reliability (often the case in behavioristic work), then even in meta-analysis no correction can be made. However, even if correction for attenuation is to be ignored, it is important to have some idea of how large the corresponding error in estimation will be. One way to do this would be to look at the reliability of similar measures.

The key to computing the effect of error of measurement on effect sizes is to measure the extent of random measurement error in the dependent variable. This is done in psychometric theory using the reliability coefficient. (See the discussion of estimation of reliability in Chapter 3.) If the reliability of the dependent measure is known, then the extent of the attenuation (downward bias) can be exactly computed. It is then possible to algebraically reverse the attenuation; this process is called "correction for attenuation."

If the true population effect size is δ, then the study population effect size would be as high as δ only if the dependent variable is perfectly measured. If the reliability of the dependent variable is less than 1.00, there will be a corresponding reduction in the study population effect size. If the reliability of the dependent variable measure is r_{YY}, the attenuated population effect size δ_o is given by

$$\delta_o = a\delta$$

where $a = \sqrt{r_{YY}}$. For example, if the reliability of the dependent variable is $r_{YY} = .64$, then the study population effect size is

$$\delta_o = .80\delta$$

that is, reduced by 20%. If we know that a number has been reduced by 20%, then we can find the original number by division. That is, if we know that $\delta_o = .80\delta$, we can divide by .80 to obtain δ, that is, $\delta = \delta_o/.80$. Thus, the population effect size δ_o could be algebraically corrected for attenuation by dividing both sides of the equation by a. That is,

$$\delta_o/a = (a\delta)/a = \delta$$

If one has the correct type of reliability (see Chapter 3), the formula for correction for attenuation works perfectly with population effect sizes. The sample effect size can also be corrected for attenuation using the same formula. That correction eliminates the systematic attenuation of the sample effect. Thus, in principle, we can use a statistical correction formula to eliminate the effects of random error of measurement. However, there is still sampling error in the corrected effect size. The crucial fact for meta-analysis is that the formula for sampling error in a corrected effect size is different from the formula for the sampling error in an uncorrected effect size. Thus, meta-analysis on corrected effect sizes uses a slightly different formula to correct the variance for sampling error.

If correction for attenuation can eliminate the attenuation produced by error of measurement, one might ask why we should bother to try to use good measurement in the first place. The answer lies in the sampling error of corrected effect sizes. A careful analysis of the correction process shows that we pay a price for statistical correction: The sampling error in a statistically corrected effect size is larger than the sampling error in a study done with perfect measurement. The higher the reliability, the less the increase in sampling error. Thus, the better the original measurement, the less the sampling error in the corrected effect size. That is, we can estimate the results for perfect measurement without being able to achieve perfect measurement in our studies, but the price for statistical correction is increased sampling error. The higher the reliability, the lower the price. The price for low reliability in an individual study is very high. However, the larger sample sizes in meta-analysis make it possible to get good estimates of effect sizes even if the individual studies in a domain have low reliability. This occurs because the sampling error in the individual studies is averaged out when the mean corrected effect size is computed.

We will now show that correcting the effect size for attenuation increases sampling error. Consider the sample effect size d_o:

$$d_o = \delta_o + e = a\delta + e \tag{7.46}$$

The attenuated sample effect size can be corrected for the effect of error of measurement. Denote the corrected effect size by d_c:

$$\begin{aligned} d_c &= d_o/a = (\delta_o + e)/a \\ &= \delta_o/a + e/a \\ &= \delta + e' \end{aligned}$$

where e' is the sampling error in the corrected effect size. The sampling error in e' is given by

$$\text{Var}(e') = \text{Var}(e)/a^2 = \text{Var}(e)/r_{YY} \tag{7.47}$$

To divide by a fraction is to increase the ratio. Thus, the increase in sampling error variance is exactly proportional to the reliability. The standard error of the corrected effect size is the square root of the variance. For the standard error, we have

$$SD_{e'} = SD_e/a \tag{7.48}$$

That is, to divide the effect size by the attenuation factor is to divide the standard error by the same factor. The lower the reliability, the greater the increase in sampling error.

For example, if the reliability of the dependent variable is .64, then the sampling error variance of the corrected effect size is

$$\text{Var}(e') = \text{Var}(e)/.64 = (1/.64)\,\text{Var}(e) = 1.56\,(e)$$

The corresponding standard error is

$$SD_{e'} = \sqrt{1.56}SD_e = 1.25\,SD_e$$

That is, if the study reliability is as low as .64, then the corrected effect size has 25% more sampling error than the uncorrected effect size. Thus, to eliminate the 20% systematic error in the uncorrected effect size, we must incur a 25% increase in the unsystematic error.

In meta-analysis, we must worry not only about the extent of reliability in single studies, but also about variation in reliability across studies. If there is variation across studies in the reliability of measures of dependent variables, then different effect sizes are attenuated by different factors. This fact will cause variation in observed d values beyond the variation due to sampling error. Thus, in a bare-bones meta-analysis, there will be artifactual variance in the effect sizes that is not subtracted when the variance is corrected for the effect of sampling error. This variation is eliminated if each effect size is individually corrected for unreliability.

Meta-Analysis of *d* Values Corrected Individually and a Worked Example

If the reliability of the dependent variable is known for all individual studies, then each effect size can be individually corrected for attenuation. If the reliability is known for almost all studies, then there is little error in using the average reliability for the missing cases. The meta-analysis is then computed on the corrected effect sizes. The steps in the meta-analysis are the same as those for a bare-bones meta-analysis: (1) Compute the mean and variance of the effect sizes, (2) compute the variance in effect sizes due to sampling error, and (3) subtract that from the variance of the sample effect sizes. However, there is one complication: The weights that are optimal for uncorrected effect sizes are not optimal for corrected effect sizes. Optimal weights are inversely related to the sampling error in the effect size. In an uncorrected effect size, sampling error is primarily determined by the sample size. In a corrected effect size, however, the sampling error also depends on the extent of the correction for attenuation. Studies that require a large correction should get less weight than studies that require only a small correction. For uncorrected effect sizes, the optimal weight for each study is its sample size N_i. For corrected effect sizes, the optimal weight for each study is

$$w_i = N_i a_i^2 = N_i r_{YY_i} \tag{7.49}$$

That is, the mean effect size is better estimated if we weight each study proportional to its reliability. The lower the reliability in the study, the lower the optimal weight for that study. (We encountered this same principle in Chapter 3.)

For each study, we compute three numbers: (1) the corrected effect size, (2) the weight to be given to the study, and (3) the sampling error variance for that study. The formula for the sampling error variance presents one small problem: It depends on the population effect size. A good approximation is to use the mean effect size in the sampling error formula (See Chapter 5; also see Hunter & Schmidt, 1994b; Law, Schmidt, & Hunter, 1994b). Thus, the sampling error in the corrected effect size is approximately

$$\mathrm{Var}(e_i') = \mathrm{Var}(e_i)/a_i^2 = \mathrm{Var}(e_i)/r_{YY_i} \tag{7.50}$$

where

$$\mathrm{Var}(e_i) = [(N_i - 1)/(N_i - 3)][4/N_i][1 + \bar{d}_o^2/8] \tag{7.51}$$

where $\bar{d}_o$ is the mean uncorrected effect size. Thus, estimation of the sampling error for the corrected effect sizes requires the computation of the average uncorrected effect size.

Let us denote the observed sample effect size by d_o and the corrected effect size by d_c. Denote the population uncorrected effect size by δ_o and the population corrected effect size by δ. Denote the sampling error variance estimate of study i by ve_i and denote the mean corrected effect size by $\bar{d}_c$. Then the three averages required for the meta-analysis are the following three weighted averages:

$$\mathrm{Ave}(d_c) = \sum w_i d_{c_i} / \sum w_i \tag{7.52}$$

$$\text{Var}(d_c) = \sum w_i (d_{c_i} - \bar{d}_c)^2 / \sum w_i \tag{7.53}$$

$$\text{Var}(e') = \sum w_i ve'_i / \sum w_i \tag{7.54}$$

The variance of population effect sizes is then estimated by subtraction:

$$\text{Var}(\delta) = \text{Var}(d_c) - \text{Var}(e') \tag{7.55}$$

Now let us consider an example. Alex Lernmor, a psychologist at New York University, developed a new method of training doppelgangers in the facts they need to operate the machinery on their jobs. His training program has been adopted by many firms in the Northeast that employ doppelgangers. So far, four studies have been done in these firms to evaluate the effectiveness of the program, and the same 100-item measure of job knowledge was used in all four studies. In all cases, there were 20 people in the trained group and 20 in the control group (see Table 7.4). Alphonso Kopikat of the University of Texas learned about this program and, in connection with his consulting work, introduced it into many Texas businesses employing doppelgangers. Four studies evaluating the method have now been completed in Texas. These studies are much the same as the earlier ones, although, to save time, a short 12-item measure of job knowledge was used instead of the lengthy 100-item scale used by Lernmor. The results for this set of studies are also shown in Table 7.4.

Kopikat felt that his studies did not replicate Lernmor's findings. Whereas all of Lernmor's findings were positive, one of Kopikat's studies went in the wrong

Table 7.4 Bare-bones meta-analyses on hypothetical studies on training doppelgangers

Research Findings *Author*	*Location*	*Sample Size*	*Effect Size*
Lernmor	NE	40	.07
Lernmor	NE	40	.36
Lernmor	NE	40	.66*
Lernmor	NE	40	.95*
Kopikat	Texas	40	−.11
Kopikat	Texas	40	.18
Kopikat	Texas	40	.48
Kopikat	Texas	40	.77*

*Significant at the .05 level.

	Within-Subset Bare-Bones Meta-Analysis	
Bare-Bones Meta-Analysis	*Texas Studies*	*Northeastern Studies*
$T = 40 + 40 + \cdots = 320$	$T = 40 + 40 + \cdots = 160$	$T = 40 + 40 + \cdots = 160$
$N = 320/8 = 40$	$N = 160/4 = 40$	$N = 160/4 = 40$
$\text{Ave}(d) = .42$	$\text{Ave}(d) = .33$	$\text{Ave}(d) = .51$
$\text{Var}(d) = .116150$	$\text{Var}(d) = .108050$	$\text{Var}(d) = .108050$
$\text{Var}(d) = .107730$	$\text{Var}(d) = .106840$	$\text{Var}(d) = .108332$
$\text{Var}\ (d) = .008420$	$\text{Var}(d) = .001210$	$\text{Var}(d) = -.000782$
$SD_\delta = .092$	$SD_\delta = .034$	$SD_\delta = 0$

direction—a finding that greatly bothered the company at which the study was done. Furthermore, where two of Lernmor's findings were significant—half the studies done—this was true for only one of Kopikat's four studies. He interpreted the difference in results in terms of a theory that postulated that Texans were slower learners.

However, a colleague warned Kopikat about sampling error and urged him to do a meta-analysis. Kopikat then did the bare-bones meta-analysis shown in Table 7.4. For the overall analysis, he found a mean of $\text{Ave}(\delta) = .42$ with a standard deviation of $SD = .09$, which, using a normal approximation, implies a middle range of $.24 < \delta < .60$. He also did the meta-analysis corresponding to his belief that the studies in Texas had different results. Those meta-analyses are also reported in Table 7.4. The mean effect was positive in Texas, as in the northeastern states, but the effect size was only a little more than half as large (i.e., .33 vs. .51). Furthermore, the within-subsets standard deviations were .03 and 0, considerably smaller than the overall standard deviation of .09. Thus, Kopikat admitted that the Texas results replicated the northeastern results in sign, but he claimed that the moderator effect confirmed his theory of regional workforce differences in learning ability. Kopikat's study was widely acclaimed as yet another convincing demonstration of the importance of moderator variables when it was published in the *Statistical Artifact Review* (2004, 66: 398–447).

Lernmor did not believe that Texans were slower learners. He was also bothered by the fact that Kopikat used only 12 items in his job knowledge test. Lernmor had found a reliability of .81 with his 100-item test. He used the reverse Spearman-Brown formula (given in the exercise at the end of this chapter and as Equation 7.67) to compute the reliability of a 12-item test and found the reliability to be only .34. So Lernmor redid Kopikat's meta-analysis, correcting for attenuation. The results are shown in Table 7.5.

Lernmor's overall meta-analysis found a mean effect size of .57 with a standard deviation of .05, an implied middle range of $.49 < \delta < .65$. Lernmor also conducted separate meta-analyses for the two regional areas. He found a mean effect size of .57 in the northeastern studies and a mean effect size of .57 in the Texas studies. He concluded that region is not a moderator variable. Instead, he concluded that Kopikat's low values had resulted from the use of a lower reliability measure of the dependent variable in the studies in Texas. The calculations performed by Lernmor are those performed by the computer program D-VALUE, part of a software package of Windows-based meta-analysis programs available for applying the methods presented in this book. This software package and its availability are discussed in the Appendix. Lernmor performed his calculations by hand. Because there is less rounding error when the program is used, results produced by the D-VALUE program are slightly more accurate than Lernmor's results. We invite the reader to apply the D-VALUE program to the data in Table 7.5. The data in Table 7.5 are included as an example data set in the software described in the Appendix.

Table 7.5 Worksheet for meta-analysis of studies in Table 7.4

Location	*N*	d_o	r_{YY}	d_c	ve'	w_i
NE	40	.07	.81	.08	.132999	32.4
NE	40	.36	.81	.40	.132999	32.4
NE	40	.66	.81	.73	.132999	32.4
NE	40	.95	.81	1.06	.132999	32.4
Texas	40	−.11	.34	−.19	.316852	13.6
Texas	40	.18	.34	.31	.316852	13.6
Texas	40	.48	.34	.83	.316852	13.6
Texas	40	.77	.34	1.33	.316852	13.6

	Within-Subset Meta-Analysis	
Overall Meta-Analysis	*Northeastern States*	*Texas Studies*
$\text{Ave}(d_c) = .568$	$\text{Ave}(d_c) = .568$	$\text{Ave}(d_c) = .570$
$\text{Var}(d_c) = .189528$	$\text{Var}(d_c) = .133669$	$\text{Var}(d_c) = .322600$
$\text{Var}(e) = .187356$	$\text{Var}(e) = .132999$	$\text{Var}(e) = .316852$
$\text{Var}(\delta) = .002172$	$\text{Var}(\delta) = .000670$	$\text{Var}(\delta) = .005748$
$SD_\delta = .047$	$SD_\delta = .026$	$SD_\delta = .076$

Artifact Distribution Meta-Analysis and a Worked Example

Reliability is sometimes available only on a sporadic basis. In that case, we cannot correct each individual effect size. However, if we can estimate the distribution of reliabilities in the research domain, we can correct the values obtained in a bare-bones meta-analysis for the effects of error of measurement. The methods for this are developed fully in Chapter 4 (for correlations) and will be only sketched here.

The Mean True Effect Size

The key to the analysis is to look at the effect of error of measurement on the statistics computed in a bare-bones meta-analysis: the mean and variance of uncorrected effect sizes. The formula relating the actual effect size and the sample effect size is

$$d_o = \delta_o + e = a\delta + e \tag{7.56}$$

where δ is the actual effect size, a is the attenuation factor (the square root of the reliability), and e is the sampling error. Across a research domain, the mean observed effect size is

$$E(d_o) = E(a\delta + e) = E(a\delta) + E(e) \tag{7.57}$$

If we ignore the slight bias in d (discussed earlier and in Chapter 6), then the mean sampling error is 0:

$$E(d_o) = E(a\delta) \tag{7.58}$$

If the level of reliability of measurement is independent of the true effect size, then the mean of the product is the product of the means:

$$E(d_o) = E(a)E(\delta) \quad (7.59)$$

The desired mean true effect size is thus attenuated by the average of the attenuation factors for individual studies. If the mean attenuation factor is known, then we can correct the observed mean effect size using the same formula we would use to correct an individual effect size:

$$E(\delta) = E(d_o)/E(a) \quad (7.60)$$

Thus, to compute the mean effect size, we do not need to know the attenuation factor for each individual study, we need only know the mean attenuation factor across studies.

Note that the factor a is not the reliability but its square root. Thus, from the distribution of reliabilities, we must extract the distribution of attenuation factors. If the reliabilities are given individually, we merely transform to square roots before computing the mean and standard deviation.

The Variance of True Effect Sizes

The variance of observed effect sizes is given by

$$\text{Var}(d_o) = \text{Var}(\delta_o + e) = \text{Var}(\delta_o) + \text{Var}(e) \quad (7.61)$$

The bare-bones meta-analysis uses this to compute the variance of study population effect sizes $\text{Var}(\delta_o)$ by subtracting the sampling error variance $\text{Var}(e)$ from the variance of observed effect sizes $\text{Var}(d_o)$. That residual variance has been corrected for sampling error, but not for error of measurement. The corrected variance from the bare-bones meta-analysis is connected to the desired variance of true effect sizes $\text{Var}(\delta)$ by

$$\text{Var}(\delta_o) = \text{Var}(a\delta) \quad (7.62)$$

If the level of reliability is independent of the true effect size across studies, then, to a close approximation,

$$\text{Var}(\delta_o) = [E(a)]^2\text{Var}(\delta) + [E(\delta)]^2\text{Var}(a) \quad (7.63)$$

This equation can be solved for the desired variance $\text{Var}(\delta)$:

$$\text{Var}(\delta) = \{\text{Var}(\delta_o) - [E(\delta)]^2\text{Var}(a)\}/[E(a)]^2 \quad (7.64)$$

The right-hand side of this equation has four entries. The entry $\text{Var}(\delta_o)$ is the corrected variance from the bare-bones meta-analysis. The entry $E(a)$ is the average attenuation factor across studies. The entry $\text{Var}(a)$ is the variance of the attenuation factor across studies. The entry $E(\delta)$ is the average true effect size as computed in the previous section. The numerator

$$\text{Var}(\delta_o) - [E(\delta)]^2\text{Var}(a) \quad (7.65)$$

shows the subtraction of the variance in observed effect sizes due to variation in reliability from the bare-bones meta-analysis estimate of variance. In Chapter 4, the resulting variance was referred to as the residual variance. That is, the variance in study effect sizes can be partitioned

$$\begin{aligned}\mathrm{Var}(\delta_o) &= [E(a)]^2\mathrm{Var}(\delta) + [E(\delta)]^2\mathrm{Var}(a) + \mathrm{Var}(e) \\ &= A + B + C\end{aligned} \tag{7.66}$$

where

A is the variance due to variation in true effect size (residual variance),
B is the variance due to variation in reliability, and
C is the variance due to sampling error.

This is the same decomposition of variance formula used in Chapter 4 for correlations.

Reliability Distribution: An Example

One of the oldest hypotheses in psychology is that a failure experience produces anxiety. For example, this is the hypothesis that links job stress to health problems, such as high blood pressure or stomach ulcers. Stress produces fear of failure, which produces anxiety, which produces autonomic arousal, which causes high levels of blood pressure and high levels of stomach acid. This has been studied in the laboratory by putting subjects in a situation where it is predetermined that they will fail, and then measuring the resulting level of state anxiety. Table 7.6 presents the database for a meta-analysis of eight hypothetical experimental studies.

Jones (1992) located the eight studies but did only a bare-bones meta-analysis of the data. Thus, Jones saw only the columns for sample size and effect size in Table 7.6. His results are given as the first meta-analysis in Table 7.7. He found a mean effect size of .31 and a standard deviation of .075. Using the normal distribution as a guide, he estimated the 95% range to be $.16 < \delta < .46$. He concluded that the effect is always positive, but that the size of the effect varied across studies by as much as 3 to 1. Jones looked for a moderator variable but found none.

Smith (1996) had read the meta-analysis book by Hunter, Schmidt, and Jackson (1982), and he worried about the reliability of the measurement of anxiety in these studies. He went back to the eight studies to see which studies reported the reliability of the dependent variable. Two studies reported reliability, the two studies with values listed in Table 7.6. He then did a meta-analysis correcting for reliability using the values found in the studies. This is the second meta-analysis shown in Table 7.7.

For the two studies that reported reliability, the attenuation factors are .77 and .81, which have a mean of .79 and a standard deviation of .02. The corrected meta-analysis yielded a mean effect size of .39 with a standard deviation of .09. The normal distribution middle 95% range would be $.21 < \delta < .57$. Smith then noted that Jones was right in asserting that the effect is always positive, but Jones

Table 7.6 Meta-analysis of hypothetical studies examining the effect of a failure experience on state anxiety

Effect Size Studies Author	*Sample Size*	*Effect Size*	*Number of Items*	*Reliability*	*Attenuation Factor*
Callous (1949)	40	.82	5	–	–
Mean (1950)	40	.23	5	.60	.77
Cruel (1951)	40	–.06	5	–	–
Sadistic (1952)	40	.53	5	.65	.81
Villainous (1983)	40	.38	1	–	–
Vicious (1984)	40	–.20	1	–	–
Fiendish (1985)	40	.68	1	–	–
Diabolical (1986)	40	.10	1	–	–

Reliability Studies Author	*Number of Items*	*Reliability*	*Reliability of One Item*
Uneasy (1964)	2	.45	.29
Nervous (1968)	2	.35	.21
Concerned (1972)	4	.60	.27
Anxious (1976)	4	.54	.23
Distressed (1980)	6	.68	.26
Paralyzed (1984)	6	.66	.24

Average reliability of one item = .25 or $a = .50$
Implied reliability of five items = .625 or $a = .79$

had underestimated the strength of the mean effect by 21%. On the other hand, Smith, too, found that the size of the effect varied by as much as 3 to 1.

Black (2002) thought that Smith was right to worry about reliability, but he worried that the two studies that reported reliability might not have been representative of the domain as a whole. Black looked at each report to see what was said about the nature of the measurement. What he found was that the four older studies were done before behavioristic methodology had had much impact on personality research. Those studies all worried about the quality of measurement and constructed multi-item scales to assess state anxiety. Each older study used a five-item scale to measure anxiety. The four later studies were done after behavioristic methodology became dominant in personality research. These studies were unconcerned with the quality of measurement and assessed state anxiety by a single response, that is, a one-item scale. Black then looked up six studies that reported the reliabilities of various scales measuring state anxiety. The reported reliabilities are shown in Table 7.6. The reliabilities are not comparable because the scales vary in the number of items. So Black used the reverse Spearman-Brown formula to compute the reliability of one item, a common reference point for all studies. This formula is

$$r_i = [r_n/n]/[1 - (1 - 1/n)r_n] \quad (7.67)$$

where n is the number of items on the scale with reliability r_n. The one-item reliabilities are reported in Table 7.6. All one-item reliabilities are close to .25, and the variation in reliabilities is no more than would be expected from sampling error. From this, it was apparent to Black that the reliability in the newer one-item

Table 7.7 Meta-analyses performed on the studies of failure and anxiety in Table 7.6

Bare-Bones Meta-Analysis (Jones, 1992)

$T = 320$
$\bar{N} = T/8 = 40$
$\text{Ave}(d) = .310$
$\text{Var}(d) = .112225$
$\text{Var}(e) = .106672$
$\text{Var}(\delta_o) = .005553$
$SD_{\delta_o} = .075$

Bare-Bones Analysis Corrected for Error of Measurement Using the Reliability Information Given in the Experimental Studies (Smith, 1996)

$\text{Ave}(a) = [.77 + .81]/2 = .79$
$\text{Var}(d) = [(.77 - .79)^2 + (.81 - .79)^2]/2 = .000400$
$\text{Ave}(\delta) = \text{Ave}(d)/\text{Ave}(a) = .31/.79 = .392$
$\text{Var}(\delta) = \{\text{Var}(\delta_o) - [\text{Ave}(\delta)]^2\text{Var}(a)\}/\{\text{Ave}(a)\}^2$
$= \{.0005553 - (.392)^2(.00040)\}/(.79)^2 = .008799$
$SD_\delta = .094$

Bare-Bones Meta-Analysis Corrected Error of Measurement Using the Information From the Reliability Studies (Black, 2002)

$\text{Ave}(a) = [.79 + .50]/2 = .645$
$\text{Var}(a) = [(.79 - .645)^2 + (.50 - .645)^2]/2 = .021025$
$\text{Ave}(\delta) = \text{Ave}(\delta_o)/\text{Ave}(a) = .310/.645 = .481$
$\text{Var}(\delta) = \{\text{Var}(\delta_o) - [\text{Ave}(\delta)]^2\text{Var}(a)\}/\{\text{Ave}(a)\}^2$
$= \{.0005553 - (.481)^2(.021025)\}/(.645)^2 = .001655$
$SD_\delta = .041$

studies was only .25. Based on this fact, he used the Spearman-Brown formula (given in the exercise at the end of this chapter) to compute a reliability of .625 for the older five-item studies, a value that agrees with the two reliabilities reported. He then used that information to do the third meta-analysis shown in Table 7.7. Black found a mean effect size of .48 with a standard deviation of .04. The normal distribution middle range would be $.40 < \delta < .56$. Black noted that Jones had underestimated the mean effect of failure by 35% while Smith had underestimated it by 19%. He also noted that both authors had very greatly overestimated the extent of variation across studies. Variation in reliability produced a variance of

$$[E(\delta)]^2\text{Var}(a) = (.481)^2(.021025) = .004864$$

in study population correlations whose variance was $S^2_{\delta_o} = .005553$. That is, variation in reliability accounts for .004864/.005553 or 88% of the variance in study effect sizes. Black noted that it would be quite possible that variation in other artifacts that could not be corrected might account for the remaining 12% of the variance. That is, it is reasonable to suspect that the actual treatment effect is actually approximately constant across studies.

The artifact distribution methods for d-value meta-analysis illustrated in this example are the basis of the computer program D-VALUE1, one of the six Windows-based interactive programs in the program package available for applying the methods described in this book. This meta-analysis software package and its availability are described in the Appendix.

Measurement Error in the Independent Variable in Experiments

The preceding section shows that error of measurement in the dependent variable can have a considerable impact on the effect size, both in terms of reducing the apparent size of the mean effect and in terms of producing artificial variation in effect sizes across studies. The analysis in Chapter 6 showed that error of measurement in the independent variable can have just as large an effect. The important point is to remember that group membership is a *nominal* designation. It represents what the experimenter *intended* to happen to the subject and may or may not represent actual processes. If the subject is not listening closely to the instructions, then an experimental difference in instructions may not apply to many of the nominally experimental group subjects. In naturalistic dichotomies, such as "schizophrenic" versus "normal," some of the nominal schizophrenics may not be psychotic and some of the nominal normals may be schizophrenic. The practical problem for meta-analysis is that in most current studies there is no information on the extent of misidentification on the independent variable. Without such information, there can be no analysis of its impact. This is unfortunate, because the fact that experimenters ignore such an error does not make the error disappear. Thus, in the typical meta-analysis, there will be no correction for error of measurement in the independent variable. It is important to remember this in the interpretation of the meta-analysis. If this artifact is ignored, then the mean treatment effect is correspondingly underestimated and the variance of treatment effects is correspondingly overstated.

If the correlation between nominal and actual identification is denoted a, then the population study effect size correlation is

$$\rho_o = a\rho \tag{7.68}$$

where ρ is the actual treatment correlation (attenuated for the other artifacts in the study). Thus, if the meta-analysis were done measuring the treatment effect as a correlation, the analysis would be directly symmetric to the analysis of the impact of error of measurement in the dependent variable. The analysis of the d statistic is complicated by the nonlinearity of the transformation from r to d:

$$d = 2r/\sqrt{(1 - r^2)} \tag{7.69}$$

In the present case, we have

$$\delta_o = 2\rho_o/\sqrt{(1 - \rho_o^2)} = 2(a\rho)/\sqrt{(1 - a^2\rho^2)} \tag{7.70}$$

where

$$\rho = \delta/\sqrt{(4 + \delta^2)} \tag{7.71}$$

In most contemporary meta-analyses, the population treatment effects are not large. Those of textbook social psychology experiments are rarely larger than $\delta = .40$. Those for more sophisticated research domains are smaller yet. We will show that, for domains where the population treatment effects are no larger than .40, we have the close approximation

$$\delta_o = a\delta \tag{7.72}$$

This approximation is perfectly symmetric to the equation for the impact of error of measurement in the dependent variable. Thus, the mathematics of the meta-analysis is the same except for the change in the meaning of the attenuation factor a. For the present case, a is the correlation between nominal and actual group membership. For the case of error in the dependent variable, a was the square root of the reliability of the dependent variable. This difference is less than it might seem. The square root of the reliability of the dependent variable is the correlation between observed dependent variable score and the dependent variable true score. Thus, the meaning of a is actually symmetric between the case of the independent variable and the case of the dependent variable.

It is important to note that the approximation is used here for population effect sizes and not for sample effect sizes. Sample effect sizes will often be larger than .40 because of sampling error. If the population effect size were $\delta = .20$ and the sample size were $N = 40$, it would not be unusual to see a sample effect size as large as $d = .64$. However, sampling error is not a part of the approximation process. Rather, sampling error is added *after* the attenuation effect. That is, the sampling error equation is additive:

$$d_o = \delta_o + e$$

Thus, the sampling error equation uses the approximation

$$d_o = \delta_o + e = a\delta + e$$

which does not alter the value of e.

In most real meta-analyses, the study population effect size is attenuated by other artifacts, such as error of measurement in the dependent variable. In this case, the extraneous attenuation has the effect of extending the range of the linear approximation. Suppose the true treatment effect is $\delta = .60$, but it is attenuated to $\delta_1 = .40$ by error of measurement in the dependent variable. The linear approximation applies to the attenuated effect size .40 rather than the unattenuated effect size .60. Thus, we have the approximation

$$\delta_o = a\delta_1 \tag{7.73}$$

which becomes

$$\delta_o = ab\delta \tag{7.74}$$

with the substitution $\delta_1 = b\delta$, where b is the attenuation factor for error of measurement in the dependent variable. Thus, in this case, the linear approximation is still quite close even though the true effect size is as large as .60.

Finally, we show that, for effect sizes no larger than .40, the impact of nonlinearity is slight. Suppose $\delta = .40$. Then

$$\rho = \delta/\sqrt{(4+\delta^2)} = .40/\sqrt{(4+.16)} = (.40/2)/\sqrt{1.04}$$

which, to a close approximation, is

$$\rho = (\delta/2)(1.02) = \delta/2 \qquad (7.75)$$

That is, for population treatment effects in the usual range, the transformation from d to ρ is approximately linear. Using this approximation, we have the approximation

$$\delta_o = [2a(\delta/2)]/\sqrt{[1 - a^2(\delta/2)^2]} \qquad (7.76)$$

$$= [a\delta]/\sqrt{[1 - .25\delta^2 a^2]} \qquad (7.77)$$

For population treatment effects no larger than $\delta = .40$, the denominator satisfies the following inequality:

$$\sqrt{[1 - .25\,\delta^2 a^2]} > \sqrt{[1 - .04a^2]}$$

$$> 1 - .02\,a^2 > 1 - .02$$

Thus, if the population treatment effect is no larger than .40, there is little error in the approximation

$$\delta_o = [a\delta]/1 = a\delta \qquad (7.78)$$

For population treatment effects no larger than .40, we have the close approximation

$$\delta_o = a\delta \qquad (7.78a)$$

Other Artifacts and Their Effects

In this chapter, we have considered the following artifacts: sampling error, random measurement error in the dependent variable, and random measurement error (causal misidentification) in the independent or treatment variable. Other artifacts were discussed in Chapter 6: imperfect construct validity of the dependent variable, imperfect construct validity (confounding) in the independent or treatment variable, dichotomization of a continuous dependent variable, variation in the strength of treatment, and attrition artifacts. Given certain information about the extent and nature of the artifact, it is possible to correct the meta-analysis for the effects of that artifact. We have shown how to do this for a meta-analysis of correlations, but we have not presented the corresponding computations for the *d* statistic. The computations can be done, although the correction formulas for the *d* statistic are usually nonlinear and more cumbersome than the formulas for

r. The simplest method is to convert the ds to rs and do the meta-analysis on r, as we noted earlier in this chapter.

We would like to emphasize that the reason that we did not present the formulas is not because the artifact effects are small. Where such artifacts have been tracked, they have often proven to be large. Of special concern is the effect of imperfect construct validity in experimental studies. Experimental studies are often metaphorical in nature. The investigator codes helping someone pick up his or her dropped papers as measuring altruism and, thus, treats that dependent variable measure as if it were equivalent to signing up for the Peace Corps. Or the investigator believes that a failure experience is an attack on self-esteem and, thus, treats failure at a laboratory problem-solving task as if it were the same as the effect of flunking out of college. In the organizational literature, there is often a considerable gap in the construct validity of lab and field studies. This has shown up in many meta-analyses conducted on organizational interventions.

It is important to correct for as many artifacts as possible, even if the formulas to do so are not given in this chapter. Finally, it is important to remember that there is an artifact that is difficult to detect and, thus, is rarely corrected: bad data. There can be error in coding raw data, error in computing statistics or recording the numbers computed, error in typing manuscripts, error in printing numbers, and, according to certain cynics, error in meta-analytic recording (especially in converting from some strange statistic to d or r). At a minimum, one should be on the lookout for extreme outliers, that is, effect sizes that are extremely different from other studies. Unfortunately, in many research domains the average sample size is so small that it is difficult to distinguish between an outlier and a large sampling error. For these reasons, it is always wise to consider residual variance with a large grain of salt. The residual variance virtually always contains the effects of uncorrected artifacts, even if the meta-analyst has convinced himself or herself that the artifact does not exist.

Correcting for Multiple Artifacts

The previous sections of this chapter treated error of measurement in the independent and dependent variable as if one or the other occurred, but not both. The fact is that both errors can occur in a given study. Furthermore, any given study may also be affected by the many artifacts listed in Chapter 6 that have not been considered in this chapter to this point. Thus, a proper meta-analysis will have to correct for multiple artifacts.

In Chapter 6, we noted that the effect of most artifacts on the effect size statistic d often requires a very complicated formula. These complicated formulas make it cumbersome to correct for the artifact individually and make it very difficult to correct for several artifacts jointly. The complicated artifact formulas also create problems for meta-analysis. In this section, we will derive an approximation formula for the correction of d for multiple artifacts. This approximation formula permits the development of very straightforward formulas for meta-analysis.

Attenuation Effect of Multiple Artifacts and Correction for the Same

The artifacts other than sampling error are systematic. At the level of population statistics, the attenuation produced by the study artifacts can be algebraically computed. That algebra can be reversed. Thus, it is possible to start with the attenuated effect size and compute the true effect size. In the form of an equation, this process would be called "correction for attenuation." The classic formulas were developed for random error of measurement, but similar correction formulas could be generated for any systematic artifact.

Observed study effect sizes are influenced not only by the systematic artifacts but by sampling error as well. The algebraic formulas that work exactly for population statistics do not work exactly for sample statistics. Instead, there is a more complicated interaction between sampling error and the systematic effect of the other artifacts. This section will describe the attenuating effect of systematic errors on population statistics. The effects of sampling error will be considered in the following section.

The complication of artifact formulas for d is in sharp contrast to the simple formulas for artifact effects on the correlation. For the artifacts currently identified, the effect on the correlation is to multiply the correlation by a constant that measures the impact of the artifact. In many of the cases in Chapter 6, we capitalized on this fact to indirectly compute the effect of an artifact on d. There are three steps to this method. First, transform the actual treatment effect d into the corresponding treatment effect correlation ρ. Second, compute the effect of the artifact on the treatment correlation, that is, compute the attenuated treatment correlation ρ_o. Third, transform the attenuated treatment correlation ρ_o back into the d statistic form as δ_o. We will now use this same strategy to compute the attenuating effect of multiple artifacts.

For correlations, it is as easy to handle multiple artifacts as it is to handle one. Each of the artifacts currently listed can be quantified in the form of a product in which the unaffected correlation is multiplied by a constant. Denote the actual population correlation by ρ and the artifactually attenuated population correlation by ρ_o. Then the effect of any one artifact is quantified as

$$\rho_o = a\rho$$

where a is an artifact multiplier (such as the square root of the reliability) that measures the effect of that artifact on the correlation. If the correlation is affected by several artifacts, then the study correlation is simply multiplied by the several corresponding artifact multipliers. For example, if three artifacts were measured by a, b, and c, then

$$\rho_o = abc\rho.$$

The net impact of the several artifacts can be combined into one artifact multiplier as in

$$\rho_o = A\rho$$

where the combined artifact multiplier A is given by the product

$$A = abc.$$

That is, the combined artifact multiplier A is the product of the individual artifact multipliers. Except for the change of notation from a to A, the math of the compound effect of several artifacts is no different from the math of a single artifact.

We will now derive a procedure to compute the attenuated study effect size δ_o from the actual treatment effect δ. This is done in three steps. First, we transform δ to ρ. Second, we use the simple multiple-artifact formulas for correlation to compute the attenuated study treatment correlation ρ_o. Third, we transform the attenuated study correlation ρ_o into the attenuated study effect size δ_o. The complexity of formulas for the d statistic stems from the nonlinearity of the relationship between d and r. Consider the true treatment effect size δ and the corresponding true treatment correlation ρ. The relationship between them is given by the conversion formulas

$$\delta = 2\rho/\sqrt{(1-\rho^2)}$$
$$\rho = \delta/\sqrt{(4+\delta^2)}$$

Note that sample size does not appear in these conversion formulas because they are formulas for population parameters.

Attenuation

To compute the attenuating effect of several artifacts, we first transform the unattenuated effect size δ to obtain the unattenuated treatment correlation ρ:

$$\rho = \delta/\sqrt{(4+\delta^2)}$$

We then compute the attenuated treatment correlation ρ_o. The combined impact of several artifacts is computed for the treatment correlation by the product

$$\rho_o = A\rho$$

where A is the combined artifact multiplier (the product of the individual artifact multipliers). We now compute the attenuated treatment effect size δ_o. The study population effect size δ_o is given by

$$\delta_o = 2\rho_o/\sqrt{(1-\rho_o^2)}$$

Correction for Attenuation

For the systematic artifacts, the attenuation effect can be computed algebraically. This algebra can be reversed to produce a formula that corrects the observed treatment effect for attenuation. That is, we can produce an algebraic procedure that takes the study effect size δ_o, which has been reduced in size by the study artifacts, and algebraically restores it to the size of the actual treatment effect δ. This is most easily done for the treatment effect statistic by transforming to treatment correlations. The steps are as follows: (1) Transform the attenuated study effect size δ_o to the attenuated study treatment correlation ρ_o; (2) correct the study treatment correlation for attenuation, that is, algebraically restore the attenuated value ρ_o to the correct treatment correlation ρ; and (3) transform the disattenuated correlation ρ into the disattenuated treatment effect δ.

Suppose we are given the attenuated study treatment effect δ_o. The attenuated study treatment correlation is computed by the conversion formula to be

$$\rho_o = \delta_o/\sqrt{(4 + \delta_o^2)}$$

From the fact that the study artifacts reduced the treatment correlation ρ to

$$\rho_o = A\rho$$

we algebraically deduce the fact that

$$\rho = \rho_o/A$$

This is the formula for the correction of the treatment correlation for attenuation due to the artifacts measured by the compound artifact multiplier A. The true treatment effect δ is then computed by transforming the true treatment correlation ρ:

$$\delta = 2\rho/\sqrt{(1 - \rho^2)}$$

Disattenuation and Sampling Error: The Confidence Interval

The causal structure of study errors has a definite order. The substantive nature of the systematic artifacts causes a reduction in the size of the study population effect size. Randomness in the sampling of people and response processes then produces sampling error in the observed study effect size. Disentangling the errors is most easily done by considering the errors in a corresponding order. To go backward from the observed effect size to the true effect size, we first "correct" for the effect of sampling error and then correct for the effect of the systematic artifacts.

In an isolated study, we cannot correct for the effect of sampling error. Instead, we use a confidence interval to generate a band of potential population values that would be reasonable given the observed value. Given the observed study value d_o, we generate the upper and lower ends of the confidence interval. Call them d_- and d_+, respectively. Thus, we deal with sampling error by generating three estimates for the study effect size δ_o. The most likely value for δ_o is the observed value d_o. The lowest reasonable estimate of δ_o is d_-. The highest reasonable value for δ_o is d_+.

If the population study effect size δ_o were known, then we would compute the actual effect size by disattenuating the effects of the systematic artifact algebraically. The sampling error analysis produces three estimates of the population study effect size. Each of these estimates can be disattenuated using the same method. This then produces a corresponding sampling error analysis of the true treatment effect. That is, because d_o is the most likely value of δ_o, the corrected value generated using d_o is the most likely value for δ. Because the lowest reasonable value for δ_o is d_-, the lowest reasonable value for δ is obtained by correcting d_- for attenuation. Because the highest reasonable value for δ_o is d_+, the highest reasonable value for δ is obtained by correcting d_+ for attenuation. The three corrected effect sizes thus provide the best estimate and the confidence interval for the true effect size δ.

A Formula for Meta-Analysis With Multiple Artifacts

The preceding procedure for computing the attenuating impact of systematic artifacts on study effect sizes works fine for isolated single-study effects. However, it is not sufficient for meta-analysis. For meta-analysis, we need a formula that enables us to compute sampling error variance and relate it to the variation in effect sizes across studies. That is, we need a formula relating the sample study d statistic to the true effect size δ. To get this formula, we need a formula for the attenuated study effect size as a function of the attenuation multiplier A and the true treatment effect d. The exact formula is untractable for meta-analysis because of the nonlinearity of the relationship of d to r. However, we will show that there are close approximations that yield formulas that can be used for meta-analysis.

The formula relating the sample study effect size d_o to the population effect size δ_o is

$$d_o = \delta_o + e \tag{7.79}$$

We then need a formula that relates the study effect size δ_o to the actual effect size δ. The exact formula will be shown to be

$$\delta_o = cA\delta \tag{7.80}$$

where δ is the true treatment effect, A is the compound attenuation multiplier, and

$$c = 1/\sqrt{(1+b)} \tag{7.81}$$

where

$$b = (1 - A^2)\delta^2/4 \tag{7.82}$$

The problem with this formula is that the number c varies from study to study in a nonlinear way. We will show that, for the typical meta-analysis, there is little error incurred by ignoring the variation in the value of c across studies. That is, there is little error in the meta-analysis if the individual study values of c are replaced by the average value of c. To show this, we will first show that c differs little from 1. In fact, there is not much error in a meta-analysis that uses the approximation

$$\delta_o = A\delta \tag{7.83}$$

In meta-analyses in which this approximation is suitable, the formulas for the meta-analysis of d would be exactly parallel to those for the correlation.

Derivation of c

The exact formula for the attenuated treatment effect δ_o is obtained by tracing the transformation method symbolically. We are given the true treatment effect δ. This is converted to the true treatment correlation ρ by

$$\rho = \delta/\sqrt{(4+\delta^2)}$$

The effect of the systematic artifacts on the treatment correlation can be measured by the compound artifact multiplier A, which is the product of the individual artifact multipliers. That is, the attenuated study treatment correlation ρ_o is

$$\rho_o = A\rho$$

The attenuated study treatment effect δ_o is then given by

$$\delta_o = 2\rho_o/\sqrt{(1-\rho_o^2)}$$

This formula states δ_o in terms of the study correlation ρ_o. What we need is a formula for the attenuated effect size that relates it directly to the true effect size. This can be done by making algebraic substitutions that trace our steps backward. The attenuated effect size can be computed from the true treatment correlation ρ. This formula is obtained by substituting $A\rho$ for ρ_o in the equation for δ_o:

$$\delta_o = 2[A\rho]/\sqrt{(1-[A\rho]^2)} \tag{7.84}$$

$$= 2A\rho/\sqrt{(1-A^2\rho^2)} \tag{7.85}$$

The attenuated effect size can then be computed from the true treatment effect size δ. This formula is obtained by substituting

$$\rho = \delta/\sqrt{(4+\delta^2)}$$

for ρ in the equation for δ_o:

$$\begin{aligned}\delta_o &= 2A[\delta/\sqrt{(4+\delta^2)}]/\sqrt{(1-A^2)[\delta^2/(4+\delta^2)]} \\ &= 2A\delta/\sqrt{[(4+[1-A^2]\delta^2)]} \\ &= A\delta/\sqrt{(1-b)}\end{aligned} \tag{7.86}$$

where

$$b = (1-A^2)\delta^2/4 \tag{7.87}$$

The numerator $A\delta$ is the same simple product that applies to compound artifacts for the correlation. However, the denominator is a highly nonlinear function of A and δ.

Thus, the denominator is a potential problem. The impact of the denominator is better seen if we convert it to a multiplier. Let c be defined by

$$c = 1/\sqrt{(1+b)} \tag{7.88}$$

Then

$$\delta_o = cA\delta \tag{7.89}$$

The potential impact of the denominator depends on how much the multiplier c differs from 1. We will show that in contemporary meta-analyses c is close to 1.00.

There are many meta-analyses in which the denominator of the effect size can simply be dropped. The key questions are as follows: (1) How large is the true effect size? (2) How large are the artifact impacts? If the true effect size is small or if the artifacts are small, then, to a close approximation, we can write

$$\delta_o = A\delta \tag{7.90}$$

and develop meta-analysis formulas for d that are exactly parallel to those for the correlation.

The analysis of the denominator starts with the approximation

$$\sqrt{(1+x)} = 1 + x/2$$

This approximation is close if x is close to 0. For example,

$$\sqrt{(1+.01)} = 1.00499 \quad \text{versus} \quad 1+.01/2 = 1.00500,$$
$$\sqrt{(1+.10)} = 1.04881 \quad \text{versus} \quad 1+.10/2 = 1.05000,$$
$$\sqrt{(1+.50)} = 1.22474 \quad \text{versus} \quad 1+.50/2 = 1.25000.$$

The approximation is not too inaccurate even for values of x as large as 1. For example,

$$\sqrt{(1+1)} = 1.414 \quad \text{versus} \quad 1+1/2 = 1.500$$

Consider then the denominator

$$\sqrt{(1+b)}$$

where

$$b = (1 - A^2)\delta^2/4$$

If b is small, then, to a close approximation,

$$\sqrt{(1+b)} = 1 + b/2$$

and, hence,

$$c = 1/\sqrt{(1+b)} = 1 - b/2$$

The effect of the denominator on the attenuated effect size would then be closely approximated by

$$\delta_o = cA\delta$$

where $c = (1 - b/2)$. That is, the numerator $A\delta$ is multiplied by the number $c = (1 - b/2)$. If b differs little from 0, then $(1 - b/2)$ would differ little from 1. If the multiplier c differs little from 1, then there would be little error incurred by dropping it.

How close is b to 0? The artifact A is a fraction. Thus,

$$1 - A^2 < 1$$

and, hence,

$$b < \delta^2/4$$

Even textbook effect sizes are rarely larger than $\delta = .50$. Thus, for a meta-analysis with $\delta = .50$,

$$b < (.50)^2/4 = .0625$$

For such cases, the reciprocal of the denominator is closer to 1 than

$$1/\sqrt{(1 + b)} = 1 - .03$$

If the attenuated effect size is about $\delta_o = .30$, then a 3% error would mean overestimating the effect size to be .31 instead of .30. In the end, this would lead to a similar sized error in the estimated mean effect size, although the error would be in the opposite direction. For example, if the true mean effect size were actually $\text{Ave}(\delta) = .50$, we would be off by 3% to generate the estimate $\text{Ave}(\delta) = .50(1 + .03) = .515$. Unless the number of studies is large, this error is smaller than sampling error. So, for small effect sizes and moderate artifact impacts, the approximation

$$\delta_o = A\delta \qquad (7.91)$$

is sufficiently accurate.

The principal problem caused by the multiplier c in developing formulas for meta-analysis is the fact that it varies from one study to the next. However, because the multiplier c does not vary much from the number 1, it cannot vary much from one study to the next. This suggests that we replace the individual multipliers by the average multiplier across studies. We compute the average attenuation multiplier A across studies. We compute the average treatment effect across studies. From these, we compute an estimate of the average value of b across studies:

$$\text{Ave}(b) = [1 - \text{Ave}(A)^2][\text{Ave}(\delta)]^2/4 \qquad (7.92)$$

The average value of c is then estimated by

$$\text{Ave}(c) = 1/\sqrt{[1 - \text{Ave}(b)]} \qquad (7.93)$$

Estimation of c

The preceding discussion of the constant c was circular. We said that to estimate c you compute the average value of A and the average value of δ across studies. However, in order to compute the average actual treatment effect (average δ), you must correct the attenuated study treatment effects for attenuation. To correct the study treatment effects for attenuation, you need the value of c. This sounds like an infinite regress, but there is an easy numerical solution.

From the previous section, we know that

$$\text{Ave}(c) = 1/\sqrt{[1 - \text{Ave}(b)]}$$

where

$$\text{Ave}(b) = [1 - \text{Ave}(A)^2][\text{Ave}(\delta)]^2/4$$

Thus, to compute Ave(c), we need to compute Ave(A) and Ave(δ). Because the artifact information is assumed to be given as part of the meta-analysis, the computation of Ave(A) presents no conceptual problem. However, Ave(δ) is the average actual effect while the original data provide only the attenuated study effects. Thus, computation of Ave(δ) is a by-product of the meta-analysis and we must estimate Ave(c) in order to compute the meta-analysis. The solution is to do a small meta-analysis before doing the main meta-analysis.

For each study in the meta-analysis, the exact equation for the study effect size is

$$\delta_o = cA\delta + e$$

Average the study effect sizes:

$$\text{Ave}(\delta_o) = \text{Ave}(cA\delta) + \text{Ave}(e)$$

For a large number of studies, the average sampling error is 0. Thus,

$$\text{Ave}(\delta_o) = \text{Ave}(cA\delta)$$

Because there is little error in ignoring the variation in c, assume that it is constant. Then it factors out of the average:

$$\text{Ave}(\delta_o) = (c)\text{Ave}(A\delta)$$

That is, to a close approximation, we have

$$\text{Ave}(\delta_o) = \text{Ave}(c)\text{Ave}(A\delta)$$

Because the substantive processes that determine the size of the artifacts are independent of the substantive processes that determine the actual treatment effect, the numbers A and δ will be independent across studies. Thus, for a large number of studies,

$$\text{Ave}(A\delta) = \text{Ave}(A)\text{Ave}(\delta)$$

Thus, we have, to a close approximation,

$$\text{Ave}(\delta_o) = \text{Ave}(c)\text{Ave}(A)\text{Ave}(\delta) \quad (7.94)$$

If c were known, then we would compute Ave(δ) by

$$\text{Ave}(\delta) = \text{Ave}(\delta_o)/[\text{Ave}(c)\text{Ave}(A)] \quad (7.95)$$

We now have two equations: one that computes Ave(c) from Ave(δ) and one that computes Ave(δ) from Ave(c). These are two equations in two unknowns. We could solve these by ordinary algebra if they were not so nonlinear. However, there is an easy iterative solution.

Start with the approximation Ave(c) = 1. Then use the equation for Ave(δ) to compute the corresponding approximation for Ave(δ). Use that value of Ave(δ) in the equation for Ave(c) to generate a new approximation for Ave(c). This new estimate of Ave(c) will be more accurate than the original approximation Ave(c) = 1. The new estimate of Ave(c) can then be used to generate a new estimate of Ave(δ) that can be used to generate a new estimate of Ave(c), and so on. This process converges rapidly to the desired estimate. A computer program to do the iteration is available from the authors.

Consider an example. Suppose the average study effect is Ave(δ_o) = .30 and the average artifact multiplier is Ave(A) = .50. From the estimate Ave(c) = 1, we obtain the estimate

$$\text{Ave}(\delta) = \text{Ave}(\delta_o)/[\text{Ave}(c)\text{Ave}(A)] = .30/[(1)(.50)] = .60$$

From the estimate Ave(δ) = .60, we generate a new estimate of Ave(c):

$$\text{Ave}(b) = [1 - \text{Ave}(A)^2]\text{Ave}(\delta)^2/4$$
$$= [1 - .50^2][.60]^2/4 = .0675$$
$$\text{Ave}(c) = 1/\sqrt{[1 + \text{Ave}(b)]} = 1/\sqrt{1.0675} = .968$$

From this new estimate of Ave(c), we obtain the new estimate

$$\text{Ave}(\delta) = \text{Ave}(\delta_o)/[\text{Ave}(c)\text{Ave}(A)]$$
$$= .30/[(.968)(.50)] = .620$$

From that, we have a new estimate of Ave(c):

$$\text{Ave}(c) = 1/\sqrt{(1 + .0721)} = .966$$

which differs little from the previous estimate of .968. The new estimate of Ave(δ) is

$$\text{Ave}(\delta) = .30/[(.966)(.50)] = .621$$

which differs only trivially from the previous estimate of .620. The next approximation of Ave(c) is

$$\text{Ave}(c) = .966$$

which is identical to the previous estimate to three digits. Thus, the process has converged to three places.

Meta-Analysis of Individually Corrected Studies

Suppose the artifact information is known for each individual study. Then the observed study values can be individually corrected and the meta-analysis can be performed on the corrected d_c statistics. For study i, we have

$$\begin{aligned} d_{oi} &= \delta_{oi} + e_i \\ &= cA_i\delta_i + e_i \end{aligned} \tag{7.96}$$

Before the correction can be carried out for each study, a preliminary meta-analysis must be done to furnish the information needed to estimate c. The two numbers to be computed are Ave(d_{oi}) and Ave(A_i). The best weights for these averages would be

$$w_i = N_i A_i^2$$

where N_i is the sample size for study i.

Once the value of c has been estimated, the corrected effect sizes can be computed by

$$d_c = d_{oi}/[cA_i] = \delta_i + e_i/[cA_i] \tag{7.97}$$

Denote the average uncorrected effect size by $\bar{d}_o$. Then the error variance for study i is

$$ve_i = \text{Var}(e_i)/[cA_i]^2 \tag{7.98}$$

where

$$\text{Var}(e_i) = [(N_i - 1)/(N_i - 3)][4/N_i][1 + \bar{d}_o^2/8] \tag{7.99}$$

Denote the mean corrected effect size by $\bar{d}_c$. Then the three averages required for the meta-analysis are the following three weighted averages:

$$\text{Ave}(d_c) = \sum w_i d_{c_i} / \sum w_i = \bar{d}_c \tag{7.100}$$

$$\text{Var}(d_c) = \sum w_i (d_{c_i} - \bar{d}_c)^2 / \sum w_i \tag{7.101}$$

$$\text{Var}(e) = \sum w_i ve_i / \sum w_i \tag{7.102}$$

The variance of population effect sizes is then estimated by subtraction:

$$\text{Var}(\delta) = \text{Var}(d_c) - \text{Var}(e) \tag{7.103}$$

Meta-Analysis With Artifact Distributions

If the artifact information is given sporadically, then the main meta-analysis is the bare-bones meta-analysis that eliminates the effect of sampling error (if the number of studies is large). It is then necessary to correct the bare-bones meta-analysis for the effect of the systematic artifacts.

Bare-Bones Meta-Analysis. The bare-bones meta-analysis is carried out using the methods given previously. Denote the average uncorrected effect size by $\bar{d}_o$ and denote the estimated variance of population study effect sizes by V_o. Denote the sampling error variance by V_e.

Artifact Distributions. If artifact information is sporadic, then the information is usually given one artifact at a time. Thus, the distribution of the compound artifact multiplier must be constructed from distributional information on the individual artifacts. This process was discussed in detail in Chapter 4 and will be presented here in very abbreviated form.

For each individual artifact a, compute three numbers: Ave(a), Var(a), and the squared coefficient of variation:

$$CV(a) = \text{Var}(a)/[\text{Ave}(a)]^2 \qquad (7.104)$$

To combine the artifact information, let us number the individual artifact multipliers $a_1, a_2, \ldots$. The compound artifact multiplier is the product of the individual multipliers:

$$A = a_1 a_2 a_3 \ldots.$$

Because the artifacts are independent, the mean of the product is the product of the means. That is,

$$\text{Ave}(A) = \text{Ave}(a_1)\text{Ave}(a_2)\text{Ave}(a_3) \ldots.$$

The variance of the product is computed from the squared coefficients of variation:

$$\text{Var}(A) = [\text{Ave}(A)]^2[CV(a_1) + CV(a_2) + CV(a_3) + \cdots] \qquad (7.105)$$

The Corrected Meta-Analysis. Because $\delta_o = cA\delta$, the mean uncorrected population effect size is

$$\text{Ave}(\delta_o) = c\text{Ave}(A\delta) = c\text{Ave}(A)\text{Ave}(\delta) \qquad (7.106)$$

Rearranging this equation, we get the formula for correcting the mean study effect size for attenuation:

$$\text{Ave}(\delta) = \text{Ave}(\delta_o)/[c\text{Ave}(A)] = \bar{d}_o/[c\text{Ave}(A)] \qquad (7.107)$$

Denote the average true effect size by $\bar{d}_c$.

The variance of uncorrected effect sizes is

$$\begin{aligned}\mathrm{Var}(\delta_o) &= c^2\mathrm{Var}(A\delta)\\ &= c^2\{[\mathrm{Ave}(A)]^2\mathrm{Var}(\delta) + [\mathrm{Ave}(\delta)]^2\mathrm{Var}(A)\} \qquad (7.108)\end{aligned}$$

Rearranging this equation, we get the formula for correcting the variance of population study effect sizes for the effect of variation in artifacts across studies:

$$\begin{aligned}\mathrm{Var}(\delta) &= \{\mathrm{Var}(\delta_o) - c^2[\mathrm{Ave}(\delta)]^2\mathrm{Var}(A)\}/\{c^2[\mathrm{Ave}(A)]^2\}\\ &= \{V_o - c^2\bar{d}_c^2\ \mathrm{Var}(A)\}/\{c^2[\mathrm{Ave}(A)]^2\} \qquad (7.109)\end{aligned}$$

Denote by V_a the amount of variance in observed effect sizes caused by variation in artifacts. That value is given by

$$V_a = c^2\bar{d}_c^2\mathrm{Var}(A) \qquad (7.110)$$

The variance of observed effect sizes can thus be partitioned into

$$V_o = \mathrm{Var}(\delta_o) + V_a + V_e \qquad (7.111)$$

If these numbers are each individually divided by V_o, then they can be called, respectively, the percentage of variance in observed effect sizes due to real variation in treatment effects, due to variation in artifacts, and due to variation in sampling error, respectively.

Summary of Meta-Analysis of *d* Values

Although statisticians have consistently warned against it, the conventional evaluation of experiments and programs has been the statistical significance test. In a two-group design, this means that the number most likely to be published is the t statistic. The value of t does not answer the most relevant question: How large was the treatment effect? Instead, the value of t answers the question: How far out is the observed treatment effect under the assumption that the population treatment effect is 0? This chapter began by presenting alternative measures of the size of the treatment effect: the raw score mean difference, the standard score mean difference (d or δ), and the point biserial correlation (r or ρ). Because different authors use different measures of the dependent variable, the raw score difference is not usually reasonable for meta-analysis. Nor is the odds ratio an appropriate statistic in most social science research. Thus, the usual statistics used to characterize the size of the treatment effect are d and r. If the point biserial correlation is used (and it is the easier of the two in terms of formulas), then the relevant chapters are Chapters 2 through 4. This chapter presented formulas for meta-analysis using the d statistic. The d statistic is influenced by a number of error factors or artifacts as listed in Chapter 6: sampling error, error of measurement in either variable, imperfect construct validity in either variable, artifactual dichotomization of the dependent variable, and so on. For each such artifact, there is artifact information that would make it possible to control for that artifact in meta-analysis. However, primary researchers are only just beginning to orient publication practices to include the collection and presentation of the information needed to control artifacts. Thus, it is often the case that the only piece of artifact information available is the sample size N, the number needed to control for the effect of sampling error.

If sample size is the only piece of artifact information available in a given research area, then the only meta-analysis that can be done is a bare-bones meta-analysis that controls for no artifact other than sampling error. Because other artifacts are not controlled, the bare-bones meta-analysis will greatly underestimate the mean treatment effect and will greatly overestimate the standard deviation of treatment effects across studies, especially in relation to the mean (i.e., the coefficient of variation of treatment effects will be greatly overestimated). The key formula for the bare-bones meta-analysis of the d statistic is the sampling error variance formula for d. The exact formula uses the gamma function and is mathematically intractable. However, approximation formulas are available, formulas that become progressively more complicated as sample size becomes smaller. Once the approximation formula is chosen, the bare-bones meta-analysis is very straightforward. The mean population d is estimated by the mean d statistic across studies, where the mean is computed weighing each study by its sample size.

The variance of population effect sizes is estimated by subtracting the sampling error variance from the observed variance of d statistics across studies. The subtraction of the sampling error variance is the statistical control for sampling error that completely eliminates the effects of sampling error once the number of studies in the meta-analysis becomes large enough. For a meta-analysis with a small number of studies, there is still sampling error in the meta-analysis values (second-order sampling error, a topic considered in Chapter 9). Thus, bare-bones meta-analysis uses the mean of sample effect size, the standard deviation of sample effect sizes, and the sample size for each study to produce an estimate of the mean and standard deviation of study population effect sizes. For most purposes, the key question is this: Is the standard deviation of effect sizes small in comparison to the effect size? If the answer is yes, then most inferences about the treatment effect will be correctly made if the mean effect size is used as "the" effect size. However, it is important to remember that the mean effect size from a bare-bones meta-analysis underestimates the actual effect size because there is no correction for attenuation due to study artifacts other than sampling error. It is also important to remember that the standard deviation of population effect sizes in a bare-bones meta-analysis is *not* corrected for variation in the other artifacts and, thus, overestimates the extent of real variation in effect sizes across studies. If some theory predicts that effect sizes will vary between certain kinds of studies, or if the standard deviation of population effect sizes is large in proportion to the mean effect size, then the meta-analysis should be extended to analyze potential moderator variables. If the theory predicts that studies of Type A will yield effect sizes larger than those of Type B, that distinction is the moderator variable. Otherwise, the moderator variable must be sought by trial and error, usually starting with some set of study characteristics that are coded for each study for descriptive purposes.

The use of bare-bones meta-analysis to study a potential moderator variable requires no new math. The potential moderator variable is used to break the studies into subsets. A bare-bones meta-analysis is then run on each subset separately. The impact of the potential moderator is registered in two ways: the difference in the mean effect size across subsets and a reduction in the standard deviation of effect sizes within subsets. Because the number of studies within subsets is smaller, the theory of second-order sampling error in Chapter 9 will show that the difference in means is better estimated than is the reduction in variance within subsets. In the case of the theoretically predicted moderator variable, the subset strategy works well. However, as discussed in Chapter 9, if multiple potential moderators are examined, it is important to avoid confounding of moderators; this can be achieved via hierarchical moderator analysis. In the case of a trial-and-error search for moderators, there is a further problem of capitalization on sampling errors. As discussed in Chapters 1 and 2, if you analyze a large number of potential moderator variables, then at least one will appear to be statistically significant by chance. If one uses regression analysis of moderators, there will always be a combination of potential moderator variables that appears to account for variation in effect size, but this "explanation" could be a result of capitalization on the specific sampling errors in specific studies.

If there is information on artifacts other than sampling error (and experience has shown that where the data are available these artifacts prove to be large and important), then the meta-analysis can be considerably more accurate than a bare-bones meta-analysis. Beyond sampling error, the artifact most commonly corrected for in meta-analyses of experiments is measurement error in the dependent variable. If artifact information is known for all or almost all studies, then each observed d value can be corrected individually for artifacts and the meta-analysis can be conducted on the corrected d values. Examples of this were presented. If artifact information is available only sporadically across studies, then artifact distribution meta-analysis can be performed. Again, examples of this were presented. If artifact information is available for some artifacts for all studies and only sporadically available for other artifacts, then a mixed meta-analysis of the type described near the end of Chapter 4 can be conducted. The principles described there for correlations apply also to d values. In all cases in which artifacts beyond sampling error are corrected for, potential moderators can be examined using the same methods described for use with bare-bones meta-analysis.

In meta-analysis of d values, when artifacts beyond sampling error and measurement error in the dependent variable are corrected for, it is usually simpler and easier to transform all d values to correlations, conduct the meta-analysis on correlations using the methods described in Chapters 3 and 4, and then transform the final results back to d values. This is because the formulas for correlations are less complicated than those for d values. Nevertheless, this chapter develops and presents formulas for multiple-artifact meta-analysis of d values. Although these formulas are of necessity approximations, they are quite accurate. Meta-analysis performed on d values using these formulas will be about as accurate as meta-analysis performed by converting all d values to correlations, conducting the meta-analysis using the methods of Chapter 3 or Chapter 4, and then converting the results back to the d-value metric. However, because this latter procedure is simpler, it is probably to be preferred.

Exercise 7.1: Meta-Analysis of *d* Values

Meta-Analysis of *d* Values
Studies of Gender Differences in Conformity

Study	Total Sample Size	Effect Size Estimate d Value	Number of Items
1	254	.35	38
2	80	.37	5
3	125	−.06	5
4	191	−.30	2
5	64	.69	30
6	90	.40	45
7	60	.47	45
8	20	.81	45
9	141	−.33	2
10	119	.07	2

A hypothetical researcher conducted a review of experimental studies of gender differences in conformity. The 10 studies summarized here are called "other conformity studies." Because all these studies use an experimental paradigm involving a nonexistent norm group, they are called "fictitious norm group" studies.

These studies measure conformity by examining the effect of knowledge of other people's responses on an individual's response. Typically, an experimental subject is presented with an opportunity to respond to a question of opinion. Before responding, the individual is shown some "data" on the responses of other individuals. The "data" are manipulated by the experimenters, and the "other individuals" are the fictitious norm group. For example, the subject might be asked for an opinion on a work of art and told that 75% of art majors liked the work "a great deal."

Positive d values indicate females were more conforming; negative values indicate males were more conforming.

Except for step 2, this exercise can be worked using the program D-VALUE, which corrects d values individually for artifacts. Alternatively, you can convert all d values to correlations and apply the program VG-6, which uses the methods presented in Chapter 3 to correct correlations individually and then performs meta-analysis of the corrected correlations. You would then convert these results back into the d-value metric using equations given in this chapter. Both these programs are included in the Windows-based package of programs available for applying the methods presented in this book. Details about this software package can be found in the Appendix. However, you will learn more if you carry out the exercise using a calculator.

Instructions for Exercise

1. Perform a bare-bones meta-analysis of these 10 studies. Correct the d values for their positive bias, as discussed in this chapter. In estimating sampling error variance, use the most accurate formula given in this chapter. Create a table

showing the mean d, the observed variance of d, the variance predicted from sampling error, the variance corrected for sampling error, and the standard deviation of the d values corrected for sampling error. In addition, present the percentage variance accounted for by sampling error variance and the 80% credibility interval.

How would these results be interpreted by someone with no knowledge of measurement error? That is, give the "face value" interpretation of these results.

From these results, in what percentage of groups would you expect males to be more conforming? Females? Note that if $\bar{d}$ were 0, males would be more conforming in 50% of the groups and the same for females. Use the properties of the normal curve to compute the percentages implied by your $\bar{d}$ value. First, compute $z = 0 - \bar{d}/SD_{\delta_{xy}}$. Then look this z value up in a normal curve table and record the percentages above and below this z value. These are the needed percentages.

2. Determine the importance of correcting the observed d values for their positive bias. Rerun the analysis in step 1 but do not correct for this bias. How different are your results? What do you conclude about the bias correction?

3. Reliabilities for the conformity measures were not given in these studies. However, the number of trials (or "items") *was* given. An example of a trial (or item) was given previously: The subjects were shown a piece of art and told that 75% of art majors liked the work "a great deal." Some studies had only two such trials; the largest number of trials was 45. (Three studies had this many.) The number of items in each study is given in the data table.

The average correlation between trials is .10 (i.e., $r = .10$). Use this information and the Spearman-Brown formula to compute the reliability of the conformity measure used in each study, based on the number of "items" (trials) used in that study. In the exercise, the Spearman-Brown formula can be written as

$$\text{Reliability} = nr/[1 + (n - 1)r]$$

where n is the number of trials and r is the average correlation between trials.

4. Use these reliability estimates to correct each d value for measurement error. (Use the d values corrected for positive bias.) Then conduct a meta-analysis of the corrected d values.

Present the same information as in the bare-bones meta-analysis, except this time for the corrected d values. That is, present the following in a table:

a. The mean corrected d value
b. The observed variance of the corrected d values
c. The sampling error variance for the corrected d values
d. The variance of the corrected d values, corrected for sampling error variance, that is, the estimated variance of the population (δ) values
e. The estimated standard deviation of δ
f. The percentage of variance accounted for by the two artifacts (sampling error and measurement error)
g. The 80% credibility interval

Interpret these findings as you did those for the bare-bones meta-analysis. Does the correction for measurement error lead to any differences in findings and conclusions? Compute the estimated percentage of groups in which males are more conforming than females and vice versa. Is the estimated percentage of groups in which males are more conforming than females different from the figures obtained in the bare-bones meta-analysis? What about the estimated percentage of groups in which the females are more conforming? Why are these percentages different from those computed from the bare-bones meta-analysis results?

8

Technical Questions in Meta-Analysis of *d* Values

This chapter discusses technical questions that arise in the meta-analysis of experimental effect sizes. The most important of these questions is the effect of different experimental designs on the properties of the resulting *d* values. We provide sources that allow the reader to correctly compute *d* values for experimental designs other than the independent-groups design addressed in Chapter 7, and we provide an extended treatment of repeated-measures designs, the most frequently used design after the independent-groups design. The other technical issues we address include threats to internal and external validity of experiments, the slight positive bias in observed *d* values, and the use of weighted regression analysis in examining potential moderators of *d* values. We discuss each of these topics in this chapter.

Alternative Experimental Designs

The methods presented in Chapter 7 are for independent-groups design. In this design, subjects are assigned randomly to experimental and control groups. Different subjects are assigned to different groups, and hence, the design is called "independent subjects," "between subjects," or "independent groups" design. This is the most commonly used design, but there are a number of other possible study designs that are sometimes used: (a) independent-groups designs with more than one level of treatment, (b) matched-group designs, (c) factorial independent-groups designs, (d) ANCOVA designs, and (e) repeated-measures designs.

In the case of each of these designs, there are two critical questions. First, how does one compute *d* values that estimate the same population parameter as is estimated by the *d* value in the independent-groups design? Second, what is the correct formula for the sampling error variance of each of these (correctly computed) *d* values? Consider the question of how to estimate the correct *d* value. In ANCOVA models, the pooled standard deviation is usually reduced by partialing out the covariates; hence, the d value is overestimated if the usual formula for a d value is used. Special formulas must be used to ensure that this does not happen. In repeated-measures designs, the standard deviation is the standard deviation of change (i.e., gain) scores, which is typically much smaller than the standard deviation of raw scores in the population. Again, special formulas are needed to ensure that the d value used represents standardized group mean differences expressed in the metric of population standard deviation units of the raw scores on the measure. If these adjustments are not made, the result can be the reporting of erroneously large mean d values in a meta-analysis. An example of this is the meta-analysis of experimenter expectancy effects by Rosenthal and Rubin (1978a). This article included a number of meta-analyses of different subareas of this literature, with mean d values (uncorrected for measurement error) often in the range of 2.00 to 4.00 for different meta-analyses. These are strikingly large mean effect sizes, especially for a subtle influence such as experimenter expectancy effects. However, they were interpreted as ordinary d values; that is, they were interpreted as if they were in the metric of the within-group standard deviation. However, many of the studies were repeated-measures designs and the d values were computed using the standard deviation of gain scores in the denominator. Hence, reported d values were much larger than actual d values. This example shows why this is a serious issue.

A number of sources are available that discuss these issues for all of these experimental study designs and present the correct formulas for computing d values and the sampling error variance of these d values for each kind of design (Cortina & Nouri, 2000; Dunlap, Cortina, Vaslow, & Burke, 1996; Morris & DeShon, 2002). For designs other than independent-groups designs, we refer the reader to these sources for the formulas needed to compute the d values and sampling error variances for each study that are needed to conduct the meta-analysis. There is also a computer program called ES (Shadish, Robinson, & Lu, 1999) that is useful for computing effect sizes (and their standard errors) from a variety of such research designs. This program is discussed in more detail in Chapter 11 (under the topic "Computer Programs for Meta-Analysis"). Once the d values and sampling error variances are computed, the meta-analysis of the resulting database proceeds in the same way as described in Chapter 7. The methods—including corrections for sampling error, measurement error, and other artifacts—are identical. The computer programs for meta-analysis of d values (D-VALUE and D-VALUE1) contained in the Windows-based software package described in the Appendix can be used to conduct such meta-analyses. However, one must be certain to enter values for sample size (N) that will lead the programs to produce correct values for sampling error variance. Given the known sampling error variance for each such d value (provided in Cortina & Nouri, 2000; Dunlap et al., 1996; Morris & DeShon, 2002), the needed value for N can be computed by solving Equation (7.30) or Equation (7.23a) for N. This value of N is then entered into the database for the computer program. This step is necessary because even when unbiased estimates of d values are obtained from repeated-measures designs, these d values do not have the same sampling error variances as d values from the independent-groups design. The programs are set up to use the sampling error variance formulas for d values from independent-groups designs.

Within-Subjects Experimental Designs

Next to the independent-groups design, the design most frequently used is the repeated-measures design. It is also the design with the greatest number of potential advantages over the independent-groups design. For these reasons, this section presents an extended discussion of the within-subjects or repeated-measures design, including a detailed examination of the role of measurement error in this design. To explain why different formulas are used, we must also discuss the derivation of the within-subjects design. That gives us the opportunity to demonstrate that, under most conditions, the within-subjects design is far superior to the between-subjects design. In particular, if the dependent variable is measured with high reliability, then the within-subjects design has much higher statistical power than the between-subjects design. This chapter presents a much more complete statistical treatment of the within-subjects design than exists in the current literature. In particular, we present formulas that are not (to our knowledge) found elsewhere in the statistical literature: (1) confidence intervals for both the raw score and the standardized treatment effect, (2) a confidence interval for the treatment by subjects interaction, and (3) confidence intervals for both the raw score and the standardized interaction variance. Finally, we describe how to incorporate the results of within-subjects studies into meta-analysis, using the appropriate formulas for d values and the sampling error variances of the d values.

Many myths have arisen concerning the within-subjects design. These myths have led many researchers to reject studies using a within-subjects design without considering the concrete details about the substantive nature of the design. For example, many researchers believe that studies that use a pre-post design should be discarded when conducting a meta-analysis. The explanation is usually something like this: "The within-subject design is fundamentally flawed by threats to internal and external validity," citing Campbell and Stanley (1963). This chapter will show that (1) this is *not* what Campbell and Stanley said, and (2) it is not true. Campbell and Stanley listed things to *think about* when evaluating a within-subjects design. They repeatedly state that one is not to *assume* that a threat is realized, but to see if there is actual evidence that the threat was realized. Thus, they were only listing *potential* problems of internal or external validity, problems to be considered concretely in each study. They did not assume the existence of such problems in advance. We will show by example that it is possible to have a pre-post study in which not a single threat to internal validity is realized. This demonstration is proof that the discard position is erroneous. On the other hand, we can offer only a statement of our own experience as to the likelihood of a violation. We have found violations of the Campbell-Stanley list to be rare. We have found few cases in which a within-subjects design could not be used.

In addition to correcting common misunderstandings of Campbell and Stanley (1963), this chapter will address other widespread misconceptions and problems concerning the within-subjects research design: (1) misunderstanding the statistical power problem for the independent-groups design, (2) misunderstanding the problem of treatment by subjects interactions and the implications for the independent-groups design, and (3) inaccessible formulas for evaluating basic statistics, especially the measurement of the treatment by subjects interaction.

This chapter urges experimenters to use the more powerful within-subjects design whenever possible. In particular, if the dependent variable is measured with high reliability, then the within-subjects design has much higher statistical precision and power than the independent-groups design.

The reason the independent-groups design is so commonly used is not because it is a good design. As we noted in the previous chapter, the independent-groups design has very low power. There are better designs. One way to create a better design is to lay out the theory of the intervention in a process model. The processes can then be mapped by various dependent variables. The full multiple-dependent-variable model can then be tested using path analysis. This approach, however, is beyond the scope of this book.

Another way to increase power is by using a within-subjects or repeated-measures design such as the pre-post design. Consider a department that produces widgets and suppose quality circles are to be introduced into the department. We could measure productivity before the intervention and then at several stages after the intervention. For simplicity, assume that we have just one post-measure of productivity. For each worker in the study, we have a pre-intervention measure called the "pretest score" and a post-intervention measure called the "posttest score." We can then check for changes in performance by subtracting the pretest score from the posttest score. That is, we can analyze changes at the level of the individual worker. These scores are variously referred to as change scores, difference scores, or gain scores. The specific term used is not important because the statistical and measurement principles and equations are identical. The main problem with such scores is error of measurement (Edwards, 1995). If the measure of productivity were perfect, then the change score would be an exact measurement of the treatment effect for that worker. However, if there is error of measurement, then the observed difference score would differ from the true difference (change) score by some random amount. If the error of measurement is large enough, and if the treatment effect is small enough, then the error in the change score may overshadow the true gain for individual subjects. In that case, the treatment effect may be reliably observed only at the level of the mean change score across subjects. In that case, the power of the within-subjects design will be no higher than the power of the between-subjects design.

The Potentially Perfect Power of the Pre-Post Design

The rule in analysis of variance is that a main effect must never be separately interpreted if there is a higher order interaction. In the case of the independent-groups design, the difference between the group means is the treatment main effect. To be certain that the interpretation of that main effect is correct, there must be no higher order interaction. In particular, this means that the conventional interpretation of the between-subjects design assumes that there is no treatment by subjects interaction. That is, the conventional independent-groups design assumes that the treatment effect is the same for every subject. We will now consider the implications of this assumption for the within-subjects design. If the treatment effect is the same for each subject, and if the dependent variable is measured perfectly, then we will see that the power of the corresponding t test on gain (or change) scores would be perfect even for very small sample sizes. That is, if there were no treatment by subjects interaction, then the use of the within-subjects design would potentially free us from the problem of sampling error. The reason it does not in practice is the presence of error of measurement. We will introduce examples that show that error of measurement reintroduces the problem of sampling error in a different form.

Suppose the introduction of quality circles increases the daily production of widgets by 5.2. Consider the production of three workers perfectly measured.

	Pretest Score	*Posttest Score*	*Change or Gain Score*
Ernesto	31.3	36.5	5.2
Horacio	41.4	46.6	5.2
Antonio	51.5	56.7	5.2

In these data, the treatment effect is reflected in the gain of any single subject. There is no need to observe a population of subjects. In these data, the fact that there is no treatment by subjects interaction is seen in the fact that the gain score is exactly the same for all subjects. Thus, both key facts about this study are shown without sampling error in a sample of subjects as small as $N = 3$!

The usual statistical analysis for the within-subjects design is a t test on the gain or change scores. The mean and standard deviation of the gain scores are

Mean gain = 5.2,
SD of gain = 0.

The t-test value is

$$t = \text{Mean}/(SD/\sqrt{N}) = 5.2/(0/\sqrt{3}) = 5.2/0 = \infty.$$

The t value of ∞ is significant at any alpha level. Thus, even for a sample of three subjects, the t test has perfect power.

Unfortunately, we will see that perfect power is lost if there is any measurement error at all, and there is always some measurement error.

Deficiencies of the Between-Subjects Design

If there is no treatment by subjects interaction, the within-subjects design potentially has perfect power. Why does the between-subjects design have such low power? The answer lies in missing data. There is a sense in which the independent-groups design has *half* the data missing, one of two scores for each subject. In fact, there is a sense in which *all* the data are missing: There is no observed *gain* score for any subject.

Consider the widget-producing department again. Suppose we organize it into two (geographically separated) subdepartments for purposes of using an independent-groups design to assess the effect of quality circles. Each worker is randomly assigned to either the quality circle group or the control group. We assume for purposes of this example that there is no measurement error in the dependent variable. Corresponding to the three-person data considered for the within-subjects design, we have six workers, three in each group.

	Productivity Score
Control Group	
Ernesto	31.3
Horacio	41.4
Antonio	51.5
Experimental Group	
Samuel	38.3
Gilberto	48.4
Alberto	58.5

The statistical analysis consists of comparing the two group means in relation to the within-groups variance.

	Control	*Experimental*
Mean	41.4	48.4
SD	10.1	10.1
Mean difference = 48.4 − 41.4 = 7.0		
Within-groups variance = 102.01		
Within-groups *SD* = 10.1		

The value of the d statistic is

$$d = 7.0/10.1 = .69$$

Because the within-groups variances were computed using $N_i - 1$ instead of N_i, the formula for the t test statistic is

$$t = \frac{\bar{Y}_E - \bar{Y}_C}{[[(N_1 - 1)\,S_1^2 + (N - 1)\,S_2^2]/[N_1 - N_2 - 2][N_1 - N_2]/[N_1 N_2]]^{1/2}},$$

$$t = .85 \tag{8.1}$$

which is not significant at the .05 level.

There are several problems with these new data. First, the treatment effect is wrong. The difference between the means is 7.0 instead of 5.2. Second, the difference is not significant, and hence, the significance test has registered a Type II error.

Where did the errors in the independent-groups design come from? Suppose that we had done a pre-post study (without a control group). Under the assumptions of our example, the data would have been

	Pretest Score	*Posttest Score*	*Gain Score*
Control Group			
Ernesto	31.3	36.5	5.2
Horacio	41.4	46.6	5.2
Antonio	51.5	56.7	5.2
Experimental Group			
Samuel	33.1	38.3	5.2
Gilberto	43.2	48.4	5.2
Alberto	53.3	58.5	5.2

Had we done a pre-post study, the gain score would have been 5.2 for every subject. (Remember that, since there was no control group, all subjects receive the treatment.) Instead, for the subjects in the control group in the independent-groups design, there was no intervention, and hence, the "posttest" score was actually the pretest score. For the subjects in the experimental group, the pretest score was not observed. Thus, the data in the independent-groups design is actually represented as follows:

	Pretest Score	*Posttest Score*	*Gain Score*
Control Group			
Ernesto	31.3	–	–
Horacio	41.4	–	–
Antonio	51.5	–	–
Experimental group			
Samuel	–	38.3	–
Gilberto	–	48.4	–
Alberto	–	58.5	–

In this table, we see that for each worker only one of his two scores is observed. In that sense, the independent-groups design is a design in which *half the data are missing*. However, there is an even more severe problem. The gain score is not observed for any subject. In that sense, for an independent-groups design, *all the data on individual treatment effects are missing.*

In the independent-groups design, we estimate the treatment difference by comparing the two group means. The experimental group mean is the experimental group posttest mean, and the control group mean is the control group pretest mean. Given within-subjects data, we could instead compare the posttest and pretest mean for each group separately. Remember that in this design all subjects receive the treatment. (There is no control group.) We would have the following:

	Pretest Mean	*Posttest Mean*	*Mean Difference*
Control group	41.4	46.6	5.2
Experimental group	43.2	48.4	5.2

For the within-subjects data, the difference between pretest and posttest means is, in fact, 5.2 for each group. That is, for the pre-post design, the mean difference between posttest and pretest is the treatment effect for either group.

What happened to sampling error? Note that, in the within-subjects design, the two subgroups do have different means. That is, by chance the pretest mean is 41.4 for the control group and 43.2 for the experimental group. This difference is sampling error. However, in the within-subjects design, the comparison of means is done within each group. That is, we compute the treatment effect mean difference for the control subgroup as the difference between their posttest mean and their pretest mean. For the experimental subgroup, we compute the mean difference using the two experimental subgroup means. Because comparisons are made within groups, the between-groups difference on the pretest does not enter into the estimation of the treatment effect.

For the independent-groups design, we estimate the treatment effect by subtracting the pretest mean for one group from the posttest mean for the other group. The sampling error difference in pretest means is $43.2 - 41.4 = 1.8$. Because the means being compared come from the two different groups, this sampling error difference enters the estimated treatment effect. That is, note that

$$5.2 + 1.8 = 7.0$$

Suppose we define

DA = Actual treatment effect,
e = Sampling error difference between pretest means,
DO = Observed treatment effect estimate.

Then

$$DO = DA + e$$

Thus, the sampling error in the conventional independent-groups design stems from a conceptual defect. Because we do not observe the treatment effect for any individual subject, we are forced to estimate the effect for individuals from data on groups. Because the groups are different, the sampling error difference between the groups is confounded with the true treatment effect. This sampling error difference can be considerable unless the number in each group is large, which is rarely the case.

The Independent-Groups Design and the Treatment by Subjects Interaction

Another key problem for the independent-groups design is the potential treatment by subjects interaction. If the treatment has different effects on different people, then there is an interaction between treatment and subjects. If so, then it is possible that the between-groups design may be rendered quite misleading. The between-groups design considers the main effect of treatment under the assumption that there is no interaction between the treatment and the subjects (Hays, 1963; Kirk, 1995; Winer, 1962). Suppose the treatment increases the dependent variable by +5 units for half the subjects, but decreases the dependent variable by −5 units for the other half of the subjects. The average treatment effect is 0, and so the mean for the experimental group will equal the mean for the control group and the usual interpretation of between-groups data would be that the treatment had no effect. This interpretation is completely false. Thus, if there is a treatment by subjects interaction, then it is possible for the between-groups design to be invalid.

A key question for the independent-groups design is this: Is it possible to run any test of the independent-groups data to see if there is a treatment by subjects interaction? The answer is, "There is no sure test." Some treatment by subjects interactions show up because the differences in treatment effects cause a difference between the standard deviation of the control and experimental groups. However, (1) this is not always true, and (2) the statistical power for detecting the difference in standard deviations may not be very high. So the between-groups design must *assume* that there is no interaction; this design does not gather the data necessary to test that assumption.

We will show that the within-subjects design does gather the data necessary to detect a treatment by subjects interaction if it occurs. Furthermore, the size of the interaction can be measured in this design. Given information on the size of the interaction, it is possible to see if the treatment effect is always in the same direction or not. That is, the within-subjects design provides a test for whether the usual treatment effect is a reasonable interpretation of the data or not.

The within-subjects design allows a treatment by subjects interaction to be detected and measured. However, the reason the change scores vary across subjects is still unknown. Thus, the interaction may be detected and measured without being identified. It is not possible to identify the interaction without data on the relevant individual difference variable that determines the subject's response to the treatment. Therefore, if the within-subjects design detects the interaction, it may be necessary to gather additional data to identify the nature of that interaction. New data would not be necessary if the individual difference variable had been measured in the first place. In the design of any study, it is important to ask whether there might be differences in the treatment effect and what variable might predict such differences. That variable can then be measured and used as a "control" variable in the final analysis. In a pre-post design, the treatment by subjects interaction can be identified as a correlation between the individual difference variable and the change scores.

The independent-groups design must *assume* that there is no treatment by subjects interaction; it does not provide the data needed to test for the interaction. Suppose the independent-groups designs were chosen after a careful theoretical consideration of the question of treatment by subjects indicated that there could be no interaction. There would then be an interaction in the study only if that theory were wrong. If the theory is empirically well grounded, then it fits a great many findings. Thus, inferences drawn about the new study design based on the theory are likely to be correct, and the theoretically justified choice of the independent-groups design is probably warranted.

However, informal interviewing shows that experimenters rarely consider the possibility of a treatment by subjects interaction. In fact, when asked if all subjects will respond to the treatment in exactly the same way, most investigators say "No." Often, they will state specific hypotheses as to individual differences in treatment response. Thus, most investigators actually expect a treatment by subjects interaction, but do not realize the significance of that expectation. Thus, use of the independent-groups design is a matter of faith, faith that is usually *not* grounded in a deliberate theoretical consideration of potential interaction and that is often contrary to the beliefs of the investigator. Most experimenters are not aware that the independent-groups design may be invalidated by the presence of such an interaction.

Error of Measurement and the Within-Subjects Design

The effect of error of measurement on the within-subjects design is quite direct: It blurs the observation of the individual treatment effect. Consider the case for Ernie.

True pretest score = 31.3
True posttest score = 36.5
True gain score = 5.2

Suppose instead that there is error of measurement. Then

Observed pretest score = 31.3 + first error
Observed posttest score = 36.5 + second error
Observed gain score = 5.2 + difference between errors

If we denote the observed gain score by OG and the errors of measurement by e_1 and e_2, respectively, then

$$OG = 5.2 + (e_2 - e_1)$$

When errors are subtracted, they do not necessarily cancel out. For example, suppose the first error is +2.3 and the second error is −2.3. We then have

Observed posttest score = 31.3 + 2.3 = 33.6
Observed posttest score = 36.5 + (−2.3) = 34.2
Observed gain score = 34.2 − 33.6 = .6
= 5.2 − 4.6
= 5.2 + ([−2.3] − [+2.3])

Half the time, the errors of measurement will have the same sign and will approximately cancel out. The other half of the time, however, the errors of measurement will have opposite signs and will thus add to each other in absolute value. Thus, error of measurement blurs the observation of the treatment effect for individual subjects. The larger the error of measurement relative to the treatment effect, the more difficult it is to detect the treatment effect in single scores.

Error of measurement does tend to cancel out in averages across subjects. Thus, the treatment effect could potentially be perfectly observed because it equals the average gain score. The word "potentially" reflects the fact that it is only the population average error that is 0; the sample mean will differ from 0 by sampling error in the measurement errors. Thus, the introduction of error of measurement into individual data causes our summary statistics to suffer from sampling error, namely, sampling error in the statistics computed based on errors of measurement. This section spells out the sampling error effects quantitatively.

Let us denote the compound error by f. That is, the error of measurement in the gain score is given by

$$f = e_2 - e_1 \tag{8.2}$$

If the gain or change true score is denoted TG, then the observed score gain score is related to the true gain score by

$$OG = TG + f \tag{8.3}$$

If we replace the notation OG by X and replace TG by T and replace f by E, this equation would be

$$X = T + E$$

the traditional equation for error of measurement. This equation would be fully justified if (1) the mean error $E(f)$ is 0, and (2) the error f is uncorrelated with the true score TG. The population mean error is

$$E(f) = E(e_2 - e_1) = E(e_2) - E(e_1) = 0 - 0 = 0 \tag{8.4}$$

To see that the error in the gain score is uncorrelated with the true gain score, consider the composition of each. Denote the true score of the pretest by T_1 and the true score of the posttest by T_2. Then

$$\begin{aligned} TG &= T_2 - T_1 \\ f &= e_2 - e_1 \end{aligned} \tag{8.5}$$

Because each of the component errors in f is uncorrelated with each of the component true scores in TG, f is uncorrelated with TG. Thus, f acts as the error of measurement in the gain score OG in exactly the manner of classical reliability theory.

How large is the error in the gain score? Because the component errors are not correlated with each other, the population variance of the gain score error is

$$\begin{aligned} \text{Var}(f) &= \text{Var}(e_1 - e_2) = \text{Var}(e_1) + \text{Var}(e_2) - 2\ \text{Cov}(e_1, e_2) \\ &= \text{Var}(e_1) + \text{Var}(e_2) - 0 \\ &= \text{Var}(e) + \text{Var}(e) \\ &= 2\ \text{Var}(e) \end{aligned} \tag{8.6}$$

That is, the error variance of the gain scores is exactly twice the error variance of the pretest and posttest scores. If the pretest and posttest scores are denoted Y_1 and Y_2, respectively, then the error variance of the dependent variable scores is

$$\text{Var}(e) = [1 - r_{YY}]\ \text{Var}(Y) \tag{8.7}$$

where r_{YY} is the reliability of the dependent variable. The gain score error variance is thus

$$\text{Var}(f) = 2\ \text{Var}(e) = 2[1 - r_{YY}]\ \text{Var}(Y) \tag{8.8}$$

Note that if the reliability were perfect ($r_{YY} = 1.00$), then the error variance would be 0, as in the perfect measurement example given previously.

What is the effect of error of measurement on sampling error? Consider the mean gain. The sample mean is given by

$$\text{Ave}(OG) = \text{Ave}(TG + f) = \text{Ave}(TG) + \text{Ave}(f) \tag{8.9}$$

If there is no treatment by subjects interaction, then each true gain score is identical, and hence,

$$\text{Ave}(TG) = TG = \text{Raw score gain} \tag{8.10}$$

That is, if there is no treatment by subjects interaction, then there is no sampling error in the average true gain score because there is no variance. (The case of the treatment by subjects interaction will be considered in the next section.) The average error of measurement is given by

$$\begin{aligned} \text{Ave}(f) &= E(f) + \text{Sampling error} = 0 + \text{Sampling error} \\ &= \text{Sampling error} \end{aligned} \tag{8.11}$$

The sample average error is not 0, but differs from 0 by sampling error. Thus, the sample average error of measurement will not be 0 unless the sample size is extremely large. The size of the potential sampling error is given by its variance

$$\text{Var}[\text{Ave}(f)] = \text{Var}(f)/N \tag{8.12}$$

where N is the sample size.

Thus, the effect of error of measurement on the observed raw score treatment effect is as follows: If there is no treatment by subjects interaction, then the sample mean gain score will differ from the raw score treatment effect by the sampling error in the mean gain score error of measurement.

Consider now the sample variance of the observed gain scores. If there is no treatment by subjects interaction, then the true gain score is constant across subjects. The population variance of observed gain scores is thus

$$\text{Var}(OG) = \text{Var}(TG + f) = \text{Var}(f) \tag{8.13}$$

That is, if there is no interaction, then the variance of observed gain scores is the variance of errors of measurement.

Thus, error of measurement introduces sampling error into both the sample mean gain score and the sample gain score variance. This causes the corresponding t test to have less than perfect power, and it introduces error of measurement into the estimate of the treatment effect from the data.

The Treatment Effect in Standard Scores

Up to now, the focus has been on the treatment effect for raw scores. For meta-analysis, results must be in a form that is the same across all studies. If all studies were done with identically the same variable, then the raw score treatment effect could be cumulated across studies. However, in most research domains the same construct is used across studies, but it is measured in different units from one study to the next. Thus, the usual measure of the treatment effect is measured in standard score units, which are in the same metric across studies. In the case of the treatment effect, the main treatment effect δ is defined in standard score units:

$$\delta = E(TG)/\sigma \tag{8.14}$$

where σ is the within-groups standard deviation for true scores. If the posttest standard deviation is the same as the pretest standard deviation (i.e., "homogeneity of variance"), then

$$\text{Var}(T_2) = \text{Var}(T_1) = \sigma^2 \tag{8.15}$$

and the within-groups standard deviation is unambiguously defined.

If the posttest standard deviation is different from the pretest standard deviation, then there are three choices for the "within-groups" standard deviation: (1) the pretest standard deviation, (2) the posttest standard deviation, and (3) an average standard deviation. In theory, the best choice is probably the pretest standard deviation. That is, the baseline level of individual differences is the level before the treatment. In practice, the best choice of standard deviation is the standard deviation that will be used in the meta-analysis. If a large portion of the studies in the domain will be independent-groups studies, then the meta-analysis will probably use the square root of the within-groups variance as its within-groups standard deviation. Thus, the best choice of within-groups standard deviation for the within-subjects design would be the corresponding average standard deviation.

Note that the desired standard deviation is the standard deviation of true scores, not the standard deviation of observed scores. However, if the reliability of the dependent variable is known, then it is easy to obtain an estimate of the true score standard deviation from the corresponding observed score standard deviation, namely,

$$\text{Var}(T) = r_{YY}\,\text{Var}(Y) \tag{8.16}$$

for the pretest, for the posttest, or for the average.

Some Conceptual Issues

Before going on to the discussion of interactions, we pause to provide a discussion of terms.

Level Scores. There are two kinds of scores: (1) the change score and (2) the pretest and posttest scores. To be able to refer to pretest and posttest by one name, we will call both "level" scores. The language is derived by thinking of the pretest and posttest as the "level" that the subject is at, while the change score measures the treatment impact.

The Pretest-Posttest Correlation. A key statistic not mentioned thus far is the correlation between pretest and posttest. This is sometimes called the "test-retest correlation," and in some contexts it can be used as an estimate of the reliability (i.e., the coefficient of stability, as discussed in Chapter 3). However, in some contexts, the test-retest correlation might be a poor estimate of the reliability. The distinction is primarily determined by whether there is a treatment by subjects interaction.

Let us first define the notation. The correlation between pretest and posttest will be denoted r_{12} while the reliability is denoted r_{YY}. For simplicity, our discussion here of error of measurement assumes that the measurement error is the sum of random response error and transient error. (See Chapter 3.) There is another kind of error called specific error. If the dependent variable has specific error, then the exact treatment of the within-subjects design is slightly more complicated. See the discussion of different types of measurement error in Chapter 3.

If there is no specific error, then the relationship between the test-retest correlation r_{12} and the reliability r_{YY} is straightforward. If there is no treatment by subjects interaction, then the population test-retest correlation equals the reliability. However, if there is a treatment by subjects interaction, then the test-retest correlation will be smaller than the reliability by an amount that is related to the size of the interaction. That is, the test-retest correlation will be lower than the reliability to the extent that the change score standard deviation σ_{TG} is large in comparison to the level score standard deviation σ_T.

Confidence Intervals. Most statistics are averages and, therefore, have approximately normal distributions except for those computed on very small sample sizes. Thus, to generate a confidence interval, we need only know the sampling error standard deviation or "standard error." Suppose the sample statistic value is denoted V and the population PV. If S is the standard error of V, then the 95% confidence interval is

$$V - 1.96S < PV < V + 1.96S \tag{8.17}$$

In this formula, it is assumed that S is the population value of the standard error. If a sample variance is used to estimate S, then the width of the confidence interval is wider because of the sampling error in S. In most cases, we merely substitute a value from the t distribution for the value 1.96 from the normal distribution. The 95% t value is

$$t = 1.96[1 + 1.2104/(N - 1)] \tag{8.18}$$

unless there are fewer than 16 subjects, in which case one should use (Kirk, 1995)

$$t = 1.96[1 + 1.2104/(N - 1) + 1.4402/(N - 1)^2] \tag{8.19}$$

The corresponding confidence interval is

$$V - tS < PV < V + tS \tag{8.20}$$

Throughout this section, we will typically present only the confidence interval for the known standard error and will make the reference "use of t," or the like, to refer to the substitution given here.

The Treatment by Subjects Interaction

If there is a treatment by subjects interaction, then the treatment effect is different for different subjects. For example, suppose that some subjects learn better techniques from quality circle discussions while other subjects are too rigid to change their work habits and, thus, gain no advantage from the new ideas expressed there. The treatment effect then varies across the population of subjects. The simplest statistical description of the raw score treatment effect would be given by the population mean and the population standard deviation of individual treatment effects. These statistics are the population mean and standard deviation of the true gain scores, that is, the gain scores free of error of measurement. On the other hand, the observed statistics will be computed on observed scores and will have components due to error of measurement. Thus, observed statistics will not only have sampling error, but error of measurement as well. It is possible to correct for the systematic effect of error of measurement in a single study, but it is possible to correct for sampling error only by conducting a meta-analysis across studies.

The significance test of the treatment main effect computed on corrected statistics is equivalent in outcome to the corresponding significance test computed on uncorrected statistics. That is, the resulting p value is identical. Thus, the tradition in analysis of variance has been to present only the test for uncorrected scores. If the null hypothesis were true—the guiding principle for traditional statistical usage—both the corrected and the uncorrected treatment main effect would be 0. Thus, if there were no treatment main effect, there would be no need to compute corrected effect sizes anyway. The failure of classic texts to mention correction formulas indirectly reflects the implicit assumption that the null hypothesis is always true. That is, the bias in classic statistics texts shows in the fact that there is no discussion of practical computations that assume that the null hypothesis might be false.

Our treatment will be more evenhanded. We will first define the treatment main effect without error of measurement. We will then relate the corresponding observed main effects to the actual main effects. Psychometrically, this is equivalent to correction for the attenuation produced by error of measurement.

There is an even greater bias in the classic statistics texts. We have shown that if there is a treatment by subjects interaction, then we must estimate two statistics: the mean and the standard deviation of treatment effects across subjects. Yet, in the conventional treatment of the within-subjects t test, there is no mention of the standard deviation at all. This corresponds to the tacit assumption of the global null hypothesis that the null hypothesis is true *for each individual subject*. If there is no treatment effect at all, then both the mean treatment effect and the standard deviation would be 0, and there would be no need to either report the standard deviation or to quantify its size. It could just be ignored. Thus, again the odd omissions of classic statistics texts can be explained by the fact that the authors implicitly assume that the null hypothesis is always true.

Perfect Measurement

Suppose there is a treatment by subjects interaction. There is variation in the treatment effect across subjects. The raw score treatment main effect is defined as the average treatment effect across subjects. If we use the notation "raw score δ" for the raw score treatment main effect, then

$$\text{Raw score } \delta = E(TG) \quad (8.21)$$

If the standard deviation of pretest true score gain scores is denoted σ_T, then the true standard score treatment effect is

$$\sigma = \text{Raw score } \delta/\sigma_T = E(TG)/\sigma_T \quad (8.22)$$

Note that the standard deviation in this formula is the standard deviation of the pretest true scores and *not* the standard deviation of the gain scores. This is an important distinction not always made clearly in conventional statistics texts. (See Cortina & Nouri, 2000; Dunlap et al., 1996; Morris & DeShon, 2002, who do make this distinction.) At the beginning of this chapter, we discussed the meta-analyses of Rosenthal and Rubin (1978a) that failed to make this distinction and, as a result, reported mean d values that were greatly inflated in comparison to the actual mean d values. Other examples of this sort can be found in the literature; see Dunlap et al. (1996) for some examples.

If there is a treatment by subjects interaction, then the extent of variation in the treatment effect can be measured in raw score form as the standard deviation of gain scores. This definition differs slightly from the definition in analysis of variance texts in that we measure the interaction by the standard deviation instead of the variance. However, this is necessary if the main effect and the interaction are to be compared, because they must be computed in the same units. Analysis of variance texts usually confuse this issue by using an ambiguous definition of the treatment main effect. In their substantive discussions and concrete examples, these texts talk about the treatment effect as the mean difference. However, in their formal analysis of variance formulas, the "treatment main effect" is defined as the *square* of the treatment difference (e.g., Hays, 1963; Kirk, 1995; Winer, 1962). By squaring the treatment main effect, they put it into the same (alas, meaningless) units as the treatment variance.

Let us denote the standard deviation of true gain scores by σ_{TG}. The quantitative measure of the interaction in raw score form is thus

$$\text{Raw score interaction} = \sigma_{TG} \quad (8.23)$$

This standard deviation can be compared with the treatment main effect directly. Suppose the raw score treatment main effect or mean gain score is 5.2 and the raw score interaction (gain score standard deviation) is 1.1. If the treatment effect were normally distributed across subjects, then the middle 95% of subjects would be described by

$$E(TG) - 1.96\sigma_{TG} < TG < E(TG) + 1.96\sigma_{TG}$$
$$5.2 - 1.96(1.1) < TG < 5.2 + 1.96(1.1)$$
$$3.04 < TG < 7.36$$

From the fact that 0 is 5.2 / 1.1 = 4.73 standard deviations below the mean, we would conclude that it is very unlikely that the treatment effect is negative for any subject. That is, it is unlikely that any subject was affected in the opposite direction from that suggested by the mean gain. This is what is called a "homogeneous interaction."

By contrast, suppose the mean is 5.2 but the standard deviation is also 5.2. According to the normal distribution, the middle 95% of the raw score effect size would be

$$5.2 - 1.96(5.2) < TG < 5.2 + 1.96(5.2)$$
$$-4.99 < TG < 15.39$$

While this interval would suggest that some people increased by 3 times as much as average, it would also suggest that some people decreased. When different subjects respond in different directions, the interaction is said to be "heterogeneous."

The normal distribution is not always the appropriate assumption for treatment effect differences. In our quality circle example, we assumed that some subjects learn from the thoughts of others, while other subjects are too rigid to change their work habits. Suppose that half the subjects are flexible and they gain 10.4 units in productivity, while the other half of the subjects are rigid and gain 0. The mean gain would be 5.2 and the standard deviation would also be 5.2. The flexible half of the subjects are exactly 1 standard deviation above mean gain at $5.2+5.2 = 10.4$. The rigid half of the subjects are exactly 1 standard deviation below mean gain at $5.2 - 5.2 = 0$. Note that in this dichotomous case the spread in effect is not 4 standard deviations, but only 2.

There are two problems with raw score treatment main effects and interactions: (1) There is no indication of whether the change is large or small in comparison to ordinary individual differences in performance, and (2) it is given in arbitrary units. Both problems are solved by using standard score units. The treatment main effect in standard score units is

$$\delta = E(TG)/\sigma_T \tag{8.24}$$

The subject by treatment interaction in standard score units is

$$s = \sigma_{TG}/\sigma_T \tag{8.25}$$

Note the distinction between the two different standard deviations in this formula: σ_{TG} is the standard deviation of *change* scores while σ_T is the standard deviation of *level* scores. If the treatment effect were the same for everyone, the standard deviation of change scores would be 0 as would the interaction. That is, the interaction can be 0 no matter how large the level score standard deviation of the dependent variable.

The raw score standard deviation of gain scores σ_{TG} measures the raw score treatment by subjects interaction. This interaction can be compared with either of the two corresponding main effects. In raw score form, the subject main effect is measured by the level score standard deviation (the "within-groups" standard deviation) σ_T. Thus, the comparison of the raw score interaction to the raw score subject main effect is the ratio σ_{TG}/σ_T, which is the standardized interaction. That is, the standardized interaction is the ratio of the treatment by subjects interaction effect to the subject main effect.

The interaction can also be compared with the treatment main effect. For raw scores, this is the ratio $E(TG)/\sigma_{TG}$, which was used earlier in discussing the identification of homogeneous versus heterogeneous interactions. Note also that the standardized mean and standard deviation have the same ratio as do the raw score mean and standard deviation. That is,

$$\delta/s = [E(TG)/\sigma_T]/[\sigma_{TG}/\sigma_T] = E(TG)/\sigma_{TG} \tag{8.26}$$

Thus, the ratio of the treatment main effect to the treatment by subjects interaction is the same for standard scores as for raw scores.

Homogeneity of Variance. It is important to compare the pretest and posttest standard deviations. If they are equal, then we have "homogeneity of variance"; otherwise, we have "heterogeneity of variance." If the treatment effect is the same for everyone, then the posttest score is related to the pretest score by

$$T_2 = T_1 + TG = T_1 + \text{Raw score } \delta \tag{8.27}$$

Because the variance is not affected by an additive constant, this means

$$\text{Var}(T_2) = \text{Var}(T_1) \tag{8.28}$$

That is, if there is no treatment by subjects interaction, then homogeneity of variance is guaranteed. In addition, if there were no treatment effect, then, because $T_2 = T_1$ for all subjects, the variances also would be equal.

Suppose an independent-groups design is used. Then the investigator is assuming that there is no interaction. If the investigator is right, then the data will satisfy homogeneity of variance. If the investigator finds heterogeneity of variance, then there must be a treatment by subjects interaction. Thus, a finding of heterogeneity of variance is a very important finding for substantive reasons. In particular, if there is heterogeneity of variance, then the mean difference is only the *mean* treatment effect, and the treatment effects for different individuals might be quite different. This will be discussed further in the section on interactions.

If the independent-groups design is used, a statistical test for heterogeneity of variance is a preliminary test for a treatment by subjects interaction. If the pretest and posttest variances are different, there is definitely an interaction. If there is homogeneity of variance, it would be nice if we could conclude that there is no interaction. However, it is easy to create hypothetical data in which there is a large interaction but no difference between variances. Consider the following data:

	Pretest	*Posttest*	*Gain*
Henry	10	6	−4
Ellen	5	5	0
Peter	6	10	+4
Average	7	7	0
SD	2.6	2.6	4

The mean difference is $7 - 7 = 0$, which suggests that there is no treatment effect. The posttest standard deviation and pretest standard deviation are both 2.6, which shows homogeneity of variance. Thus, there is nothing in the independent-groups data to suggest that there is an interaction and that the mean difference is misleading. However, if we consider the individual gain scores, a different pattern becomes clear. The mean treatment effect is 0, which suggests that there is no treatment effect. However, the finding of "no treatment effect" is true only for Ellen. Peter went up by 4 units (more than a standard deviation) and Henry went down by 4 units (more than a standard deviation). Thus, the treatment had large effects for 2 out of 3 subjects; the effects were just in opposite directions.

The first step in the analysis of independent-groups data should be a check for homogeneity of variance. If the variances are different, then there is a treatment by subjects interaction, and the mean treatment effect may be a very misleading picture of the typical treatment effect for individual subjects. If the variances are not different, then there may or may not be an interaction. It is not possible to tell. The key conclusion is that, with the independent-groups design, it is never possible to rule out the possibility of a treatment by subjects interaction.

Error of Measurement

Traditional analysis of variance has ignored error of measurement. The observed score statistics are treated as if they were unaffected by error of measurement. Why is this true?

Some of the confusion stems from considering only the raw score main effect. Because the population mean error of measurement is 0, the population mean observed score is the same as the population mean true score. Thus, the raw score treatment main effect for observed scores equals (in expectation) the raw score treatment main effect for true scores. That is, error of measurement does not alter the population raw score treatment main effect.

However, the treatment effect parameter that is crucial for statistical precision and power calculations and that is crucial to meta-analysis is not the raw score treatment effect but the standard score treatment effect. The standardized treatment effect (also called the "power parameter" in advanced texts; e.g., Kirk, 1995; Winer, 1962) is the mean gain divided by a standard deviation. Error of measurement does not alter the population mean, but it increases the population variance. Thus, to divide by the enlarged standard deviation is to reduce the ratio. That is, error of measurement reduces the size of the power parameter and, hence, reduces power and leads to wider confidence intervals. It also reduces the size of the observed standardized effect size (the effect size needed for meta-analysis).

Ideally, error of measurement would be reduced, if not eliminated, by better experimental measurement techniques. However, some imperfection will always remain. Thus, we need a method of correcting the observed treatment statistics for error of measurement. In this section, we will derive correction formulas using population statistics.

There are four key statistics in a within-subjects design: (1) the raw score treatment effect, (2) the raw score interaction, (3) the standardized treatment effect, and (4) the standardized interaction. Each is affected by error of measurement in a different way.

At the level of population statistics, the mean error of measurement across the population of subjects is 0. Thus, for population statistics, the mean observed gain score is the same as the mean true gain score, and the population raw score treatment effect is not changed by error of measurement.

The raw score interaction is measured by the standard deviation of gain scores. This standard deviation is increased by error of measurement, sometimes dramatically increased. In particular, the error variation in gain scores can cause the appearance of a treatment by subjects interaction where there is none. The error variance is directly added to the true score variance. That is,

$$\mathrm{Var}(OG) = \mathrm{Var}(TG + f) = \mathrm{Var}(TG) + \mathrm{Var}(f) \tag{8.29}$$

Thus, we correct the raw score interaction variance by subtracting the error of measurement variance:

$$\begin{aligned}\mathrm{Var}(TG) &= \mathrm{Var}(OG) - \mathrm{Var}(f)\\ &= \mathrm{Var}(OG) - 2[1 - r_{YY}]\mathrm{Var}(Y)\end{aligned} \tag{8.30}$$

The square root of the corrected variance is the corrected standard deviation.

The standard score treatment effect is the ratio of the mean raw score effect size to the level standard deviation. The numerator of this ratio is the raw score treatment effect that is not affected by error of measurement. Thus, the numerator need not be corrected. However, the denominator is the level score standard deviation. Because the observed score standard deviation is inflated by error of measurement, it must be corrected before it can be used in the denominator of the standard score treatment effect. Error of measurement variance is directly added to true score variance. Thus, we have

$$\mathrm{Var}(Y) = \mathrm{Var}(T + e) = \mathrm{Var}(T) + \mathrm{Var}(e) \tag{8.31}$$

We correct the observed level score variance by subtracting the error variance:

$$\begin{aligned}\mathrm{Var}(T) &= \mathrm{Var}(Y) - \mathrm{Var}(e)\\ &= \mathrm{Var}(Y) - [1 - r_{YY}]\,\mathrm{Var}(Y)\\ &= r_{YY}\,\mathrm{Var}(Y)\end{aligned} \tag{8.32}$$

That is, by algebraic identity, to subtract the error variance from the observed level score variance is to multiply the level score variance by the level score reliability. The corrected standard deviation is then obtained by taking the square root of the corrected variance:

$$\sigma_T = \sqrt{r_{YY}}\sigma_Y \tag{8.33}$$

The corrected standardized treatment effect is

$$\begin{aligned}\delta &= E(TG)/\sigma_T = E(OG)/[\sqrt{r_{YY}}\sigma_Y]\\ &= [E(OG)/\sigma_Y]/\sqrt{r_{YY}}\\ &= d/\sqrt{r_{YY}}\end{aligned} \tag{8.34}$$

Thus, the standard score treatment effect is corrected by dividing the observed standard score treatment effect by the square root of the level score reliability.

The standard score interaction is the ratio of two standard deviations, each of which is inflated by error of measurement. Thus, both the numerator and the denominator must be corrected before the correct ratio can be computed. Because variances are more easily corrected than standard deviations, we first square the interaction ratio. The squared interaction ratio is the ratio of the variance of true gain scores to the variance of true level scores, that is,

$$\text{Interaction}^2 = \text{Var}(TG)/\text{Var}(T) \tag{8.35}$$

The correction of each variance has been given before:

$$\begin{aligned}\text{Var}(TG) &= \text{Var}(OG) - \text{Var}(f)\\ &= \text{Var}(OG) - 2[1 - r_{YY}]\,\text{Var}(Y)\end{aligned} \tag{8.36}$$

$$\begin{aligned}\text{Var}(T) &= \text{Var}(Y) - \text{Var}(e)\\ &= \text{Var}(Y) - [1 - r_{YY}]\,\text{Var}(Y)\\ &= r_{YY}\,\text{Var}(Y)\end{aligned} \tag{8.37}$$

The square root of the corrected variances is the desired standard score interaction measure.

Consider an example. Assume population means and variances are known and suppose the pretest mean observed level score is 20, the standard deviation of observed level scores is 7 for both pretest and posttest, the mean observed gain score is 5.2, the standard deviation of observed gain scores is 5.94, and the reliability of the observed level scores is .81. Because the population mean error of measurement is 0, the raw score treatment main effect is the same as the treatment effect for raw scores, that is,

$$\text{Raw score } \delta = E(TG) = E(OG) = 5.2$$

The apparent interaction is the raw score interaction computed on observed scores:

$$\text{Apparent raw score interaction} = \sigma_{OG} = 5.94$$

This apparent interaction is not 0 and, thus, suggests that there might be a true interaction. If this apparent interaction is compared to the raw score treatment effect, we have

$$\text{Apparent relative interaction} = 5.94/5.2 = 1.14$$

which suggests a heterogeneous interaction. That is, it suggests that some individuals are responding positively and some negatively with the treatment, because the interaction is large relative with the treatment effect. However, the standard deviation of observed scores is inflated by error of measurement. The corrected variance is

$$\begin{aligned}\mathrm{Var}(TG) &= \mathrm{Var}(OG) - 2[1 - r_{YY}]\,\mathrm{Var}(Y)\\ &= 5.94^2 - 2[1 - .64]7^2\\ &= 35.2836 - 35.28\\ &= .0036\end{aligned}$$

This number is so close to 0 as to potentially be rounding error (the actual fact in this example). However, let us take the value at face value. The square root is the raw score true gain standard deviation $\sigma_{TG} = .06$. If this is compared with the treatment main effect, we find

$$\text{True relative interaction} = .06/5.2 = .01$$

Thus, while the observed score gain standard deviation suggested a heterogeneous interaction, the true score gain standard deviation reveals the fact that there was virtually no interaction and that different individuals were responding essentially the same to the treatment.

To compute the standardized treatment main effect, we must compute the level true score standard deviation σ_T. This is computed from the level observed score standard deviation:

$$\mathrm{Var}(T) = r_{YY}\,\mathrm{Var}(Y) = (.81)7^2 = 39.69$$

The level true score standard deviation is $\sigma_T = \sqrt{39.69} = 6.3$. The true standard score treatment main effect is thus

$$\delta = E(TG)/\sigma_T = 5.2/6.3 = .83$$

The true standard score interaction is

$$s = \sigma_{TG}/\sigma_T = .06/6.3 = .0095$$

If the true relative interaction is computed on standard score effect sizes, we have

$$\text{Relative interaction} = .0095/.83 = .01$$

which is the same value obtained using raw scores.

Sampling Error

No Error of Measurement and No Interaction

If there is no error of measurement and no treatment by subjects interaction, then there is no sampling error in the observed mean gain score. It is equal to the observed gain score for each individual subject, which is equal to the raw score treatment effect. There is also no sampling error in the standard deviation of gain scores because the sample standard deviation is always 0 if the population standard deviation is 0. The null hypothesis is directly testable. If there is no treatment effect, then the gain score will be 0 for every individual subject, and hence, the mean gain score will also be 0 without sampling error. Thus, if there is no error of measurement and no treatment by subjects interaction, then the null hypothesis is perfectly tested by inspection. Either the mean gain is 0 or it is not.

If there is no treatment by subjects interaction and there is no error of measurement, then the raw score treatment effect is measured without sampling error because it is observed and is the same for every subject. However, the standard score effect size δ uses the population within-groups standard deviation in its definition:

$$\delta = E(TG)/\sigma \tag{8.38}$$

Because the within-groups standard deviation σ is not known, the standardized effect size will be estimated with sampling error. There are two difference estimates of the population within-groups variance that could be used: the sample variance of the pretest score $\text{SV}(Y_1)$ and the average variance:

$$\text{SV} = [\text{SV}(Y_1) + \text{SV}(Y_2)]/2 \tag{8.39}$$

Note that, because there is no error of measurement, the observed score Y is the true score T. Because there is no interaction, the posttest variance is equal to the pretest variance. Thus, in this case, the average variance is equal to the pretest variance, and there is no sampling error advantage in using the average variance. Using the chi-square distribution, we obtain a confidence interval for the population within-groups variance. To a close approximation for $N > 30$ and a good approximation for $N > 4$, the confidence interval can be written as

$$b^2\text{SV}(T) < \sigma^2 < B^2\text{SV}(T) \tag{8.40}$$

where

$$b = \sqrt{(2N-2)}/[\sqrt{(2N-3)} + 1.96\sqrt{(1 - 1/4\{N-2\})}]$$
$$B = \sqrt{(2N-2)}/[\sqrt{(2N-3)} - 1.96\sqrt{(1 - 1/4\{N-2\})}]$$

From this, we obtain the confidence interval for the standardized effect size:

$$d/B < \delta < d/b$$
$$\text{where } d = \text{Ave}(OG)/\sqrt{\text{SV}}$$

Error of Measurement but No Interaction

If there is no treatment by subjects interaction, then the treatment effect is the same for all subjects. Thus, it makes sense to talk about "the treatment effect" without referring to some particular subject. In this case, "the treatment effect" is the treatment main effect and the interaction standard deviation is 0.

If there were no error of measurement, then the treatment effect and the zero treatment effect standard deviation would be directly observable without sampling error. However, if there is error of measurement, then there is sampling error in both the mean observed change score and the standard deviation of observed change scores. This sampling error is due to the sampling of errors of measurement, not to the sampling of subjects. That is, the sampling error is due to sampling error in the mean and standard deviation of the measurement error scores. There will be a sampling error band around any treatment parameter that we estimate. Ideally, we would like confidence intervals about each of those parameter estimates. If 0 were included in the confidence interval for the treatment effect, then the actual treatment effect could be 0. The use of a significance test without computing a confidence interval is a very biased way of looking at the data because only sampling error in one direction is considered, and sampling error in the other direction (probability, one-half) is ignored and, thus, implicitly (and falsely) assumed to be nonexistent.

The Treatment Effect. Consider the sample mean gain score:

$$\text{Ave}(OG) = \text{Ave}(TG + f) = \text{Ave}(TG) + \text{Ave}(f) \quad (8.41)$$

If there is no interaction, the true gain score is the same for each individual subject and, hence,

$$\text{Ave}(TG) = TG = \text{Raw score } \delta \quad (8.42)$$

without sampling error. If we denote the raw score treatment effect by δ^*, then

$$\text{Ave}(OG) = \delta^* + \text{Ave}(f) \quad (8.43)$$

The average error of measurement will converge to 0 only if many errors are averaged. Thus, on a finite sample, there will be sampling error in the average error. Denote the sampling error variance in Ave(f) by V_f. Then the sampling error in the average error is given by

$$V_f = \text{Var}(f)/N \quad (8.44)$$

where N is the number of subjects and Var(f) is the population variance of the gain error scores. Denote the square root of V_f by S. If the population variance were known, then the confidence interval for the raw score treatment effect would be

$$\text{Ave}(OG) - 1.96S < \text{Raw score } \delta < \text{Ave}(OG) + 1.96S \quad (8.45)$$

If the population variance of level scores Var(Y) were known, then the variance of errors could be computed using reliability theory:

$$\text{Var}(f) = 2[1 - r_{YY}]\,\text{Var}(Y) \quad (8.46)$$

However, the population variance of level scores is usually unknown. If we use the notation SV(Y) for sample variance, then one estimate of the error variance would be

$$\text{Est Var}(f) = 2[1 - r_{YY}]\,\text{SV}(Y) \quad (8.47)$$

However, because there is no subject by treatment interaction, there is a better estimate that stems from the identity

$$\mathrm{SV}(f) = \mathrm{SV}(OG) \tag{8.48}$$

That is, we estimate the sampling error standard deviation S by

$$\text{Est } S = \sqrt{[\mathrm{SV}(OG)/N]} \tag{8.49}$$

(This number will itself have sampling error whose extent could be estimated using the chi-square distribution.) The sampling error in the estimate of S renders the normal curve confidence interval slightly too narrow. A more precise interval requires use of the noncentral t distribution, which is beyond the scope of our work here. To a good first approximation, the implication of the sampling error in our estimate of S is captured by replacing 1.96 by the t value, as noted in the section on confidence intervals.

The standard score treatment effect is obtained by dividing the raw score treatment effect by the level true score standard deviation. Because true scores are not observed, there is also no direct estimate of the true score standard deviation. Instead, we estimate the true score standard deviation indirectly using reliability theory. From the fact that

$$\mathrm{Var}(T) = r_{YY}\,\mathrm{Var}(Y) \tag{8.50}$$

we obtain the sample estimate

$$\text{Est SV}(T) = r_{YY}\mathrm{SV}(Y) \tag{8.51}$$

Denote the square root of that estimate by $S(T)$. Then the sample estimate of the standard score treatment effect is

$$\text{Est } \delta = \mathrm{Ave}(OG)/S(T) \tag{8.52}$$

This estimate of the effect size is very similar to the d_t statistic of the independent-groups design (i.e., the d value corrected for measurement error in the dependent variable; see Chapter 7). It is so similar that we will abuse our notation by using the notation d_t for this estimate of the standard score treatment effect. That is, for the within-subjects design, we define d_t by

$$d_t = \text{Est } \delta = \mathrm{Ave}(OG)/S(T) \tag{8.53}$$

There is sampling error in both the numerator and the denominator.

Because of error of measurement, the posttest variance will differ from the pretest variance because errors are independently sampled. Thus, the best estimate of the within-group variance is the average variance. If we define $\mathrm{SV}(Y)$ by

$$\mathrm{SV}(Y) = [\mathrm{SV}(Y_1) + \mathrm{SV}(Y_2)]/2 \tag{8.54}$$

then the confidence interval for d_t is

$$d_t - 1.96S < \delta < d_t + 1.96S \tag{8.55}$$

where

$$S^2 = [2(1 - r)/N] + [\delta^2(1 + r^2)/\{4(N - 1)\}] \quad (8.56)$$

where for this case (because there is no subject by treatment interaction)

$$r = r_{12} = r_{YY}$$

In using d_t to denote the sample effect size, it is important to note that d_t is *not* related to the t statistic that tests the null hypothesis that the treatment is 0. If we divide the test statistic by the square root of the sample size, then

$$t/\sqrt{N} = \text{Ave}(OG)/\sqrt{\text{SV}(OG)} \quad (8.57)$$

versus

$$d_t = \text{Ave}(OG)/\sqrt{[r_{YY}\,\text{SV}(Y)]} \quad (8.58)$$

These numbers differ in two ways. First, the d_t value contains the reliability r_{YY} so as to correct for attenuation due to measurement error. However, the two variances also differ. SV(OG) is the sample variance of *change* scores, whereas SV(Y) is the sample variance of *level* scores. Thus, in the within-groups design, there is no simple transformation from t to d as is true for the independent-groups design.

The Apparent Treatment Interaction. In this case, we have assumed that there is no actual treatment by subjects interaction. However, because of error of measurement, there will be a large apparent interaction. The formula for the inflation is

$$\text{Var}(TG) = 0 \quad (8.59)$$

$$\text{Var}(OG) = \text{Var}(f) = 2\,\text{Var}(e) = 2[1 - r_{YY}]\,\text{Var}(Y) \quad (8.60)$$

Even for moderately large reliability, this will be a very substantial inflation. This inflation must be corrected so that the true value of 0 is observed.

The variance of gain scores will be inflated from 0 to twice the error variance of level scores. If there were no sampling error, this algebraic effect could be simply subtracted, and there would be no room for doubt that the apparent interaction is actually nonexistent. However, error of measurement not only introduces a systematic error into the estimate of the interaction, it introduces sampling error as well.

If there were an interaction, then

$$\text{Var}(OG) = \text{Var}(TG) + \text{Var}(f) \quad (8.61)$$

The true raw score interaction variance would be

$$\text{Var}(TG) = \text{Var}(OG) - \text{Var}(f) \quad (8.62)$$

To subtract, we need an estimate of the error variance that is independent of the gain scores. That estimate is

$$\text{Var}(f) = 2[1 - r_{YY}]\ \text{Var}(Y_1) \tag{8.63}$$

where Var (Y_1) is the pretest variance. (If there is an interaction, then the posttest variance may differ from the pretest variance.)

The sample estimate of the true raw score interaction variance is thus given by

$$\text{Est SV}(TG) = \text{SV}(OG) - \text{Est Var}(f) \tag{8.64}$$

where

$$\text{Est Var}(f) = 2[1 - r_{YY}]\,\text{SV}(Y_1) \tag{8.65}$$

If there is no actual interaction, then this estimate of the interaction will differ from 0 by sampling error. With probability one-half, sampling error will cause the estimate to be negative, and there will be little doubt that there is no true interaction. However, with probability one-half sampling error will cause the estimate to be positive and will falsely suggest a true interaction. However, if this value is small, it will be correctly attributed to sampling error.

Consider the null hypothesis that there is no treatment effect. If there were no interaction, then every subject would have a gain score of 0. Because of error of measurement, the individual gain scores will depart randomly from 0. Because individual gain scores would be as likely to be negative as positive, we might also change terminology from "gain score" to "change score." For simplicity, we will continue to use the phrase "gain score" with the understanding that a negative gain score represents a decrease.

Because there is sampling error, the null hypothesis is not directly testable. Even if there were no treatment effect, the mean gain score would differ from 0 by sampling error (the sampling error in the mean error score). There are then two ways to test the null hypothesis statistically. One way is to compute the confidence interval as noted previously. The more risky way is to compute a significance test without generating the confidence interval. Suppose we first compute the confidence interval. The significance test is obtained by checking to see if the confidence interval contains 0 or not. This test is unbiased in that the investigator can see how far the confidence interval extends in both directions and, thus, interpret the significance test with the required degree of skepticism.

On the other hand, it is common practice in the field to ignore confidence intervals. This leads to the test of the null hypothesis by a "dependent group" t test or—equivalently—by the "treatment by subject" or "repeated measure" analysis of variance. The statistical power is the same in either case. However, the person who looks at a wide confidence interval can tell when there is quite a stretch down to 0. The person who never sees a confidence interval has no concrete way of knowing how tenuous that null hypothesis may be.

Interaction but No Error of Measurement

If there is no error of measurement, the treatment effect is directly observed for each individual subject. However, if there is a treatment by subjects interaction, then that treatment effect will differ from one subject to the next. Thus, the phrase "the treatment effect," has no meaning if separated from some individual subject. The conventional practice in this case is to create a single number to represent the treatment effects by averaging the treatment effect across a population of subjects. This average treatment effect is the *treatment main effect* of analysis of variance. Thus, if there is an interaction, we must be careful to always describe the average treatment effect as the "treatment main effect," and we must avoid the phrase "treatment effect."

If there is no error of measurement, then the treatment effect is exactly observed for each individual subject. However, the mean treatment effect is known only for the sample of subjects at hand. The sample average treatment effect will differ from the population average treatment effect by sampling error. In this case, the sampling error is traditional sampling error: One sample of subjects will differ randomly from another sample. Thus, we would like to have a confidence interval to estimate the potential error band around the sample mean treatment effect. In fact, we need two confidence intervals: one for the raw score treatment main effect and one for the standard score treatment main effect.

The treatment by subjects interaction is the population standard deviation of gain scores. The sample standard deviation will differ from the population standard deviation by sampling error. Thus, we would like a confidence interval around our sample estimate of the interaction standard deviation. We would like two confidence intervals: one for the raw score interaction and one for the standard score interaction.

The Treatment Main Effect. Because in this example we assume that there is no error of measurement, the gain scores observed in the study are the true gain scores. Thus, we can directly observe the sample mean true gain score and, hence, the sample raw score treatment effect. Denote the sample average by $\text{Ave}(TG)$. The sample average is related to the population average $E(TG)$ by

$$\begin{aligned}\text{Ave}(TG) &= E(TG) + \text{Sampling error} \\ &= \text{Raw score } \delta + \text{Sampling error}\end{aligned} \tag{8.66}$$

The sampling error variance in the mean gain score is determined by the population variance of gain scores. If we denote the sampling error standard deviation by S, then

$$S^2 = \text{Var}(TG)/N \tag{8.67}$$

where N is the sample size. If the population variance of gain scores were known, then S would be known and the confidence interval would be

$$\text{Ave}(TG) - 1.96S < E(TG) < \text{Ave}(TG) + 1.96S \tag{8.68}$$

Because the population variance is not known, we instead estimate S using the sample variance of gain scores. That is,

$$\text{Est } S^2 = \text{SV}(TG)/N \tag{8.69}$$

The sampling error in this estimate of S further increases the width of the corresponding confidence interval. We replace the 1.96 by the corresponding value of t as noted in the section on confidence intervals.

To estimate the standard score treatment effect, we must estimate the level score standard deviation. Because there is an interaction, the pretest and posttest standard deviation may be different. Thus, we define the desired standard deviation to be the pretest standard deviation. That is, we would like to know the population variance $\text{Var}(T_1)$. Because there is no error of measurement, the level scores observed in the study are level true scores. Thus, the sample standard deviation of level true scores is directly observable. The obvious estimate of the standard score treatment effect is obtained by dividing the sample treatment main effect by the pretest standard deviation:

$$\text{Est } \delta = \text{Ave}(TG)/S(T_1) \tag{8.70}$$

It is tempting to obtain the confidence interval the same way. We could just take the two endpoints of the confidence interval for the raw score treatment main effect and divide each by the level score pretest standard deviation. This is not entirely accurate because it does not take into account the sampling error in the pretest standard deviation, but it is a good first approximation.

The Treatment by Subjects Interaction. The raw score interaction is measured by the standard deviation of true gain scores. If there is no error of measurement, the gain scores observed are the true gain scores. The null hypothesis of no treatment by subjects interaction would be directly testable. Either the standard deviation of gain scores is 0 or it is not. If the standard deviation is greater than 0, then there is a treatment by subjects interaction.

The sample standard deviation of gain scores is the sample standard deviation for the treatment by subjects interaction. The sample standard deviation differs from the population interaction by sampling error. The confidence interval can be computed using the chi-square distribution.

If the sample standard deviation is computed using N in the denominator, then define the statistic Q by

$$Q = N \text{ SV}(TG)/\text{Var}(TG) \tag{8.71}$$

If the less accurate formula for the standard deviation using $N - 1$ is used, then compute Q by

$$Q = (N - 1)\text{SV}(TG)/\text{Var}(TG) \tag{8.72}$$

If the gain scores have a normal distribution, then Q has a chi-square distribution with $N - 1$ degrees of freedom, and the confidence interval can be derived from that distribution. Let L and U be the lower and upper 97.5% points of that distribution. The 95% confidence interval for the raw score interaction standard deviation is

$$S(TG)/\sqrt{U} < \sigma_{TG} < S(TG)/\sqrt{L} \tag{8.73}$$

To a close approximation for $N > 30$ and a good approximation for $N > 4$, the confidence interval can also be written as

$$bS(TG) < \sigma_{TG} < BS(TG) \tag{8.74}$$

where

$$b = \sqrt{(2N-2)}/[\sqrt{(2N-3)} + 1.96\sqrt{(1 - 1/4\{N-2\})}],$$

$$B = \sqrt{(2N-2)}/[\sqrt{(2N-3)} + 1.96\sqrt{(1 - 1/4\{N-2\})}].$$

The standard score interaction is defined as the ratio σ_{TG}/σ_T. To estimate this ratio, we must estimate the standard deviation of level scores. Because there is an interaction, the pretest and posttest standard deviation may be different. Thus, we define the desired standard deviation to be the pretest standard deviation. That is, we would like to know the population variance $\text{Var}(T_1)$. Because there is no error of measurement, the level scores observed in the study are level true scores. Thus, the sample standard deviation of level true scores is directly observable. The obvious estimate of the standard score interaction is obtained by dividing the sample raw score treatment by subjects interaction by the pretest standard deviation.

$$\text{Est } s = S\,(TG)/S\,(T_1) \tag{8.75}$$

It is again tempting to obtain the confidence interval the same way. We could take the two endpoints of the confidence interval for the raw score treatment main effect and divide each by the level score pretest standard deviation. Again, this is not entirely accurate because it does not take into account the sampling error in the pretest standard deviation, but it is a good first approximation.

The Null Hypothesis. Consider the null hypothesis that there is no treatment effect. This statement is ambiguous. If we mean that there is no treatment effect for any subject, then there is also no treatment by subjects interaction. We treated this case earlier. However, it is also possible to define a null hypothesis by the possibility that the treatment *main* effect is 0 even though the treatment by subjects interaction is not 0. If the mean treatment effect is 0 and the variance is not, then some subjects must have positive gain scores while other subjects have negative gain scores. Thus, the interaction is necessarily heterogeneous.

If there were no interaction, then every subject would have a gain score of 0. If there is an interaction, then the individual gain scores will depart from 0 in both directions. Because individual gain scores would be as likely to be negative as positive, we might also change terminology from "gain score" to "change score." For simplicity, we will continue to use the phrase "gain score" with the understanding that a negative gain score represents a decrease.

Because subjects differ in their true gain scores, there is sampling error in the average gain score. Because there is sampling error, the null hypothesis is not directly testable. Even if there were no treatment main effect, the mean gain score would differ from 0 by sampling error in the sampling of people. There are then two ways to test the null hypothesis statistically. One way is to compute the confidence interval as noted previously. The riskier way is to compute a significance test without generating the confidence interval. Suppose we first compute the confidence interval. The significance test is obtained by checking to see if the confidence interval contains 0 or not. This test is unbiased in that the investigator can see how far the confidence interval extends in both directions and thus take the appropriate skeptical attitude toward the significance test.

A word of warning to those tempted to use significance tests despite the preceding statements: If there is a treatment by subjects interaction, then *the conventional* t *test does not work, even within the limitations of significance tests*. The conventional t test and the conventional repeated-measures analysis of variance use the nominal interaction term as an error term to test the main effect. In doing this, they assume homogeneity of variance and independence between the interaction and the subject level scores. These assumptions are justified if the apparent interaction is actually error of measurement. However, for real interactions, these assumptions are usually false. Thus, the conventional F test cannot be trusted. There have been experimental tests—the "quasi-F"—for such cases, but these, too, make independence assumptions that are quite implausible for most common interactions (such as a multiplicative treatment effect). These procedures are beyond the scope of the present text. Thus, if there is a treatment by subjects interaction, the confidence interval approach appears to be the only approach available.

Error of Measurement and an Interaction

If there is both error of measurement and an interaction, then there are two sources of sampling error: sampling of errors of measurement and sampling of different levels of treatment effect (i.e., sampling of subjects). If there is error of measurement, then the treatment effect is only imperfectly observed at the level of individuals. Thus, we must rely heavily on indirect statistics, especially our estimate of the treatment main effect and our estimate of the treatment interaction standard deviation. In both cases, we must adjust observed score statistics for the effects of error of measurement, especially the apparent interaction standard deviation.

The Treatment Main Effect. The treatment main effect is the population mean true gain score. Our estimate is the sample mean observed gain score. The sample mean observed gain score suffers from two sources of sampling error:

$$\text{Ave}(OG) = \text{Ave}(TG + f) = \text{Ave}(TG) + \text{Ave}(f) \tag{8.76}$$

where

$$\text{Ave}(TG) = E(TG) + \text{Sampling error}$$
$$\text{Ave}(f) = 0 + \text{Sampling error}$$

The sampling error in the average true gain score stems from variation in the treatment effect across subjects. The sampling error in the average error of measurement stems from variation in errors of measurement across subjects. The error of measurement can be pooled, as in

$$\text{Ave}\,(OG) = E(TG) + \text{Sampling error} \tag{8.77}$$

If we denote the pooled sampling error standard deviation by S, then that variance is determined by the population variance of observed gain scores:

$$S^2 = \text{Var}(OG)/N \tag{8.78}$$

The corresponding confidence interval is

$$\text{Ave}(OG) - 1.96S < \text{Raw score } \delta < \text{Ave}(OG) + 1.96S \tag{8.79}$$

If the population variance must be estimated by the sample variance SV(OG), the underlying distribution for the confidence interval is no longer the normal distribution but the t distribution with $N - 1$ degrees of freedom. Thus, the "1.96" must be replaced by the corresponding values from the 95% two-tailed column of the t table. To a close approximation for $N > 14$, we replace 1.96 by

$$1.96\,[1 + 1.2104/(N - 1)]$$

and for $14 > N > 5$ by

$$1.96\,[1 + 1.2104/(N - 1) + 1.4402/(N - 1)^2 + 1.3041/(N - 1)^2]$$

The standard score treatment main effect is the ratio of the mean raw score effect size to the level standard deviation. Because there is an interaction, the standard deviation used is the pretest standard deviation. The numerator of the ratio is the raw score treatment main effect, which is not changed by error of measurement. Thus, the numerator need not be corrected. However, the denominator is the level score standard deviation. Because the observed score standard deviation is inflated by error of measurement, it must be corrected before it can be used in the denominator of the standard score treatment main effect. Error of measurement variance is directly added to true score variance. Thus, we have

$$\text{Var}(Y_1) = \text{Var}(T_1 + e_1) = \text{Var}(T_1) + \text{Var}(e_1) \tag{8.80}$$

We correct the observed level score variance by subtracting the error variance:

$$\begin{aligned} \text{Var}(T) &= \text{Var}(Y) - \text{Var}(e) \\ &= \text{Var}(Y) - [1 - r_{YY}]\,\text{Var}(Y) \\ &= r_{YY}\,\text{Var}\,(Y) \end{aligned} \tag{8.81}$$

That is, by algebraic identity, to subtract the error variance from the observed level score variance is to multiply the level score variance by the level score reliability. The corrected standard deviation is then obtained by taking the square root of the corrected variance:

$$\sigma_T = \sqrt{r_{YY}}\,\sigma_Y \tag{8.82}$$

The corrected standardized treatment main effect is thus

$$\delta = E(TG)/\sigma_T = E(OG)/[\sqrt{r_{YY}}\sigma_Y] \tag{8.83}$$

It is also possible to compute an observed score treatment main effect "δ" defined by

$$\text{“}\delta\text{”} = E(OG)/\sigma_Y \tag{8.84}$$

The true score or actual treatment main effect is related to the observed score treatment effect by

$$\begin{aligned} \delta &= [E(OG)/\sigma_Y]/\sqrt{r_{YY}} \\ &= [\text{Observed score “}\delta\text{”}]/\sqrt{r_{YY}} \end{aligned} \tag{8.85}$$

This is the conventional formula for correcting a main effect for the error of measurement in the dependent variable. Thus, the actual standard score treatment main effect is corrected by dividing the observed standard score treatment main effect by the square root of the level score reliability.

The confidence interval for the standard score treatment main effect is most easily approximated by dividing the endpoints of the confidence interval for the raw score treatment main effect by the level score standard deviation. This would ignore the sampling error in the level score main effect. The exact formula for the standard error can be computed. Estimate the raw score treatment effect by

$$\text{Est } E(TG) = \text{Ave}(OG) = \text{Ave}(Y_2) - \text{Ave}(Y_1) \tag{8.86}$$

and estimate the pretest level true score standard deviation by

$$\text{Est } \sigma_T = \sqrt{r_{YY}\text{SV}(Y_1)} \tag{8.87}$$

The standard score treatment main effect is then estimated by

$$d = \text{Est } \delta = \text{Est } E(TG)/\text{Est } \sigma_T \tag{8.88}$$

The bias in this formula is given by

$$E(d) = \delta/J(N-1) \tag{8.89}$$

where

$$J(N) = \Gamma(N/2)/\sqrt{(N/2)}\,\Gamma(\{N-1\}/2)$$

which is closely approximated by

$$J(N-1) = 1 - .75/(N-2) \tag{8.90}$$

That is,

$$E(d) = a\delta \tag{8.91}$$

where

$$a = 1 + .75/(N-2)$$

This bias is very small even for sample sizes as low as 50 (although not so small for sample sizes of 20 or less). The bias can be corrected by dividing the estimate of d by the multiplier a.

The large-sample sampling error variance of d is given by

$$\mathrm{Var}(d) = [4/N][\mu + \delta^2/8] \tag{8.92}$$

where

$$\mu = [1 - r_{12}]/[4 r_{YY}]$$

if there might be an interaction, and by

$$\mu = [1 - r_{YY}]/[4\ r_{YY}]$$

if there is no interaction. For small samples, the sampling variance is more closely computed by

$$\mathrm{Var}(d) = [(N-1)/(N-3)][4/N][\mu + (\delta^2/8)(N/\{N-1\})] \tag{8.93}$$

Let the square root of this variance be denoted by S. Then, to a close approximation, the confidence interval for δ is

$$d - 1.96S < \delta < d + 1.96S \tag{8.94}$$

The Treatment by Subjects Interaction. The treatment by subjects interaction is measured by the population true gain score standard deviation. The corresponding observed gain score standard deviation is greatly inflated by error of measurement. Thus, it must be corrected before it becomes an unbiased estimate of the actual interaction.

Consider first the inflation of the interaction variance by error of measurement. The formula for the inflation is

$$\mathrm{Var}(OG) = \mathrm{Var}(TG) + \mathrm{Var}(f) \tag{8.95}$$

where

$$\mathrm{Var}(f) = 2\,\mathrm{Var}(e) = 2[1 - r_{YY}]\,\mathrm{Var}(Y_1)$$

Even for moderately large reliability, this will be a very substantial inflation, especially if there is no interaction.

The true raw score interaction variance can be computed by subtraction:

$$\mathrm{Var}(TG) = \mathrm{Var}(OG) - \mathrm{Var}(f) \tag{8.96}$$

To subtract, we need an estimate of the error variance that is independent of the gain scores. That estimate is

$$\mathrm{Var}(f) = 2[1 - r_{YY}]\,\mathrm{Var}(Y_1) \tag{8.97}$$

where $\mathrm{Var}(Y_1)$ is the pretest variance. If there is an interaction, then the posttest variance may differ from the pretest variance.

Using the notation $\mathrm{SV}(Y)$ for sample variance, the sample estimate of the true raw score interaction variance is given by

$$\text{Est Var}(TG) = \mathrm{SV}(OG) - \text{Est Var}(f) \tag{8.98}$$

where

$$\text{Est Var}(f) = 2[1 - r_{YY}]\,\text{SV}(Y_1) \tag{8.99}$$

If there is no actual interaction, then this estimate of the interaction will differ from 0 by sampling error. With probability one-half, sampling error will cause the estimate to be negative, and there will be little doubt that there is no true interaction. However, with probability one-half, sampling error will cause the estimate to be positive and will falsely suggest a true interaction.

The estimate of the standard score interaction is the raw score interaction divided by the level true score standard deviation. The corresponding variance is estimated by

$$\text{Est Var}(T_1) = r_{YY}\,\text{SV}(Y_1) \tag{8.100}$$

That is,

$$\begin{aligned}\text{Est } s^2 &= \text{Est Var}(TG)/\text{Est Var}(T_1)\\ &= [\text{SV}(OG) - \text{Est Var}(f)]/\text{Est Var}(T_1)\end{aligned} \tag{8.101}$$

where

$$\text{Est Var}(f) = 2[1 - r_{YY}]\text{SV}(Y_1)$$

To generate a confidence interval for s, we note first that

$$\text{Est } s^2 = [1/r_{YY}][\text{SV}(OG)/\text{SV}(Y_1)] - [2(1 - r_{YY})/r_{YY}] \tag{8.102}$$

That is, the estimated interaction square has the form

$$\text{Est } s^2 = \beta[\text{SV}(OG)/\text{SV}(Y_1)] - \alpha \tag{8.103}$$

where α and β are constants. The variance ratio $\text{SV}(OG)/\text{SV}(Y_1)$ would have an approximate F ratio if it were not for the fact that the numerator and denominator population variances are different. There is a modified ratio that does have an approximate F distribution:

$$F = [\text{Var}(Y_1)/\text{Var}(OG)]\,[\text{SV}(OG)/\text{SV}(Y_1)] \tag{8.104}$$

with degrees of freedom $(N - 1, N - 1)$. The corresponding endpoints for the confidence interval are obtained from the F endpoint tabled under $p = .025$, although few tables have that value for the degrees of freedom characteristic of most studies. To a close approximation, the upper endpoint is given by

$$U = e^{2w} \tag{8.105}$$

where

$$w = 1.96/\sqrt{(N - 2)}$$

The lower endpoint is given by the reciprocal, that is,

$$L = 1/U \tag{8.106}$$

Define the constant β by

$$\beta = 2(1 - r_{YY})/r_{YY} \quad (8.107)$$

Then the confidence interval for the squared interaction is

$$[\text{Est } s^2 + \beta]/U - \beta < s^2 < [\text{Est } s^2 + \beta]/L - \beta \quad (8.108)$$

The confidence interval for the interaction s is obtained by taking the square root of each endpoint.

Meta-Analysis and the Within-Subjects Design

The *d* Statistic

Studies that report standard deviations are easy to code for meta-analysis. We estimate the true score level standard deviation σ_{T_1} by

$$S^2 = r_{YY}\text{SV}(Y_1) \quad (8.109)$$

We define d by

$$d = \text{Ave}(OG)/S = [\text{Ave}(Y_2) - \text{Ave}(Y_1)]/S \quad (8.110)$$

We can relate this sample estimate to the population δ by the sampling error formula:

$$d = \delta + e \quad (8.111)$$

The sampling error variance in d is given by

$$\text{Var}(e) = [(N-1)/(N-3)]\,[1/N]\,[\beta + \{\delta^2/2\}\,\{N/(N-1)\}] \quad (8.112)$$

where

$$\beta = [\sigma_{OG}/\sigma_T]^2 = 2[1 - r_{12}]/r_{YY}$$

where r_{12} is the pretest-posttest correlation. If there is no treatment by subjects interaction, the test-retest correlation is equal to the reliability, that is,

$$r_{12} = r_{YY}$$

For large samples,

$$\text{Var}(e) = [\beta + \delta^2/2]/N \quad (8.113)$$

For small samples,

$$\text{Var}(e) = [(N-1)/(N-3)]\,[\beta + (\delta^2/2)(N/\{N-1\})]/N \quad (8.114)$$

Note that the sampling error in this d statistic is not the same as the sampling error of d for the independent-groups design. Thus, if the meta-analysis is mixing within-subjects and between-subjects designs, the sampling error must be computed separately for the two sets of studies. See Morris & DeShon, 2002, for illustrations of this. See page 280 for a hint on how to use our d-value meta-analysis programs with d-values of this sort. The programs compute sampling error based on the independent groups design. One must start with the sampling error from the Equation (8.114) and solve the independent groups sampling error equation for N. This N is then entered into the program.

The Treatment by Subjects Interaction

The independent-groups design assumes no treatment by subjects interaction. Furthermore, as we saw earlier, there is no way to test that assumption in an independent-groups design. For the within-groups design, a significance test is available for the interaction, namely,

$$\begin{aligned} F &= \text{SV}(OG)/\text{Est Var}(f) \\ &= \text{SV}(OG)/[2(1 - r_{YY})\text{SV}(Y_1)] \end{aligned} \tag{8.115}$$

with degrees of freedom $(N - 1,\ N - 1)$. However, confidence intervals are also available for this interaction and should be used in preference to the significance test. (In the case of independent-groups design, neither a confidence interval nor a significance test is available for the interaction.)

The standard score interaction is defined by

$$s = \sigma_{TG}/\sigma_T$$

which is estimated by

$$\begin{aligned} \text{Est } s^2 &= \text{Est Var}(TG)/\text{Est Var}(T_1) \\ &= [\text{SV}(OG) - \text{Est Var}(f)]/\text{Est Var}(T_1) \end{aligned} \tag{8.116}$$

where

$$\text{Est Var}(f) = 2[1 - r_{YY}]\text{SV}(Y_1)$$

$$\text{Est Var}(T_1) = r_{YY}\text{SV}(Y_1)$$

To generate a confidence interval for s, we note first that

$$\text{Est } s^2 = [1/r_{YY}]\,[\text{SV}(OG)/\text{SV}(Y_1)] - [2(1 - r_{YY})/r_{YY}] \tag{8.117}$$

That is, the estimated interaction square has the form

$$\text{Est } s^2 = \beta[\text{SV}(OG)/\text{SV}(Y_1)] - \alpha \tag{8.118}$$

where α and β are constants. The variance ratio $\text{SV}(OG)/\text{SV}(Y_1)$ would have an approximate F ratio if it were not for the fact that the numerator and denominator population variances are different. There is a modified ratio that does have an approximate F distribution:

$$F = [\text{Var}(Y_1)/\text{Var}(OG)][\text{SV}(OG)/\text{SV}(Y_1)] \tag{8.119}$$

with degrees of freedom $(N - 1,\ N - 1)$. The corresponding endpoints for the confidence interval are obtained from the F endpoint tabled under $p = .025$, although few tables have that value for the degrees of freedom characteristic of most studies. To a close approximation, the upper endpoint is given by

$$U = e^{2w} \tag{8.120}$$

where

$$w = 1.96/\sqrt{(N - 2)}$$

The lower endpoint is given by the reciprocal, that is,

$$L = 1/U \tag{8.121}$$

Define the constant β by

$$\beta = 2(1 - r_{12})/r_{YY} \tag{8.122}$$

Then the confidence interval for the squared interaction is

$$[\text{Est } s^2 + \beta]/U - \beta < s^2 < [\text{Est } s^2 + \beta]/L - \beta \tag{8.123}$$

The confidence interval for the interaction s is obtained by taking the square root of each endpoint.

To estimate the standard error of this estimate of s, compute the width of the final confidence interval. The corresponding standard error is the width divided by $2(1.96) = 3.92$. The sampling error variance is the square of the standard error. That is, if we write the equation defining sampling error e as

$$\text{Est } s = s + e \tag{8.124}$$

then

$$\text{Var}(e) = \{[\text{Est } s^2 + \beta]/L - [\text{Est } s^2 + \beta]/U\}/1.96^2 \tag{8.125}$$

The t *Statistic.* The preceding discussion assumed that the study reported standard deviations. However, standard deviations are often left out of the report. Instead, authors report significance test statistics such as t. By analogy with the independent-groups case, we might search for a way to transform the value of t to provide an estimate of δ. Without standard deviations, there is no way to estimate the interaction s.

Consider now the t test for within-subjects designs:

$$t = \text{Ave}(OG)/\sqrt{[\text{SV}(OG)/N]} \tag{8.126}$$

If there were no treatment main effect, then this t statistic would have a central t distribution with $N - 1$ degrees of freedom and its value could be compared with those in the conventional t table in the conventional manner. If there is a treatment main effect, then this t statistic will have a noncentral t distribution whose noncentrality parameter depends on the size of the treatment main effect relative to the standard deviation of observed gain or change scores (Smithson, 2001, 2003, in press).

Note that the relevant standard deviation for sampling is the standard deviation of gain scores rather than the standard deviation of level scores. This means that transforming this value of t to the conventional within-subjects power parameter creates a ratio with the wrong denominator see also Kulik & Kulik, 1986). To see this, divide t by the square root of the sample size and consider the value for very large samples:

$$\text{limit } [t/\sqrt{N}] = E(OG)/\sigma_{OG} \tag{8.127}$$

Because $E(OG) = E(TG)$, we have

$$\delta = E(TG)/\sigma_T = E(OG)/\sigma_T \tag{8.128}$$

Thus, the t statistic has the wrong standard deviation (σ_{OG} instead of σ_T). We can relate the t statistic to δ by a ratio

$$\text{limit } [t/\sqrt{N}] = \alpha\ \delta \quad (8.129)$$

where

$$\alpha = \sigma_T/\sigma_{OG} \quad (8.130)$$

For the case of no interaction and no error of measurement, $\sigma_{OG} = 0$ and the ratio is infinite! If there is error of measurement but no interaction, then the ratio α can be computed from the reliability of the dependent variable. The square of α is given by

$$\alpha^2 = r_{YY}/[2(1 - r_{YY})] \quad (8.131)$$

Consider now the formula used to convert the independent-groups t to d, that is,

$$\text{“}d\text{”} = 2t/\sqrt{N} \quad (8.132)$$

In our repeated-measures case, the limit for large sample sizes is

$$\text{limit “}d\text{”} = \alpha\delta \quad (8.133)$$

where

$$\alpha^2 = r_{YY}/(1 - r_{YY})$$

This ratio would be 1 only for the special case $r_{YY} = .50$. For any other reliability, the independent-groups formula would be inaccurate.

The desired formula transforming t to d is

$$d = at/\sqrt{N} \quad (8.134)$$

where

$$a = \sqrt{[2(1 - r_{12})/r_{YY}]}$$

if there is an interaction and

$$a = \sqrt{[2(1 - r_{YY})/r_{YY}]}$$

if there is no interaction. (The approximation $r_{12} = r_{YY}$ can be used if there is an interaction but the test-retest correlation is not reported.) If we define sampling error e for this d by

$$d = \delta + e \quad (8.135)$$

then the sampling error variance is

$$\text{Var}(e) = [1/N]\ [(N - 1)/(N - 3)]\ [a^2 + \delta^2/2] \quad (8.136)$$

The corresponding large-sample formula is

$$\text{Var}(e) = [a^2 + \delta^2/2]/N \tag{8.137}$$

To compare this with the formula for the independent-groups d sampling error variance, consider the independent-groups large-sample formula

$$\text{“Var}(e)\text{”} = [4/N]\,[1 + \delta^2/8] \tag{8.138}$$

The within-groups large-sample formula can be written as

$$\text{Var}(e) = [4/N]\,[\beta^2 + \delta^2/8] \tag{8.139}$$

where

$$\beta^2 = a^2/4 = [1 - r_{YY}]/[2\,r_{YY}] \tag{8.140}$$

The two formulas will agree only in the special case $\beta^2 = 1$, that is, for the special case $r_{YY} = .33$. For higher reliabilities, the independent-groups formula will overstate the sampling error in d.

Statistical Power in the Two Designs

We have given a substantive argument showing that the within-subjects design with high reliability of measurement has higher statistical power than the independent-groups design. However, we have given neither formulas nor examples showing how much higher the power is. We will present such formulas in this section. For ease of presentation, we will assume that the independent-groups design is justifiable; that is, we will assume that if there is a treatment by subjects interaction, then that interaction is small enough to ignore. That is, like the conventional textbooks, we will assume that there is no treatment by subjects interaction.

A key question in matching designs is to match the sample sizes. There are two different ways to do this: matching the number of subjects or matching the number of scores. In the independent-groups design, the number of scores equals the number of people. That is, N_1 people in group 1 get N_1 scores on the dependent variable, while N_2 people in group 2 get N_2 scores. Thus, there are $N_1 + N_2$ people and $N_1 + N_2$ scores. However, in the within-subjects design, there are N people and $2N$ scores because each person gets two scores, a score for the first condition and a score for the second condition (in our discussion a pretest and a posttest score). Thus, in matching designs to enable comparisons, we can either match or equate on number of people (subjects) or match or equate on number of scores (measurement taken).

The choice is not simple. In practice, the matching will be determined by a “resource match.” There are two extreme cases. In most field studies, the sample size is set by the number of people available for study. For example, if we want to study the introduction of quality circles into the machinist department of Acme Manufacture, then our sample will contain at most the 32 people who work there at this time. However, in most lab studies, the sample size is set by the number of hours the lab is available (or the number of assistant-hours available). If the lab is available for 40 hours and it takes 30 minutes to run a subject through a condition, then the study will have 80 scores.

Consider the typical field study. We have N subjects available. Our design choice is this: (1) Run all N subjects in a pre-post design or (2) randomly split the N subjects into two half-samples of $N/2$ persons each and assign one-half of the sample to the control group and the other half-sample to the experimental group. Thus, we end up matching the designs by number of subjects, but we get twice as many scores in the pre-post design as in the independent-groups design.

Consider the typical lab study. We have N units of observation time available. Our choice then is (1) to run $N/2$ subjects through each of the two conditions or (2) to run one randomly chosen set of subjects in one condition and to run a second randomly chosen set of subjects in the other condition. Thus, we end up matching the designs on number of scores, but the independent-groups design has twice as many people in it.

Designs Matched for Number of Subjects

Consider then the choice between the two designs with the same number of subjects. In the within-subjects design, all N subjects are observed in both conditions. In the independent-groups design, the N subjects are randomly divided into two half-samples, with subjects in one sample observed in one condition and the subjects in the other sample observed in the other condition. Consider the power of the t test in each design.

First, we note that there will be a trivial difference in the degrees of freedom: $N-1$ for the within-subjects design and $N-2$ for the independent-groups design. This difference does not matter and will be ignored here (assume $N > 19$).

If there were no treatment effect, then the only possible statistical error would be a Type I error. In both designs, the t statistic and t tables are designed so that the probability of a Type I error is .05. Thus, if the null hypothesis were true, then it would not matter which design is chosen.

Assume then that there is a treatment effect. Define the size by

$$\delta = E(TG)/\sigma_T = [E(T_2) - E(T_1)]/\sigma_T \tag{8.141}$$

where T stands for the actual dependent variable, that is, the dependent variable scores that would have been observed had there been no error of measurement. For either design, the t test has a noncentral t distribution. Thus, it can be written as

$$t = (\mu + z)/c \tag{8.142}$$

where z has a standard normal distribution, c is the square root of a chi square divided by its degrees of freedom, z and c are independent, and μ is the impact of the treatment effect. If the degrees of freedom are denoted v, then

$$E(t) = \mu/J(v) \tag{8.143}$$

$$\text{Var}(t) = v/(v-2) + \mu^2[v/(v-2) - 1/J(v)] \tag{8.144}$$

To a close approximation,

$$E(t) = (1 + .75/v)\mu \qquad (8.145)$$

$$\text{Var}(t) = [v/(v-2)]\,[1 + (\mu^2/2v)(1 + 3/\{v-1\})] \qquad (8.146)$$

If the study designs are matched for the number of subjects, the designs differ only trivially in degrees of freedom. Thus, it is the parameter μ that differs between designs and that determines the relative power of the t test. In either design, we can write

$$\mu = \delta\sqrt{(N\, r_{YY}/b)} \qquad (8.147)$$

where b—the divisor under the radical—differs between the designs.

For the within-subjects design, we have

$$b = 2(1 - r_{YY}) \qquad (8.148)$$

and, hence,

$$\mu_w = \delta\sqrt{[Nr_{YY}/(2\{1 - r_{YY}\})]} \qquad (8.149)$$

For the independent-groups design, we have

$$b = 4$$

and, hence,

$$\mu_i = \delta\sqrt{[Nr_{YY}/4]} \qquad (8.150)$$

The relative size of the parameters is the ratio

$$\mu_w/\mu_i = \sqrt{[4/2(1 - r_{YY})]} = \sqrt{[2/(1 - r_{YY})]} \qquad (8.151)$$

The higher the reliability, the greater the relative advantage of the within-subjects design. As measurement nears perfection, the ratio nears ∞. This reflects the fact that if there is no interaction and no error of measurement, the within-subjects design always has perfect power (an infinite value of t), as shown earlier in this chapter. The lower the reliability, the lower the relative advantage. However, even as the reliability approaches 0, there is still a relative advantage of $\sqrt{2} = 1.41$, a 41% advantage. This reflects the fact that, as the level scores approach perfect unreliability, the gain scores still represent twice as much data as the independent-groups data because each subject has two measurements rather than one.

The mapping from power parameter to power is highly nonlinear. Thus, the power advantage is not proportional to the relative advantage in the power parameter. In part, this reflects the fact that, as sample size increases, power tends to its upper bound of 1.00 in both designs. As both tests approach perfect power, there is no room for the power of the within-subjects design to be more than slightly higher than that for the independent-groups design.

A power comparison is presented in Table 8.1. In the top part of the table, the effect size is always the same: $\delta = .40$. This is the typical effect size of

Table 8.1 Power of the within-subjects and independent-groups designs for two effect sizes when the number of subjects is the same in both designs

I. $\delta = .40$: *Textbook Examples*

	Within-Subjects Reliability					*Independent-Groups Reliability*				
N	*.25*	*.36*	*.49*	*.64*	*.81*	*.25*	*.36*	*.49*	*.64*	*.81*
10	8	10	14	22	44	6	7	7	8	9
20	11	16	24	39	71	7	8	10	11	13
30	15	22	33	53	87	9	10	12	14	17
40	18	27	42	65	94	10	12	14	17	21
50	22	32	50	75	98	11	14	17	21	25
60	25	38	57	82	99	12	15	20	24	29
70	28	43	63	87	100	13	17	22	27	33
80	31	47	69	91	100	15	20	24	30	36
90	34	52	74	94	100	16	21	27	33	40
100	37	56	79	96	100	17	23	29	36	44

II. $\delta = .20$: *Sophisticated Research*

	Within-Subjects Reliability					*Independent-Groups Reliability*				
N	*.25*	*.36*	*.49*	*.64*	*.81*	*.25*	*.36*	*.49*	*.64*	*.81*
10	6	6	7	9	15	5	5	6	6	6
20	7	8	10	13	26	6	6	6	6	7
30	7	9	12	18	36	6	6	7	7	8
40	8	10	14	23	45	6	7	7	8	9
50	9	12	17	27	54	6	7	8	9	10
60	10	13	20	31	61	7	8	8	10	11
70	10	14	22	35	68	7	8	9	10	12
80	11	16	24	39	74	7	8	10	11	13
90	12	17	26	43	78	8	9	10	12	14
100	13	19	29	47	82	8	9	11	13	15

NOTE: N is the sample size, the effect size is δ, and the power is given as the percentage of times the null hypothesis would be rejected, based on a two-tailed t test with alpha = .05.

major textbook examples (Cooper, 1984). The test is a two-tailed t test with alpha = .05. Power is tabulated for varying values of sample size N and reliability r_{YY}. Because five levels of reliability are shown, there are five columns for each design. Counting sample size as column 1, there are 11 columns in Table 8.1. The five columns for the within-subjects design are columns 2 to 6, while the five columns for the independent-groups design are columns 7 to 11. Corresponding columns represent the same level of measurement error.

Consider the row for a sample size of $N = 100$. As the reliability rises from .25 (the average reliability of a single response or a single item) to .81 (the reliability of professionally developed scales), the power of the independent-groups design rises from 17% to 44%. That is, the error rate for the independent-groups significance test drops from 83% to 56%. For the within-subjects design, the corresponding power values rise from 37% to 100%. That is, the error rate drops from 63% to 0. For a sample size of $N = 100$, the within-subjects design attains perfect power for reliabilities as low as .81, while the independent-groups design never attains perfect power.

Consider the two columns for reliability $r_{YY} = .81$. The smaller the sample size, the greater the relative power advantage for the within-subjects design. At the extremely low sample size of $N = 10$, the relative power is $44/9 = 4.89$; the within-subjects design is nearly 5 times more likely to detect the treatment effect than is the independent-groups design. When the sample size reaches $N = 70$, the power of the within-subjects design reaches 100%—perfect power—and can grow no further. At $N = 70$, the relative power is $100/33 = 3.03$, or 3 to 1. From that point on, the power of the within-subjects design remains fixed at 100%, while the power of the independent-groups design climbs to 44% at $N = 100$. At a sample size of 100, the relative power has dropped correspondingly to $100/44 = 2.27$, which is only a 2 to 1 advantage.

For more sophisticated research, the effect size is usually a contrast between versions of a treatment rather than the contrast of treatment versus control. Thus, effect sizes are much smaller. The bottom part of Table 8.1 illustrates sophisticated research; the effect size is $\delta = .20$. For $\delta = .20$, sample sizes up to $N = 100$, and reliability up to .81, the within-subjects design does not reach perfect power. Thus, in the table corresponding to the smaller effect size of sophisticated research, there is no ceiling effect for the within-subjects design, and it retains a massive relative advantage in all cells.

Confidence Intervals. The advantage of the within-subjects design over the between-subjects design can also be illustrated in terms of narrower confidence intervals. As discussed in Chapters 1 to 3, confidence intervals have many advantages over significance tests in analyzing data in individual studies (see, e.g., Schmidt, 1996). Higher statistical power and narrower (more precise) confidence intervals are produced by the same cause: smaller sampling error standard errors. Hence, in Table 8.1, higher statistical power means narrower confidence intervals; that is, the within-subjects design not only has higher statistical power, it also produces estimates of the d value that are more precise.

Designs Matched for Number of Measurements or Scores

Consider the choice between two designs with the same number of scores. In the independent-groups design, the N subjects are randomly divided into two half-samples, with subjects in one sample observed in one condition and subjects in the other sample observed in the other condition. There will be $N/2 + N/2 = N$ scores measured. In the within-subjects design, there will be only $N/2$ subjects, each of whom is observed in both conditions. There will be $2(N/2) = N$ scores measured. Thus, if measurement is expensive, then resource matching will match on number of scores rather than on number of subjects. Consider the power of the t test in each design.

First, we note that there will be a nontrivial difference in the degrees of freedom: $df = (N/2 - 1)$ for the within-subjects design and $N - 2$ for the independent-groups design. The ratio of degrees of freedom for the independent-groups design over the within-subjects design is

$$df_i/df_w = (N-2)/(\{N/2\} - 1) = 2(N-2)/(N-2) = 2$$

That is, the independent-groups design has a 2 to 1 advantage in degrees of freedom. Note, however, that it is the square root of sample size that counts and, hence, the relative advantage is the square root of 2, a 41% advantage in degrees of freedom. Furthermore, the number of degrees of freedom governs the extent of sampling error in the denominator of the t test. We will see, however, that the relative sampling error in the numerator is much greater.

If there were no treatment effect, then the only possible statistical error would be a Type I error. In both designs, the t statistic and t tables are designed so that the probability of a Type I error is .05. Thus, if the null hypothesis were true, then it would not matter which design is chosen.

Assume then that there is a treatment effect. Define the size by

$$\delta = E(TG)/\sigma_T = [E(T_2) - E(T_1)]/\sigma_T \tag{8.152}$$

where T stands for the actual dependent variable, that is, the dependent variable scores that would have been observed had there been no error of measurement. For either design, the t test has a noncentral t distribution. Thus, it can be written as

$$t = (\mu + z)/c \tag{8.153}$$

where z has a standard normal distribution, c is the square root of a chi square divided by its degrees of freedom, z and c are independent, and μ is the systematic impact of the treatment effect.

The parameter μ differs between designs. In either design, we can write

$$\mu = \delta\sqrt{N\,r_{YY}/4b} \tag{8.154}$$

where b—the divisor under the radical—differs between the designs.

For the within-subjects design, we have

$$b = 1 - r_{YY} \tag{8.155}$$

and, hence,

$$\mu_w = \delta\sqrt{[Nr_{YY}/4\{1 - r_{YY}\}]} \tag{8.156}$$

For the independent-groups design, we have

$$b = 1$$

and, hence,

$$\mu_i = \delta\sqrt{[Nr_{YY}/4]} \tag{8.157}$$

The relative size of the parameters is the ratio

$$\mu_w/\mu_i = \sqrt{[1/(1 - r_{YY})]} \tag{8.158}$$

The higher the reliability, the greater the relative advantage of the within-subjects design. As measurement nears perfection, the ratio nears ∞. This reflects the fact that if there is no interaction and no error of measurement, the within-subjects design always has perfect power (an infinite value of t). The lower the reliability, the lower the relative advantage. As the reliability approaches 0, the relative advantage vanishes. This reflects the fact that as the level scores approach perfect unreliability, the gain scores still represent exactly the same amount of data as the independent-groups scores because there are the same number of measurements in each design.

If the designs are matched for the number of scores, the advantage lies in opposite directions for the power parameter and for the degrees of freedom. The 2 to 1 advantage in degrees of freedom means that there is less sampling error in the denominator for the independent-groups design than for the within-subjects design. The within-subjects advantage in the power parameter means that there will be less sampling error in the numerator of the within-subjects design than in the numerator of the independent-groups design. The question is: Which has the greater impact, sampling error in the numerator or sampling error in the denominator? Table 8.2 shows that sampling error in the numerator is more important.

A power comparison is presented in Table 8.2. In the top part of the table, the effect size is always the same: .40. Consider the row for 100 measurements. As the reliability rises from .25 (the average reliability of a single response or a single item) to .81 (the reliability of professionally developed tests), the power of the independent-groups design rises from 17% to 44%. That is, the error rate for the independent-groups significance test drops from 83% to 56%. For the within-subjects design, the corresponding power values rise from 22% to 98%. That is, the error rate drops from 78% to 2%. Note that the power is always higher for the within-subjects design.

Consider the two columns for reliability $r_{YY} = .81$. The smaller the number of measurements, the greater the relative power advantage for the within-subjects design. At 10 measurements, the relative power is $25/9 = 2.78$; the within-subjects design is nearly 3 times more likely to detect the treatment effect than is the independent-groups design. When the number of measurements reaches $N = 100$, the relative power is $98/44 = 2.28$, or still better than 2 to 1. Because the within-subjects design does not reach the 100% ceiling in this table, the high relative advantage is largely maintained across the sample sizes displayed.

The bottom part of Table 8.2 illustrates sophisticated research; the effect size is $\delta = .20$. For $\delta = .20$, sample sizes up to $N = 100$, and reliability up to .81, the within-subjects design does not approach perfect power. Thus, in the table corresponding to the smaller effect size of sophisticated research, there is no ceiling effect for the within-subjects design, and it retains a massive relative power advantage in all cells.

For every cell in Table 8.2, the power is at least as large for the within-subjects design as for the independent-groups design. Thus, there is no case in this table

Table 8.2 Power of the within-subjects and independent-groups designs for two effect sizes when the number of measurements is the same in both designs

I. $\delta = .40$: *Textbook Examples*

	Within-Subjects Reliability					*Independent-Groups Reliability*				
No. Msmts.	*.25*	*.36*	*.49*	*.64*	*.81*	*.25*	*.36*	*.49*	*.64*	*.81*
10	7	8	10	14	25	6	7	7	8	9
20	8	10	14	22	44	7	8	10	11	13
30	10	13	19	31	59	9	10	12	14	17
40	11	16	24	39	71	10	12	14	17	21
50	13	19	29	46	80	11	14	17	21	25
60	15	22	33	53	87	12	15	20	24	29
70	16	25	37	60	91	13	17	22	27	33
80	18	27	42	65	94	15	20	24	30	36
90	20	30	46	70	96	16	21	27	33	40
100	22	32	50	75	98	17	23	29	36	44

II. $\delta = .20$: *Sophisticated Research*

	Within-Subjects Reliability					*Independent-Groups Reliability*				
No. Msmts.	*.25*	*.36*	*.49*	*.64*	*.81*	*.25*	*.36*	*.49*	*.64*	*.81*
10	5	6	6	7	10	5	5	6	6	6
20	6	6	7	9	15	6	6	6	6	7
30	6	7	8	1	20	6	6	7	7	8
40	7	8	10	13	26	6	7	7	8	9
50	7	8	11	16	31	6	7	8	9	10
60	7	9	12	18	36	7	8	8	10	11
70	8	10	13	21	41	7	8	9	10	12
80	8	10	14	23	45	7	8	10	11	13
90	9	11	15	25	50	8	9	10	12	14
100	9	12	17	27	54	8	9	11	13	15

NOTE: The effect size is δ and the power is given as the percentage of times the null hypothesis would be rejected, based on a two-tailed t test with alpha = .05.

where the advantage in degrees of freedom outweighs the advantage in the power parameter.

Confidence Intervals. The advantage of the within-subjects design over the between-subjects design can also be illustrated in terms of narrower confidence intervals. As discussed in Chapters 1 to 3, confidence intervals have many advantages over significance tests in analyzing data in individual studies (see, e.g., Schmidt, 1996). Higher statistical power and narrower (more precise) confidence intervals are produced by the same cause: smaller sampling error standard errors. Hence, in Table 8.2, higher statistical power means narrower confidence intervals; that is, the within-subjects design not only has higher statistical power in most of the cells of Table 8.2, it also produces estimates of the *d* value that are more precise.

Threats to Internal and External Validity

There are many who reject the within-subjects design before even considering issues such as the low power of the independent-groups design. This rejection is philosophical in nature and stems primarily from a misreading of the deservedly famous monograph by Campbell and Stanley (1963). In Table 1 of that monograph, they listed "sources of invalidity" for various designs, including seven sources for the within-subjects design. However, at the bottom of the table is the reminder that these are only *potential* threats to validity and that they may not apply to any given study. Many have dropped the adjective "potential" in the phrase "potential threats to validity" and, thus, state that the within-subjects design has "threats to validity." Worse yet, some researchers have lost the word "threat" and interpret Campbell and Stanley as having said that the within-subjects design is "fundamentally flawed because it lacks internal and external validity." Nothing could be further from what Campbell and Stanley wrote, and they themselves said so several times. Yet the topic of within-subjects designs can hardly come up in a group without someone citing Campbell and Stanley as stating that the within-subjects design is riddled with uncontrolled sources of internal and external invalidity.

Campbell and Stanley (1963) viewed potential threats to validity as source ideas of possible rival theories to explain an observed effect. They stipulated, however, that one must argue for the rival hypothesis—the claim that a threat was realized—with carefully documented evidence of the same sort that is used for the original hypothesis. For example, on page 7 they say, "To become a *plausible* rival hypothesis, such an event should have occurred to most of the students in the group under study. . . ." Note that they are interested only in *plausible* threats, not in vague hypothetical possibilities, and that they cast their argument in terms of a specific concrete event, not as an abstract argument such as "the within-subject design is flawed by failure to control for history."

The purpose of this section is not to criticize Campbell and Stanley, but to remind researchers of what Campbell and Stanley actually said. Their intention was this: If you are planning to do a within-subjects design, check these potential problems to see if any apply to that study. If so, then change the study procedures to eliminate that problem (or abandon the study design). The frequent false conclusion is that their checklist is a statement of problems that apply to every within-subjects design. We will attempt to dispel these false beliefs by presenting a series of examples. On the one hand, we will take a typical example of a pre-post study in organizational psychology and show that not one of the Campbell-Stanley threats actually exists for that study. On the other hand, for each threat, we will cite a study for which that threat would exist. Thus, we will be true to the actual content of Campbell and Stanley: a checklist of *possible* problems, not a list of charges in an indictment of the design.

Some would argue that showing that a given example is free of the threats listed by Campbell and Stanley does not save the within-subjects design. They would say that only a rare study would be free of flaws, and thus, it is a waste of time to consider such a design in the first place. It is true that the logical conclusions that can be drawn from an example are limited. Not all within-subjects studies are ruled out by the Campbell-Stanley list. However, we believe that the probability implication in this argument is wrong. In our experience, the probability of each threat on the Campbell-Stanley list is actually very low. In fact, we have rarely seen a study in which the within-subjects design could not be used. Our combined experience covers 60 years of scientific work in the field. So we do not believe that our opinion is based on limited experience.

Campbell and Stanley (1963, p. 8) listed the following potential threats to the internal validity of the within-subjects design: history, maturation, testing, instrumentation, regression (they put a question mark after this one), and interactions of these factors. They listed the following potential threats to the external validity of the within-subjects design: interaction of testing and treatment, interaction of selection and treatment, and reactive arrangements (with a question mark). We will show by example that a within-subjects design could indeed suffer from a flaw of each kind. However, we will also show by example that there can be a study that suffers from none of these potential problems. The Campbell-Stanley list is intended to be a list of potential problems to consider, not a list of problems to assume.

The part of the psychological literature in which the within-subjects design is most commonly used is field studies of interventions, that is, program evaluation. In most such studies, the subjects are adults who understand the program's objectives and who know that they are part of an intervention. However, it is also true that the dependent variable in most interventions is a behavior or event that is very difficult to change without intervention. These aspects of the study usually rule out all the Campbell-Stanley potential threats to validity.

Consider a management training program. Supervisors are to be given a training experience that explains how to apply certain skills, such as active listening, to supervisor problems. The dependent variable is the performance rating of the supervisor by the manager who is the supervisor's immediate superior. The pre-post design compares performance ratings before and after the training experience.

History

The experimenter interprets the change in the dependent variable as being caused by the intervention. But perhaps there was some concurrent event outside the scope of the study that actually caused the improvement. For example, suppose that we introduce goal setting to a group of small-car salesmen. During the test interval, there is a massive oil price increase in the Middle East that drives buyers from the large cars they had bought before to smaller cars. An increase in sales could be due to the oil price increase rather than to the goal-setting intervention. Thus, there could be a study in which history made the interpretation of the study result false.

How often are there natural events that produce a large change in important dependent variables? How often would such an event be overlooked by a seasoned scientific researcher working in an area that he knows well? Consider the skills training study. There is a long history of supervisory behavior study, which has found that even with intervention it is difficult to produce change in supervisory social behavior. What real event could change these supervisors that the experimenter would not be aware of?

Maturation

Perhaps the change observed in the study could be due to some internal process in the subject that would have taken place whether the intervention was done or not. Consider a psychologist studying psychomotor skills training in children. He argues that the change he observed between ages 5 and 6 was due to the special training program that he administered. However, psychomotor systems between the ages of 5 and 6 improve because of brain maturation. In this study, we would need some additional evidence to show that the increase in skills was not due to maturation rather than training.

How often would a psychologist overlook the process of maturation? For most dependent variables, there is ample evidence showing that the variable changes little for adults unless there is some major event that causes a reorganization of that behavior domain. Consider the social skills training example. Most people change their basic social behavior little over the adult years. Thus, we know before doing the study that there is no maturation process for the behavior in question.

Testing

Perhaps the observed change could be due to the pretest rather than to the intervention. For example, suppose we believe that teaching mathematical reasoning will improve a person's problem-solving skills. We create a problem-solving test to assess skills. We see if the test score improves from before the reasoning module to after the reasoning module. The problem is memory. If people remember how they solved the problem the first time, they can use that same method of solution much more rapidly. So it is possible that the observed improvement was due to memory for the specific problems rather than due to the use of the skills taught. Thus, it is possible for the results of a study to be due to testing rather than to the intervention.

How often does a psychologist have so little understanding of the dependent variable being used that he would overlook practice effects? In some social psychology experiments, subjects are deceived or misled as to the purpose of the study, and it is critical to the study that they not figure out that purpose. In such cases, the testing is a clue to the purpose and, hence, produces undesired effects. In field studies, however, the subject is usually told the purpose of the intervention, and hence, there is no secret to be revealed. Thus, testing rarely alerts the subject to anything not already known and provides no opportunity for practice.

Consider the social skills training example. The supervisors in the study have had performance ratings all of their working lives. Why should the performance rating before the training program change their fundamental social behavior? Testing is not a plausible rival theory for change in that study.

Instrumentation

Perhaps the change in a value is due to a change in the measuring instrument. If a spring is used to weigh a very heavy object, it will not spring all the way back to its original position. Consider studies in which the dependent variable is obtained from the subjective judgment of an observer. The observer may be tired or may have different standards after the study than he or she had before the study. For example, suppose that, unlike in our example, both the supervisor and his manager are put through the same training experience. Suppose the supervisor does not change, but the manager now has new standards for proper procedure. The manager evaluates the unchanged supervisor behavior negatively against the new standards and gives lower ratings after the training. So it is possible that a change in the instrument could produce a change in value, which is falsely attributed to the intervention.

In many studies, the instrument is not a subjective observer. In such studies, it is not likely that the instrument will change. If the dependent variable is a judgment, is it likely that a scientist familiar with the research area would overlook the possibility of change in the observer? In most studies with human observers, researchers go to a great deal of trouble to train the observers. One typical criterion for training is that the observer learn to give consistent responses to equivalent stimuli. Thus, even with subjective judgment, change in the instrument is rarely a plausible hypothesis.

Consider our social skills training study example. Managers usually have long experience in making performance ratings. They are not likely to change their standards because of a study in which they do not participate. In fact, studies have shown that it is difficult to change performance ratings even with extensive training on the rating process. Thus, in our example, change in the instrument is not a threat to validity.

Regression to the Mean

Suppose that people are preselected for the study. Perhaps the preselection biases the pretest scores and causes a false change effect when unbiased scores are obtained after the study. One such change is regression to the mean due to error of measurement. Consider an example from therapy to reduce anxiety about public speaking. The study begins by giving a public speaking anxiety test to a large class of subjects. The top 20 of 100 students are put into a special lab that uses stimulus desensitization to reduce the anxiety. At the end of the class period, the same anxiety instrument is used to assess change. The problem is this: No instrument is without error of measurement. In particular, the anxiety test has less than perfect reliability. To pick out unusually high scores is to select people for positive errors of measurement. Thus, the selected group will not have an average error of 0 on the pretest; the average error will be positive. Suppose there is no change in anxiety produced by the desensitization. After the study, each subject will have the same true score on anxiety. However, the new measurement will produce new errors of measurement. For each subject, the new error of measurement is as likely to be negative as positive. Thus, for the group of subjects, the average posttest error of measurement is 0. The change in average error of measurement from positive to 0 produces a negative change in mean score that could be falsely attributed to therapy. Thus, regression to the mean could cause a change to be falsely interpreted.

On the other hand, there is no preselection of subjects in most studies and, hence, no possibility of regression effects. If there is preselection, then there is an easy way to eliminate a possible regression effect: Use a double pretest. That is, use a first pretest for selection. Then use a second pretest to assess the preintervention level. The errors of measurement will be resampled on the second pretest, and hence, the mean error will be 0 on the second pretest, as on the posttest, thus eliminating the regression problem. Also, if the reliability of the dependent variable is known, and if the extent of selection is known, then it is possible to use a procedure similar to range restriction correction to correct the observed change for regression to the mean (Allen, Hunter, & Donohue, 1989), even without a double pretest.

Consider the social skills training study. All supervisors are to be given the training. There is no preselection and, hence, no possibility of a regression effect.

Reactive Arrangements

Reactive arrangements are interventions in which some seemingly trivial aspect of the treatment procedure causes a change that is not anticipated in the interpretation of the treatment as such. There are two possibilities: reactive measurement and reactive procedure.

Consider an example of potential reactive measurement. Suppose we believe that a certain dramatic movie (*Guess Who's Coming to Dinner?*) will produce altruistic thoughts on racial issues. We use a sentence completion test to assess racial imagery. A typical item is "Black people are . . ." We see if the person expresses more racial altruism after the movie than before the movie. The problem is this: What will the person think when she (1) is given a test that taps attitudes toward blacks and (2) is then presented with a movie about prejudice? It may be that the person would then try to do a self-evaluation in the form of, "I'm not that prejudiced, am I?" The person would search her memory for instances of nonprejudiced behavior. These biased memories might then form the substance of the apparently altruistic thoughts that register in the posttest. This would then lead the experimenter to a false conclusion.

Consider an example of reactive procedure. As part of a quality circle experiment, randomly selected workers are taken to a room off the factory floor. They might wonder what this is for and might form paranoid theories about assessment for labor union sympathies or dislike of their supervisor, or whatever. They might then be preset to have a negative reaction to the quality circle presentation. Thus, reactive procedure could produce a spurious change.

Consider the question of reactive measurement. Most field studies in political, organizational, or clinical psychology use measurements of important dependent variables, variables that are well-known to the experimenters and are reasonably well understood by the participants. Thus, reactive measurement is rare in these fields.

Consider the question of reactive procedure. In laboratory experiments that depend critically on deception, this is a serious problem. In most field studies, however, the subjects are told the objectives of the study, and the nature of the measurements is obviously related to those objectives. Thus, the measurement cannot reveal secrets and cannot produce bizarre subject theories as to the experimenter's unknown objectives. That is, reactive procedures are rare in most areas of psychological research.

Consider the social skills training example. The subjects are told that they will be participating in a training exercise. They are told that the objective is to improve their skills as supervisors. The training exercise tells them what they are supposed to do, and successful instructors tell them why. Thus, both reactive measurement and reactive procedures are unlikely or impossible.

Interaction Between Testing and Treatment

What Campbell and Stanley called "interaction between testing and treatment" has been called "reactive measurement" here. This was covered in the preceding paragraphs on "reactive arrangements."

Interaction Between Selection and Treatment

The problem discussed by Campbell and Stanley (1963) under the rubric "interaction between selection and treatment" is not a problem of false interpretation of the results of the study itself. That is, it is not a threat to "internal validity." Rather, they were worried about a generalization from the results of the study to some other context that might turn out to be wrong, that is, a threat to "external validity." The interaction in question represents the assumption that the effect of a treatment might differ from one setting to the next. If there is such variation, then an experimenter who generalizes from one setting to another may make a false inference. However, if there is variation in results across settings, the independent-groups design will *not* work any better than the within-subjects design. If people in a given setting are randomly assigned to control and experimental groups, the mean difference will be the same as if a pre-post study had been done in that same setting. Thus, variation in treatment effects across settings creates the same logical problem for single-setting studies—usually the only feasible study—for between-subjects designs as for within-subjects designs.

Meta-analysis is essential if there is variation in results across studies. That variation would not show in a single study, but that variation can be detected and identified in a meta-analysis. However, detailed consideration of this issue shows that identification of the interaction is often critically dependent on the statistical power of single studies. For this reason, consideration of meta-analysis shows that within-subjects designs are to be preferred when feasible.

Bias in Observed *d* Values

Hedges (1981, 1982a) and Rosenthal and Rubin (1982a) showed that there is a slight positive bias in the *d*-value statistic presented in Chapters 6 and 7. That is, the computed *d* value is slightly larger on average than the population value (δ). The size of this bias depends on δ (the population value) and N (the sample size). This bias is typically small enough to be ignored. For example, if $\delta = .70$ and $N = 80$, the bias is .007. Rounded to two places, this would be .01, a bias of no practical or theoretical significance. (Also, if the d value is converted to a correlation using the formulas given in Chapter 7, the bias in the correlation will be only about half as large.) The bias is large enough to be of concern only when the sample size is quite small. Green and Hall (1984) stated that the bias can be ignored unless the sample size for a study is 10 or less. In the previous example, if N were 20 instead of 80, the computed d value would average approximately .03 too large, that is, about a 4% upward bias. Both Hedges (1981) and Rosenthal and Rubin (1982a) presented formulas that provide approximate corrections for this bias. We also present such a correction in Chapters 6 and 7, and this correction is built into our computer programs for meta-analysis of d values. If study sample sizes are very small, these corrections should be used. Otherwise, this tiny bias can safely be ignored. This upward bias is small in comparison to the ever-present downward bias created by measurement error in the dependent variable. For example, if the reliability of the measure of the dependent variable were .75 in our example in which $\delta = .70$, then the average observed d value would be $(.75)^{1/2}(.70) = .61$; then if no correction were made for measurement error (often the case in published meta-analyses), the negative bias would be .09. This is 9 times greater than the upward bias of .01 identified by Hedges (1981) and Rosenthal and Rubin (1982a) when $N = 80$, and 3 times larger than the bias when $N = 20$. This places the upward bias in d values in its proper perspective.

Use of Multiple Regression in Moderator Analysis of *d* Values

Glass (1977) was the first to advocate use of ordinary least squares multiple regression to identify moderator variables in meta-analysis. The procedure is conceptually simple: The d values from a set of studies are regressed on the coded study characteristics, and those study characteristics with statistically significant regression weights are considered to be moderators of the effect size. This procedure has been used in meta-analyses of psychotherapy outcome studies (Smith & Glass, 1977) and the effects of class size (Smith & Glass, 1980), among other meta-analyses. Hedges and Olkin (1985, pp. 11–12, 167–169) argued against this procedure on grounds that the assumption of homogeneity of sampling error variances is usually not met in meta-analysis data sets. The (sampling) variance of each "observation" (i.e., each d value) depends on the sample size on which it is based (and on the size of the observed d value). If these sample sizes vary substantially, as they often do, then different effect size estimates will have very different sampling error variances. Heterogeneity of variances can affect the validity of significance tests; actual alpha levels may be larger than nominal levels (e.g., .15 vs. the nominal .05). Estimates of regression weights on moderators and multiple correlations can also be affected. Hedges and Olkin (1985, Chap. 8) presented a weighted least squares (WLS) regression procedure that circumvents this problem by weighting each study by the inverse of its sampling error variance. However, when Hedges and Stock (1983) used this method to reanalyze the Glass-Smith (1980) studies on class size, they obtained results that were quite similar to the original results, suggesting that the problem identified by Hedges and Olkin (1985) may not be serious. The general finding has been that most statistical tests are robust with respect to violations of the assumption of homogeneity of variance (see, e.g., Glass, Peckham, & Sanders, 1972, or Kirk, 1995).

In an attempt to address this question, Steel and Kammeyer-Mueller (2002) compared ordinary least squares (OLS) and weighted least squares (WLS) using computer simulation. They focused only on continuous moderators and only on the accuracy of the multiple R resulting from predicting observed effect sizes from the continuous moderator variables. They did not look at the accuracy of the standardized regression weights, which are a more informative index of the size and leverage of a moderator variable. They found that when the distribution of study sample sizes (N) was approximately normal, there was little difference in the accuracy of OLS and WLS. However, when the distribution of study Ns was skewed to the right, WLS produced more accurate estimates of the multiple R. However, the level of skew they examined was somewhat extreme (skew $= 2.66$) and might occur only infrequently in real research literatures.

There are reasons to be cautious about the use of WLS. If there is an outlier (in either direction) with an extremely large N, the WLS estimates will be distorted. Hence, with WLS, it is especially important to be concerned with outliers. There are also potential problems in the weighting of studies with small Ns. When N is small, very large r or d values can occur due to large sampling errors. The observed value of r or d affects the computed sampling error variance (as can be seen by inspecting the formulas for sampling error variance for r and d) and, therefore, affects the weight the study gets. As Steel and Kammeyer-Mueller (2002) noted, a study based on $N = 20$ with an r of .99 would be given the same weight as a study based on $N = 20{,}000$ but with an r of .60! One solution to this latter problem is to use mean r or d in the sampling error variance formulas for r and d, in place of the r and d values from the individual study, as discussed and recommended in Chapters 3, 4, and 7. An alternative solution that is simpler and statistically equivalent is to weight studies by the inverse of their sample size. Because both OLS and WLS regression methods have (different) problems, Overton (1998) recommended applying both and comparing the results. If they are similar, one's confidence in the results is supported.

With these cautions in mind, it is probably advisable in typical cases to emphasize WLS methods in preference to OLS methods when moderators are continuous. However, it is important to remember that both WLS and OLS will work poorly when the d or r values have not been corrected for measurement error. While all the values will be biased downward by measurement error, some will be biased more than others, undercutting the construct validity of the observed ds or rs as measures of the real effects and, hence, artifactually reducing the apparent strength of all moderators. Even if the d or r values are corrected for measurement error, there is still the problem created by the fact that much or most (or all) of the variance in the d values or rs is due to sampling error, creating low reliability for the dependent variable and, hence, downwardly biased estimates of moderator effects (as discussed in Chapter 2). Also, the correction for measurement error will cause the estimated standard errors for standardized regression coefficients to be inaccurate with most computer programs. Hunter (1995) developed special software that yields accurate standard error values when the data have been corrected for measurement error. The study of Steel and Kammeyer-Mueller (2002) did not address these issues.

If moderators are dichotomous or categorical (e.g., sex or race), the subgrouping approach to moderator analysis may be superior. However, it is important to bear in mind that moderators are often correlated and that it is important to use hierarchical moderator analysis (discussed in Chapter 9) to avoid confounding of correlated moderators. When moderators are continuous, the subgrouping method has the disadvantage of requiring dichotomization of the continuous variables to produce the subgroups, thus losing information. When there is only one moderator to be examined and it is continuous, simple correlation can be used, as described in Chapters 3, 4, and 7. When there is more than one continuous moderator, simple correlation is maximally informative only if the moderators are uncorrelated. If the moderators are correlated, OLS or WLS should be used to assess the moderators.

The problem of potential distortion of regression results pointed out by Hedges and Olkin (1985, Chap. 8) pales in comparison to other, more serious problems that plague the use of multiple regression to identify moderators: capitalization on chance and low statistical power. As described graphically in Chapter 2, these latter problems can completely destroy the interpretability of the results of such moderator analyses. By comparison, the violation of the assumption of homogeneity of sampling error variances is almost academic. Finally, we note that although this discussion appears in a chapter devoted to d values, it applies equally to meta-analyses based on correlations.

PART IV

General Issues in Meta-Analysis

9

General Technical Issues in Meta-Analysis

This chapter discusses technical issues that are general to meta-analysis. That is, these issues apply whether meta-analysis is applied to correlations, to d values, or to other statistics (e.g., odds ratios). Also, these issues apply whether the methods used are those presented in this book, those of Hedges and Olkin (1985), those of Rosenthal (1984, 1991), or any other methods.

Whether to use random- or fixed-effects models in meta-analysis is the first such issue. This issue was first broached in Chapter 5 and is covered in somewhat more conceptual detail here.

The second technical issue is second-order sampling error in meta-analysis. We first present a conceptual overview of this phenomenon; then, near the end of the chapter, we present the technical treatment and the equations. This topic includes the impact of second-order sampling error on the difficult task of detecting moderators that are not hypothesized a priori.

The third technical issue is second-order meta-analysis: the meta-analysis of meta-analyses. This topic includes a discussion of whether it is better to have a single large-sample study or a meta-analysis of many small-sample studies.

Finally, we present the reader with an exercise: conducting a second-order meta-analysis.

Fixed-Effects Versus Random-Effects Models in Meta-Analysis

Within meta-analysis methods, there is a distinction between fixed-effects (FE) models (Hedges & Olkin, 1985, Chap. 7) and random-effects (RE) models (Hedges & Olkin, 1985, Chap. 9). These models lead to different significance tests and confidence intervals for mean effect sizes (mean r, mean d, etc.). They also yield different significance tests for moderator variables (interactions) in meta-analysis, that is, different significance tests for the relationship between study characteristics and study outcomes (effect sizes) (National Research Council, 1992;

Overton, 1998). Hedges (1992b, pp. 284–292) provided a succinct overview of the differences between these two models in meta-analysis. Other treatments of this distinction can be found in Hedges (1994a, 1994b), National Research Council (1992), Raudenbush (1994), and Shadish and Haddock (1994).

Application of FE significance tests and confidence intervals is based on the assumption that the studies being analyzed are homogeneous at the level of study population effect sizes. For example, if the effect size index used is the d value, the FE model assumes that δ, the population value of d, is the same in all studies included in the meta-analysis. RE models do not make this assumption (Hedges, 1992b; Hedges & Olkin, 1985, Chap. 9; National Research Council, 1992). RE models allow for the possibility that the population parameter values (δs or ρs) vary from study to study (Becker, 1996; Cook et al., 1992, Chap. 7; Hedges, 1992b).

The methods described in Hunter, Schmidt, and Jackson (1982), Hunter and Schmidt (1990a), Callender and Osburn (1980), and Raju and Burke (1983) are RE models (Hedges & Olkin, 1985, Chap. 9, p. 242; National Research Council, 1992, pp. 94–95). These methods have been extensively applied to substantive questions in the published literature (see, e.g., Schmidt, 1992). The methods described in Hedges (1988), Hedges and Olkin (1985, Chap. 9), Raudenbush and Bryk (1985), and Rubin (1980, 1981) are also RE methods. These latter methods have been used less frequently in meta-analysis. For example, although *Psychological Bulletin*, the major review journal in psychology, has published many meta-analyses, we could locate no meta-analyses published in that journal that employed these methods. Cooper (1997) stated: "In practice, most meta-analysts opt for the fixed effects assumption because it is analytically easier to manage" (p. 179). The National Research Council (1992) report stated that many users of meta-analysis prefer FE models because of "their conceptual and computational simplicity" (p. 52).

RE formulas for statistical significance of mean effect sizes and moderator relationships have the appropriate Type I error rate (e.g., 5% for a designated alpha of .05), both when population parameter values (ρ or δ) are the same across all studies and when the population parameters vary across studies. However, when population parameters vary across studies, the FE formulas have Type I error rates that are higher than the nominal values—often much higher (Hunter & Schmidt, 2000). In addition, if confidence intervals are used based on the FE standard errors, the confidence intervals are too narrow. For example, a nominal 95% confidence interval may actually be a 60% confidence interval (Hunter & Schmidt, 2000), a substantial inaccuracy, and a substantial overstatement of the precision of the meta-analysis results. Hunter and Schmidt (2000) presented numerous examples of errors of this sort produced by FE models.

The fact that FE models produce inaccurate results unless population effect sizes are constant across studies is important because it is likely that there is at least some variation in study population parameters in all research domains. Many would argue that for theoretical or substantive reasons there is always some variation in population parameter values across studies. That is, they would argue that there are always at least some real (i.e., substantive, not methodological) moderator variables that create differing values of δ_i or ρ_i across studies (National Research Council, 1992). We do not argue for this position, because, based on our experience, some study domains do appear to be homogeneous at the level of substantive population parameters (see, e.g., Schmidt et al., 1993). However, whether this is true can be ascertained only by using RE models to estimate the level of heterogeneity. FE models do not allow for an estimate of S_ρ^2 or S_δ^2, because they assume homogeneity a priori. That is, they assume $S_\rho^2 = 0$ and $S_\delta^2 = 0$.

Even if there are no substantive moderators causing variation in population parameters, there are methodological variations across studies that cause variation in study population ρ_i or δ_i. For example, if the amount of measurement error in the measures used varies across studies, this variation creates differences in study population parameters; studies with more measurement error will have smaller study population values of δ_i or ρ_i. So, even if there is no substantive variation in population parameters, differences across studies in such methodological factors as reliability of measurement, range variation, or dichotomization of continuous variables (Hunter & Schmidt, 1990b) will create differences in study population parameters (Osburn & Callender, 1992). Such variation will typically exist; hence, the assumption of homogeneous study population effect sizes or correlations will usually be false for this reason alone.

The formulas for statistical significance used in published applications of the Hedges-Olkin (1985) and Rosenthal-Rubin (1982a, 1982b) meta-analysis methods are almost invariably FE formulas. The following meta-analyses, all of which appeared in *Psychological Bulletin*, the premier general review journal in psychology, are some recent examples: Bettencourt and Miller (1996), Bond and Titus (1983), Burt, Zembar, and Niederehe (1995), Collins and Miller (1994), Eagly and Carli (1981), Eagly and Johnson (1990), Eagly, Karau, and Makhijani (1995), Eagly, Makhijani, and Klonsky (1992), Erel and Burman (1996), Feingold (1994), Herbert and Cohen (1995), Ito, Miller, and Pollock (1996), Jorgensen, Johnson, Kolodziej, and Scheer (1996), Knight, Fabes, and Higgins (1996), Newcomb and Bagwell (1995), Polich, Pollock, and Bloom (1994), Symons and Johnson (1997), Van Iizendorn (1995), Voyer, Voyer, and Bryden (1995), Wood (1987), and Wood, Lundgren, Ouellette, Busceme, and Blackstone (1994).

Hedges and Olkin (1985) specified that a chi-square test for homogeneity should precede the test for the significance of the mean correlation or d value. This chi-square test is the same for both the FE and RE models (Hedges, 1992b; Hedges & Olkin, 1985, Chap. 9). If this test is nonsignificant, then the chi-square test cannot reject the hypothesis of homogeneity. However, a nonsignificant homogeneity test does not support a conclusion of homogeneity of study population values of ρ and δ. Unless the number of studies is large, this chi-square test typically has low power to detect variation in study population parameters (Hedges & Olkin, 1985; Mengersen, Tweedie, & Biggerstaff, 1995; Morris & DeShon, 1997; National Research Council, 1992, p. 52), resulting in frequent Type II errors. That is, the chi square is often nonsignificant in the presence of real variation in study population parameters (Hedges & Olkin, 1985). As a result, FE significance tests are often applied to heterogeneous study domains, resulting in inflated Type I error rates and confidence intervals (around mean effect sizes) that are substantially narrower than the actual confidence intervals.

In addition, even if the chi-square test of homogeneity *is* significant (indicating heterogeneity of population effect sizes), users of FE methods nevertheless often apply FE formulas for statistical significance of mean effect sizes (or compute confidence intervals using the FE standard error of the mean effect size). This practice ensures distorted results and conclusions. Examples of meta-analyses that have been done this way include Bettencourt and Miller (1996), Bond and Titus (1983), Burt et al. (1995), Collins and Miller (1994), Eagly and Johnson (1990), Eagly et al. (1995), Eagly et al. (1992), Erel and Burman (1996), Feingold (1994), Ito et al. (1996), Knight et al. (1996), Newcomb and Bagwell (1995), Polich et al. (1994), Symons and Johnson (1997), Van Iizendorn (1995), Wood (1987), and Wood et al. (1994). These meta-analyses all focus on substantive research questions that are quite important. With these practices, it is even more likely that FE significance tests will have substantially inflated Type I error rates and will report falsely narrow confidence intervals, overestimating the precision of the findings. (In some of these meta-analyses, the authors specify that FE confidence intervals for mean effect sizes are first computed and presented and only after this are tests of homogeneity conducted! See, e.g., Collins & Miller, 1994, p. 462; Feingold, 1994, p. 432.)

The National Research Council (1992, p. 147) stated that the use of FE models in meta-analysis is "the rule rather than the exception" and that FE models "tend to understate actual uncertainty" in research findings. The National Research Council recommended "an increase in the use of RE models in preference to the current default of FE models" (p. 2; see also pp. 185–187 of that report). Cook et al. (1992, Chap. 7) also recommended random models over fixed models. Others have also warned that use of FE models can lead to inflated Type I error rates and erroneously narrow confidence intervals (e.g., Hedges, 1994a; Raudenbush, 1994; Rosenthal, 1995b). However, FE models have continued to be "the rule rather than the exception" in the published literature in psychology and other disciplines.

Erez, Bloom, and Wells (1996) called for increased use of RE models in preference to FE models. However, they did not discuss the most widely used FE models, those of Hedges and Olkin (1985). Nor did they discuss the FE methods of Rosenthal and Rubin (Rosenthal, 1991; Rosenthal & Rubin, 1982a, 1982b). They also misidentified the methods in Hunter et al. (1982), Hunter and Schmidt (1990a), Callender and Osburn (1980), and Raju and Burke (1983) as FE methods; these methods are all RE methods.

What rationales have been offered for the FE model? The initial rationale was that scientists may sometimes not be interested in the mean effect size for the full domain of studies, but rather may be interested only in the specific effect sizes represented in the studies included in a meta-analysis (Hedges, 1992b, 1994a, 1994b; Raudenbush, 1994; Shadish & Haddock, 1994). Under this rationale, researchers do not regard the studies in their meta-analysis as a sample from a potentially larger population of studies, but rather as the entire universe of studies of interest. Under this assumption, there is no possibility of sampling error due to this sampling of study effect sizes, because all possible study effect sizes are, by definition, included in the meta-analysis. Overton (1998) showed that the FE model has the appropriate level of Type I error under this assumption. However, the key question is whether this assumption is ever realistic or appropriate.

The major problem with this assumption is that it is difficult (and perhaps impossible) to conceive of a situation in which a researcher would be interested only in the specific studies included in the meta-analysis and would not be interested in the broader task of estimation of the population effect sizes for the research domain as a whole. For example, suppose 16 studies have been conducted relating the personality trait of Openness to Experience to job performance, but those studies have been published in widely varying journals. Suppose, as a result, the meta-analyst locates only 8 of the 16 studies to include in his or her meta-analysis. Consider this question in a hypothetical survey of personality researchers: Which would you as a researcher find more informative: (a) meta-analysis means and confidence intervals that generalize to the entire domain of studies in this research area (RE model results) or (b) meta-analysis means and confidence intervals that describe only the specific studies located for this meta-analysis and cannot be generalized to the research domain as a whole (FE model)? It seems clear that substantive researchers would (rightly) prefer the random-effects results. Science is about generalization, and the purpose of research is the identification of generalizable conclusions (Overton, 1998). Conclusions limited to a specific subset of studies are not scientifically informative.

Consider the same reasoning applied at the broader study domain level. Would a researcher rather have the results of a meta-analysis that describes only the first several studies conducted in a domain or the outcome of a meta-analysis that generalizes to all studies that could or might be conducted in the future in that domain? That is, would he or she prefer for the meta-analysis results and conclusions to generalize to future replication studies or would he or she prefer results that do not generalize to future replication studies? Most researchers would judge that conclusions about the broader study domain are of more scientific value. That is, the information produced by RE models is the information most researchers expect a meta-analysis to convey (Overton, 1998), whereas the information produced by FE models is of very limited scientific value.

This rationale in support of the fixed-effects model sprang from an analogy with FE models in analysis of variance (ANOVA). In ANOVA, an FE design is one in which all levels of the treatment that are of interest are included in the design, while an RE model in ANOVA is one in which only a sample of treatment levels of interest is included in the study. By analogy with this distinction in ANOVA, Hedges and Olkin (1985) labeled the two different approaches to meta-analysis as FE and RE models. Hence, in FE meta-analysis models, the studies included in the meta-analysis are assumed to constitute the entire universe of relevant studies, whereas in RE models the studies are taken to be a sample of all possible studies that might be conducted or might exist on the subject. The National Research Council report (1992, pp. 46 and 139) indicated that there are problems with this analogy. As the report stated:

> The manner in which the terms "fixed effects" and "random effects" are used in the meta-analysis literature is somewhat different from the classical definitions used in other techniques of statistics such as analysis of variance, where "fixed effects" is the term required to deny the concept of a distribution of the true effects, $\delta_1, \ldots, \delta_k$, and "random effects" supposes that the δ_1's are sampled from a population and therefore have a distribution. (p. 46)

As an aid in interpreting this statement, consider research on the effects of drugs on patients. A researcher might include the dosages 0 mg, 10 mg, and 20 mg. In

FE ANOVA, these treatments (dosages) are fixed at these levels, which are the only ones considered of interest, and the idea that there is a naturally occurring distribution of dosages from which these three dosages are sampled is denied. This is different from the FE model in meta-analysis in two important ways. First, in meta-analysis, the researcher does not specify (or fix) the parameter values (ρ_1 or δ_1) in the individual studies included in the FE meta-analysis. Instead, these are merely accepted as they happen to occur in the sample of studies. That is, they are merely observed and are not manipulated. The second difference flows from the first: Because the researcher does not fix the parameter values in the studies included in the meta-analysis, but rather merely accepts them as they happen to have occurred, there is no basis or rationale for postulating or assuming that these parameter values do not have a distribution across studies—the key assumption of the fixed model in ANOVA. These are the reasons the National Research Council report (1992) rejected the analogy between FE models in ANOVA and FE models in meta-analysis. These considerations led to the conclusion (stated earlier) that the FE model in meta-analysis is legitimate only in study sets in which S_ρ^2 (or S_δ^2) $= 0$. In these (rare) circumstances, study parameter values are indeed fixed—although all at the same value, unlike FE ANOVA designs. As discussed earlier, the National Research Council report concluded that, whenever this condition is not met, the FE meta-analysis model leads to elevated Type I error rates and unrealistically narrow confidence intervals.

Hedges and Vevea (1998, p. 488) abandoned the rationale discussed here for the FE model in favor of the conclusion that there is no statistical rationale or justification for the FE model in meta-analysis. However, they stated that there can be a rationale based on subjective judgment by the researcher. They began by acknowledging that FE results are of little value or interest if they cannot be generalized beyond the specific studies included in the meta-analysis, and they concluded that such generalization is "not justified by a formal sampling argument." However, they argued that a researcher can make a subjective "extrastatistical" or "extraempirical" judgment that generalization of FE estimates to the whole research domain is justified: "Specifically, inferences may be justified if the studies are judged *a priori* to be sufficiently similar to those in the study sample" (p. 488). This judgment is the judgment that the new studies (to which generalization is to be extended) have study parameters (ρ_1 or δ_1) that exactly reproduce, study for study, those in the original study set included in the FE meta-analysis. It is difficult to see how such a subjective judgment could be justified. What basis could a researcher have for such knowledge?

Although Hedges and Vevea (1998) provided computational examples applying the FE model, they give no substantive example (even a hypothetical one) of a case in which such a subjective judgment would be appropriate as a rationale for use of the FE model. Nor did they provide any guidelines or suggestions for when this might be appropriate.

Hedges and Vevea (1998) recognized that the FE model in meta-analysis has no statistical justification, and this is a step forward. However, their attempt to provide a subjective rationale based on questionable judgments by researchers appears to be weak. If a procedure has no statistical justification, replacing it with one that does would seem preferable to constructing a subjective, nonstatistical justification. The

RE model has a clear statistical justification, requires no subjective judgments, and can be used in all applications of meta-analysis.

Second-Order Sampling Error: General Principles

The outcome of any meta-analysis based on a small number of studies depends to some extent on which studies randomly happen to be available; that is, the outcome depends in part on study properties that vary randomly across studies. This is true even if the studies analyzed are all that exist at that moment. This phenomenon is called "second-order sampling error." It affects meta-analytic estimates of standard deviations more than it affects estimates of means. This is also the case with ordinary, or first-order, sampling error and ordinary statistics: Ordinary sampling error affects standard deviations more than means. Ordinary, or first-order, sampling error stems from the sampling of subjects within a study. Second-order sampling error stems from the sampling of studies in a meta-analysis.

Consider a hypothetical example. Suppose there were only 10 studies available estimating the relationship between trait A and job performance. Even if the mean sample size per study were only 68 (the median for published validity studies reviewed by Lent, Auerbach, & Levin, 1971a, 1971b), the mean validity would be based on $N = 680$ and would be reasonably stable. The observed variance across studies would be based on only 10 studies, however, and this variance, which we compare to the amount of variance expected from sampling error, would be based on only 10 data points. Now suppose sampling error were, in fact, the only factor operating to produce between-study variance in observed correlations (validities). Then, if we randomly happened to have one or two studies with large positive sampling errors, the observed variance across studies would likely be larger than the predicted variance, and we might falsely wind up concluding, for example, that sampling error accounts for only 50% of the observed variance of validities across studies. On the other hand, if the observed validity coefficients of, say, five or six of the studies randomly happened to be very close to the expected value (population mean), then the observed variance across studies would likely be very small and would underestimate the amount of variance one would typically (or on the average) observe across 10 such randomly drawn studies (from the population of such hypothetical studies that could be conducted). In fact, the observed variance might be smaller than the variance predicted from sampling error. The computed percentage variance accounted for by sampling error would then be some figure greater than 100%, for example, 150%. Of course, in this case, the correct conclusion would be reached: All the observed variance could be accounted for by sampling error. However, some people have been troubled by such outcomes. They are taken aback by results indicating that sampling error can account for more variance than is actually observed. Sometimes they are led to question the validity of the formula for sampling error variance (see, e.g., Thomas, 1988, and the reply by Osburn & Callender, 1990). This formula correctly predicts the amount of variance sampling error will produce on average. However, sampling error randomly produces more than this amount in some samples and less in other samples. The larger the number of studies (other things being equal), the smaller the deviations of observed from expected variance. If the number of studies is small, however, these deviations can be quite large *on a percentage basis* (although *absolute* deviations are usually small, even in such cases).

Negative estimates of variances occur using other methods of statistical estimation. In one-way analysis of variance (ANOVA), for example, the variance of sample means is the sum of two components: the variance of population means and the sampling error variance. This is directly analogous to the meta-analytic breakdown of the observed variance of sample correlations across studies into the variance of population correlations (the real variance) and the sampling error variance (the false or spurious variance). In estimating the variance of population means in ANOVA, the first step is to subtract the within-group mean square from the between-group mean square. This difference can be, and sometimes is, negative, as a result of sampling error. Consider a case in which the null hypothesis is true; the population means are then all equal and the variance of population means is 0. The variance of observed means (i.e., sample means) is then determined entirely by sampling error. This observed between-group variance will vary randomly from one study to another. About half the time the within-group mean square will be larger than the between-group mean square, while half the time the within-group mean square will be smaller. That is, if the variance of population means is 0, then in half of the observed samples the estimated variance of population means will be negative. This is exactly the same as the situation in meta-analysis if all the population correlations are equal: The estimated variance will lie just above 0 half the time and will lie just below 0 half the time. The key here is to note that the variance of population correlations is estimated by subtraction: The known error variance is subtracted from the variance of sample correlations, which estimates the variance of sample correlations across a population of studies. Because the number of studies is never infinite, the observed variance of sample correlations will depart by sampling error from the expected value. Thus, when the variance of population correlations is 0, the difference will be negative half the time.

Another example is the estimation of variance components in generalizability theory. Cronbach and his colleagues (Cronbach, Gleser, Nanda, & Rajaratnam, 1972) proposed generalizability theory as a liberalization of classical reliability theory, and it is now widely used to assess the reliability of measuring instruments in situations where the techniques of classical reliability theory are considered inadequate. Generalizability theory is based on the well-known ANOVA model and requires estimated variance components for its application. One or more of the estimated variance components may be negative, as noted by Cronbach et al. (1972, pp. 57–58) and Brennan (1983, pp. 47–48), even though, by definition, population variance components are nonnegative. The same phenomenon was also noted by Leone and Nelson (1966). Cronbach et al. (1972) recommended substituting 0 for the negative variance, and Brennan (1983) agreed with this recommendation.

Negative estimated variances are not uncommon in statistical estimation. The occurrence of negative estimates of variance in empirical research does not call into question a statistical theory such as ANOVA or a psychometric theory such as meta-analysis or validity generalization. As described previously, existing statistical sampling theory provides a sound rationale for observed negative estimates of variance in meta-analysis when the actual variance of true validities is 0 or close to 0.

Detecting Moderators Not Hypothesized a Priori

When the moderator variable is not specified or hypothesized in advance by theory, the statistical power of a meta-analysis with respect to the variance of ρ or δ is the probability that the meta-analysis will detect variation in ρ or δ values across studies when such variation does, in fact, exist. One minus this probability is the probability of a Type II error: concluding that all the variance across studies is due to artifacts when, in fact, some of it is real. When all variance is indeed artifactually caused, there is no possibility of a Type II error, and there can be no statistical power question. Just as second-order sampling error becomes more of a problem as the number of studies becomes smaller, statistical power also becomes lower. A number of statistical tools have been used to make the decision about whether any of the observed variance is real. In our meta-analytic research on test validities, we have used the 75% rule: If 75% or more of the variance is due to artifacts, we conclude that all of it is, on grounds that the remaining 25% is likely to be due to artifacts for which no correction has been made. Another method is the chi-square test of homogeneity. As pointed out in Chapter 5 and again in this chapter, this test has low power under most realistic circumstances (Hedges & Pigott, 2001). In addition, it has all the other disadvantages of significance tests, as discussed in Chapter 2. Callender and Osburn (1981) presented another method, one based on simulation.

Extensive computer simulation studies have been conducted to estimate the statistical power of meta-analyses to detect variation in ρ using these decision rules (Osburn, Callender, Greener, & Ashworth, 1983; Sackett, Harris, & Orr, 1986; Spector & Levine, 1987). These estimates have been obtained for different combinations of (1) numbers of studies, (2) sample size of studies, (3) amount of variation in ρ, (4) mean ρ values, and (5) levels of measurement error. The findings of the Sackett et al. (1986) study are probably the most relevant to meta-analysis in general. Sackett et al. found that, under all conditions, the 75% rule had "statistical power" greater than (or equal to) the other methods (although it also showed a higher Type I error rate: concluding there was a moderator when there was not). The term statistical power is placed in quotation marks here because that term applies only to significance tests, and the 75% rule is not a significance test, but rather a simple "rule of thumb" decision rule. This advantage in statistical power was relatively the greatest when the number of studies was small (4, 8, 16, 32, or 64) and the sample size of each study was small (50 or 100). However, when the assumed population variance to be detected (s^2_ρ) was small, and both the number of studies and the sample size of the studies were small, all methods had relatively low statistical power. For example, if there were four studies ($N = 50$ each) with $\rho = .25$, and four studies ($N = 50$ each also) with $\rho = .35$ (corresponding to $s^2_\rho = .01$) and if $r_{xx} = r_{yy} = .80$ in all studies, statistical power was .34 for the 75% rule (and only .08 for the other methods). However, a total sample size of 8(50) = 400 is very small, and 8 is a small number of studies for a meta-analysis. Also, a difference of .10 is very small. If the difference in this example is raised to .30, power rises to .75. This difference between ρs is more representative of the moderators that it would be theoretically and practically important to study. Nevertheless, it is true that individual meta-analyses have less than optimal statistical power in some cases. As the reader of this book is by now aware, we recommend against the use of significance tests (see, e.g., Chapter 2). These simulation studies show that our simple 75% rule typically is more accurate than significance tests used to assess homogeneity. However, no decision rule for judging homogeneity versus heterogeneity in meta-analyses of realistic sets of studies has perfect accuracy.

The preceding discussion applies to "omnibus" tests for moderator variables—moderator variables that are not specified in advance by theories or hypotheses. In such cases, the existence of moderators must be detected by determining whether the variance of study effect sizes is larger than can be accounted for by the presence of variance-generating artifacts. The story is very different when the moderator hypotheses are specified in advance. In such cases, the studies in the meta-analysis can be subgrouped based on the moderator hypothesis (e.g., studies done on blue- vs. white-collar employees), and confidence intervals can be placed around the means ($\bar{\delta}$ or $\bar{\rho}$) of the subgroup meta-analyses, as described in Chapter 5 (and later in this chapter for bare-bones meta-analysis). This procedure is much more effective in identifying moderators than operating without a priori moderator hypotheses and attempting to assess the presence of moderators by testing for heterogeneity in observed d or r values.

In most areas of research, there should be sufficient development of theory to generate hypotheses about moderators. However, in one major meta-analytic research area—the generalizability of employment test validities—this has not been the case. It has not been possible to use the subgrouping approach to test the "situational specificity" hypothesis in personnel selection. To use this approach, the moderators must be specified. There must be a theory, or at least a hypothesis, that is specific enough to postulate that, for example, correlations will be larger for females than for males, or larger for "high-growth-need" individuals than for "low-growth-need" individuals, or larger in situations where supervisors are high in "consideration" than where supervisors are low in consideration. The situational specificity hypothesis does not meet this criterion; it postulates merely that there are unspecified subtle but important differences from job to job and setting to setting in what constitutes job performance, and that job analysts and other human observers are not proficient enough as information processors to detect these critical elusive differences (Albright, Glennon, & Smith, 1963, p. 18; Lawshe, 1948, p. 13). When the operative moderators are actually unknown and unidentifiable, it is not possible to subgroup studies by hypothesized moderators. However, if one can show that all observed validity variance is due to artifacts, one has shown that no moderators can possibly be operating. This approach does not require that the postulated moderators be identified or even identifiable. Given that there is a broad and heterogeneous range of situations represented in one's validity generalization meta-analysis, one can show that the postulated moderators do not exist, even without knowing what the moderators are. One would hope that situational specificity would be the first and only hypothesis of this nature to be tested using meta-analysis. We hope that theories and hypotheses tested in the future using meta-analysis will be far better specified and definite in the predictions they make. If so, they will allow use of the second approach to identifying moderators.

However, critics of particular theories or conclusions sometimes make statements like the following: "There are many factors that could affect outcomes. Supervisory style may have important effects; group membership, geographical location, type of industry, and many other variables would be expected to be moderators." Such critiques are usually not based on theoretical reasoning or empirical evidence. They are usually just vague speculations and, thus, are not scientifically useful. However, they do occur, and because the number of hypothesized potential moderators is essentially unlimited, it will never be possible to test them all using the second, more effective, procedure. However, the first procedure—the omnibus procedure we have used to test the situational specificity hypothesis—can be used to test all such moderators simultaneously, even those that have not (yet) been named by the critic. If the meta-analysis is based on a *large* group of studies that is heterogeneous across all potential moderators, then a finding that artifacts account for all between-study variance in correlations or effect sizes indicates that none of the postulated moderators are, in fact, moderators. Even when all the variance is not accounted for by artifacts, the remaining variance may often be small, demonstrating that even if some moderators might exist, their effect is far more limited in scope than implied by the critic. In fact, the results may often indicate that the moderators have at best only trivial effects (Schmidt et al., 1993). In this connection, it should always be remembered that the variance remaining after correction for artifacts indicates the *upper bound* of the effects of the moderators. This will almost always be true because, as described in Chapter 5, there will almost always be some artifacts operating to create variance for which no corrections will be possible.

The facts of second-order sampling error and less than perfect "statistical power" in individual meta-analyses point to another reason for the importance of a principle we stated in Chapters 1 and 2. The results of a meta-analysis should not be interpreted in isolation but rather in relation to a broader set of linked findings from other meta-analyses that form the foundation for theoretical explanations. Estimating a particular relationship is only the immediate objective of a meta-analysis; the ultimate objective is to contribute pieces of information that can be fitted into a wider developing mosaic of theory and understanding. However, just as the results of a meta-analysis can contribute to this bigger picture understanding, so also can the resulting bigger picture understanding contribute to the interpretation of particular meta-analysis results. Results of "small" meta-analyses (those based on few studies and small-sample studies) that are inconsistent with the broader cumulative picture of knowledge thereby become suspect, and the credibility of those that are consistent is likewise enhanced. This is the universal pattern of reciprocal causation between data and theory in science.

Some have worried that the inadequate ability of meta-analysis to detect moderators might be an almost insurmountable problem limiting scientific progress (even while admitting that better alternatives to meta-analysis do not appear to be available). The critical difficulty with this argument is that it focuses on single meta-analytic studies. Just as earlier researchers focused on the individual study, failing to realize that single studies cannot be interpreted in isolation, this position focuses on single meta-analyses—in particular, on the sometimes weak ability of single meta-analyses to identify moderators—not seeing that it is the overall pattern of findings from many meta-analyses that is important in revealing the underlying reality.

Consider an example in which the overall pattern of findings was critical. In personnel selection, the theory of situational specificity holds that the true (population) validity of any employment test varies substantially from one organization to another even for highly similar or identical jobs. This is the hypothesis that $S_{\rho}^2 > 0$. In meta-analysis (called validity generalization when used in personnel selection), this hypothesis is tested by determining whether artifacts such as sampling error account for the variation of observed validity coefficients across studies conducted in different organizations on similar jobs using measures of the same ability (e.g., arithmetic reasoning). In the initial validity generalization studies, the average percentage of the observed validity variance accounted for by artifacts was less than 100%. However, these meta-analyses were based on published and unpublished studies from a wide variety of sources and researchers, and we pointed out in all our studies that there were several sources of between-study variance that we could neither control for nor correct for (e.g., programmer errors, transcriptional errors; see Schmidt et al., 1993). When all studies going into a validity generalization analysis are conducted by the same research team, strong efforts can be made to control these sources of errors. In two large-scale, nationwide consortium studies, such efforts were made (Dunnette et al., 1982; Peterson, 1982). In both cases, these studies found that, on average, all variance across settings (i.e., companies) was accounted for by artifacts. The same was found to be true in data from studies conducted in 16 companies by Psychological Services, Inc. (Dye, 1982). Thus, our prediction that improved control of sources of error variance would show that all between-study variance is due to artifacts was borne out. These findings are strong evidence that there is no situational specificity in the validity of employment tests of cognitive ability.

There were more aspects to the pattern of evidence against situational specificity, however. The situational specificity hypothesis predicts that if the situation is held constant and the tests, criteria, and job remain unchanged, validity findings should be constant across different studies conducted in that setting. That is, because the setting is constant, observed validities should be constant because it is differences between settings that are hypothesized to cause differences in observed validities. Meta-analytic principles predict that such observed validities will vary substantially, mostly because of sampling error. We tested these predictions in two studies (Schmidt & Hunter, 1984; Schmidt, Ocasio, Hillery, & Hunter, 1985) and found that observed validities within the same situation varied markedly, disconfirming the situational specificity hypothesis. In the second of these studies, the data from a large-sample validity study ($N = 1{,}455$) were divided into smaller, randomly identical studies (21 studies of $n = 68$ each). Because situational variables were controlled, the specificity hypothesis predicted that all the smaller studies would show the same observed validity. This was not the case, however. Instead, there was great variance among studies in both magnitude of validity and significance level, as predicted by the theory of artifacts, which is the basis of meta-analysis and validity generalization. A key finding was that the variation in validities was as great as that typically found across studies conducted in entirely different settings.

The final piece of evidence that fits into this framework is this: Recent refinements in validity generalization methods have led to the conclusion that published validity generalization studies substantially underestimate the percentage of observed validity variance that is due to artifacts, further undercutting the situational specificity hypothesis. There are three such refinements. First, non-Pearson validity coefficients are removed, because the sampling error formula for Pearson correlations substantially underestimates the sampling error in non-Pearson correlations such as the biserial and the tetrachoric (see Chapter 5). Second, within each meta-analysis, the population observed correlation used in the sampling error formula is estimated by the mean observed validity instead of the individual observed validity from the study at hand. This provides a more accurate estimate of sampling error (see Chapter 5). Third, the problem created by nonlinearity in the range restriction correction (cf. Chapter 5 and Law, Schmidt, & Hunter, 1994a, 1994b) is solved by a new set of computational procedures. Schmidt et al. (1993) applied these improvements in the massive validity database in Pearlman, Schmidt, and Hunter (1980), which consisted of approximately 3,600 validity coefficients from published and unpublished studies from many organizations, researchers, and time periods. Each of these methodological refinements resulted in increases in the percentage of validity variance accounted for and/or smaller estimates of SD_{ρ}. Even in this heterogeneous group of studies, almost all validity variance (nearly 90%) was found to be due to artifacts. This research is discussed in more detail in Chapter 5.

All these pieces of interlocking evidence point in the same direction: toward the conclusion that, for employment tests of cognitive abilities, the situational specificity hypothesis is false. The only conclusion consistent with the total pattern of evidence is that there is no situational specificity (or that situational effects are so tiny that it is reasonable to consider them to be 0; some prefer this latter conclusion, which we regard as scientifically identical).

In some research areas, there may be no related meta-analyses with which one's meta-analytic results can be cross-referenced and checked for consistency. In such cases, one's results should be compared with the broader pattern of general research findings. Where even this is not possible, meta-analyses based on small numbers of studies should indeed be interpreted with caution, even though the meta-analysis provides the most accurate summary possible of existing research knowledge. We stress that, in cases such as this, the problem is created not by meta-analysis methods, but by the limitations of the research literature. These limitations do not have to be permanent. Consider an example. McDaniel, Schmidt, and Hunter (1988a) found that only 15 criterion-related studies had ever been conducted on the validity of the behavioral consistency method of evaluating applicants' past job-related achievements and accomplishments. Based on these 15 studies, mean true validity is estimated at .45 (SD = .10; 90% credibility value = .33; percentage variance accounted for = 82%). The appropriate interpretation of these findings is different from the interpretation that would be appropriate for exactly the same findings based on exactly the same number of studies in a meta-analysis of cognitive ability. There are literally hundreds of meta-analyses of cognitive abilities and job performance to which the latter findings could be cross-referenced to check for consistency. In the case of the behavioral consistency method, there are no other meta-analyses. Further, we have very little information as to precisely what the behavioral consistency procedure measures. For example, there are no reported correlations between cognitive ability test scores and behavioral consistency scores. Behavioral consistency scores are not yet part of a rich, structured, complex, and elaborated network of established knowledge as cognitive abilities are. Therefore, this meta-analysis must stand alone to a much greater extent. We cannot be really certain that the results are not substantially influenced by outliers or by second-order sampling error. (For example, the actual amount of variance due to artifacts may be 100%, or it may be 50%.) For these reasons, McDaniel et al. (1988a) stated that these findings must be considered preliminary and recommended that additional validity studies be conducted, not to estimate "local validities" from local studies for local settings, but to have more studies to combine into the meta-analysis.

There are other areas of research in industrial-organizational psychology completely outside the area of personnel selection where (1) the number of studies now available is small, and (2) there is no elaborated structure of empirical and theoretical knowledge against which the meta-analytic results can be checked. When meta-analytic results have less evidentiary value because the number of individual studies in the meta-analysis is small *and* there is no related structure of empirical and theoretical knowledge against which the meta-analytic results can be checked, the alternative is neither reversion to reliance on the single study nor a return to the narrative review method of integrating study findings; both are vastly inferior to meta-analysis in information yield. The appropriate reaction is to accept the meta-analysis provisionally while conducting (or awaiting) additional studies, which are then incorporated into a new and more informative meta-analysis. During this time, other forms of evidence bearing on the hypothesis in question may appear—forms of evidence analogous to the within-setting studies (Schmidt & Hunter, 1984; Schmidt, Ocasio, et al., 1985) in the area of situational specificity, in that they represent different approaches to the same question. Such evidence then allows the beginning of the construction of the kind of structured pattern of evidence described previously.

Second-Order Meta-Analyses

In the research program described previously, results in the form of percentage variance accounted for were combined across different meta-analyses, in particular, meta-analyses of different abilities used to predict job performance. In cases like this in which the same theoretical considerations apply to a number of meta-analyses, the problem of second-order sampling error can be addressed using a meta-analysis of meta-analyses, or a *second-order meta-analysis*. Validity generalization research on cognitive ability tests is an example. Under the situational specificity hypothesis, the hypothesized situational moderators would be essentially the same for different abilities, and under the alternate hypothesis, all variance would be hypothesized to be artifactual for all abilities. The second-order meta-analysis would involve computing the average percentage of variance accounted for across the several meta-analyses. For example, in a large consortium study conducted by Psychological Services, Inc., in 16 companies, the percentage of variance accounted for by sampling error ranged from about 60% to over 100% for the various abilities examined. The average percentage accounted for across abilities was 99%, indicating that once second-order sampling error was considered, all variance of validities across the 16 companies was accounted for by sampling error for all the abilities studied.

In particular, such a finding indicates that the meta-analyses with less than 100% of the observed variance accounted for are explained as cases of second-order sampling error (specifically, secondary second-order sampling error, as defined later in this chapter). The same is true of meta-analyses with more than 100% of the observed variance accounted for. It should be clear that in conducting a second-order meta-analysis, figures greater than 100% should not be rounded down to 100%. Doing so would obviously bias the mean for these figures, because those that are randomly lower than 100% are not rounded upward.

There is a very important technical issue in second-order meta-analysis: The average percentage of variance accounted for must be computed in a particular way or it will be inaccurate. This technical issue is best illustrated by a study conducted by Spector and Levine (1987).

Spector and Levine (1987) conducted a computer simulation study aimed at evaluating the accuracy of the formula for the sampling error variance of r. In their study, the value of ρ was always 0, so the formula for the sampling error variance of observed rs was $S_e^2 = 1/(N - 1)$. They conducted simulation studies for various values of N, ranging from 30 to 500. The number of observed rs per meta-analysis was varied from 6 to 100. For each combination of N and number of rs, they replicated the meta-analysis 1,000 times and then evaluated the average value of S_e^2/S_r^2 across 1,000 meta-analyses. That is, they focused their attention on the average ratio of variance predicted from the sampling error formula to the average observed variance of the rs across studies. They did not look at $S_r^2 - S_e^2$, the difference between predicted and observed variances. They found that for all numbers of rs less than 100, the ratio S_e^2/S_r^2 averaged more than 1.00. For example, when there were 10 rs per meta-analysis and $N = 75$ in each study, the average ratio was 1.25. Kemery, Mossholder, and Roth (1987) obtained similar results in their simulation study. The smaller the number of rs per meta-analysis, the more the ratio exceeded 1.00. They interpreted these figures as demonstrating that the formula S_e^2 overestimates sampling variance when the number of correlations in a meta-analysis is less than 100. Their assumption was that if the S_e^2 formula were accurate, the ratio S_e^2/S_r^2 would average 1.00.

The Spector-Levine (1987) study was critiqued by Callender and Osburn (1988), who showed that if one assessed accuracy by the difference $S_r^2 - S_e^2$, the sampling error variance formula was shown to be extremely accurate, as had also been demonstrated in their numerous previous simulation studies. There was no bias. They also demonstrated why the average ratio S_e^2/S_r^2 is greater than 1.00 despite the fact that S_e^2 is an unbiased estimate of sampling variance. When the number of correlations in a meta-analysis is small, then, by chance, the S_r^2 will sometimes be very small; that is, by chance, all observed rs will be very similar to each other. Because S_r^2 is the denominator of the ratio, these tiny S_r^2 values lead to very large values for S_e^2/S_r^2, sometimes as large as 30 or more. Furthermore, if S_r^2 should, by chance, be 0, the ratio is *infinitely large*. These extreme values raise the mean ratio above 1.00; the *median* ratio is very close to 1.00. The analysis by Callender and Osburn (1988) fully explains the startling conclusions of Spector and Levine (1987) and demonstrates that the fundamental sampling variance formula for the correlation is, in fact, accurate.

It should be noted that Spector and Levine would not have reached this same conclusion had they used the reciprocal of their ratio. That is, if they had used S_r^2/S_e^2 instead of S_e^2/S_r^2, they would have found that the mean ratio was 1.00. With this reversed ratio, the most extreme possible value is 0 (rather than ∞), and the distribution of ratios is much less skewed. This point has important implications for second-order meta-analyses, that is, meta-analyses of meta-analyses. As noted earlier, second-order meta-analysis is conducted by averaging the percentage of variance accounted for by artifacts over similar meta-analyses. In any given meta-analysis, this percentage is the ratio of artifact-predicted variance (sampling variance plus that due to other artifacts) to the observed variance. One over this ratio is the reversed ratio, S_r^2/S_e^2. In second-order meta-analysis, this reversed ratio should be averaged across studies, and then the reciprocal of that average should be taken. This procedure prevents the upward bias that appeared in the Spector-Levine study and results in an unbiased estimate of the average percentage of variance across the meta-analyses that is due to artifacts. For an example application, see Rothstein, Schmidt, Erwin, Owens, and Sparks (1990).

Meta-analysis has made clear how little information there is in single studies because of the distorting effect of (first-order) sampling error. An examination of second-order sampling error shows that even several studies combined meta-analytically contain limited information about between-study variance (although they provide substantial information about means). Accurate analyses of between-study variance require either meta-analyses based on a substantial number of studies (we have had up to 882; cf. Pearlman et al., 1980) or meta-analyses of similar meta-analyses (second-order meta-analyses). These are the realities and inherent uncertainties of small-sample research in the behavioral and social sciences (or in any other area, e.g., medicine). There is no perfect solution to these problems, but meta-analysis is the best available solution. As the number of studies increases, successive meta-analyses will become increasingly more accurate.

Large-*N* Studies and Meta-Analysis

Some have argued that the need for meta-analysis is merely a consequence of small-sample studies with their typically low levels of statistical power. The argument is made that researchers should conduct only large-sample studies and that such studies, with their higher statistical power, would make meta-analysis unnecessary (see, e.g., Bobko & Stone-Romero, 1998; Murphy, 1997). We question this position for three reasons: (1) It leads to a reduction in the total amount of information available in the literature for the calibration of correlations and effect sizes, (2) it reduces the ability to detect the presence of potential moderators, and (3) it does not eliminate the need for meta-analysis.

Loss of Information. For practical reasons, many researchers cannot obtain large sample sizes, despite their best efforts. If a requirement for large Ns is imposed, many studies that would otherwise be conducted and published will not be conducted—studies that could contribute useful information to subsequent meta-analyses (Schmidt, 1996). This is what has happened in the area of validity studies in personnel psychology. After publication of the study by Schmidt, Hunter, and Urry (1976) showing that statistical power in traditional validity studies averaged only about .50, the average sample sizes of published studies increased from around 70 to more than 300. However, the *number* of studies declined dramatically, with the result that the total amount of information created per year or per decade (expressed as Ns in a meta-analysis) for entry into validity generalization studies decreased. That is, the total amount of information generated in the earlier period from a large number of small-sample studies was greater than that generated in the later period for a much smaller number of large-sample studies. Hence, there was a net loss in ability to calibrate validities.

Reduced Ability to Detect Potential Moderators. The situation described previously creates a net loss of information *even if there are no moderator variables* to be detected, that is, even if $SD_\rho = 0$ in all validity domains studied. Although $SD_\rho = 0$ is a viable hypothesis in the predictor domains of ability and aptitude tests (Schmidt et al., 1993), this hypothesis may not be viable in some other predictor domains (e.g., assessment centers, college grades). And it is certainly not viable in many research areas outside personnel selection. If $SD_\rho = 0$, the total number of studies does not matter; all that matters in determining the accuracy of the VG study is the total N across all studies in the VG analysis. As described previously, this total N has been reduced in recent years. If $SD_\rho > 0$, however, it is critical to have an accurate estimate of SD_ρ. In estimating SD_ρ, N is *the number of studies.* Hence, holding the total N in the meta-analysis constant, a small number of large studies provides a less accurate estimate of SD_ρ than a large number of small studies. A large number of small studies samples a much more numerous array of potential moderators—in fact, each small study samples different potential moderators that might contribute to $SD_\rho > 0$. For example, suppose total N for the VG study is 5,000. If this total N consists of four studies each with $N = 1{,}250$, then the estimate of SD_ρ is based on *only four data points:* four samples from the distribution of ρ. On the other hand, if this total N consists of 50 studies of $N = 100$ each, then the estimate of SD_ρ is based on 50 data points sampled from the ρ distribution—and is therefore likely to be much more accurate. This greatly increases what Cook and Campbell (1976, 1979) called "external validity."

Bobko and Stone-Romero (1998) argued that this same level of precision of estimation for SD_ρ can be obtained with a single large-N study by, in effect, dividing the one large study into many smaller ones. This is unlikely to be true. The single large study reflects the way a single researcher or set of researchers conducted that one study: same measures, same population, same analysis procedures, and so forth. It is unlikely to contain within itself the kinds of variations in the methods and potential moderator variables that are found in 50 independently conducted studies. Another way to see this is to consider the continuum of different types of replications of studies (Aronson, Ellsworth, Carlsmith, & Gonzales, 1990). In a literal replication, the same researcher conducts the new study in exactly the same way as in the original study. In an operational replication, a different researcher attempts to duplicate the original study. In systematic replication, a second researcher conducts a study in which many features of the original study are maintained but some aspects (e.g., types of subjects) are changed. Literal and operational replications contribute in only a limited way to external validity (generalizability) of findings, but systematic replications are useful in assessing the generalizability of findings across different types of subjects, measures, and so on. Finally, in the case of constructive replications, the researcher attempts to vary most of the aspects of the initial study's methods, including subject type, measures, and manipulations. Successful constructive replication adds greatly to the external validity of a finding. Breaking up a large study into "pieces" is similar to the creation of several smaller literal replications and does not contribute much to external validity or generalizability of findings. However, in a meta-analysis of a large number of small studies, the studies in the meta-analysis constitute systematic or constructive replications of each other; that is, many study aspects vary across studies. In these circumstances, a finding of a small SD_ρ (or a small SD_δ) provides strong support for generalizability—that is, this result is strong evidence of external validity of the finding. If the number of studies in the meta-analysis is small, even if each study is a large-sample study, the meta-analysis is weaker because the number of systematic or constructive replications underlying the final results is smaller, and hence, external validity is more questionable. This is another approach to understanding why a large number of small studies is better than a small number of large studies.

Meta-Analysis Still Necessary. Finally, even if all studies conducted are large-sample studies, it is still necessary to integrate findings across studies to ascertain the meaning of the set of studies as a whole. Because meta-analysis is the statistically optimal method for doing this, meta-analysis is still necessary. In concluding that meta-analysis would no longer be necessary, advocates of the position we are critiquing appear to be thinking of the fact that large-N studies, with their high statistical power, will show agreement on statistical significance tests: If there is an effect, all studies should detect it as statistically significant. However, this does not mean meta-analysis is unnecessary. What is important is the estimates of effect size magnitudes. Effect size estimates will still vary across studies, and meta-analysis is still necessary to integrate these findings across studies. Hence, we cannot escape the need for meta-analysis.

We conclude therefore that a movement to a smaller number of larger N studies would not contribute to the advancement of cumulative knowledge in any area of research. In fact, it would be detrimental to knowledge generation and discovery.

Second-Order Sampling Error: Technical Treatment

This section presents a more technical and analytical treatment of second-order sampling error and statistical power in meta-analysis. For the sake of simplifying the presentation, the results are presented for "bare-bones" meta-analyses, that is, meta-analyses for which sampling error is the only artifact that occurs and for which a correction is made. However, the principles apply to the more complete forms of meta-analysis presented in this book.

If a meta-analysis is based on a large number of studies, then there is little sampling error in the meta-analytic estimates. However, if the meta-analysis is based on only a small number of studies, there will be sampling error in the meta-analytic estimates of means and standard deviations. This is called second-order sampling error. There are potentially two kinds of second-order sampling error: sampling error due to incompletely averaged sampling error in the primary studies and sampling error produced by variation in effect sizes across studies. We will call unresolved sampling error from the primary studies "secondary second-order sampling error," or "secondary sampling error" for short. We will call sampling error due to variation in effect sizes primary second-order sampling error." Table 9.1 shows the circumstances in which the two types of second order sampling errors occur. The key to this table is whether we have the homogeneous or heterogeneous case in the population. In the homogeneous case, there is no variance in ρ or δ in the population. In the heterogeneous case, the population values of ρ or δ do vary. As we noted in Chapter 5 and earlier in this chapter in the discussion of fixed- versus random-effects meta-analysis models, the heterogeneous case is much more common in real data. Note that regardless of whether the set of studies is homogeneous or heterogeneous, there is always secondary second-order sampling error. This occurs because, in real data sets, it is never the case that the number of studies is infinite or that all studies have infinite sample size—the only conditions that can completely eliminate secondary second-order sampling error. However, primary second-order sampling error occurs only in the heterogeneous case. That is, when there is variance in ρ or δ, then primary second-order sampling error will be produced by the sampling of particular values of ρ_i or δ_i in individual studies. This cannot happen in the homogeneous case, because different values of ρ or δ cannot be sampled, because there is only a single value of ρ or δ in all studies. Because the homogeneous case is rare in real data, however, there will typically be both kinds of second-order sampling error in real meta-analyses. That is, typical real-world meta-analyses fall into the bottom row of Table 9.1.

For simplicity, the following discussion will be written for analyses of the d statistic, but analyses based on correlations or other statistics are also subject to second-order sampling error when the number of studies is not large. In particular, second-order sampling error for correlations is directly analogous to that for d values.

Consider secondary sampling error. Meta-analytic estimates are averages. Thus, the sampling error in individual studies is averaged across studies. If enough studies are averaged, then the average sampling error effects become exactly computable and, hence, exactly correctable. However, if the number of studies is small, then the average sampling error effects will still be partly random. For example, consider

Table 9.1 Second-order sampling error: Schematic showing when the two types of second-order sampling error occur

	Secondary Second-Order Sampling Error	*Primary Second-Order Sampling Error*
Homogeneous Case ($S_p^2 - 0$; $S_\delta^2 = 0$)	Yes	No
Heterogeneous Case ($S_p^2 > 0$; $S_\delta^2 > 0$)	Yes	Yes

the mean effect size. Ignoring the small bias in the d statistic (see Chapters 7 and 8), the average d for the meta-analysis is

$$\text{Ave}(d) = \text{Ave}(\delta) + \text{Ave}(e) \tag{9.1}$$

If the number of studies is large, then the average sampling error across studies, Ave(e), will equal its population value of 0. That is, if we average across a large number of particular sampling errors, the sampling errors will cancel out exactly and yield an average of 0. If Ave(e) = 0, then

$$\text{Ave}(d) = \text{Ave}(\delta) \tag{9.2}$$

That is, if the average sampling error in the meta-analysis is 0, then the average observed effect size in the meta-analysis is equal to the average population effect size in the meta-analysis. If Ave(e) differs from 0, that is the effect of secondary sampling error.

If secondary sampling error were 0, then the average effect size in the meta-analysis would equal the average population effect size in the studies included in the meta-analysis. The number that we want to know, however, is the average population effect size across the entire research domain. The average effect size in the meta-analysis might differ from the average for the whole domain. If there were no variance in effect sizes across studies (the homogeneous case), then Ave(δ) $= \delta$ for any meta-analysis, and there can be no difference between the mean for the meta-analysis and the mean for the research domain. If there is variation across studies (the heterogeneous case), however, then the mean in the meta-analysis could differ by chance from the mean in the domain as a whole. This is primary second-order sampling error.

If the number of studies is large and if the studies are representative of the research domain, then the average population effect size in the meta-analysis, Ave(δ), will differ little from the average effect size across the research domain. That is, if the number of studies is large, then the Ave(d) value in the meta-analysis will be almost exactly equal to the average across the entire potential research domain. Thus, for a large number of studies, there will be no primary second-order sampling error in the meta-analysis mean.

To summarize, if the number of studies is small, then there will be second-order sampling error in the mean effect size. Ave(d) will differ somewhat from the mean population effect size because the sampling errors in the individual studies will not have an average that is exactly 0 (secondary sampling error) and possibly because of chance variation in the mean population effect size in the meta-analysis (potential primary second-order sampling error). In this section, we will derive a confidence interval to estimate the potential range of second-order sampling error in the meta-analysis mean.

Both the mean (i.e., $\hat{\bar{\rho}}$ or $\hat{\bar{\delta}}$) and the standard deviation (i.e., SD_ρ or SD_δ) estimated in meta-analysis have second-order sampling error, although the exact relationship is more complicated in the case of standard deviations than it is for means. If the number of studies is large, then the variance of the particular sampling errors in the meta-analysis, Var(e), will equal the value predicted from statistical theory. If the number of studies is small, then the observed sampling error variance may differ from the statistically expected value. Similarly, if the number of studies is large, then the variance in the particular effect sizes included in the meta-analysis, Var(δ), will equal the variance for the research domain as a whole. However, if the number of studies is small, then the variance of study population effect sizes in the meta-analysis may differ by chance from the variance of population effect sizes. This can also be stated as follows: If the number of studies is large, then the covariance between effect size and sampling error will be 0, but if the number of studies is small, then the covariance in the meta-analysis may differ by chance from 0.

Let us consider primary second-order sampling error in more detail. One key question is whether there is any primary second-order sampling error. There are two possible cases. First, there is the "homogeneous case" in which the population effect sizes do not differ from one study to the next (i.e., $S_\delta^2 = 0$). Second, there is the "heterogeneous case" where there is variation in population effect sizes across studies (i.e., $S_\delta^2 > 0$). Consider first the case in which the population study effect, δ_i, does not vary across studies. That is, in the homogeneous case, we have

$$\delta_i = \delta \text{ for each study } i \text{ in the domain}$$

As discussed in Chapter 5 and earlier in this chapter, the homogeneous case is probably rare in real data. In the homogeneous case, it is possible to speak of "the" population effect size δ. Because δ_i is the same for each study,

$$\text{Ave}(\delta_i) = \delta \text{ for any set of studies from the domain,}$$

$$\text{Var}(\delta_i) = 0 \text{ for any set of studies from the domain.}$$

The meta-analysis mean observed effect size is

$$\begin{aligned}\text{Ave}(d_i) &= \text{Ave}(\delta_i) + \text{Ave}(e_i)\\ &= \delta + \text{Ave}(e_i) \qquad (9.3)\end{aligned}$$

Thus, the meta-analytic average effect size differs from the effect size δ only to the extent that the average of the sampling errors in the meta-analysis differs from 0. That is, the only second-order sampling error in the mean effect size in the meta-analysis is the secondary sampling error, the sampling error resulting from primary sampling errors that by chance do not average to exactly 0.

In the homogeneous case, the population effect size is constant across studies. Thus,

$$\text{Var}(d_i) = \text{Var}(e_i)$$

If the number of studies were large, then the variance of the particular sampling errors in the meta-analysis would equal the variance predicted by the statistical theory for the research domain as a whole. However, if the particular sampling errors in the meta-analysis have a variance that is different by chance from the domain variance, then that unresolved primary sampling error will not have been eliminated from the meta-analysis. Thus, in the homogeneous case, the only second-order sampling error in the variance of observed effect sizes will be secondary sampling error, that is, unresolved first-order study sampling error.

Now let us consider the heterogeneous case in which population effect sizes *do* differ from one study to the next (i.e., $S_\delta^2 > 0$). The average observed effect size in a meta-analysis is

$$\text{Ave}(d_i) = \text{Ave}(\delta_i) + \text{Ave}(e_i) \tag{9.4}$$

If the number of studies is small, then there can be error in each of the two terms: the average sampling error, $\text{Ave}(e_i)$, and the average population effect size, $\text{Ave}(\delta_i)$. Consider the average sampling error, $\text{Ave}(e_i)$. By chance, the average sampling error for that meta-analysis, $\text{Ave}(e_i)$, is likely to depart from 0 by at least some small amount. That is secondary sampling error. Secondary sampling error always converges to 0 if the number of studies is large enough. However, it is possible for secondary sampling error to be small even if the number of studies is small. If the sample sizes in the primary studies were all very large—an unlikely event in psychological research—the average of the individual sampling errors would be near 0. The average sampling error would then be near 0 even though the number of studies is small.

Now consider the other term in the average effect size, $\text{Ave}(\delta_i)$, the average population effect size for the meta-analysis. If the number of studies is large, then the average population effect size in the meta-analysis will differ little from the average population effect size for the whole research domain. However, if the number of studies is small, then the particular values of δ_i observed in the meta-analysis are only a sample of the effect sizes from the domain as a whole. Thus, by chance, the average effect size in the meta-analysis may differ by some amount from the average effect size for the entire research domain. This departure is primary second-order sampling error. Even if all primary studies were done with an infinite number of subjects (i.e., even if every primary study sampling error e_i were 0), then the particular effect sizes in the meta-analysis need not have an average that is exactly equal to the domain average.

Thus, in the heterogeneous case, both the mean and the standard deviation of population effect sizes in the meta-analysis will depart from the research domain values because the studies observed are only a sample of studies. This is "primary second-order sampling error."

The Homogeneous Case

In defining the word "homogeneity," it is important to distinguish between actual treatment effects and study population treatment effects. There are few studies that are methodologically perfect and, thus, few studies in which the study population treatment effect is equal to the actual treatment effect. In a research domain in which the actual treatment effect is the same for all studies, artifact variation across studies (e.g., varying levels of measurement error in different studies) will produce artifactual differences in study effect sizes. In most current textbooks on meta-analysis, the definition of "homogeneous" is obscured by implicit statistical assumptions. The definition of homogeneity requires that the study population effect sizes be exactly uniform across studies. In particular, most current chi-square homogeneity tests thus assume not only that the actual treatment effect is constant across studies, but also that there is no variation in artifact values (e.g., measurement error) across studies. This assumption is very unlikely to hold in real data.

Most contemporary meta-analyses of experimental treatments have been bare-bones meta-analyses; no correction has been made for error of measurement or variation in strength of treatment, or variation in construct validity, or other artifacts. For a bare-bones meta-analysis, it is very unlikely that the study population effect sizes would be exactly equal for all studies. To have uniformity in the study effect sizes, the studies would not only have to be uniform in actual effect size, but they would have to be uniform in artifact values as well. All studies would have to measure the dependent variable with exactly the same reliability and the same construct validity. All studies would have to have the same degree of misidentification—inadvertent treatment failure—in group identification, and so on. (See the discussion of fixed vs. random meta-analysis models in Chapter 5 and earlier in this chapter; fixed-effects meta-analysis models assume the homogeneous case; see also Chapters 2 and 6.) However, it may be useful in some cases to think of the homogeneous case as an approximation.

For purposes of this exposition of second-order sampling error, we assume homogeneity, and we denote the uniform study effect size by δ. Assume the average sample size to be 50 or more so that we can ignore bias in mean d values. Then, for each study individually, the treatment effect differs from δ only by sampling error. That is,

$$d_i = \delta + e_i \tag{9.5}$$

We then have

$$\text{Ave}(d) = \delta + \text{Ave}(e_i) \tag{9.6}$$

$$\text{Var}(d) = \text{Var}(e_i) \tag{9.7}$$

The average differs from δ only if the average sampling error is not the expected value of 0, that is, only if the number of studies is too low for errors to average out to the expected value (to within rounding error). The variance of observed effect sizes differs from Var(e) only if the variance of sampling errors Var(e_i) differs from the expected variance Var(e). This would not occur for a meta-analysis on a large number of studies. However, the sampling error in the variance estimate ($\hat{S}^2_{\delta}$) is larger than the sampling error in the estimate of the mean ($\hat{\bar{\delta}}$). Thus, in most meta-analyses, the sampling error in the estimate of the variance of effect sizes is much more important than the sampling error in the estimate of the average effect size.

In the homogeneous case, the sampling error in the mean effect size for a bare-bones meta-analysis is obtained from the sampling error equation

$$\bar{d} = \delta + \varepsilon$$

where $\bar{d}$ is the mean effect size and ε is the average sampling error. The distribution of meta-analytic sampling error ε is described by

$$E(\varepsilon) = 0$$

$$\text{Var}(\varepsilon) = \text{Var}(e)/K \qquad (9.8)$$

where K is the number of studies and Var(e) is the average sampling error variance across the studies in the meta-analysis. $\text{Var}(\varepsilon)^{\frac{1}{2}} = SD_{\varepsilon}$. Thus, under the assumption of homogeneity, the confidence interval for the mean effect size in a *bare-bones meta-analysis* is

$$\text{Ave}(d) - 1.96SD_{\varepsilon} < \delta < \text{Ave}(d) + 1.96\,SD_{\varepsilon}$$

(See Chapter 5 for methods of computing this confidence interval when artifacts beyond sampling error are corrected for.)

The sampling error in the estimated variance of effect sizes for a bare-bones meta-analysis is obtained by considering a variance ratio. For a large number of studies, the condition of homogeneity could be identified by computing the following ratio:

$$\text{Var}(d)/\text{Var}(e) = 1$$

For a small number of studies, this ratio will depart from 1 by sampling error. Many writers recommend that a chi-square test be used to assess the extent to which there is variance beyond sampling error variance. Define the statistic Q by

$$Q = K\ \text{Var}(d)/\text{Var}(e)$$

Q is the comparison variance ratio multiplied by the number of studies. Under the assumption of homogeneity, Q has a chi-square distribution with $K - 1$ degrees of freedom. This is the most commonly used "homogeneity test" of contemporary meta-analysis.

The homogeneity test has all the flaws of any significance test. If the number of studies is small, then a real moderator variable must be enormous to be detected by this test. That is, the power of the test is low unless the moderator effect (interaction) is very large (National Research Council, 1992). On the other hand, if the number of studies is large, then any trivial departure from homogeneity, such as departures from artifact uniformity across studies, will suggest the presence of a moderator variable where there may be none. Because of these problems, we recommend against use of the homogeneity test.

The Heterogeneous Case

If the research domain is heterogeneous (i.e., $S_\delta^2 > 0$), then there can be primary second-order sampling error—error due to the fact that the number of studies is not infinite. In a real meta-analysis in the heterogeneous case, there will therefore be two kinds of error: secondary sampling error and primary second-order sampling error. For purposes of discussion, we will focus first on just primary second-order sampling error. To do this, we will make a very unrealistic assumption: We will assume either (1) that all studies are done with infinite size or (2) (which is the same thing) that all study population effect sizes are known. After consideration of the special case, we will return to the realistic case of primary as well as second-order sampling error.

To make primary second-order sampling error clearly visible, let us eliminate primary sampling error. Suppose population effect sizes do vary across studies (i.e., $S_\delta^2 > 0$). The individual study effect size is δ_i. Meta-analysis will compute the average and variance of the study effect sizes in the studies located:

$$\text{Ave}(d) = \text{Ave}(\delta_i)$$

$$\text{Var}(d) = \text{Var}(\delta_i)$$

However, if the number of studies is small, the average population effect size in the studies in the meta-analysis is only a sample average of the population effect sizes across all possible studies in the research domain.

The simplest case of a moderator variable is the binary case, for example, studies done with males versus studies done with females. The statistical description of a binary variable includes four pieces of information: the two values that are taken on by the binary variable and the probability of each value. Denote the two values by X_1 and X_2 and denote the respective probabilities by p and q. Because the sum of probabilities is 1, $p + q = 1$ and, hence, $q = 1 - p$. The mean value is

$$E(X) = pX_1 + qX_2 \tag{9.9}$$

Let D denote the difference between the values; that is, define D by

$$D = X_1 - X_2$$

The variance of the binary variable is

$$\text{Var}(X) = pqD^2 \tag{9.10}$$

Suppose a research domain has a moderator variable such that for 50% of studies the effect size is $\delta = .20$, while for the other 50% of studies the effect size is $\delta = .30$. For the research domain as a whole, the mean effect size is

$$\text{Ave}(\delta) = .50(.20) + .50(.30) = .25$$

The variance is given by

$$\text{Var}(\delta) = pqD^2 = (.50)(.50)(.30 - .20)^2 = .0025$$

Thus, the standard deviation is $SD_\delta = .05$. Consider a meta-analysis with $K = 10$ studies. If the studies are split 5 and 5, then for that meta-analysis the mean effect size would be .25 and the standard deviation would be .05. Suppose, however, the studies by chance are split 7 and 3. The mean would be

$$\text{Ave}(d) = (7/10)(.20) + (3/10)(.30) = .23$$

rather than .25. The variance would be

$$\text{Var}(d) = (7/10)(3/10)(.30 - .20)^2 = (.21)(.01) = .0021$$

instead of .0025. That is, the standard deviation would be .046 rather than .05. These deviations in the mean and standard deviation of effect sizes are primary second-order sampling error, variation due to the fact that the sample of studies has chance variations from the research domain, which is the study population.

How large is primary second-order sampling error? The answer is simple for the mean effect size:

$$\text{Var}[\text{Ave}(\delta)] = \text{Var}(\delta)/K \quad (9.11)$$

The primary second-order sampling error variance of the variance estimate ($\hat{S}_\delta^2$) depends on the shape of the effect size distribution. That discussion is beyond the scope of the present book.

Consider now the case of a real meta-analysis with a small number of heterogeneous studies. There will be both primary and second-order sampling error. For the mean effect size in a bare-bones meta-analysis, each can be computed separately and easily:

$$\begin{aligned} \text{Var}[\text{Ave}(d)] &= \text{Var}[\text{Ave}(\delta)] + \text{Var}[\text{Ave}(e)] \\ &= \text{Var}(\delta)/K + \text{Var}(e)/K \\ &= [\text{Var}(\delta) + \text{Var}(e)]/K \\ &= \text{Var}(d)/K \end{aligned} \quad (9.12)$$

The square root of this quantity is the standard error of $\bar{d}$ and is used to create confidence intervals around $\bar{d}$. This formula holds for whatever set of weights is used in the basic estimation equations (see also Hunter & Schmidt, 2000; Schmidt, Hunter, & Raju, 1988). (Equation [9.12] applies to bare-bones meta-analysis; see Chapter 5 for methods of computing confidence intervals for $\hat{\bar{\delta}}$ or $\hat{\bar{\rho}}$ in the heterogeneous case (random-effects model) when measurement error and other artifacts in addition to sampling error are corrected for.)

The standard error of the standard deviation (or of $\hat{S}_\delta^2$) is much more complex and is beyond the scope of this book (cf. Raju & Drasgow, 2003).

A Numerical Example

Consider the first numerical example presented in Chapter 7:

N	d
100	.01
90	.41*
50	.50*
40	−.10

*Significant at the .05 level.

The meta-analysis using the more accurate formula found the following:

$$T = 280$$
$$K = 4$$
$$\bar{N} = 70$$
$$\text{Ave}(d) = .20$$
$$\text{Var}(d) = .058854$$
$$\text{Var}(e) = .059143$$

Anyone using the chi-square test for homogeneity (which we do not recommend) would calculate the following:

$$Q = K\text{Var}(d)/\text{Var}(e) = 4[.058854/.059143] = 3.98$$

with 3 degrees of freedom. This is far below the value required for statistical significance. Thus (ignoring the low statistical power of this test here), this test suggests the research domain to be homogeneous. Suppose this is, in fact, the case.

If the domain is considered to be homogeneous, then the standard deviation of effect sizes is 0 and need not be estimated. That is, the researcher would apply the fixed-effects meta-analysis model (see Chapter 5 and the discussion earlier in this chapter). Thus, the only second-order sampling error would be the secondary sampling error in the mean effect size. As described earlier, for the homogeneous case, the sampling error in the mean for a bare-bones meta-analysis is given by

$$\text{Var}[\text{Ave}(d)] = \text{Var}(e)/K = .059143/4 = .014786$$

and, thus, the standard error of the mean is .12. The confidence interval for the effect size δ is

$$.20 - 1.96(.12) < \delta < .20 + 1.96(.12)$$
$$-.04 < \delta < .44$$

Thus, the sampling error in this meta-analysis is substantial. We cannot be sure that the effect size is actually positive.

The problem in the previous meta-analysis is the total sample size. A total sample size of 280 would be a small sample size even for a single study. Thus, this meta-analysis can be expected to have considerable sampling error. To make this very explicit, suppose the number of studies was $K = 40$ rather than $K = 4$. The total sample size would then be $T = 2{,}800$, which is far from infinite but still substantial. The sampling error variance would be

$$\text{Var}[\text{Ave}(d)] = \text{Var}(e)/K = .059143/40 = .001479$$

and the standard error would be .04. The confidence interval would be

$$.20 - 1.96(.04) < \delta < .20 + 1.96(.04)$$

$$.12 < \delta < .28$$

Thus, assuming the fixed-effects model and given 40 studies with an average sample size of 70, the average value of δ is known to be positive and the width of the 95% uncertainty interval shrinks from .48 to .16.

If the number of studies were 400, the total sample size would be 28,000 and the confidence interval would shrink to

$$.18 < \delta < .22$$

Thus, under these assumptions, meta-analysis will eventually yield very accurate estimates of effect sizes in all research domains. However, if the average sample size in the primary studies is very small, the number of studies required may be quite large.

The Leadership Training by Experts Example

Consider the leadership bare-bones meta-analysis from Table 7.1 in Chapter 7. Let us illustrate the computation of confidence intervals about those estimates. We cannot assume the homogeneous case here, so we must use Equation (9.12) to compute the sampling error variance of our estimate of the mean. The sampling error variance in the mean effect size is

$$\text{Var}[\text{Ave}(d)] = \text{Var}(d)/K = .106000/5 = .021200$$

and the corresponding standard error is .146. The 95% confidence interval for the mean effect size is thus

$$.20 - 1.96(.146) < \text{Ave}(\delta) < .20 + 1.96(.146)$$

$$-.09 < \text{Ave}(\delta) < .49$$

This is a random-effects standard error and a random-effects confidence interval. Thus, with a total sample size of only 200, the confidence interval for the mean effect size is very wide.

This would also be true, however, for a single study with a sample size of only 200. For a single study with sample size 200 and an observed d of .20, the sampling error variance would be

$$\text{Var}(e) = [199/197]\,[4/200]\,[1 + .20^2/8] = .020304$$

The corresponding standard error would be .142, and the 95% confidence interval would be

$$.20 - 1.96\,(.142) < \delta < .20 + 1.96\,(.142)$$

$$-.08 < \delta < .48$$

The key to accuracy in the estimate of the mean effect size is to gather enough studies to generate a large total sample size.

For this example with a total sample size of 200, the confidence interval for the mean effect size is $-.09 < \text{Ave}(\delta) < .49$. In particular, because the confidence interval extends below 0, we cannot be sure that the mean effect size is positive. On the other hand, it is equally likely to be off in the other direction. Just as the mean effect size might be .00 rather than the observed mean of .20, so with equal likelihood it could be .40 rather than the observed value of .20.

The estimated variation in effect size is very small. Anyone using the homogeneity test would find that the chi-square test for homogeneity yields

$$Q = 5[.106000/.105932] = 5.00$$

with 4 degrees of freedom. This value is far from significant. Thus, the test suggests that there is no variance in population effect sizes at all. However, with only five studies, its power is low.

Assume now that we obtained similar results not for 5 studies but for 500 studies. For 500 studies with an average sample size of 40, the total sample size would be 500(40) = 20,000. There would be little sampling error in the meta-analysis estimates. The sampling error in the mean effect size would be

$$\text{Var}[\text{Ave}(d)] = \text{Var}(d)/K = .106000/500 = .000212$$

and the standard error would be .015. The 95% confidence interval for the mean effect size would be

$$.20 - 1.96(.015) < \text{Ave}(\delta) < .20 + 1.96(.015)$$

$$.17 < \text{Ave}(\delta) < .23$$

The Skills Training Moderator Example

Consider the overall bare-bones meta-analysis of the studies in Table 7.2 of Chapter 7. We have

$$T = 40 + 40 + \cdots = 400$$

$$K = 10$$

$$\bar{N} = T/10 = 40$$

$$\text{Ave}(d) = .30$$

$$\text{Var}(d) = .116000$$

$$\text{Var}(e) = [39/37][4/40][1 + .30^2/8] = .106591$$

$$\text{Var}(\delta) = .116000 - .106591 = .009409$$

$$SD_\delta = .097$$

The estimated standard deviation of effect sizes is .097, which is large relative to the mean of .30. However, the total sample size is only 400. The chi-square test for homogeneity is

$$Q = 10[.116000/.106591] = 10.88$$

with 9 degrees of freedom. This value is not significant. Thus, the chi-square test failed to detect the moderator variable present in this meta-analysis. Remember that with 5 studies in each subset, the total sample sizes are only 200 in each subset meta-analysis. Hence, the statistical power of the chi-square test is even lower than usual.

Because the total sample size is only 400, we should worry about the sampling error in the mean effect size. Because the test for homogeneity is untrustworthy with such small total sample size, we ignore the results of the chi-square test and assume the heterogeneous (random effects) case. The sampling error in the mean effect size is thus

$$\text{Var}[\text{Ave}(d)] = \text{Var}(d)/K = .116000/10 = .011600$$

and the standard error is .108. The confidence interval for the mean effect size is thus

$$.30 - 1.96(.108) < \text{Ave}(\delta) < .30 + 1.96(.108)$$

$$.09 < \text{Ave}(\delta) < .51$$

That is, with a total sample size of 400, there is a large amount of sampling error in the mean effect size.

On the other hand, suppose we obtained these results not with 10 studies but with 1,000 studies. The total sample size would be 1,000(40) = 40,000, and there would be very little sampling error in the mean effect size. The confidence interval for the mean effect size would be

$$.30 - 1.96(.0108) < \text{Ave}(\delta) < .30 + 1.96(.0108)$$

$$.28 < \text{Ave}(\delta) < .32$$

The chi-square test for homogeneity would yield

$$Q = 1{,}000\,[.116000/.106591] = 1{,}088.27$$

with 999 degrees of freedom. This value is statistically significant.

What is the minimum number of studies required for the chi-square test to be significant? In this example, the minimum number of studies is $K = 671$. This shows that the chi-square test has very low power in this example: 671 studies are required for a power of 50%. This example is similar to many real situations in meta-analysis.

The power of the chi-square test depends sharply on the average sample size in the primary studies. In this example, we considered a moderator with effect sizes $\delta = .20$ versus $\delta = .40$ and an average sample size of $N = 40$. The number of studies required for the power to be 50% is $K = 671$. Had the average sample size been $N = 68$, the number of studies required for power of .50 would have been $K = 189$. Had the average sample size been $N = 100$, this number would have been $K = 82$. Had the average sample size been $N = 200$, the minimum number of studies would have been only $K = 17$. Had the average sample size been $N = 236$, the minimum number of studies would have been only $K = 10$. That is, had the sample size in the primary studies been $N = 236$ rather than

$N = 40$, the chi-square test would have been significant for the present example. However, remember that these figures give the number of studies required for statistical power of 50%—an unacceptably low level of power. The number of studies required for power of, say, 90%, is much larger.

The problems of low statistical power of the chi-square test of homogeneity were discussed by the National Research Council (1992) report on meta-analysis. This report recommended that it not be used to decide whether the data are homogeneous. (See the discussion of fixed versus random meta-analysis models in Chapter 5 and earlier in this chapter.) The low power of the chi-square test to detect a moderator variable stands in sharp contrast to the high power for the comparison of the means for the two moderator groups. However, we recommend confidence intervals, not significance tests, in such an analysis. Hence, *precision of estimation*, and not statistical power, becomes the relevant concept.

The Detection of Moderator Variables: Summary

The presence of second-order sampling error in meta-analysis means that under certain conditions it will be difficult to distinguish between sampling error and real variation in the population effect size. How, then, is a moderator variable to be detected? The most common case is the binary moderator. For a binary moderator variable, the research domain can be split into two subdomains so that the mean effect size is different in each subdomain.

In every statistical domain, there is a trade-off between substantive knowledge and statistical precision and power. That is, it is always possible for a clever data analyst to use substantive knowledge about the statistic in question to reduce the effect of sampling error on inferences to be drawn. This is strikingly true of meta-analysis in the case of the binary moderator variable. Consider the substantively extreme cases: the theoretically predicted moderator variable versus the unsuspected moderator variable. The statistical power to detect the theoretically predicted moderator is far higher than the power to detect the unsuspected moderator variable. This was demonstrated in detail in the last edition of this book (Hunter & Schmidt, 1990a, Chap. 9).

Consider the theoretically predicted moderator variable. Because this moderator variable is predicted, it can be coded in the meta-analysis. The test for this moderator variable will be the comparison of subgroup meta-analyses in the two subgroups of studies in the original overall meta-analysis. We recommend that this be done using confidence intervals. The methods for computing such confidence intervals for bare-bones meta-analysis were presented earlier in this chapter and are given in Chapter 5 for more complete methods of meta-analysis.

Consider the unsuspected moderator variable. Because it is unsuspected, it will not be coded in the meta-analysis. Thus, it must be detected in the form of residual variation left after all identifiable artifacts have been controlled. In some current textbooks on meta-analysis, this detection takes on the form of a chi-square test for homogeneity. The leadership training example illustrates the fact that this chi-square test typically has low power. An alternative to the chi-square test is to take the estimated residual standard deviation at face value. Another alternative is to use our 75% rule, discussed earlier in this chapter. However, if the moderator is hypothesized a priori, then one can place confidence intervals around subgroup mean values. This is the most informative statistical analysis in such cases, and this is what we recommend.

Hierarchical Analysis of Moderator Variables

In searching for moderator variables using meta-analysis, some authors have used a partially hierarchical breakdown. First, all studies are included in an overall meta-analysis. The studies are then broken out by one key moderator variable, then they are broken out by another key moderator variable, and so on. The meta-analysis of assessment center validities by Gaugler, Rosenthal, Thornton, and Bentson (1987) is an example of this approach. This type of analysis, however, is not fully hierarchical because the moderator variables are not considered in combination, which can result in major errors of interpretation. These errors are analogous to problems in analysis of variance due to confounding and interaction. Consider the case of two large moderator variables. An analysis of each moderator separately may lead to quite misleading results. In a meta-analysis of the effects of management by objectives (MBO) on productivity by Rodgers and Hunter (1986), the initial analysis suggested two moderator variables: top-level-management commitment and length of time horizon. Their initial analysis suggested that MBO programs with the strong support of top management increased productivity by an average of 40%, while programs without the strong support of top management had little effect. Their initial analysis also suggested that studies based on an assessment period of more than 2 years showed much larger effects than studies based on less than 2 years. However, when the studies were broken down by the two moderator variables together, the effect of time period virtually vanished. Most of the long-term studies were studies with strong top-management commitment, while most of the short-term studies were studies with weak top-management commitment. Thus, the apparent impact of time horizon as a moderator variable was due to the fact that it was confounded with managerial commitment. The difficulty in conducting fully hierarchical moderator analyses in meta-analysis is that there are often too few studies to yield adequate numbers of studies in cells beyond the two-way breakout. This simply means that it is not possible to address all moderator hypotheses at that time. As more studies accumulate over time, more complete moderator analyses can be performed.

The MBO meta-analysis illustrates the potential problems of confounding between moderators, that is, "spurious" (in the language of path analysis) mean differences for one potential moderator produced by real differences on another. Thus, confounding results from the fact that the moderators are correlated. The second problem is potential interaction between moderator variables. Suppose two moderator variables A and B have been found to moderate effect sizes when analyzed separately, and assume the moderator variables are independent (uncorrelated) across studies. Can we then conclude that A and B always moderate effect size? We cannot. Consider an example. Suppose the mean effect size is .30 when *A* is present versus .20 when *A* is absent, and suppose the mean effect size is .30 when *B* is present versus .20 when *B* is absent. Assume that the frequency of *A* is 50% and the frequency of *B* is 50% and that *A* and *B* are independent. Then each of the four cells obtained by considering *A* and *B* together will have a 25% frequency. Consider the mean effect sizes in the following joint breakdown table:

		Moderator B		
		Present	*Absent*	*Ave.*
Moderator *A*	Present	.40	.20	.30
	Absent	.20	.20	.20
	Ave.	.30	.20	.25

Consider the 50% of studies in which moderator *B* is absent. Within those studies, the presence or absence of *A* does not matter; the mean effect size is .20 in either case. Thus, *A* is a moderator variable only for the studies in which *B* is present. The statement that "*A* moderates the effect of *X* on *Y*" is false for the 50% of the studies where *B* is absent. Consider the 50% of studies in which moderator *A* is absent. Within those studies, the presence or absence of *B* does not matter; the mean effect size is .20 in either case. Thus, *B* is a moderator variable only for the studies in which *A* is present. To say "*B* moderates the effect of *X* on *Y*" is false for the 50% of the studies where *A* is absent. This means that *A* and *B* are inextricably linked as moderator variables. Within the 75% of studies in which one or the other is absent, the mean effect size is .20, regardless of whether either variable is present or absent. The only moderating effect is that studies in which both *A* and *B* are present together differ from the other studies.

There is a rule in analysis of variance that states, "If there is an interaction between two or more factors in the design, then interpretation of lower order main effects or interactions may be quite erroneous." This same rule applies to interaction between moderators. If moderators have interacting effects, then the interpretation of separate effects may be erroneous.

If the hierarchical breakdown reveals moderator variables, then the overall analysis without moderator variables is likely to be misleading. If the hierarchical analysis shows that moderator variables are correlated and/or interact, then the analysis of moderator variables separately is likely to be misleading. Thus, if a hierarchical breakdown is presented, it is critical to focus the interpretation solely on the lowest level—the final breakdown of the data.

Consider the partially hierarchical analysis in the meta-analysis of personnel selection validities by Schmitt, Gooding, Noe, and Kirsch (1984). These researchers first pooled correlations across all predictors (biodata, tests, interviews, and more) and all criterion measures (performance ratings, tenure, advancement, etc.). They then broke the data down by predictor and criterion separately, and finally by the two together. The combinatorial breakdown showed a strong interaction between predictor and criterion variables as moderators—as had been found in past analyses. Had they based their conclusions solely on that last analysis, they would have made no error of interpretation. Unfortunately, they based some of their conclusions on the earlier global analyses. For example, they claimed that their meta-analysis yielded results at odds with the comparable meta-analysis done by Hunter and Hunter (1984). However, Hunter and Hunter broke their data down by both predictor variable and criterion variable from the beginning. Thus, the only table in Schmitt et al. comparable to the analysis of Hunter and Hunter is their final table, the combinatorial breakdown. There is no contradiction between their results in that analysis and that of Hunter and Hunter (1984). This was brought out in a side-by-side presentation in Hunter and Hirsh (1987) that showed the analyses to be in agreement.

We have no fundamental objection to a hierarchical presentation of a meta-analysis. However, it is important to avoid two common errors in this procedure. First, many studies do not complete the analysis. If there are two large moderator variables, it is critical to consider them together and not just separately. Second, it is critical to focus the main interpretation of the data on the final breakdown and not on the earlier potentially confounded global averages.

The analysis of multiple moderator variables separately will be correct only if one makes two assumptions: One must assume that (1) the moderator variables are independent and (2) the moderator variables are additive in their effects. In the MBO analysis of Rodgers and Hunter (1986), the commitment and time moderator variables were correlated across studies. Thus, the large difference due to the commitment variable produced a "spurious" mean difference between studies of different time lengths. If the two potential moderator variables had been independent, there could have been no spurious effect for time produced by commitment. The *AB* combination example showed that interactive moderators must always be considered together to generate correct conclusions.

If a fully hierarchical analysis is presented, it is critical to base conclusions on the highest level of interaction. Schmitt et al. (1984) made an error of interpretation because they went back to an analysis with confounded interactions for one of their conclusions. Finally, it is important to recognize that one often will not have enough studies to conduct a fully hierarchical moderator analysis. If the number of studies in the cells of the fully hierarchical analysis is very small, the conclusions about moderators can only be tentative. Firmer conclusions must await the accumulation of a larger number of studies.

Exercise 9.1

Second-Order Meta-Analysis

This exercise is based on the data used in the exercise at the end of Chapter 4. That exercise required you to conduct separate bare-bones meta-analyses for each of six tests. This results in an estimate of the percentage of variance accounted for by sampling error for each test. These are the first set of figures needed for this exercise. We hope you have retained them.

These data meet the requirements for a second-order meta-analysis, as described in this chapter. That is, the six meta-analyses are very similar substantively, and there is no reason to believe that there are different nonartifactual sources of variance (i.e., moderators) for the different tests.

Conduct a second-order meta-analysis across these six tests using the methods described in this chapter.

What is the average percentage of variance accounted for by sampling error across these six tests? What is your interpretation of this finding?

In the exercise at the end of Chapter 4, you also computed the percentage of variance accounted for by *all* artifacts—sampling error plus the other artifacts. This was computed not as part of the bare-bones meta-analysis but as part of the full meta-analyses, which corrected for measurement error and range restriction, as well as for sampling error. There were two such meta-analyses—one correcting for direct and one correcting for indirect range restriction. Conduct a separate second-order meta-analysis for each of these sets of percentage of variance figures.

Are these values different from those computed earlier based only on sampling error variance? Why is this difference in this particular set of data not larger than it is? What is your interpretation of these values?

10

Cumulation of Findings Within Studies

It is often possible to obtain more than one correlation or estimate of effect size from within the same study. Should these estimates be included in the meta-analysis as independent estimates? Or should they be combined somehow within the study so that only one value is contributed? There is no single answer to these questions because there are several different kinds of replications that can take place within studies. This chapter surveys the most frequent cases.

Many single studies have replication of observation of a relationship within the study. Thus, there can be cumulation of results within, as well as across, studies. However, the method of cumulation depends on the nature of the replication process used in the study. Three kinds of replication will be considered here: fully replicated designs, conceptual replication, and analysis of subgroups.

Fully Replicated Designs

A fully replicated design occurs in a study if that study can be broken into parts that are conceptually equivalent but statistically independent. For example, if data are gathered at several different organizations, then statistics calculated within organizations can be regarded as replicated across organizations. The outcome measures from each organization are statistically independent and can be treated as if they were values from different studies. That is, the cumulation process for these values is the same as that for cumulation across entirely different studies. This is the statistical definition of independence: If statistics (e.g., rs or d values) are computed on different samples, then their sampling errors cannot be correlated. Some writers go further and state that, even if the samples are different, the studies are not independent because they were all conducted by the same researcher, who may have biases that could have affected the results of all three studies. This is not the typically accepted definition of independence and is certainly not the definition of statistical independence. Also, this concept of independence is subject to being carried to extremes. For example, one could contend that the studies included in a meta-analysis were not independent because they were all carried out during one time period (e.g., 1980–2002) or because they were all conducted in English-speaking countries. That is, this concept of independence is so vaguely defined that it is subject to indefinite expansion. In this chapter, we focus only on the statistical concept of independence.

Conceptual Replication

Conceptual replication occurs within a study when more than one observation that is relevant to a given relationship is made on each subject. The most common example is replicated measurement, the use of multiple indicators to assess a given variable: for example, the use of several scales to assess job satisfaction; the use of training grades, selection test scores, and job knowledge to assess cognitive ability for work performance; or the use of peer ratings, supervisor ratings, and production records to assess job performance. The second most common example is observation in multiple situations. For example, a participant in an assessment center may be asked to show problem-solving skills in Task A, Task B, and so on. The observation in the various situations can be regarded as replicated measurements of problem-solving skills.

The replication within the study can be used in either of two ways: (1) Each conceptual replication can be represented by a different outcome value, and these separate outcome values can either be cumulated within the study or contributed as a set to a larger cumulation, or (2) the measurements can be combined, and the resulting single-outcome measure can be used to assess the relationship in question.

Suppose three variables are used as indicators of job performance: peer rating, supervisor rating, and a job sample measure. Any potential test could then have three correlations that are conceptually all validity coefficients: the correlation between test and peer rating, the correlation between test and supervisor rating, and the correlation between test and job sample measure. These values could contribute to a larger cumulative study in two ways: (1) The three correlations could be contributed as three separate values, or (2) the three correlations could be averaged and the average could be contributed as the one value representing the study.

If the set of correlations is contributed to the larger study, then there is a problem for the cumulation formulas presented in Parts II and III of this book. These formulas assume that the values used are statistically independent of each other. This is guaranteed if the values come from different studies, but is only true in the present example if the correlations between peer rating, supervisor rating, and job sample test are all 0 (as population values for that study), which is impossible if the measures are even approximately equivalent measures, as they are assumed to be. If the number of correlations or d values contributed by each study is small in comparison to the total number of correlations or d values, then there is little error in the resulting cumulation. However, if a very large number of values are contributed from one small study, then the result can be undercorrection for sampling error in the meta-analysis.

To the extent that a meta-analysis contains groups of correlations or d values that come from the same study samples, the formulas for sampling error presented in Chapters 3 and 7 will underestimate the sampling error variance component in the observed variance of effect sizes (S_r^2 or S_d^2). This means that there will be an undercorrection for sampling error and that the final estimate of S_ρ^2 or S_δ^2 will be too large. To this extent, the obtained meta-analysis results will be conservative; that is, they will underestimate the degree of agreement (or generalizability) across studies.

One way to understand how violations of statistical independence cause sampling error variance to be larger than predicted by sampling error variance formulas is as follows. If sampling errors are uncorrelated across two independent samples (i.e., $r_{e_1 e_2} = 0$), then

$$\text{Total sampling variance } = \sum S_{e_i}^2 = S_{e_1}^2 + S_{e_2}^2 \tag{10.1}$$

$$\bar{S}_e^2 = \frac{\sum S_{e_i}^2}{k} \tag{10.2}$$

where k is the number of independent samples or studies ($k = 2$ here) and $\bar{S}_e^2$ is the size of the sampling error component in the variance of observed rs or ds in the meta-analysis (S_r^2 or S_d^2).

If the r or d values are computed on the same sample, however, sampling errors *are* correlated (i.e., $r_{e_1 e_2} > 0$). Then

$$\text{Total sampling variance} = S_{e_1}^2 + S_{e_2}^2 + 2r_{e_1 e_2} S_{e_1} S_{e_2} \tag{10.3}$$

and

$$\bar{S}_e^2 = [S_{e_1}^2 + S_{e_2}^2 + 2r_{e_1 e_2} S_{e_1} S_{e_2}]/2 \tag{10.4}$$

The standard formulas for sampling error variance are Equations (10.1) and (10.2) to estimate the amount of sampling error variance in S_r^2 or S_d^2. When independence is violated, however, the actual amount of sampling error is the larger amount given by Equation (10.4). Hence, sampling error is underestimated. Note that it is not possible to estimate the correlation $r_{e_1 e_2}$, and so it is not possible to avoid the underestimation for sampling error by just using Equation (10.4) in conducting the meta-analysis.

In our own earlier research on the validity of ability tests in personnel selection, whenever it was the ability (e.g., verbal ability) that had multiple measures, we included the individual correlations in the meta-analysis. Most studies contained only one measure of each ability and, thus, contributed only one correlation to the meta-analysis for that ability. A minority of studies had two measures (e.g., two measures of spatial ability). Therefore, this decision rule contributed only a slight conservative bias to our estimates of SD_ρ. Whenever a study contained multiple measures of job performance, these measures were combined into a composite as described later; if that was not possible, then the correlations were averaged and only the average correlation was entered into the meta-analysis. This decision rule ensured complete independence on the job performance side of the correlation.

It should be noted that while violations of the assumption of independence affect (inflate) the observed variance of effect sizes across studies, such violations have no systematic effect on the mean d or mean r values in a meta-analysis. Thus, violations of independence cause no bias in estimates of mean values in meta-analysis. However, the methods described in this book focus strongly on estimating the true (population) variance (and *SD*) of study effects. The accuracy of estimates of SD_δ and SD_ρ is important because these estimates play a critical role in the interpretation of the results of the meta-analysis. Because violations of independence create an upward bias in estimates of SD_δ and SD_ρ, the question of statistical independence in the data deserves careful attention in applications of our meta-analysis methods.

If the average correlation is used to represent the study, then there is no violation of the independence assumption. However, what are we to use for the sample size of the average correlation? If we use the total number of observations that go into the average correlation (i.e., the product of sample size times the number of correlations averaged), then we greatly underestimate the sampling error because this assumes that we have averaged independent correlations. On the other hand, if we use the sample size of the study, then we overestimate the sampling error because the average correlation will have less sampling error than a single correlation. In most studies, there is much less error in assuming the simple sample size for the average correlation.

There is another potential problem with the average correlation. In those rare cases in which there is a strong moderator variable, that is, cases in which there is a large, real, corrected standard deviation across studies, the moderator variable may vary within studies as well as across studies. In such a case, the average correlation would be conceptually ambiguous. For example, there is strong evidence that measures of ability have higher true score correlations with job sample measures than with supervisory ratings (Hunter, 1983f; Nathan & Alexander, 1988). Identification of this difference in any meta-analysis would require that these two measures not be combined.

Conceptual Replication and Confirmatory Factor Analysis

Multiple measurements can be used to generate correlations with smaller measurement error or to estimate correlations corrected for measurement error (Hunter & Gerbing, 1982). The crucial question is the extent to which measures believed to be equivalent are, in fact, measures of the same underlying trait. If the replicated measures are equivalent in the sense of reliability theory (i.e., randomly equivalent measures; Nunnally & Bernstein, 1994), then measurement error can be reduced by using a composite score formed by averaging the standard scores (or by just adding the raw scores if the standard deviations are all about the same). If the correlations for this composite score are corrected for attenuation, then the bias created by measurement error is eliminated altogether. In the case of the items in a scale, the composite score is the test score, and the true score is the underlying factor measured without error.

In confirmatory factor analysis, the same distinction is made in terms of the language of factor analysis. If the analysis is done "with 1s in the diagonal," then the factor is the composite score. If the analysis is done "with communalities," then the factor is the underlying trait measured without error. If the alternate indicators are equivalent in the sense of reliability theory (i.e., they differ only by measurement error), then the computations of confirmatory factor analysis are identical to those of reliability theory. However, confirmatory factor analysis is valid in certain situations in which reliability theory fails. Hunter and Gerbing (1982) noted that if the indicator variables define a general factor, and if the specific factors are irrelevant to the other variables being considered, then, at the level of second-order factor analysis, the indicator variables satisfy the assumptions of reliability theory, and confirmatory factor analysis generates the correct correlation between the general factor that was intended to be measured and the other variable. For example, it is quite likely that peer rating, supervisor rating, and job sample test each measure specific factors in addition to the general factor of job performance. However, if these specific factors are uncorrelated with each other and with the selection test (independent variable), then confirmatory factor analysis will generate a correct correlation between the test and job performance. However, in the case of second-order analysis, the correction for attenuation is not made with the reliability of the composite score, but with a slightly smaller number. The reliability of the composite is given by Mosier's (1943) formula (discussed later in this chapter) with indicator reliabilities in the numerator diagonal, whereas the equivalent correction formula for second-order analysis is Mosier's formula with communalities in the numerator diagonal. Thus, second-order factor analysis correctly treats the specific factors as error.

There is a strong algebraic relationship between the average correlation and the correlation for the composite score. Let the indicator variables be denoted by $y_1, y_2, \ldots, y_n$, let the composite score be denoted by Y, and let the other variable be denoted by x. Let $\bar{r}_{xy}$ be the average correlation between the individual indicators and x; that is, let $\bar{r}_{xy}$ be the average of r_{xy_1}, r_{xy_2}, and so on. Let $\bar{r}_{yy}$ be the average correlation between the indicator variables; that is, let $\bar{r}_{yy}$ be the average of $r_{y_1y_2}, r_{y_1y_3}, r_{y_2y_3}$, and so on. Let $\bar{c}_{yy}$ be the average covariance between the indicators; that is, let $\bar{c}_{yy}$ be defined by

$$\bar{c}_{yy} = \frac{1 + (n-1)\bar{r}_{yy}}{n} \tag{10.5}$$

Then the relationship between the average correlation $\bar{r}_{xy}$ and the composite score correlation r_{xY} is given by

$$r_{xY} = \frac{\bar{r}_{xy}}{\sqrt{\bar{c}_{yy}}} \tag{10.6}$$

The number $\bar{r}_{yy}$ is a fraction; $0 \leq \bar{r}_{yy} \leq 1$. The number $\bar{c}_{yy}$ is a weighted average of $\bar{r}_{yy}$ and 1 and, hence, is between them; that is,

$$0 \leq \bar{r}_{yy} \leq \bar{c}_{yy} \leq 1 \tag{10.7}$$

Because $\bar{c}_{yy}$ is a fraction, its square root is also a fraction and it lies between $\bar{c}_{yy}$ and 1; that is,

$$0 \leq \bar{r}_{yy} \leq \bar{c}_{yy} \leq \sqrt{\bar{c}_{yy}} \leq 1 \tag{10.8}$$

To divide $\bar{r}_{xy}$ by a fraction is to increase its size. Thus, for positive correlations, we have

$$r_{xY} \geq \bar{r}_{xy} \tag{10.9}$$

That is, the composite score correlation is always equal to or larger in size than the average correlation. It is the composite correlation whose sampling error is given by the conventional formula with the study sample size. That is, entering r_{xY} and the study N into the sampling error variance formula for the correlation yields the sampling error variance of r_{xY}. Thc standard error of the average correlation is smaller than that by exactly the multiplicative factor $\sqrt{\bar{c}_{yy}}$. Thus, the composite score correlation enters into a larger cumulation in exact accordance with the assumptions about sampling error made by the cumulation formulas in Chapters 2 to 4, while the average correlation does not. In fact, the sampling error variance of $\bar{r}_{xy}$ cannot even be computed unless one can first compute $\bar{c}_{yy}$. If the information needed to compute $\bar{c}_{yy}$ is available, however, then one can compute r_{yX}. If the conceptual assumptions of the study are correct, then the composite score correlation r_{xY} is also more accurate numerically.

From a conceptual point of view, the number we really want is the correlation for the composite without measurement error, that is, the correlation obtained from confirmatory factor analysis with communalities. This number will be larger than the composite score correlation (and, hence, larger than the average correlation). However, a corrected correlation does not have the same standard error as an uncorrected correlation; the standard error is larger by the same multiplicative factor of correction (as shown in Chapter 3). If the correlations are corrected for attenuation or generated using confirmatory factor analysis with communalities, then the cumulative variance should be corrected using the formulas given in Chapter 3.

Consider an example. Suppose peer rating, supervisor rating, and a job sample test are each correlated .60 with each other. Then

$$\bar{r}_{yy} = .60, \quad \bar{c}_{yy} = .73, \quad \sqrt{\bar{c}_{yy}} = .86,$$

and, hence,

$$r_{xY} = 1.16\bar{r}_{xy}$$

That is, the composite score correlation would be about 16% larger than the average correlation. If Y_t is job performance measured without error, then the trait correlation r_{xY_t} is related to the others by

$$r_{xY_t} = \frac{r_{xY}}{\sqrt{r_{yy}}} = 1.10r_{xY} = 1.28\bar{r}_{xy}$$

where r_{yy} is the "reliability" of the composite score calculated using Mosier's (1943) formula (see Equation [10.15] later in this chapter) with communalities in the numerator diagonal (which is also equal to coefficient alpha [Cronbach, 1951] calculated using the correlations between the scales). (Here $r_{yy} = .82$.) Thus, the correlation for actual job performance is 10% larger than the composite score correlation, and 28% larger than the average correlation. If we correct for measurement error in x (the independent variable), the correlation will again increase somewhat.

Conceptual Replication: An Alternative Approach

Because the methods of confirmatory factor analysis may not be familiar to all readers, it is worthwhile noting that the correlation of a variable with the sum of other variables can be computed using more familiar formulas for the correlation of variables with composites (Nunnally, 1978, Chap. 5). The basic formula for the Pearson correlation between any two variables a and b is

$$r_{ab} = \frac{\text{Cov}(a, b)}{SD_a SD_b} \tag{10.10}$$

If one variable, say b, is a composite, then we need only replace SD_b with the expression for the standard deviation of a composite and replace Cov(a, b) with the expression for the covariance of a variable with a composite. Suppose we want to compute r_{xY}, where x is a single variable and Y is a composite that is the sum of the measures y_1, y_2, and y_3. Then, if the y_i measures are all in z-score form (i.e., if $SD = 1$ for all y_is), the value S_Y^2, the variance of the composite, is merely the sum of all the values in the intercorrelation matrix of the y_i measures. This sum is denoted by $\underline{1}'R_{yy}\underline{1}$ in matrix algebra, where R_{yy} is the correlation matrix among the y_i measures (including the 1.00s in the diagonal). The $\underline{1}$s are vectors that indicate that values in R_{yy} are to be summed. The square root of this value is SD_Y, that is, $(\underline{1}'R_{yy}\underline{1})^{1/2} = SD_Y$.

The covariance of a variable with a composite is the sum of the covariances of the variable with each of the component measures of the composite. In our example, this would be $\text{Cov}(xy_1) + \text{Cov}(xy_2) + \text{Cov}(xy_3)$. Because all variables are standardized, however, this is $r_{xy_1} + r_{xy_2} + r_{xy_3}$. This is denoted in matrix algebra as $\underline{1}'r_{xy_i}$. Thus, we have

$$r_{xY} = \frac{\underline{1}'r_{xy_i}}{SD_x\sqrt{\underline{1}'R_{yy}\underline{1}}} = \frac{\sum r_{xy_i}}{(1)\sqrt{n + n(n-1)\bar{r}_{y_iy_j}}} \tag{10.11}$$

where $\bar{r}_{y_iy_j}$ is the average off-diagonal correlation in the correlation matrix R_{yy}.

Suppose, for example, a measure of perceptual speed (x) were correlated in the same sample of people with three measures of job performance: supervisory ratings of job performance ($r = .20$), peer ratings of job performance ($r = .30$), and records of output ($r = .25$). Suppose the correlations among the job performance measures are reported and the average of these is .50, that is, $\bar{r}_{y_iy_j} = .50$. Then

$$r_{xY} = \frac{(.20 + .30 + .25)}{\sqrt{3 + 3(2)(.50)}} = .31$$

The obtained value of .31 is larger than the average r ($\bar{r}_{xy_i} = .25$), as expected. Also, the sampling error variance of r_{xY} is known; it is $S_e^2 = (1-.31^2)^2/(N-1)$. If the meta-analysis is to be based on artifact distributions (see Chapter 4), this value of .31 should be entered directly into the meta-analysis. However, the reliability of the composite measure of job performance should be computed, using the methods discussed below, and entered into the artifact distribution for reliabilities. If the meta-analysis is to be based on correlations individually corrected for unreliability (see Chapter 3), then the correction for unreliability (and range restriction if appropriate) should be applied to the .31 value before it is entered into the meta-analysis. In theoretically oriented meta-analyses, r_{xY} would also be corrected for unreliability in x (using the appropriate estimate of r_{xx}).

The formula given previously assumes that the y_i measures are to be weighted equally. All weights are unity and all variables are in standard score form; therefore, each y_i measure has the same effect on the final Y composite. If you make the calculations with the variance-covariance matrix instead of the correlation matrix, the y_i measures will be weighted by their standard deviations. If you make the calculations with the correlation matrix, you can still weight the y_i measures differentially, by assigning unequal weights instead of unity weights. For example, suppose that, based on construct validity considerations, you decide to assign twice as much weight to production records as to supervisory ratings and three times as much weight to peer ratings as to supervisory ratings. This leads to the weight vector $w' = [1\ 3\ 2]$. The correlation between the independent variable x and the weighted composite Y is then

$$r_{xY_2} = \frac{\underline{w}'\, r_{xyi}}{\sqrt{\underline{w}'\, R_{yy}\underline{w}}} = \frac{[1\ 3\ 2]\begin{matrix}.20\\.30\\.25\end{matrix}}{\sqrt{[1\ 3\ 2]\begin{matrix}1.00 & .50 & .50\\ .50 & 1.00 & .50\\ .50 & .50 & 1.00\end{matrix}\begin{bmatrix}1\\3\\2\end{bmatrix}}}$$

$$= \frac{(1)(.20)\ +\ (3)(.30)\ + 2(.25)}{\sqrt{[3.5\ 4.5\ 4.0]\begin{bmatrix}1\\3\\2\end{bmatrix}}} = \frac{1.6}{5.0} = .32$$

Thus, the weighted correlation is .32, while the unweighted correlation was .31. This is a typical result; when measures in a composite are substantially positively correlated, weighting usually has little effect on the correlation of the composite with other variables. If some measures in a composite have higher construct validity, however, differential weighting should be considered. The weighted mean correlation is

$$\bar{r}_w = \frac{(1)(.20) + (3)(.30) + 2(.25)}{1 + 3 + 2} = .26$$

Again, the mean correlation is smaller than the composite correlation.

Sometimes a study sample will have multiple measures of both the independent and dependent variables. If the correlations among all measures are given, you can compute the correlation between the sum of the independent variable measures (composite X) and the sum of the dependent variable measure (composite Y). The measure within each composite can be weighted equally or differentially. If the k measures in the independent variable composite are $x_1, x_2 \ldots x_i \ldots x_k$ and the measures in the dependent variable composite are $y_1, y_2 \ldots y_i \ldots y_m$, then the correlation between the two composites when all variables are equally weighted is

$$r_{XY} = \frac{\underline{1}' R_{xy} \underline{1}}{\sqrt{\underline{1}' R_{xx} \underline{1}} \sqrt{\underline{1}' R_{YY} \underline{1}}} \tag{10.12}$$

Note that the first term in the denominator is SD_X and the second is SD_Y; these are the SDs of the two composites. R_{xy} is the matrix of cross-correlations between the x_i measures and the y_i measures. The sum of these correlations is the covariance of composite X with composite Y. Thus, this formula corresponds to the fundamental formula for the Pearson r, that is,

$$r_{XY} = \frac{\mathrm{Cov}(X, Y)}{SD_X SD_Y}$$

The measures contained in each composite can also be differentially weighted. If the vector of (unequal) weights to be applied to the y_i is $\underline{w}$, as before, and the vector of weights for the x_i measures is $\underline{v}$, then the correlation between the two weighted composites is

$$r_{XY} = \frac{\underline{v}' R_{xy} \underline{w}}{\sqrt{\underline{v}' R_{xx} \underline{v}} \sqrt{\underline{w}' R_{YY} \underline{w}}} \tag{10.13}$$

If the measures in one composite are to be weighted unequally, but not the measures in the other composite, then the differential weights can be replaced by a vector of 1s for the composite whose measures are to be equally weighted. For example, if the x_is are to be equally weighted, then $\underline{v}$ should be replaced by 1.

The formulas for the correlation of variables with composites and composites with other composites can often be used to compute a better estimate of the correlation from a study with conceptual replications. Entering these correlations into the meta-analysis instead of the individual measure correlations, or the mean r, improves the precision of the meta-analysis. We have used these formulas repeatedly in our work; typically the composite correlations can be computed with a hand calculator when one is reading and coding data from the study. These formulas are also useful in data interpretation in general. For example, suppose you are reading a journal research report that employs three measures of job satisfaction that are all correlated with a measure of organizational commitment. It may be clear that the best measure of job satisfaction would be the sum of the three measures. If the study reports the correlations among measures, you can use the formulas in this section to quickly compute the correlation between the job satisfaction composite and the organizational commitment measure, thus extracting an important piece of information not reported by the study's authors. If the study does not report the correlations among the measures, you can often get estimates of these correlations from other studies and use these to compute the composite correlation; McDaniel, Schmidt, and Hunter (1988a) presented an example of this. You can also check reported research for errors. If the study reports correlations for composites, these rs should be as large or larger than the rs for individual measures. If they are not, that indicates an error in the reported results.

If you compute composite correlations, then you should compute the reliability of the composite measure. If you are using the meta-analysis procedure that corrects each correlation individually (see Chapter 3), you should use this reliability to correct the correlation computed. If you are using artifact distribution meta-analysis (see Chapter 4), then you should enter this reliability into the distribution of reliabilities.

The Spearman-Brown formula can be used to compute the reliability of the composite, based on the $\bar{r}$ among the measures in the composite. In our example, this would be

$$r_{yy} = \frac{n\bar{r}_{yy}}{1 + (n - 1)\bar{r}_{yy}}$$

$$= \frac{3(.50)}{1 + (3 - 1)(.50)} = .75 \qquad (10.14)$$

An identical estimate of reliability would be produced by Cronbach's alpha. The corrected correlation is then

$$r_{xY_T} = \frac{.31}{\sqrt{.75}} = .36$$

In most meta-analyses, one would correct for unreliability in the x measure also. This would further increase the correlation.

Use of Spearman-Brown or alpha reliabilities assumes that the specific factors measured by each component measure in the composite are unrelated to the construct measured by the other variable (in this case x, a measure of perceptual speed) and can be treated as random error. In our example, this would be the assumption that the specific factors in supervisory ratings, peer ratings, and production records are unrelated to perceptual speed (as well as unrelated to each other). It also assumes that these specific factors are not part of true job performance, that is, are irrelevant to the construct of job performance. If either or both of the assumptions appear to be implausible, then each measure in the composite may be measuring some aspect of actual or true job performance that is not measured by the other y_i measures. If so, then a different measure of reliability must be used, one that treats specific factor variance as true variance. The appropriate formula is given by Mosier (1943):

$$r_{yy} = \frac{\underline{1}'(R_{yy} - D + D_{\text{rel}})\,\underline{1}}{\underline{1}'\,R_{yy}\,\underline{1}} \qquad (10.15)$$

The denominator of this formula is the total variance of the composite, as explained earlier. Because reliability is always the ratio of true to total variance, the numerator is true variance. The matrix D is a k-by-k diagonal matrix with 1s in the diagonal (all other values are 0). Subtracting D from R_{yy} just takes all the 1s out of the diagonal of R_{yy}. Then adding the matrix D_{rel} (also k by k) back in replaces all the diagonal values with the reliabilities of the individual y_i measures. D_{rel} is a diagonal matrix that contains only these reliabilities.

Suppose in our example the reliability of the y_is is as follows:

$$\text{Supervisory ratings: } r_{y_1 y_1} = .70$$

$$\text{Peer ratings: } r_{y_2 y_2} = .80$$

$$\text{Production records: } r_{y_3 y_3} = .85$$

Then the Mosier reliability is

$$r_{yy} = \frac{\underline{1}' \left(\begin{bmatrix} 1.00 & .50 & .50 \\ .50 & 1.00 & .50 \\ .50 & .50 & 1.00 \end{bmatrix} - \begin{bmatrix} 1 & 0 & 0 \\ 0 & 1 & 0 \\ 0 & 0 & 1 \end{bmatrix} + \begin{bmatrix} .70 & 0 & 0 \\ 0 & .80 & 0 \\ 0 & 0 & .85 \end{bmatrix} \right) \underline{1}}{\underline{1}' \begin{bmatrix} 1.00 & .50 & .50 \\ .50 & 1.00 & .50 \\ .50 & .50 & 1.00 \end{bmatrix} \underline{1}}$$

$$r_{yy} = \frac{.70 + .80 + .85 + 6(.50)}{3 + 6(.50)}$$

$$r_{yy} = \frac{5.35}{6.00} = .89$$

Because the Mosier reliability considers specific factor variance as true variance, the reliability estimate is larger than our Spearman-Brown estimate of .75. Therefore, the correlation corrected for unreliability is smaller:

$$r_{xY_T} = \frac{.31}{\sqrt{.89}} = .33$$

This value is 8% smaller than the previous value of .36. Thus, you should give careful consideration to the question of whether specific factors should be treated as random error variance or true construct variance. In general, the larger the number of measures contained in a composite, the less likely it will be that specific factor variance should be treated as true variance. However, the final answer depends on the definition and theory of the construct being measured, and so no general answer can be given. In many cases, however, theory does provide fairly clear answers. For example, verbal ability may be *defined* as what different measures of verbal ability have in common, thus implying that specific factor variance is error variance. Other constructs, for example, job satisfaction and role conflict, are often defined theoretically in the same way. In most cases that we have encountered, specific factor variance should be treated as measurement error.

Analysis of Subgroups

For many, it has now become routine to compute correlations separately by race and sex, even though there is usually no reason to believe that either will act as a moderator. This practice stems in part from a common confusion between additive and moderator effects. For example, some have hypothesized that the technology of an organization sets limits on its managerial philosophy. For example, large-scale manufacturing requires rigid coordination of work and, hence, provides fewer opportunities for power sharing with subordinates. This leads to the prediction that the level of consideration will be lower in manufacturing organizations. Even if this is true, however, within such organizations it may still be true that those who bring workers into their decision-making structure will have higher production. Thus, the *correlation* need not be lower in such plants even though the mean is.

If there is reason to believe that demographic membership is a real and substantial moderator, then the subgroup correlations can be entered into the larger cumulation as independent outcome values. Statistically, outcome values for nonoverlapping groups have the same properties as values from different studies.

Subgroups and Loss of Power

The analysis of subgroups exacts a price. Consider an example in which 100 persons are evenly split by race and by sex. There will then be four subgroups: 25 black females, 25 black males, 25 white females, and 25 white males. An outcome value for a sample size of 25 has much more sampling error than an outcome based on 100 cases. In fact, the confidence interval for 25 cases is about twice as wide as that for 100 cases. For example, for the full sample, an observed correlation of .20 would have a confidence interval of $.00 \leq \rho \leq .40$. For each subsample, the confidence interval would be $-.20 \leq \rho \leq .60$. There is actually very little information in an observed correlation based on as few as 25 cases (although it can be cumulated with other small-sample correlations and make a contribution in this way).

The immense statistical uncertainty and sampling error in subgroup analysis leads to massive capitalization on chance. For simplicity, suppose there is no moderating effect. If the population correlation is 0, then there are four opportunities to make a Type I error instead of one, and the actual Type I error rate would not be .05 but .19. If the population correlation is not 0, then there are four opportunities to make a Type II error rather than just one. However, the situation is worse than that. The probability of a Type I error is always .05 for each individual test regardless of the sample size, but the probability of a Type II error increases drastically with a decrease in sample size. For example, if the population correlation is .20 and the sample size is 100, then the probability of statistical significance and a correct inference is only .50. If the sample size is 25, however, then the probability of significance drops to .16; that is, the investigator will be wrong 84% of the time. Furthermore, the probability of correctly concluding significance in all four subgroups is $(.16)^4 = .0007$, which is less than 1 in 1,000. That is, analysis by subgroups for a population correlation of .20 raises the Type II error rate from 50% to 99.9%.

Subgroups and Capitalization on Chance

The situation is even worse for the many investigators who select the data to present using significance tests. If there were 10 variables in the study, then the correlation matrix would have 45 entries. If all population correlations were 0, then the analysis of the whole sample would provide for a search through 45 entries to capitalize on sampling error. At least 2 such correlations would be expected to be significant, and it would not be incredibly unlucky to get 5. For a sample size of 100, the largest correlation in a chance matrix would be expected to be .23. However, for a subgroup, the largest correlation among 45 would be expected to be .46. Furthermore, the analysis by subgroups provides a search list of $4(45) = 180$ elements on which to capitalize on sampling error and, hence, a greater expected error and an expected 8 and possibly 20 false significant readings.

Even if the null hypothesis were false for every correlation (in which case every failure to find significance would be Type II error of about 84% frequency), the handful pulled out would be completely unrepresentative of the population correlations. The true value of each correlation is .20, but with a sample size of 25, only correlations of .40 or greater will be significant (two-tailed test, $p \leq .05$). Therefore, only those correlations that by chance are much larger than the population value will be statistically significant. The conclusion that these correlations are not 0 will be correct; that is, in this 16% of cases there will be no Type II error. However, these significant observed correlations will greatly overestimate actual population correlations. The significant observed correlations will, in fact, be about twice as large as the actual value.

Subgroups and Suppression of Data

There is a current practice in journals that acts to restrict publication of data. Under current pressures, it is likely that an author who analyzed four subgroups would be allowed to publish only one-fourth as much data on each group. From the point of view of future cumulation, this is a disaster. There are too many missing values as it is.

Subgroups and the Bias of Disaggregation

If the moderator effect is nonexistent or trivial in magnitude, then the desired correlation for cumulation is the total group correlation. For practical purposes, however, it is the average correlation that is entered into the larger cumulation. That is, if there is no moderator effect, then the larger cumulation will ultimately average all entries and, hence, implicitly average the entries for each study. As it happens, the average correlation in this case may be quite "biased" as an estimate of the total sample correlation. This bias is always in the direction of the average correlation being smaller in magnitude than the total sample correlation. This bias is produced by restriction in range in the subgroups.

Assume that the covariance structures are the same in each subgroup; that is, assume that the regression line is the same in all groups. Then the correlation is smaller in a subgroup to the extent that the standard deviation in the subgroup is smaller than the total population standard deviation. Let u be the ratio of standard deviations; that is, let u be defined by

$$u = \frac{\sigma_{\text{subgroup}}}{\sigma_{\text{total}}}$$

Let r_t be the correlation in the total group and let r_s be the correlation in the subgroup. Then the formula for direct restriction in range yields

$$r_s = \frac{u r_1}{((u^2 - 1)\, r_t^2 + 1)^{1/2}}$$

For small correlations, this formula differs little from $r_s = ur$; that is, the subgroup correlation is lower by a factor of u. To show that u is less than 1, we note that

$$u^2 = \frac{\sigma^2_{\text{subgroup}}}{\sigma^2_{\text{total}}} = 1 - \eta^2 \qquad (10.16)$$

where η^2 is the correlation ratio between the grouping variable and the causally prior variable of the two being correlated. If the range restriction is indirect, then, for the same value of u, the downward bias in the subgroup correlations will be greater. (See Chapters 3–5.)

Conclusion: Use Total Group Correlations

If the moderating effect of the demographic variable is to be studied, then, of course, subgroup correlations should be entered into the cumulation. However, once the demographic variable is known to have little or no moderator effect, the major cumulative analysis should be done with total group correlations.

Summary

There are three common forms of replication within studies: fully replicated designs, conceptual replication, and analysis of subgroups. Each requires a different strategy for meta-analysis.

A fully replicated design is a study in which there are subparts that are independent replications of the study design. For example, the same study design might be carried out in three organizations. Results from each organization can then be entered into the meta-analysis as if the results were from three separate studies. If results are averaged rather than entered separately, then the average should be treated as if the sample size were the sum of the sample sizes across the three organizations.

Conceptual replication is multiple measurement. Either the independent or the dependent variable could be measured by several instruments or methods. Each such measure then produces its own correlation or effect size. Ideally, these alternate measures should be combined by using confirmatory factor analysis or formulas for the correlations of composites, to yield a single correlation or effect size. The study then contributes one value to the meta-analysis with a minimum error of measurement. If the study does not report the between-measure correlations needed to do a confirmatory factor analysis or to compute composite correlations, and if estimates of these correlations cannot be obtained from other studies, then the best alternative is to average the conceptually equivalent correlations or effect sizes. The average value will be an underestimate of the value that would have been produced by confirmatory factor analysis or by use of composite correlations.

Analysis of subgroups may be either important or frivolous. If the subgroups are defined by what is believed to be a moderator variable, then there should be a corresponding meta-analysis of these subgroups across studies. However, if the analysis of subgroups simply stems from a ritual analysis by sex, race, or other subgrouping, then the total group correlation should be the only contribution to the meta-analysis. In any case, the total group correlation should be used for the main meta-analysis across studies. If the total group correlation is not given and cannot be computed from the information in the report, the subgroup correlations can be used individually in the meta-analysis. Alternatively, the subgroup correlations can be averaged and the average correlation used in the meta-analysis with the total group sample size. This average correlation will usually be slightly smaller than the total group correlation and, hence, will underestimate the relationship of interest.

11

Methods of Integrating Findings Across Studies and Related Software

This chapter presents and discusses 10 different methods for integrating study results across studies. These methods are presented and discussed in their approximate order of efficacy (from least to most efficacious) in extracting the information needed from the studies reviewed. Available computer programs for applying these methods are discussed at the end of this chapter.

The Traditional Narrative Procedure

The oldest procedure is the narrative review. The narrative review has been described as "literary," "qualitative," "nonquantitative," and "verbal." In this procedure, the reviewer takes the results reported in each study at face value and attempts to find an overarching theory that reconciles the findings. If there are few studies to be interpreted, this integration might be feasible. If the number of studies is large (50 to 1,000), however, the studies will almost never be precisely comparable in design, measures, and so forth, and findings will typically vary across studies in seemingly bizarre ways. As a result, the information-processing task becomes too taxing for the human mind. The result is usually one of three outcomes. First, the result may be "pedestrian reviewing where verbal synopses of studies are strung out in dizzying lists" (Glass, 1976, p. 4). That is, the reviewer may not even attempt to integrate findings across studies. Second, the reviewer may simplify the integration task by basing his or her conclusions on only a small subset of the studies. Reviewers often reject all but a few of the available studies as deficient in design or analysis and then "advance the one or two acceptable studies as the truth of the matter" (Glass, 1976, p. 4). This approach unjustifiably wastes much information and, in addition, may base conclusions on unrepresentative studies. Third, the reviewer may actually attempt the task of mentally integrating findings across all studies—and fail to do an adequate job. Cooper and Rosenthal

(1980) showed that even when the number of studies reviewed is as small as seven, reviewers who use narrative-discursive methods and reviewers who use quantitative methods reach different conclusions.

The Traditional Voting Method

The traditional voting method was one of the first techniques developed to ease the information-processing burden on the reviewer. In its simplest form, it consists merely of a tabulation of significant and nonsignificant findings. Light and Smith (1971) described this approach as follows:

> All studies which have data on a dependent variable and a specific independent variable of interest are examined. Three possible outcomes are defined. The relationship between the independent and dependent variable is either significantly positive, significantly negative, or there is no significant relationship in either direction. The number of studies falling into each of these three categories is then simply tallied. If a plurality of studies falls into any of these three categories, with fewer falling into the other two, the model category is declared the winner. This model categorization is then assumed to give the best estimates of the direction of the true relationship between the independent and dependent variable. (p. 433)

The voting method is sometimes also used in an attempt to identify correlates of study outcomes. For example, the proportion of studies in which training method A was superior to training method B might be compared for males and females.

An example of a review based on this method is Eagly (1978). The voting method is biased in favor of large-sample studies that may show only small effect sizes. Even where variation in sample size does not cause problems in interpreting significance levels, and where the voting method correctly leads to the conclusion that an effect exists, the critical question of the size of the effect is still left unanswered. However, the most important problem with the voting method is that it can and does lead to false conclusions. Consider an example. Based on a meta-analysis of 144 studies, Pearlman, Schmidt, and Hunter (1980) found the correlation of general intelligence and proficiency in clerical work to be .51. That is, if a perfect study were done using the entire applicant population and a perfectly reliable measure of job proficiency, then the correlation between measured intelligence and performance would be .51. However, proficiency measures cannot be obtained on applicants; performance can be measured only on those who are hired. Most organizations hire fewer than half of those who apply. Suppose those hired are those in the top half of the distribution on intelligence. Then, because of restriction in range, the correlation between test and performance will only be .33, rather than .51. It is also impossible to obtain perfect measures of job performance. Typically, the best feasible measure is the rating of the single supervisor who knows the person's work well enough to rate it. According to the review of Viswesvaran, Ones, and Schmidt (1996), the average inter-rater reliability of a rating by a single supervisor using a multi-item rating scale is .50. This means that the correlation between test and performance would drop to $(.50)^{1/2}(.33) = .23$. With an underlying population correlation of $\rho_{xy} = .23$, the average statistical power in a series of studies can easily be less than .50. Suppose it were .45. Then, in expectation, 55% of the studies—a majority—would find no significant relationship, and the traditional voting method would falsely conclude there was no relationship—despite the fact that the relationship is $\rho_{xy} = .23$ in every study.

Hedges and Olkin (1980) showed that if there is a true effect, then in any set of studies in which mean statistical power is less than about .50, the probability of a false conclusion using the voting method increases as the number of studies increases. That is, the more data examined, the greater the certainty of a false conclusion about the meaning of the data! Thus, the traditional voting method is fatally flawed statistically and logically. The typical conclusion of reviewers using the voting method is that the research literature is in deplorable shape. Some researchers get results; others do not. Sometimes a given researcher gets significant results, sometimes not. These reviewers almost invariably conclude that more research is needed and issue calls for better research designs, better experimental controls, better measures, and so on (Glass, 1976).

Cumulation of *p* Values Across Studies

This procedure attempts to cumulate significance levels across studies to produce an overall p value (significance level) for the set of studies as a whole. If this value is small enough, the reviewer concludes that existence of the effect has been established. These methods were developed by Mosteller and Bush (1954) from earlier work by Stouffer, Suchman, DeVinney, Star, and Williams (1949). The most recent advocates of this method have been Rosenthal and his associates (Cooper & Rosenthal, 1980; Rosenthal, 1978a). As discussed in Chapter 13, in this method, the p value from a one-tailed significance test from each study is converted to a standardized normal deviate, denoted z. These z values are either summed directly or used to compute a weighted sum of the zs. Then the average of these zs is computed and the significance level (p value) of the average z value is determined. This is the p value for the set of studies as a whole.

An important problem with this method is that it assumes the homogeneous case (Hunter & Schmidt, 2000, pp. 286–287). That is, it assumes that $S_\rho^2 = 0$ (or that $S_\delta^2 = 0$). This means that it is a fixed-effects model and, therefore, has all the problems of fixed-effects meta-analysis methods, as discussed in Chapters 5 and 9. In particular, if the fixed-effects assumption does not hold and $S_\rho^2 > 0$ (or $S_\delta^2 > 0$), then the alpha level of the test is inflated. For example, the combined p value for a set of studies might be computed as $p = .01$ when, in fact, it is .10. As noted in Chapters 5 and 9, the fixed-effects assumption of homogeneity is rarely met in real studies.

Another major problem with this method is that in most sets of studies the combined p value will be significant, but that fact tells nothing about the magnitude of the effect. Obviously, the practical and theoretical implications of an effect depend at least as much on its size as on its existence. Rosenthal (1978a, p. 192) recognized the necessity for analysis of effect sizes along with p values, and in his later substantive reviews he used a combination of p value and effect size analysis.

This method—cumulation of p values along with computation of the mean effect size ($\bar{r}$ or $\bar{d}$)—has been labeled the combined probability method by Bangert-Drowns (1986). Bangert-Drowns noted that the combined probability method is best regarded as a "transitional" form of meta-analysis. The introduction of the mean effect size resulted from the recognition by Rosenthal and his colleagues (Rosenthal, 1978a; Rosenthal & Rubin, 1982a, 1982b) of the need for an index of the magnitude of study outcomes; at the same time, however, the method provides no information about the variability of effect sizes across studies and, therefore, lacks an important component available in some other forms of meta-analysis. With the introduction of the combined probability method, the method of cumulating p values alone was left with no major advocates. Rosenthal (1984) provided an extensive discussion of methods for cumulating p values across studies. Additional information can be found in Rosenthal (1983) and Rosenthal and Rubin (1979a, 1983). In Chapter 13, we present a discussion of the specific method of combining p values favored by Rosenthal (the Stouffer method), but we do not emphasize these methods in this book because of the problems just discussed. Others have also discussed problems with the combined p-value methods (see, e.g., Becker, 1987; Becker & Schram, 1994; National Research Council, 1992). As a result of these problems, the National Research Council (1992) report recommended that the use of p-value methods "be discontinued" (p. 182). In fact, these methods are rarely used in the literature today.

In passing, we note a technique developed by Rosenthal as a result of his work in cumulating p values across studies. This technique was developed to address the so-called "file drawer problem." Suppose a researcher has demonstrated that the combined p value across the studies reviewed is, say, .0001, and concludes that a real effect exists. A critic could then argue that this finding is due to non-representativeness of the studies reviewed, on grounds that studies not showing an effect are much less likely to have been located by the reviewer. That is, the studies with negative findings are apt to have been tucked away in file drawers rather than circulated or published. Using Rosenthal's (1979) technique, the researcher can calculate the number of missing studies showing zero effect size that would have to exist in order to bring the combined p value down to .05, .10, or any other level. This number typically turns out to be very large, for example, 65,000 (Rosenthal & Rubin, 1978a). It is highly unlikely that there are 65,000 "lost" studies on any topic. The statistical formulas and the rationale for this form of file drawer analysis are given in Chapter 13. However, the file drawer technique, like the combined p-value method, is a fixed-effects model and, therefore, yields accurate results only if the underlying correlation (or d value) is identical in all studies. If population values of ρ and δ vary across studies (which is usually the case, as noted in Chapters 5 and 9), the number of studies needed to make the combined p-value just barely significant is much smaller than the number provided by the file drawer analysis. Another source of inaccuracy is the fact that the initially computed p value for the set of studies also depends on the fixed-effects assumption and, therefore, is typically inaccurate also. Other important criticisms of the Rosenthal file drawer analysis are given by Begg (1994, p. 406). These problems reduce the usefulness of the file drawer analysis.

Statistically Correct Vote-Counting Procedures

Although the traditional vote-counting method is statistically and logically deficient, there are methods of cumulating research findings across studies based on vote counting that are statistically correct. These methods fall into two categories: (1) those that yield only a statistical significance level for the body of studies and (2) those that provide a quantitative estimate of the mean effect size.

Vote-Counting Methods Yielding Only Significance Levels

If the null hypothesis is true, then the population correlation or effect size is, in fact, 0. Thus, when study results are given in the form of *p* values, half would be expected to be larger than .50 and half smaller than .50. The sign test can be used to test whether the observed frequencies of findings in the positive and negative directions depart significantly from the 50–50 split expected under the null hypothesis (Hedges & Olkin, 1980; Rosenthal, 1978a). Alternatively, the reviewer can use a count to determine the proportion of studies reporting statistically significant findings supporting the theory (positive significant results) and test this proportion against the proportion expected under the null hypothesis (typically, .05 or .01). The binomial test or the chi-square statistic can be used for this test (Brozek & Tiede, 1952; Hedges & Olkin, 1980; Rosenthal, 1978a). Hedges and Olkin (1980) noted that some reviewers believe that most, if not the majority, of studies should show a positive significant result if the true effect size or true correlation is nonzero. In fact, this is typically not true. When the true effect size or true correlation is in the range of magnitude typically encountered, only a minority of studies will usually report significant positive findings because of low statistical power in the individual studies (National Research Council, 1992). Hedges and Olkin (1980) also pointed out that the proportion of positive significant findings required to reject the null hypothesis is much smaller than is commonly believed. For example, if 10 studies are run using alpha = .05, the probability of three or more positive significant findings is less than .01. That is, three positive significant findings out of ten are sufficient to reject the null hypothesis.

These vote-counting methods, however, are most useful when the null hypothesis is true, not when it is false. For example, Bartlett, Bobko, Mosier, and Hannan (1978) and Hunter, Schmidt, and Hunter (1979) showed that the frequency of significant differences in employment test validities for blacks and whites did not differ from the chance frequencies expected under the null hypothesis and the alpha levels used. Bartlett et al., for example, examined over 1,100 such tests at the alpha = .05 level and found that 6.2% were significant. Coward and Sackett (1990) examined thousands of ability-performance relationships and found that the frequency of statistically significant departures from linearity at the .05 alpha level was about 5%. When the null hypothesis is not rejected in cumulative studies with high statistical power, this method does provide an estimate of population effect size or population correlation: 0. However, when the null hypothesis is false (the usual case), the binomial or sign tests provide no estimate of effect size.

This is a serious disadvantage. In addition, because they are statistical significance tests, the binomial and sign tests have all the disadvantages of significance tests, as discussed in detail in Chapter 1. However, it is possible to use these correct vote-counting methods without using a significance test. For example, in the studies of Bartlett et al. (1978) and Coward and Sackett (1990), the numerical findings make it perfectly apparent what the conclusion should be without using a significance test.

Vote-Counting Methods Yielding Estimates of Effect Sizes

The probability of a positive result and the probability of a positive significant result are both functions of the population effect size and study sample size. If sample sizes are known for all studies, then the mean effect size underlying a set of studies can be estimated from either the proportion of positive results or from the proportion of positive significant results. Hedges and Olkin (1980) derived formulas for both of these methods of estimating effect size. They also presented formulas that can be used to compute confidence intervals around the mean effect size estimate. These confidence intervals are, in general, wider than those resulting when effect sizes can be and are computed individually for each study and then averaged. In the latter case, confidence intervals are based on the standard error of the mean. Confidence intervals are wider for the Hedges-Olkin estimates of the mean effect size because estimation of effect sizes from counts of positive results (regardless of statistical significance) or positive significant results uses less information from the studies than the usual direct procedure. Therefore, vote-counting-based estimates of effect sizes should typically only be used when the information needed to determine effect sizes in individual studies is not available or retrievable.

Most studies provide either r or d values or enough information to compute these values. If a few studies do not, ordinarily one would just omit these studies from the meta-analysis. If the entire set does not, one would have to use one of the methods presented by Hedges and Olkin; however, that would be unusual. It would be more likely that one would have a subset of studies (say 10 studies) that do not provide enough information to compute r or d. One could then use the Hedges-Olkin method to derive an estimate of $\bar{d}$ for this subset of studies and thereby avoid losing these studies. Also, if you are reading a traditional review that gives only statistical significance and the direction of significance for each study, you can use one of these methods to get an estimate of the $\bar{d}$ for the studies in the review; in effect, this would be an incomplete and less precise—but quick and convenient—meta-analysis of these studies.

Counting Positive Significant Findings

Suppose one has 10 studies in which $N_E = N_C = 12$ in each study and suppose 6 of the 10 have significant positive results ($\hat{p} = 6/10 = .60$). Then, from Table A2 of Hedges and Olkin (1980), one can determine that the estimated $\hat{\delta} = .80$. The researcher can also derive an estimate of the standard error of this $\hat{\delta}$ using the formula given by Hedges and Olkin for the confidence intervals for the p value. The 90% confidence interval for $\hat{p}$ is

$$\frac{(2m\hat{p} + c_\alpha^2) \pm \sqrt{c_\alpha^4 + 4mc_\alpha^2 \hat{p}(1 - \hat{p})}}{2(m + c_\alpha^2)} \tag{11.1}$$

where m is the number of studies (10 here) and $c_\alpha = 1.645$. The 90% confidence interval in our example is then

$$\frac{\{2(10)(.6) + 1.645^2\} \pm \sqrt{1.645^4 + 4(10)(1.645)^2(.60)(1 - .60)}}{2(10 + 1.645^2)}$$

$$= .35 < \hat{p} < .81$$

This confidence interval applies to $\hat{p}$. We must next transform the endpoints of this confidence interval to $\hat{\delta}$ values, again using Table A2 of Hedges and Olkin (1980). By linear interpolation, $\hat{\delta}$ for $\hat{p} = .81$ is 1.10 and $\hat{\delta}$ for $\hat{p} = .35$ is .53. The approximate standard error of $\hat{\delta}$ is then

$$SE_{\hat{\delta}} = \frac{1.10 - .53}{2(1.645)} = .1733$$

and the sampling error variance of $\hat{\delta}$ is $(.1733)^2$ or .03003. Thus, for the 10 studies combined, there is only one entry into the meta-analysis: $\hat{\delta} = .80$ and $S_e^2 = .03003$.

Note that the $SE_{\hat{\delta}}$ here is the SE of the $\bar{d}$, not the standard error of ds from each individual study. This SE is analogous to the standard error of the mean (i.e., $SE_{\bar{d}} = SD_d/\sqrt{m}$) from an ordinary meta-analysis of observed (and uncorrected) ds. (Recall that m is the number of studies in the Hedges-Olkin notation.) The analogous estimate of SE_d for individual d values would be $\sqrt{m}SE_{\bar{d}}$, which here is $\sqrt{10}(.1733) = .548$. This is the estimate of the observed SD of individual d values across the 10 studies, when the estimate of $\bar{d}$ is based only on the significance information. Here we have, in effect, combined the 10 studies into one "study" for entry into the meta-analysis. Hence the sampling error variance value that should be used is $S_{e_{\hat{\delta}}}^2$, which is .03003 here. This estimate, like the Hedges-Olkin vote-counting methods in general, assumes that d does not vary across studies. If δ does vary, the estimate of SE_δ is only approximate.

This procedure allows us to salvage some, but not all, of the information potentially in the 10 studies. We can compute how much information is lost by our inability to compute a d value for each study. The actual total N in the 10 studies is $10(12)(2) = 240$. We can solve the following equation for N to determine the effective N in this analysis:

$$S_e^2 = \frac{4}{N}\left(1 + \frac{\bar{d}^2}{8}\right)$$

$$.03003 = \frac{4}{N}\left(1 + \frac{.8^2}{8}\right)$$

$$N = 144$$

Thus, the effective N, when only significance is known, is reduced from 240 to 144; 40% of the information in the studies is lost because the researchers did not report enough information to allow computation of d values.

This example assumed that $N_E = N_C =$ some constant across all studies. This will virtually never be true. If sample sizes vary, some form of the average sample size should be used. Hedges and Olkin (1980) suggested the geometric mean, the square mean root, or the simple average sample size. The geometric mean is

$$GM = \sqrt[m]{N_1 N_2 \ldots N_m} \tag{11.2}$$

The square mean root is

$$SMR = \left[\sum_{1}^{m}\left[\frac{\sqrt{N_i}}{m}\right]\right]^2 \tag{11.3}$$

If sample sizes do not vary dramatically across studies, the simple average N will be reasonably accurate. The reader should note that in Hedges and Olkin's Table A2, n is the number in the control *or* experimental group. Total N is $2n$. Thus, when sample sizes are not equal, one should average both the N_E and N_C values together.

Hedges and Olkin did not provide a separate table for correlations. However, their Table A2 will yield approximately correct values for r if (1) one converts the δ values at the top of the table to r (actually ρ), using Equation (7.9) in Chapter 7, and (2) one remembers to use one-half of the N in entering the table.

Counting Positive Results

An estimate of $\bar{d}$ or $\bar{r}$ for a group of studies that does not provide enough information to compute d and r in individual studies can also be derived from the number of outcomes that favor the experimental group—whether or not they are significant. If the null hypothesis is true, and there are no differences between experimental and control groups, this expected frequency is 50%. This method uses departures from the expected 50% to estimate $\bar{d}$ or $\bar{r}$. Suppose you have 10 studies for which $N_C = N_E = 14$ in each study, and 9 of 10 results are in the positive direction (i.e., favor the experimental group whether they are significant or not). Entering this information into Table A1 of Hedges and Olkin (1980) yields $\hat{\delta} = .50$. Confidence intervals and the *SE* and S_e^2 of $\hat{\delta}$ are computed in the same way as illustrated previously for counts of positive significant results.

Counting Positive and Negative Results

This method is more useful than the previous two methods when you suspect that publication or other availability bias is distorting the sample of studies, that is, when you believe that significant results—both positive and negative—are being published or located and nonsignificant results are not being published or located. This means the available set of studies is unrepresentative of all studies that have been conducted. This method is based on the proportion of all significant findings that are *positive* significant results, that is,

$$\hat{p} = \frac{\text{Number of positive significant results}}{\text{Number of positive plus negative significant results}}$$

If the null hypothesis is true, the expected value of $\hat{p}$ is .50. Departures from .50 are the basis for the estimate $\hat{\delta}$. For example, suppose you have 20 studies, each with $N_E = N_C = 10$. Ten studies report significant results, and of the 10, 8 are significant positive findings. Thus, $\hat{p} = .80$. Table A3 of Hedges and Olkin (1980) shows that $\hat{\delta}$ is then .15. Confidence intervals and standard errors can be estimated in the same way as described previously for counts of positive significant results. This method should be used only when (1) publication bias based on significance only (not direction) is suspected, and (2) the studies do not allow computation of d or r values.

The Hedges-Olkin (1980) methods of estimating effect size based on vote counting assume that the population effect size (δ) does not vary across studies. If δ varies substantially across studies, these methods yield only approximate estimates of mean effect size and variance of effect sizes.

Meta-Analysis of Research Studies

In this book, we have limited the term "meta-analysis" to methods that focus on the cumulation of effect sizes, rather than significance levels, across studies. Much early systematic work on combining p values across studies can be found in the literature (e.g., Fisher, 1932, 1938; Pearson, 1938). Although systematic methods for meta-analysis have been presented and advocated only recently, many of the basic concepts underlying meta-analysis have been employed by individual researchers and research teams over the decades. Thorndike (1933) cumulated test-retest reliability coefficients for the Binet intelligence test from 36 studies and even went so far as to correct the observed variance of these coefficients for the effects of sampling error. He found that not all the observed variance could be explained by sampling error; some of the variation was due to the length of the interval between test and retest. Ghiselli (1949, 1955, 1966) cumulated validity coefficients from numerous studies for different types of tests and different jobs, presenting the results in the form of median values. Although he did not systematically analyze the variances of coefficients, he did cumulate a vast amount of information, which he presented in his 1966 book, followed by an update later (Ghiselli, 1973). Despite his later emphasis on the cumulation of significance levels across studies, Rosenthal was computing and publishing mean correlations as early as 1961 (Rosenthal, 1961, 1963). Bloom (1964) averaged correlation coefficients to summarize the large number of studies that had accumulated on the stability (and instability) of human traits and abilities. Erlenmeyer-Kimling and Jarvik (1963) used kinship correlations for intelligence test scores from many studies to piece together a picture of hereditary influences on mental ability. Fleishman and Levine and their associates cumulated effect sizes across experimental studies to determine the relationship between alcohol intake and decrements in task performances dependent on different abilities (Levine, Kramer, & Levine, 1975) and to determine the effectiveness of an abilities classification system in the vigilance area of human performance (Levine, Romashko, & Fleishman, 1973). None of these authors, however, advanced a systematic body of meta-analysis methodology for use in solving the general problem of integrating findings across studies to produce cumulative knowledge. It was not until the 1970s that systematic quantitative techniques for integrating research findings across studies were introduced. Glass (1976) advanced the first such set of procedures. Unaware of Glass's work, we published our first article on meta-analysis methods the following year (Schmidt & Hunter, 1977). Glass coined the term "meta-analysis" to refer to the analysis of analyses (studies). One reason he introduced this term was to distinguish such analyses from secondary analysis. In secondary analysis, the researcher obtains and reanalyzes the original data on which an earlier study was based (Light & Smith, 1971). Meta-analysis is the quantitative cumulation and analysis of effect sizes and other descriptive statistics across studies. It does not require access to original study data.

Meta-analysis methods fall into three broad categories, as depicted graphically in Figure 11.1. The purely descriptive methods (the Glass methods and study effects meta-analysis methods) paint a descriptive picture of what is in the research literature but do not attempt to analyze, correct for, or otherwise address any of the artifacts that distort study findings. Next are meta-analysis methods that address only the artifact of sampling error. These include the homogeneity test–based methods of Hedges and Olkin (1985) and Rosenthal and Rubin (1982a, 1982b) and also the "bare-bones" meta-analysis methods described in the early part of Chapter 3. These methods do not address the effects of artifacts other than sampling error. In particular, they do not address measurement error. Finally, there are meta-analysis methods that address and correct for the effects of not only sampling error but also a variety of other artifacts that distort study results. These methods estimate the results that would have been obtained had all the studies been conducted in a methodological unflawed manner. That is, they attempt to reveal the scientific reality underlying a group of imperfect real-world studies. This is the purpose that Rubin (1990) stated meta-analysis methods should serve. These methods, called psychometric meta-analysis methods, are the focus of this book. In addition to the methods that we have presented, beginning in 1977 (Schmidt & Hunter, 1977), Callender and Osburn (1980) and Raju and his associates (e.g., Raju & Drasgow, 2003) have also made important contributions, as noted in Chapters 4 and 5 and elsewhere in this book.

Descriptive Meta-Analysis Methods: Glassian and Related Methods

Glassian Meta-Analysis Methods and Criticisms

For Glass, the purpose of meta-analysis is descriptive; the goal is to paint a very general, broad, and inclusive picture of a particular research literature (Glass, 1977; Glass, McGaw, & Smith, 1981). The questions to be answered are very general; for example, does psychotherapy—regardless of type—have an impact on the kinds of outcomes that therapy researchers consider important enough to measure, regardless of the nature of these outcomes (e.g., self-reported anxiety, count of emotional outbursts, etc.)? Thus, Glassian meta-analysis often combines studies with somewhat different independent variables (e.g., different kinds of

Figure 11.1 Schematic illustrating methods of meta-analysis

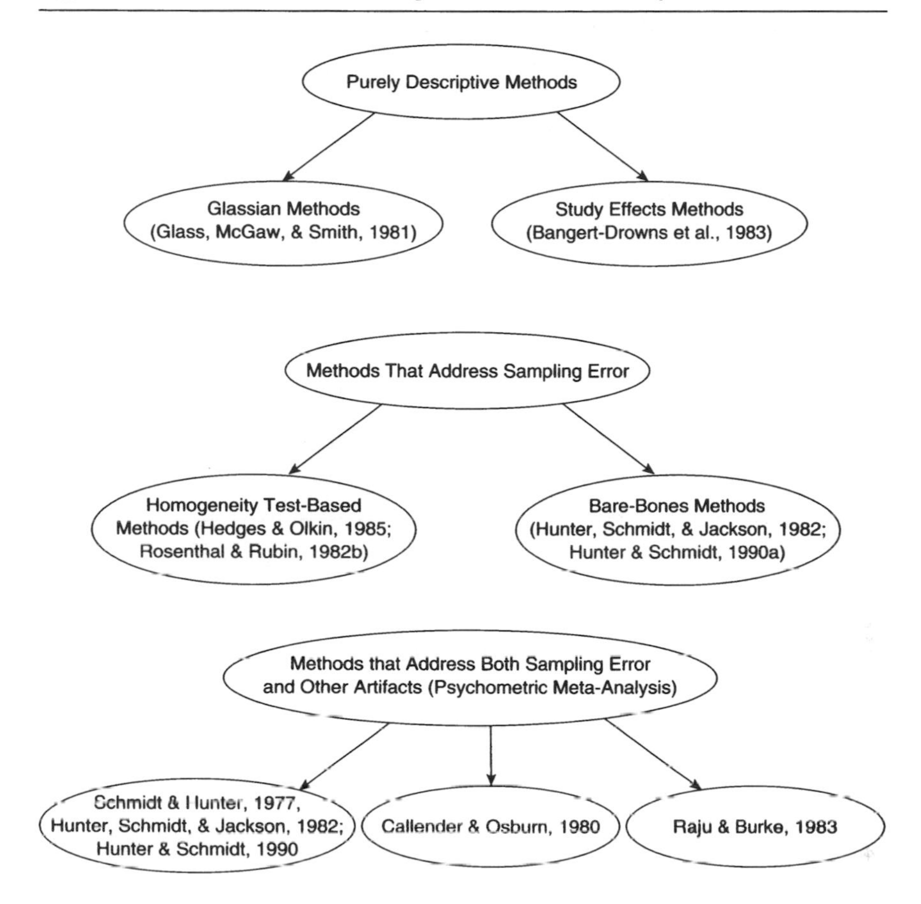

therapy) and different dependent variables. As a result, some have criticized these methods as combining apples and oranges. Glassian meta-analysis has three primary properties:

1. *A strong emphasis on effect sizes rather than significance levels.* Glass believed the purpose of research integration is more descriptive than inferential and that the most important descriptive statistics are those that indicate most clearly the magnitude of effects. Glassian meta-analysis typically employs estimates of the Pearson r or estimates of d. The initial product of a Glassian meta-analysis is the mean and standard deviation of observed effect sizes or correlations across studies.

2. *Acceptance of the variance of effect sizes at face value.* Glassian meta-analysis implicitly assumes that the observed variability in effect sizes is real and should have some substantive explanation. There is no attention to sampling error variance in the effect sizes. The substantive explanations are sought in the varying characteristics of the studies (e.g., sex or mean age of subjects, length of treatment, and more). Study characteristics that correlate with study effects are examined for their explanatory power. The general finding in applications

of Glassian meta-analysis has been that few study characteristics correlate significantly with study outcomes. Problems of capitalization on chance and low statistical power associated with this step in meta-analysis were discussed in Chapter 2.

3. *A strongly empirical approach to determining which aspects of studies should be coded and tested for possible association with study outcomes.* Glass (1976, 1977) felt that all such questions are empirical questions, and he de-emphasized the role of theory in determining which variables should be tested as potential moderators of study outcome (see also Glass, 1972).

In later sections of this chapter, we argue that Glassian meta-analysis is incomplete in important respects and that the methods presented in this book extend and complete Glass's methods. However, others have also advanced criticisms of Glass's methods. As a result of these criticisms, new approaches to meta-analysis have been advanced, approaches that are essentially variations on the Glass methods. These new approaches are discussed later. The major criticisms of Glassian methods are the following:

1. In Glassian meta-analysis, the study effect size estimate is the unit of analysis. Studies based on a single research sample often report several (sometimes numerous) estimates of effect sizes; in such cases, Glass and his associates typically include all such estimates in the meta-analysis, resulting in violations of the assumption of statistical independence (see Chapter 10). The effect of this is to cast doubt on the validity of any inferential statistical tests that might be applied in the meta-analysis, for example, tests of the significance of the $\bar{d}$ value. This criticism is statistically correct, but it overlooks the important fact that, for Glassian meta-analysis, the purpose of research integration is more descriptive than inferential. Although statistical tests are usually used, they are secondary to the descriptive purpose. We agree with the de-emphasis of significance testing in Glassian meta-analysis. As shown in Chapters 1 and 2, overreliance on statistical significance tests in psychology and the other social sciences has led to extreme difficulties in drawing correct conclusions from research literatures. Also, in most cases, violations of independence have a conservative effect on meta-analysis outcomes; they lead to overestimates of what the observed variance of study outcomes would be if all study effects were independent. Another important consideration is that violations of independence can be expected to have no systematic effect on $\bar{d}$ or $\bar{r}$ values, and the main focus of the Glass method is on these two summary statistics. Nevertheless, when a very small percentage of studies contributes a large percentage of the effect sizes, the credibility of the meta-analysis is called into question. Technical issues related to this problem are discussed in Chapter 10.

2. The second criticism holds that Glass is mistaken in including all studies in the meta-analysis regardless of methodological quality (Bangert-Drowns, 1986; Slavin, 1986). Slavin (1986), for example, called for replacement of Glass's method by what he referred to as "best evidence synthesis," in which all but the studies judged to be methodologically strongest are excluded from the meta-analysis. We discuss this question in more detail in Chapter 12. Glass's

position—one that we agree with—is that judgments of overall methodological quality are often very subjective, and inter-evaluator agreement is often low. Therefore, the question should be decided empirically by meta-analyzing separately the studies judged methodologically strong and weak and comparing the results. If they differ, one should rely on the "strong" studies; if they do not, then all studies should be used.

3. The third criticism is that the Glass methods mix very different independent variables in the meta-analysis, thereby masking important differences in the mean outcomes for different independent variables. For example, the Smith-Glass (1977) meta-analysis of the effects of psychotherapy included 10 different kinds of therapy (e.g., rational-emotive along with behavior modification therapies). The argument is that if some of these therapy methods are more effective than others, such a meta-analysis would never reveal that fact. This criticism ignores the fact that application of Glass's methods usually includes separate meta-analysis for each independent variable type as a second step, allowing any such differences in treatment effects to emerge. However, Glass correctly argued that whether such finer grained meta-analyses are necessary depends on the purpose of the meta-analysis. If the research question is, "What is the relative effectiveness of different types of therapy?" clearly they are. However, if the research question is whether therapy in general is effective, then the overall analysis may be more appropriate (Wortman, 1983). Glass's critics are theoretically and analytically oriented and, therefore, find it hard to see why anyone would ever ask such a broad research question. In our research, we have typically asked narrower questions, and, therefore, our independent variables have been quite homogeneous.

4. The last major criticism is that Glassian methods mix measures of very different *dependent* variables. For example, in studies of educational interventions, *d* values for measures of attitudes, beliefs, disciplinary behavior, and academic achievement may all be included in the same meta-analysis. The critics are correct in contending that the results of such meta-analysis are difficult or impossible to interpret. It does not seem likely that the impact of, say, the open classroom would be the same on such conceptually diverse dependent variables. Again, however, there is nothing inherent in Glass's methods that precludes conducting separate meta-analyses for each dependent variable construct. The problem is that this has often not been done. In our research, we have confined the dependent variable measures within a single meta-analysis to measures of a single construct. In our validity generalization research, for example, the dependent variable has always been a measure of overall job performance.

Most of these criticisms do not stem from the nature of the Glassian statistical methods for meta-analysis per se. Instead, they are criticisms of the applications of these methods made by Glass, his associates, and some others. The criticisms stem from the fact that Glass and his critics have very different concepts of the purpose of meta-analysis. For Glass, the purpose of meta-analysis is to paint a very general, broad, and inclusive picture of a research literature. The questions to be answered are very general; for example, does psychotherapy—regardless of type—have an impact in general on the kinds of things that therapist-researchers consider important enough to measure, regardless of the nature of the construct (e.g., self-reported anxiety and counts of emotional outbursts and . . .). His critics believe meta-analysis must answer much narrower, more specific questions if it is to contribute to cumulative knowledge, understanding, and theory development. Actually, meta-analysis can be used for both purposes. A more general quantitative summary may be useful as a first step. For those who believed that there was no cumulativeness—and indeed no order whatsoever other than randomness—in social science research literatures, the results of such meta-analysis could be (and probably have been) a heartening step back from epistemological despair. However, they can only be a first step; further advances in scientific understanding do require that meta-analysis answer more specific questions. For example, we must look separately at the impact of a given organizational intervention on job satisfaction and job knowledge.

Study Effects Meta-Analysis Methods as a Response to Criticisms

One variation on Glass's methods has been labeled study effects meta-analysis by Bangert-Drowns (1986). It attempts to address some of the criticisms directed against Glassian methods. These methods differ from Glass's procedures in several ways. First, only one effect size from each study is included in the meta-analysis, thus assuring statistical independence within the meta-analysis. If a study has multiple dependent measures, those that assess the same construct are combined (usually averaged), and those that assess different constructs are assigned to different meta-analyses. These steps are similar to those we have followed in our research. Second, this procedure calls for the meta-analyst to make at least some judgments about study methodological quality and to exclude studies with deficiencies judged serious enough to distort study outcomes. In reviewing experimental studies, for example, the experimental treatment must be at least similar to those judged by experts in the research area to be appropriate, or the study will be excluded. This procedure seeks to determine the effect of a particular treatment on a particular outcome (construct), rather than to paint a broad Glassian picture of a research area. Some of those instrumental in developing and using this procedure are Mansfield and Busse (1977), Kulik and his associates (Bangert-Drowns, Kulik, & Kulik, 1983; Kulik & Bangert-Drowns, 1983/1984), Landman and Dawes (1982), and Wortman and Bryant (1985).

Meta-Analysis Methods Focusing Only on Sampling Error: Hedges's Methods, Rosenthal's Methods, and Bare-Bones Methods

As noted earlier, numerous artifacts produce the deceptive appearance of variability in results across studies. The artifact that typically produces more false variability than any other is sampling error variance. Glassian meta-analysis and study effects meta-analysis implicitly accept variability produced by sampling error variance as real variability. There are two types of meta-analyses that move beyond Glassian methods in that they attempt to control for sampling error variance.

Homogeneity Test–Based Meta-Analysis: Hedges's Methods and Rosenthal's Methods

The first of these methods is homogeneity test–based meta-analysis. This approach has been advocated independently by Hedges (1982c; Hedges & Olkin, 1985) and by Rosenthal and Rubin (1982a, 1982b).

Hedges (1982a) and Rosenthal and Rubin (1982a, 1982b) proposed that chi-square statistical tests be used to decide whether study outcomes are more variable than would be expected from sampling error alone. If these chi-square tests of homogeneity are not statistically significant, then the population correlation or effect size is accepted as constant across studies and there is no search for moderators. Use of chi-square tests of homogeneity to estimate whether findings in a set of studies differ more than would be expected from sampling error variance was originally proposed by Snedecor (1946).

The chi-square test of homogeneity typically has low power to detect variation beyond sampling error (Hedges & Pigott, 2001; National Research Council, 1992). Hence, the meta-analyst will often conclude that the studies being examined are homogeneous when they are not; that is, the meta-analyst will conclude that the value of ρ_{xy} or δ_{xy} is the same in all the studies included in the meta-analysis when, in fact, these parameters actually vary across studies (Hedges & Pigott, 2001). A major problem is that, in these circumstances, the fixed-effects model of meta-analysis (see Chapters 5 and 9) is then used in almost all cases. Unlike random-effects meta-analysis models, fixed-effects models assume zero between-study variability in ρ_{xy} or δ_{xy} in computing the standard error of $\bar{r}$ or $\bar{d}$, resulting in underestimates of the relevant standard errors of the mean. This, in turn, results in confidence intervals around $\bar{r}$ or $\bar{d}$ that are erroneously narrow—sometimes by large amounts. This creates an erroneous impression that the meta-analysis findings are much more precise than they really are. This problem also results in Type I biases in all significance tests conducted on $\bar{r}$ or $\bar{d}$, and these biases are often quite large (Hunter & Schmidt, 2000). As a result of this problem, the National Research Council (1992) report on data integration recommended that fixed-effects models be replaced by random-effects models, which do not suffer from this problem. We have also made that recommendation (Hunter & Schmidt, 2000). However, the majority of published meta-analyses using the Rosenthal-Rubin methods and the Hedges-Olkin methods have used their fixed-effects models. For example, as noted in Chapters 5 and 9, most of the meta-analyses that have appeared in *Psychological Bulletin* are fixed-effects meta-analyses. Most of these analyses used the Hedges-Olkin (1985) fixed-effects meta-analysis model.

Both Rosenthal and Rubin and Hedges and Olkin presented random-effects meta-analysis models as well as fixed-effects methods, but meta-analysts have rarely employed their random-effects methods. The methods presented in this book are all random-effects methods.

Hedges (1982b) and Hedges and Olkin (1985) extended the concept of homogeneity tests to develop a more general procedure for moderator analysis based on significance testing. It calls for breaking the overall chi-square statistic down into the sum of within- and between-group chi-squares. The original set of effect sizes in the meta-analysis is divided into successively smaller subgroups until the chi-square statistics within the subgroups are nonsignificant, indicating that sampling error can explain all the variation within the last set of subgroups.

Homogeneity test–based meta-analysis represents a return to the practice that originally led to the great difficulties in making sense out of research literature's reliance on statistical significance tests. As noted previously, the chi-square test typically has low power. (Perhaps somewhat ironically, Hedges & Olkin, 1985, Chap. 1, warned against the dangers of reliance on significance tests under conditions of low power. They directed this warning to those conducting primary studies, not to those conducting meta-analyses, but it is equally applicable in both cases.) Another problem is that the chi-square test has a Type I bias (Schmidt & Hunter, 2003). Under the null hypotheses, the chi-square test assumes that all between-study variance in study outcomes (e.g., rs or ds) is sampling error variance; but there are other purely artifactual sources of variance between studies in effect sizes. As discussed earlier, these include computational, transcriptional, and other data errors; differences between studies in reliability of measurement and in levels of range restriction; and others (see, e.g., Chapters 2 and 6). Thus, even when true study effect sizes are actually the same across studies, these sources of artifactual variance will create variance beyond sampling error, sometimes causing the chi-square test to be significant and, hence, to falsely indicate heterogeneity of effect sizes. This is especially likely when the number of studies is large, increasing statistical power to detect small amounts of such artifactual variance. Another problem is that, even when the variance beyond sampling error is not artifactual, it often will be small in magnitude and of little or no theoretical or practical significance. Hedges and Olkin (1985) recognized this fact and cautioned that researchers should not merely look at significance levels but should evaluate the actual size of the variance; unfortunately, however, once researchers are caught up in significance tests, the usual practice is to assume that if it is statistically significant it is important (and if it is not, it is 0). Once the major focus is on the results of significance tests, effect sizes are usually ignored.

Bare-Bones Meta-Analysis

The second approach to meta-analysis that attempts to control only for the artifact of sampling error is what we referred to earlier as bare-bones meta-analysis (see, e.g., Chapters 3 and 4). This approach can be applied to correlations, d values, or any other effect size statistic for which the standard error is known. For example, if the statistic is correlations, $\bar{r}$ is first computed. Then the variance of the set of correlations is computed. Next the amount of sampling error variance is computed and subtracted from this observed variance. If the result is 0, then sampling error accounts for all the observed variance, and the r value accurately summarizes all the studies in the meta-analysis. If not, then the square root of the remaining variance is the index of variability remaining around the mean r after sampling error variance has been removed. Chapters 3 and 4 present examples of bare-bones meta-analysis.

Because there are always other artifacts (such as measurement error) that should be corrected for, we have consistently stated in our writings that the bare-bones meta-analysis method is incomplete and unsatisfactory. It is useful primarily as the first step in *explaining* and *teaching* meta-analysis to novices. However, meta-analyses based on bare-bones methods alone have been published; the authors of these studies have invariably claimed that the information needed to correct for artifacts beyond sampling error was unavailable to them. In our experience, this is rarely the case. Estimates of artifact values (e.g., reliabilities of scales) are usually available from the literature, from test manuals, or from other sources, as indicated earlier. These values can be used to create distributions of artifacts for use in artifact distribution–based meta-analysis (described in Chapter 4), thus correcting for the biasing effects of measurement error and other artifacts in addition to sampling error.

Psychometric Meta-Analysis: Correction for Multiple Artifacts

The third type of meta-analysis is psychometric meta-analysis. These methods correct not only for sampling error (an unsystematic artifact) but for other, systematic artifacts, such as measurement error, range restriction or enhancement, dichotomization of measures, and so forth. These other artifacts are said to be systematic because, in addition to creating artifactual variation across studies, they also create systematic downward biases in the results of all studies. For example, measurement error systematically biases all correlations downward. Psychometric meta-analysis corrects not only for the artifactual variation across studies, but also for the downward biases. Psychometric meta-analysis is the only meta-analysis method that takes into account both statistical and measurement artifacts. Two variations of these procedures were described earlier in Chapters 3, 4, and 7. In the first, each r or d value is corrected individually for artifacts; in the second, correction is accomplished using artifact distributions. Callender and Osburn (1980) and Raju and Burke (1983) also developed methods for psychometric meta-analysis. These methods differ slightly in computational details but have been shown to produce virtually identical results (Law, Schmidt, & Hunter, 1994a, 1994b).

Every method of meta-analysis is of necessity based on a theory of data. It is this theory (or understanding of data) that determines the meta-analysis methods used to analyze the data. A complete theory of data includes an understanding of sampling error, measurement error, biased sampling (range restriction and range enhancement), dichotomization and its effects, data errors, and other causal factors that distort the raw data we see in research studies. Once a theoretical understanding of how these factors affect data is developed, it becomes possible to develop methods for correcting for their effects. In the language of psychometrics, the first process—the process by which these factors (artifacts) influence data—is modeled as the attenuation model. The second process—the process of correcting for these artifact-induced biases—is called the disattenuation model. If the theory of data on which a method of meta-analysis model is based is incomplete, that method will fail to correct for some or all of these artifacts and will thus produce biased results. For example, a theory of data that fails to recognize measurement error will lead to methods of meta-analysis that do not correct for measurement error. Such methods will then perforce produce biased meta-analysis results. As discussed in this chapter, some current methods of meta-analysis do not, in fact, correct for measurement error.

Sampling error and measurement error have a unique status among the statistical and measurement artifacts with which meta-analysis must deal: They are always present in all real data. Other artifacts, such as range restriction, artificial dichotomization of continuous variables, or data transcription errors, may be absent in a particular set of studies being subjected to meta-analysis. There is always sampling error, however, because sample sizes are never infinite. Likewise, there is always measurement error, because there are no perfectly reliable measures. In fact, it is the requirement of dealing simultaneously with both sampling error and measurement error that makes even relatively simple psychometric meta-analyses seem complicated. We are used to dealing with these two types of errors separately. For example, when psychometric texts (e.g., Lord & Novick, 1968; Nunnally & Bernstein, 1994) discuss measurement error, they assume an infinite (or very large) sample size, so that the focus of attention can be on measurement error alone, with no need to deal simultaneously with sampling error. When statistics texts discuss sampling error, they implicitly assume perfect reliability (the absence of measurement error), so that they and the reader can focus solely on sampling error. Both assumptions are highly unrealistic, because all real data simultaneously contains both types of errors. It is admittedly complicated to deal with both types of errors simultaneously, yet this is what meta-analysis must do to produce accurate results (Cook et al., 1992, pp. 315–316, 325–328).

The question of what theory of data underlies a method of meta-analysis is strongly related to the question of what the general purpose of meta-analysis is. Glass (1976, 1977) stated that the purpose is simply to summarize and describe the studies in a research literature. Our view, the alternative view, is that the purpose is to estimate as accurately as possible the construct-level relationships in the population (i.e., to estimate population values or parameters), because these are the relationships of scientific interest. This is an entirely different task; this is the task of estimating what the findings would have been if all studies had been conducted perfectly (i.e., with no methodological limitations). Doing this requires correction for sampling error, measurement error, and other artifacts (if present) that distort study results. Simply describing the contents of studies in the literature requires no such corrections but does not allow estimation of parameters of scientific interest.

Rubin (1990) critiqued the common, descriptive concept of the purpose of meta-analysis and proposed the alternative offered in this book. He stated that, as scientists, we do not really care about the population of imperfect studies per se; hence, an accurate description or summary of these studies is not really important. Instead, he argued that the goal of meta-analysis is to estimate the true effects or relationships—defined as "results that would be obtained in an infinitely large, perfectly designed study or sequence of such studies." According to Rubin,

> Under this view, we really do not care *scientifically* about summarizing this finite population (of observed studies). We really care about the underlying scientific process—the underlying process that is generating these outcomes that we happen to see—that we, as fallible researchers, are trying to glimpse through the opaque window of imperfect empirical studies. (p. 157; emphasis in original)

This is an excellent summary of the purpose of meta-analysis as we see it and as embodied in the methods presented in this book—the methods of psychometric meta-analysis.

Unresolved Problems in Meta-Analysis

In all forms of meta-analysis, including psychometric meta-analysis, there are unresolved problems. First, when effect size estimates are correlated with or regressed on multiple-study characteristics, capitalization on chance operates to increase the apparent number of significant associations for those study characteristics that have no actual associations with study outcomes. Because the sample size is the *number of studies* and many study properties may be coded, this problem is potentially severe (see discussion in Chapter 2). There is no purely statistical solution to this problem. The problem can be mitigated, however, by basing choice of study characteristics and final conclusions not only on the statistics at hand, but also on other theoretically relevant findings (which may be the result of other meta-analyses) and on theoretical considerations. Results should be examined closely for substantive and theoretical meaning. Capitalization on chance is a threat whenever the (unknown) correlation or regression weight is actually 0 or near 0. Second, when there is, in fact, a relationship, there is another problem: Statistical power to detect the relationship may be low (see discussion in Chapter 2). Thus, true moderators of study outcomes (to the extent that such exist) may have only a low probability of showing up as statistically significant. In short, this step in meta-analysis is often plagued with all the problems of small-sample studies. For a discussion of these problems, see Schmidt, Hunter, and Urry (1976) and Schmidt and Hunter (1978). Other things being equal, conducting separate meta-analyses on subsets of studies to identify a moderator does not avoid these problems and may lead to additional problems of confounding (see Chapter 9).

Summary of Methods of Integrating Studies

We have reviewed 10 different methods for integrating research findings across studies. These methods form a rough continuum of efficacy in revealing hidden facts that can be proven by the cumulative weight of previous studies. The narrative method is unsystematic, haphazard, and imposes an impossible information-processing burden on the reviewer. The traditional voting method uses only part of the available information, provides no information about effect size, and, worst of all, logically leads to false conclusions under circumstances that are quite common. Cumulating p values across studies does not logically lead to false conclusions, but has all the other disadvantages of the traditional voting method. Statistically correct vote-counting methods that yield only an overall statistical significance level (p value) for the group of studies reviewed have all the disadvantages of cumulating p values across studies. In particular, these methods provide no estimate of effect size. Other vote-counting procedures presented by Hedges and Olkin

(1980, 1985) do provide estimates of effect size, but the uncertainty in such estimates is substantial because these methods are based on only a part of the information that individual studies should present. These methods require the assumption that effect sizes are equal across studies; if this assumption is not met, then these methods yield only approximate estimates.

Glassian meta-analysis is a quantum improvement over these research integration methods. It uses more of the available information from the individual studies and provides a more accurate estimate of mean effect size; it does not require the assumption that effect sizes are constant across studies; and it provides an estimate of the variance of effect sizes. It also provides for correlating study effect sizes with study characteristics in an attempt to determine the causes of variation in study findings.

For most purposes of scientific research, study effects meta-analysis is an improvement over Glassian meta-analysis. It allows clearer conclusions about relationships between specific independent and dependent variable constructs, permitting finer tests of scientific hypothesis. Homogeneity test–based meta-analysis and bare-bones meta-analysis have the additional advantage of addressing sampling error in study findings. However, these methods fail to address or correct for the effects of any artifacts beyond sampling error. In particular, they ignore the biases created by measurement error, which are present in all studies. In this respect, they are based on an incomplete, and therefore erroneous, theory of data, as noted earlier.

Only psychometric meta-analysis methods are based on a complete theory of data—that is, an understanding of data that includes not only the effects of sampling error on data but also the effects of measurement error and other artifacts such as range restriction, dichotomization, imperfect construct validity, and others discussed in this book. Psychometric meta-analysis corrects not only for the artifactual variation across studies created by these artifacts, but also for the downward biases created by them on the mean correlation or mean d value. Psychometric meta-analysis can be accomplished either by correcting each r or d individually or by use of distributions of artifacts when artifact values are not available for each r or d value. Psychometric meta-analysis estimates what research findings would have been had it been possible to conduct studies without methodological flaws. As Rubin (1990) noted, this is what we, as scientists, want to know, and, therefore, the production of such estimates should be the purpose of meta-analysis.

Computer Programs for Meta-Analysis

In conducting their meta-analyses, many researchers prefer to write their own programs, often using spreadsheet programs. Others prefer to use commercially available programs for the PC. There are many programs available today for conducting the different types of meta-analysis discussed in this chapter. There are undoubtedly also many we are not aware of, including many of the "free" programs in the public domain. Public-domain programs are usually more limited in features. In any event, their number is great enough to preclude discussion of them here because of space considerations. In this section, we briefly discuss some of the commercially available programs for the PC. A more complete description of available software for meta-analysis is given in Rothstein, McDaniel, and Borenstein (2001).

We are not aware of any commercially available programs for Glass meta-analysis or study effects meta-analysis. However, the key statistical step in these methods is the computation of effect sizes. A program called ES is available (Shadish, Robinson, & Lu, 1999) that computes effect sizes from a wide variety of reported statistics and study designs. As we noted in Chapter 8, this program is useful for computing effect sizes from repeated-measures designs, ANOVA factorial designs (both between- and within-subjects designs), and a variety of other research designs. Marketed by Assessment Systems Corporation, this program also allows computation of effect sizes from studies that report limited information—for example, studies that report only specific significance tests. The program includes over 40 different methods of computing effect sizes. The utility of this program is by no means limited to applications of Glass or study effects meta-analysis. The program is a useful adjunct in preparing a database for any type of meta-analysis.

We are aware of three commercially available programs for homogeneity test–based meta-analysis. The first is D-Stat (Johnson, 1989), marketed by Lawrence Erlbaum. This program is based on the Hedges-Olkin (1985) meta-analysis methods. The second is Advanced BASIC Meta-Analysis (Mullen, 1989), also marketed by Lawrence Erlbaum. This program is oriented more toward the Rosenthal-Rubin methods of meta-analysis, although it can be used to conduct Hedges-Olkin meta-analyses. These two programs are limited to fixed-effects meta-analysis models. Finally, there is Meta-Win (Rosenberg, Adams, & Gurevitch, 1997; www.sinauer.com). Unlike D-Stat and Advanced BASIC Meta-Analysis, this program allows for both fixed- and random-effects meta-analysis models in the Hedges-Olkin framework. It also has a number of other additional features.

There are several programs available for psychometric meta-analysis. The first is the software package written to accompany this book: Hunter-Schmidt Meta-Analysis Programs (see the Appendix). This Windows-based program package is available commercially from Frank Schmidt and Huy Le. It includes six programs that implement the methods presented in this book. The first two programs are for correlations corrected individually (discussed in Chapter 3). The first subprogram here is for studies in which range restriction is direct, while the second is for data in which range restriction is indirect. (If there is no range restriction in one's study set, either program can be used; the programs will produce identical output.) The second two programs conduct artifact distribution meta-analysis for correlations, based on the interactive method described in Chapter 4. The first of these is for studies in which range restriction is direct; the second, for studies with indirect range restriction. (Again, if there is no range restriction in one's studies, either program can be used.) The fifth program is for *d* values corrected individually, while the sixth program is for artifact distribution meta-analysis of *d* values. Both these approaches to meta-analysis of *d* values are discussed in Chapter 7. Data files for data analyzed as examples in Chapters 3, 5, and 7 are included in the program and the user can run these analyses to become familiar with the programs.

All these programs include the accuracy-enhancing procedures discussed in Chapter 5 and other chapters. In addition to psychometric meta-analysis results, all six programs also report bare-bones meta-analysis results. For all these programs, the Windows format allows for easy data input on the screen or from stored data files. Output can be printed or presented on the screen. Output and data files can be saved on the program site. The program set also includes a number of utility programs for computing statistics for entry into meta-analysis (e.g., a program for converting point biserial correlations to biserial correlations and a program for computing correlations of sums [composites] and reliabilities of composites—see Chapter 10). More detail on this software package and its availability is presented in the Appendix.

The computer program MAIN (Raju & Fleer, 1997) corrects correlations individually and applies psychometric meta-analysis to the corrected correlations. This method, described in Raju, Burke, Normand, and Langlois (1991), takes into account sampling error in the reliability estimates, as well as in the correlations. It is set up for use only with direct range restriction, although it may be modified in the future to also handle indirect range restriction. This program does not conduct artifact distribution meta-analysis for correlations, nor does it perform meta-analysis of *d* values. However, Raju has noncommercial programs available for artifact distribution psychometric meta-analysis of correlations based on the Taylor series approximation (TSA) procedures (Raju & Burke, 1983) discussed in Chapter 4. As of this writing, these programs are limited to studies with direct range restriction. They are quite accurate for data with direct range restriction (as shown in Law et al., 1994a, 1994b).

Finally, there is one program that comes close to being an all-purpose meta-analysis program. This Windows-based program, Comprehensive Meta-Analysis, is marketed by Biostat (www.Meta-Analysis.com). Considerably more costly than the other programs discussed here, this program performs psychometric meta-analysis, Hedges-Olkin (1985) homogeneity test–based meta-analysis (both fixed- and random-effects models), and a variety of additional types of meta-analysis used in medical research and other areas. It has a large number of features for calculation of effect sizes, confidence intervals for individual study results, and other statistics from individual studies. The resulting data can be displayed in a variety of clarifying and informative ways, and there are features that allow for the creation, management, and updating of the resulting databases. As of this writing, this program does not allow for psychometric meta-analysis of correlations corrected individually, although there are plans to introduce this feature later. The program allows for artifact distribution meta-analysis of correlations based on the interactive method (discussed in Chapter 4). However, this subprogram handles only direct range restriction. A program for meta-analysis of studies with indirect range restriction may be added in the future. Psychometric meta-analysis of *d* values may be conducted in both ways: either correcting each *d* value individually or using artifact distribution meta-analysis.

This discussion of software for meta-analysis is by no means comprehensive. New programs for meta-analysis appear with some frequency, and we have undoubtedly missed some existing programs. Readers interested in a fuller picture will probably find that an internet search turns up additional programs of interest.

12

Locating, Evaluating, Selecting, and Coding Studies

Because of the explosive expansion over the last 15 years, no single book can today cover all aspects of meta-analysis. The primary focus of this book is on statistical and psychometric methods for data analysis in meta-analysis. However, the less quantitative processes of locating, selecting, evaluating, and coding studies are also important. We cannot cover these topics in detail but fortunately good published treatments of these topics are readily available. The material in this chapter is selective rather than comprehensive. It is intended to supplement other published discussions of this topic. We have included in this chapter mostly material we have found to be absent from other published treatments.

Conducting a Thorough Literature Search

Many topics not addressed in detail in this book are covered in detail in Cooper (1998). For this reason, we recommended Cooper (1998) as a supplement to this book in graduate courses in meta-analysis. Chapter 3 of the Cooper book presents considerable detail on how to conduct a thorough literature search, including discussion of the following methods for locating studies: the World Wide Web, conference papers, personal journals, libraries, electronic journals, research report reference lists, research bibliographies, and reference databases (such as PsycINFO, ERIC, Dissertation Abstracts International, and Social Sciences Citation Index). Cooper also provides a discussion of the limitations of computer-based literature searches and gives methods for assessing the adequacy and completeness of a literature search. Other useful sources include Cook et al. (1992, pp. 289–305), Reed and Baxter (1994), M. C. Rosenthal (1994), Rothstein (2003), and White (1994).

What to Do About Studies With Methodological Weaknesses

Many reviewers wish to eliminate from their analyses studies that they perceive as having methodological inadequacies (Slavin, 1986). This often is not as reasonable and desirable as it may seem. The assertion of "methodological inadequacy" always depends on theoretical assumptions about what *might* be true in a study. These assumptions may well be false and are rarely tested in their own right. Those who believe the assumptions usually feel no need to test them. That is, the hypothesis of "methodological inadequacy" is rarely tested empirically. No research study can be defended against all possible counterhypotheses; hence, no study can be "without methodological inadequacy." However, methodological inadequacies do not always cause biased findings, and, prior to the analyses of the full set of studies on the topic, it is difficult to determine reliably when methodological inadequacies have caused biased findings and when they have not.

Some reviewers are inclined to use the simple strategy of eliminating all studies believed to have methodological inadequacies. (See "The Myth of the Perfect Study" in Chapter 1.) Because most studies have some weaknesses, these reviewers often end up reporting inferences based on only a few studies. When there is good a priori evidence that the eliminated studies had substantially biased results, this strategy would be justified, but that seldom is the case.

The hypothesis of methodological inadequacy should be tested only after two prior hypotheses have been rejected. First, one should determine if the variation across all studies can be accounted for by sampling error and other artifacts, such as differences in reliability. If the variation is due solely to artifacts, then there can be no variance due to methodological inadequacy. Second, if there is substantial variation across studies, then theoretically plausible moderator variables should be tested. If the moderator variables account for nonartifactual variance, there can be no variance across studies due to methodological inadequacy. If the theoretically plausible moderator variables do not explain the variance, methodological inadequacies may be present. One can then rate the internal and external validity of the studies or code the characteristics that might produce inadequacy and test these characteristics as moderator variables.

It is important to recognize that the actual threat to the internal and external validity of a study is not determined exclusively or even primarily by the design of the study. Campbell and Stanley's monograph (1963) on experimental and quasi-experimental design shows which threats are controlled by various research designs if none of the controlled factors interact. However, the monograph does not indicate which threats are likely to be trivial in a given study or which threats can be reasonably controlled by other means (see the discussion at the end of Chapter 8).

Some have suggested that there is a counterexample to our argument: violations of construct validity across studies. The fact that the same variable name is used in different studies does not mean that the same variable is measured in those studies. We believe that construct validity is potentially an empirical question, as well as a theoretical question. Ideally, one would do an empirical study in which alternative instruments or methods are used to measure the independent and dependent variables. Confirmatory factor analysis could then be used to see if the alternate measures differ by more than error of measurement. That is, do the different measures correlate approximately 1.00 after correcting for measurement error? An inferior test of the construct invalidity hypothesis can be run within a meta-analysis. If several instruments are really measuring different things, then it would be unlikely that they would have the same correlation with the second variable of the meta-analysis (or that the treatment effect would be identical across the different variables). If the meta-analysis shows no variance across studies, then that would suggest that the alternate measures are substantially equivalent. On the other hand, if the meta-analysis does find variance across studies, the hypothesized nonequivalence of variables can be tested as a moderator variable. If this moderator variable does explain the variance across studies, this finding is confirmation of the hypothesis of construct invalidity. In any case, it is our belief that the *assertion* of construct invalidity is not the same as the *fact* of construct invalidity. We believe that methodological hypotheses are less likely to be true than substantive hypotheses because they are usually based on a much weaker database.

If meta-analysis shows that the studies evaluated as methodologically superior yield different results from the studies rated methodologically poorer, then final conclusions can be based on the "good" studies. If there is no difference in results, this finding disconfirms the methodological hypotheses. In such cases, all studies should be retained and included in the final meta-analysis to provide the largest possible database.

Cooper (1998, pp. 81–84) pointed out another reason for caution in attempts to exclude methodologically weak studies. To make such decisions, evaluators must judge and rate each study on methodological quality. Cooper (1998) noted that research on inter-rater agreement for judgments of research quality shows that the average correlation between experienced evaluators is at best about .50, illustrating the subjectivity of assessments of methodological quality. Based on the Spearman-Brown formula, it would require use of six evaluators to yield a reliability of approximately .85. Most meta-analyses will not be able to draw on the considerable time and effort of six experienced judges. Use of fewer judges would usually result in the erroneous elimination of a prohibitive number of acceptable studies.

The question of methodological weaknesses must be separated from the question of relevant and irrelevant studies. Relevant studies are those that focus on the relationship of interest. For example, if one is interested in the relationship between role conflict and job satisfaction, studies that report only correlations between measures of role conflict and organizational identification should be excluded because they are irrelevant. (If enough such studies are encountered, one can, of course, conduct a separate meta-analysis of the relationship between role conflict and organizational identification.) Measures of different dependent variable constructs should ordinarily not be combined in the same meta-analysis (see Chapter 11), but if they are, separate meta-analyses should also be reported for each conceptually different dependent variable. Glass and his associates do combine different dependent variable constructs, and they have been severely criticized on this account (see, e.g., Chapter 11 and Mansfield & Busse, 1977). While it is true that meta-analyses that "mix apples and oranges" are difficult to interpret, no harm is done as long as separate meta-analyses are presented later for each dependent variable construct. In general, meta-analyses that do not mix different *independent* variables are also more likely to be informative. However, the question is not a simple one. For example, in our meta-analyses of the relationship between verbal ability and job performance, we excluded job performance correlations based on other abilities (e.g., quantitative ability measures). For our purposes, such correlations were irrelevant. However, we later found that the mean and standard deviation of correlations for verbal ability were very similar to the mean and standard deviation for quantitative ability (see, e.g., Pearlman, Schmidt, & Hunter, 1980). We also found that the validity of both kinds of measures stemmed entirely from the fact that they were both measures of general mental ability (see, e.g., Hunter, 1986; Schmidt, 2002). Although we have not conducted such an analysis, these findings provide a rationale for a meta-analysis that includes both kinds of measures—a meta-analysis of the relationship between "g-loaded" tests and job performance. The point is that measures that assess different constructs from one theoretical perspective may assess the same construct from the perspective of another theory. Furthermore, the second theory may represent an advance in understanding. Thus, the question of how varied the independent and dependent variable measures included in a meta-analysis should be is a more complex and subtle one than it appears to be at first glance. The answer depends on the specific hypotheses, theories, and purposes of the investigator. Glass has stated that there is nothing objectionable about mixing apples and oranges if the focus of the research interest is fruit. This statement is consistent with our position. However, Glass goes beyond the theory-based rationale presented here in arguing that it may be appropriate to include in the same meta-analysis independent and dependent variable measures that appear to be different constructs. Specifically, he argues that such broad, mixed meta-analyses may be justified and useful in summarizing a research literature in broad strokes (see Chapter 11). However, most researchers—ourselves included—do not usually find such broad-brush research summaries as informative as more focused meta-analyses. At least initially, meta-analyses in a given research area should probably be narrow and focused enough to correspond to the major constructs recognized by researchers in that area. Then, as understanding develops, later meta-analyses may become broader in scope if that is shown to be theoretically appropriate.

Additional considerations in evaluating studies for meta-analysis can be found in Chapter 7 of Cook et al. (1992), Chapter 4 of Cooper (1998), and in Wortman (1994).

Coding Studies in Meta-Analysis

The process of coding data from primary studies can often be complex, tedious, and time-consuming. Nevertheless, it is a critical component of meta-analysis, and it is essential that it be done appropriately and accurately. Stock (1994) and Orwin (1994) presented detailed discussions of the many considerations, decisions, and subtasks that can be involved in coding information from primary studies. Chapter 4 of Cooper (1998) presents a shorter discussion of some issues in coding.

The complexity of the needed coding depends on the hypotheses and purposes underlying the meta-analysis, making any general detailed discussion of coding issues difficult. If studies differ on many dimensions, the meta-analysis focuses on several different relationships, and there is reason to believe many study characteristics may affect study results, the coding task will usually be quite complex. On the other hand, coding can be relatively simple in research literatures in which studies are quite similar, the focus is on a single bivariate relationship, and there is reason to believe that there will be few, if any, moderators of this relationship. In such a case, few study characteristics need to be coded, greatly reducing the scope of the coding task. This distinction bears on the issue of coder agreement. Whetzel and McDaniel (1988) found that, for studies of the latter type, inter-coder agreement and inter-coder reliability were virtually perfect. The conclusion of this study was that for such research literatures there was no need to report inter-coder agreement or reliability. Even in more complex coding tasks, the general finding has been that coder agreement and reliability have typically been quite good (Cooper, 1998, pp. 95–97). However, these findings apply to the coding of more objective aspects of studies. As noted previously, subjective evaluations such as assessments of overall study methodological quality produce much lower agreement. However, one study (Miller, Lee, & Carlson, 1991) found that coders could reliably make inferential judgments about psychological mediators in studies based on reading the methods sections of studies and that these judgments revealed important moderator variables in the meta-analyses.

As discussed in Chapters 3 and 4, the initial application of the methods presented in this book was to the area of personnel selection, specifically, to the estimation of the validity of selection methods such as ability tests, structured interviews, and personality tests. The coding schemes needed in research of this sort are usually closer to the simple end of the continuum than has been the case for many subsequent applications of these methods to other research literatures. However, even these coding schemes can be somewhat complex. To illustrate this, the Appendix to this chapter presents the coding scheme used by the U.S. Office of Personnel Management for validity generalization meta-analyses, along with the instructions and decision rules for the coding task. Despite the apparent complexity of the instructions, this coding scheme is far simpler than many used in meta-analyses in organizational behavior and other areas today. There is no such thing as the perfect illustrative coding scheme, because each coding scheme must be tailor-made to the purposes of the particular meta-analysis. However, we hope that this coding scheme nevertheless provides some general guidance for approaching the task of constructing a coding scheme.

What to Include in the Meta-Analysis Report

A widely held precept in all the sciences is that reports of research ought to include enough information about the study so that the reader can critically examine the evidence and, if desired, replicate the study. At a minimum, it is held that the report ought to describe the research design, sampling, measurement, analyses, and findings. Where unusual procedures have been used, it is expected that they will be described in some detail.

Researchers are never more acutely aware of the importance of these reporting standards than when they are reviewing a set of studies. Inadequate reports of primary research tremendously increase the burden of doing any kind of review. Narrative reviews probably violate these precepts more often than do reports of primary research. Jackson's (1978) analysis of 36 review articles in top-tier journals found that only 4 reported major aspects of the search for relevant studies; only 7 indicated whether the full set of located studies on the topic was analyzed; only half of the 36 reported the direction and magnitude of the findings of *any* of the primary studies; and only 3 cited the mean, range, or another summary of the magnitude of the primary study's findings.

The consequences of such reporting omissions are serious. There are two reasons for carefully describing the literature search process in a review article. First, it helps the reader to judge the comprehensiveness and representativeness of the sources that are the subject of the review. Second, briefly detailing the literature search process in a review article allows future reviewers of the topic to extend the review without duplicating it. If it is known that most of the articles included in the review were those listed under certain descriptors of certain years of certain indexes, or found in the bibliographies of specified sources, it is easy for a subsequent reviewer to broaden or deepen the search for relevant sources without duplicating the earlier work.

Excluding some located studies on a given topic from the analysis of the review can seriously affect the inferences drawn from the review. Readers need to know whether there may be such an effect. Furthermore, if some studies are excluded, the criteria for exclusion, the number of studies excluded, and the citations of the excluded studies are useful to the critical reader.

The direction and magnitude of each primary study finding or of the mean or variance of the set of findings is important information. Without it, the reader often cannot make even a preliminary judgment about the validity of a review's conclusions unless he or she laboriously consults the original reports of each study. Many meta-analyses do not cover more than 40 or 50 studies. In such cases, it is often possible to provide substantial data on each study in a single-page table. The table should include the author and date of each study, the sample size, and the standardized effect score. This is, in fact, often done today in published meta-analyses. If sources of spurious variance do not account for most of the variation in the standardized effect scores, other characteristics of each study should be included, such as the status characteristics of the subjects, subjects' average pretreatment scores on the criterion (when applicable), level and duration or scope conditions (such as region of the country, occupations of subjects, and the like), strength of the study design with respect to internal and external validity, and other study characteristics. If there is not enough space for this table in the publication, there should be a reference indicating where it can be obtained.

Additional issues to consider in preparing the final report of a meta-analysis are presented in Cooper (1998, Chap. 6), Halvorsen (1994), Rothstein (2003), and Light, Singer, and Willett (1994).

Information Needed in Reports of Primary Studies

Meta-analysis procedures require certain kinds of data from each primary study that is to be included in the cumulation. Unfortunately, some of those data are usually missing from at least a few of the studies being reviewed. This forces the reviewer to track down authors and try to secure the data from them and, when this fails, to attempt to estimate the data using statistical approximations of the sort recommended by Glass, McGaw, and Smith (1981). Often, the missing data would lengthen the report of the study by only one-fourth to one-half a page, and in all cases these data would provide the readers important information about the study as well as provide a basis for valid meta-analyses. Large correlation matrices may be awkward to include in some reports, but these primary data can often be reported in appendixes. At the very least, they should be preserved for later analysis and referenced in the report.

Correlational Studies

Consider first correlation studies. If reported study findings are to be usable in cumulative studies, then the mean, standard deviation, and reliability of each variable should be published. The mean is necessary for the cumulation of norms, for the cumulation of regression lines (or for the assessment of possible nonlinearity over extreme ranges), or for the identification of very special populations. The standard deviation is necessary for the same reasons and for an additional one. If the relationship between two variables is linear, then there is little variation in the correlation produced by variation in the mean from study to study. However, this is quite different for the standard deviation. Differences in variability from study to study can have dramatic effects on intercorrelations between variables. If a study is being done in a homogeneous population in which the standard deviation is only half the size of the standard deviation in other studies, then, in that population, the correlations for that variable will be much smaller than the correlations observed in other populations. Similarly, if the variance is inflated by observing only high and low extreme groups on a given variable, then correlations for that study will be larger than those in populations with the middle range included. This is the problem of range restriction and range enhancement discussed in detail in Chapters 3 to 5. Estimates of reliability of the measures used are needed for two reasons. First, variations in standard deviation produce differences in reliability. Second, and more important, the variable used in the study may not be identical to that used in published norm studies. For example, a study might include a measure of "authoritarianism," but that scale might consist of a subset of eight items chosen by the investigator; the reliability of this subscale may be quite different from the reliability of the complete scale published in norm studies. In the case of new scales, reliabilities may not have been established on large norm populations; in such cases, the reliabilities can be established by cumulating reliability estimates across studies.

It is imperative that the entire matrix of zero-order correlations between all variables be published (the means, standard deviations, and reliabilities can be easily appended as extra rows or columns of this matrix). Each entry in this table may be used in entirely unrelated cumulation studies. Correlations that are not statistically significant should still be included; one cannot average a "—" or an "ns" or a "..." or whatever. If only significant correlations are printed, then cumulation is necessarily biased. This is even more the case for correlations that are not even mentioned because they are not significant.

Moreover, there is a prevalent misperception concerning "nonsignificant" correlations. Many believe that "nonsignificant" means that no statistically significant finding could be associated with those variables in that study. This is not, in fact, the case. The size of a correlation is relative to the context in which it is considered; partial correlations and beta weights may be much larger than zero-order correlations. For example, suppose we find a nonsignificant correlation of .10 between performance of supervisor and subordinate performance. If cognitive ability of subordinates were correlated .70 with their performance but correlated 0 with quality of supervision, then the partial correlation between quality of supervision and subordinate performance with subordinate ability held constant would rise to .14, which might then be statistically significant. If motivation of subordinates were correlated .70 with their performance but were uncorrelated with their abilities, then the double partial correlation of quality of supervision and subordinate performance with both ability and motivation controlled would be .71, which would almost certainly be highly significant. Thus, although quality of supervision might not be significantly correlated with subordinate performance at a zero level, it might be highly correlated when extraneous variables are controlled. In brief, even though an independent variable is not significantly correlated with a dependent variable, its beta weight in multiple regression might be large and highly statistically significant. This is another important reason why all zero-order correlations should be included in published studies.

Experimental Studies

What about experimental studies in which analysis of variance is used instead of correlation? In a two-group design, the F value that is conventionally computed is an exact transformation of the point biserial correlation, as noted in Chapter 7. The significance test on the point biserial correlation is exactly equivalent to the F test. In a 2-by-2-by-2-by ... design, every effect in the analysis of variance is the comparison of two means and could thus be represented by a point biserial correlation. In fact, the square of that point biserial correlation is the "eta square," or percentage of variance accounted for by that effect. In designs with more than two categories for a facet, the categories are frequently ordered (indeed frequently quantitative). In such cases, there is rarely any important effect beyond the linear trend. In such cases, the square root of eta can be used as a correlation between the corresponding variables, after assignment of the appropriate positive or negative sign to eta. Thus, everything stated previously, including considerations of restrictions in range and reliability, applies to experimental as well as correlational studies.

Studies Using Multiple Regression

A multiple regression analysis of a primary study is based on the full zero-order correlation (or covariance) matrix for the set of predictor variables and the criterion variable. Similarly, a cumulation of multiple regression analyses must be based on a cumulative zero-order correlation matrix (as shown in Chapter 5). However, many reports of multiple regression fail to report the full correlation matrix, often omitting the zero-order correlations among the predictors and sometimes even the zero-order correlations between each predictor and the criterion. Reporting practices are sometimes even worse. Some studies report only the multiple regression weights for the predictors. However, cumulation leading to optimal estimates of multiple regression weights requires cumulation of the predictor intercorrelations as well as of the predictor-dependent variable correlations. That is, the formula for each multiple regression weight uses all the correlations between the predictors, and hence, they must be cumulatively estimated.

The practice of ignoring the predictor intercorrelations is extremely frustrating even if large samples are used. Given the predictor intercorrelations, path analysis can be used to test hypotheses about direct and indirect causes. If the predictor intercorrelations are not given, one cannot distinguish between a predictor that makes no contribution and a predictor that makes a strong but indirect contribution. In short, one cannot do the desired path analysis unless the predictor intercorrelations are given as well as the predictor-criterion correlations.

Finally, it should be noted that, as discussed in Chapter 5, regression weights are typically not suitable for cumulation. Suppose y is to be predicted from $X_1, X_2, \ldots, X_m$. The beta weights for X_1 depend not only on the variables X_1 and Y, but on all the other variables $X_2, X_3, \ldots, X_m$ contained in the same regression equation. That is, beta weights are relative to the set of predictors considered and will replicate across studies only if the exact set of predictors is considered in each. If any predictor is added or subtracted from one study to the next, then the beta weights for all variables may change. Although it may be worthwhile to calculate beta weights within a study, it is crucial for cumulation purposes that the zero-order correlations be included in the published study. *After* cumulation of zero-order correlations, a multiple regression can be run using a set of predictors that may never have occurred together in any one study. (See Collins et al., 2003, for an example of this.)

For example, suppose we wanted to predict job performance from three abilities, a, b, and c. To cumulate beta weights, we would have to find multiple studies that computed beta weights for the a, b, and c combination. There may be few such studies. On the other hand, cumulation from zero-order correlations greatly expands the set of studies that can contribute estimates of one or more of the needed correlations. In fact, any predictive study containing any combination of two of these variables (a and b, a and c, or b and c) would contain a correlation of interest. In order for r_{ab} to be estimated, there must be at least one study with both a and b; estimation of r_{ac} requires at least one study with both a and c; and estimation of r_{bc} requires at least one study with both b and c. However, there need be no study in which all three predictors occur together. See Chapter 1 for a more complete discussion of this process.

Studies Using Factor Analysis

Factor analyses are often published with the zero-order correlation matrix omitted, presumably to conserve journal space. However, zero-order correlations can be meta-analyzed across studies while factor loadings cannot be. First, the factors that appear in a given study are not determined by the single variables that appear, but by the sets or clusters of variables that occur. For example, suppose a study contains one good measure of motivation and ten cognitive ability measures. Then it is likely that the communality of the motivation variable will be 0, and a motivation factor will not appear in the factor analysis. Factors are defined by *redundant* measurement; no factor will appear unless it is measured by at least two redundant indicators (and preferably by three or more). Second, the factors in an exploratory factor analysis (such as principal axis factors followed by VARIMAX rotation) are not defined independently of one another. For example, suppose that in the initial output one cluster of variables defines G_1 and another cluster defines G_2 and the correlation between G_1 and G_2 is r. Then, if factor scores are standardized, the VARIMAX factors will be defined by

$$F_1 = G_1 - \alpha G_2$$

$$F_2 = G_2 - \alpha G_1$$

where

$$\alpha = \frac{1 - \sqrt{1 - r^2}}{r}$$

Thus, each orthogonal factor is defined as a discrepancy variable between natural clusters, and the loading of an indicator of G_1 on factor F_1 will depend not only on the other indicators of G_1 in its own set but also on what other factors appear in the same study (Hunter & Gerbing, 1982). Cluster analysis results and confirmatory factor analysis results present a somewhat different picture. If a cluster analysis or confirmatory factor analysis model fits the data (Hunter, 1980a; Hunter & Gerbing, 1982), then the factor loading of an indicator on its own factor is the square root of its reliability and is independent of the rest of the variables and is thus subject to cumulation. However, high-quality confirmatory factor analyses are still quite rare in the literature.

Studies Using Canonical Correlation

Canonical correlation begins with a set of predictor variables and a set of dependent measures and is thus conceptually a situation suitable for multiple regression. In canonical correlation, however, two *new* variables are formed: a weighted combination of the predictor variables and a weighted combination of the dependent measures. These combinations are formed in such a way as to maximize the correlation between the two weighted composites.

Canonical correlations cannot be cumulated across studies. Neither can the canonical weights. In multiple regression, each beta weight depends on the dependent variable and on the specific set of predictors. Thus, it generalizes only to other studies in which exactly the same set of predictors is used (which is rare indeed). However, each canonical regression weight depends not only on the exact set of predictors in the study, but on the exact set of dependent measures as well. Thus, it will be very rare that the results of canonical regression can be compared or cumulated. On the other hand, the zero-order correlation matrices of such studies can be cumulated across studies.

Studies Using Multivariate Analysis of Variance (MANOVA)

Statistically, MANOVA is a canonical regression, with the treatment contrast variables as "independent" variables and with measured variables as "dependent" measures. Consequently, the data needed for cumulation across studies are the set of zero-order correlations between contrasts, between contrasts and other measured variables, and between other measured variables. These data should be reported but rarely are. Hence, data from studies using MANOVA can rarely be meta-analyzed.

General Comments on Reporting in Primary Studies

For multiple regression, factor analysis, and canonical correlation analyses, the zero-order correlation matrices are essential for cumulation across studies. Once these data are secured, the reviewer is able to analyze the cumulative correlation matrix using any appropriate statistical procedure. For example, data gathered for multiple regression can be used in path analysis.

If journals required the publication of confidence intervals in place of levels of statistical significance, three benefits would ensue. First, researchers would be alerted to how much uncertainty there is in estimates derived from most individual social science studies. The common small-sample studies will generally have wide confidence intervals. Second, the results across studies would correctly appear to be in greater agreement than they usually do when focusing on the proportions of studies that are statistically significant (Schmidt, 1996). For instance, if there are five studies, each with a sample size of 50 and with correlations of .05, .13, .24, .33, and .34, only two of the five are statistically significant at the .05 level, but the 95% confidence intervals of all five correlations would overlap substantially. Finally, in the case of two-sample tests, reports of the confidence interval and sample sizes are all that is needed for computing standardized effect scores.

When measures of variables with less than perfect reliability are used, should the correlations between such measures be corrected for attenuation due to error of measurement? It is clear from measurement theory that the reduction in correlations due to the use of imperfect measurement is purely a matter of artifact. Reliability of measurement is a matter of feasibility and practicality independent of the theoretical and psychological meaning of the variables measured. Therefore, it is correlations between perfectly measured variables that are of theoretical importance; that is, it is the corrected correlations that should be used in multiple regression or path analysis when theories are being tested. If the reliability of each variable is published, those cumulating findings across studies can analyze the data using appropriate methods. Meta-analysis should ideally be performed on corrected correlations (although, as shown in Chapter 4, this correction can be made when necessary after the cumulation, using artifact distribution meta-analysis methods). As noted earlier (see Chapter 3), correction increases the sampling error in the estimated correlation, and therefore, the formulas for the correction of variance due to sampling error in uncorrected correlation coefficients are not appropriate for correlations corrected for attenuation. Instead, the formulas given in Chapter 3 for corrected correlations should be used to compute the sampling error in corrected correlations.

Appendix

Coding Sheet for Validity Studies

Validity Coding Sheet
U.S. Office of Personnel Management

1. Study ID — 1 2 3 4 5

Sample Information

2. Sample Within Study (applies to subgroups) — 6 7 8
3. Race Subgroup? (Y if yes, blank otherwise) — 9
4. Sex Subgroup? (Y if yes, blank otherwise) — 10
5. Race — 11
   1. American Indian or Alaskan Native
   2. Asian or Pacific Islander
   3. Black, not Hispanic
   5. Hispanic
   6. Unspecified Minority
   7. Mixed
   8. Other (specify) ________
6. Sex — 12
   1. Female
   2. Male
   3. Mixed
7. Sample Size (total) — 13 14 15 16 17
8. Occupational Code (DOT Edition IV) — 18 19 20 21 22 23 / 24 25 26

Validity Information

9. Validity Coefficient (Uncorrected) Include sign if negative. — 27 . 28 29
10. Validity Coefficient (Corrected for Range Restriction) Code only if included in study. — 30 . 31 32
11. Validity Coefficient (Corrected for Criterion Unreliability) Code only if included in study. — 33 . 34 35
12. Validity Coefficient (Corrected for Criterion Unreliaiblity and Range Restriction) Code only if included in study. — 36 . 37 38
13. Type of Coefficient — 39 40
   01 Biserial
   02 Partial (tenure held constant)
   03 Pearson product-moment
   04 Ptm
   05 Point-biserial
   06 Rho
   07 Tetrachonc
   08 Triserial
   09 Shrunken R
   10 Other (specify) ________
14. Sample Size for Mean r — 41 42 43 44 45
15. Study Type — 46
16. Time in months Between Collection of Predictor and Criterion Data — 47 48 49

Predictor Information

17. Predictor Code — 50 51 52 53

Variable and Scale

Employee Group

18. Predictor Reliability Coefficient — 54 55
19. Predictor Mean — 56 57 58 . 59 60
20. Predictor Standard Deviation — 61 62 . 63 64
21. Type of Predictor Reliability — 65
   1. Alternate forms
   2. Internal consistency or corrected split half
   3. Test-retest
   4. Inter-rater
   9. Other (specify) ________
22. Time Interval Between Testing for Predictor Reliability Estimate (in Weeks) — 66 67 68

Applicant Group

23. Predictor Reliability Coefficient — 69 70
24. Predictor Mean — 71 72 73 . 74 75
25. Predictor Standard Deviation — 76 77 . 78 79
26. Type of Predictor Reliability — 80
   1. Alternate forms
   2. Internal consistency or corrected split half
   3. Test-retest
   4. Inter-rater
   9. Other (specify) ________
27. Time Interval Between Testing for Predictor Reliability Estimates (in Weeks) — 81 82 83
28. Ratio Restricted/Unrestricted SD Code only if provided in study — 84 85

Criterion Information

29. Criterion Content — 86
    1. Job performance
    2. Training performance
    3. Tenure
    4. Wage
    5. Promotion/demotion
    6. Commendations/reprimands
    8. Mixture of above
    9. Unknown

30. Criterion Measurement Method — 87
    1. Supervisor/instructor rating
    2. Peer rating
    3. Other rating
    4. Work sample
    5. Written test
    6. Production data
    8. Mixture of above
    9. Unknown

31. Criterion: Administrative vs. Research — 88
    1. Administrative
    2. Research

32. Criterion Reliability — 89 90

33. Type of Criterion Reliability — 91
    1. Inter-rater (not Spearman-Brown corrected)
    2. Inter-rater (Spearman-Brown corrected)
    3. Internal consistency or corrected split half
    4. Rate-rerate (not Spearman-Brown corrected)
    5. Rate-rerate (Spearman-Brown corrected)
    9. Other (specify) __________

34. Total Number of Raters for Reliability Estimate (if ratings or rankings) — 92 93 94

35. Time Interval for Testing Between Criterion Ratings (in Weeks) — 95 96 97

Race and Gender Predictor Data if Separate Validity Data Is Not Available

Employee Group

37. Caucasian Mean — 113 114 115 . 116 117
38. Caucasian *SD* — 118 119 . 120 121
39. Black Mean — 122 123 124 . 125 126
40. Black *SD* — 127 128 . 129 130
41. Hispanic Mean — 131 132 133 . 134 135
42. Hispanic *SD* — 136 137 . 138 139
43. Asian Mean — 140 141 142 . 143 144
44. Asian *SD* — 145 146 . 147 148
45. Male Mean — 149 150 151 . 152 153
46. Male *SD* — 154 155 . 156 157
47. Female Mean — 158 159 160 . 161 162
48. Female *SD* — 163 164 . 165 166

Applicant Group

49. Caucasian Mean — 167 168 169 . 170 171
50. Caucasian *SD* — 172 173 . 174 175
51. Black Mean — 176 177 178 . 179 180
52. Black *SD* — 181 182 . 183 184
53. Hispanic Mean — 185 186 187 . 188 189
54. Hispanic *SD* — 190 191 . 192 193
55. Asian Mean — 194 195 196 . 197 198
56. Asian *SD* — 199 200 . 201 202
57. Male Mean — 203 204 205 . 206 207
58. Male *SD* — 208 209 . 210 211
59. Female Mean — 212 213 214 . 215 216
60. Female *SD* — 217 218 . 219 220

Other Data

61. Does the Study Report Intercorrelations Among Predictors? (1 = yes 2 = no) — 221
62. Additional Information #1 — 222 223 224 225 226
63. Additional Information #2 — 227 228 229 230 231
64. Additional Information #3 — 232 233 234 235 236

ITEM-BY-ITEM INSTRUCTIONS FOR VALIDITY CODING SHEET

1. STUDY ID

The study ID is the ID number assigned to a research report. This ID number is also referenced in the bibliography data file. If the study has not been entered into the bibliography data file, it needs to be entered. This field cannot be blank. Use leading zeros as needed.

2. SAMPLE WITHIN STUDY

The "SAMPLE WITHIN STUDY" number assigns a number to each sample within the research report. Samples are numbered consecutively starting with number 1. If validity data are available for a sample and for one or more racial or gender subgroups of the sample, a separate coding sheet should be completed for the total sample and for each racial or gender subgroup that reports a validity coefficient. The assigned number for the "SAMPLE WITHIN STUDY" for a racial/gender subgroup is the *same* as the number assigned to the total sample. This field cannot be blank. This allows the data analyst to know which race or gender subsample is a subset of which total sample.

EXAMPLE: The validity for a clerical test is given for two samples of stenographers. For the first sample, validity coefficients are available for the total sample and separately by gender. For the second sample, only the validity coefficient for the total sample is reported. A value of 1 is assigned as the SAMPLE WITHIN STUDY number for the three coefficients for the first sample. A value of 2 is assigned for the coefficient from the second sample.

EXAMPLE: A validity study has two criteria for one sample. It is judged that it is best to consider the two criteria as separate. Two coding sheets are completed, one for each criterion. The SAMPLE WITHIN STUDY code for each coding sheet is 1.

EXAMPLE: A validity study has two predictors for one sample. It is judged that it is best to consider the two predictors as separate. Two coding sheets are completed, one for each predictor. The SAMPLE WITHIN STUDY code for each coding sheet is 1.

3. RACE SUBGROUP?

If a validity coefficient for a sample is given for the total sample, and given separately for racial subgroups, leave this field blank on the coding sheet for the total sample and enter Y (Y for "Yes, this is a race subsample.") on the coding sheets for the racial subsamples. If a validity coefficient is only available for a racial subgroup and not for a total sample, leave this field blank. If the total sample is composed of individuals who all have the same race, leave this field blank.

4. SEX SUBGROUP?

If a validity coefficient for a sample is given for the total sample, and given separately for gender subgroups, leave this field blank on the coding sheet for the total sample and enter Y (Y for "Yes, this is a gender subsample.") on the coding sheets for the gender subsamples. If a validity coefficient is only available for a gender subgroup and not for a total sample, leave this field blank. If the total sample is composed of individuals who all have the same gender, leave this field blank.

5. RACE

Code the race of the sample or subsample for which the sheet is completed. If unknown, leave blank.

6. SEX

Code the sex of the sample or subsample for which the sheet is completed. If unknown, leave blank.

7. SAMPLE SIZE

Enter the sample size of the sample or subsample for which the sheet is completed. This is the actual sample size and not an adjusted sample size. This field cannot be blank. If the coefficient is a mean or a composite of several coefficients, use the mean of the sample sizes.

EXAMPLE: A study contains two criteria for one sample. The first criterion is a performance rating on quantity of work, and the second criterion is a performance rating on quality of work. A decision was made to consider the two performance ratings as subscales of one criterion. Thus, the reported *r* is the correlation between one predictor and a composite of the two criteria. The sample size for the first performance rating is 100. Data on only 90 of these 100 people were available for the second performance rating. An average (e.g., 95) of these two sample sizes was coded.

8. OCCUPATIONAL CODE

Enter the occupational code for the sample. Use the fourth edition of the DOT. This field cannot be blank.

9. VALIDITY COEFFICIENT (UNCORRECTED)

Enter the uncorrected validity coefficient. See "Sign Reversal" under "Other Notes." This field cannot be blank.

EXAMPLE: A coefficient of .50 is coded *0. 5 0.*

A coefficient of −.50 is coded *− .5 0.*

10. VALIDITY COEFFICIENT (CORRECTED FOR RANGE RESTRICTION)

Code this coefficient only if it is reported in the study. Do not compute this coefficient. Leave blank if missing.

11. VALIDITY COEFFICIENT (CORRECTED FOR CRITERION UNRELIABILITY)

Code this coefficient only if it is reported in the study. Do not compute this coefficient. Leave blank if missing.

12. VALIDITY COEFFICIENT (CORRECTED FOR CRITERION UNRELIABILITY AND RANGE RESTRICTION)

Code this coefficient only if it is reported in the study. Do not compute this coefficient. Leave blank if missing.

13. TYPE OF COEFFICIENT

Enter the type of coefficient. If the coefficient is a composite or a mean coefficient enter the type of coefficient used to compute it. If the type of correlation coefficient is not specified, the coefficient is probably a Pearson correlation coefficient. Note that a rank coefficient is a Rho. This field cannot be blank.

EXAMPLE: The validity coefficient is a Pearson correlation coefficient. Code 03.

EXAMPLE: The validity coefficient is the mean of four Pearson correlation coefficients. Code 03.

14. SAMPLE SIZE FOR MEAN *r*

If the reported validity coefficient is a *mean* of several coefficients, code the sum of the sample sizes for the several coefficients. Leave this field blank unless the validity coefficient coded in item 10 is a mean of two or more coefficients. If the validity coefficient is a composite, leave this field blank.

EXAMPLE: The validity coefficient reported in item 10 is a mean of two coefficients. While data on 200 individuals were available for one of the coefficients, data on only 199 of the 200 individuals were available for the second coefficient. The sample size for the mean *r* is reported as 399.

15. STUDY TYPE

There are two types of predictive studies: (1) predictive studies where the predictor is not used in the selection of the employees and (2) predictive studies where the predictor is used in the selection of employees. Code 1 for the first case and 2 for the second case. Code 3 if the study is predictive, but one does not know if the predictor was used in the selection of employees. Code 4 for a concurrent study.

16. TIME IN MONTHS BETWEEN COLLECTION OF PREDICTOR AND CRITERION DATA

If the study is predictive, enter the number of months between the collection of predictor and criterion data. If the time varies across the subjects in a sample, report the mean or median time. Leave blank if missing.

17. PREDICTOR CODE

Enter the four-digit predictor code.

18. PREDICTOR RELIABILITY COEFFICIENT—EMPLOYEE GROUP

If the predictor reliability computed on the employee (restricted) group is given, code it here.

EXAMPLE: A reliability of .95 is coded *9 5*.

If the predictor is the sum of the mean of two or more measures, you may need to adjust the reliability with the Spearman-Brown formula.

EXAMPLE: The predictor is an interview. The predictor score is the sum of ratings by two independent raters. The inter-rater reliability coefficient is .80. This coefficient is the reliability of scores for one rater. Because the predictor is the sum of two independent raters, the Spearman-Brown formula is used to boost the reliability to reflect this fact. The coded reliability is .89.

19. PREDICTOR MEAN—EMPLOYEE GROUP

Code the predictor mean for the employee (restricted) group. Leave blank if not given.

20. PREDICTOR STANDARD DEVIATION—EMPLOYEE GROUP

Code the predictor standard deviation for the employee (restricted) group. Leave blank if missing.

21. TYPE OF PREDICTOR RELIABILITY—EMPLOYEE GROUP

Code the type of reliability. Note that coefficient alpha is an internal consistency reliability.

22. TIME INTERVAL BETWEEN TESTING FOR PREDICTOR RELIABILITY ESTIMATE (in weeks)—EMPLOYEE GROUP

For reliabilities using two ratings (e.g., rate-rerate or inter-rater), code the number of weeks between the two ratings.

23. PREDICTOR RELIABILITY COEFFICIENT—APPLICANT GROUP

If the predictor reliability computed on the applicant (unrestricted) group is given, code it here.

EXAMPLE: A reliability 95 is coded *9 5*.

If the predictor is the sum or the mean of two or more measures, you may need to adjust the reliability with the Spearman-Brown formula.

EXAMPLE: The predictor is an interview. The predictor score is the sum of two independent ratings. The inter-rater reliability coefficient is .80. This coefficient is the reliability of scores for one rater. Because the predictor is the sum of ratings by two independent raters, the Spearman-Brown formula is used to boost the reliability to reflect this fact. The coded reliability is .89.

24. PREDICTOR MEAN—APPLICANT GROUP

Code the predictor mean for the applicant (unrestricted) group. Leave blank if not given.

25. PREDICTOR STANDARD DEVIATION—APPLICANT GROUP

Code the predictor standard deviation for the applicant (unrestricted) group. Leave blank if missing.

26. TYPE OF PREDICTOR RELIABILITY—APPLICANT GROUP

Code the type of reliability. Note that the coefficient alpha is an internal consistency reliability.

27. TIME INTERVAL BETWEEN TESTING FOR PREDICTOR RELIABILITY ESTIMATE (in weeks)—APPLICANT GROUP

For reliabilities using two ratings (e.g., rate-rerate or inter-rater), code the number of weeks between the two ratings.

28. RATIO RESTRICTED/UNRESTRICTED *SD*

If the ratio of the restricted to unrestricted standard deviation of the predictor is given, code it. Do not compute this statistic. If not given, leave it blank.

29. CRITERION CONTENT

Code the type of criterion content. If the criterion is wages, promotion/demotion, or commendations/reprimands, code it as such; do not code it as job performance. Note: Grade level is not a criterion unless it reflects promotion/demotion decisions.

30. CRITERION MEASUREMENT METHOD

Code the measurement method used to collect the criterion data. Typically, this item is relevant only when the criterion content is job performance or training performance. If this item is not relevant to the criterion, leave it blank.

EXAMPLE: If the criterion content is wages, none of the measurement categories is relevant. This item is left blank.

Production data include counts of quantity (e.g., widgets produced), error counts, and amount of time to process a given quantity of product (time to complete 10 widgets).

31. CRITERION: ADMINISTRATIVE VS. RESEARCH

If a criterion is collected solely for a validity study, it should be coded as a "research" criterion. If the criterion is collected as part of a routine administrative procedure, code it as an "administrative" procedure.

EXAMPLE: Supervisors rate each of their employees as part of a concurrent validity study. This criterion is coded as "research."

EXAMPLE: Performance evaluations that are routinely completed every year are used as criteria in a validity study. Code this criterion as "administrative."

EXAMPLE: A tenure or wage criterion is always administrative.

32. CRITERION RELIABILITY

Code the criterion reliability if it is given. If the criterion is missing, leave items 33 to 35 blank. If the criterion is a composite, and the reliabilities of the components are given, one should compute the reliability of the composite. Note that this reliability may need to be boosted. See the examples for details.

EXAMPLE: A reliability of .95 is coded *9 5*.

EXAMPLE: The criterion is a performance appraisal. Only one rater's evaluation is used as the criterion. The reliability is an inter-rater reliability. This reliability is not boosted via the Spearman-Brown formula.

EXAMPLE: The criterion is a performance appraisal. The criterion is the sum of two raters' evaluations. The reliability is an inter-rater reliability. This reliability is boosted ($k = 2$) via the Spearman-Brown formula.

33. TYPE OF CRITERION RELIABILITY

Code the type of criterion reliability.

34. TOTAL NUMBER OF RATERS FOR RELIABILITY ESTIMATE (if ratings or rankings)

Code the number of raters who rated each subject.

EXAMPLE: If the criterion reliability applies to ratings by two supervisors (i.e., each ratee was rated by two raters), item 34 is coded *0 0 2*.

EXAMPLE: The criterion reliability is the correlation between the same supervisor's ratings made one week apart. There is only one rater, so item 34 is coded *0 0 1*.

35. TIME INTERVAL BETWEEN CRITERION RATINGS (in weeks)

If the criterion rating used two or more ratings (e.g., rate-rerate or inter-rater), code the time interval in weeks between the two ratings.

36. IDS OF OTHER STUDIES COVERING SAME DATA (not shown on coding sheet)

If the data in a particular study are reported in more than one report, code the other study IDs. This will prevent the data from being coded twice.

37–60. RACE AND GENDER PREDICTOR DATA

These items request means and standard deviations for racial and gender subgroups. Code these data here only if a validity for the subgroup is not reported. If subgroup data are reported, the subgroup information is placed on its own coding sheet and the mean and standard deviation data are coded in items 19, 20, 24, and 25.

61. DOES THE STUDY REPORT INTER-CORRELATIONS AMONG PREDICTORS?

If the study reports intercorrelations between two or more predictors, code 1(1 = yes). Then complete the intercorrelation coding sheet.

62–64. ADDITIONAL INFORMATION #1, #2, #3.

This space is left for future information needs whose content is at present unanticipated.

At present, this space is only used when coding interviews. See the separate instruction sheets for additional information.

DECISION RULES FOR CODING VALIDITY STUDIES

Multiple Correlations in Each Study: Introduction

One goal of this coding scheme is to code one validity coefficient for each predictor/job combination using the entire study sample. In addition, when validity data are available, separate coding sheets should be completed for each racial or gender subgroup.

A problem arises when there are separate validity coefficients for multiple predictors or multiple criteria. A judgment is needed as to whether multiple predictors are truly separate predictors or are repeated measures of the same predictor. Likewise, when there are two or more criteria, one must decide if a separate coefficient is warranted for each criterion or if the several validity coefficients are best expressed as one coefficient. To assist in making these judgments, a set of decision rules is provided.

Refer to "Multiple Predictor Decision Rules" for guidelines and examples of multiple predictor problems. Refer to "Multiple Criterion Decision Rules" for guidelines and examples of multiple criterion problems. Once a decision has been made to combine coefficients, refer to "Combining Coefficients Decision Rules."

Multiple Predictor Decision Rules

General Rule: When in doubt, consider multiple predictors to be separate predictors and code each coefficient separately.

Examples of predictors to be viewed as subscales of the same predictors:

- A performance score and a time-to-completion score from an MT&E (miniature training and experience)
- Assessment center dimensions

Examples of predictors to be viewed as separate predictors:

- Predictors with the same item type (e.g., if the study involved two reading comprehension tests, two coefficients would be coded)
- Predictors measuring different construct types
- An interview conducted by one person and an interview conducted by a panel

Multiple Criterion Decision Rules

General Rule: When in doubt, combine the coefficients for different criteria in order to report one coefficient.

Note the criterion categories in item 29. Do not combine across these categories. While wages, promotions, and commendations can be considered job performance measures, they probably have different reliability distributions than job performance ratings.

If multiple coefficients are reported for the same sample for the same criteria at two or more points in time, code the coefficients separately. If these data are reported for many points in time, use judgment.

EXAMPLE: Two validity coefficients are reported for the same sample. The two criteria are training ratings made at 3 months and 6 months into training. Complete two coding sheets. Note that the sheets will have the same SAMPLE WITHIN STUDY code and will have different values for TIME IN MONTHS BETWEEN COLLECTION OF PREDICTOR AND CRITERION DATA.

Examples of criteria to be viewed as subscales of the same criterion:

- Subscales of a performance appraisal form. If there is an overall performance rating that is the sum (or composite) of the subscales, use the overall performance rating. If the overall performance rating is a single rating, consider it a subscale and combine with the other subscale coefficients.

Examples of criteria to be viewed as separate criteria:

- A performance measure and a training measure
- A performance appraisal rating and a work simulation exercise

Combining Coefficients Decision Rules

Note that combining coefficients is acceptable only when it is appropriate to view multiple predictors as subscales of the same predictor or when it is appropriate to view multiple criteria as subscales of the same criterion. When separate validity coefficients are reported and a decision has been made to report only one coefficient, select the best choice available:

First choice: Use a composite correlation. Unless the author presents a meaningful reason for unequal weighting of components, the composite correlation should be based on equally weighted components. If two or more components are to be unequally weighted, and a composite is to receive very little weight, examine the component. It may be reasonable to exclude the component from the composite.

To compute a composite correlation, use the composite correlation program in the SPSS software or in the computer program described in the Appendix to this book. For small calculations, one might calculate the composite by hand (using the methods presented in Chapter 10).

Second choice: Shrink the multiple R. Use the formulas described in Cattin (1980).

Third choice: Use the one coefficient that best represents the correlation between the overall test performance and the overall job performance.

Fourth choice: Compute a mean validity.

OTHER NOTES

Clerical Tests

Written examinations, labeled "clerical," are often composites of verbal, quantitative, and perceptual speed items. If so, code them as a combination ($V+Q+PS$). If not, determine what construct(s) the test is measuring and code them accordingly.

Right-Justify, Leading Zeros

Right-justify and use leading zeros for all codes that do not fill up the entire item field.

EXAMPLE: The value for item 2, SAMPLE WITHIN STUDY, is 1. Code it as *0 0 1.*

Sign Reversal

One may need to reverse the sign of a correlation. A positive correlation should indicate that a high score on a measure is associated with better job performance.

EXAMPLE: The criterion is a count of errors. A correlation is reported as −.2, indicating that the higher the predictor score the lower the number of errors. This coefficient is coded as +.2.

Who Is an Employee, What Is a Job?

Coding sheets are to be completed for predictors of job or training performance for employees.

Examples of studies that should be coded:

- Subjects are interns in an agency
- Subjects are employees in an agency

Examples of studies that should not be coded:

- Subjects are students
- Subjects are psychiatric patients
- The criterion measure is job satisfaction

INSTRUCTION SHEET
FOR CODING INTERCORRELATIONS AMONG PREDICTORS

Intercorrelations among predictors are being recorded for subsequent data analysis. These intercorrelations are needed to estimate the validity of a composite selection system.

1. PREDICTOR CODE—FIRST PREDICTOR

   Enter the predictor code for the first of two predictors.

2. RELIABILITY—FIRST PREDICTOR

   Enter the reliability of the first predictor.

3. PREDICTOR CODE—SECOND PREDICTOR

   Enter the predictor code for the second predictor.

4. RELIABILITY—SECOND PREDICTOR

   Enter the reliability for the second predictor.

5. OBSERVED CORRELATION

   Code the observed correlation between the two predictors.

6. CORRECTED CORRELATION

   If reported, code the corrected correlation between the two predictors. Do not compute this value, only code if it is reported.

7. SAMPLE SIZE

   Code the sample size for the correlation coefficient.

8. STUDY ID

   Code the study ID.

13

Availability and Source Bias in Meta-Analysis

Questions, issues, and criticisms of meta-analysis that are technical in nature were discussed in Chapter 5 for meta-analyses of correlations, and in Chapter 8 for meta-analyses of *d* values. This chapter explores the general issue of availability bias in meta-analysis. One of the most frequent criticisms leveled against meta-analysis is the argument that the studies available for analysis will typically be a biased sample of all existing studies. This is often referred to as "publication bias," defined as existing when published studies are a biased sample of all existing studies. However, publication bias is not necessarily the only source of bias. Even among unpublished studies, those that are retrievable may not be representative of all unpublished studies. So we favor the more general term "availability bias." (Comparable terms used by others are "retrieval bias" and "selection bias"). In particular, it is often suspected that published studies will show results that are more often statistically significant and have larger effect sizes than unpublished studies (see, e.g., Begg, 1994; Coursol & Wagner, 1986; McNemar, 1960). Thus, it is contended, effect size estimates from meta-analysis will be biased upward. The first thing to note about this criticism is that it applies equally well to the narrative review, the usual alternative to meta-analysis. The fact that the narrative review is not quantitative in no way mitigates the effects of any bias in the sample of studies. Thus, to the extent that source or availability bias is a problem, it is a completely general one and is not limited to meta-analysis.

There is evidence that availability bias may not exist in some literatures. Also, apparent differences in mean effect sizes by source (e.g., journals, books, and unpublished reports) may at least in part reflect the artifactual effects of differences in average methodological quality among sources. If so, then a meta-analysis that corrects for methodological weaknesses (such as measurement error) will correct for these differences. Finally, if there is reason to suspect availability or reporting biases, methods are now available to help detect and control for these effects. We now examine each of these points in turn.

Some Evidence on Publication Bias

The publication bias hypothesis holds that unpublished studies have two important properties: (1) They have smaller effect sizes, and (2) they are less frequently available to be included in meta-analysis. If the first of these were not true, then even if the second were true, no bias would be introduced into meta-analysis results. The question of whether effect sizes are smaller in unpublished studies can be addressed empirically.

Based on data presented in Glass, McGaw, and Smith (1981), Rosenthal (1984, pp. 41–45) examined the effect sizes from 12 meta-analyses on different topics to determine whether mean effect sizes differed depending on their sources. Based on several hundred effect sizes, he found there was virtually no difference on the average between those published in journals and those from unpublished reports. The mean d value was .08 *larger* for the unpublished reports; the median d value was .05 larger for the published journal articles. Thus, the mean and median differences were in the opposite directions, and neither was statistically or practically significant. His overall conclusion was that the effect sizes from journal articles, unpublished reports, and books are "essentially indistinguishable from each other" (p. 44). On the other hand, Rosenthal did find that doctoral dissertations and master's theses yielded average d values that were 40% or more smaller than those from other sources. The problem created by this difference for theses and dissertations is mitigated by the fact that most dissertations are retrievable by meta-analysts through *Dissertation Abstracts*.

In our meta-analytic research on the validity of employment tests (see Chapter 4), we have examined that vast literature to determine whether correlations (validities) from published and unpublished studies differ. We found that they do not. Where it was possible to compare data sets like that of Pearlman, Schmidt, and Hunter (1980) to other large data sets, the two data sets were found to be very similar. For example, the data of Pearlman et al. is very similar to the unpublished U.S. Department of Labor GATB data set used by Hunter (1983b) in terms of validity means and variances (controlling for sample sizes) of observed validity coefficients. The same is true when the comparison is with large-sample military data sets. Military researchers routinely report all data, and the reported validity means and variances correspond closely to those from other data sets for the same criterion measures. Also, mean observed validities in our data sets are virtually identical to Ghiselli's (1966) reported medians, based on decades of careful gathering of both published and unpublished studies.

There are other indications of a lack of source bias in validity generalization data sets. For example, in the Pearlman et al. (1980) data set for measures of performance on the job, 349 of the 2,795 observed validities (12.5%) were 0 or negative; 737 (26.4%) were .10 or less. Further, 56.1% of the 2,795 observed validities were nonsignificant at the .05 level. This figure is consistent with our estimate (Schmidt, Hunter, & Urry, 1976) that the average criterion-related validity study has statistical power no greater than .50. If selectivity or bias in reporting were operating, many of the nonsignificant validities would have been omitted, and the percentage significant would have been much higher than 43.9%.

Even more striking was the close comparability of the percentage of observed validities that were nonsignificant in the published studies reviewed by Lent, Auerbach, and Levin (1971a, 1971b)—57%—and the percentage nonsignificant in the mostly unpublished data set (68% of the sources were unpublished) of Pearlman et al. (1980)—56.1%. The Pearlman et al. data almost perfectly match the published data, an empirical indication that the unpublished data were not different from the published data. (Note: To provide comparability with Lent et al., 1971b, all figures for Pearlman et al., 1980, are for two-tailed tests. Using one-tailed tests, 49.1% of the Pearlman et al. proficiency coefficients are nonsignificant at the .05 level.)

We have examined many hundreds of unpublished studies in the personnel selection research domain and have found no evidence that data were suppressed or omitted. It has been our experience that studies typically reported results for all tests tried out (even poorly constructed experimental instruments with well below average reliabilities). In the typical scenario, the study is an exploratory one designed to determine the optimal test battery. A multitest battery is tried out on a variety of jobs and/or criteria. Full tables of validities against all criteria for all jobs were reported. We found no evidence that reporting the full set of results (usually including many low and nonsignificant validities) was viewed negatively by the sponsoring organization, or that it allowed or encouraged either their own psychologists or outside consultants to partially or fully suppress the results. Thus, this evidence also indicates that the results of unpublished studies are essentially identical to those of published studies, indicating that there is no problem of availability bias in this literature.

Effects of Methodological Quality on Mean Effect Sizes From Different Sources

If published studies do have larger observed effect sizes than unpublished studies in a particular research literature, that fact need not indicate the existence of a publication bias in favor of large or significant effect sizes. Instead, the publication "bias" could be in favor of methodologically stronger research studies. Reviewers are often selected by journal editors based on their judged methodological expertise, and it is therefore to be expected that their evaluations will focus heavily on the methodological quality of the study. Many methodological weaknesses have the effect of artifactually reducing the expected study effect size. For example, unreliability of measurement reduces study effect sizes in both correlational and experimental studies. Thus, publication decisions based on methodological quality alone would be expected to produce, as a side effect, differences in mean study effect sizes between published and unpublished studies, given only that the null hypothesis of no relationship is false, the usual case today (see, e.g., Lipsey & Wilson, 1993). This would be expected to be the case even though the actual effect size is exactly the same in published and unpublished studies.

Table 13.1 shows the approximate mean observed d values found by Smith and Glass (1977) for books (.80), journals (.70), dissertations (.60), and unpublished

Table 13.1 Hypothetical example of observed and true mean effect sizes for four sources of effect sizes

Source	*Observed Mean* ($\bar{d}$)	*Mean Dependent Variable Reliability* ($\bar{R}_{yy}$)	*True Mean d Value* $\bar{\delta}$
Books	.8	.90	.84
Journals	.7	.70	.84
Dissertations	.6	.51	.84
Unpublished	.5	.35	.84

reports (.50) in studies on the effectiveness of psychotherapy. The difference between the largest and smallest $\bar{d}$ is .80 − .50 = .30, a considerable difference. Suppose, however, the mean reliabilities of the dependent variables were as indicated in the second column of numbers in Table 13.1. Then the true effect sizes (effect sizes corrected for the attenuating effects of measurement error) would be the same in all sources, and the apparent "source effect" on study outcomes would be shown to be entirely artifactual. The point is that the effects of methodological quality on study outcomes should be carefully examined before accepting the conclusion that real study findings differ by study source. This example also clearly illustrates the importance and necessity of making the appropriate corrections for measurement error in conducting meta-analyses.

If the null hypothesis is true, and there is no effect or relationship, publication bias can lead to a Type I error in meta-analysis—a conclusion that a relationship exists when it does not. However, as noted in Chapter 2 and elsewhere in this book, there is much evidence that the null hypothesis is rarely true. For example, Lipsey and Wilson (1993) found that less than 1% of psychological interventions (2 out of 302) produced no effect. Even allowing for the possibility of some Type I errors produced by publication bias in the 302 meta-analyses they reviewed, it would still appear that the null hypothesis is rarely true. Hence, the usual effect of publication bias would be to inflate the size of mean correlations and *d* values, rather than producing Type I errors. Hence, the conclusions of meta-analyses affected by publication or other availability bias would be qualitatively correct but quantitatively incorrect. However, it is typically important to have accurate estimates of the size of effects; it is rarely sufficient merely to know that such effects exist. Hence, availability bias is a potentially serious problem—not specifically for meta-analysis, but for all scientific efforts to attain cumulative knowledge. For this reason, availability bias, especially publication bias, has been the subject of much attention over the last decade.

Multiple Hypotheses and Other Considerations in Availability Bias

An important consideration in understanding availability bias was pointed out by Cooper (1998, p. 74) and earlier by Schmidt, Hunter, Pearlman, and Hirsh

(1985). Most studies examine multiple hypotheses, and, hence, there are multiple significance tests. This reduces (and may eliminate) the possibility of publication bias based on statistical significance, because the probability that all such tests would be significant is quite low. Likewise, the probability that all such tests will be nonsignificant is also low. Hence, the vast majority of studies register in the minds of evaluators not as "significant" or "nonsignificant," but as "mixed," making it difficult to create publication bias based on statistical significance. If only studies with all significant results were published, only a tiny fraction of studies would be published. Likewise, if only studies with no significant results were not published, only a tiny fraction of all studies would not be published. Most discussions of publication bias—and most methods for detecting and correcting for this bias—appear to ignore these facts. In effect, they assume that there is only one significance test per study or at least that there is only one important significance test.

A related consideration is that many meta-analyses focus on questions that were not central to the primary studies from which data are taken. For example, sex differences (in traits, abilities, attitudes, etc.) are rarely the central focus of a study; instead, they tend to be reported on an incidental basis, as supplementary analysis. Hence, these results tend not to be subject to publication bias because they are close to irrelevant to the central hypotheses of the research study (Cooper, 1998, p. 74).

Nevertheless, many authors have concluded that there is much evidence that publication bias or other forms of availability bias are important problems (see, e.g., summaries in Begg, 1994; Hedges, 1992a; Rothstein, McDaniel, & Borenstein, 2001). However, this evidence calls for critical evaluation in light of the fact that almost all studies today—at least in psychology and the social sciences—examine and test multiple hypotheses. In fact, there has been a trend over time in many research areas for the number of hypotheses tested per study to increase.

The first type of evidence offered for the importance of publication bias consists of surveys of the beliefs and attitudes of researchers, reviewers, and editors about the role of statistical significance in making decisions about manuscripts. In these surveys, most researchers say they are more likely to submit a study if the results are statistically significant. Also, most reviewers say they are more likely to evaluate a study favorably if the results are significant. Finally, many editors state that they are more likely to accept a paper if the results are significant. Studies reporting findings of this sort include Chase and Chase (1976), Coursol and Wagner (1986), and Greenwald (1975). The questions in these surveys are worded in terms of a significant versus nonsignificant study outcome. Essentially, they measure the attitude a researcher, reviewer, or editor would have if (a) the study tested only one hypothesis (a rare event today) and the result was either significant or nonsignificant, or (b) multiple hypotheses were tested but the result was either that all tests were nonsignificant or all were significant (again, a highly improbable event). To our knowledge, no studies of this sort on publication bias have attempted to assess what the role of statistical significance in decisions about manuscripts would be for typical real-world studies—studies in which several hypotheses are tested and some tests are significant and some are nonsignificant. Hence, surveys of this sort are of questionable evidentiary value in illuminating the extent of publication bias.

The second type of evidence offered in support of the proposition that publication bias is a serious problem consists of reports that the frequency of statistical significance in published articles is suspiciously high. For example, Sterling (1959) and Bozarth and Roberts (1972) found that 92% to 97% of published articles reported significant results. Given the evidence (discussed in Chapter 1) that the average level of statistical power in psychological research is somewhere around 50%, these percentages would seem to suggest massive publication bias. However, if most studies test multiple hypotheses, and hence report multiple significance tests, then, even in the absence of publication bias, we would expect almost all studies to report some significant statistical test results. Hence, studies of this sort are of limited value in clarifying the scope of publication bias.

What about studies that directly compare the effect sizes of published and unpublished studies (such as those discussed in an earlier section of this chapter)? There are apparently few, if any, such studies that examine this comparison for the most common type of study—studies that examine and test several hypotheses. It is possible that an examination of such studies would show that effect sizes for published and unpublished studies do not differ beyond differences explainable by differences in measurement error, range restriction, and other correctable artifacts.

In the health sciences areas, particularly in medical research, studies frequently examine only one hypothesis—or at least only one hypothesis that is considered important. This is especially true for randomized controlled trials (RCTs) in medical research. In the typical RCT study, either a treatment is compared with a placebo or with no treatment, or two treatments are compared with each other. Hence, there is essentially only one hypothesis of interest—and therefore the protection against publication bias afforded by multiple hypotheses is absent. In fact, the evidence for publication bias is quite strong for RCTs: When the results of the single hypothesis are nonsignificant, they are far less likely to be submitted for publication and also less likely to be accepted if they are published (see, e.g., Dickerson, Min, & Meinert, 1992; Easterbrook, Berlin, Gopalan, & Matthews, 1991). This evidence is not based on surveys of attitudes or statements of what researchers and editors say they would do; it is based on the empirical history of actual RCT studies. While this suggests that publication bias can be severe in literatures in which studies test only one hypothesis, there are few—and increasingly fewer—such literatures in psychology and the social sciences.

Methods for Detecting Availability Bias

If there is reason to suspect that availability bias might be a problem for a set of studies, methods are available for addressing this problem. Rosenthal (1979) advanced his "file drawer analysis" as one approach; this method focuses only on statistical significance, ignoring effect sizes. An alternative file drawer method is available that is based on effect sizes. In addition, funnel plots can be used to assess whether availability bias is present. Finally, more statistically sophisticated and complex methods of detecting and correcting for availability bias have been developed recently. Although not yet widely used, these methods may become important in the future. We now discuss each of these approaches in turn.

File Drawer Analysis Based on *p* Values

Rosenthal's (1979) file drawer analysis estimates the number of unlocated ("file drawer") studies averaging null results (i.e., $\bar{d} = 0$ or $\bar{r} = 0$) that would have to exist to bring the significance level for a set of studies down to the "just significant" level, that is, to $p = .05$. The required number of studies is often so large as to have very little likelihood of existing, thus supporting the conclusion that the study findings, taken as a whole, are indeed unlikely to have resulted from biased sampling of studies. The first step in applying file drawer analysis is computation of the overall significance level for the set of studies. One first converts the p value for each of the k effect sizes to its corresponding z value using ordinary normal curve tables, for example,

Study	*p Value*	*z Value*
1	.05	1.645
2	.01	2.330
3	.50	.000
.	.	.
.	.	.
.	.	.

This test is directional (one-tailed), so the researcher must determine the direction of the hypothesized difference. For example, if females are hypothesized to have higher average levels of perceptual speed than males, then a finding that favors *males* at the .05 level (one-tailed) would be entered with a p value of $1.00 - .05 = .95$ and its z value would be -1.645.

When variables are uncorrelated, the variance of the sum is the sum of the variances. If the z values are from k independent studies, then each has a variance of 1.00, and the variance of the sum of the zs across the k studies is k. Because the variance of $\sum z_k$ is k, the $SD = \sqrt{k}$. The z_c, the z score corresponding to the significance level of the total set of studies, is then

$$z_c = \frac{\sum z_k}{\sqrt{k}} = \frac{k\bar{z}_k}{\sqrt{k}} = \sqrt{k}\,\bar{z}_k.$$

For example, if there were 10 studies ($k = 10$) and $\bar{z}_k = 1.35$, then $z_c = \sqrt{10}(1.35) = 4.27$, a highly significant z_c value ($p = .0000098$).

In the file drawer analysis, we want to compute the number of additional unlocated studies averaging $z = 0$ needed to bring z_c down to 1.645 (or $p = .05$). Denote this additional number of studies by x. Because these studies have $\bar{z} = 0$, $\sum z_{k+x} = \sum z_k$. However, the number of studies will increase from k to $k + x$. Thus, the new SD for $\sum z_{k+z}$ will be $\sqrt{k + x}$. If we set $z_c = 1.645$, the desired value, we can then solve the following equation for x:

$$1.645 = \frac{k\bar{z}_k}{\sqrt{k + x}}$$

Solving for x,

$$x = k/2.706[k(\bar{z}_k)^2 - 2.706] \tag{13.1}$$

This is the file drawer formula when the critical overall significance level is $p =$ .05. Returning to our earlier example where $k = 10$ and $\bar{z}_k = 1.35$, we obtain

$$x = \frac{10}{2.706}[10(1.35)^2 - 2.706] = 57$$

Thus, there would have to be 57 unlocated studies averaging null results to bring the combined probability level for the group of studies up to .05. If in this example there were originally 100 studies ($k = 100$) instead of 10, then $x = 6{,}635$! Over 6,000 studies would be required to raise the combined p value to .05. In most research areas, it is inconceivable that there could be over 6,000 "lost" studies.

An important problem with this method is that it assumes the homogeneous case (Hunter & Schmidt, 2000, pp. 286–287). That is, it assumes $S^2_\rho = 0$ (or that $S^2_\delta = 0$). This means it is a fixed-effects model and therefore has all the problems of fixed-effects meta-analysis methods, as discussed in Chapters 5 and 9. In particular, if the fixed-effects assumption does not hold (and it rarely does), then the number of missing studies needed to make the combined p value just barely significant is much smaller than the number yielded by the file drawer analysis (Iyengar & Greenhouse, 1988). Another source of inaccuracy is the fact that the initially computed p values for individual studies also depend on the fixed-effects assumption and therefore are typically inaccurate also, as discussed in Chapter 11. Other important criticisms of the Rosenthal file drawer analysis are given by Begg (1994, p. 406) and Iyengar and Greenhouse (1988, pp. 111–112).

File Drawer Analysis Based on Effect Size

Another problem with the file drawer analysis of Rosenthal (1979) is that, even accepted at face value, it yields a very weak conclusion. The combined study results can be highly significant statistically even though the mean effect size is small or even tiny. Neither the combined probability method in general (see Chapter 11) nor the file drawer analysis in particular provides any information on effect size. It would be more informative to know how many missing studies averaging null findings would have to exist to bring $\bar{d}$ or $\bar{r}$ down to some specific level. The formulas given here for this calculation were derived by the authors in 1979 and used extensively by Pearlman (1982). Later, we learned that Orwin (1983) had independently derived the same formulas. These equations do not depend on the fixed-effects assumption; in effect, they represent a random-effects model.

If k is again the number of studies, then

$$\bar{d}_k = \frac{\Sigma d_k}{k}.$$

We want to know how many "lost" studies (x) must exist to bring $\bar{d}_k$ down to $\bar{d}_c$, the critical value for mean d (which may be the smallest mean value that we would consider theoretically or practically significant). Thus, the new total number of studies will again be $k + x$. Σd_k will remain unchanged, because $\Sigma d = 0$ for the x new studies. We again set $\bar{d}_k$ equal to $\bar{d}_c$ and solve for x:

$$\bar{d}_c = \frac{\Sigma d_k}{k + x}$$

$$x = k\bar{d}_k/\bar{d}_c - k$$

$$x = k(\bar{d}_k/\bar{d}_c - 1) \quad (13.2a)$$

The corresponding formula for $\bar{r}$ is

$$x = k(\bar{r}_k/\bar{r}_c - 1) \quad (13.2b)$$

For example, if $\bar{d}_k = 1.00$, $k = 10$, and $\bar{d}_c = .10$, then

$$x = 10(1.00/.10 - 1)$$

$$x = 90 \text{ studies}$$

If $k = 100$ but the other numbers remain the same, then $x = 900$. The number of missing studies averaging null results needed to reduce the effect size to some specified level is usually much smaller than the number required to reduce the combined probability value to $p = .05$. Nevertheless, in many research areas, it is unlikely that there are even 90 "lost" studies, and it is highly unlikely that there are 900. McNatt (2000) provided an example of the use of this procedure in a published meta-analysis. He found that it would take 367 missing studies averaging zero effect size to reduce his observed $\bar{d}$ of 1.13 (a large effect) to $\bar{d} = .05$ (a trivial effect).

A Graphic Method for Detecting Availability Bias: The Funnel Plot

Light and Pillemer (1984) introduced a simple graphic method of detecting publication or other availability bias. This technique is based on the fact that, in the absence of availability bias, the average effect size is expected to be the same in large- and small-sample studies, while varying more widely in small-sample studies due to greater sampling error. In applying this technique, one graphs effect sizes (d values or correlations) against study sample size (or the standard error of the study estimate, which is an inverse function of sample size). In the absence of bias, the resulting figure should take the form of an inverted funnel, as shown in Figure 13.1. Note that in Figure 13.1 the average effect size is approximately the same regardless of study sample size. However, if there is publication or other availability bias based on the statistical significance (p value) of the studies, then small-sample studies reporting small effect sizes will be disproportionately absent, because these are the studies that will fail to attain statistical significance. These are the studies in the lower left hand corner of the funnel plot. Figure 13.2 shows a funnel plot that suggests the presence of availability bias. Note that in Figure 13.2 the average effect size of the small-sample studies is larger than that for the large-sample-size studies.

Figure 13.1 Example of funnel plot showing no evidence of availability bias

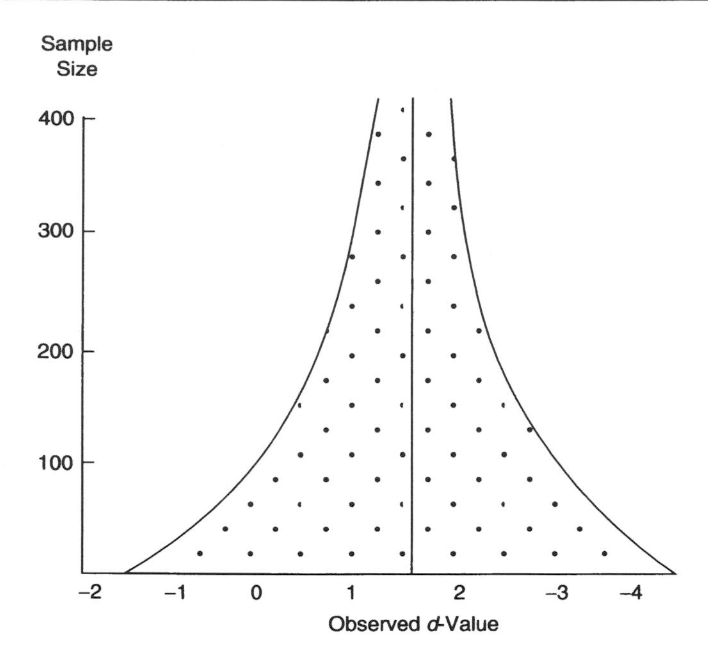

Figure 13.2 Example of funnel plot showing evidence of availability bias

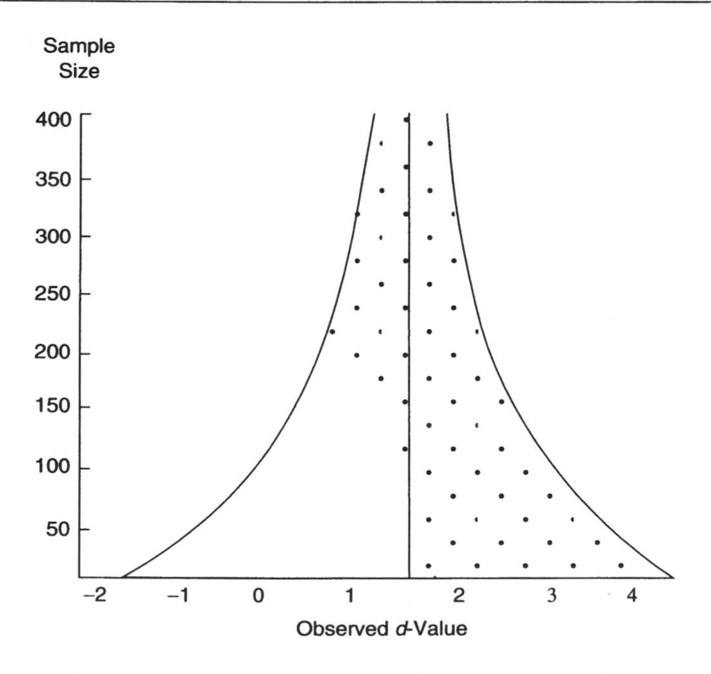

Although the concept underlying the funnel plot method is simple and direct, it has a problematic aspect. If all nonsignificant studies are unavailable due to publication or other availability bias, it is easy to see the evidence of bias. However, if only some of them are missing (say, 20%–60%), it is much harder to detect the bias (Greenhouse & Iyengar, 1994). This is especially true if the number of studies is not large (perhaps the usual case). It is highly unlikely that 100% of all nonsignificant studies will be missing. Significance tests are available as a substitute for judgment in evaluating the funnel plot, but these tests have all the problems of significance tests discussed in Chapter 1. In particular, they have low power.

When the funnel plot suggests availability bias, some have suggested basing the meta-analysis only on the large-N studies (e.g., Begg, 1994), under the assumption that all or nearly all of these would have been statistically significant (and therefore published), and hence, these studies would provide an unbiased estimate of the mean effect size. This is probably the case if the underlying mean effect size is large and there is little real variance in this parameter. (These two conditions together contribute to high statistical power in the larger N studies, helping to ensure the larger N studies will not be a biased sample of studies.) Otherwise, this prescription is questionable. Note also that the bias shown in Figure 13.2 appears larger than it actually would be in the meta-analysis, because studies are weighted by their sample size, and so the small-N studies (which have the biased estimates) receive little weight in the meta-analysis average.

Applications of the funnel plot typically do not suggest evidence of availability bias. This may well be explained by two facts mentioned earlier in this chapter. First, most studies test multiple hypotheses, making it difficult for publication to be contingent on statistical significance for the test of any one hypothesis. Second, many meta-analyses examine relationships that were not the central focus of the primary studies, making it unlikely that availability or publication bias could have occurred. This line of reasoning suggests that failure of the funnel plot to detect bias often leads to a correct conclusion that there is no bias.

Methods for Correcting for Availability Bias

Starting in the mid-1980s and continuing up to the present, statisticians have developed statistical methods for correcting meta-analysis results for the effects of availability bias. Over time, these methods have become increasingly sophisticated statistically (and increasingly complex). However, all these methods are based on the p values of the primary studies; that is, they all assume that the probability of publication depends (via some weight function) on the p value of that study. There is no provision for the possibility that other properties of studies affect the probability of publication (e.g., the effect size reported, methodological qualities of the study, the reputation of the authors, etc.). This would appear to make these methods somewhat unrealistic (Duval & Tweedie, 2000). However, perhaps a more serious problem is that all these methods seem to implicitly assume that each study tests only one hypothesis (and hence has only one relevant p value to be considered). As a result, the applicability of these methods to studies in which several hypotheses are tested, resulting in several significance tests and p values, is questionable. As noted earlier, studies of this sort make up the vast majority in most of the research literatures today. Beyond these broad assumptional problems, these methods depend on a variety of additional statistical assumptions that may or may not hold in real data (see, e.g., Hedges, 1992a).

Nevertheless, because publication bias, if it exists, has the potential to seriously distort conclusions from research reviews, including meta-analytic reviews, these methods have received considerable attention. It is possible that they will become substantially more important in meta-analysis in the future. These methods have evolved over time, and in the following presentation we present these methods in the approximate chronological order in which they appeared. Because of the highly technical nature of these methods and because of space constraints, we present only overviews and summary descriptions of these methods.

The Original Hedges-Olkin (1985) Method

The initial method presented by Hedges (1984) and Hedges and Olkin (1985) was based on the assumption that all significant studies were published (regardless of the direction of significance) and none of the nonsignificant studies was published. That is, they started with the simplest of "weight functions": All significant studies were weighted 1 and all nonsignificant studies were weighted 0. Later methods employed more complex—and less unrealistic—assumptions and weighting functions.

If, in a given research literature, only published studies were available and only studies reporting significant results were published, then, if the null hypothesis were true, there would be approximately equal numbers of statistically significant positive and negative d or r values in the published literature, and $\bar{r}$ and $\bar{d}$ would, on the average, be 0, and there would be no effect of publication bias on estimates of $\bar{r}$ and $\bar{d}$ (although estimates of S_ρ^2 and S_δ^2 would be biased). Significant and extreme results in either direction would be equally likely. However, if the null hypothesis were false (e.g., $\bar{\delta} > 0$), the mean effect size computed from such studies would not equal its true value, but instead would be biased upward. The amount of this bias would depend on the underlying δ and on study sample size.

Based on maximum likelihood methods, Hedges and Olkin (1985) estimated and tabled the estimates of δ for different study sample sizes and values of g^*, where g^* is the observed value of d from a study in a set of studies from which all nonsignificant ds have been eliminated (censored). In a set of studies that excludes all nonsignificant ds, there is a bias in each d value. These biased d values (symbolized g^*) can be converted to approximately unbiased estimates of δ by use of Hedges and Olkin's Table 2 (pp. 293–294). For example, if $N_E = N_C = 20$ and $g^* = .90$, this table shows that the maximum likelihood estimate of δ ($\hat{\delta}$) is .631. This conversion from g^* to $\hat{\delta}$ can be made for each of the g^* values in the set of studies. The table is based on the assumption that $N_E = N_C$, but Hedges and Olkin (p. 292) noted that when the experimental and control group sample sizes are unequal, one can use the average of the two to enter the table with minimal loss of accuracy. Once all observed d values have been corrected for the bias induced by the reporting of only significant results, Hedges and Olkin recommended that the resulting $\hat{\delta}$ values be weighted by study sample sizes and averaged to estimate the (almost) unbiased mean effect size ($\bar{\delta}$). Thus, it is possible to obtain an unbiased estimate of mean effect size even when only studies that report significant effect sizes are available for analysis. Note that this estimate, $\bar{\delta}$, will be considerably smaller than the observed mean effect size, $\bar{g}^*$. The formulas for this method were derived under the assumption that the population effect size δ does not vary across studies (i.e., it is a fixed-effects model). If δ varies substantially across studies, this method yields only an approximate estimate of the mean effect size ($\bar{\delta}$).

The sampling error variance of the $\hat{\delta}$ values is considerably larger than that given for ordinary d values in the formula in Chapter 7. This is true unless the actual δ is less than about .25 or both sample size and δ are "large" (e.g., $N_E = N_C = 50$ and $\delta = 1.50$). For most data sets that occur in meta-analysis, the sampling error variance formulas in Chapter 7 would underestimate actual sampling error variance by about one-third to one-half. Thus, the resulting estimate of SD_δ would be too large. However, as noted previously, the estimate of $\bar{\delta}$ should be approximately unbiased.

Ordinarily, the censoring of studies is not complete. Some nonsignificant studies will be found among the significant ones. In these cases, Hedges and Olkin (1985) suggested that the researcher eliminate the nonsignificant studies and then proceed to use the methods described here. However, methods developed subsequently allow for less than total publication bias. That is, they allow for the possibility that some nonsignificant studies are published and some significant studies are not published. This eliminates the need to exclude nonsignificant studies from the analysis.

The Iyengar-Greenhouse (1988) Method

Iyengar and Greenhouse (1988) extended the original Hedges-Olkin method to allow for nonzero probabilities of publication for nonsignificant studies. They retained the assumption that all significant studies would be published, regardless of direction of significance (i.e., their selection model was two-tailed, like the Hedges-Olkin model). Their method assumes that all nonsignificant studies have the same nonzero probability of being published, although it can be extended to include different probabilities of publication for nonsignificant studies with different p values. Similar to the Hedges-Olkin method, this method uses maximum likelihood (ML) methods to estimate the values of $\bar{\rho}$ or $\bar{\delta}$ that would have been observed had there been no publication bias. Sensitivity analyses can be conducted to determine whether different weights for different p values have large or small effects on the final estimates of $\bar{\rho}$ or $\bar{\delta}$. Although more realistic than the original Hedges-Olkin method, this method, like that one, is a fixed-effects model and, hence, will rarely be appropriate for real data (as noted by several commentators in the same issue of the journal). Also, the assumption of two-tailed publication bias is probably unrealistic in many cases.

The Begg-Mazumdar (1994) Method

Begg and Mazumdar (1994) assumed that small-sample studies tend to be published only if they yield a correlation or d value of large magnitude (which is required for statistical significance, given the small N), while large-sample studies tend to be published regardless of the size of their r or d values (because their results will almost always be statistically significant). This is the assumption underlying the funnel plot, and Figure 13.2 illustrates the expected outcome under this assumption: The missing studies are those with both small Ns and small d values. They therefore suggested a simple test for publication bias: the rank order correlation between the d (or r) values and their standard errors. In the absence of publication bias, this correlation should be 0. A positive correlation indicates publication bias. This procedure can be viewed as a way of quantifying the outcome of a funnel plot as a substitute for subjective interpretation of the funnel plot. McDaniel and Nguyen (2002) provided an example of use of this procedure.

Further Work by Hedges and Associates

Hedges (1992a) generalized the Iyengar-Greenhouse method to include study weights reflecting probabilities of publication that are based on research findings about how researchers view p values. For example, researchers see little difference between p values of .05 and .04, but view the difference between .06 and .05 as very important. Hedges used this information to create a discrete step function of study weights based on p values. Again using ML methods, these initial weight estimates are iterated to refine the estimates, and the refined weight estimates are then used to produce estimates of the values of $\bar{\rho}$ or $\bar{\delta}$ that would have been observed had there been no publication bias. This is a random-effects model and so estimates of S_ρ^2 and S_δ^2 are also produced. Based on these estimates, this method can estimate the distribution of p values that would be expected in the absence of publication bias. This distribution can then be compared with the observed distribution of p values in the set of studies. Discrepancies indicate the presence of publication bias. In addition to the improved methods for estimating study weights, this method is more realistic in being a random-effects model. However, it still assumes two-tailed selection based on p values.

In this study and in another (Vevea, Clements, & Hedges, 1993), this method was applied to the 755-study database of validity studies for the General Aptitude Test Battery (GATB) of the U.S. Department of Labor. Although the two applications were slightly different in detail, both indicated there was essentially no availability bias in this data set. This is exactly what would be expected when multiple hypotheses are tested. Each GATB study estimates the validity of the 12 different tests in the battery and also estimates the validity of 9 different abilities measured by different combinations of these 12 tests. (Almost no studies reported only partial results.) As discussed earlier, under these conditions it is highly unlikely that there could be any availability bias based on p values. The probability of all 21 significance tests being nonsignificant is vanishing small, as is the probability that all would be significant. Almost all studies must have a mixture of significant and nonsignificant results, which would make the attainment of availability bias difficult even for someone deliberately intent on producing such a bias. Hence, we would not expect to see availability bias in such a literature, and this was the conclusion of the Hedges bias detection and correction method.

Vevea and Hedges (1995) further refined the preceding set of methods. Recognizing that the assumption of two-tailed publication bias is probably unrealistic in most situations, they modified the method to assume one-tailed publication bias. The major improvement, however, is the provision for moderator variables that might be correlated with study effect sizes (and hence with study *p* values). For example, one type of psychotherapy might be particularly effective (large effect sizes) and, at the same time, typically be studied with small sample sizes. This situation calls for a random-effects model with weighted least squares used to predict study outcomes from study characteristics (coded moderators) to (in effect) partial out the effect of the moderators on the bias-corrected estimates of $\bar{\rho}$ and S_{ρ}^2 (or $\bar{\delta}$ and S_{δ}^2). That is, this method allows one to distinguish between publication bias and the effects of moderators of study outcomes. Vevea and Hedges (1995) illustrated this method by applying it to a subset of Glass's studies on psychotherapy. The two moderators were type of therapy (behavioral vs. desensitization) and type of phobia (simple vs. complex). Even after controlling for these moderators, their analysis still detected publication bias; the bias-corrected estimates of $\bar{\delta}$ were 15% to 25% smaller than the original uncorrected estimates. The reason availability bias was detected in these studies, and not in the GATB studies, may be that most of the psychotherapy studies focused on a single hypothesis (or a single important hypothesis) rather than on multiple hypotheses, as in the GATB study set. Although smaller, the bias-corrected mean effect sizes were still substantial, ranging from .48 to .76.

(In this analysis, there was no correction for measurement error in the measure of the dependent variable [the therapy outcome measure]. Correction of the publication bias-corrected mean *d* values for measurement error would likely raise them to values larger than the original mean *d* values [uncorrected for publication bias]. Hence, as estimates of the actual effects of psychotherapy, the original reported values might have been fairly accurate—and might be more accurate than the bias-corrected values of Vevea and Hedges. There is no recognition of the importance of measurement error as a bias-creating effect in the discussions of publication bias.)

Although this procedure appears to remove the effects of publication bias, the price is an increased standard error (*SE*) of the mean estimate. In this application, the average *SE* more than doubled, increasing from .07 to .15. This is similar to what we saw in the case of corrections for measurement error and range restriction: The correction removes the bias but increases the uncertainty in the estimate of the mean.

Hedges and Vevea (1996) used computer simulation to test the accuracy of the basic methods presented in Hedges (1992a), modified from two-tailed to one-tailed publication bias. These methods were derived as large-sample methods, and one question was whether they were accurate with small samples. The methods assume that the random-effects distribution of ρ or δ is normal. When these distributions were normal, the model generated fairly accurate corrected estimates of $\bar{\rho}$ and $\bar{\delta}$ in the presence of publication bias, even when sample sizes were small. When these distributions were not normal, these estimates were less accurate but still more accurate than the uncorrected estimates. However, their significance test for the presence of publication bias showed a large Type I bias. In the absence of publication bias, it falsely indicated significant publication bias up to 50% of the time. Except for the significance test, the results from this study were mostly supportive of the accuracy of these methods. However, one must remember that the publication bias scenarios simulated were those assumed by the model: a step function of increasing probabilities of publication as study p values decrease. As noted earlier, this assumption may not describe reality in many research literatures.

The Duval-Tweedie (2000) Trim-and-Fill Method

The methods of Hedges and his associates and of Iyengar and Greenhouse (1988) are all statistically very complex. Duval and Tweedie (2000) noted that they are highly computer intensive to run and are rarely used, probably for that reason. They present a simpler, nonparametric method based on the properties of the Wilcoxon distribution. This method estimates the number of missing studies, assumed to be from the lower left corner of the funnel plot. They present three different nonparametric estimators of the number of missing studies, all of which seem to provide similar estimates. The method is first presented for the simple case in which the $\bar{\rho}$ and $\bar{\delta}$ are 0. They then present an iterative procedure that allows the method to be used when $\bar{\rho} > 0$ or $\bar{\delta} > 0$. Based on the estimate of the number of missing studies, their method provides an estimate of what $\bar{\rho}$ and $\bar{\delta}$ would have been had there been no availability bias. This is done by "filling in" the missing studies and then recomputing $\bar{\rho}$ and $\bar{\delta}$. For example, it can be seen in Figure 13.2 that small-sample studies are missing in the lower left-hand corner. In Figure 13.1, these missing studies have been "filled in" to create a mirror image of the lower right-hand corner of the figure. This is a method for adjusting for the effects of publication bias, not a method for determining whether it exists. It is assumed that determination will be made by examination of the funnel plot or by other means. If there are actually no missing studies, this method should indicate that the number of missing studies is 0. This method is suitable for random-effects data as well as fixed-effects data.

Duval and Tweedie (2000) presented examples showing that their method gives results very similar to more complex methods. (In particular, they showed that both their method and the more complex methods indicate that, after the adjustment for availability [publication] bias, there is little evidence that second-hand smoke [environmental tobacco smoke] is harmful.) This method would be much easier to program for use by meta-analysts than the other methods of adjusting for availability bias discussed here. However, to our knowledge this has not yet been done.

Terrin, Schmid, Lau, and Olkin (2002) stated that the Duval-Tweedie trim-and-fill method does not provide accurate results if the data contain moderator variables. This is probably true to some extent for all the procedures described here with the exception of the Vevea-Hedges (1995) procedure (described previously). Examples of application of the Duval-Tweedie method in the medical literature include Sutton, Duval, Tweedie, Abrams, and Jones (2000) and Song, Khan, Dinnes, and Sutton (2002). This procedure is also beginning to be used in social science research.

Summary of Methods for Correcting Availability Bias

The area of availability bias is one of the most difficult and complex in meta-analysis. It is often difficult to determine whether such bias exists in a set of studies, and, if it does, most methods of correcting for it are complex and not easy to use. In addition, some of the assumptions on which many of them are based may be questionable. Nevertheless, the issue is an important one and will undoubtedly continue to receive attention. In fact, an edited book devoted to this subject will soon become available (Rothstein, Sutton, & Borenstein, in press).

There is evidence that availability bias may be relatively unimportant in some literatures used in meta-analysis. In particular, if the primary studies examine multiple hypotheses or if the meta-analysis examines relationships that were not the major focus of interest in the primary studies, there may be little publication bias or any other form of availability bias. This may include the majority of meta-analyses. In other cases, it may be necessary to look closely at the possibility of availability bias and to consider some of the methods for detecting and correcting such bias that we have discussed in this chapter.

14

Summary of Psychometric Meta-Analysis

Meta-Analysis Methods and Theories of Data

Every method of meta-analysis is of necessity based on a theory of data. It is this theory (or understanding of data) that determines the nature of the resulting meta-analysis methods. A complete theory of data includes an understanding of sampling error, measurement error, biased sampling (range restriction and range enhancement), dichotomization and its effects, data errors, and other causal factors that distort the raw data we see in research studies. Once a theoretical understanding of how these factors affect data is developed, it becomes possible to develop methods for correcting for their effects. In the language of psychometrics, the first process—the process by which these factors (artifacts) influence data—is modeled as the attenuation model. The second process—the process of correcting for these artifact-induced biases—is called the disattenuation model. If the theory of data on which a method of meta-analysis is based is incomplete, that method will fail to correct for some or all of these artifacts and will thus produce biased results. For example, a theory of data that fails to recognize measurement error will lead to methods of meta-analysis that do not correct for measurement error. Such methods will then perforce produce biased meta-analysis results. Most current methods of meta-analysis do not, in fact, correct for measurement error, as noted in Chapter 11.

Sampling error and measurement error have a unique status among the statistical and measurement artifacts with which meta-analysis must deal: They are always present in all real data. Other artifacts, such as range restriction, artificial dichotomization of continuous variables, or data transcription errors, may be absent in a particular set of studies being subjected to meta-analysis. There is always sampling error, however, because sample sizes are never infinite. Likewise, there is always measurement error, because there are no perfectly reliable measures. In fact, it is the requirement of dealing simultaneously with both sampling error and measurement error that makes even relatively straightforward psychometric meta-analyses seem complicated to many. Most of us are used to dealing with these two types of errors separately. For example, when psychometric texts (e.g., Lord & Novick, 1968; Nunnally & Bernstein, 1994) discuss measurement error, they assume an infinite (or very large) sample size, so that the focus of attention can be on measurement error alone, with no need to deal simultaneously with sampling error. When statistics texts discuss sampling error, they implicitly assume perfect reliability (the absence of measurement error), so that they and the reader can focus solely on sampling error and can ignore issues of measurement error. Both assumptions are highly unrealistic, because all real data simultaneously contain both sampling error and measurement error. It is admittedly more complicated to deal with both types of error simultaneously, yet this is what meta-analysis must do to be successful, as the thrust of this book has made clear. In an important statement, Cook et al. (1992, pp. 315–316, 325–328) also acknowledged this necessity.

Another critical component of a complete theory of data capable of providing a foundation for meta-analysis methods is recognition of the fact that it is highly likely that study population correlations or effect sizes will vary from study to study. The assumption that these parameters are identical across all studies in a meta-analysis—the assumption made by all fixed-effects meta-analysis models—is unrealistic and highly likely to be erroneous, as discussed in Chapters 5 and 9. Fixed-effects and random-effects models are both (partial) theories of the nature of data. Evidence and observation disconfirm the fixed-effects theory and support the random-effects theory. Fixed-effects models can lead to serious errors in meta-analytic results, and this is not the case for random-effects models. Therefore, the theory of data underlying meta-analysis methods should include the random-effects model but not the fixed-effects model.

What Is the Ultimate Purpose of Meta-Analysis?

The question of what theory of data underlies a method of meta-analysis is strongly related to the question of what the general purpose of meta-analysis is. As discussed in Chapter 11, Glass (1976, 1977) stated that the purpose is simply to summarize and describe in a general way the studies in a research literature. In the Hedges-Olkin (1985) and the Rosenthal (1984, 1991) approaches to meta-analysis, the purpose of meta-analysis is more analytic: The focus is on examination of relationships between measures of particular constructs or between measures of specific types of treatments and measures of specific outcomes. However, the purpose is still to summarize the findings reported in a specific research literature (Rubin, 1990). Our view of the purpose of meta-analysis is different: The purpose is to estimate as accurately as possible the construct-level relationships in the population (i.e., to estimate population values or parameters), because these are the relationships of scientific interest. This is an entirely different task; this is the task of estimating what the findings would have been if all studies had been conducted perfectly (i.e., with no methodological limitations). Doing this requires correction for sampling error, measurement error, and other artifacts (when present) that distort study results. Simply quantitatively summarizing and describing the contents of studies in the literature requires no such corrections and does not allow estimation of parameters of scientific interest.

Rubin (1990, pp. 155–166) critiqued the common, descriptive concept of the purpose of meta-analysis and proposed the alternative offered in this book. He stated that, as scientists, we are not really interested in the population of imperfect studies per se; hence, an accurate description or summary of these studies is not really important. Instead, he argued that the goal of meta-analysis should be to estimate the true effects or relationships—defined as "results that would be obtained in an infinitely large, perfectly designed study or sequence of such studies." According to Rubin,

> Under this view, we really do not care *scientifically* about summarizing this finite population (of observed studies). We really care about the underlying scientific process—the underlying process that is generating these outcomes that we happen to see—that we, as fallible researchers, are trying to glimpse through the opaque window of imperfect empirical studies. (p. 157; emphasis in original)

Rubin stated that all studies in the finite population of existing studies, or in a hypothetical population of studies from which these studies are drawn, are flawed in various ways. Therefore, in order to understand the underlying scientific realities, our purpose should not be to summarize their typical reported effect sizes or correlations but rather to use the flawed study findings to estimate the underlying unobserved relationships among constructs. This is an excellent statement of the purpose of meta-analysis as we see it and as embodied in the methods presented in this book.

Psychometric Meta-Analysis: Summary Overview

The goal of research in any area is the production of an integrated statement of the findings of the many pieces of research done in that area. This means an analysis of how the many facts fit together, that is, the development of theory. However, this broad theoretical integration cannot be put on a sound footing until a narrower integration of the literature has taken place. We must first establish the basic facts about relationships before those facts can be integrated. The purpose of meta-analysis is to calibrate these basic relationships at the construct level. That is, the purpose is to estimate what these relationships would be found to be in perfectly conducted studies.

Consider a theoretical question such as, "Does job satisfaction increase organizational commitment?" Before we can answer such a question, we must consider the more mundane question, "Is there a correlation between satisfaction and commitment?" Such questions cannot be answered in any one empirical study. Results must be pooled across studies to eliminate sampling error. Furthermore, the correlation between satisfaction and commitment might vary across studies. That is, we must compare the population correlations in different settings. If there is variation across settings that is large enough to be theoretically important, then we must identify the moderator variables that produce this variation. To compare correlations across settings, we must correct these correlations for other artifacts such as measurement error or range variation.

Consider error of measurement. Job satisfaction can be measured in many ways. These different methods may not measure exactly the same thing, or they may differ in the extent of measurement error. Differences in measurement error can be assessed by differences in the appropriate reliability coefficients. If the reliability of each measure is known in each study, then the effect of error of measurement can be eliminated from each study by correcting the correlation for attenuation and performing the psychometric meta-analysis on these corrected correlations. If only the distribution of reliability coefficients across studies is known, then the effect of random error of measurement can be eliminated using the artifact distribution methods of psychometric meta-analysis.

Systematic differences between measures with the same name require examination of the construct validity of the different methods. If there are large systematic differences between measures, then these must be assessed in multimeasure studies using techniques such as confirmatory factor analysis or path analysis. These studies have replication of results within studies as well as across studies and require special treatment.

Range variation on the independent variable produces differences of an artifactual nature in correlations and in effect size statistics. Even if the basic relationship between variables is the same across studies, variation in the size of the variance on the independent variable will produce variation in the correlation with the dependent variable. The larger the variance on the independent variable, the higher will be the correlation. Range variation (or range restriction) can be either direct or indirect. Indirect range restriction is by far the more common type in all literatures and produces more severe data distortions than direct range restriction. In experimental studies, range variation is produced by differences in the strength of the treatment. If the range size in each study is known (i.e., if standard deviations are published or if treatment strengths are measured), then all correlations or effect sizes can be corrected to the same standard value, eliminating the impact of range variation across studies. Psychometric meta-analysis can then be carried out on these corrected correlations or d values. If only the distribution of range variation is known, then this effect can be eliminated using artifact distribution meta-analysis methods.

Meta-analysis begins with all studies that an investigator can find that provide empirical evidence that bears on some particular fact, such as the relationship between organizational commitment and job satisfaction. The key findings of each study are expressed in a common statistic, such as the correlation between commitment and satisfaction or such as the d statistic, which measures the difference between experimental and control groups for the treatment of interest. Each such statistic can be examined across studies. The mean value of the statistic across studies is a good estimate of the mean attenuated population value across studies. However, the variance across studies is inflated by sampling error. Thus, the first task in artifact distribution meta-analysis is to correct the observed variance across studies to eliminate the effect of sampling error. Then the mean and variance of population values are corrected for the effect of error of measurement and range variation. This mean and standard deviation have thus been corrected for three sources of artifactual variation across studies: sampling error, error of measurement, and range variation. The largest source of variation not corrected for is often reporting errors, such as incorrect computations, typographical errors, failure to reverse score, and the like. However, there are numerous other potential sources of artifactual variation.

In many studies, we have found essentially no variance in results across studies once artifacts have been eliminated. In such cases, the theorist is provided with a very straightforward fact to weave into the overall picture. In such a case, one way to reveal theoretical implications is to review all the reasons that have been cited as explanations for the apparent but artifactual variation across studies. Most such explanations are based on more general theoretical considerations. Hence, the disconfirmation of the explanation leads to disconfirmation of the more general theoretical propositions behind the explanation. For example, meta-analysis has shown that the correlation between cognitive ability factors and job performance essentially does not vary across settings for a given job or for different jobs with the same mental complexity level. This means that it is unnecessary and wasteful for those in personnel research to conduct detailed behavioristic job analyses to equate jobs in different organizations on the specific tasks performed in those jobs, because meta-analysis has disconfirmed the theory that specific task differences cause validity differences.

If there is variation across studies, it may not be large enough to warrant an immediate search for moderator variables. For example, suppose meta-analysis had shown the mean effect of interpersonal skills training on supervisor performance to be $\bar{\delta} = .50$ with a standard deviation of .05. It would be wise for an employer to institute a program of training immediately rather than wait to find out which programs work best. On the other hand, if the mean effect were $\bar{\delta} = .10$ with a standard deviation of .10, then the arbitrary choice of program might incur a loss. There is a 16% chance that the program would be counterproductive, and another 34% chance that the program would cause a positive but nearly trivial improvement.

If there are large differences between studies, then moderator variables are often not difficult to identify. For example, by the time the first meta-analysis was done on the effects of incentives on work performance, there were already interactive studies available clearly showing that incentives increase performance only if the worker has or is given specific information about what aspects of performance will be rewarded.

Meta-analysis provides a method for establishing the relevance of a potential moderator variable. The moderator variable is used to split the studies into subsets, and meta-analysis is then applied to each subset separately. Mean differences will appear if a moderator is present. If there are large differences in subset means, then there will be a corresponding reduction in within-subset variation across studies. Meta-analysis shows how much of any remaining variation is due to artifacts.

The extent of variation is in part a question of the scope of the research review. If we start with all studies on psychotherapy, it is no surprise to find moderator effects. However, if we consider only studies using desensitization on simple phobias, then we might expect to find no differences. However, this is an empirical question. The a priori assumption that there are no differences—made by all fixed-effects meta-analysis methods—is virtually never justifiable. For meta-analysis, scope is an empirical question. If we have the resources for a wide scope, then meta-analysis can be used to assess the scope of the results. If meta-analysis shows only small differences over a very wide set of studies, that finding indicates that many moderator hypotheses are at most of only minor importance. If the wide-scope study shows large differences, then meta-analysis can be applied to subsets of studies with smaller scope. Meta-analysis then shows which aspects of scope (i.e., which potential moderators) are truly important and which are only erroneously thought to be important. The general finding of meta-analysis studies is that true differences across studies are much smaller than researchers believe them to be. These beliefs derive in large part from the cumulative psychological effects of sampling error, that is, repeated observation of large but spurious differences in the observed results from small-sample studies.

Restriction of scope in meta-analysis should be theory based rather than methodological. The most misleading reviews are those in which the author cites only "key" studies selected based on the author's judgments of methodological quality. First, reviews that selectively ignore studies with contrary findings may falsely suggest that there are no moderator variables. Second, even if there are no real variations across studies, there are still spurious variations due to sampling error. Studies selected because they have particularly "sharp" findings are likely to be studies that capitalize on between-study variation that meta-analysis shows to be due to sampling error. In particular, consideration of only studies with statistically significant findings leads to great bias in the estimate of correlations or effect sizes.

Many authors justify selective reviews on the basis of the "methodological deficiencies" in the studies not considered. However, the assertion of "deficiency" is usually based on a personal theory that is itself empirically untested. Agreement between researchers on overall methodological quality is typically quite low. Two reviewers could select mutually exclusive sets of "best studies" from the same literature on the basis of "methodological quality." Meta-analysis provides an empirical procedure for the identification of methodological deficiencies if there are any. First, one should gather a comprehensive set of studies. Second, one should identify those believed to be "methodologically flawed." Third, one should apply meta-analysis to all studies. If there is no nonartifactual variation across studies, then there is no difference between the "defective" studies and the "competent" studies. Fourth, if there is variation across all studies, then that variation may or may not be explained by separate meta-analyses of the "defective" and "nondefective" studies, the next analysis to be conducted.

It is our belief that many real methodological problems beyond sampling error are captured by the rubrics "error of measurement" and "range variation." Error of measurement, in particular, is universal, although some studies may have much poorer measurement than others. The solution to these methodological problems is to *measure* the deficiency and correct for it rather than to discard the data.

Appendix Windows-Based Meta-Analysis Software Package

The Hunter-Schmidt Meta-Analysis Programs Package includes six programs that implement all basic types of Hunter-Schmidt psychometric meta-analysis methods. Information on how to obtain this program package is provided at the end of the Appendix. Brief descriptions of the six programs are provided in the section "Types of Analyses." More detailed descriptions are provided in the text of this book. These programs are intended to be used in conjunction with this book (henceforth referred to as "the text").

The programs are provided on a CD and are compatible with Microsoft Windows® operating systems (Windows 95, 98, 98SE, ME, 2000, and XP). Program interface is logically and intuitively arranged so that people with basic familiarity with Windows-based applications can easily learn to use the program functions. Navigating through the different steps (pages) of the programs is achieved by single-clicking appropriate buttons or icons. Throughout all the steps (pages), there are built-in help functions in the form of roll-over pop-ups (i.e., help statements that appear when the cursor is rolled over certain predetermined areas) explaining the options and instructing the user in how to execute his or her desired tasks.

1. What Is in the CD?

The CD contains (1) the Setup file (Setup Meta Program.exe), (2) the Readme.doc file (the file you are now reading), and (3) two utility programs in the form of Microsoft® Excel templates (Composites.xls and Point-Biserial.xls; details of these programs are described in the "Extras" section) that help users convert correlations in the primary studies to appropriate forms before inputting them into the meta-analysis programs.

2. Installation

If you have an earlier version (Beta version) of the program, you should uninstall it before installing the current version. (Note: The earlier Beta versions contain errors and should no longer be used.) Uninstallation can easily be done by using the "Remove Hunter-Schmidt Meta Analysis Programs" option available in the Windows Programs taskbar.

The installation process starts by double-clicking the Setup file in the CD. You will be asked to provide a serial number to continue. The main programs and all the supporting files will be copied to folder "C:\Meta Analysis Programs" on your hard drive (unless you specify a different drive).

3. Starting the Program

The programs can be activated by selecting the "Hunter & Schmidt Meta Analysis Programs" in the Windows Programs taskbar. Alternatively, you can start the programs by using the icon "Hunter & Schmidt MA" on your desktop. You will be presented with the Start Page, where you can access the Readme file by clicking on the book icon at the upper right corner of the page. To move on to the next page, in which you can select types of meta-analyses to be used, click on the red arrow icon at the lower right corner of the page (if you do not click on the icon, the program will automatically move to the next page after 5 minutes). The "Type of Analyses" page will appear, presenting you with four options of analyses (described next).

4. Types of Analyses

The programs in this package do the following types of meta-analysis:

1. Meta-analysis of correlations corrected individually for the effects of artifacts. (These two programs are collectively referred to in the text as VG6.) These programs are used when (1) the user desires to estimate the correlation between variables and (2) information on the statistical and measurement artifacts (i.e., range restriction, reliabilities on both variables) is available in all (or the majority) of the primary studies.

There are two subprograms under this type of meta-analysis:

A. Program that corrects for direct range restriction: To be used when range restriction is direct (i.e., selection occurs on one of the two variables being correlated). (This program is referred to in the text as VG6-D; see Chapter 3.)

B. Program that corrects for indirect range restriction: To be used when range restriction is indirect (i.e., selection occurs on a third variable that is correlated with both the variables of interest). (This program is referred to in the text as VG6-I; see Chapter 3.)

(Note: The program will ask you if there is any range restriction. When there is no range restriction, results provided by the subprograms 1A and 1B are identical.)

2. Meta-analysis of correlations using artifact distributions. These programs are used when (1) the user desires to estimate the correlation between variables and (2) information on the statistical and measurement artifacts is *not* available in most of the primary studies. (These two programs are collectively referred to in the text as INTNL; see Chapter 4.)

This meta-analysis program also includes two subprograms:

A. Program that corrects for direct range restriction: To be used when range restriction is direct (i.e., selection occurs on one of the two variables being correlated). (This program is referred to in the text as INTNL-D; see Chapter 4.)

B. Program that corrects for indirect range restriction: To be used when range restriction is indirect (i.e., selection occurs on a third variable that is correlated with both the variables of interest). (This program is referred to in the text as INTNL-I; see Chapter 4.)

(Note: The program will ask you if there is any range restriction. When there is no range restriction, results provided by the subprograms 2A and 2B are identical.)

3. Meta-analysis of *d* values corrected individually for measurement error.

This program is used when (1) the user desires to estimate the effect size (*d* value; standardized difference between groups) and (2) information on the reliability of the measure of the dependent variable is available in all (or most) of the primary studies. (This program is referred to in the text as D-VALUE; see Chapter 7.)

4. Meta-analysis of *d* values using artifact distributions.

This program is used when (1) the user is interested in estimating the effect size (*d* value; standardized difference between groups) and (2) information on the reliability of the measure of the dependent variable is *not* available in most of the primary studies. (This program is referred to in the text as D-VALUE1; see Chapter 7.)

The "Type of Analyses" page of the program shows four types of meta-analysis (1–4 listed previously), and the user selects the most appropriate analysis. If the user selects option 1 or 2, the subprograms (1A and 1B or 2A and 2B) will appear on subsequent pages (under the Analysis section) for further choice of the exact program to be used (depending on whether range restriction is direct or indirect).

5. Data Management

After selecting the appropriate type of analysis, the user is presented with the "Setting up the data" page. Here the user can opt either to input (enter) new data or to load existing (previously saved) data files.

a. Entering Data:

For meta-analysis type 1 (i.e., meta-analysis for correlations, with information on statistical and measurement artifacts available in most primary studies; VG6 programs), the user need only enter data into one general data file. The "Enter data from primary studies" page has a spreadsheet-like layout with five fields (spaces) so that relevant information (i.e., correlation, sample size, reliability of variable X [independent variable reliability, R_{xx}], reliability of variable Y [dependent variable reliability, R_{yy}], and range restriction ratio [u]) can be entered accordingly. Data are entered sequentially for each study. When corrections are needed, the user can click on the "Modification" buttons available in front of the data holder for each study. All the data fields must be filled. When there is no range restriction in a study, "1" should be entered in the range restriction (u) cell. Similarly, when a variable is assumed to be perfectly measured (very rare case), "1" should be entered in the corresponding reliability cell. In situations where information on an artifact (R_{xx}, R_{yy}, or u) of a study is not available, the user can simply enter "99" into the corresponding cell. The program will then automatically use the mean of all the relevant artifact values provided in other studies to replace the missing value.

There are spaces to enter data for eight studies in each page. After entering the data for each page, the user clicks on the "Continue" button to proceed to the next page. The two buttons, "Back" and "Continue," can be used to navigate through the pages to modify and/or enter data. (At present, the maximum number of studies is 200.) After completing data entry, the user can press the "Done" button to exit to the previous page and start analysis (or choose other options, such as printing, saving, or modifying the data, as described later).

For meta-analysis type 2 (i.e., meta-analysis for correlations when information on statistical and measurement artifacts is *unavailable* in most primary studies; INTNL programs), the user enters data separately into several data files: The first data file consists of the correlations and the corresponding sample sizes of the primary studies (R and N). The second data file consists of the distribution of reliability coefficients of the independent variable (R_{xx} and freq). The third data file consists of the distribution of reliability coefficients of the dependent variable (R_{yy} and freq). And the fourth data file consists of the distribution of range restriction (u and freq). If information is not available (or the artifact is not applicable) for an artifact distribution (e.g., when there is no range restriction), the program will assume that such artifacts have values fixed at 1.00 and automatically place 1.00s in the relevant data file(s). This means no correction will be made for these artifacts.

For meta-analysis type 3 (i.e., meta-analysis for effect sizes [d values], with information on statistical and measurement artifacts available in most primary studies; D-VALUE program), the procedures are similar to those of the type 1 meta-analysis described previously, except that the user enters only information on dependent variable reliability (R_{yy}); information on independent variable reliability (R_{xx}) and range restriction (u) is not required.

For meta-analysis type 4 (i.e., meta-analysis for effect sizes [d values] when information on statistical and measurement artifacts is *unavailable* in most primary studies; D-VALUE1 program), the procedures are similar to those of the type 2 meta-analysis described previously, except that the user enters only information on the distribution of dependent variable reliability (R_{yy}); information on distributions of independent variable reliability (R_{xx}) and range restriction (u) is not required. (Hence, there are only two data files rather then the four data files required for meta-analysis type 2.)

b. Saving Data

After completing the entry of the data (by clicking on the "Done" button), the user is taken back to the previous page where several options are presented: "Save," "Print," "Analysis," and "Exit." Selecting the "Save" option allows the user to save the data file he or she has just entered. The user will be asked to provide the name for the data set so that it can be easily retrieved when needed. The data will then be saved at the following location: C:\Meta Analysis Programs\Data*i*\"datasetname", with i being the number corresponding to the type of meta-analysis.

Alternatively, the user can simply start analyzing the data. After the meta-analysis results are presented, the user is given another opportunity to save the current data set.

c. Loading Previously Saved Data

To load the previously saved data, select the "Load" option in the "Setting Up Data" page. The user will be presented with names of all the previously saved data sets. He or she can select the appropriate data set to load into the program by typing the name of that data set into the space provided and then pressing "Enter." (It will soon be possible for users to merely click on the selected data file.)

d. Viewing/Modifying Saved Data

After loading/entering data, the user can view the data by selecting the "Entering/Modifying" option. Data will be presented in the spreadsheet-like layout. Modifications (corrections) can be made by clicking the icon in front of each individual study.

e. Printing Data

The user can print the current data set (i.e., the data that have just been entered or loaded) for easy reviewing by selecting the "Print" option.

6. Analyzing Data

After entering/loading/modifying the data, the user can start analyzing the data by clicking on the "Analyzing the Data" button. For correlation-based meta-analysis (i.e., types 1 and 2; VG6 and INTNL programs), the user will next be asked to indicate the nature of range restriction existing in his or her data (i.e., direct or indirect, which means selecting between type 1A [VG6-D program] or 1B [VG6-I program] or selecting between 2A [INTNL-D program] or 2B [INTNL-I program]).

Both direct range restriction programs (VG6-D and INTNL-D) automatically assume that the independent variable reliabilities (R_{xx}) are from the unrestricted samples, and the dependent variable reliabilities (R_{yy}) are from the restricted samples. These assumptions agree with the nature of data available in research and practice. (See the text, Chapters 3, 4, and 5, for a more detailed discussion.)

Both indirect range restriction programs (VG6-I and INTNL-I) require the user to specify whether (1) the independent variable reliabilities (R_{xx}) are from the restricted or unrestricted samples and (2) whether the range restriction ratios are for true scores (u_T) or observed scores (u_X). For all cases, the program assumes that the dependent variable reliabilities are from the restricted samples. (See the text, Chapters 3, 4, and 5, for a more detailed discussion.)

When there is no range restriction, it does not matter which type of analysis (A or B) the user chooses; the programs will provide identical results.

The user will be asked to provide the title for the analysis (e.g., "Interviews and job performance—Meta-analysis 1") and the name of the output file where results will be saved.

7. Reporting Results

Results of the analyses are provided three different ways: (1) on screen (partial output), (2) on disk (at C:\Meta Analysis Programs\Output\"filename", with "filename" being the name the user provided for the current analysis), and (3) print out (optional; which can be activated by clicking on the "Printer" option). Due to space limitations, only partial output is presented on the screen. Complete output is saved to disk and printed with the print-out option.

A full listing and description of the output of each program is given later. The following are *some* of the items provided as output of the analysis:

1. Number of correlations (or d values) and total sample size.

2. Mean true score correlation (or mean fully corrected d value), the corresponding standard deviation (true score correlation SD_ρ or true effect size SD_δ), and the corresponding variances. These values are corrected for the biasing effects of all the artifacts considered in the meta-analysis. These values are estimates of mean construct-level relationships. Credibility values for this distribution are also provided.

3. Weighted mean observed correlation (or d values), observed variance and observed standard deviation, and variance and standard deviation corrected for sampling error only.

4. Sampling error variance, percentage of the observed variance due to sampling error variance, variance accounted for by all artifacts combined, and percentage of the observed variance due to all the artifacts combined.

5. For types 1 and 2 analyses (i.e., correlation-based meta-analyses), certain output is provided that is relevant to employment or educational selection research. The VG6 and INTNL programs provide the mean true validity and its standard deviation. Credibility values for this distribution are also provided. The true validity (also called operational validity) is the correlation between the predictor (X) and the criterion (Y) corrected for all the artifacts except for the attenuating effect of measurement error in the predictor X. This value represents the mean correlation of the predictor *measures* with the criterion of interest. (In contrast, the true score correlation represents the mean construct-level correlation between the independent variable and the dependent variable.)

8. *Illustrating Examples*

The programs include several data sets used as examples in Chapters 3, 4, and 7. There are examples representing all six types of meta-analyses discussed previously. The user can practice doing analyses based on these data sets to familiarize him- or herself with the programs.

9. *Extras*

There are two utility programs in the form of Microsoft Excel® templates that aid in processing data before entering data into the meta-analysis programs. The user must have Microsoft Excel to use these programs. During the process of installing the main (meta-analysis) programs, these two utility programs will be automatically copied onto your hard drive at the following location: "C:\Meta Analysis Programs\Extras." The first program ("Composite.xls") combines correlations within a study; it computes the correlation between a composite (summed) independent or dependent variable and the other variable. This program also computes the reliability of the composite measure. (Both these procedures are described in Chapter 10 of the text.) The second program ("Formula to compute biserial r.xls") computes the biserial correlation from a point biserial correlation provided in a primary study. This conversion should be carried out when a continuous (and normally distributed) variable has been artificially dichotomized in a primary study (as described in Chapters 6 and 7 of the text). To activate these programs, go to the folder "C:\Meta Analysis Programs\Extras," then double-click on the program name ("Composite.xls" or "Formula to compute biserial r.xls") found therein.

10. Full Description of Output of Individual Programs

Program output is divided into three sections: (1) Main Meta-Analysis Output, which presents results corrected for all artifacts; (2) Bare Bones Meta-Analysis Output, which presents results corrected for sampling error only; and (3) Validity Generalization Output, which presents validity results relevant to tests and other procedures used in employment and educational selection. Section 3 is provided only for meta-analyses of correlations (i.e., type 1 meta-analysis [based on the VG6 programs] and type 2 meta-analyses [based on the INTNL programs]). It is not provided for meta-analyses of *d* values (type 3 meta-analysis [based on the D-VALUE program] and type 4 meta-analysis [based on the D-VALUE1 program]). The sections of program output always appear in the same order: The Main Output is always presented first, followed by the Bare Bones Output, followed by the Validity Generalization Output (if applicable).

A. *Bare Bones Output for VG6 (type 1 meta-analysis) and INTNL (type 2 meta-analysis).* (Bare Bones Output is identical for these two types of meta-analysis.)

   1. Sample-size-weighted mean observed correlation.
   2. Variance of correlations after removing sampling error variance.
   3. Standard deviation (*SD*) of correlations after removing sampling error variance. (This is the square root of item 2.)
   4. Sample-size-weighted variance of observed correlations.
   5. Sample-size-weighted *SD* of observed correlations. (This is the square root of item 4.)
   6. Variance due to sampling error variance.
   7. *SD* predicted from sampling error alone. (This is the square root of item 6.)
   8. Percentage variance of observed correlations due to sampling error variance.

B. *Main Output for VG6 programs (type 1 meta-analysis)*

   1. Number of correlations in the meta-analysis.
   2. Total sample size. (Sum of study sample sizes.)
   3. Mean true score correlation ($\bar{\rho}$).
   4. Variance of true score correlations (S^2_ρ).
   5. *SD* of true score correlations (SD_ρ). (This is the square root of item 4.) Note: For most purposes, the key output is items 3 and 5.

6. 80% credibility interval for true score correlation distribution. (See Chapter 5.)
7. Observed variance of the corrected correlations ($S^2_{r_c}$). (Each correlation is first corrected for measurement error and other artifacts; then the variance of these corrected correlations is computed. This is the variance of the corrected correlations before sampling error variance is removed. As described in Chapter 3, the corrections for artifacts, while eliminating systematic downward biases, increase sampling error.)
8. *SD* of the corrected correlations SD_{r_c}. (This is the square root of item 7.)
9. Variance in corrected correlations due to sampling error. [Note: This figure is larger than the variance in *uncorrected* (*observed*) correlations due to sampling error variance, which is presented in the Bare Bones Output section. This is because the artifact corrections, while removing systematic downward biases, increase sampling error variance.]
10. *SD* of corrected correlations predicted from sampling error. (This is the square root of item 9.)
11. Percentage variance in corrected correlations due to sampling error.

C. *Validity Generalization Output for VG6 programs (type 1 meta-analysis)*

1. Mean true validity. (Same as mean true score correlation, except it is not corrected for the attenuating effects of measurement error in the independent variable; see Chapter 3 of text.)
2. Variance of true validities.
3. *SD* of true validities. (This is the square root of item 2.)
4. 80% credibility interval for true validity distribution. (See Chapter 5.)

D. *Main Output for INTNL programs (type 2 meta-analysis)*

1. Number of correlations in the meta-analysis.
2. Total sample size. (Sum of study sample sizes.)
3. Mean true score correlation ($\bar{\rho}$).
4. Variance of true score correlations (S^2_ρ).
5. *SD* of true score correlations (SD_ρ). (This is the square root of item 4.) Note: For most purposes, the key output is items 3 and 5.
6. 80% credibility interval for true score correlation distribution. (See Chapter 5.)
7. Variance in observed correlations due to all artifacts combined. (See Chapter 4.)
8. *SD* of observed correlations predicted from all artifacts. (This is the square root of item 7.)
9. Variance of observed correlations after removal of variance due to all artifacts (residual variance [SD_{res}]; see Chapter 4).
10. Percentage variance of observed correlations due to all artifacts.

E. *Validity Generalization Output for INTNL programs (type 2 meta-analysis)*

1. Mean true validity. (Same as mean true score correlation, except not corrected for the attenuating effects of measurement error in the independent variable.)
2. Variance of true validities.

3. *SD* of true validities. (This is the square root of item 2.)
4. 80% credibility interval of true validity distribution. (See Chapter 5.)
5. Variance of observed validities due to all artifacts combined. (See Chapter 4.)
6. *SD* of observed validities predicted from all artifacts. (This is the square root of item 5.)
7. Variance in observed validities after removal of variance due to all artifacts (residual variance [SD_{res}]; see Chapter 4).
8. Percentage variance in observed validities due to all artifacts.

F. *Bare Bones Output for D-VALUE and D-VALUE1 programs (meta-analysis types 3 and 4).* (Bare Bones Output is identical for these two types of meta-analyses.)

1. Sample-size-weighted mean effect size (mean *d* value).
2. Variance of *d* values after removing sampling error variance.
3. *SD* of *d* values after removing sampling error variance. (This is the square root of item 2.) 4. Sample-size-weighted variance of observed *d* values.
5. Sample-size-weighted standard deviation of observed *d* values.
6. Variance is observed *d*-values due to sampling error variance.
7. *SD* predicted from sampling error variance alone. (This is the square root of item 6.)
8. Percentage variance in observed *d* values due to sampling error variance.

G. *Main Output for D-VALUE program (type 3 meta-analysis)*

1. Number of effect sizes (*d* values) in the meta-analysis.
2. Total sample size. (Sample sizes summed across studies.)
3. Mean true effect size ($\bar{\delta}$).
4. True variance of effect sizes (S_{δ}^2).
5. *SD* of delta (SD_{δ}). (This is the square root of item 4.) Note: For most purposes, the key output is items 3 and 5.
6. 80% credibility interval for delta distribution. (See Chapter 5.)
7. Observed variance of corrected *d* values ($S_{d_c}^2$). (Each *d* value is corrected for measurement error in the dependent variable; then the variance of these corrected *d* values is computed. This is the variance of the corrected *d* values before sampling error variance is removed. As described in Chapter 7, the correction for measurement error, while eliminating the systematic downward bias, increases sampling error variance.)
8. Observed *SD* of the corrected *d* values (SD_{d_c}). (This is the square root of item 7.)
9. Variance in corrected *d* values due to sampling error. (Note: This figure is larger than the variance in *uncorrected* [*observed*] *d* values due to sampling error variance, which is presented in the Bare Bones Output section. This is because the correction for measurement error, while removing the systematic downward biases, increases the sampling error variance.)
10. *SD* of corrected *d* values predicted from sampling error variance. (This is the square root of item 9.)
11. Percentage variance in corrected *d* values due to sampling error variance.

H. Main Output for D-VALUE1 program (type 4 meta-analysis)

1. Number of effect sizes (d values) in the meta-analysis.
2. Total sample size. (Sample sizes summed across studies.)
3. Mean true effect size ($\bar{\delta}$).
4. True variance of effect sizes (S_δ^2).
5. SD of delta (SD_δ). (This is the square root of item 4.) Note: For most purposes, the key output is items 3 and 5.
6. 80% credibility interval for delta distribution. (See Chapter 5.)
7. Variance in observed d values due to all artifacts. (See Chapter 7.)
8. SD of observed d values predicted from all artifacts. (This is the square root of item 7.)
9. Variance in observed d values after removal of variance due to all artifacts (residual variance [S_{res}^2]; see Chapter 7).
10. Percentage variance in observed d values due to all artifacts.

This program package can be ordered by contacting Frank Schmidt or Huy Le, Department of Management and Organization, Tippie College of Business, University of Iowa, Iowa City, IA 52242. Electronic mail: frank-schmidt@uiowa.edu, flschmidt@mchsi.com, or huy-le@uiowa.edu. A Web site for this program is being prepared and will be available soon.

References

AERA-APA-NCME. (1985). *Standards for educational and psychological testing* (4th ed.). Washington, DC: American Educational Research Association.

AERA-APA-NCME. (1999). *Standards for educational and psychological testing* (5th ed.). Washington, DC: American Educational Research Association.

Aguinis, H. (2001). Estimation of sampling variance of correlations in meta-analysis. *Personnel Psychology, 54,* 569–590.

Aguinis, H., & Pierce, C. A. (1998). Testing moderator variable hypotheses meta-analytically. *Journal of Management, 24,* 577–592.

Aguinis, H., & Whitehead, R. (1997). Sampling variance in the correlation coefficient under indirect range restriction: Implications for validity generalization. *Journal of Applied Psychology, 82,* 528–538.

Albright, L. E., Glennon, J. R., & Smith, W. J. (1963). *The use of psychological tests in industry.* Cleveland, OH: Howard Allen.

Alexander, R. A. (1988). Group homogeneity, range restriction, and range enhancement effects on correlations. *Personnel Psychology, 41,* 773–777.

Alexander, R. A., Carson, K. P., Alliger, G. M., & Carr, L. (1987). Correcting doubly truncated correlations: An improved approximation for correcting the bivariate normal correlation when truncation has occurred on both variables. *Educational and Psychological Measurement, 47,* 309–315.

Alexander, R. A., Carson, K. P., Alliger, G. M., & Cronshaw, S. F. (1989). Empirical distributions of range restricted SDx in validity studies. *Journal of Applied Psychology, 74,* 253–258.

Allen, M., Hunter, J. E., & Donahue, W. A. (1988). *Meta-analysis of self report data on the effectiveness of communication apprehension treatment techniques.* Unpublished manuscript, Department of Communication, Wake Forest University.

Allen, M., Hunter, J. E., & Donahue, W. A. (1989). Meta-analysis of self-report data on the effectiveness of public speaking anxiety treatment techniques. *Communication Education, 38,* 54–76.

American Psychological Association, Division of Industrial and Organizational Psychology (Division 14). (1987). *Principles for the validation and use of personnel selection procedures* (3rd ed.). College Park, MD: Author.

American Psychological Association. (2001). *Publication manual of the American Psychological Association* (5th ed.). Washington, DC: Author.

Anastasi, A. (1986). *Psychological testing* (6th ed.). New York: Macmillan.

Anastasi, A. (1988). *Psychological testing* (7th ed.). New York: Macmillan.

Antman, E. M., Lau, J., Kupelnick, B., Mosteller, F., & Chalmers, T. C. (1992). A comparison of results of meta-analyses of randomized control trials and recommendations of clinical experts. *Journal of the American Medical Association, 268,* 240–248.

Aronson, E., Ellsworth, P., Carlsmith, J., & Gonzales, M. (1990). *Methods of research in social psychology* (2nd ed.). New York: McGraw-Hill.

Baker, P. C. (1952). Combining tests of significance in cross validation. *Educational and Psychological Measurement, 12,* 300–306.

Bangert-Drowns, R. L. (1986). Review of developments in meta-analysis method. *Psychological Bulletin, 99,* 388–399.

Bangert-Drowns, R. L., Kulik, J. A., & Kulik, C.-L. C. (1983). Effects of coaching programs on achievement test performance. *Review of Educational Research, 53,* 571–585.

Bangert-Drowns, R. L., Kulik, J. A., & Kulik, C.-L. C. (1984, August). *The influence of study features on outcomes of educational research.* Paper presented at the 92nd Annual Meeting of the American Psychological Association, Toronto.

Barnett, V., & Lewis, T. (1978). *Outliers in statistical data.* New York: Wiley.

Barrick, M. R., & Mount, M. K. (1991). The Big Five personality dimensions and job performance: A meta-analysis. *Personnel Psychology, 44,* 1–26.

Bartlett, C. J., Bobko, P., Mosier, S. B., & Hannan, R. (1978). Testing for fairness with a moderated multiple regression strategy: An alternative to differential analysis. *Personnel Psychology, 31,* 233–241.

Baum, M. L., Anish, D. S., Chalmers, T. C., Sacks, H. S., Smith, H., & Fagerstrom, R. M. (1981). A survey of clinical trials of antibiotic prophylaxis in colon surgery: Evidence against further use of no-treatment controls. *New England Journal of Medicine, 305,* 795–799.

Becker, B. J. (1987). Applying tests of combined significance in meta-analysis. *Psychological Bulletin, 102,* 164–171.

Becker, B. J. (1989, March). *Model-driven meta-analysis: Possibilities and limitations.* Paper presented at the annual meeting of the American Educational Research Association, San Francisco.

Becker, B. J. (1992). Models of science achievement: Forces affecting male and female performance in school science. In Cook T. D., Cooper, H., Cordray, D. S., Hartmann, H., Hedges, L. V., et al. (Eds.), *Meta-analysis for explanation: A casebook* (pp. 209–282). New York: Russell Sage.

Becker, B. J. (1996). The generalizability of empirical research results. In C. P. Benbow & D. Lubinski (Eds.), *Intellectual talent: Psychological and social issues* (pp. 363–383). Baltimore: Johns Hopkins University Press.

Becker, B. J., & Schram, C. M. (1994). Examining explanatory models through research synthesis. In H. Cooper & L. V. Hedges (Eds.), *The handbook of research synthesis* (pp. 357–382). New York: Russell Sage.

Begg, C. B. (1994). Publication bias. In H. Cooper & L. V. Hedges (Eds.), *The handbook of research synthesis* (pp. 399–409). New York: Russell Sage.

Begg, C. B., & Mazumdar, M. (1994). Operating characteristics of a rank order correlation for publication bias. *Biometrics, 50,* 1088–1101.

Bettencourt, B. A., & Miller, N. (1996). Gender differences in aggression as a function of provocation: A meta-analysis. *Psychological Bulletin, 119,* 422–427.

Bloom, B. S. (1964). *Stability and change in human characteristics.* New York: Wiley.

Bobko, P. (1983). An analysis of correlations corrected for attenuation and range restriction. *Journal of Applied Psychology, 68,* 584–589.

Bobko, P., & Reick, A. (1980). Large sample estimators for standard errors of functions of correlation coefficients. *Applied Psychological Measurement, 4,* 385–398.

Bobko, P., Roth, P. L., & Bobko, C. (2001). Correcting the effect size of *d* for range restriction and unreliability. *Organizational Research Methods, 4,* 46–61.

Bobko, P., & Stone-Romero, E. F. (1998). Meta-analysis may be another useful research tool but it is not a panacea. In G. R. Ferris (Ed.), *Research in personnel and human resources management* (Vol. 16, pp. 359–397). Greenwich, CT: JAI Press.

Bond, C. F., & Titus, L. J. (1983). Social facilitation: A meta-analysis of 241 studies. *Psychological Bulletin, 94,* 265–292.

Borenstein, M. (1994). The case for confidence intervals in controlled clinical trials. *Controlled Clinical Trials, 15,* 411–428.

Borenstein, M., & Rothstein, H. R. (2000). *Comprehensive meta-analysis.* Englewood, NJ: Biostat, Inc.

Boudreau, J. W. (1983). Economic considerations in estimating the utility of human resource productivity improvement programs. *Personnel Psychology, 36,* 551–576.

Boudreau, J. W. (1984). Decision theory contributions to human resource management research and practice. *Industrial Relations, 23,* 198–217.

Bozarth, J. D., & Roberts, R. R. (1972). Signifying significant significance. *American Psychologist, 27,* 774–775.

Bradley, J. V. (1968). *Distribution free statistical tests.* Englewood Cliffs, NJ: Prentice Hall.

Brannick, M. T. (2001). Implications of empirical Bayes meta-analysis for test validation. *Journal of Applied Psychology, 86,* 468–480.

Brennan, R. L. (1983). *Elements of generalizability theory.* Iowa City, IA: ACT Publications.

Brogden, H. E. (1946). On the interpretation of the correlation coefficient as a measure of predictive efficiency. *Journal of Educational Psychology, 37,* 65–76.

Brogden, H. E. (1949). When testing pays off. *Personnel Psychology, 2,* 171–183.

Brogden, H. E. (1968). *Restriction in range.* Unpublished manuscript, Department of Psychology, Purdue University, Lafayette, IN.

Brogden, H. E. (1972). Some observations on two methods in psychology. *Psychological Bulletin, 77,* 431–437.

Brown, S. A. (1990). Studies of educational interventions and outcomes in diabetic adults: A meta-analysis revisited. *Patient Education and Counseling, 16,* 189–215.

Brown, S. P. (1996). A meta-analysis and review of organizational research. *Psychological Bulletin, 120,* 235–255.

Brozek, J., & Tiede, K. (1952). Reliable and questionable significance in a series of statistical tests. *Psychological Bulletin, 49,* 339–344.

Bullock, R. J., & Svyantek, D. J. (1985). Analyzing meta-analysis: Potential problems, an unsuccessful replication, and evaluation criteria. *Journal of Applied Psychology, 70,* 108–115.

Burt, D. B., Zembar, M. J., & Niederehe, G. (1995). Depression and memory impairment: A meta-analysis of the association, its pattern, and specificity. *Psychological Bulletin, 117,* 285–303.

Bushman, B. J., & Wang, M. C. (1995). A procedure for combining sample correlation coefficients and vote counts to obtain an estimate and a confidence interval for the population correlation coefficient. *Psychological Bulletin, 117,* 530–546.

Bushman, B. J., & Wang, M. C. (1996). A procedure for combining sample standardized mean differences and vote counts to estimate the population standardized mean difference in fixed effect models. *Psychological Methods, 1,* 66–80.

Callender, J. C. (1978). *A Monte Carlo investigation of the accuracy of two models for validity generalization.* Unpublished doctoral dissertation, University of Houston.

Callender, J. C. (1983, March). *Conducting validity generalization research based on correlations, regression slopes, and covariances.* Paper presented at the I/O and OB Graduate Student Convention, Chicago.

Callender, J. C., & Osburn, H. G. (1980). Development and test of a new model for validity generalization. *Journal of Applied Psychology, 65,* 543–558.

Callender, J. C., & Osburn, H. G. (1981). Testing the constancy of validity with computer generated sampling distributions of the multiplicative model variance estimate: Results for petroleum industry validation research. *Journal of Applied Psychology, 66,* 274–281.

Callender, J. C., & Osburn, H. G. (1988). Unbiased estimation of the sampling variance of correlations. *Journal of Applied Psychology, 73,* 312–315.

Callender, J. C., Osburn, H. G., & Greener, J. M. (1979). *Small sample tests of two validity generalization models.* Paper presented at the meeting of the American Psychological Association, New York.

Callender, J. C., Osburn, H. G., Greener, J. M., & Ashworth, S. (1982). Multiplicative validity generalization model: Accuracy of estimates as a function of sample size and mean, variance, and shape of the distribution of true validities. *Journal of Applied Psychology, 67,* 859–867.

Campbell, D. T., & Stanley, J. C. (1963). *Experimental and quasi-experimental designs for research.* Chicago: Rand McNally.

Carlson, K. D., Scullen, S. E., Schmidt, F. L., Rothstein, H. R., & Erwin, F. W. (1999). Generalizable biographical data validity: Is multi-organizational development and keying necessary? *Personnel Psychology, 52,* 731–756.

Carver, R. P. (1978). The case against statistical significance testing. *Harvard Educational Review, 48,* 378–399.

Cattin, P. (1980). The estimation of the predictive power of a regression model. *Journal of Applied Psychology, 65,* 407–414.

Chalmers, I., & Altman, D. G. (1995). *Systematic reviews.* London: BJM.

Chase, L. J., & Chase, R. B. (1976). Statistical power analysis of applied psychological research. *Journal of Applied Psychology, 61,* 234–237.

Chelimsky, E. (1994, October). *Use of meta-analysis in the General Accounting Office.* Paper presented at the Science and Public Policy Seminars, Federation of Behavioral, Psychological and Cognitive Sciences, Washington, DC.

Clarke, K., & Oxman, A. D. (Eds.). (1999). *Cochrane Reviewers' Handbook 4.0* (updated July 1999). In Review Manager (RevMan) (computer program), Version 4.0. Oxford, UK: The Cochrane Collaboration.

Coggin, T. D., & Hunter, J. E. (1983, May/June). Problems in measuring the quality of investment information: The perils of the information coefficient. *Financial Analysts Journal,* 25–33.

Coggin, T. D., & Hunter, J. E. (1987). A meta-analysis of pricing of "risk" factors in APT. *The Journal of Portfolio Management, 14,* 35–38.

Cohen, J. (1962). The statistical power of abnormal-social psychological research: A review. *Journal of Abnormal and Social Psychology, 65,* 145–153.

Cohen, J. (1977). *Statistical power analysis for the behavior sciences* (Rev. ed.). New York: Academic Press.

Cohen, J. (1983). The cost of dichotomization. *Applied Psychological Measurement, 7,* 249–253.

Cohen, J. (1988). *Statistical power analysis for the behavioral sciences* (2nd ed.). Hillsdale, NJ: Lawrence Erlbaum.

Cohen, J. (1990). Things I learned (so far). *American Psychologist, 45,* 1304–1312.

Cohen, J. (1992). Statistical power analysis. *Current Directions in Psychological Science, 1,* 98–101.

Cohen, J. (1994). The earth is round ($p < .05$). *American Psychologist, 49,* 997–1003.

Coleman, J. S., et al. (1966). *Equality of educational opportunity.* Washington, DC: U.S. Government Printing Office.

Collins, J. M., Schmidt, F. L., Sanchez-Ku, M., Thomas, L., McDaniel, M. A., & Le, H. (2003). Can individual differences shed light on the construct meaning of assessment centers? *International Journal of Selection and Assessment, 11,* 17–29.

Collins, N. L., & Miller, L. C. (1994). Self-disclosure and liking: A meta-analytic review. *Psychological Bulletin, 116,* 457–475.

Colquitt, J. A., LePine, J. A., & Noe, R. A. (2002). Toward an integrative theory of training motivation: A meta-analytic path analysis of 20 years of research. *Journal of Applied Psychology, 85,* 678–707.

Conway, J. M., & Huffcutt, A. I. (1997). Psychometric properties of multisource performance ratings: A meta-analysis of subordinate, supervisor, peer, and self-ratings. *Human Performance, 10*(4), 331–360.

Cook, T., & Campbell, D. T. (1976). The design and conduct of quasi-experiments and true experiments in field settings. In M. Dunnette (Ed.), *Handbook of industrial and organizational psychology* (pp. 223–236). Chicago: Rand McNally.

Cook, T., & Campbell, D. T. (1979). *Quasi-experiments and true experimentation: Design and analysis for field settings.* Chicago: Rand McNally.

Cook, T. D., Cooper, H., Cordray, D. S., Hartmann, H., Hedges, L. V., et al. (1992). *Meta-analysis for explanation: A casebook.* New York: Russell Sage.

Cook, T. D., & Leviton, L. C. (1980). Reviewing the literature: A comparison of traditional methods with meta-analysis. *Journal of Personality, 48,* 449–472.

Cooper, H. (1984). *The integrative research review: A systematic approach.* Beverly Hills, CA: Sage.

Cooper, H. (1997). Some finer points in meta-analysis. In M. Hunt (Ed.), *How science takes stock: The story of meta-analysis* (pp. 169–181). New York: Russell Sage.

Cooper, H. (1998). *Synthesizing research: A guide for literature reviews.* Thousand Oaks, CA: Sage.

Cooper, H., DeNeve, K., & Charlton, K. (1997). Finding the missing science: The fate of studies submitted for review by a human subjects committee. *Psychological Methods, 2,* 447–452.

Cooper, H., & Hedges, L. V. (1994a). Research synthesis as a scientific enterprise. In H. Cooper and L. V. Hedges (Eds.), *The handbook of research synthesis* (pp. 3–14). New York: Russell Sage.

Cooper, H., & Hedges, L. V. (Eds.). (1994b). *The handbook of research synthesis.* New York: Russell Sage.

Cooper, H. M., & Rosenthal, R. (1980). Statistical versus traditional procedures for summarizing research findings. *Psychological Bulletin, 87,* 442–449.

Cooper, W. W., Ho, J. L. Y., Hunter, J. E., & Rodgers, R. C. (1985). The impact of the Foreign Corrupt Practices Act on internal control practices (a meta-analysis). *Journal of Accounting, Auditing, and Finance, 9,* 22–39.

Cortina, J. M., & Nouri, H. (2000). *Effect size for ANOVA designs.* Thousand Oaks, CA: Sage.

Coursol, A., & Wagner, E. E. (1986). Effect of positive findings on submission and acceptance rates: A note on meta-analysis bias. *Professional Psychology, 17,* 136–137.

Coward, W. M., & Sackett, P. R. (1990). Linearity of ability-performance relationships: A reconfirmation. *Journal of Applied Psychology, 75,* 297–300.

Cowles, M. (1989). *Statistics in psychology: An historical perspective.* Hillsdale, NJ: Lawrence Erlbaum.

Cronbach, L. J. (1947). Test "reliability": Its meaning and determination. *Psychometrika, 12,* 1–16.

Cronbach, L. J. (1951). Coefficient alpha and the internal structure of tests. *Psychometrika, 16,* 297–334.

Cronbach, L. J. (1975). Beyond the two disciplines of scientific psychology revisited. *American Psychologist, 30,* 116–127.

Cronbach, L. J., & Gleser, G. C. (1965). *Psychological tests and personnel decisions* (2nd ed.). Urbana: University of Illinois Press.

Cronbach, L. J., Gleser, G. C., Nanda, H., & Rajaratnam, N. (1972). *The dependability of behavioral measurements: Theory of generalizability for scores and profiles.* New York: Wiley.

Cureton, E. E. (1936). On certain estimated correlation functions and their standard errors. *Journal of Experimental Education, 4,* 252–264.

Cuts raise new social science query: Does anyone appreciate social science? (1981, March 27). *Wall Street Journal,* p. 54.

Dickerson, K. (1994). Research registers. In H. Cooper & L. V. Hedges (Eds.), *The handbook of research synthesis* (pp. 71–84). New York: Russell Sage.

Dickerson, K., Min, Y., & Meinert, C. (1992). Factors influencing the publication of research results: Follow-up of applications submitted to two institutional review boards. *Journal of the American Medical Association, 267,* 374–378.

Dillard, J. P., Hunter, J. E., & Burgoon, M. (1984). Sequential requests, persuasive message strategies: A meta-analysis of foot-in-door and door-in-the-face. *Human Communication Research, 10,* 461–488.

DiMatteo, M. R., Lepper, H. S., & Croghan, T. W. (2000). Depression is a risk factor for noncompliance with medical treatment: A meta-analysis of the effects of anxiety and depression on patient adherence. *Archives of Internal Medicine, 160,* 2101–2107.

Dimson, E., & Marsh, P. (1984). An analysis of brokers' and analysts' unpublished forecasts of UK stock returns. *Journal of Finance, 39*(5), 1257–1292.

Dunlap, W. P., Cortina, J. M., Vaslow, J. B., & Burke, M. J. (1996). Meta-analysis of experiments with matched groups or repeated measures designs. *Psychological Methods, 1,* 170–177.

Dunnette, M. D., & Borman, W. C. (1979). Personnel selection and classification. In M. R. Rosenzweig & L. W. Porter (Eds.), *Annual review of psychology* (Vol. 30). Palo Alto, CA: Annual Reviews.

Dunnette, M. D., Houston, J. S., Hough, L. M., Touquam, J., Lamnstein, S., King, K., Bosshardt, M. J., & Keys, M. (1982). *Development and validation of an industry-wide electric power plant operator selection system.* Minneapolis, MN: Personnel Decisions Research Institute.

Durlak, J. A., Fuhrman, R., & Lampman, C. (1991). Effectiveness of cognitive behavior therapy for maladapting children: A meta-analysis. *Psychological Bulletin, 110,* 204–214.

Duval, S., & Tweedie, R. (2000). Trim and fill: A simple funnel plot based method of testing and adjusting for publication bias in meta-analysis. *Biometrics, 56,* 276–284.

Dye, D. (1982). *Validity generalization analysis for data from 16 studies participating in a consortium study.* Unpublished manuscript, Department of Psychology, George Washington University, Washington, DC.

Dye, D., Reck, M., & Murphy, M. A. (1993). The validity of job knowledge measures. *International Journal of Selection and Assessment, 1,* 153–157.

Eagly, A. H. (1978). Sex differences in influenceability. *Psychological Bulletin, 85,* 86–116.

Eagly, A. H., Ashmore, R. D., Makhijani, M. G., & Longo, L. C. (1991). What is beautiful is good, but . . . : A meta-analysis review of research on the physical attractiveness stereotype. *Psychological Bulletin, 110,* 109–128.

Eagly, A. H., & Carli, L. L. (1981). Sex of researchers and sex-typical communications as determinants of sex differences in influenceability: A meta-analysis of social influence studies. *Psychological Bulletin, 90,* 1–20.

Eagly, A. H., & Johnson, B. T. (1990). Gender and leadership style: A meta-analysis. *Psychological Bulletin, 108,* 233–256.

Eagly, A. H., Karau, S. J., & Makhijani, M. G. (1995). Gender and the effectiveness of leaders: A meta-analysis. *Psychological Bulletin, 117,* 125–145.

Eagly, A. H., Makhijani, M. G., & Klonsky, B. G. (1992). Gender and the evaluation of leaders: A meta-analysis. *Psychological Bulletin, 111,* 3–22.

Easterbrook, P. J., Berlin, J. A., Gopalan, R., & Matthews, D. R. (1991). Publication bias in clinical research. *Lancet, 337,* 867–872.

Edwards, J. R. (1995). Alternatives to difference scores as dependent variables in the study of congruence in organizational research. *Organizational Behavior and Human Decision Processes, 64,* 307–327.

Egger, M., Smith, G., Schneider, M., & Minder, C. (1997). Bias in meta-analysis detected by a simple, graphical test. *British Medical Journal, 315,* 629–634.

Erel, O., & Burman, B. (1996). Interrelatedness of marital relations and parent-child relations: A meta-analytic review. *Psychological Bulletin, 118,* 108–132.

Erez, A., Bloom, M. C., & Wells, M. T. (1996). Using random rather than fixed effects models in meta-analysis: Implications for situational specificity and validity generalization. *Personnel Psychology, 49,* 275–306.

Erlenmeyer-Kimling, L., & Jarvik, L. F. (1963). Genetics and intelligence: A review. *Science, 142,* 1477–1479.

Eysenck, H. J. (1978). An exercise in mega-silliness. *American Psychologist, 33,* 517.

Feingold, A. (1994). Gender differences in personality: A meta-analysis. *Psychological Bulletin, 116,* 429–456.

Field, A. P. (2001). Meta-analysis of correlation coefficients: A Monte Carlo comparison of fixed- and random-effects methods. *Psychological Methods, 6,* 161–180.

Fisher, C. D., & Gittelson, R. (1983). A meta-analysis of the correlates of role conflict and ambiguity. *Journal of Applied Psychology, 68,* 320–333.

Fisher, R. A. (1932). *Statistical methods for research workers* (4th ed.). London: Oliver & Boyd.

Fisher, R. A. (1935). *The design of experiments.* London: Oliver & Boyd.

Fisher, R. A. (1938). *Statistical methods for research workers* (7th ed.). London: Oliver & Boyd.

Fisher, R. A. (1973). *Statistical methods and scientific inference* (3rd ed.). Edinburgh: Oliver & Boyd.

Fiske, D. W. (1978). The several kinds of generalization. *The Behavioral and Brain Sciences, 3,* 393–394.

Fleishman, E. A. (1975). Toward a taxonomy of human performance. *American Psychologist, 30,* 1127–1149.

Fleishman, E. A., & Hempel, W. E., Jr. (1954). Changes in factor structure of a complex psychomotor test as a function of practice. *Psychometrika, 19,* 239–252.

Fleishman, E. A., & Hempel, W. E., Jr. (1955). The relation between abilities and improvement with practice in a visual discrimination reaction test. *Journal of Experimental Psychology, 49,* 301–312.

Fleiss, J. L. (1994). Measures of effect size for categorical data. In H. Cooper & L. V. Hedges (Eds.), *The handbook of research synthesis* (pp. 245–260). New York: Russell Sage.

Foley, P. P., & Swanson, L. (1985). *An investigation of validity generalization of Navy selector composites* (Technical Report). San Diego, CA: Navy Personnel Research and Development Center.

Forsyth, R. A., & Feldt, L. S. (1969). An investigation of empirical sampling distributions of correlation coefficients corrected for attenuation. *Educational and Psychological Measurement, 29,* 61–71.

Gaugler, B. B., Rosenthal, D. B., Thornton, G. C., & Bentson, C. (1987). Meta-analysis of assessment center validity. *Journal of Applied Psychology, 72,* 493–511.

Gergen, K. J. (1982). *Toward transformation in social knowledge.* New York: Springer-Verlag.

Ghiselli, E. E. (1949). The validity of commonly employed occupational tests. *University of California Publications in Psychology, 5,* 253–288.

Ghiselli, E. E. (1955). The measurement of occupational aptitude. *University of California Publications in Psychology, 8,* 101–216.

Ghiselli, E. E. (1966). *The validity of occupational aptitude tests.* New York: Wiley.

Ghiselli, E. E. (1973). The validity of aptitude tests in personnel selection. *Personnel Psychology, 26,* 461–477.

Glass, G. V. (1972). The wisdom of scientific inquiry on education. *Journal of Research in Science Teaching, 9,* 3–18.

Glass, G. V. (1976). Primary, secondary and meta-analysis of research. *Educational Researcher, 5,* 3–8.

Glass, G. V. (1977). Integrating findings: The meta-analysis of research. *Review of Research in Education, 5,* 351–379.

Glass, G. V., Cahen, L. S., Smith, M. L., & Filby, N. N. (1982). *School class size: Research and policy.* Beverly Hills, CA: Sage.

Glass, G. V., & Kliegl, R. M. (1983). An apology for research integration in the study of psychotherapy. *Journal of Consulting and Clinical Psychology, 51,* 28–41.

Glass, G. V., McGaw, B., & Smith, M. L. (1981). *Meta-analysis in social research.* Beverly Hills, CA: Sage.

Glass, G. V., Peckham, P. D., & Sanders, J. R. (1972). Consequences of failure to meet assumptions underlying fixed effects analysis of variance and covariance. *Review of Educational Research, 42,* 237–288.

Gottfredson, L. S. (1985). Education as a valid but fallible signal of worker quality. *Research in Sociology of Education and Socialization, 5,* 123–169.

Green, B. F., & Hall, J. A. (1984). Quantitative methods for literature reviews. *Annual Review of Psychology, 35,* 37–53.

Greenhouse, J. B., & Iyengar, S. (1994). Sensitivity analysis and diagnostics. In H. Cooper & L. V. Hedges (Eds.), *Handbook of research synthesis* (pp. 383–398). New York: Russell Sage.

Greenwald, A. G. (1975). Consequences of prejudice against the null hypothesis. *Psychological Bulletin, 82,* 1–20.

Gross, A. L., & McGanney, M. L. (1987). The range restriction problem and nonignorable selection processes. *Journal of Applied Psychology, 72,* 604–610.

Grubbs, F. E. (1969). Procedures for detecting outliers. *Technometrics, 11,* 1–21.

Gulliksen, H. (1986). The increasing importance of mathematics in psychological research (Part 3). *The Score, 9,* 1–5.

Guttman, L. (1985). The illogic of statistical inference for cumulative science. *Applied Stochastic Models and Data Analysis, 1,* 3–10.

Guzzo, R. A., Jackson, S. E., & Katzell, R. A. (1986). Meta-analysis analysis. In L. L. Cummings & B. M. Staw (Eds.), *Research in organizational behavior* (Vol. 9). Greenwich, CT: JAI Press.

Guzzo, R. A., Jette, R. D., & Katzell, R. A. (1985). The effects of psychologically based intervention programs on worker productivity: A meta-analysis. *Personnel Psychology, 38,* 275–292.

Hackett, R. D., & Guion, R. M. (1985). A re-evaluation of the absenteeism-job satisfaction relationship. *Organizational Behavior and Human Decision Processes, 35,* 340–381.

Hackman, J. R., & Oldham, G. R. (1975). Development of the Job Diagnostic Survey. *Journal of Applied Psychology, 60,* 159–170.

Haddock, C., Rindskopf, D., & Shadish, W. (1998). Using odds ratios as effect sizes for meta-analysis of dichotomous data: A primer on methods and issues. *Psychological Methods, 3,* 339–353.

Hall, J. A. (1978). Gender effects in decoding nonverbal clues. *Psychological Bulletin, 85,* 845–857.

Hall, J. A., & Rosenthal, R. (1995). Interpreting and evaluating meta-analysis. *Evaluation and the Health Professions, 18,* 393–407.

Hall, S. M., & Brannick, M. T. (2002). Comparison of two random effects methods of meta-analysis. *Journal of Applied Psychology, 87,* 377–389.

Halvorsen, K. T. (1986). Combining results from independent investigations: Meta-analysis in medical research. In J. C. Bailar & F. Mosteller (Eds.), *Medical uses of statistics.* Waltham, MA: NEJM Books.

Halvorsen, K. T. (1994). The reporting format. In H. Cooper & L. V. Hedges (Eds.), *Handbook of research synthesis* (pp. 425–438). New York: Russell Sage.

Hamilton, M. A., & Hunter, J. E. (1987). *Two accounts of language intensity effects.* Paper presented at the International Communication Association Convention, New Orleans.

Hardy, R. J., & Thompson, S. G. (1998). Detecting and describing heterogeneity in meta-analysis. *Statistics in Medicine, 17,* 841–856.

Harter, J. K., Schmidt, F. L., & Hayes, T. L. (2002). Business unit level relationships between employee satisfaction/engagement and business outcomes: A meta-analysis. *Journal of Applied Psychology, 87,* 268–279.

Hartigan, J. A., & Wigdor, A. K. (Eds.). (1989). *Fairness in employment testing: Validity generalization, minority issues, and the General Aptitude Test Battery.* Washington, DC: National Academy Press.

Harwell, M. (1997). An investigation of the Raudenbush (1988) test for studying variance heterogeneity. *Journal of Experimental Education, 65*(2), 181–190.

Hays, W. L. (1963). *Statistics.* New York: Holt, Rinehart & Winston.

Hedges, L. V. (1980). *Combining the results of experiments using different scales of measurement.* Unpublished manuscript, Center for Educational Research, Stanford University, Stanford, CA.

Hedges, L. V. (1981). Distribution theory for Glass's estimator of effect size and related estimators. *Journal of Educational Statistics, 6,* 107–128.

Hedges, L. V. (1982a). Estimation of effect size from a series of independent experiments. *Psychological Bulletin, 92,* 490–499.

Hedges, L. V. (1982b). Fitting categorical models to effect sizes from a series of experiments. *Journal of Educational Statistics, 7,* 119–137.

Hedges, L. V. (1982c). Fitting continuous models to effect size data. *Journal of Educational Statistics, 7,* 245–270.

Hedges, L. V. (1983a). Combining independent estimators in research synthesis. *British Journal of Mathematical and Statistical Psychology, 36*(1), 123–131.

Hedges, L. V. (1983b). A random effects model for effect sizes. *Psychological Bulletin, 93,* 388–395.

Hedges, L. (1984). Estimation of effect size under non-random sampling: The effects of censoring studies yielding statistically mean differences. *Journal of Educational Statistics, 9,* 61–85.

Hedges, L. V. (1987). How hard is hard science, how soft is soft science: The empirical cumulativeness of research. *American Psychologist, 42,* 443–455.

Hedges, L. V. (1988). The meta-analysis of test validity studies. In H. Wainer & H. I. Braun (Eds.), *Test validity* (pp. 191–212). Hillsdale, NJ: Lawrence Erlbaum.

Hedges, L. V. (1992a). Modeling publication selection effects in meta-analysis. *Statistical Science, 7,* 246–255.

Hedges, L. V. (1992b). Meta-analysis. *Journal of Educational Statistics, 17,* 279–296.

Hedges, L. V. (1994a). Statistical considerations. In H. Cooper & L. V. Hedges (Eds.), *Handbook of research synthesis* (pp. 29–38). New York: Russell Sage.

Hedges, L. V. (1994b). Fixed effects models. In H. Cooper & L. V. Hedges (Eds.), *Handbook of research synthesis* (pp. 285–300). New York: Russell Sage.

Hedges, L. V., & Olkin, I. (1980). Vote counting methods in research synthesis. *Psychological Bulletin, 88,* 359–369.

Hedges, L. V., & Olkin, I. (1982). Analyses, reanalyses, and meta-analyses. *Contemporary Education Review, 1,* 157–165.

Hedges, L. V., & Olkin, I. (1983a). Clustering estimates of effect magnitude from independent studies. *Psychological Bulletin, 93,* 563–573.

Hedges, L. V., & Olkin, I. (1983b). Regression models in research synthesis. *The American Statistician, 37,* 137–140.

Hedges, L. V., & Olkin, I. (1985). *Statistical methods for meta-analysis.* Orlando, FL: Academic Press.

Hedges, L. V., & Olkin, I. (in press). *Statistical methods for meta-analysis* (2nd ed.).

Hedges, L. V., & Pigott, T. D. (2001). The power of statistical tests in meta-analysis. *Psychological Methods, 6,* 203–217.

Hedges, L. V., & Stock, W. (1983). The effects of class size: An examination of rival hypotheses. *American Educational Research Journal, 20,* 63–85.

Hedges, L. V., & Vevea, J. L. (1996). Estimating effect size under publication bias: Small sample properties and robustness of a random effects selection model. *Journal of Educational and Behavioral Statistics, 21,* 299–333.

Hedges, L. V., & Vevea, J. L. (1998). Fixed- and random-effects models in meta-analysis. *Psychological Methods, 3,* 486–504.

Heinsman, D. T., & Shadish, W. R. (1996). Assignment methods in experimentation: When do nonrandomized experiments approximate the answers from randomized experiments? *Psychological Methods, 1,* 154–169.

Hembree, R. (1988). Correlates, causes, effects, and treatment of test anxiety. *Review of Educational Research, 58,* 44–77.

Herbert, T. B., & Cohen, S. (1995). Depression and immunity: A meta-analytic review. *Psychological Bulletin, 113,* 472–486.

Hill, T. E. (1980, September). Development of a clerical program in Sears. In V. J. Benz (Chair), *Methodological implications of large scale validity studies of clerical occupations.* Symposium conducted at the meeting of the American Psychological Association, Montreal, Canada.

Hirsh, H. R., & McDaniel, M. A. (1987). *Decision rules in applications of the Schmidt-Hunter meta-analysis technique: Some critical considerations.* Unpublished manuscript, Baruch College, City University of New York.

Hirsh, H. R., Northrop, L. C., & Schmidt, F. L. (1986). Validity generalization results for law enforcement occupations. *Personnel Psychology, 39,* 399–420.

Hirsh, H. R., Schmidt, F. L., Pearlman, K., & Hunter, J. E. (1985). *Improvements and refinements in validity generalization methods: Implications for the situational specificity hypothesis.* Paper presented at the 93rd Annual Convention of the American Psychological Association, Los Angeles.

Hoffert, S. P. (1997). Meta-analysis is gaining status in science and policymaking. *The Scientist, 11*(18), 1–6.

Hom, P. W., Caranikas-Walker, F., Prussia, G. E., & Griffeth, R. W. (1992). A meta-analytic structural equations analysis of a model of employee turnover. *Journal of Applied Psychology, 77,* 890–909.

Hotelling, H. (1953). New light on the correlation coefficient and its transforms. *Journal of the Royal Statistical Society, B, 15,* 193–225.

Hoyt, W. T. (2000). Rater bias in psychological research: When it is a problem and what we can do about it? *Psychological Methods, 5,* 64–86.

Huber, P. J. (1980). *Robust statistics.* New York: Wiley.

Huffcutt, A. I., & Arthur, W. A. (1995). Development of a new outlier statistic for meta-analytic data. *Journal of Applied Psychology, 80,* 327–334.

Hunt, M. (1997). *How science takes stock.* New York: Russell Sage.

Hunter, J. E. (1977, August). *Path analysis: Longitudinal studies and causal analysis in program evaluation.* Invited address presented at the 85th American Psychological Association Convention, San Francisco.

Hunter, J. E. (1979, September). *Cumulating results across studies: A critique of factor analysis, canonical correlation, MANOVA, and statistical significance testing.* Invited address presented at the 86th Annual Convention of the American Psychological Association, New York.

Hunter, J. E. (1980a). Factor analysis. In P. Monge (Ed.), *Multivariate techniques in human communication research.* New York: Academic Press.

Hunter, J. E. (1980b). Validity generalization and construct validity. In *Construct validity in psychological measurement: Proceedings of a colloquium on theory and application in education and measurement.* Princeton, NJ: Educational Testing Service.

Hunter, J. E. (1983a). *The dimensionality of the general aptitude tests battery (GATB) and the dominance of the general factors over specific factors in the prediction of job performance for USES* (Test Research Rep. No. 44). Washington, DC: U.S. Department of Labor, U.S. Employment Services.

Hunter, J. E. (1983b). *Test validation for 12,000 jobs: An application of job classification and validity generalization analysis to the general aptitude test battery (GATB)* (Test Research Rep. No. 45). Washington, DC: U.S. Department of Labor, U.S. Employment Service.

Hunter, J. E. (1983c). *Fairness of the general aptitude test battery (GATB): Ability differences and their impact on minority hiring rates* (Test Research Rep. No. 46). Washington, DC: U.S. Department of Labor, U.S. Employment Service.

Hunter, J. E. (1983d). *The economic benefits of personnel selection using ability tests: A state of the art review including a detailed analysis of the dollar benefit of U.S. employment service placements and a critique of the low cut off method of test use* (Test Research Rep. No. 47). Washington, DC: U.S. Department of Labor, U.S. Employment Service.

Hunter, J. E. (1983e). *The prediction of job performance in the military using ability composites: The dominance of general cognitive ability over specific aptitudes.* Report for Research Applications, Inc., in partial fulfillment of DOD Contract No. F41689–83-C-0025.

Hunter, J. E. (1983f). A causal analysis of cognitive ability, job knowledge, job performance, and supervisory ratings. In F. Landy, S. Zedeck, & J. Cleveland (Eds.), *Performance measurement and theory* (pp. 257–266). Hillsdale, NJ: Lawrence Erlbaum.

Hunter, J. E. (1984). *The validity of the Armed Forces Vocational Aptitude Battery (ASVAB) High School Composites.* Report for Research Applications, Inc., in partial fulfillment of DOD Contract No. F41689–83-C-0025.

Hunter, J. E. (1985). *Differential validity across jobs in the military.* Report for Research Applications, Inc., in partial fulfillment of DOD Contract No. F41689–83-C-0025.

Hunter, J. E. (1986). *Multiple dependent variables in experimental design.* Monograph presented at a workshop at the University of Iowa.

Hunter, J. E. (1987). Multiple dependent variables in program evaluation. In M. M. Mark & R. L. Shotland (Eds.), *Multiple methods in program evaluation.* San Francisco: Jossey-Bass.

Hunter, J. E. (1988). *A path analytic approach to analysis of covariance.* Unpublished manuscript, Department of Psychology, Michigan State University.

Hunter, J. E. (1995). *PACKAGE: Software for data analysis in the social sciences.* Unpublished suite of computer programs. (Available from Frank Schmidt, University of Iowa.)

Hunter, J. E. (1997). Needed: A ban on the significance test. *Psychological Science, 8,* 3–7.

Hunter, J. E., Crosson, J. J., & Friedman, D. H. (1985). *The validity of the Armed Services Vocational Aptitude Battery (ASVAB) for civilian and military job performance.* Final report for Research Applications, Inc., in fulfillment of Contract No. F41689–83-C-0025.

Hunter, J. E., & Gerbing, D. W. (1982). Unidimensional measurement, second order factor analysis and causal models. In B. M. Staw & L. L. Cummings (Eds.), *Research in organizational behavior* (Vol. 4). Greenwich, CT: JAI Press.

Hunter, J. E., & Hirsh, H. R. (1987). Applications of meta-analysis. In C. L. Cooper & I. T. Robertson (Eds.), *International review of industrial and organizational psychology 1987.* London: Wiley.

Hunter, J. E., & Hunter, R. F. (1984). Validity and utility of alternate predictors of job performance. *Psychological Bulletin, 96,* 72–98.

Hunter, J. E., & Schmidt, F. L. (1977). A critical analysis of the statistical and ethical implications of various definitions of test fairness. *Psychological Bulletin, 83,* 1053–1071.

Hunter, J. E., & Schmidt, F. L. (1978). Differential and single group validity of employment tests by race: A critical analysis of three recent studies. *Journal of Applied Psychology, 63,* 1–11.

Hunter, J. E., & Schmidt, F. L. (1982a). Fitting people to jobs: Implications of personnel selection for national productivity. In E. A. Fleishman &

M. D. Dunnette (Eds.), *Human performance and productivity: Vol. 1. Human capability assessment* (pp. 233–284). Hillsdale, NJ: Lawrence Erlbaum.

Hunter, J. E., & Schmidt, F. L. (1982b). Ability tests: Economic benefits versus the issue of fairness. *Industrial Relations, 21*(3), 293–308.

Hunter, J. E., & Schmidt, F. L. (1982). Quantifying the effects of psychological interventions on employee job performance and work force productivity. *American Psychologist, 38,* 473–478.

Hunter, J. E., & Schmidt, F. L. (1987a). *Error in the meta-analysis of correlations: The mean correlation.* Unpublished manuscript, Department of Psychology, Michigan State University.

Hunter, J. E., & Schmidt, F. L. (1987b). *Error in the meta-analysis of correlations: The standard deviation.* Unpublished manuscript, Department of Psychology, Michigan State University.

Hunter, J. E., & Schmidt, F. L. (1990a). *Methods of meta-analysis: Correcting error and bias in research findings* (1st ed.). Newbury Park, CA: Sage.

Hunter, J. E., & Schmidt, F. L. (1990b). Dichotomizing continuous variables: The implications for meta-analysis. *Journal of Applied Psychology, 75,* 334–349.

Hunter, J. E., & Schmidt, F. L. (1994a). Correcting for sources of artifactual variance across studies. In H. Cooper & L. V. Hedges (Eds.), *The handbook of research synthesis* (pp. 323–338). New York: Russell Sage.

Hunter, J. E., & Schmidt, F. L. (1994b). The estimation of sampling error variance in meta-analysis of correlations: The homogeneous case. *Journal of Applied Psychology, 79,* 171–177.

Hunter, J. E., & Schmidt, F. L. (1996). Cumulative research knowledge and social policy formulation: The critical role of meta-analysis. *Psychology, Public Policy, and Law, 2,* 324–347.

Hunter, J. E., & Schmidt, F. L. (2000). Fixed effects vs. random effects meta-analysis models: Implications for cumulative knowledge in psychology. *International Journal of Selection and Assessment, 8,* 275–292.

Hunter, J. E., & Schmidt, F. L. (2001). *Sequential meta-analysis: Correcting for artifacts one at a time.* Unpublished manuscript, University of Iowa.

Hunter, J. E., Schmidt, F. L., & Coggin, T. D. (1996). *Meta-analysis of correlations: Bias in the correlation coefficient and the Fisher z transformation.* Unpublished manuscript, University of Iowa.

Hunter, J. E., Schmidt, F. L., & Hunter, R. (1979). Differential validity of employment tests by race: A comprehensive review and analysis. *Psychological Bulletin, 31,* 215–232.

Hunter, J. E., Schmidt, F. L., & Jackson, G. B. (1982). *Meta-analysis: Cumulating research findings across studies.* Beverly Hills, CA: Sage.

Hunter, J. E., Schmidt, F. L., & Le, H. (2002). *Implications of direct and indirect range restriction for meta-analysis methods and findings.* Manuscript submitted for publication.

Hunter, J. E., Schmidt, F. L., & Raju, N. S. (1986). *Analysis of Hoben Thomas' critique of validity generalization.* Unpublished manuscript, Department of Psychology, Michigan State University.

Iaffaldono, M. T., & Muchinsky, P. M. (1985). Job satisfaction and job performance: A meta-analysis. *Psychological Bulletin, 97,* 251–273.

Ito, T. A., Miller, N., & Pollock, V. E. (1996). Alcohol and aggression: A meta-analysis of the moderating effects of inhibitory cues, triggering events, and self-focused attention. *Psychological Bulletin, 120,* 60–82.

Iyengar, S., & Greenhouse, J. (1988). Selection models and the file drawer problem. *Statistical Science, 3,* 109–135.

Jackson, G. B. (1978, April). *Methods for reviewing and integrating research in the social sciences.* Final reports to the National Science Foundation for Grant #DIS 76–20398. Washington, DC: George Washington University, Social Research Group. (NTIS No. PB 283 747/AS)

Jackson, G. B. (1980). Methods for integrative reviews. *Review of Educational Research, 50,* 438–460.

Jackson, S. E. (1984, August). *Can meta-analysis be used for theory development in organizational psychology?* Paper presented at the meeting of the American Psychological Association, Toronto.

Jackson, S. E., & Schuler, R. S. (1985). A meta-analysis and conceptual critique of research on role ambiguity and role conflict in work settings. *Organizational Behavioral and Human Decision Processes, 36,* 16–78.

James, L. R., Demaree, R. G., & Mulaik, S. A. (1986). A note on validity generalization procedures. *Journal of Applied Psychology, 71,* 440–450.

James, L. R., Demaree, R. G., Mulaik, S. A., & Ladd, R. T. (1992). Validity generalization in the context of situational models. *Journal of Applied Psychology, 77,* 3–14.

Jensen, A. R. (1980). *Bias in mental testing.* New York: Free Press.

Johnson, B. T. (1989). *D-Stat: Software for the meta-analytic review of research literatures.* Hillsdale, NJ: Lawrence Erlbaum.

Jones, L. V., & Fiske, D. W. (1953). Models for testing the significance of combined results. *Psychological Bulletin, 50,* 375–382.

Joreskog, K. G., & Sorbom, D. (1979). *Advances in factor analysis and structural equation models.* Cambridge, MA: Abt Books.

Jorgensen, R. S., Johnson, B. T., Kolodziej, M. E., & Scheer, G. E. (1996). Elevated blood pressure and personality: A meta-analytic review. *Psychological Bulletin, 120,* 293–320.

Judge, T. A., & Bono, J. E. (2000). Relationship of core self-evaluations traits—self-esteem, generalized self-efficacy, locus of control, and emotional stability—with job satisfaction and job performance: A meta-analysis. *Journal of Applied Psychology, 86,* 80–92.

Judge, T. A., Thorensen, C. J., Bono, J. E., & Patton, G. K. (2001). The job satisfaction–job performance relationship: A qualitative and quantitative review. *Psychological Bulletin, 127,* 376–401.

Kalaian, H. A., & Raudenbush, S. W. (1996). A multivariate mixed linear model for meta-analysis. *Psychological Methods, 1,* 227–235.

Katzell, R. A., & Dyer, F. J. (1977). Differential validity revived. *Journal of Applied Psychology, 62,* 137–145.

Kelly, T. L. (1947). *Fundamentals of statistics.* Cambridge, MA: Harvard University Press.

Kemery, E. R., Dunlap, W. P., & Griffeth, R. W. (1988). Correction for unequal proportions in point biserial correlations. *Journal of Applied Psychology, 73,* 688–691.

Kemery, E. R., Mossholder, K. W., & Dunlap, W. P. (1989). Meta-analysis and moderator variables: A cautionary note on transportability. *Journal of Applied Psychology, 74,* 168–170.

Kemery, E. R., Mossholder, K. W., & Roth, L. (1987). The power of the Schmidt and Hunter additive model of validity generalization. *Journal of Applied Psychology, 72,* 30–37.

King, L. M., Hunter, J. E., & Schmidt, F. L. (1980). Halo in multidimensional forced choice performance evaluation scale. *Journal of Applied Psychology, 65,* 507–516.

Kirk, R. E. (1995). *Experimental design: Procedures for the behavioral sciences.* New York: Brooks/Cole.

Kirk, R. (1996). Practical significance: A concept whose time has come. *Educational and Psychological Measurement, 56,* 746–759.

Kirk, R. E. (2001). Promoting good statistical practices: Some suggestions. *Educational and Psychological Measurement, 61,* 213–218.

Knight, G. P., Fabes, R. A., & Higgins, D. A. (1996). Concerns about drawing causal inferences from meta-analyses: An example in the study of gender differences in aggression. *Psychological Bulletin, 119,* 410–421.

Kondrasuk, J. N. (1981). Studies in MBO effectiveness. *Academy of Management Review, 6,* 419–430.

Kraiger, K., & Ford, J. K. (1985). A meta-analysis of race effects in performance ratings. *Journal of Applied Psychology, 70,* 56–65.

Kulik, J. A. (1984, April). *The uses and misuses of meta-analysis.* Paper presented at the meeting of the American Educational Research Association, New Orleans.

Kulik, J. A., & Bangert-Drowns, R. L. (1983/1984). Effectiveness of technology in precollege mathematics and science teaching. *Journal of Educational Technology Systems, 12,* 137–158.

Kulik, C. C., & Kulik, J. A. (1986). *Estimating effect sizes in quantitative research integration.* Manuscript submitted for publication.

Kulik, J. A., Kulik, C. C., & Cohen, P. A. (1979). A meta-analysis of outcome studies of Keller's personalized system of instruction. *American Psychologist, 34,* 307–318.

Laczo, R. M., Sackett, P. R., Bobko, P., & Cortina, J. M. (in press). A comment on sampling error in *d* with unequal *N*s: Avoiding potential errors in meta-analytic and primary research. *Journal of Applied Psychology.*

Ladd, R. T., & Cornwell, J. M. (1986, April). *The accuracy of meta-analysis estimates.* Paper presented at the First Annual Conference of the Society for Industrial and Organizational Psychology, Inc., Chicago.

Lamb, W. K., & Whitla, D. K. (1983). *Meta-analysis and the integration of research findings: A trend analysis and bibliography prior to 1983.* Unpublished manuscript, Harvard University, Cambridge, MA.

Landman, J. T., & Dawes, R. M. (1982). Psychotherapy outcome: Smith and Glass' conclusions stand up under scrutiny. *American Psychologist, 37,* 504–516.

Law, K. S., Schmidt, F. L., & Hunter, J. E. (1994a). Nonlinearity of range corrections in meta-analysis: A test of an improved procedure. *Journal of Applied Psychology, 79,* 425–438.

Law, K. S., Schmidt, F. L., & Hunter, J. E. (1994b). A test of two refinements in meta-analysis procedures. *Journal of Applied Psychology, 79,* 978–986.

Lawshe, C. H. (1948). *Principles of personnel selection.* New York: McGraw-Hill.

Le, H. A. (2003). *Correcting for indirect range restriction in meta-analysis: Testing a new meta-analysis method.* Unpublished doctoral dissertation, University of Iowa, Iowa City.

Le, H., Schmidt, F. L., & Lauver, K. (2003). *The multi-faceted nature of measurement error and its implications for measurement error corrections: The case of job satisfaction.* Manuscript submitted for publication.

Lee, R., Miller, K. J., & Graham, W. K. (1982). Corrections for restriction of range and attenuation in criterion-related validation studies. *Journal of Applied Psychology, 67,* 637–639.

Lent, R. H., Auerbach, H. A., & Levin, L. S. (1971a). Research design and validity assessment. *Personnel Psychology, 24,* 247–274.

Lent, R. H., Auerbach, H. A., & Levin, L. S. (1971b). Predictors, criteria and significant results. *Personnel Psychology, 24,* 519–533.

Leone, F. C., & Nelson, L. S. (1966). Sampling distributions of variance components: I. Empirical studies of balanced nested designs. *Technometrics, 8,* 457–468.

Levine, J. M., Kramer, G. G., & Levine, E. N. (1975). Effects of alcohol on human performance: An integration of research findings based on an abilities classification. *Journal of Applied Psychology, 60,* 285–293.

Levine, J. M., Romashko, T., & Fleishman, E. A. (1973). Evaluation of an abilities classification system for integration and generalizing human performance research findings: An application to vigilance tasks. *Journal of Applied Psychology, 58,* 149–157.

Light, R. J. (Ed.). (1983). *Evaluation studies review annual* (Vol. 8). Beverly Hills, CA: Sage.

Light, R. J., & Pillemer, D. B. (1984). *Summing up: The science of reviewing research.* Cambridge, MA: Harvard University Press.

Light, R. J., Singer, J. D., & Willett, J. B. (1994). The visual presentation and interpretation of meta-analyses. In H. Cooper & L. V. Hedges (Eds.), *The handbook of research synthesis* (pp. 439–453). New York: Russell Sage.

Light, R. J., & Smith, P. V. (1971). Accumulating evidence: Procedures for resolving contradictions among different research studies. *Harvard Educational Review, 41,* 429–471.

Lilienthal, R. A., & Pearlman, K. (1983). *The validity of federal selection tests for aid/technicians in the health, science, and engineering fields.* Washington,

DC: U.S. Office of Personnel Management, Office of Personnel Research and Development.

Linn, R. L. (1968). Range restriction problems in the use of self-selected groups for test validation. *Psychological Bulletin, 69,* 69–73.

Linn, R. L. (in press). The Pearson selection formulas: Implications for studies of predictive bias and estimates of educational effects in selected samples. *Journal of Educational Measurement.*

Linn, R. L., & Dunbar, S. B. (1985). Validity generalization and predictive bias. In R. A. Burk (Ed.), *Performance assessment: State of the art.* Baltimore: Johns Hopkins University Press.

Linn, R. L., Harnisch, D. L., & Dunbar, S. B. (1981a). Validity generalization and situational specificity: An analysis of the prediction of first year grades in law school. *Applied Psychological Measurement, 5,* 281–289.

Linn, R. L., Harnisch, D. L., & Dunbar, S. B. (1981b). Corrections for range restriction: An empirical investigation of conditions resulting in conservative corrections. *Journal of Applied Psychology, 66,* 655–663.

Lipsey, M. W., & Wilson, D. B. (1993). The efficacy of psychological, educational, and behavioral treatment: Confirmation from meta-analysis. *American Psychologist, 48,* 1181–1209.

Lipsey, M. W., & Wilson, D. B. (2001). *Practical meta-analysis.* Thousand Oaks, CA: Sage.

Locke, E. A. (1986). Generalizing from laboratory to field: Ecological validity or abstraction of elements? In E. A. Locke (Ed.), *Generalizing from laboratory to field settings.* Lexington, MA: Lexington Books.

Lockhart, R. S. (1998). *Statistics and data analysis for the behavioral sciences.* New York: W. H. Freeman.

Loftus, G. R. (1996). Psychology will be a much better science when we change the way we analyze data. *Current Directions in Psychological Science, 5,* 161–171.

Loher, B. T., Noe, R. A., Moeller, N., & Fitzgerald, M. P. (1985). A meta-analysis of the relationship of job characteristics to job satisfaction. *Journal of Applied Psychology, 70,* 280–289.

Lord, F., & Novick, M. (1968). *Statistical theories of mental test scores.*

Mabe, P. A., III, & West, S. G. (1982). Validity of self evaluations of ability: A review and meta-analysis. *Journal of Applied Psychology, 67,* 280–296.

MacCallum, R. C., Zhang, S., Preacher, K. J., & Rucker, D. D. (2002). On the practice of dichotomization of quantitative variables. *Psychological Methods, 7,* 19–40.

Mackenzie, B. D. (1972). Behaviorism and positivism. *Journal of History of the Behavioral Sciences, 8,* 222–231.

Mackenzie, B. D. (1977). *Behaviorism and the limits of scientific method.* Atlantic Highlands, NJ: Humanities Press.

Madigan, R. M., Scott, K. D., Deadrick, D. L., & Stoddard, J. A. (1986, September). Employment testing: The U.S. Job Service is spearheading a revolution. *Personnel Administrator,* 103–112.

Maloley et al. v. Department of National Revenue. (1986, February). Canadian Civil Service Appeals Board, Ottawa, Canada.

Mann, C. (1990, August 3). Meta-analysis in the breech. *Science, 249,* 476–480.

Mansfield, R. S., & Busse, T. V. (1977). Meta-analysis of research: A rejoinder to Glass. *Educational Researcher, 6,* 3.

McDaniel, M. A. (1985). *The evaluation of a causal model of job performance: The interrelationships of general mental ability, job experience and job performance.* Unpublished doctoral dissertation, Department of Psychology, George Washington University, Washington, DC.

McDaniel, M. A., & Hirsh, H. R. (1986, April). Methods of moderator detection in meta-analysis. In M. A. McDaniel (Chair), *An overview and new directions in the Hunter-Schmidt-Jackson meta-analysis technique.* Symposium conducted at the annual conference of the Society for Industrial/Organizational Psychology, Chicago.

McDaniel, M. A., & Nguyen, N. T. (2002, December 5). *A meta-analysis of the relationship between* in vivo *brain volume and intelligence.* Paper presented at the Third Annual Conference of the International Society for Intelligence Research, Nashville, TN.

McDaniel, M. A., Schmidt, F. L., & Hunter, J. E. (1988a). A meta-analysis of the validity of training and experience ratings in personnel selection. *Personnel Psychology, 41,* 283–314.

McDaniel, M. A., Schmidt, F. L., & Hunter, J. E. (1988b). Job experience correlates of job performance. *Journal of Applied Psychology, 73,* 327–330.

McDaniel, M. A., Whetzel, D. L., Schmidt, F. L., & Maurer, S. D. (1994). The validity of employment interviews: A comprehensive review and meta-analysis. *Journal of Applied Psychology, 79,* 599–616.

McEvoy, G. M., & Cascio, W. F. (1985). Strategies for reducing employee turnover: A meta-analysis. *Journal of Applied Psychology, 70,* 342–353.

McEvoy, G. M., & Cascio, W. F. (1987). Do poor performers leave? A meta-analysis of the relation between performance and turnover. *Academy of Management Journal, 30,* 744–762.

McKinney, M. W. (1984). *Final report: Validity generalization pilot study.* Raleigh, NC: U.S. Department of Labor, U.S. Employment Service, Southern Test Development Field Center.

McNatt, D. B. (2000). Ancient Pygmalion joins contemporary management: A meta-analysis of the result. *Journal of Applied Psychology, 85,* 314–322.

McNemar, Q. (1960). At random: Sense and nonsense. *American Psychologist, 15,* 295–300.

Meehl, P. E. (1978). Theoretical risks and tabular asterisks: Sir Karl, Sir Ronald and the slow progress of soft psychology. *Journal of Consulting and Clinical Psychology, 46,* 806–834.

Mendoza, J. L., & Mumford, M. (1987). Correction for attenuation and range restriction on the predictor. *Journal of Educational Statistics, 12,* 282–293.

Mendoza, J. L., & Reinhardt, R. N. (1991). Validity generalization procedures using sample-based estimates: A comparison of six procedures. *Psychological Bulletin, 110,* 596–610.

Mendoza, J. L., Stafford, K. L., & Stauffer, J. M. (2000). Large sample confidence intervals for validity and reliability coefficients. *Psychological Methods, 5,* 356–369.

Mengersen, K. L., Tweedie, R. L., & Biggerstaff, B. (1995). The impact of method choice on meta-analysis. *Australian Journal of Statistics, 37,* 19–44.

Miller, K., & Monge, P. (in press). Participation, satisfaction, and productivity: A meta-analysis. *Academy of Management Review.*

Miller, N., & Carlson, M. (1990). Valid theory-testing meta-analyses further question the negative state relief model of helping. *Psychological Bulletin, 107,* 215–225.

Miller, N., Lee, S., & Carlson, M. (1991). The validity of inferential judgments when used in theory-testing meta-analysis. *Personality and Social Psychology Bulletin, 17,* 335–343.

Millsap, R. (1988). Sampling variance in attenuated correlation coefficients: A Monte Carlo study. *Journal of Applied Psychology, 73,* 316–319.

Millsap, R. (1989). The sampling variance in the correlation under range restriction: A Monte Carlo study. *Journal of Applied Psychology, 74,* 456–461.

Moher, D., & Olkin, I. (1995). Meta-analysis of randomized controlled trials: A concern for standards. *Journal of the American Medical Association, 274,* 1962–1964.

Morris, S. B., & DeShon, R. P. (1997). Correcting effect sizes computed from factorial analysis of variance for use in meta-analysis. *Psychological Methods, 2,* 192–199.

Morris, S. B., & DeShon, R. P. (2002). Combining effect size estimates in meta-analysis with repeated measures and independent groups designs. *Psychological Methods, 7,* 105–125.

Mosier, C. I. (1943). On the reliability of a weighted composite. *Psychometrika, 8,* 161–168.

Mosteller, F. M., & Bush, R. R. (1954). Selected quantitative techniques. In G. Lindzey (Ed.), *Handbook of social psychology: Vol. I. Theory and method.* Cambridge, MA: Addison-Wesley.

Mosteller, F., & Colditz, G. A. (1996). Understanding research synthesis (meta-analysis). *Annual Review of Public Health, 17,* 1–17.

Mosteller, F., & Moynihan, D. (1972). *On equality of educational opportunity.* New York: Vintage Books.

Mosteller, F., & Tukey, J. W. (1977). *Data analysis and regression: A second course in statistics.* Reading, MA: Addison-Wesley.

Mount, M. K., & Barrick, M. R. (1995). The big five personality dimensions: Implications for research and practice in human resources management. In G. R. Ferris (Ed.), *Research in personnel and human resources management* (Vol. 13, pp. 153–200). Greenwich, CT: JAI Press.

Mullen, B. (1989). *Advanced BASIC meta-analysis.* Hillsdale, NJ: Lawrence Erlbaum.

Mullen, B., Salas, E., & Miller, N. (1991). Using meta-analysis to test theoretical hypotheses in social psychology. *Personality and Social Psychology Bulletin, 17*(3), 258–264.

Mullen, P. D., Mains, D. A., & Velez, R. (1992). A meta-analysis of controlled trials of cardiac patient education. *Patient Education and Counseling, 19,* 143–162.

Murphy, K. R. (1997). Meta-analysis and validity generalization. In N. Anderson & P. Herriott (Eds.), *International handbook of selection and assessment* (pp. 323–342). Chichester, UK: Wiley.

Murphy, K. R. (Ed.). (2003). *Validity generalization: A critical review.* Mahwah, NJ: Lawrence Erlbaum.

Murphy, K. R., & DeShon, R. (2000). Interrater correlations do not estimate the reliability of job performance ratings. *Personnel Psychology, 53,* 873–900.

Myers, D. G. (1991). Union is strength: A consumer's view of meta-analysis. *Personality and Social Psychology Bulletin, 17,* 265–266.

Nathan, B. R., & Alexander, R. A. (1988). A comparison of criteria for test validation: A meta-analytic investigation. *Personnel Psychology, 41,* 517–535.

National Research Council. (1992). *Combining information: Statistical issues and opportunities for research.* Washington, DC: National Academy of Sciences Press.

Newcomb, A. F., & Bagwell, C. L. (1995). Children's friendship relations: A meta-analytic review. *Psychological Bulletin, 117,* 306–347.

Nicol, T. S., & Hunter, J. E. (1973). *Mathematical models of the reliability of the semantic differential.* Paper presented at the Psychometric Society, Chicago.

Novick, M. R. (1986, April). *The limits of validity generalization: The future of prediction generalization.* Paper presented at the First Annual Meeting of the Society for Industrial/Organizational Psychology, Chicago.

Nunnally, J. (1978). *Psychometric theory.* New York: McGraw-Hill.

Nunnally, J. C., & Bernstein, I. H. (1994). *Psychometric theory* (3rd ed.). New York: McGraw-Hill.

Oakes, M. (1986). *Statistical inference: A commentary for the social and behavioral sciences.* New York: Wiley.

O'Connor, E. J., Wexley, K. N., & Alexander, R. A. (1975). Single group validity: Fact or fallacy? *Journal of Applied Psychology, 60,* 352–355.

Ones, D. S., & Viswesvaran, C. (2003). Job-specific applicant pools and national norms for personality scales: Implications for range restriction corrections in validation research. *Journal of Applied Psychology, 88,* 570–577.

Ones, D. S., Viswesvaran, C., & Schmidt, F. L. (1993). Meta-analysis of integrity test validities: Findings and implications for personnel selection and theories of job performance. *Journal of Applied Psychology Monograph, 78,* 679–703.

Orwin, R. G. (1983). A fail-safe *N* for effect size. *Journal of Educational Statistics, 8,* 147–159.

Orwin, R. G. (1994). Evaluating coding decisions. In H. Cooper & L. V. Hedges (Eds.), *Handbook of research synthesis* (pp. 139–162). New York: Russell Sage.

Orwin, R. G., & Cordray, D. S. (1985). Effects of deficient reporting on meta-analysis: A conceptual framework and reanalysis. *Journal of Applied Psychology, 97,* 134–147.

Osburn, H. G. (1978). Optimal sampling strategies for validation studies. *Journal of Applied Psychology, 63,* 602–608.

Osburn, H. G., & Callender, J. C. (1990). Accuracy of the validity generalization sampling variance estimate: A reply to Hoben Thomas. *Journal of Applied Psychology, 75,* 328–333.

Osburn, H. G., & Callender, J. (1992). A note on the sampling variance of the mean uncorrected correlation in meta-analysis and validity generalization. *Journal of Applied Psychology, 77,* 115–122.

Osburn, H. G., Callender, J. C., Greener, J. M., & Ashworth, S. (1983). Statistical power of tests of the situational specificity hypothesis in validity generalization studies: A cautionary note. *Journal of Applied Psychology, 68,* 115–122.

Ostroff, C., & Harrison, D. A. (1999). Meta-analysis, level of analysis, and best estimates of population correlations: Cautions for interpreting meta-analytic results in organizational behavior. *Journal of Applied Psychology, 84,* 260–270.

Oswald, F., & Johnson, J. (1998). On the robustness, bias and stability of statistics from meta-analysis of correlation coefficients: Some initial Monte Carlo findings. *Journal of Applied Psychology, 83,* 164–178.

Overton, R. C. (1998). A comparison of fixed effects and mixed (random effects) models for meta-analysis tests of moderator variable effects. *Psychological Methods, 3,* 354–379.

Oxman, A. (1995). Checklists for review articles. In I. Chalmers & D. Altman (Eds.), *Systematic reviews.* London: BMJ Publishing Group.

Paese, P. W., & Switzer, F. S., III. (1988). Validity generalization and hypothetical reliability distributions: A test of the Schmidt-Hunter procedure. *Journal of Applied Psychology, 73,* 267–274.

Paese, P. W., & Switzer, F. S., III. (1989). *Validity generalization and hypothetical reliability distributions: A reexamination.* Unpublished manuscript, Psychology Department, University of Missouri, St. Louis.

Pearlman, K. (1979). *The validity of tests used to select clerical personnel: A comprehensive summary and evaluation.* Washington, DC: U.S. Office of Personnel Management.

Pearlman, K. (1980a, September). Seeing the whole picture: Application of cumulated validity data to issues in clerical selection. In V. J. Benz (Chair), *Methodological implications of large-scale validity studies of clerical occupations.* Symposium conducted at the meeting of the American Psychological Association, Montreal.

Pearlman, K. (1980b). Job families: A review and discussion of their implications for personnel selection. *Psychological Bulletin, 87,* 1–28.

Pearlman, K. (1982). *The Bayesian approach to validity generalization: A systematic examination of the robustness of procedures and conclusions.* Unpublished doctoral dissertation, Department of Psychology, George Washington University, Washington, DC.

Pearlman, K., & Schmidt, F. L. (1981, August). Effects of alternate job grouping methods on selection procedure validity. In E. L. Levine (Chair), *Job analysis/job families: Current perspectives on research and application.* Symposium conducted at the meeting of the American Psychological Association, Los Angeles.

Pearlman, K., Schmidt, F. L., & Hunter, J. E. (1980). Validity generalization results for tests used to predict job proficiency and training success in clerical occupations. *Journal of Applied Psychology, 65,* 373–406.

Pearson, E. S. (1938). The probability integral transformation for testing goodness of fit and combining tests of significance. *Biometrika, 30,* 134–148.

Pearson, K. (1904). Report on certain enteric fever inoculation statistics. *British Medical Journal, 2,* 1243–1246.

Peters, L. H., Harthe, D., & Pohlman, J. (1985). Fiedler's contingency theory of leadership: An application of the meta-analysis procedures of Schmidt and Hunter. *Psychological Bulletin, 97,* 274–285.

Peterson, N. G. (1982, October). *Investigation of validity generalization in clerical and technical/professional occupations in the insurance industry.* Paper presented at the Conference on Validity Generalization, Personnel Testing Council of Southern California, Newport Beach, CA.

Petty, M. M., McGee, G. W., & Cavender, J. W. (1984). A meta-analysis of the relationship between individual job satisfaction and individual performance. *Academy of Management Review, 9,* 712–721.

Pinello, D. R. (1999). Linking party to judicial ideology in American courts: A meta-analysis. *The Justice System Journal, 20,* 219–254.

Polich, J., Pollock, V. E., & Bloom, F. E. (1994). Meta-analysis of P300 amplitude from males at risk for alcoholism. *Psychological Bulletin, 115,* 55–73.

Premack, S., & Wanous, J. P. (1985). Meta-analysis of realistic job preview experiments. *Journal of Applied Psychology, 70,* 706–719.

Raju, N. S., Anselmi, T. V., Goodman, J. S., & Thomas, A. (1998). The effects of correlated artifacts and true validity on the accuracy of parameter estimation in validity generalization. *Personnel Psychology, 51,* 453–465.

Raju, N. S., & Brand, P. A. (2003). Determining the significance of correlations corrected for unreliability and range restriction. *Applied Psychological Methods, 27,* 52–72.

Raju, N. S., & Burke, M. J. (1983). Two new procedures for studying validity generalization. *Journal of Applied Psychology, 68,* 382–395.

Raju, N. S., Burke, M. J., & Normand, J. (1983). *The asymptotic sampling distribution of correlations corrected for attenuation and range restriction.* Unpublished manuscript, Department of Psychology, Illinois Institute of Technology, Chicago.

Raju, N. S., Burke, M. J., Normand, J., & Langlois, G. M. (1991). A new meta-analysis approach. *Journal of Applied Psychology, 76,* 432–446.

Raju, N. S., & Drasgow, F. (2003). Maximum likelihood estimation in validity generalization. In K. R. Murphy (Ed.), *Validity generalization: A critical review* (Chap. 9). Hillsdale, NJ: Lawrence Erlbaum.

Raju, N. S., & Fleer, P. G. (1997). *MAIN: A computer program for meta-analysis.* Chicago: Illinois Institute of Technology.

Raju, N. S., Fralicx, R., & Steinhaus, S. D. (1986). Covariance and regression slope models for studying validity generalization. *Applied Psychological Measurement, 10,* 195–211.

Ramamurti, A. S. (1989). A systematic approach to generating excess returns using a multiple variable model. In F. J. Fabozzi (Ed.), *Institutional investor focus on investment management.* Cambridge, MA: Ballinger.

Raudenbush, S. W. (1994). Random effects models. In H. Cooper & L. V. Hedges (Eds.), *The handbook of research synthesis* (pp. 301–322). New York: Russell Sage.

Raudenbush, S. W., & Bryk, A. S. (1985). Empirical Bayes meta-analysis. *Journal of Educational Statistics, 10,* 75–98.

Reed, J. G., & Baxter, P. M. (1994). Using reference databases. In H. Cooper & L. V. Hedges (Eds.), *Handbook of research synthesis* (pp. 57–70). New York: Russell Sage.

Rodgers, R. C., & Hunter, J. E. (1986). *The impact of management by objectives on organizational productivity.* Unpublished manuscript, Management Department, University of Texas at Austin.

Rodgers, R. C., & Hunter, J. E. (1989). *The impact of false methodological hypotheses in reviews of management research: The case of management by objectives.* Unpublished manuscript.

Rosenberg, M. S., Adams, D. C., & Gurevitch, J. (1997). *MetaWin: Statistical software for meta-analysis with resampling tests.* Sunderland, MA: Sinauer Associates.

Rosenthal, M. C. (1994). The fugitive literature. In H. Cooper & L. V. Hedges (Eds.), *The handbook of research synthesis* (pp. 85–94). New York: Russell Sage.

Rosenthal, R. (1961, September). On the social psychology of the psychological experiment: With particular reference to experimenter bias. In H. W. Riecken (Chair), *On the social psychology of the psychological experiment.* Symposium conducted at the meeting of the American Psychological Association, New York.

Rosenthal, R. (1963). On the social psychology of the psychological experiment: The experimenter's hypothesis as unintended determinant of experimental results. *American Scientist, 51,* 268–283.

Rosenthal, R. (1978a). Combining results of independent studies. *Psychological Bulletin, 85,* 185–193.

Rosenthal, R. (1978b). How often are our numbers wrong? *American Psychologist, 33,* 1005–1008.

Rosenthal, R. (1979). The "file drawer problem" and tolerance for null results. *Psychological Bulletin, 86,* 638–641.

Rosenthal, R. (1983). Assessing the statistical and social importance of the effects of psychotherapy. *Journal of Consulting and Clinical Psychology, 51,* 4–13.

Rosenthal, R. (1984). *Meta-analysis procedures for social research.* Beverly Hills, CA: Sage.

Rosenthal, R. (1991). *Meta-analytic procedures for social research* (2nd ed.). Newbury Park, CA: Sage.

Rosenthal, R. (1994). Parametric measures of effect size. In H. Cooper & L. V. Hedges (Eds.), *The handbook of research synthesis* (pp. 231–244). New York: Russell Sage.

Rosenthal, R. (1995a). Progress in clinical psychology: Is there any? *Clinical Psychology: Scientific Practice, 2,* 133–150.

Rosenthal, R. (1995b). Writing meta-analytic reviews. *Psychological Bulletin, 118,* 183–192.

Rosenthal, R., & Rubin, D. B. (1978a). Interpersonal expectancy effects: The first 345 studies. *The Behavioral and Brain Sciences, 3,* 377–386.

Rosenthal, R., & Rubin, D. B. (1978b). Issues in summarizing the first 345 studies of interpersonal expectancy effects. *The Behavioral and Brain Sciences, 3,* 410–415.

Rosenthal, R., & Rubin, D. B. (1979a). Comparing significance levels of independent studies. *Psychological Bulletin, 86,* 1165–1168.

Rosenthal, R., & Rubin, D. B. (1979b). A note on percent variance explained as a measure of the importance of effects. *Journal of Applied Psychology, 9,* 395–396.

Rosenthal, R., & Rubin, D. B. (1980). Further issues in summarizing 345 studies of interpersonal expectancy effects. *The Behavioral and Brain Sciences, 3,* 475–476.

Rosenthal, R., & Rubin, D. B. (1982a). Comparing effect sizes of independent studies. *Psychological Bulletin, 92,* 500–504.

Rosenthal, R., & Rubin, D. B. (1982b). Further meta-analytic procedures for assessing cognitive gender differences. *Journal of Educational Psychology, 74,* 708–712.

Rosenthal, R., & Rubin, D. B. (1982c). A simple, general purpose display of magnitude of experiment effect. *Journal of Educational Psychology, 74,* 166–169.

Rosenthal, R., & Rubin, D. B. (1983). Ensemble-adjusted *p* values. *Psychological Bulletin, 94,* 540–541.

Rosenthal, R., & Rubin, D. B. (1994). The counternull value of an effect size: A new statistic. *Psychological Science, 5,* 329–334.

Roth, P. L., BeVier, C. A., Bobko, P., Switzer, F. S., III, & Tyler, P. (2001). Ethnic group differences in cognitive ability in employment and educational settings: A meta-analysis. *Personnel Psychology, 54,* 297–330.

Roth, P. L., BeVier, C. A., Switzer, F. S., & Shippmann, J. S. (1996). Meta-analyzing the relationship between grades and job performance. *Journal of Applied Psychology, 81,* 548–556.

Roth, P. L., Bobko, P., Switzer, F. S., & Dean, M. A. (2001). Prior selection causes biased estimates of standardized ethnic group differences: Simulation and analysis. *Personnel Psychology, 54,* 297–330.

Rothstein, H. R. (1990). Interrater reliability of job performance ratings: Growth to asymptote level with increasing opportunity to observe. *Journal of Applied Psychology, 75,* 322–327.

Rothstein, H. R. (2003). Progress is our most important product: Contributions of validity generalization and meta-analysis to the development and communication of knowledge in I/O psychology. In K. R. Murphy (Ed.), *Validity generalization: A critical review* (pp. 115–154). Mahwah, NJ: Lawrence Erlbaum.

Rothstein, H. R., McDaniel, M. A., & Borenstein, M. (2001). Meta-analysis: A review of quantitative cumulation methods. In N. Schmitt & F. Drasgow (Eds.), *Advances in measurement and data analysis.* San Francisco: Jossey-Bass.

Rothstein, H. R., Schmidt, F. L., Erwin, F. W., Owens, W. A., & Sparks, C. P. (1990). Biographical data in employment selection: Can validities be made generalizable? *Journal of Applied Psychology, 75,* 175–184.

Rothstein, H. R., Sutton, A., & Borenstein, M. (Eds.). (in press). *Publication bias in meta-analysis: Prevention, assessment, and adjustments.* London: Wiley.

Rozeboom, W. W. (1960). The fallacy of the null hypothesis significance test. *Psychological Bulletin, 57,* 416–428.

Rubin, D. B. (1980). Using empirical Bayes techniques in the law school validity studies. *Journal of the American Statistical Association, 75*(372), 801–827.

Rubin, D. B. (1981). Estimation in parallel randomized experiments. *Journal of Educational Statistics, 6,* 337–400.

Rubin, D. B. (1990). A new perspective on meta-analysis. In K. W. Wachter & M. L. Straf (Eds.), *The future of meta-analysis.* New York: Russell Sage.

Russell, C. J., & Gilliland, S. W. (1995). Why meta-analysis doesn't tell us what the data really mean: Distinguishing between moderator effects and moderator processes. *Journal of Management, 21,* 813–831.

Sackett, P. R., Harris, M. M., & Orr, J. M. (1986). On seeking moderator variables in the meta-analysis of correlational data: A Monte Carlo investigation of statistical power and resistance to Type I error. *Journal of Applied Psychology, 71,* 302–310.

Sackett, P. R., Laczo, R. M., & Arvey, R. D. (2002). The effects of range restriction on estimates of criterion interrater reliability: Implications for validation research. *Personnel Psychology, 55,* 807–825.

Sackett, P. R., Schmitt, N., Tenopyr, M. L., Kehoe, J., & Zedeck, S. (1985). Commentary on forty questions about validity generalization and meta-analysis. *Personnel Psychology, 38,* 697–798.

Sackett, P. R., & Wade, B. E. (1983). On the feasibility of criterion related validity: The effects of range restriction assumptions on needed sample size. *Journal of Applied Psychology, 68,* 374–381.

Sacks, H. S., Berrier, J., Reitman, D., Ancona-Berk, V. A., & Chalmers, T. C. (1987). Meta-analysis of randomized controlled trials. *New England Journal of Medicine, 316,* 450–455.

Sanchez-Meca, J., & Marin-Martinez, F. (1997). Homogeneity tests in meta-analysis: A Monte-Carlo comparison of statistical power and Type I error. *Quality and Quantity, 31*(4), 385–399.

Schlagel, R. H. (1979). *Revaluation in the philosophy of science: Implications for method and theory in psychology.* Invited address presented at the meeting of the American Psychological Association, New York.

Schmidt, F. L. (1984, August). *Meta-analysis: Implications for cumulative knowledge in the behavioral and social sciences.* Invited address presented at the 92nd Annual Meeting of the American Psychological Association, Toronto.

Schmidt, F. L. (1985, April). From validity generalization to meta-analysis: The development and application of a new research procedure. In M. J. Burke (Chair), *Validity generalization as meta-analysis.* Symposium conducted at the annual meeting of the American Educational Research Association, Chicago.

Schmidt, F. L. (1988). Validity generalization and the future of criterion-related validity. In H. Wainer & H. Braun (Eds.), *Test validity* (pp. 173–189). Hillsdale, NJ: Lawrence Erlbaum.

Schmidt, F. L. (1992). What do data really mean? Research findings, meta-analysis, and cumulative knowledge in psychology. *American Psychologist, 47,* 1173–1181.

Schmidt, F. L. (1996). Statistical significance testing and cumulative knowledge in psychology: Implications for the training of researchers. *Psychological Methods, 1,* 115–129.

Schmidt, F. L. (2002). The role of general cognitive ability in job performance: Why there cannot be a debate. *Human Performance, 15,* 187–210.

Schmidt, F. L. (2003). John E. Hunter, 1939–2002. *American Psychologist, 58,* 238.

Schmidt, F. L., Berner, J. G., & Hunter, J. E. (1973). Racial differences in validity of employment tests: Reality or illusion? *Journal of Applied Psychology, 58,* 5–9.

Schmidt, F. L., Caplan, J. R., Bemis, S. E., Decuir, R., Dunn, L., & Antone, L. (1979). *The behavioral consistency method of unassembled examining* (Technical Publication No. 79–21). Washington, DC: U.S. Office of Personnel Management, Personnel Research and Development Center.

Schmidt, F. L., Gast-Rosenberg, I., & Hunter, J. E. (1980). Validity generalization results for computer programmers. *Journal of Applied Psychology, 65,* 643–661.

Schmidt, F. L., & Hunter, J. E. (1977). Development of a general solution to the problem of validity generalization. *Journal of Applied Psychology, 62,* 529–540.

Schmidt, F. L., & Hunter, J. E. (1978). Moderator research and the law of small numbers. *Personnel Psychology, 31,* 215–232.

Schmidt, F. L., & Hunter, J. E. (1980). The future of criterion related validity. *Personnel Psychology, 33,* 41–60.

Schmidt, F. L., & Hunter, J. E. (1981). Employment testing: Old theories and new research findings. *American Psychologist, 36,* 1128–1137.

Schmidt, F. L., & Hunter, J. E. (1983). Individual differences in productivity: An empirical test of estimates derived from studies of selection procedure utility. *Journal of Applied Psychology, 68,* 407–415.

Schmidt, F. L., & Hunter, J. E. (1984). A within setting test of the situational specificity hypothesis in personnel selection. *Personnel Psychology, 37,* 317–326.

Schmidt, F. L., & Hunter, J. E. (1992). Development of causal models of job performance. *Current Directions in Psychological Science, 1,* 89–92.

Schmidt, F. L., & Hunter, J. E. (1995). The impact of data analysis method on cumulative knowledge: Statistical significance testing, confidence intervals, and meta-analysis. *Evaluation and the Health Professions, 18,* 408–427.

Schmidt, F. L., & Hunter, J. E. (1996). Measurement error in psychological research: Lessons from 26 research scenarios. *Psychological Methods, 1,* 199–223.

Schmidt, F. L., & Hunter, J. E. (1997). Eight common but false objections to the discontinuation of significance testing in the analysis of research data. In L. Harlow, S. Muliak, & J. Steiger (Eds.), *What if there were no significance tests?* (pp. 37–64). Mahwah, NJ: Lawrence Erlbaum.

Schmidt, F. L., & Hunter, J. E. (1998). The validity and utility of selection methods in personnel psychology: Practical and theoretical implications of 85 years of research findings. *Psychological Bulletin, 124,* 262–274.

Schmidt, F. L., & Hunter, J. E. (1999a). Comparison of three meta-analysis methods revisited: An analysis of Johnson, Mullen, and Salas (1995). *Journal of Applied Psychology, 84,* 114–148.

Schmidt, F. L., & Hunter, J. E. (1999b). Theory testing and measurement error. *Intelligence, 27,* 183–198.

Schmidt, F. L., & Hunter, J. E. (2002). Meta-analysis. In J. Schinka & W. Velicer (Eds.), *Comprehensive handbook of psychology: Vol. 2. Research methods in psychology.* New York: Wiley.

Schmidt, F. L., & Hunter, J. E. (2003). History, development, evolution, and impact of validity generalization and meta-analysis methods, 1975–2001. In K. R. Murphy (Ed.), *Validity generalization: A critical review* (pp. 31–66). Mahwah, NJ: Lawrence Erlbaum.

Schmidt, F. L., Hunter, J. E., & Caplan, J. R. (1981a). Validity generalization results for two job groups in the petroleum industry. *Journal of Applied Psychology, 66,* 261–273.

Schmidt, F. L., Hunter, J. E., & Caplan, J. R. (1981b). *Selection procedure validity generalization (transportability) results for three job groups in the petroleum industry.* Washington, DC: American Petroleum Institute.

Schmidt, F. L., Hunter, J. E., McKenzie, R. C., & Muldrow, T. W. (1979). The impact of valid selection procedures on work-force productivity. *Journal of Applied Psychology, 64,* 609–626.

Schmidt, F. L., Hunter, J. E., & Outerbridge, A. N. (1986). Impact of job experience and ability on job knowledge, work sample performance, and supervisory ratings of job performance. *Journal of Applied Psychology, 71,* 432–439.

Schmidt, F. L., Hunter, J. E., Outerbridge, A. N., & Goff, S. (1988). Joint relation of experience and ability with job performance: Test of three hypotheses. *Journal of Applied Psychology, 73,* 46–57.

Schmidt, F. L., Hunter, J. E., Outerbridge, A. M., & Trattner, M. H. (1986). The economic impact of job selection methods on the size, productivity, and payroll costs of the federal workforce: An empirical demonstration. *Personnel Psychology, 39,* 1–29.

Schmidt, F. L., Hunter, J. E., & Pearlman, K. (1981). Task differences and validity of aptitude tests in selection: A red herring. *Journal of Applied Psychology, 66,* 166–185.

Schmidt, F. L., Hunter, J. E., & Pearlman, K. (1982). Progress in validity generalization: Comments on Callender and Osburn and further developments. *Journal of Applied Psychology, 67,* 835–845.

Schmidt, F. L., Hunter, J. E., Pearlman, K., & Caplan, J. R. (1981). *Validity generalization results for three occupations in Sears, Roebuck and Company.* Chicago: Sears, Roebuck and Company.

Schmidt, F. L., Hunter, J. E., Pearlman, K., & Hirsh, H. R. (1985). Forty questions about validity generalization and meta-analysis. *Personnel Psychology, 38,* 697–798.

Schmidt, F. L., Hunter, J. E., Pearlman, K., & Shane, G. S. (1979). Further tests of the Schmidt-Hunter Bayesian validity generalization procedure. *Personnel Psychology, 32,* 257–381.

Schmidt, F. L., Hunter, J. E., & Raju, N. S. (1988). Validity generalization and situational specificity: A second look at the 75% rule and the Fisher's *z* transformation. *Journal of Applied Psychology, 73,* 665–672.

Schmidt, F. L., Hunter, J. E., & Urry, V. E. (1976). Statistical power in criterion-related validation studies. *Journal of Applied Psychology, 61,* 473–485.

Schmidt, F. L., Law, K. S., Hunter, J. E., Rothstein, H. R., Pearlman, K., & McDaniel, M. (1989). *Refinements in validity generalization methods (including outlier analysis).* Unpublished paper, Department of Management and Organization, University of Iowa.

Schmidt, F. L., Law, K. S., Hunter, J. E., Rothstein, H. R., Pearlman, K., & McDaniel, M. (1993). Refinements in validity generalization methods: Implications for the situational specificity hypothesis. *Journal of Applied Psychology, 78,* 3–13.

Schmidt, F. L., Le, H., & Ilies, R. (2003). Beyond Alpha: An empirical examination of the effects of different sources of measurement error on reliability estimates for measures of individual differences constructs. *Psychological Methods, 8,* 206–234.

Schmidt, F. L., Mack, M. J., & Hunter, J. E. (1984). Selection utility in the occupation of U.S. Park Ranger for three modes of test use. *Journal of Applied Psychology, 69,* 490–497.

Schmidt, F. L., Ocasio, B. P., Hillery, J. M., & Hunter, J. E. (1985). Further within-setting empirical tests of the situational specificity hypothesis in personnel selection. *Personnel Psychology, 38,* 509–524.

Schmidt, F. L., Ones, D., & Hunter, J. E. (1992). Personnel selection. *Annual Review of Psychology, 43,* 627–670.

Schmidt, F. L., Pearlman, K., & Hunter, J. E. (1980). The validity and fairness of employment and educational tests for Hispanic Americans: A review and analysis. *Personnel Psychology, 33,* 705–724.

Schmidt, F. L., & Rothstein, H. R. (1994). Application of validity generalization methods of meta-analysis to biographical data scores in employment selection. In G. S. Stokes, M. D. Mumford, & W. A. Owens (Eds.), *The biodata handbook: Theory, research, and applications* (pp. 237–260). Chicago: Consulting Psychologists Press.

Schmidt, F. L., Viswesvaran, C., & Ones, D. S. (2000). Reliability is not validity and validity is not reliability. *Personnel Psychology, 53,* 901–912.

Schmidt, F. L., & Zimmerman, R. (in press). A counter-intuitive hypothesis about interview validity and some supporting evidence. *Journal of Applied Psychology.*

Schmitt, N., Gooding, R. Z., Noe, R. A., & Kirsch, M. (1984). Meta-analysis of validity studies published between 1964 and 1982 and the investigation of study characteristics. *Personnel Psychology, 37,* 407–422.

Schwab, D. P., Olian-Gottlieb, J. D., & Heneman, H. G., III. (1979). Between subject's expectancy theory research: A statistical review of studies predicting effort and performance. *Psychological Bulletin, 86,* 139–147.

Sechrest, L., & Yeaton, W. H. (1982). Magnitudes of experimental effects in social science research. *Evaluation Review, 6,* 579–600.

Sedlmeier, P., & Gigerenzer, G. (1989). Do studies of statistical power have an effect on the power of studies? *Psychological Bulletin, 105,* 309–316.

Shadish, W. R. (1996). Meta-analysis and the exploration of causal mediating processes: A primer of examples, methods, and issues. *Psychological Methods, 1,* 47–65.

Shadish, W. R., & Haddock, C. K. (1994). Combining estimates of effects size. In H. Cooper & L. V. Hedges (Eds.), *Handbook of research synthesis* (pp. 261–282). New York: Russell Sage.

Shadish, W. R., Matt, G. E., Navarro, A. M., & Phillips, G. (2000). The effects of psychological therapies under clinically representative conditions: A meta-analysis. *Psychological Bulletin, 126,* 512–529.

Shadish, W. R., & Ragsdale, K. (1996). Random versus nonrandom assignment in psychotherapy experiments: Do you get the same answer? *Journal of Consulting and Clinical Psychology, 64,* 1290–1305.

Shadish, W. R., Robinson, L., & Lu, C. (1999). *ES: A computer program and manual for effect size calculation.* St. Paul, MN: Assessment Systems Corporation.

Shapiro, D. A., & Shapiro, D. (1982). Meta-analysis of comparative therapy outcome studies: A replication and refinement. *Psychological Bulletin, 92,* 581–604.

Shapiro, D. A., & Shapiro, D. (1983). Comparative therapy outcome research: Methodological implications of meta-analysis. *Journal of Consulting and Clinical Psychology, 51,* 42–53.

Sharf, J. (1987). Validity generalization: Round two. *The Industrial-Organizational Psychologist, 25,* 49–52.

Slavin, R. (1984). Meta-analysis in education: How has it been used? *The Educational Researcher, 3*(18), 6–15.

Slavin, R. E. (1986). Best-evidence synthesis: An alternative to meta-analytic and traditional reviews. *The Educational Researcher, 15,* 5–11.

Smith, M. L., & Glass, G. V. (1977). Meta-analysis of psychotherapy outcome studies. *American Psychologist, 32,* 752–760.

Smith, M., & Glass, G. (1980). Meta-analysis of research on class size and its relationship to attitudes and instruction. *American Educational Research Journal, 17,* 419–433.

Smith, M. L., Glass, G. V., & Miller, T. I. (1980). *The benefits of psychotherapy.* Baltimore: Johns Hopkins University Press.

Smithson, M. (2000). *Statistics with confidence.* London: Sage.

Smithson, M. (2001). Correct confidence intervals for various regression effect sizes and parameters: The importance of noncentral distributions in computing intervals. *Educational and Psychological Measurement, 61,* 605–632.

Smithson, M. (2003). *Confidence intervals.* Thousand Oaks, CA: Sage.

Smithson, M. (in press). Confidence intervals and power for heterogeneity statistics in meta-analysis. *Educational and Psychological Methods.*

Snedecor, G. W. (1946). *Statistical methods* (4th ed.). Ames: Iowa State College Press.

Song, F., Khan, K. S., Dinnes, J., & Sutton, A. J. (2002). Asymmetric funnel plots and publication bias in meta-analysis of diagnostic accuracy. *International Journal of Epidemiology, 31,* 88–95.

Spector, P. E., & Levine, E. L. (1987). Meta-analysis for integrating study outcomes: A Monte Carlo study of its susceptibility to Type I and Type II errors. *Journal of Applied Psychology, 72,* 3–9.

Stanley, J. C. (1971). Reliability. In R. L. Thorndike (Ed.), *Educational measurement* (2nd ed., pp. 356–442). Washington, DC: American Council on Education.

Stanley, T. D. (1998). New wine in old bottles: A meta-analysis of Ricardian equivalence. *Southern Economic Journal, 64,* 713–727.

Stanley, T. D. (2001). Wheat from chaff: Meta-analysis as quantitative literature review. *Journal of Economic Perspectives, 15,* 131–150.

Stanley, T. D., & Jarrell, S. B. (1989). Meta-regression analysis: A quantitative method of literature surveys. *Journal of Economic Surveys, 3,* 161–169.

Stanley, T. D., & Jarrell, S. D. (1998). Gender wage discrimination bias? A meta-regression analysis. *Journal of Human Resources, 33,* 947–973.

Stauffer, J. M. (1996). *The proper sequence for correcting correlations for range restriction and unreliability.* Unpublished manuscript, University of Iowa.

Stauffer, J. M., & Mendoza, J. L. (2001). The proper sequence for correcting correlation coefficients for range restriction and unreliability. *Psychometrika, 66,* 63–68.

Steel, P. D., & Kammeyer-Mueller, J. D. (2002). Comparing meta-analytic moderator estimation techniques under realistic conditions. *Journal of Applied Psychology, 87,* 96–111.

Steele, R. P., & Ovalle, N. K. (1984). A review and meta-analysis of research on the relationship between behavioral intentions and employee turnover. *Journal of Applied Psychology, 69,* 673–686.

Steering Committee, Physicians' Health Study Research Group. (1998). Preliminary report: Findings from the aspirin component of the ongoing physicians' health study. *New England Journal of Medicine, 318,* 262–264.

Sterling, T. C. (1959). Publication decisions and their possible effects on inferences drawn from tests of significance or vice versa. *Journal of the American Statistical Association, 54,* 30–34.

Sterling, T., Rosenbaum, W., & Weinkam, J. (1995). Publication decisions revisited: The effect of the outcome of statistical tests on the decision to publish and vice versa. *American Statistician, 49,* 108–112.

Stewart, D. W. (1984). *Secondary research.* Beverly Hills, CA: Sage.

Stock, W. A. (1994). Systematic coding for research synthesis. In H. Cooper & L. V. Hedges (Eds.), *Handbook of research synthesis* (pp. 125–138). New York: Russell Sage.

Stoffelmeyr, B. E., Dillavou, D., & Hunter, J. E. (1983). Premorbid functioning and recidivism in schizophrenia: A cumulative analysis. *Journal of Consulting and Clinical Psychology, 51,* 338–352.

Stouffer, S. A., Suchman, E. A., DeVinney, L. C., Star, S. A., & Williams, R. M., Jr. (1949). *The American soldier: Adjustment during Army life* (Vol. 1). Princeton, NJ: Princeton University Press.

Sutton, A. J., Duval, S. J., Tweedie, R. L., Abrams, K. R., & Jones, D. R. (2000). Empirical assessment of effect of publication bias on meta-analysis. *British Medical Journal, 320,* 1574–1577.

Symons, C. S., & Johnson, B. T. (1997). The self-reference effect in memory: A meta-analysis. *Psychological Bulletin, 121,* 371–394.

Taveggia, T. (1974). Resolving research controversy through empirical cumulation. *Sociological Methods and Research, 2,* 395–407.

Terborg, J. R., & Lee, T. W. (1982). Extension of the Schmidt-Hunter validity generalization procedure to the prediction of absenteeism behavior from knowledge of job satisfaction and organizational commitment. *Journal of Applied Psychology, 67,* 280–296.

Terpstra, D. E. (1981). Relationship between methodological rigor and reported outcomes in organization development evaluation research. *Journal of Applied Psychology, 66,* 541–543.

Terrin, N., Schmid, C. H., Lau, J., & Olkin, I. (2002, May 10). *Adjusting for publication bias in the presence of heterogeneity.* Paper presented at the Meta-Analysis Symposium, Mathematical Research Institute, University of California, Berkeley.

Tett, R. P., Meyer, J. P., & Roese, N. J. (1994). Applications of meta-analysis: 1987–1992. In *International review of industrial and organizational psychology* (Vol. 9, pp. 71–112). London: Wiley.

Thomas, H. (1988). What is the interpretation of the validity generalization estimate $S_p^2 = S_r^2 - S_c^2$? *Journal of Applied Psychology, 73,* 679–682.

Thompson, B. (1999). Journal editorial policies regarding statistical significance tests: Heat is to fire as *p* is to importance. *Educational Psychology Review, 11,* 157–169.

Thompson, B. (2002, April). What future quantitative social science research could look like: Confidence intervals for effect sizes. *Educational Researcher,* 25–32.

Thorndike, R. L. (1933). The effect of the interval between test and retest on the constancy of the IQ. *Journal of Educational Psychology, 25,* 543–549.

Thorndike, R. L. (1949). *Personnel selection.* New York: Wiley.

Thorndike, R. L. (1951). Reliability. In E. F. Lindquist (Ed.), *Educational measurement* (pp. 560–620). Washington, DC: American Council on Education.

Timmreck, C. W. (1981). *Moderating effect of tasks on the validity of selection tests.* Unpublished doctoral dissertation, Department of Psychology, University of Houston.

Tukey, J. W. (1960). A survey of sampling from contaminated distributions. In I. Olkin, J. G. Ghurye, W. Hoeffding, W. G. Madoo, & H. Mann (Eds.), *Contributions to probability and statistics.* Stanford, CA: Stanford University Press.

Tukey, J. (1977). *Exploratory data analysis.* Reading, MA: Addison-Wesley.

U.S. Department of Labor. (1970). *Manual for the U.S.E.S. General Aptitude Test Battery. Section III: Development.* Washington, DC: U.S. Employment Service.

U.S. Equal Employment Opportunity Commission, U.S. Civil Service Commission, U.S. Department of Labor, and U.S. Department of Justice. (1978). Uniform guidelines on employee selection procedures. *Federal Register, 43*(166), 38295–38309.

Van Iizendorn, M. H. (1995). Adult attachment representations, parental responsiveness, and infant attachment: A meta-analysis on the predictive validity of the adult attachment interview. *Psychological Bulletin, 117,* 387–403.

Vevea, J. L., Clements, N. C., & Hedges, L. V. (1993). Assessing the effects of selection bias on validity data for the General Aptitude Test Battery. *Journal of Applied Psychology, 78,* 981–987.

Vevea, J. L., & Hedges, L. V. (1995). A general linear model for estimating effect size in the presence of publication bias. *Psychometrika, 60,* 419–435.

Viswesvaran, C., & Ones, D. S. (1995). Theory testing: Combining psychometric meta-analysis and structural equation modeling. *Personnel Psychology, 48,* 865–885.

Viswesvaran, C., Ones, D. S., & Schmidt, F. L. (1996). Comparative analysis of the reliability of job performance ratings. *Journal of Applied Psychology, 81,* 557–560.

Viswesvaran, C., Schmidt, F. L., & Ones, D. S. (2002). The moderating influence of job performance dimensions on convergence of supervisory and peer ratings of job performance. *Journal of Applied Psychology, 87,* 345–354.

Viswesvaran, C., Schmidt, F. L., & Ones, D. S. (in press). Is there a general factor in job performance ratings? A meta-analytic framework for disentangling substantive and error influences. *Journal of Applied Psychology.*

Voyer, D., Voyer, S., & Bryden, M. P. (1995). Magnitude of sex differences in spatial abilities: A meta-analysis and consideration of critical variables. *Psychological Bulletin, 117,* 250–270.

Wachter, K. W., & Straf, M. L. (Eds.). (1990). *The future of meta-analysis.* New York: Russell Sage.

Whetzel, D. L., & McDaniel, M. A. (1988). Reliability of validity generalization data bases. *Psychological Reports, 63,* 131–134.

Whetzel, D. L., McDaniel, M. A., & Schmidt, F. L. (1985). The validity of employment interviews: A review and meta-analysis. In H. R. Hirsh (Chair), *Meta-analysis of alternative predictors of job performance.* Symposium conducted at the 93rd Annual Convention of the American Psychological Association, Los Angeles.

White, H. D. (1994). Scientific communication and literature retrieval. In H. Cooper & L. V. Hedges (Eds.), *Handbook of research synthesis* (pp. 41–56). New York: Russell Sage.

Whitener, E. M. (1990). Confusion of confidence intervals and credibility intervals in meta-analysis. *Journal of Applied Psychology, 75,* 315–321.

Whiteside, M. G., & Becker, B. J. (2000). Parental factors and the young child's postdivorce adjustment: A meta-analysis with implications for parenting arrangements. *Journal of Family Psychology, 14,* 5–26.

Wigdor, A. K., & Garner, W. R. (Eds.). (1982a). *Ability testing: Uses, consequences and controversies. Part I: Report of the committee.* Washington, DC: National Academy Press.

Wigdor, A. K., & Garner, W. R. (Eds.). (1982b). *Ability testing: Uses, consequences and controversies. Part II: Documentation section.* Washington, DC: National Academy Press.

Wilkinson, L., & The APA Task Force on Statistical Inference. (1999). Statistical methods in psychology journals: Guidelines and explanations. *American Psychologist, 54,* 594–604. (Reprint available through the APA home page: http://www.apa.org/journals/amp/amp548594.html)

Winer, B. J. (1962). *Statistical principles in experimental design.* New York: McGraw-Hill.

Wolf, F. M. (1986). *Meta-analysis: Quantitative methods for research synthesis.* Beverly Hills, CA: Sage.

Wolins, L. (1962). Responsibility for raw data. *American Psychologist, 17,* 657–658.

Wood, W. (1987). Meta-analytic review of sex differences in group performance. *Psychological Bulletin, 102,* 53–71.

Wood, W., Lundgren, S., Ouellette, J. A., Busceme, S., & Blackstone, T. (1994). Minority influence: A meta-analytic review of social influence processes. *Psychological Bulletin, 115,* 323–345.

Work America. (1986a, May). Validity generalization: Employment Service is doing new tricks with an old aptitude test (1–4). National Alliance of Business.

Work America. (1986b, May). New Jersey zealots just scratch the surface with validity generalization (3). National Alliance of Business.

Work America. (1986c, May). Taking the load off GM: Hiring 2,000 is easy with validity generalization (4). National Alliance of Business.

Wortman, P. M. (1983). Evaluation research: A methodological perspective. *Annotated Review of Psychology, 34,* 223–260.

Wortman, P. M. (1994). Judging research quality. In H. Cooper & L. V. Hedges (Eds.), *Handbook of research synthesis* (pp. 97–110). New York: Russell Sage.

Wortman, P. M., & Bryant, F. B. (1985). School desegregation and black achievement: An integrative review. *Sociological Methods and Research, 13,* 289–324.

Wunder, R. S., & Herring, J. W. (1980). *Interpretive guide for the API test validity generalization project.* Human Resources Series, American Petroleum Institute, Publication 755.

Wunder, R. S., Herring, J. W., & Carron, T. J. (1982). *Interpretive guide for the API test validity generalization project.* Human Resources Series, American Petroleum Institute, Publication 755.

Yusuf, S., Simon, R., & Ellenberg, S. S. (1986). Preface to proceedings of the workshop on methodological issues in overviews of randomized clinical trials, May 1986. *Statistics in Medicine, 6,* 217–218.

Name Index

Subject Index

About the Authors

John E. (Jack) Hunter (1939–2002) was a professor in the Department of Psychology at Michigan State University. He received his Ph.D. in psychology from the University of Illinois. Jack coauthored two books and authored or coauthored over 200 articles and book chapters on a wide variety of methodological topics, including confirmatory and exploratory factor analysis, measurement theory and methods, statistics, and research methods. He also published numerous research articles on such substantive topics as intelligence, attitude change, the relationship between attitudes and behavior, validity generalization, differential validity/selection fairness, and selection utility. Much of his research on attitudes was in the field of communications, and the American Communications Association named a research award in his honor. Professor Hunter received the Distinguished Scientific Award for Contributions to Applied Psychology from the American Psychological Association (APA) (jointly with Frank Schmidt) and the Distinguished Scientific Contributions Award from the Society for Industrial/Organizational Psychology (SIOP) (also jointly with Frank Schmidt). He was a Fellow of the APA, the American Psychological Society, and the SIOP, and was a past president of the Midwestern Society for Multivariate Experimental Psychology. For the story of Jack's life, see Schmidt (2003).

Frank L. Schmidt is the Ralph Sheets Professor in the Department of Management and Organization in the Tippie College of Business at the University of Iowa. He received his Ph.D. in industrial/organizational psychology from Purdue University and has been on the faculties of Michigan State and George Washington Universities. He has authored or coauthored several books and over 150 articles and book chapters on measurement, statistics, research methods, individual differences, and personnel selection. He headed a research program in the U.S. Office of Personnel Management in Washington, D.C., for 11 years, during which time he published numerous research studies in personnel psychology, primarily with John Hunter. Their research on the generalizability of employment selection method validities led to the development of the meta-analysis methods presented in this book. Professor Schmidt has received the Distinguished Scientific Award for Contributions to Applied Psychology from the American Psychological Association (APA) (jointly with John Hunter) and the Distinguished Scientific Contributions Award from the Society for Industrial/Organizational Psychology (SIOP) (also jointly with John Hunter). He has also received the Distinguished Career Award for

Contributions to Human Resources and the Distinguished Career Achievement Award for Contributions to Research Methods, both from the Academy of Management. He is a Fellow of the APA, the American Psychological Society, and the SIOP, and is past president of Division 5 (Measurement, Statistics, & Evaluation) of the APA.

Printed in Germany
by Amazon Distribution
GmbH, Leipzig